# FRESH PAINT NYC

Billy Schon

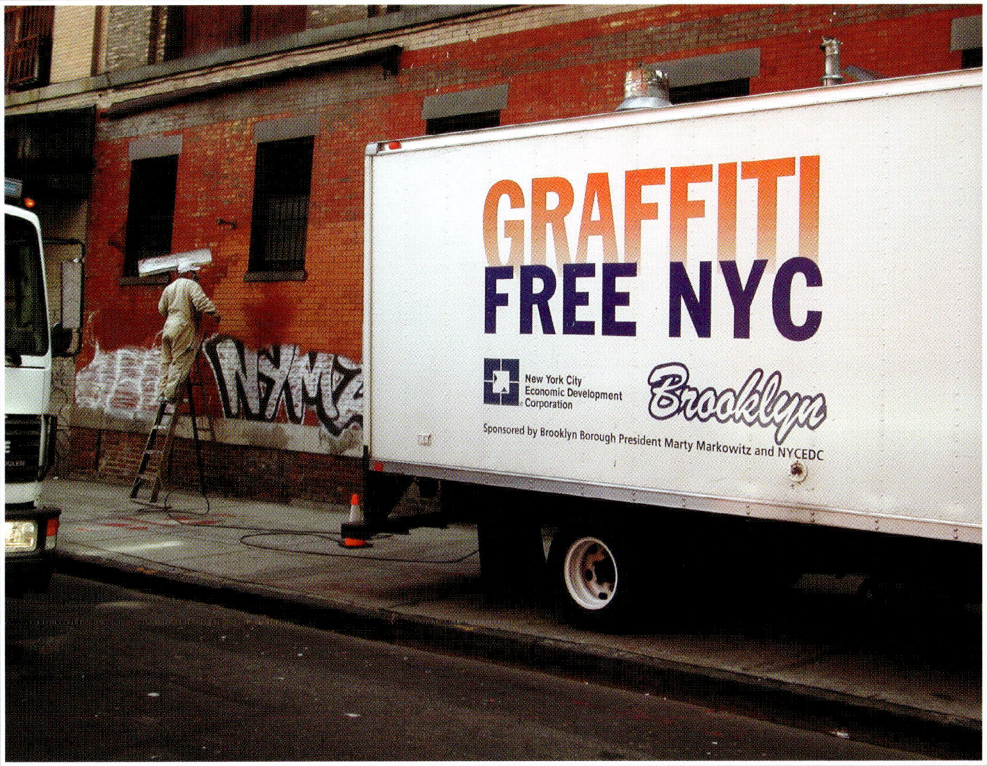


Schiffer Publishing Ltd

4880 Lower Valley Road Atglen, Pennsylvania 19310

Printed in China

# CREDITS

**Cover:** Ques 718
**Back Cover:** Outline by Keo X-Men
**Photography:** Billy Schon
**Special Thanks:** Meres (5 Pointz) and all the TD4 family, Tuff City Styles, Oil City Skate Park, Pete (Special Sauce), Leif (Alphabeta), Tats Cru, Jesse (New Design High School), Albus Cavus, Rebel NSA, Ink76, Jaes, Teknyc, Clark and Erotica Fly-ID, Tatu X-Men, Dezo TC-5, Cope2, Wane COD, Ket, Keo, Ques 718, Doves, Host18 and Tenz DYM, Part TDS, Jim & Karla Murray, Ros TPA, Peek and Diva, Stae2 and Uend, Faust, Gusto, Omni 156, Ewok 5MH, Trap IF, DJ Charm, Roman, Sen2 and Beond, James Top, Stay High 149, Chain3, Mark and Gio (Scrap Yard).

Special thanks to Ironlak Paint, www.ironlak.com

For the latest news and updates please visit **www.freshpaintnyc.blogspot.com**



Library of Congress Control Number: 2010920461



Type set in Zurich BT

ISBN: 978-0-7643-3495-5
Printed in China

Schiffer Books are available at special discounts for bulk purchases for sales promotions or premiums. Special editions, including personalized covers, corporate imprints, and excerpts can be created in large quantities for special needs. For more information contact the publisher:

Published by Schiffer Publishing Ltd.
4880 Lower Valley Road
Atglen, PA 19310
Phone: (610) 593-1777; Fax: (610) 593-2002
E-mail: Info@schifferbooks.com

For the largest selection of fine reference books on this and related subjects please visit our web site at **www.schifferbooks.com**
We are always looking for people to write books on new and related subjects. If you have an idea for a book please contact us at the above address.

This book may be purchased from the publisher.
Include $5.00 for shipping.
Please try your bookstore first.
You may write for a free catalog.

In Europe, Schiffer books are distributed by
Bushwood Books
6 Marksbury Ave.
Kew Gardens
Surrey TW9 4JF England
Phone: 44 (0) 20 8392 8585; Fax: 44 (0) 20 8392 9876
E-mail: info@bushwoodbooks.co.uk
Website: www.bushwoodbooks.co.uk

# NTRO

I first noticed graffiti in the streets of Long Island and Queens, New York, in 1987. The first graffiti writer to catch my attention was AVE SWK, aka "The Running Man." He was up everywhere. Although graffiti wasn't my main focus then, I was always aware of it and always knew someone who had a tag. In the 1990s, I was into reading magazines such as *On The Go, Stress, Rap Pages, The Source,* and various underground graffiti magazines. These magazines played a big part in creating a foundation for understanding how different letter styles and color schemes worked.

In the summer of 1999, I moved to the Lower East Side with a friend who skated with me. He wrote the tag Foes 501. I began to learn about graffiti history from him and by meeting and hanging out with older writers.

In early 2001, I began photographing graffiti in the streets and organizing a collection. I have had many rewarding experiences by getting off at random train stops in the Bronx and just walking around neighborhoods where I have never been before. When I was shooting on film, I was always careful not to use all the film before a neighborhood mission was over.

Once, downtown Manhattan parking lots were among my favorite spots for graffiti. On weekend mornings, the parking lots were empty and I would visit some repeatedly. Their walls were filled with layers of history and I always noticed some old, faded tag that I hadn't seen the last time I was there. Parking lots were the first walls that I attempted to shoot panoramically to capture the lots and their graf in their entirety. I also loved walking the streets early in the morning, before the businesses opened, and seeing all the graffiti on roll-down gates that were often hidden in the daytime.

In time, the parking lots and roll-down gates took the same "anti-graffiti" path that the trains had: the graffiti disappeared and it is all pretty much a thing of the past now. Beginning in 2007, the city of New York moved into action with a program that forced property owners to sign a contract allowing the city to clean off any graffiti on their property. If they did not do this, the owners were responsible for removing the graffiti themselves or risking a large fine from the city.

As part of all the change and development going on in the city today, graffiti is rapidly disappearing. The ongoing anti-graffiti program includes painting over production walls that many consider respectable art. As a result of this new attitude, graffiti artists, who, as sometimes happens, have been commissioned to paint walls for businesses, are subject to harassment by police patrols at any given time, especially in high impact zones. I feel fortunate to have witnessed the last days of the "plague" of graffiti-covered walls in the streets of New York.

Gentrification, quality of life concerns, technology, and the law have left those who are dedicated to graffiti art with a whole new batch of challenges as well as opportunities. The selection of photos featured in this book consists of current graffiti art by artists both old and new. It is valuable contribution to the history and style in New York City.

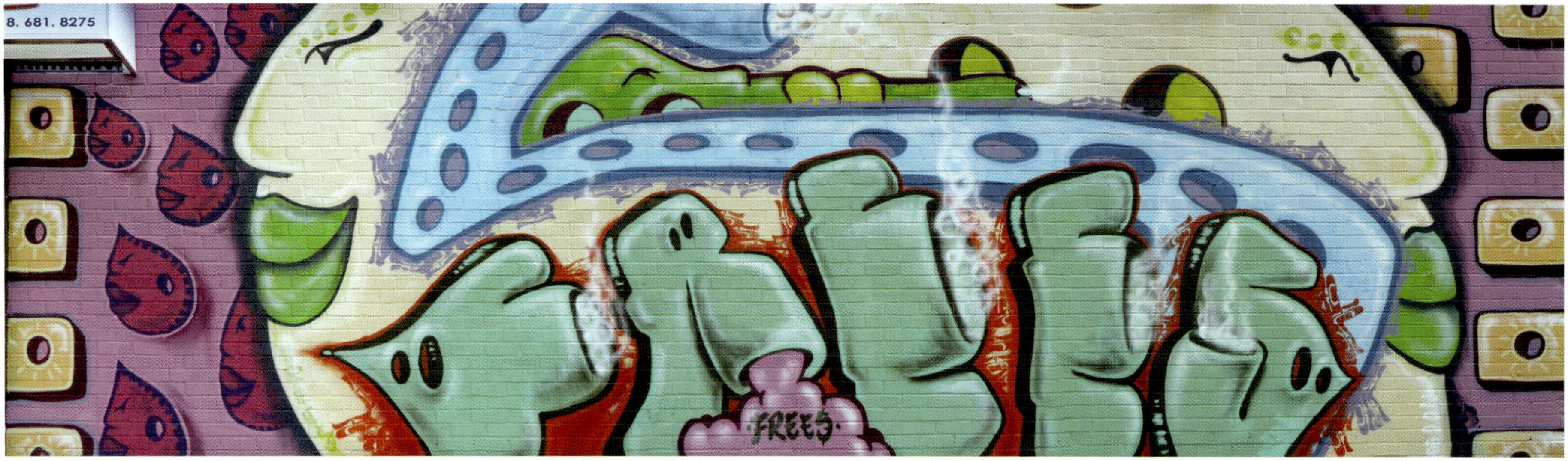

Free5, Bronx, NY

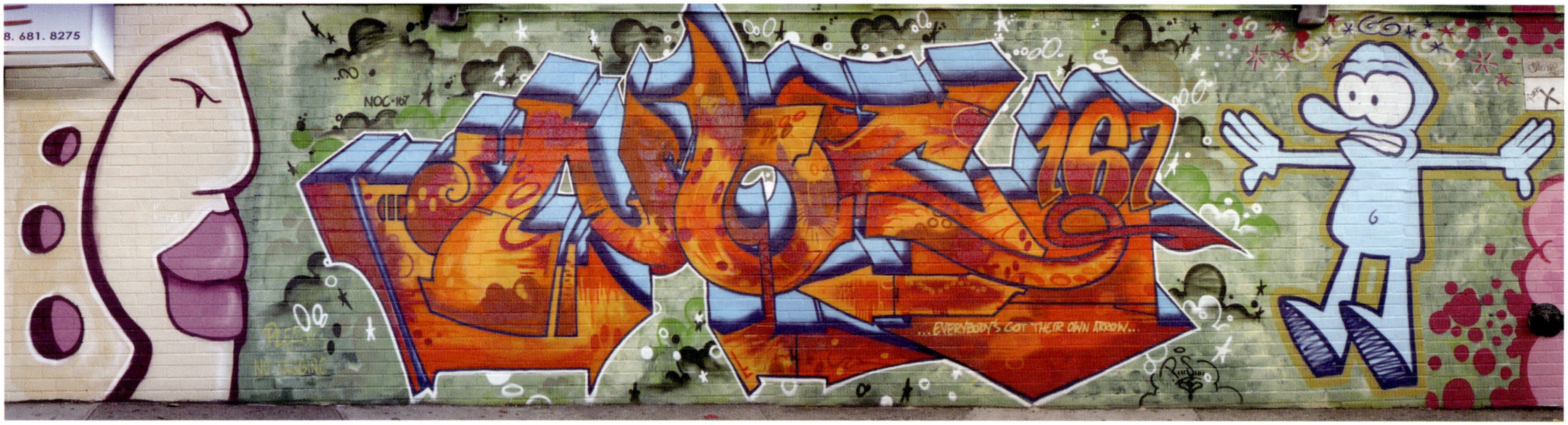

Noc167 (Smith), Bronx, NY

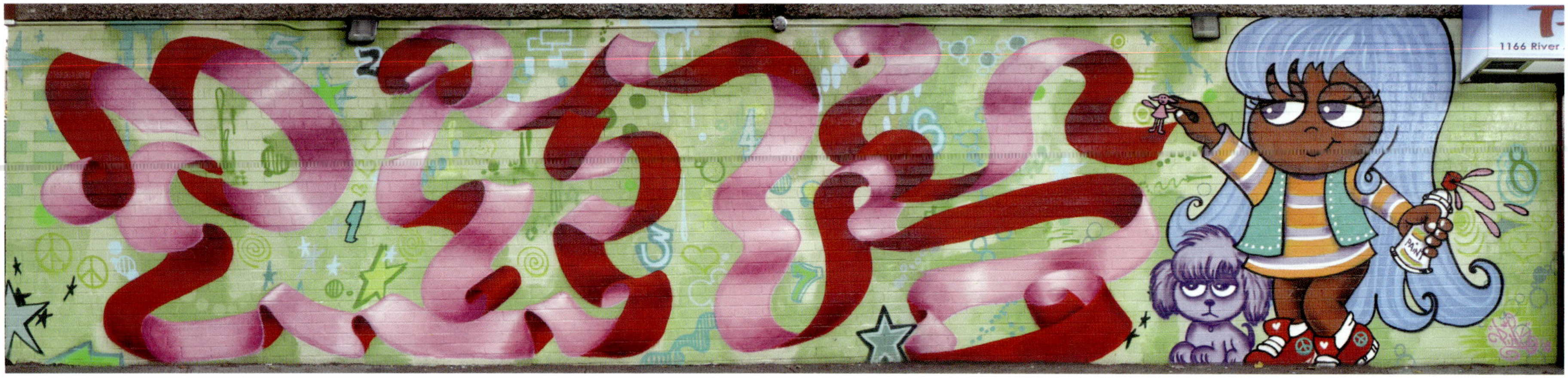

Lady Pink, Bronx, NY

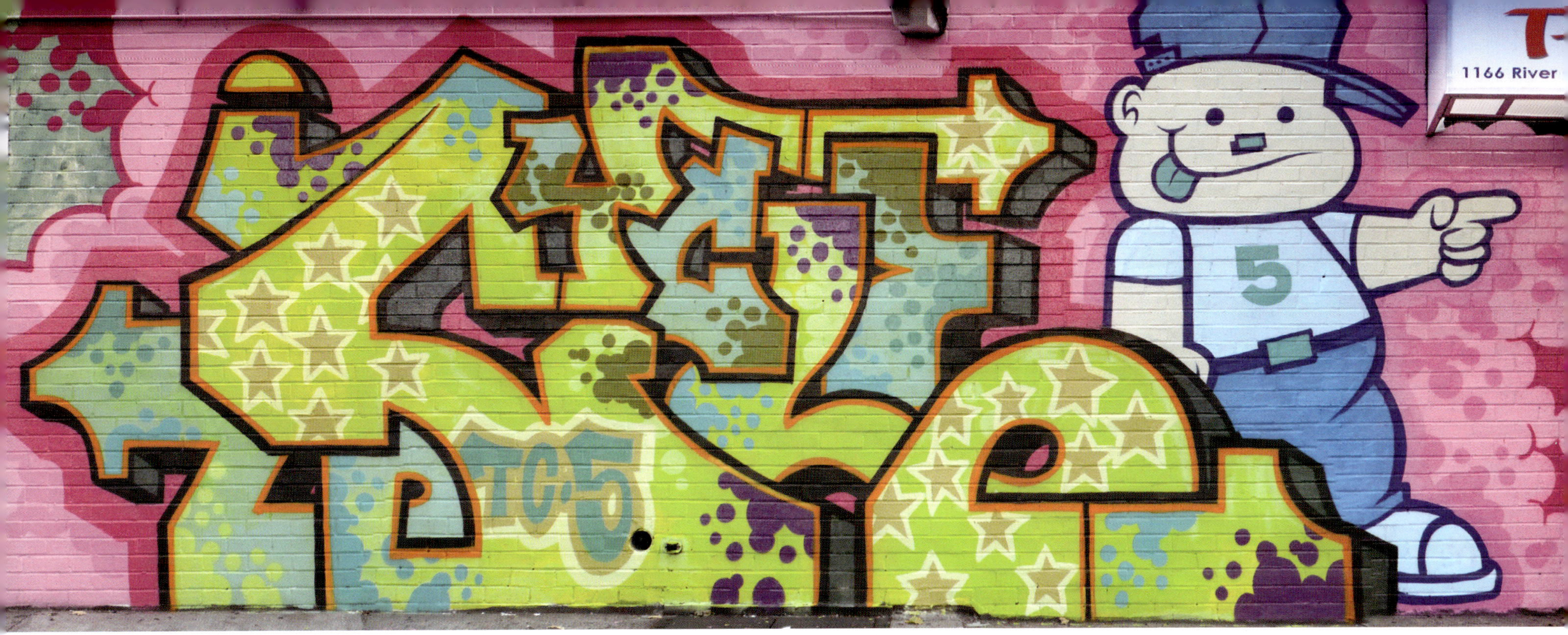


Cycle, Bronx, NY

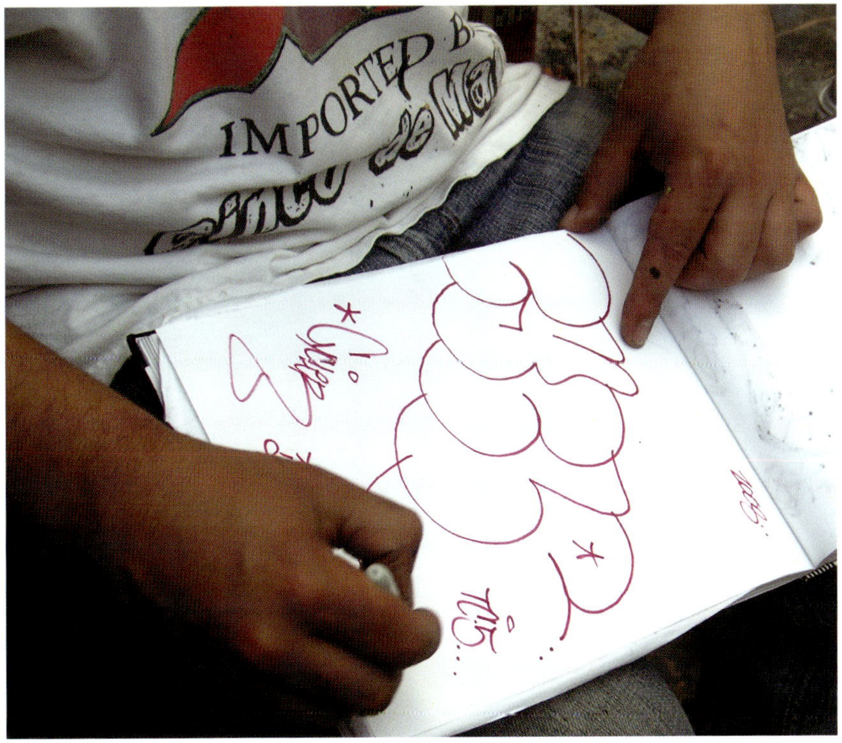


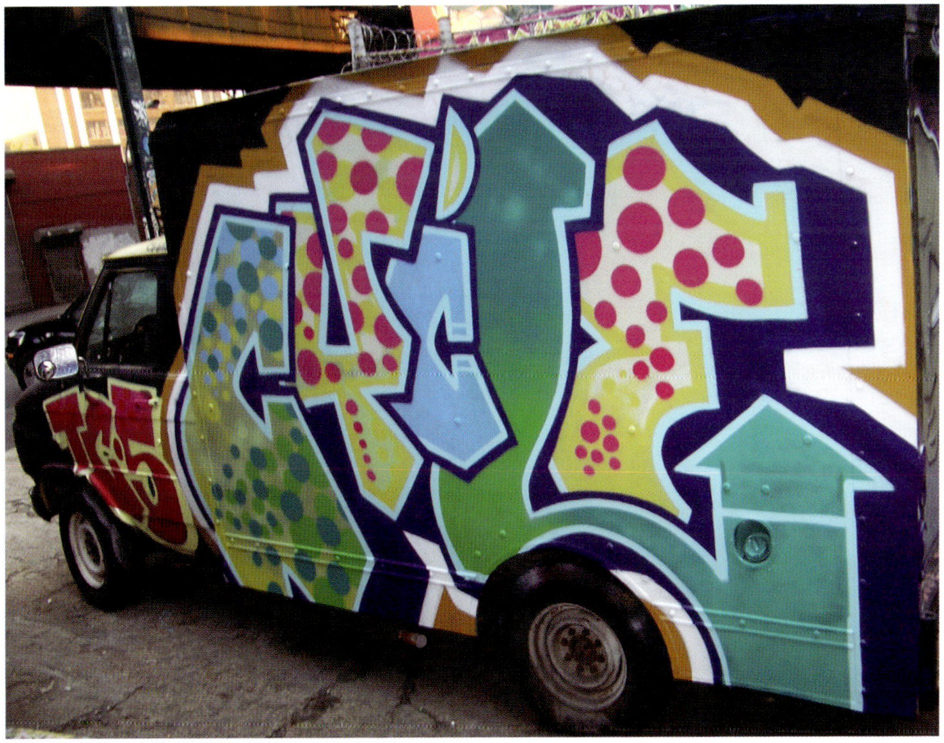

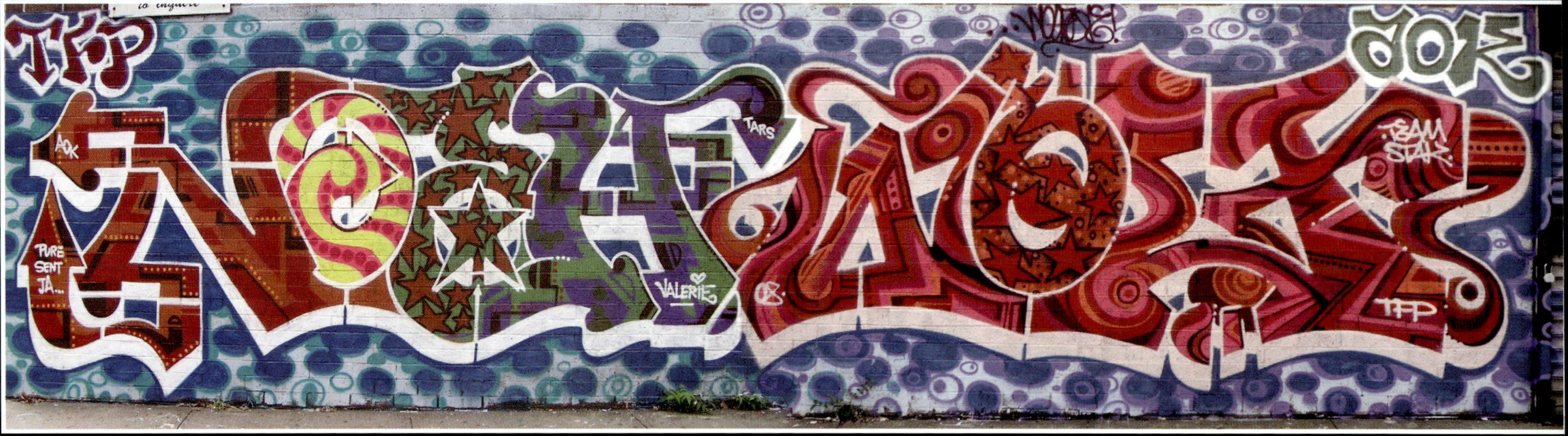

Noah, Wolf, Queens, NY

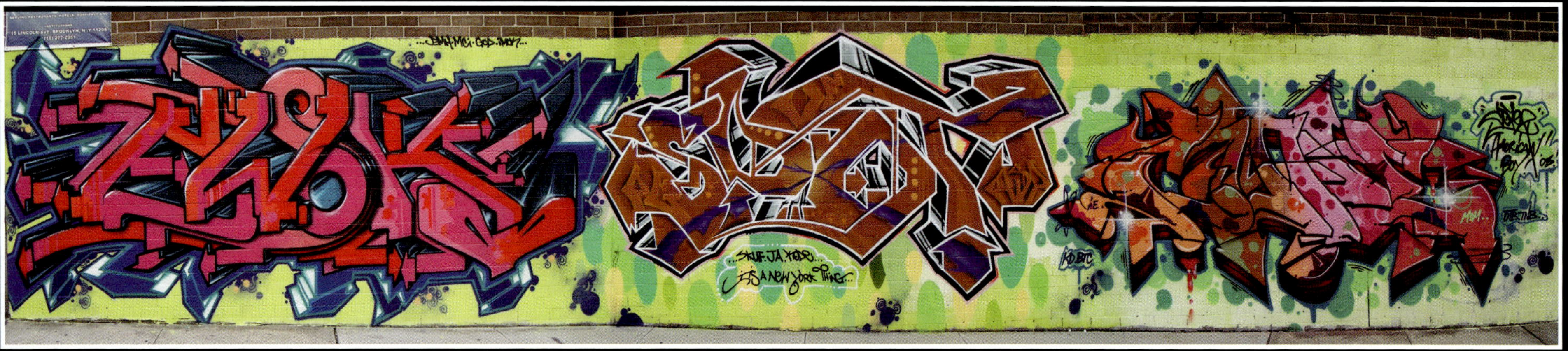

Ewok, Spot, Cope2, Queens, NY

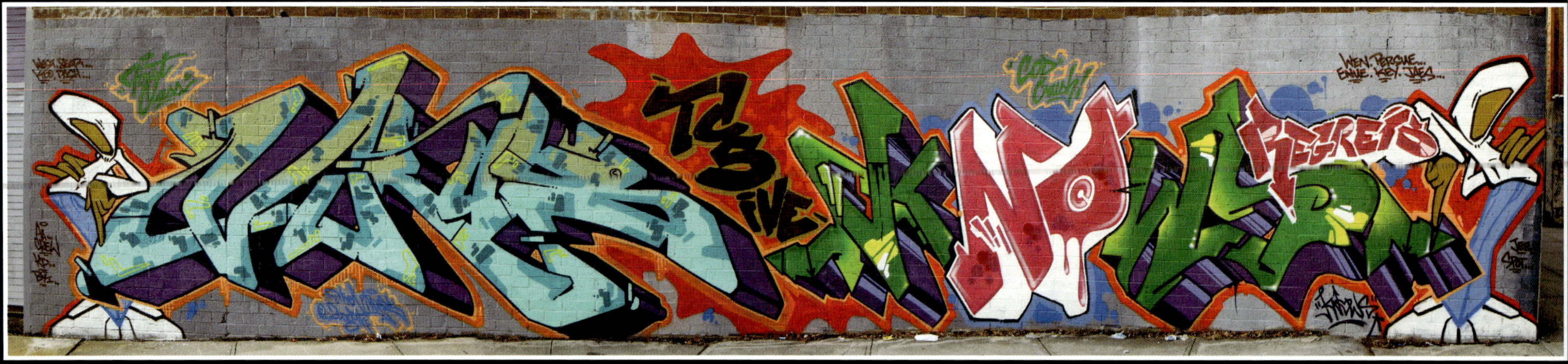

Virus, Knows, Queens, NY

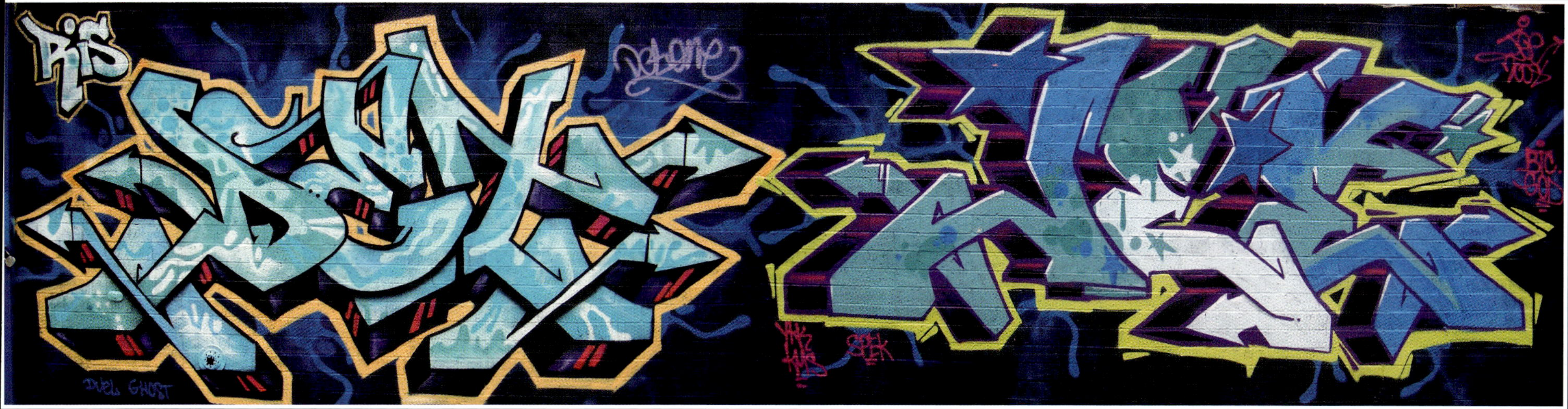

Det, Jee, Queens, NY

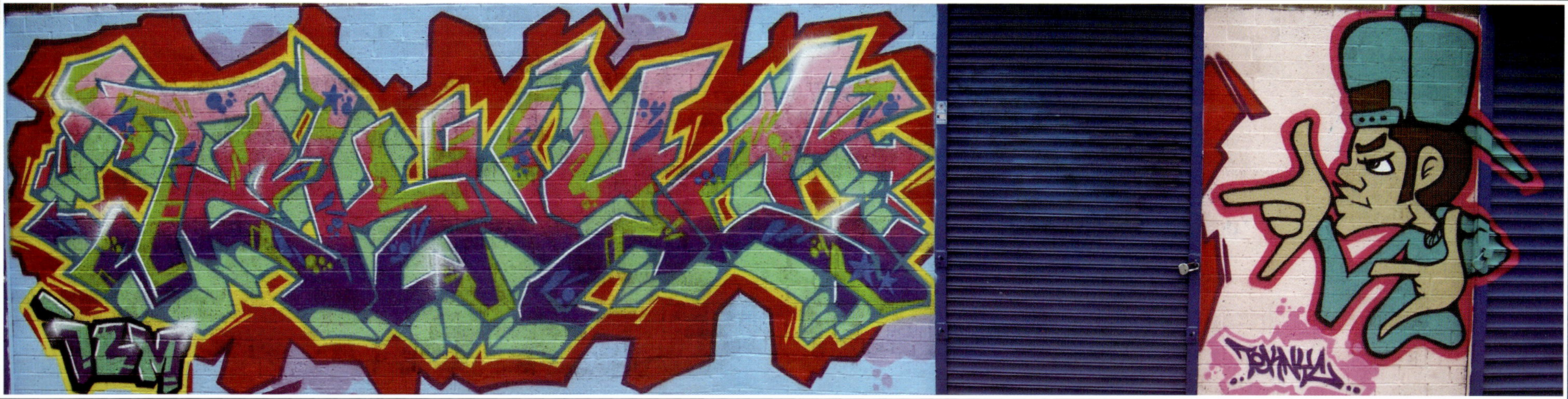

Teknyc, Queens, NY

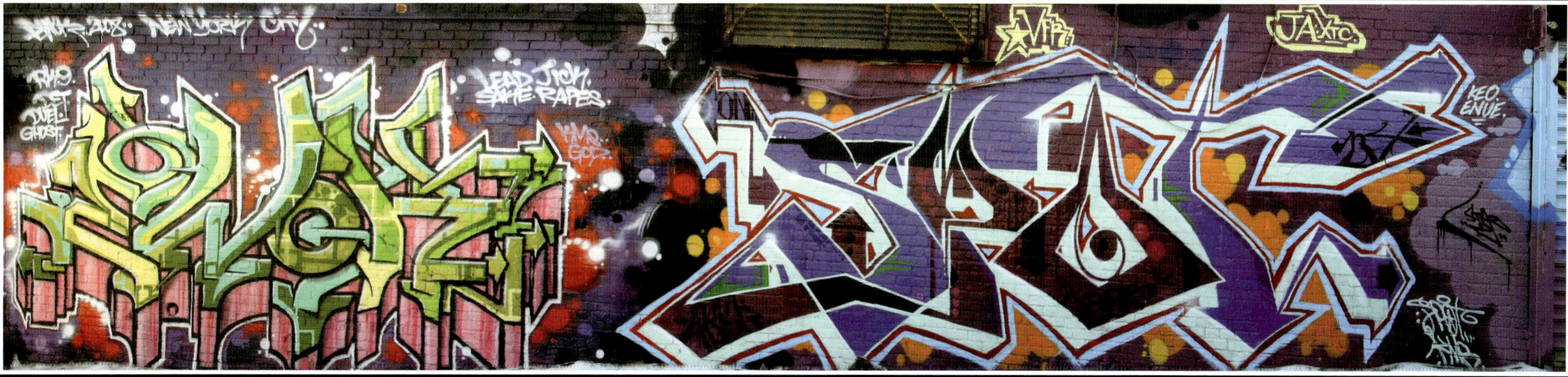

Ewok, Spot, Bronx, NY

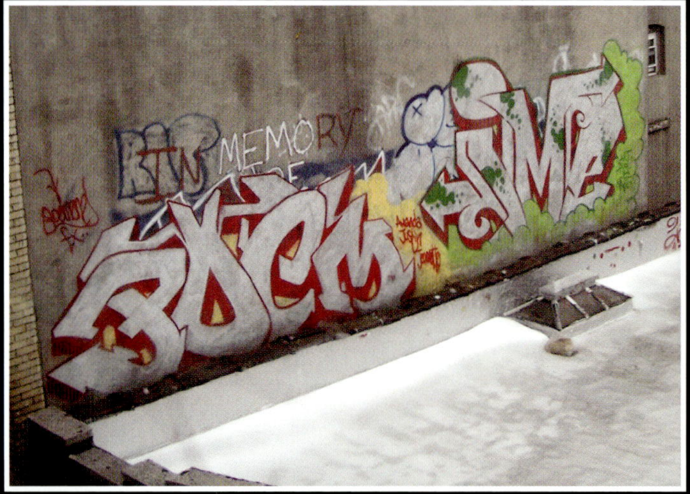

Poem, Brooklyn, NY

Per, Such, Bronx, NY

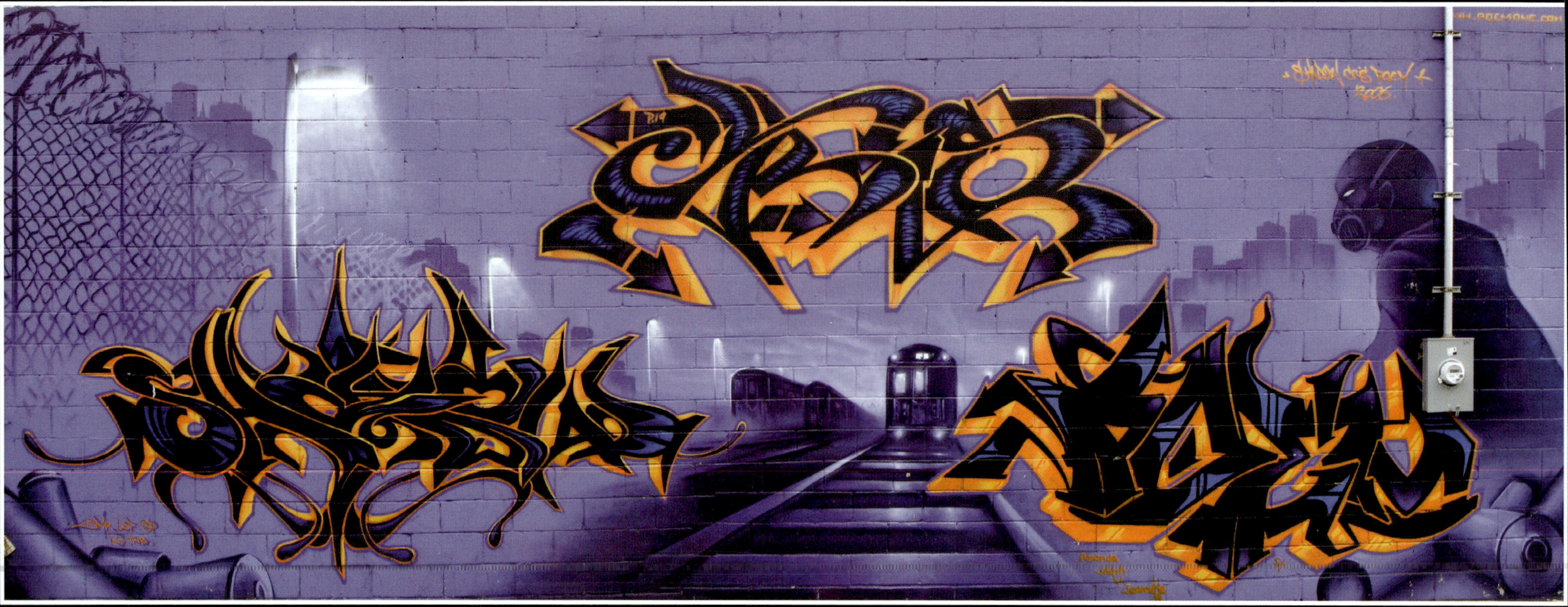

Cris, Shadow, Poem, Queens, NY

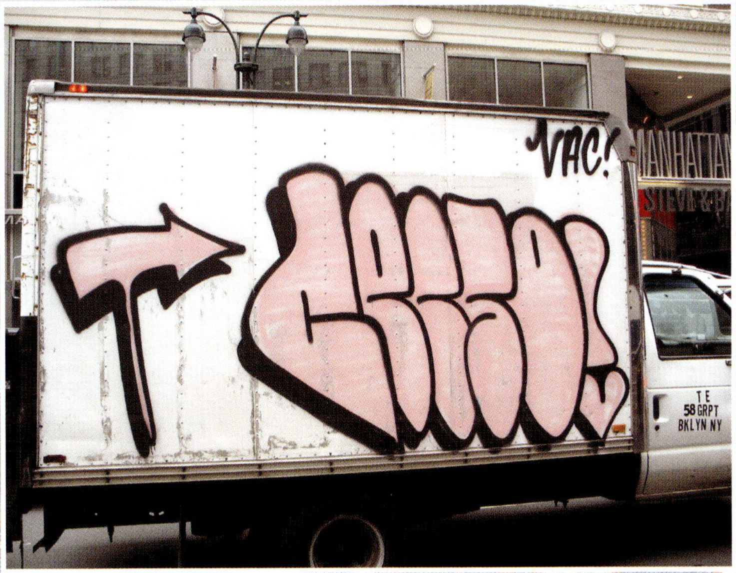

Cecs, 2006

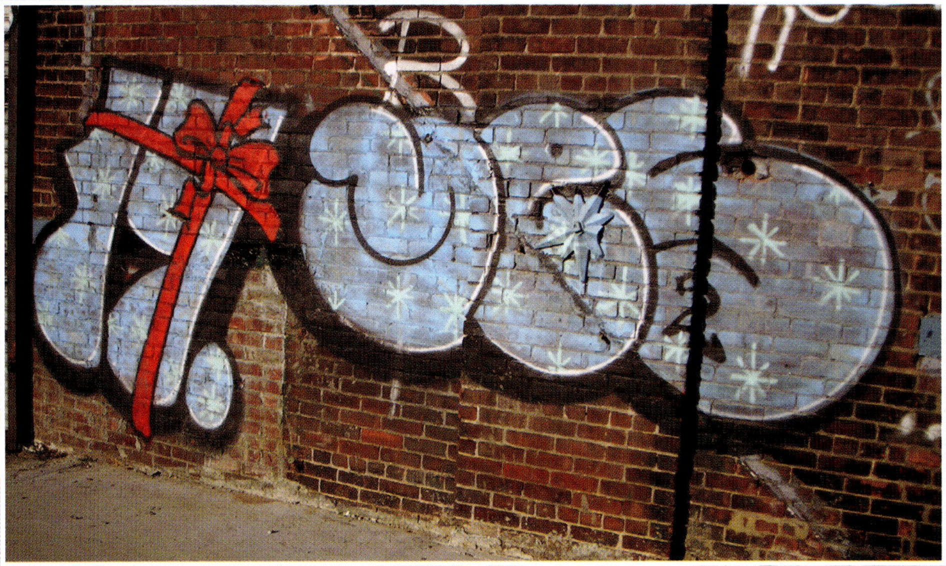

Miss17, Yes2, 2006

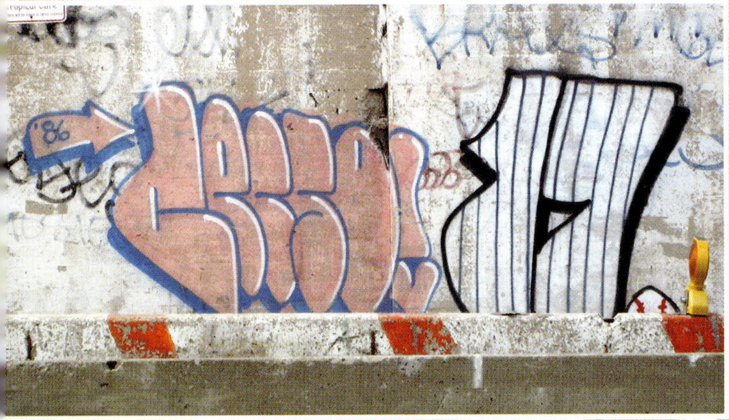

Cecs, Miss17, 2006

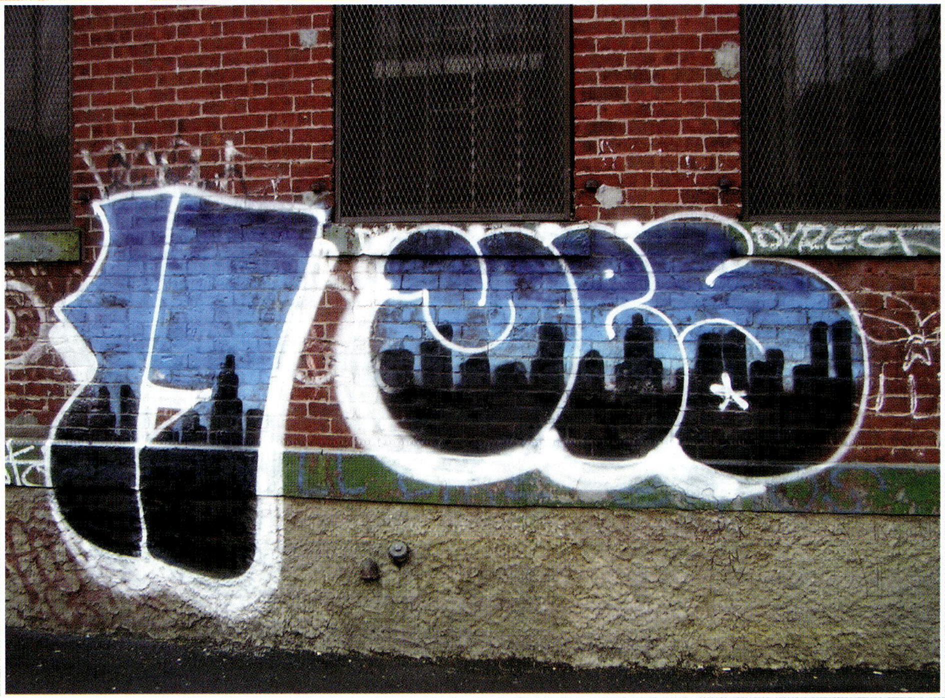

Miss17, Yes2, 2006

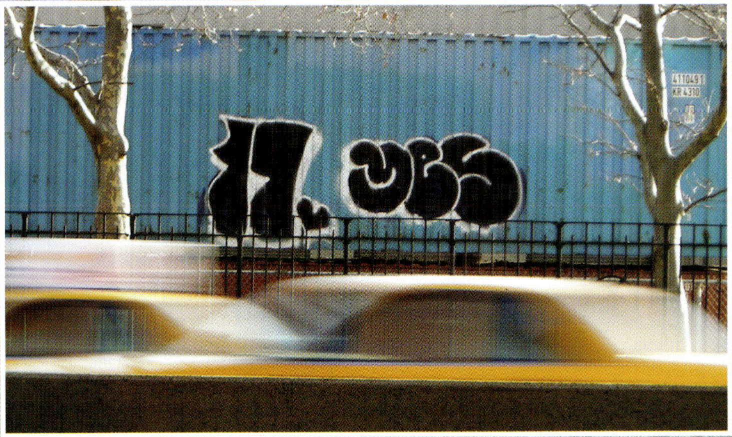

Miss17, Yes2, 2006

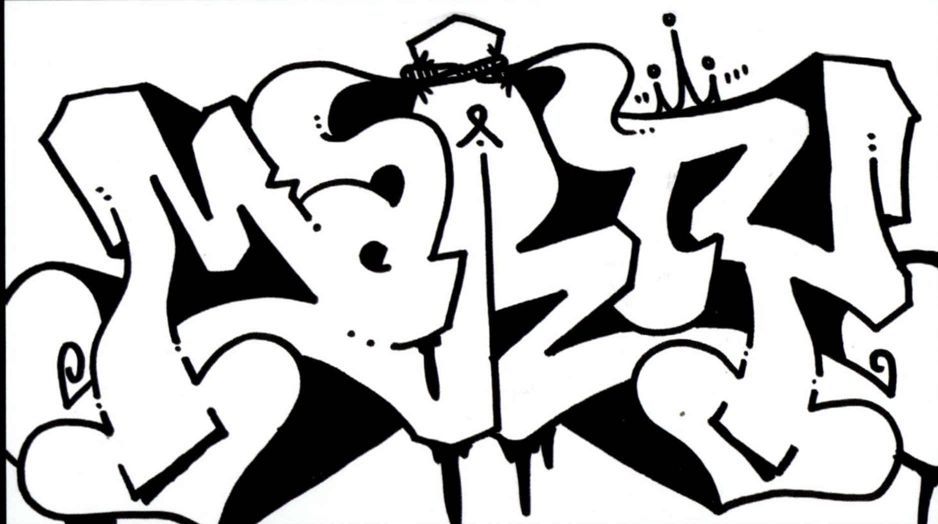

Marty–Outline, 2007

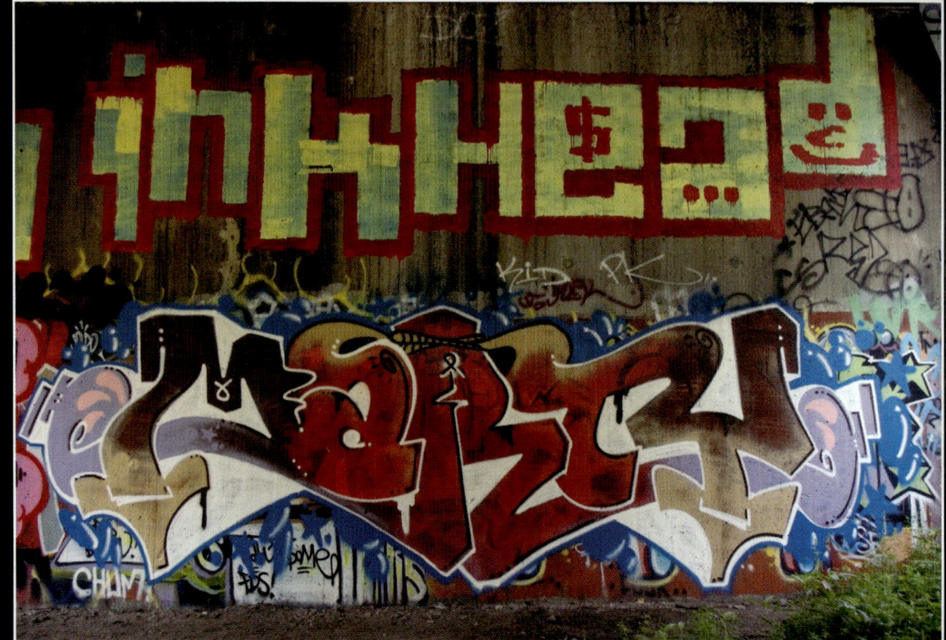

Marty–Inkhead, New Jersey

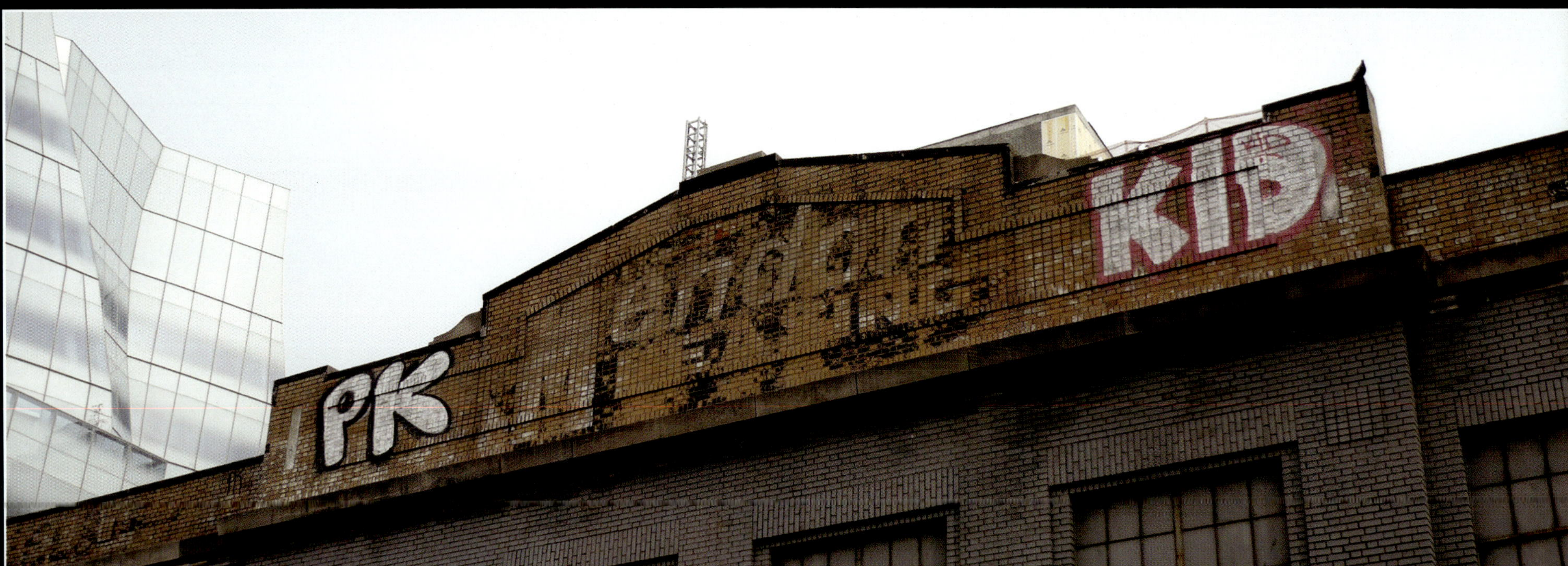


PK, KID, New York, NY

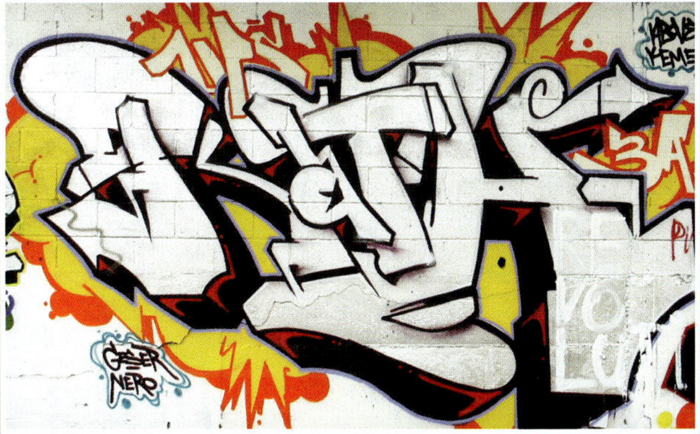

Rath, New Jersey

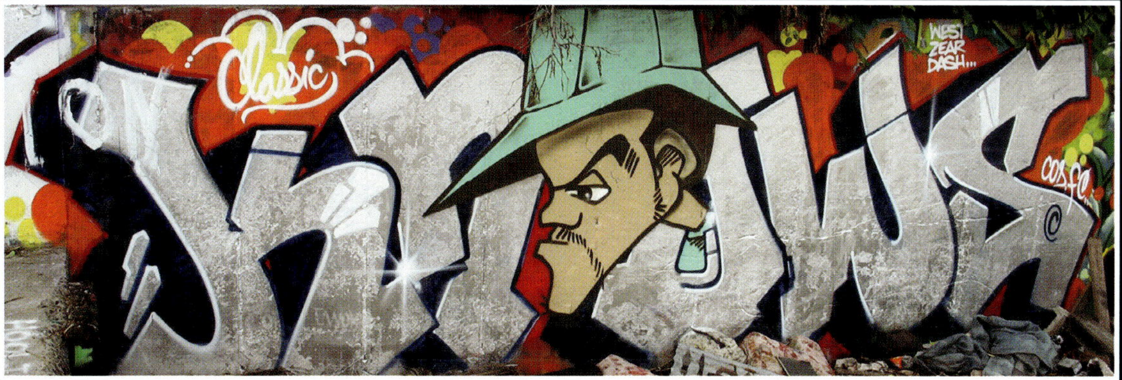

Knows, New Jersey

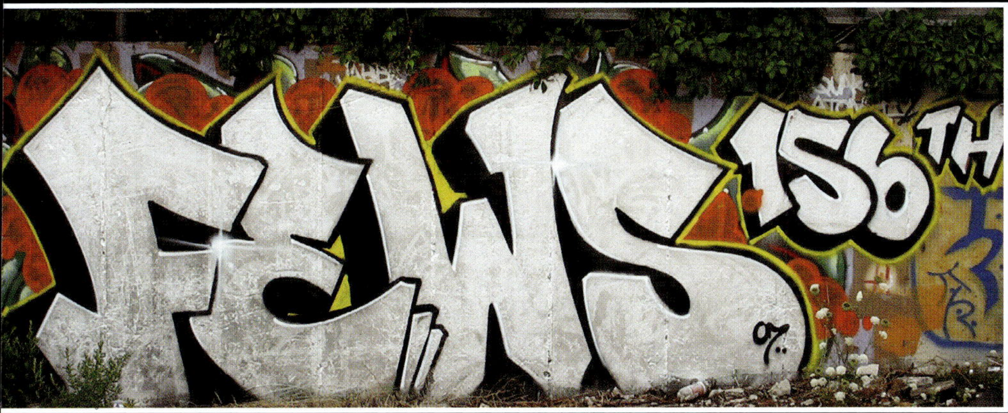

ws, New Jersey

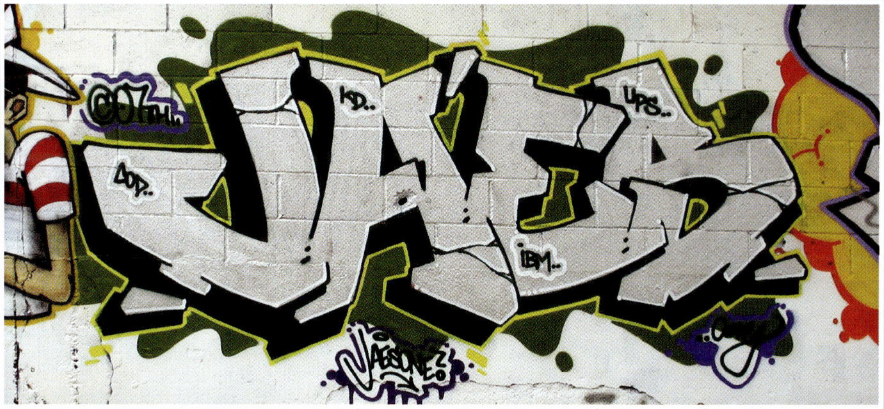

Jaes, New Jersey

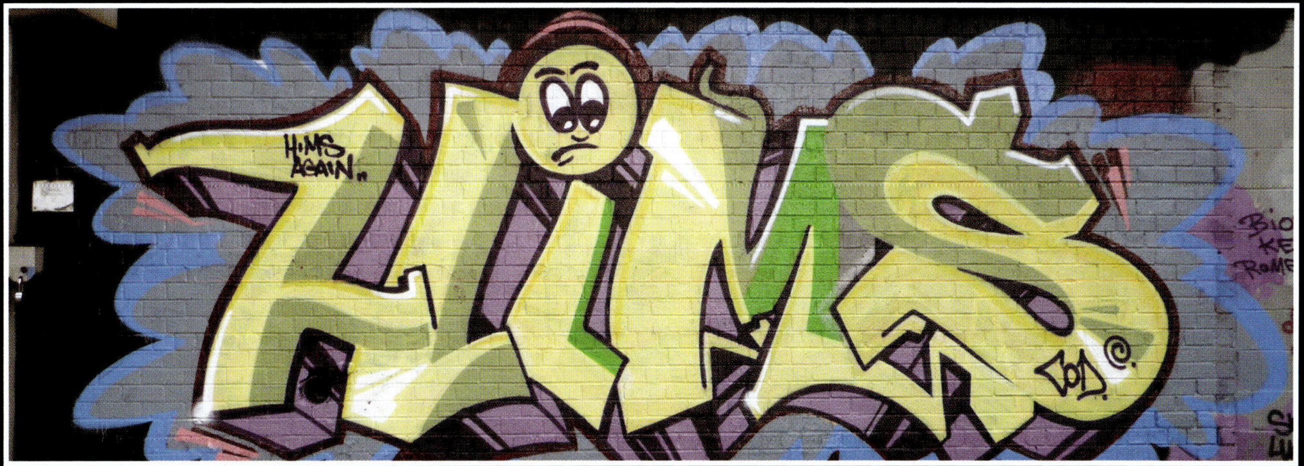

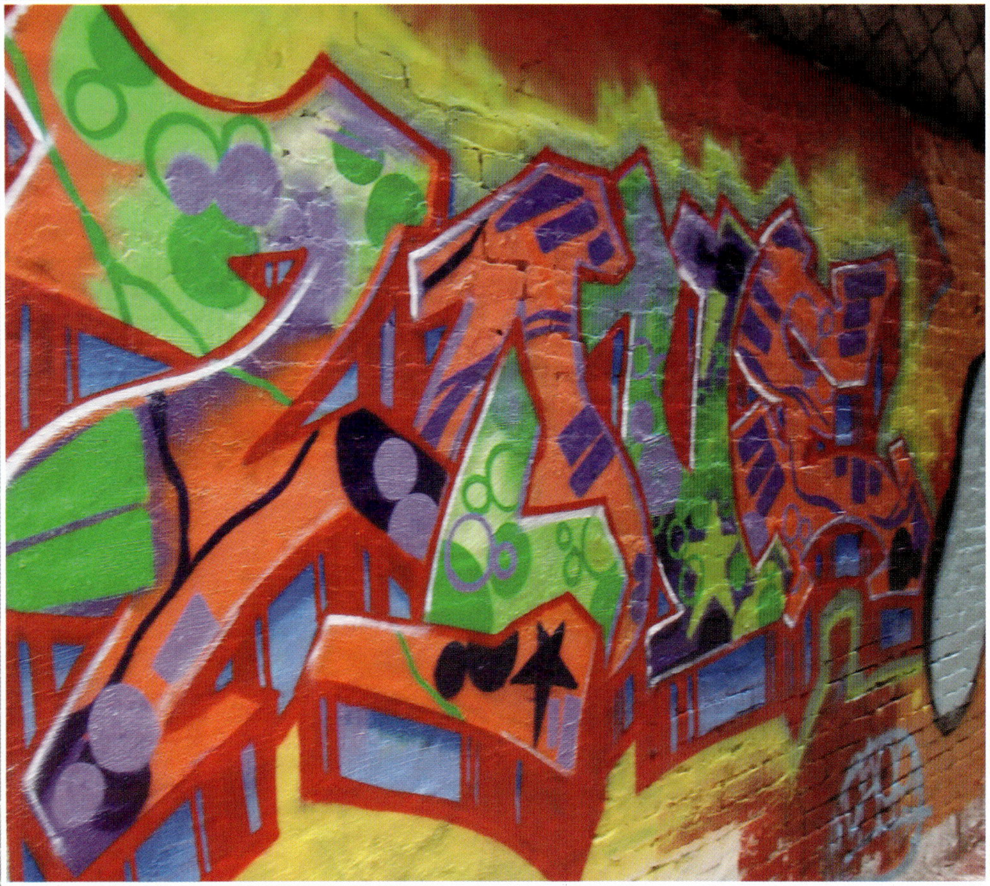

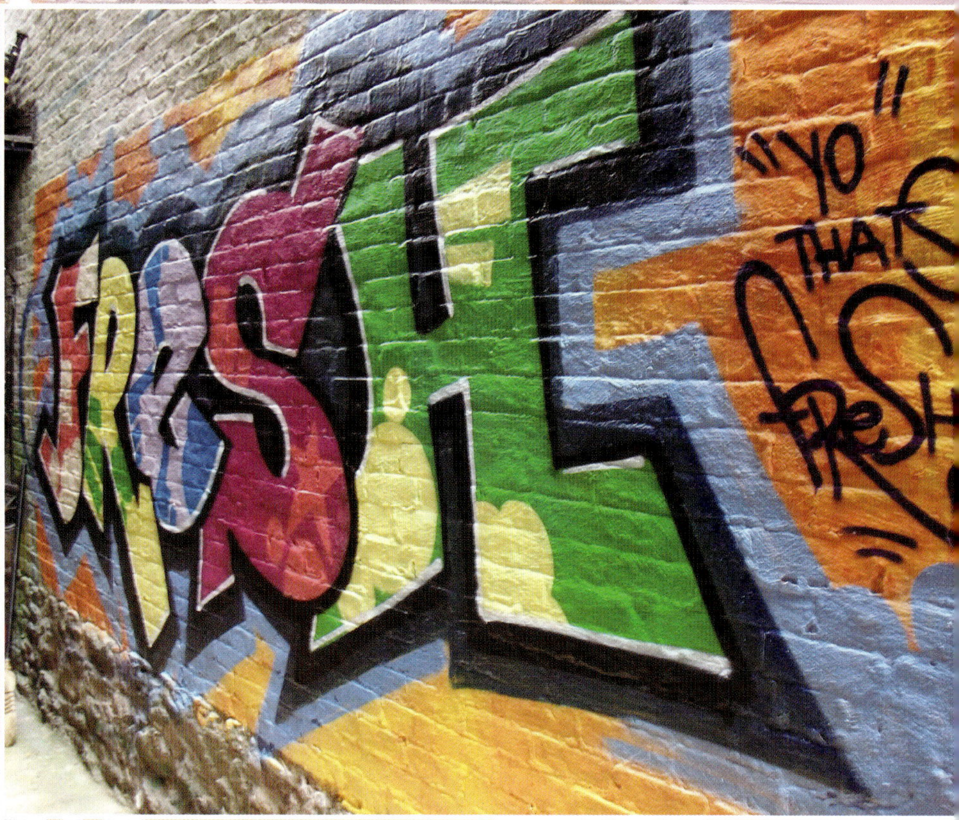
FRESH
"YO"
FRESH

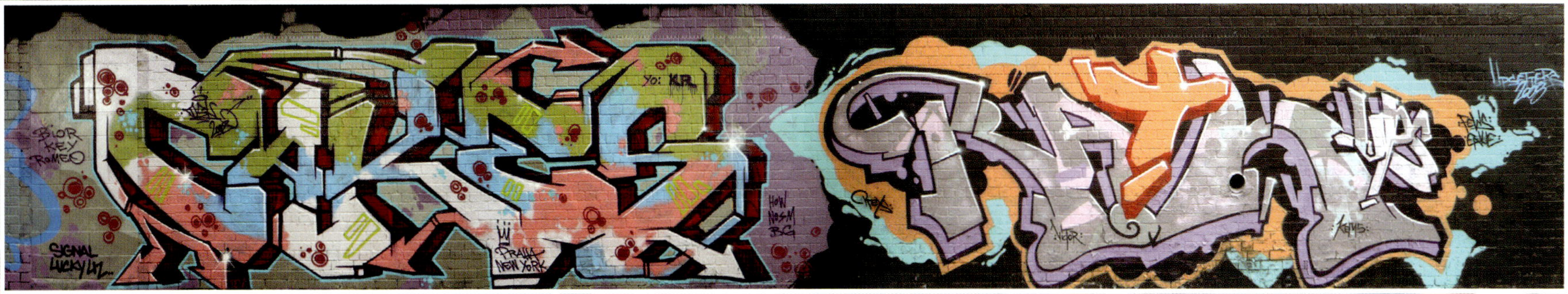
Cakes, Rath, Queens, NY

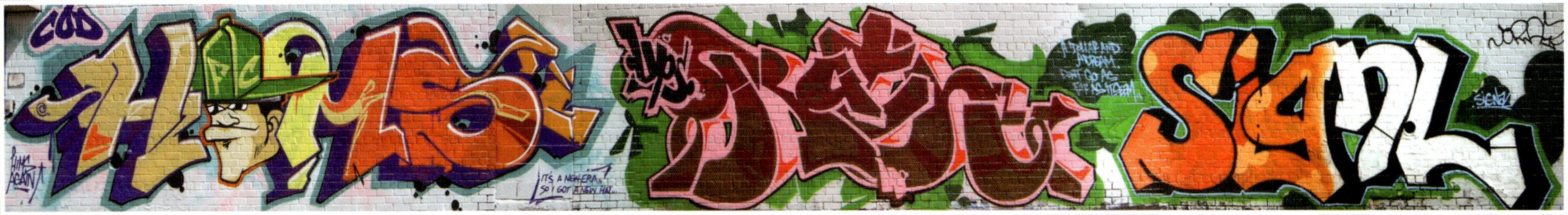
Hims, Rath, Signl, Queens, NY

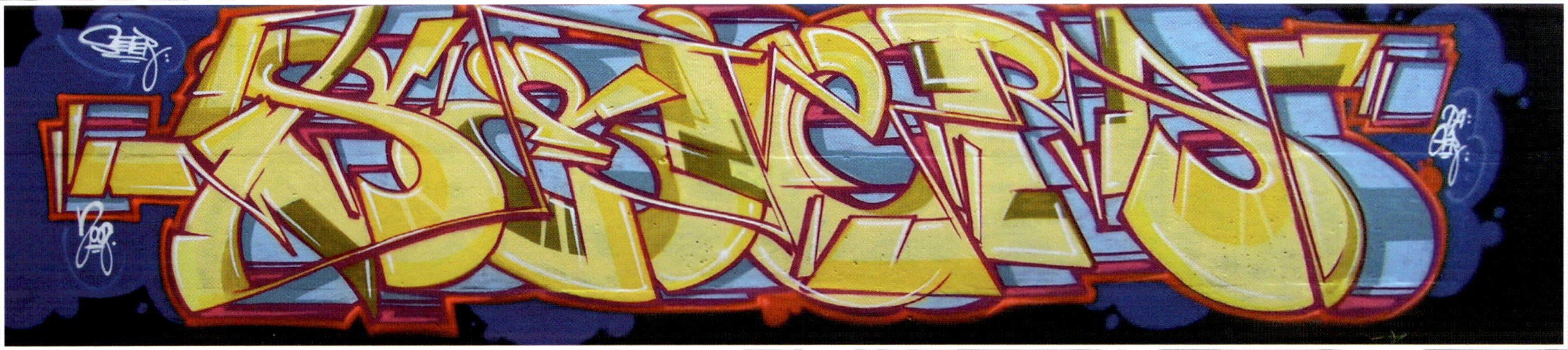
Seter, Brooklyn, NY

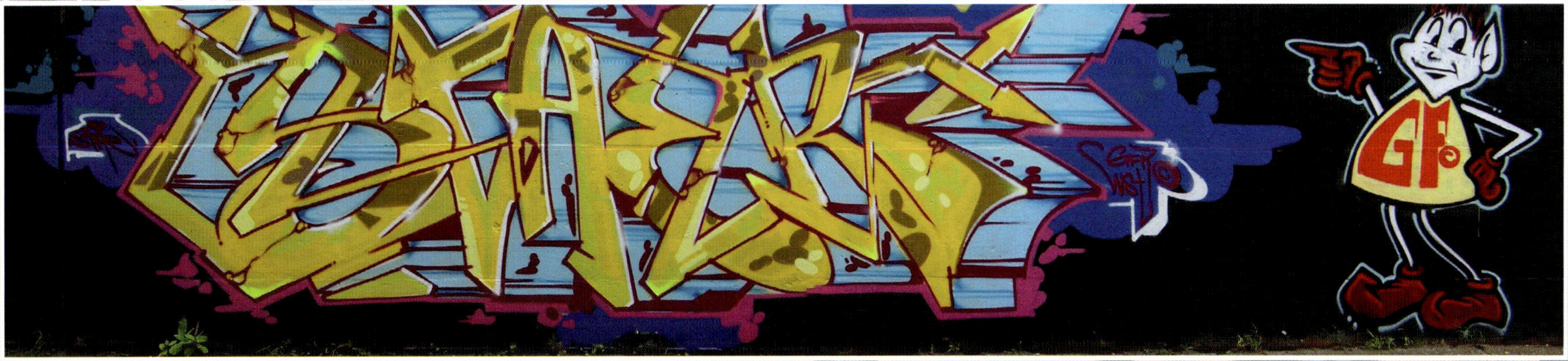
Stae2, Brooklyn, NY

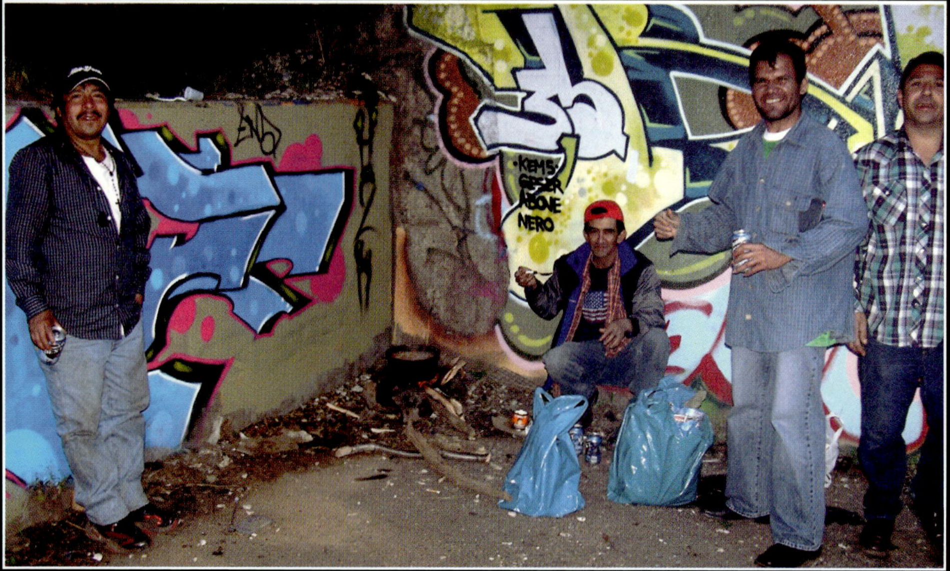

Rath, New Jersey

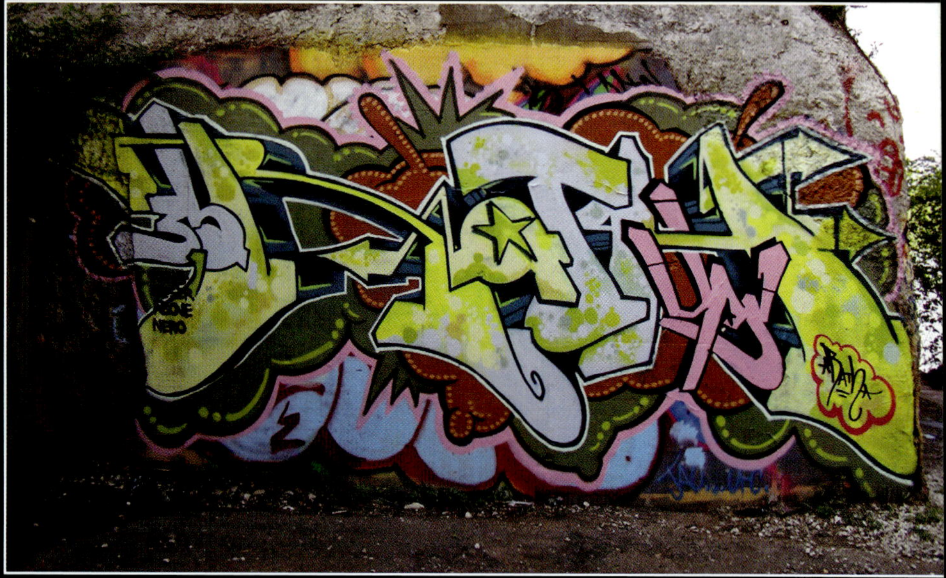

Rath, New Jersey

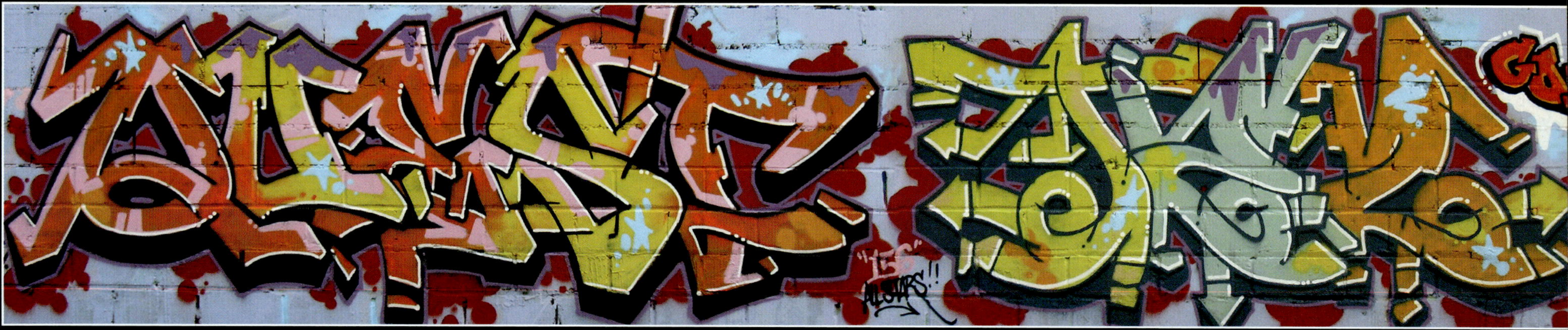

Ques, Jez, Bronx, NY

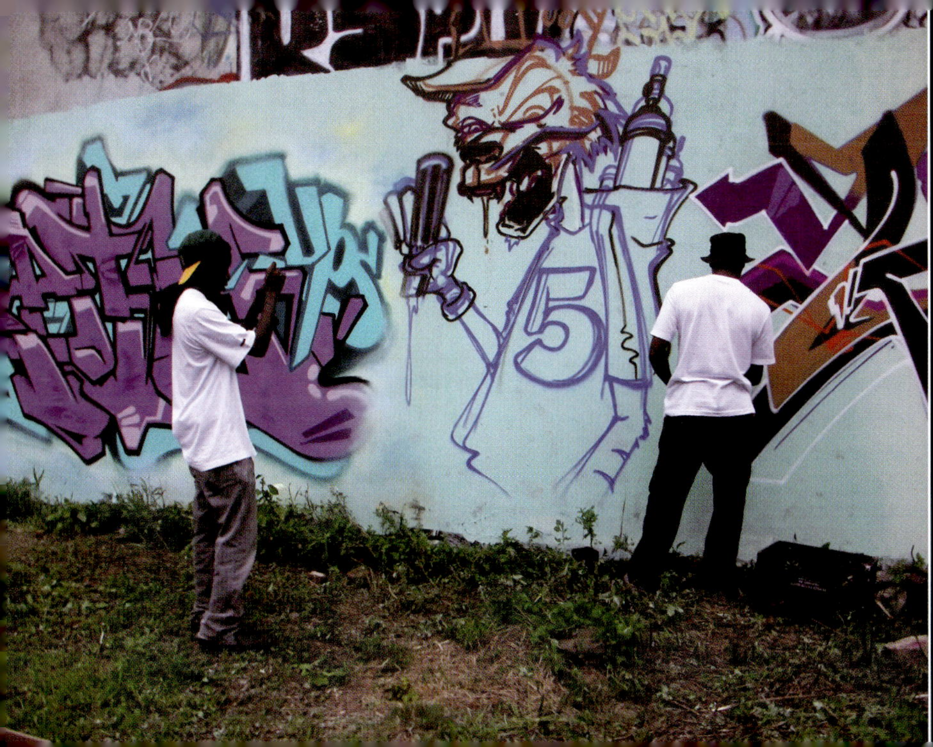

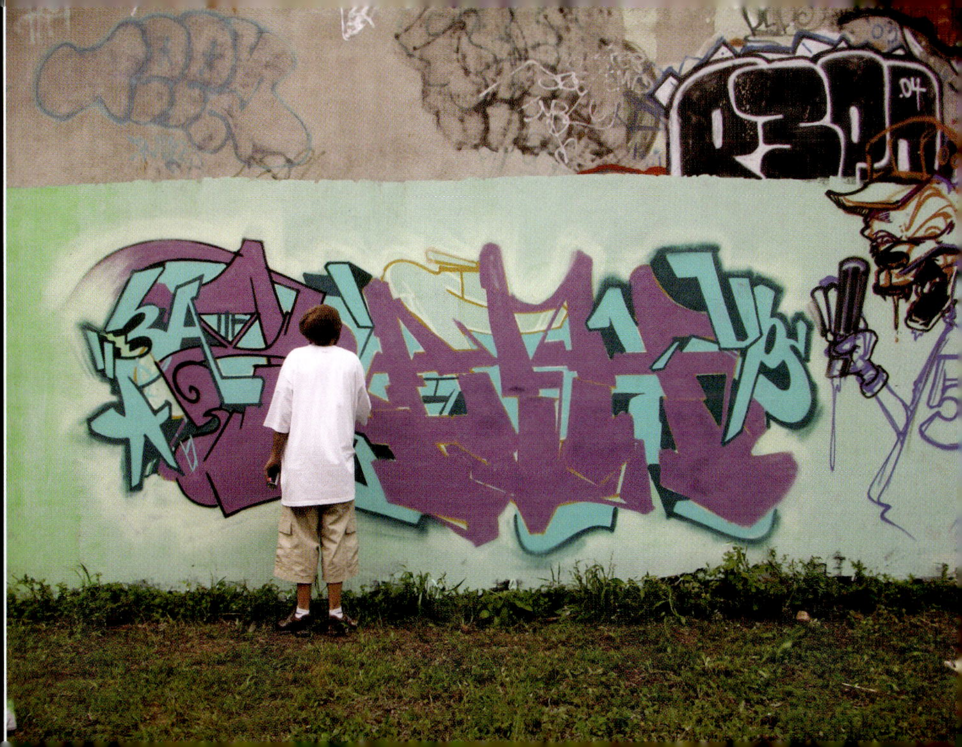

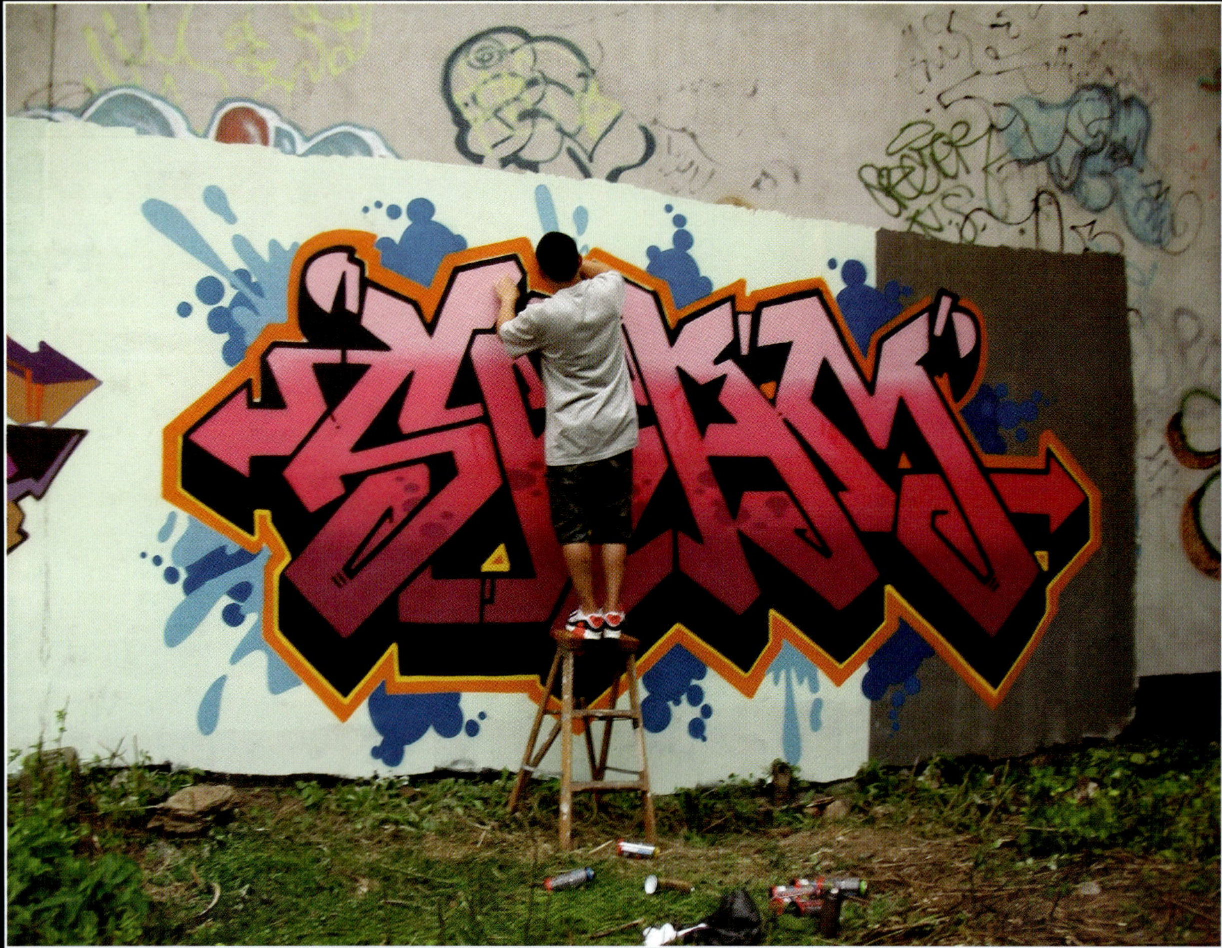

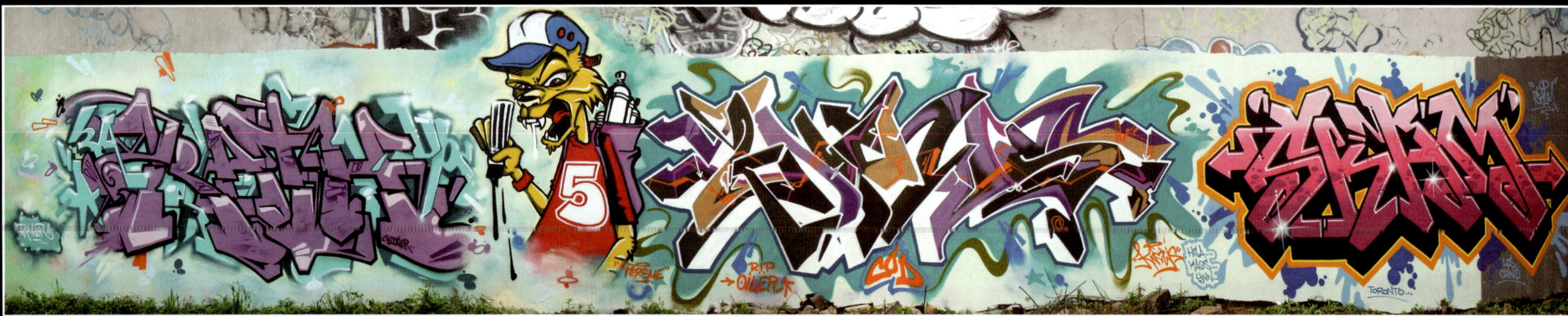

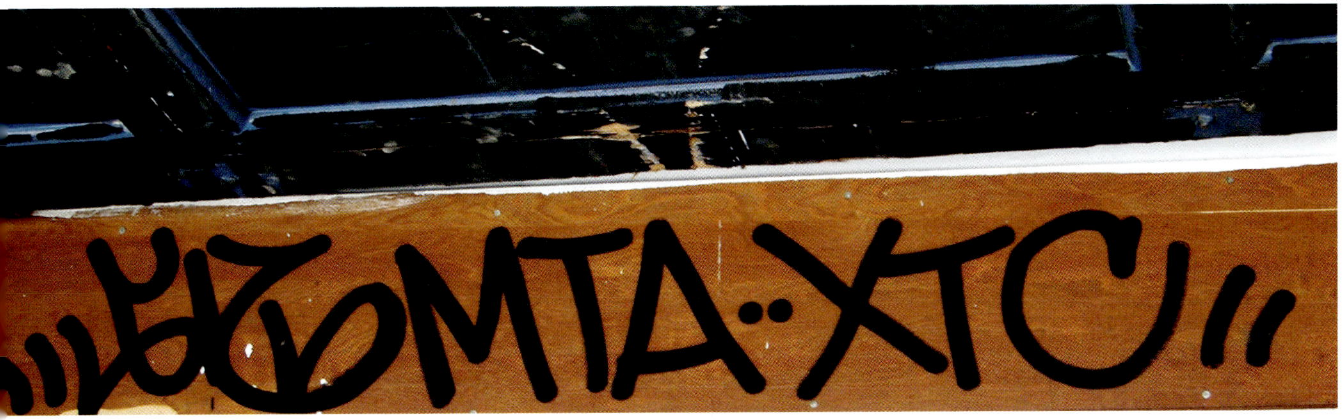
MTA-XTC

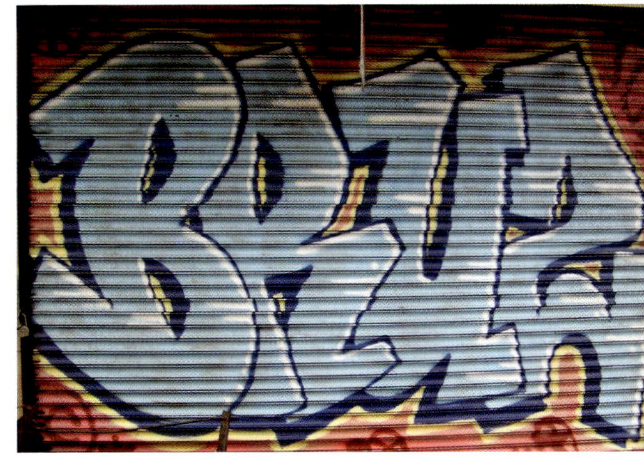

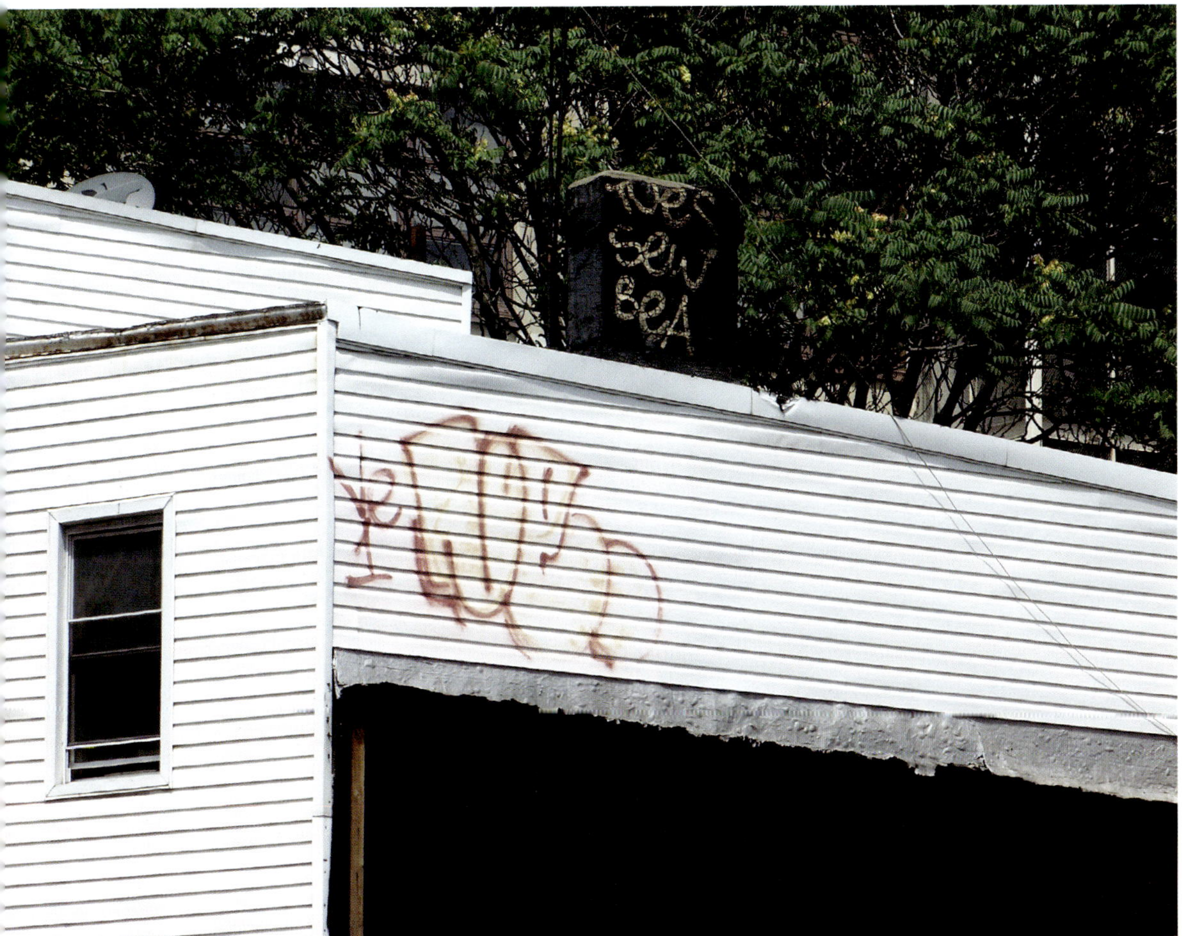

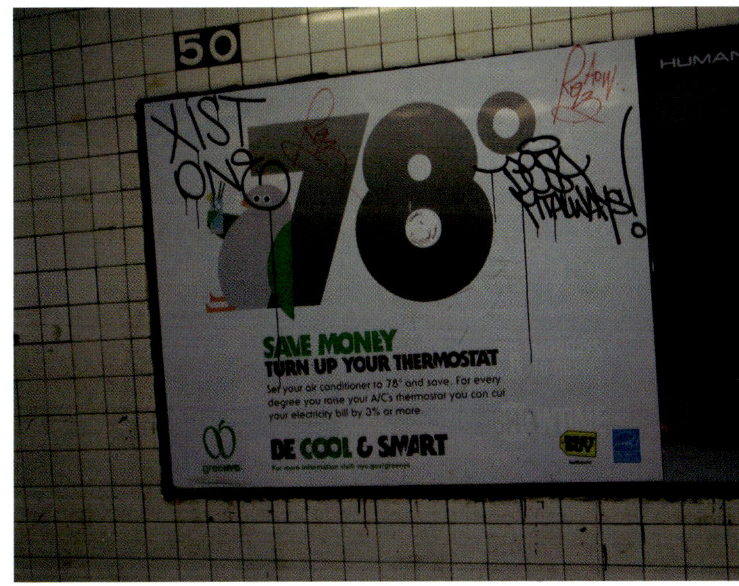
50
78°
SAVE MONEY
TURN UP YOUR THERMOSTAT
Set your air conditioner to 78° and save. For every degree you raise your A/C's thermostat you can cut your electricity bill by 3% or more.
BE COOL & SMART

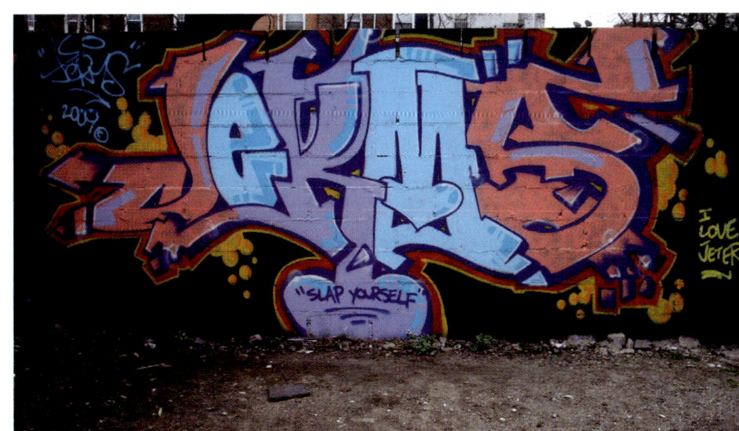
"SLAP YOURSELF"
I LOVE JETER

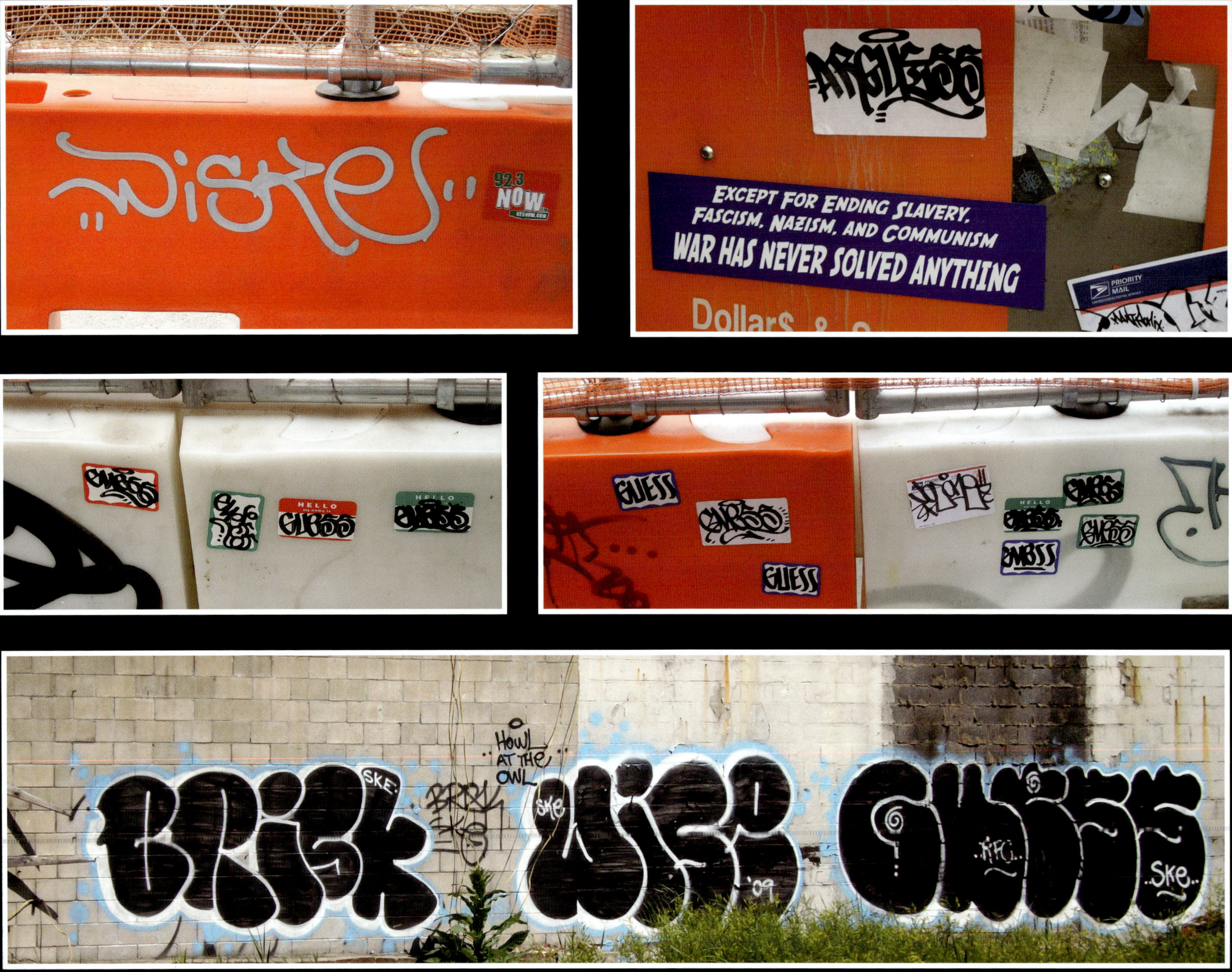


Brisk, Wise, Guess, Manhattan, NY

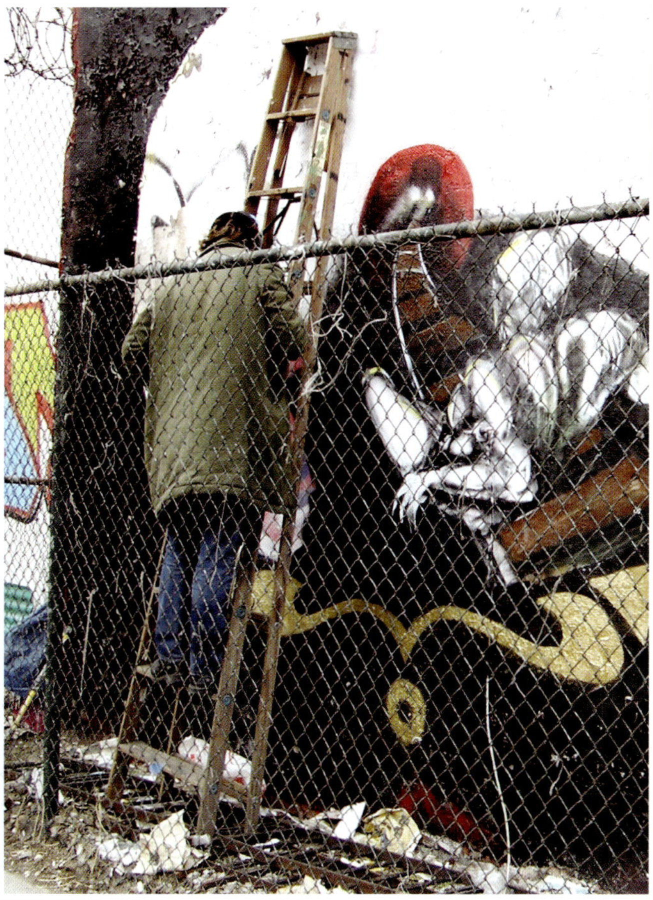

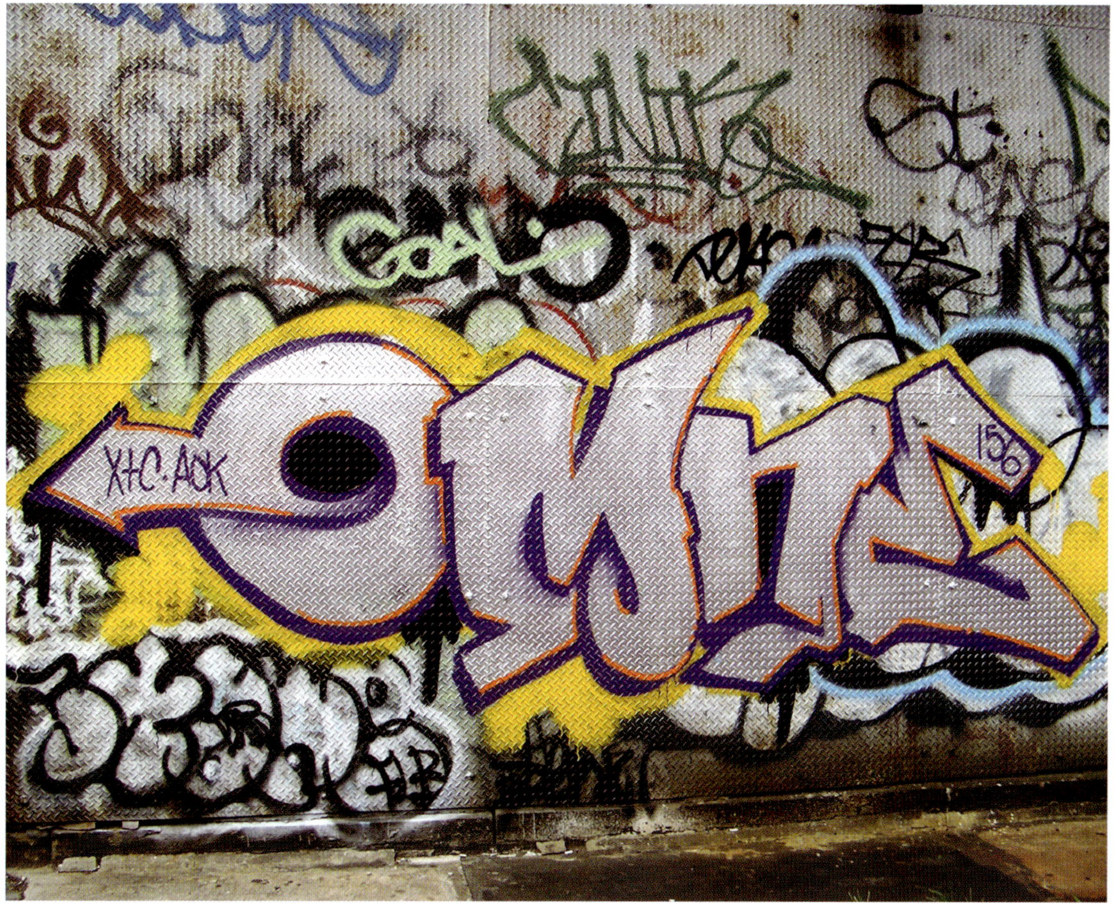


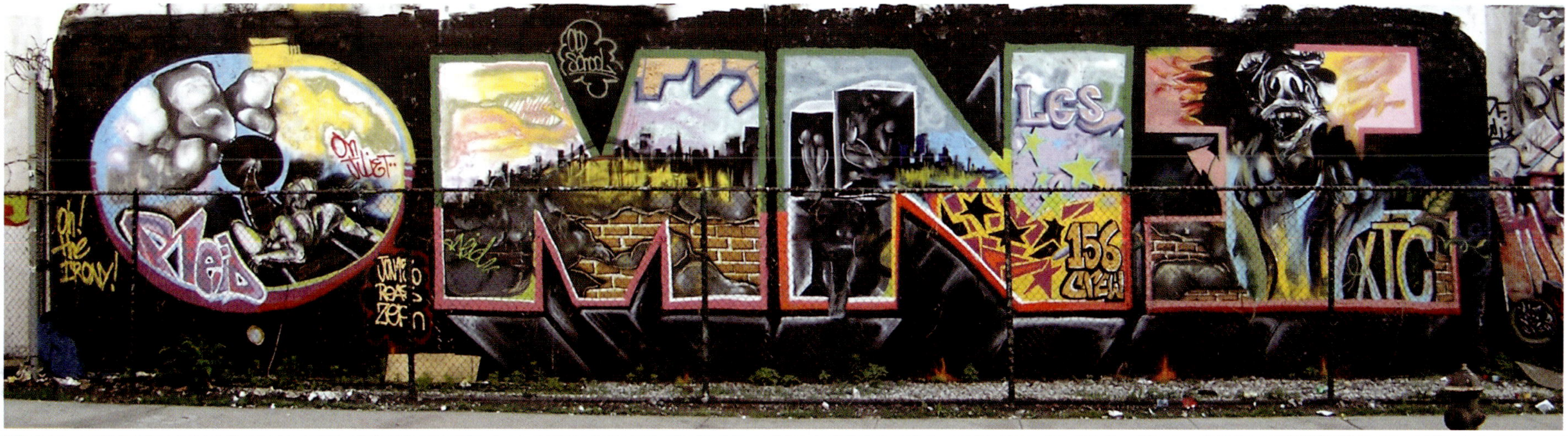


Omni, Manhattan, NY

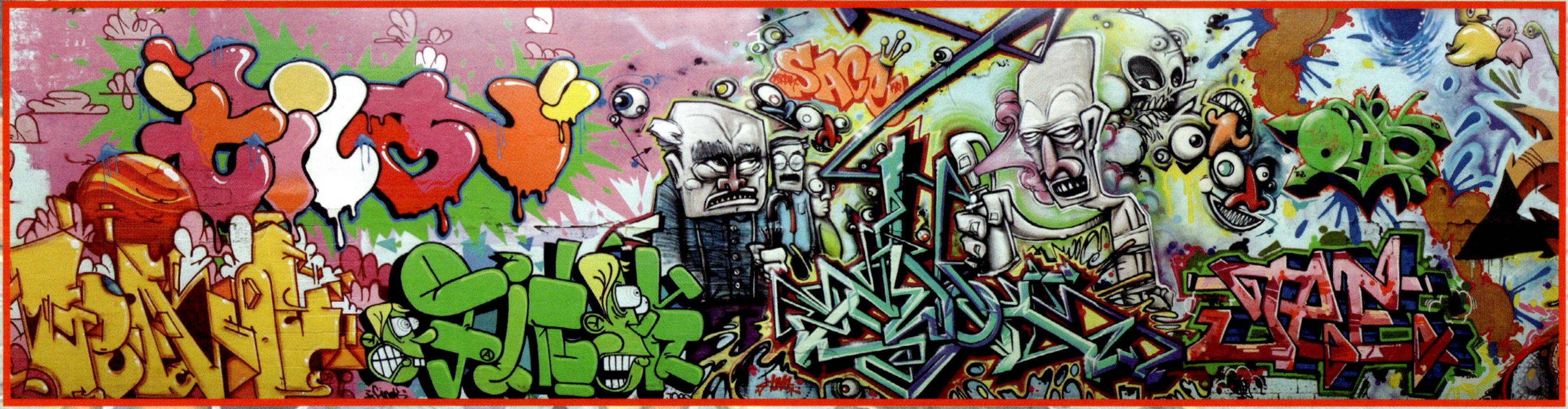

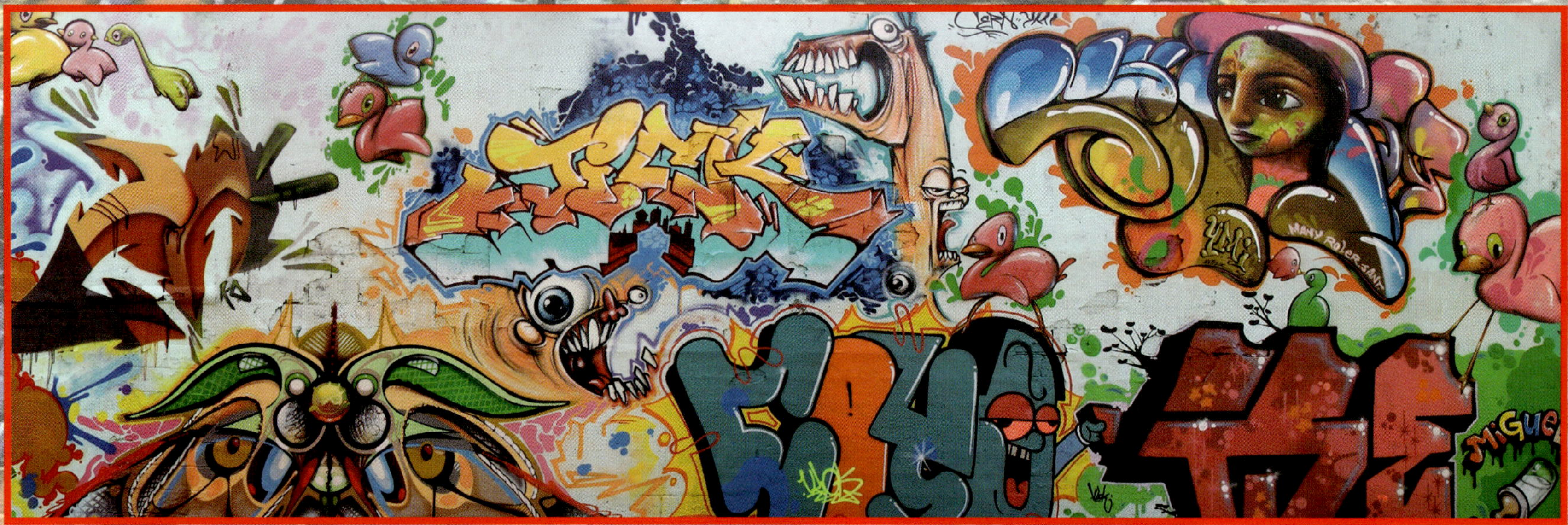

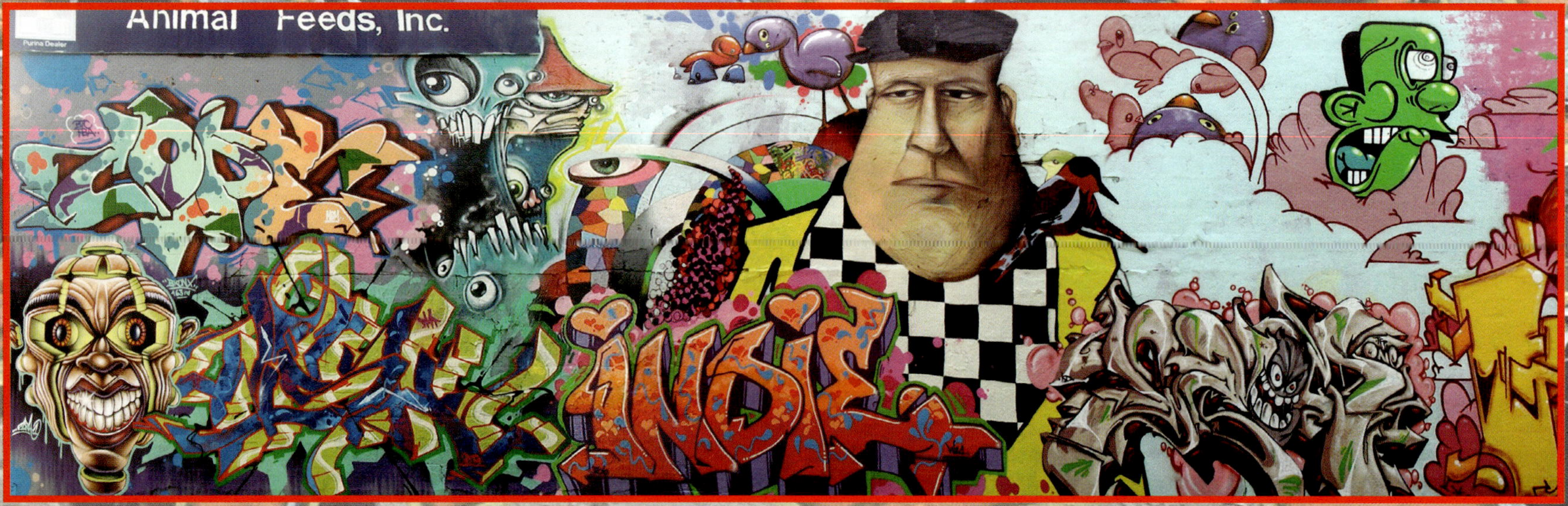
Animal Feeds, Inc.

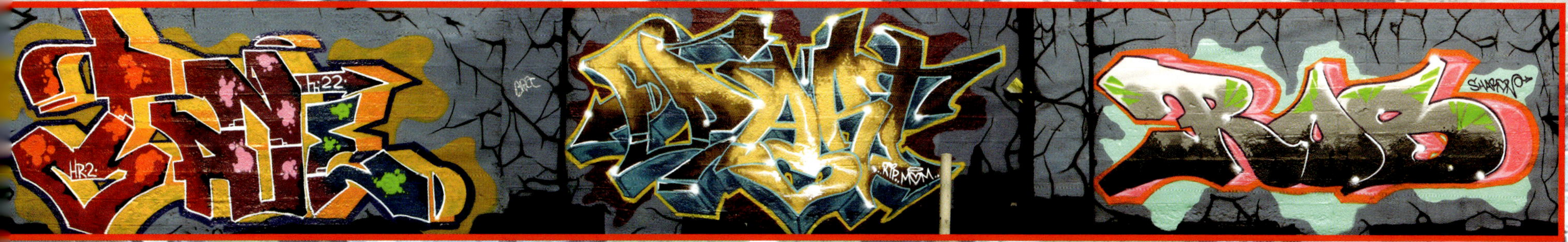

Pane22, Part, Ros, Long Island, NY

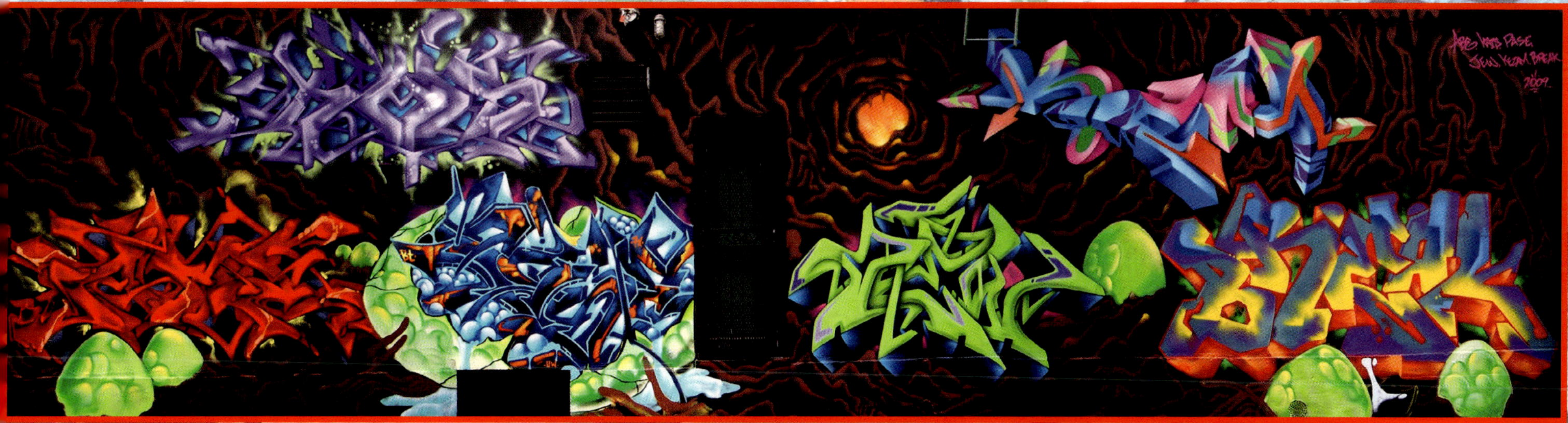

Abe, Kais, Pase, Jew, Kezam, Break, Brooklyn, NY

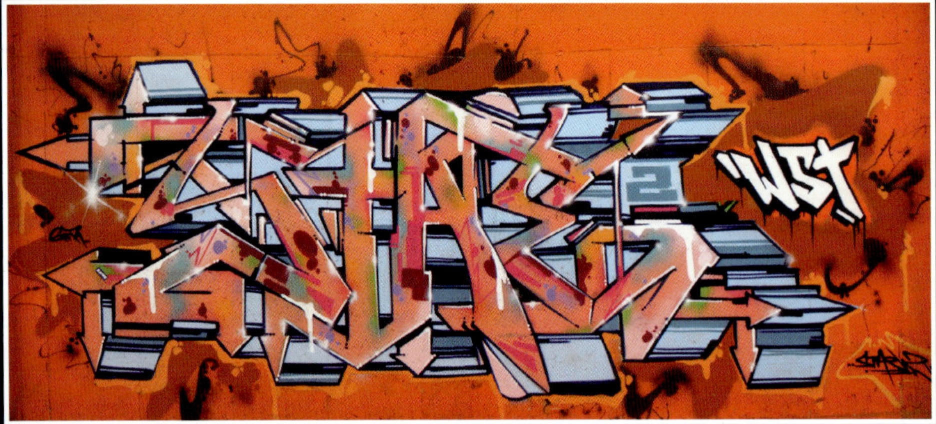


Stae2, Long Island, NY

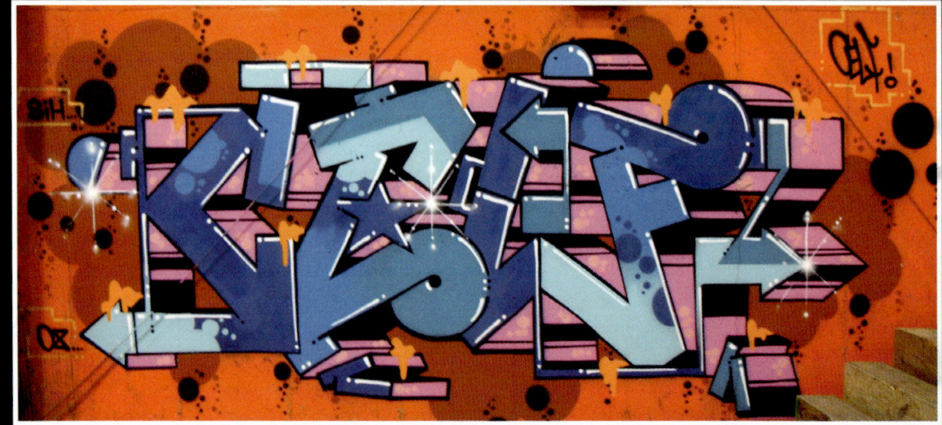

Celf, Long Island, NY

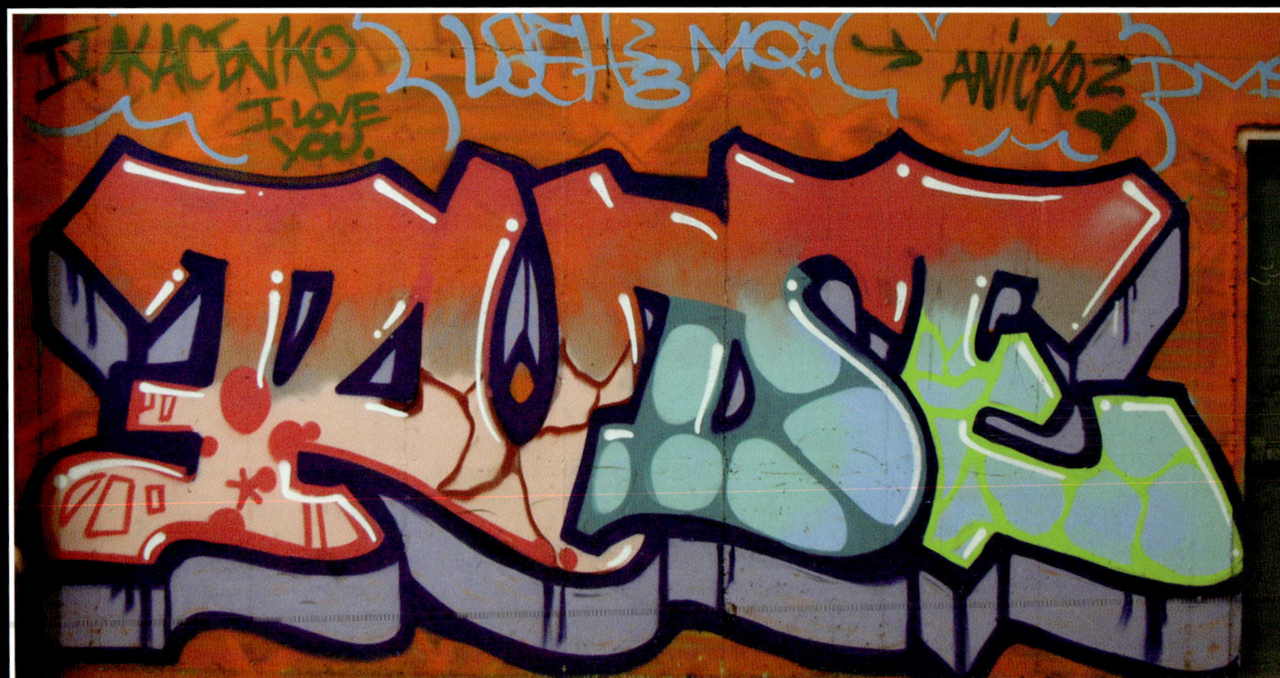

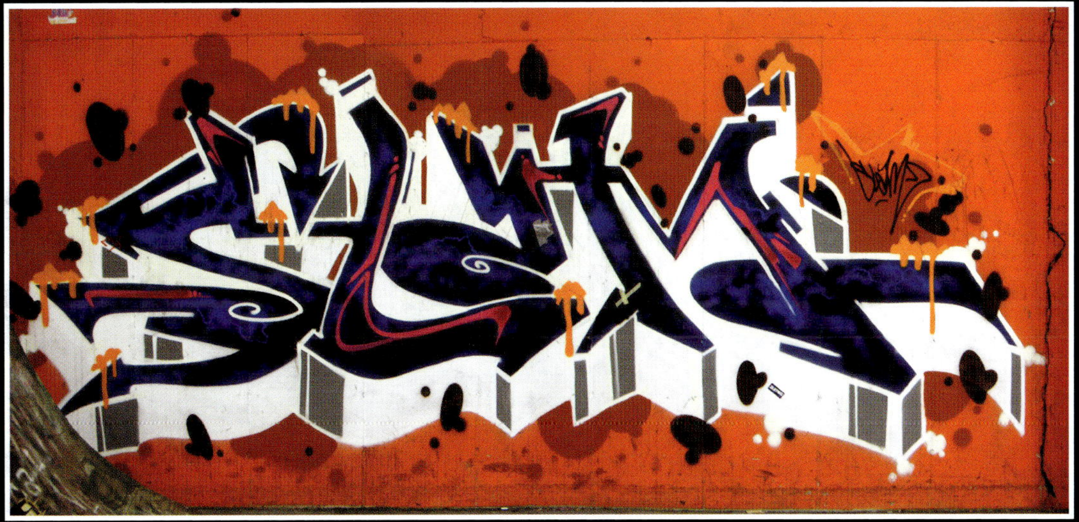

Slam, Long Island, NY

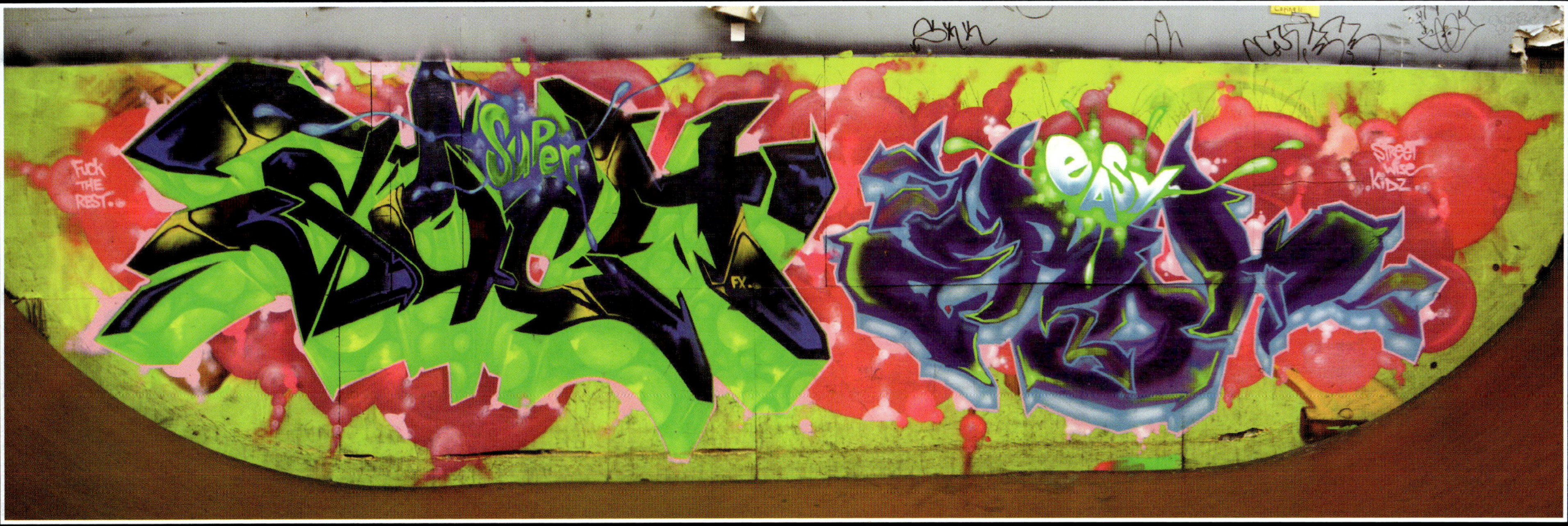


Such, Erok, Long Island, NY

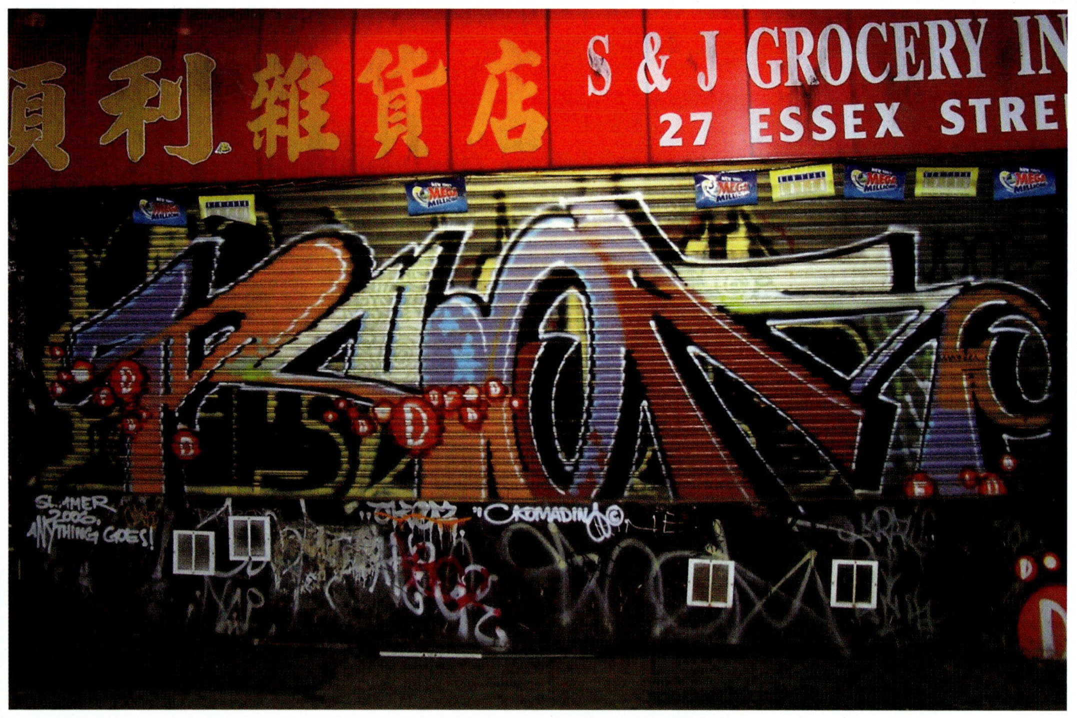


Scope, Manhattan, NY

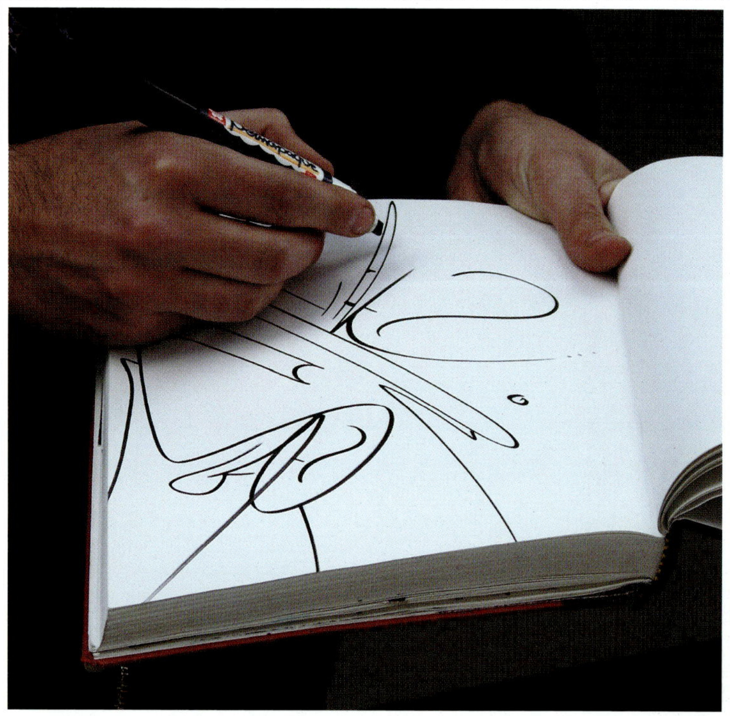

Rime, Manhattan, NY

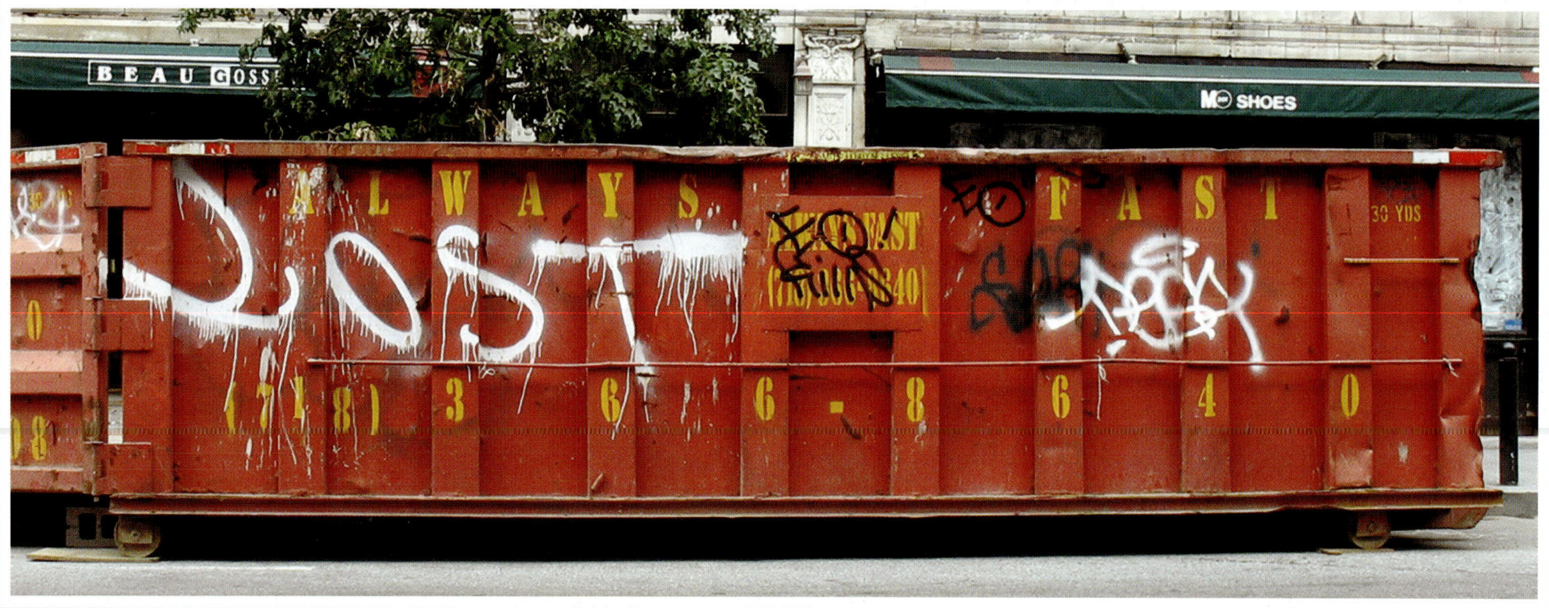


Cost, Desa, Manhattan, NY

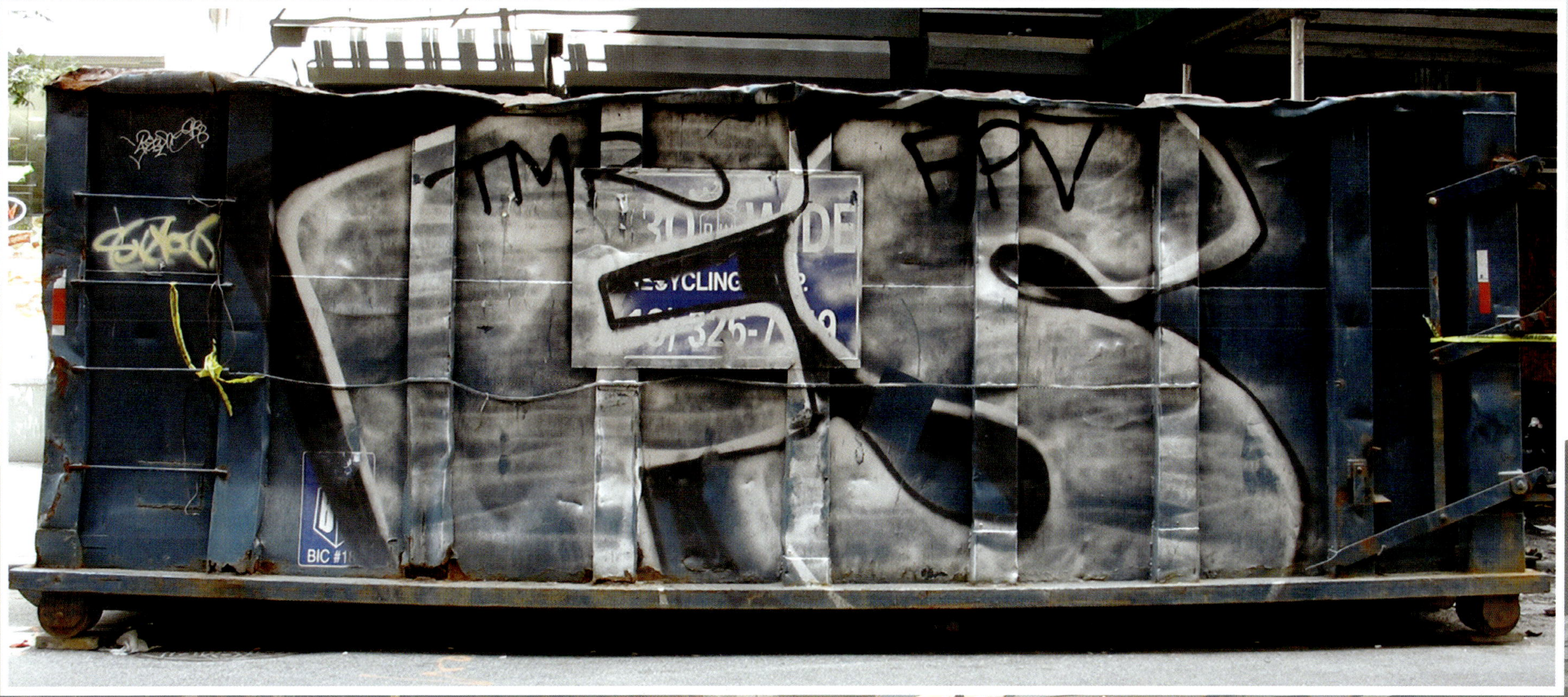

FS, Manhattan, NY

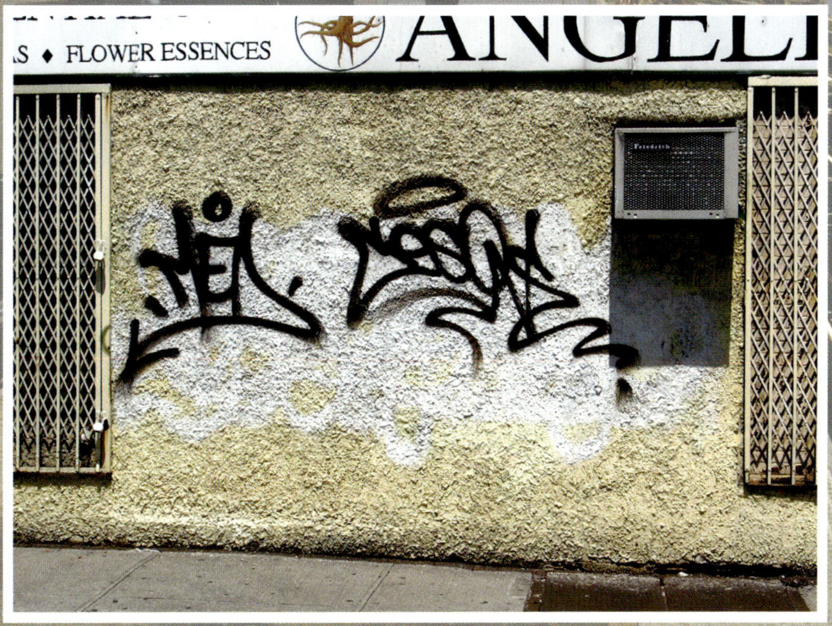


Med, Ces, Manhattan, NY

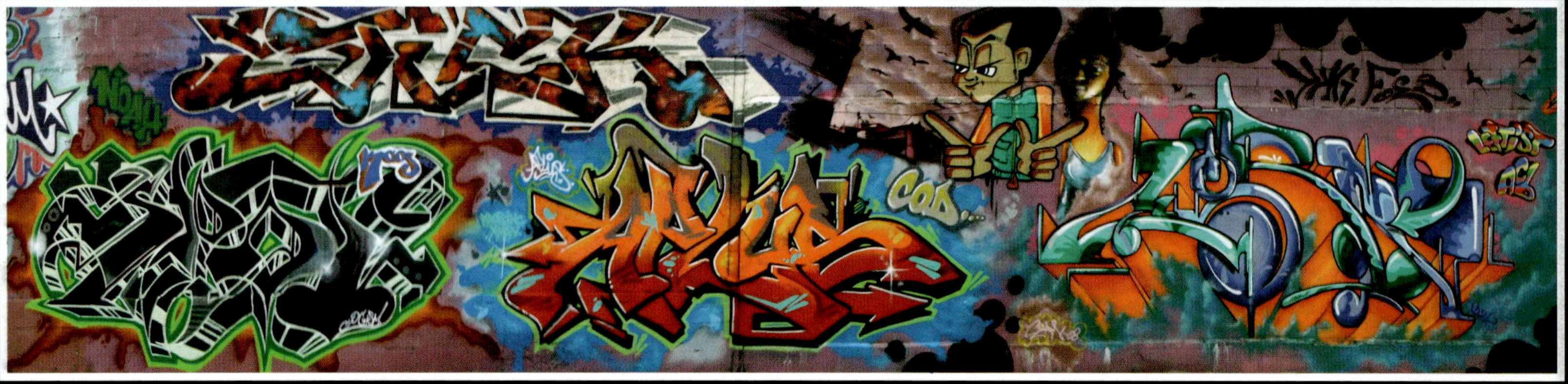

Spot, Jick, APlus (Enue), Cern, Brooklyn, NY

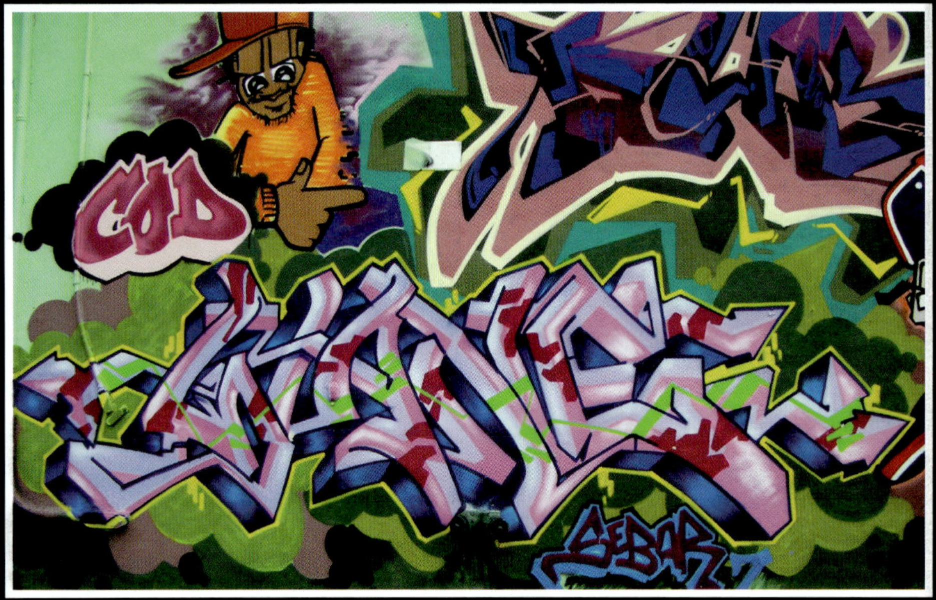


Wane, Bronx, NY

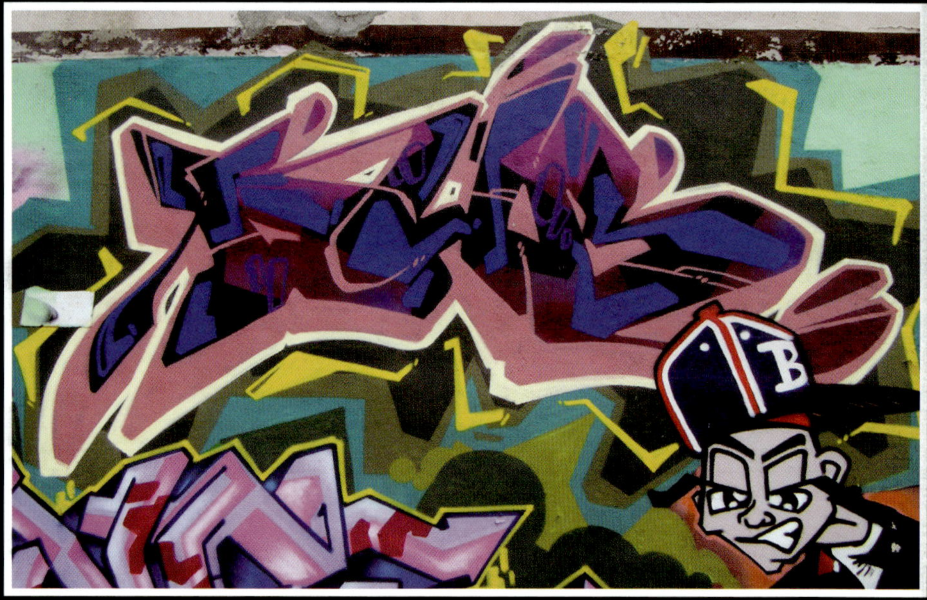

Dub, Bronx, NY

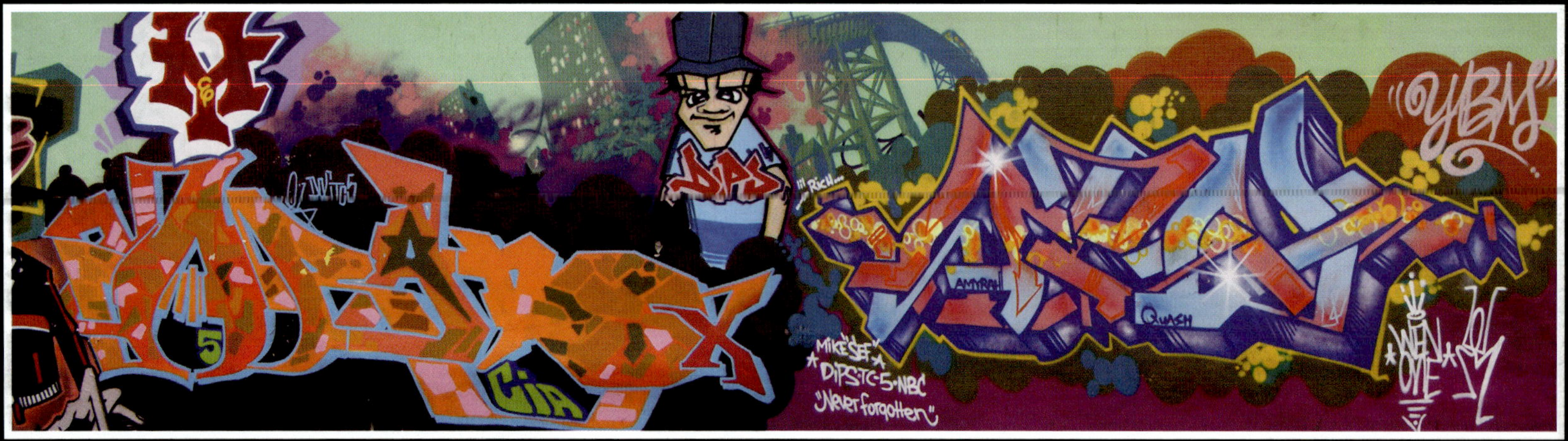


Arab (Doc), Wen, Bronx, NY

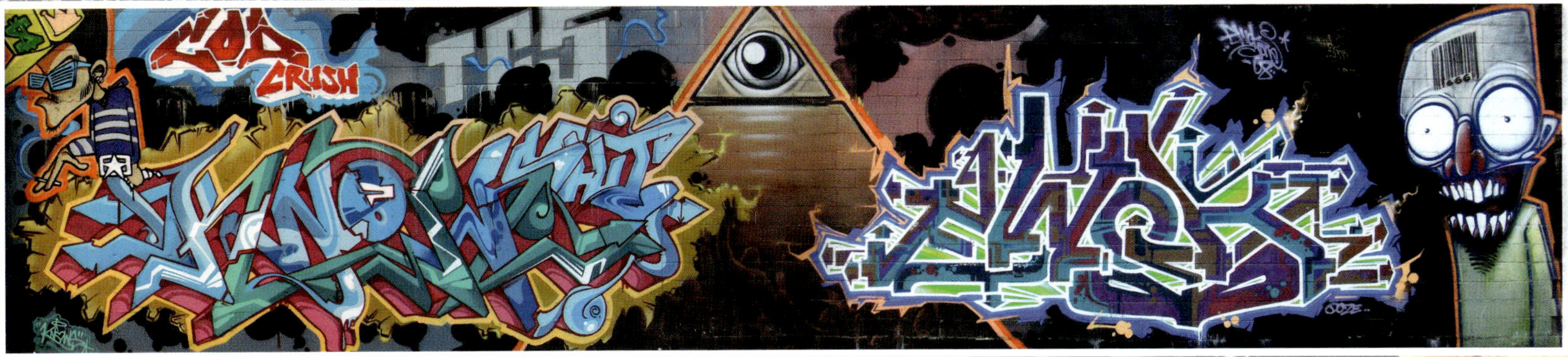


Knows, Ewok, Brooklyn, NY

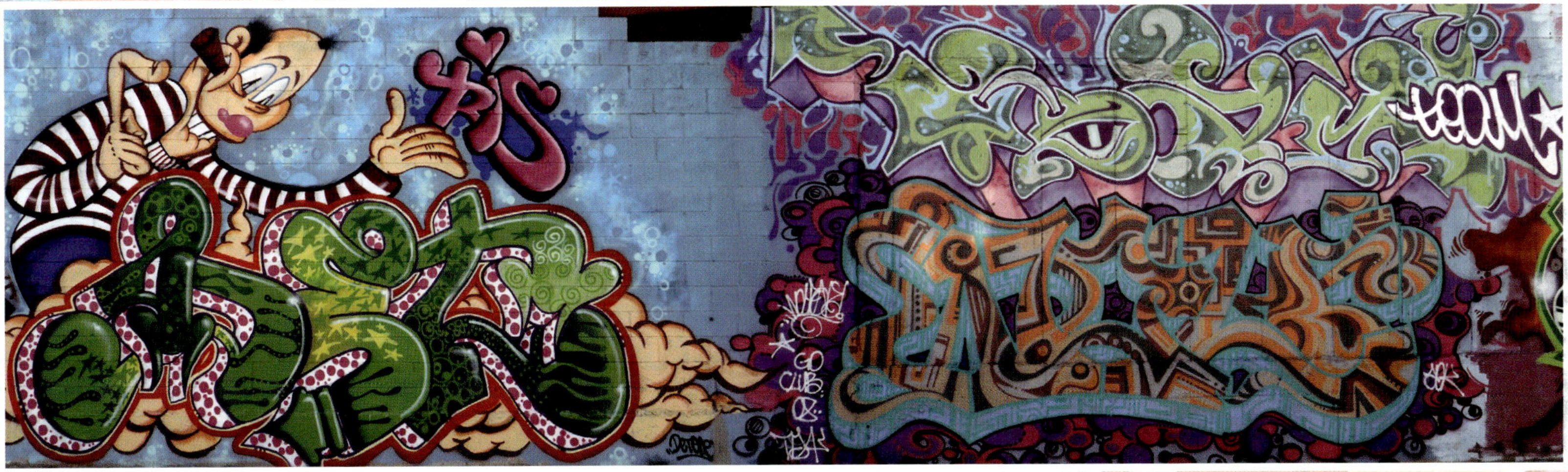

Det, Team, Wolf, Brooklyn,NY

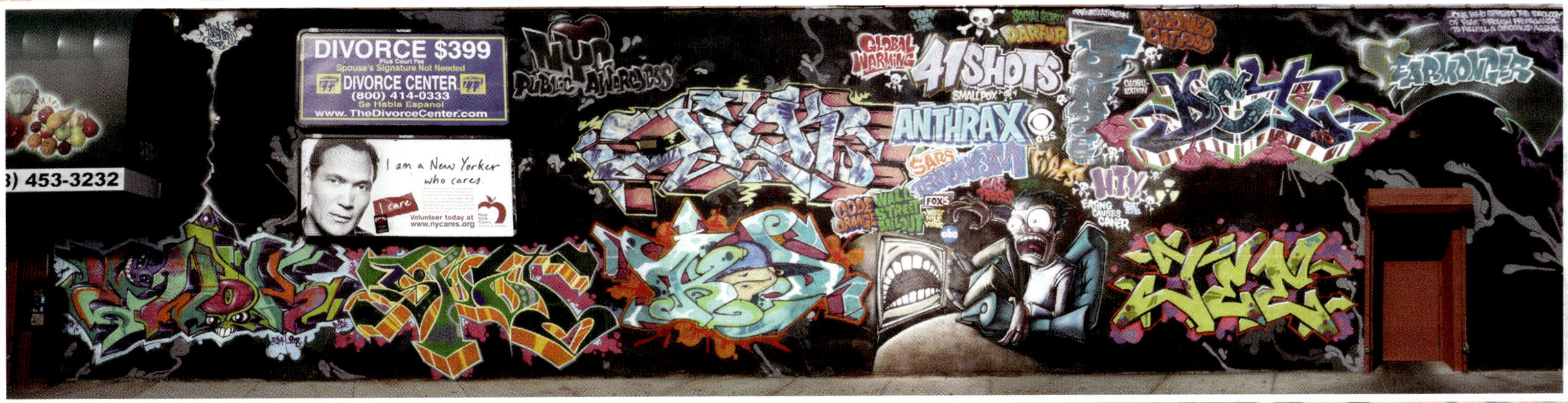


Ewok, Spot, Jick, T-Kid, Det, Jee, Brooklyn,NY

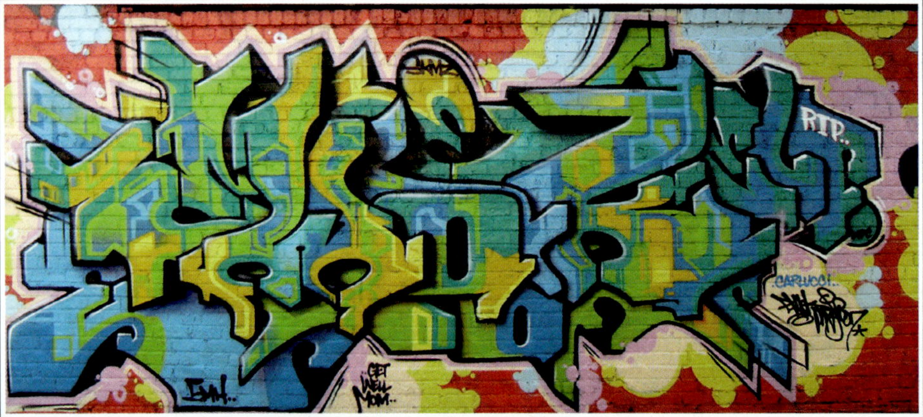

Ewok, Brooklyn, NY

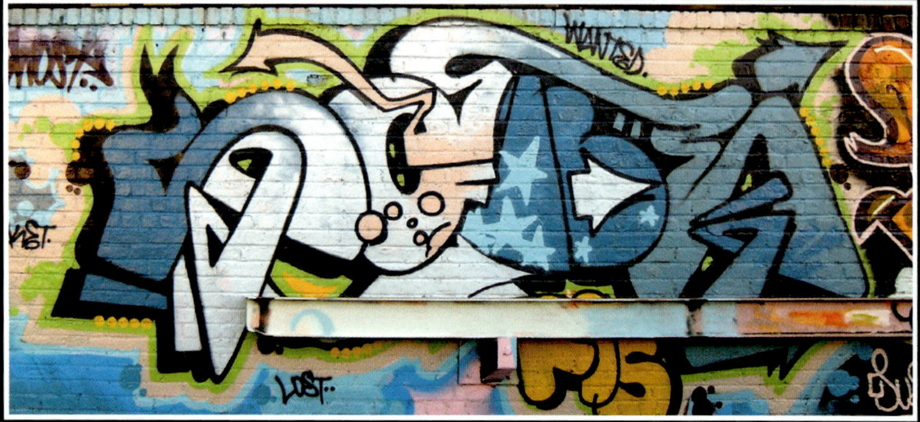

Sabe (Ghost), Brooklyn, NY

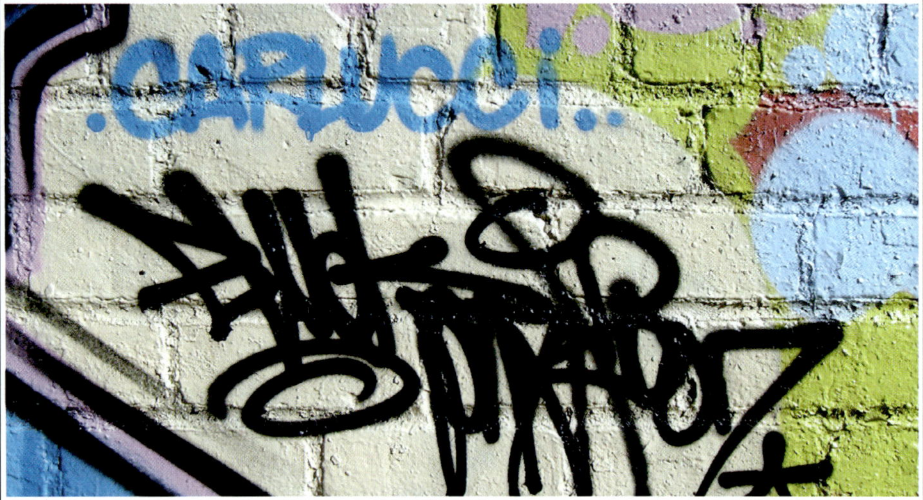


Ewok One, Brooklyn, NY

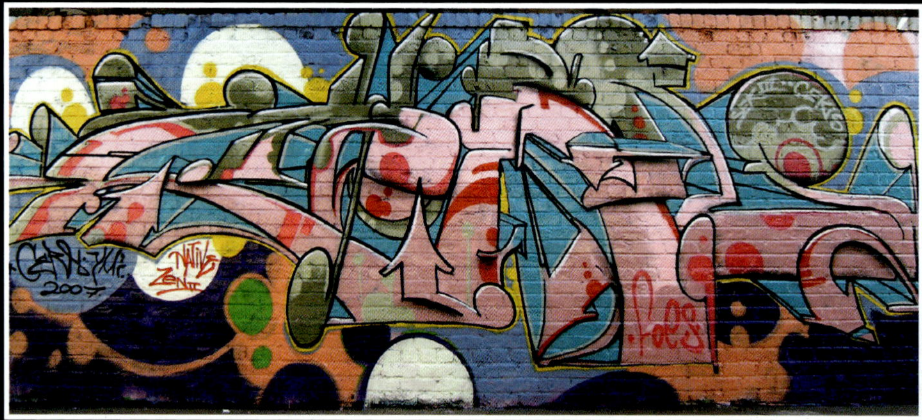

Cern, Brooklyn, NY

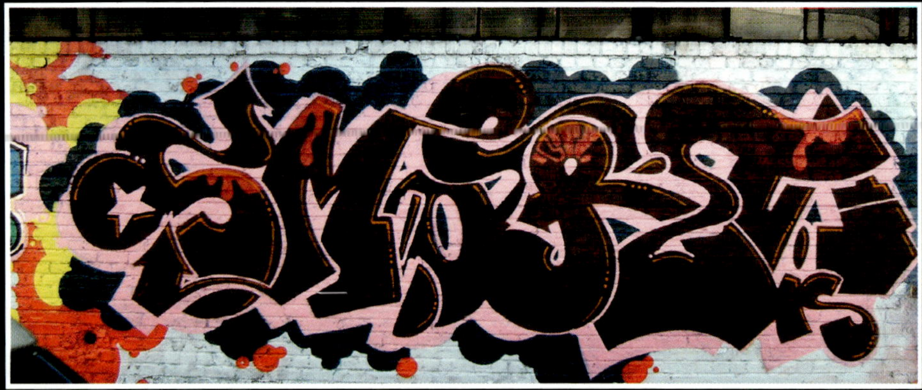

Smart, Brooklyn, NY

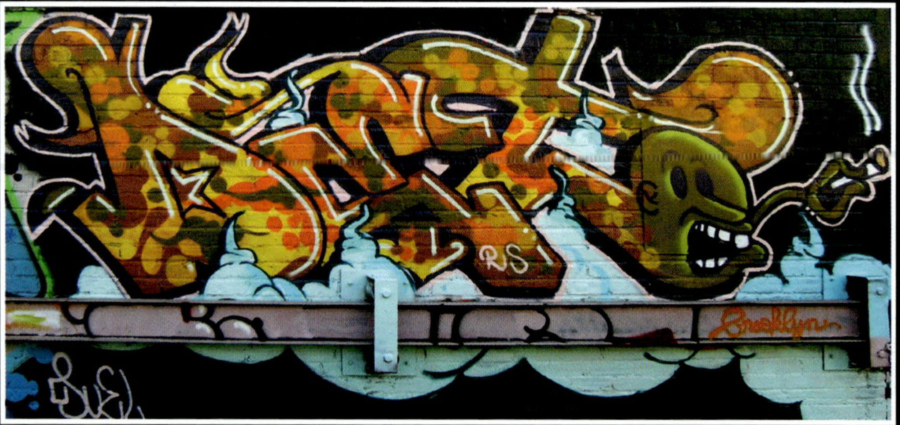

Det, Brooklyn, NY

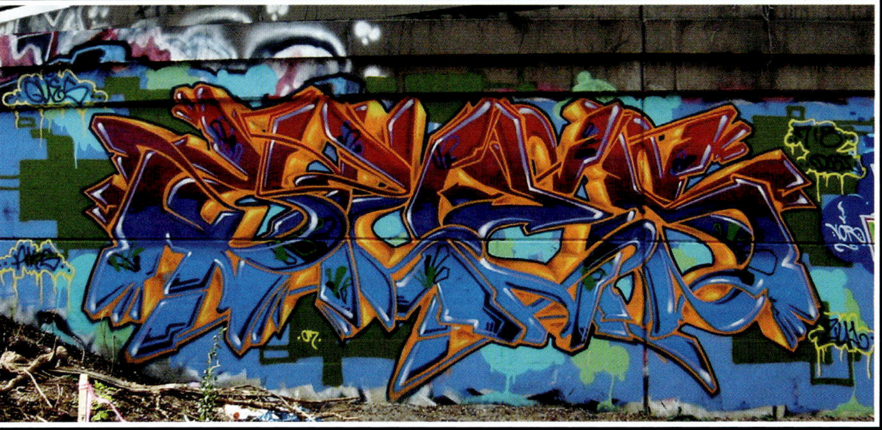

Ques, New Jersey

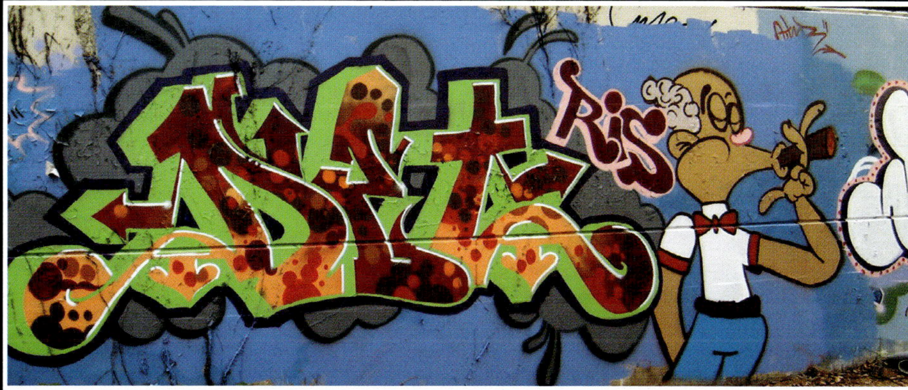

Det, New Jersey

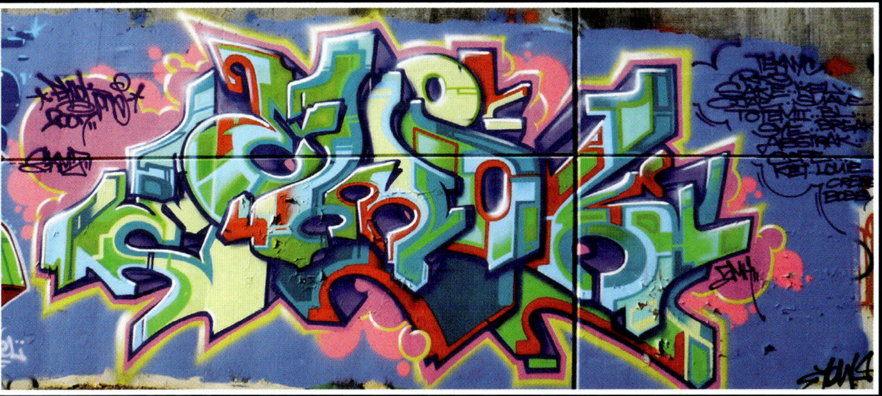

Ewok, New Jersey

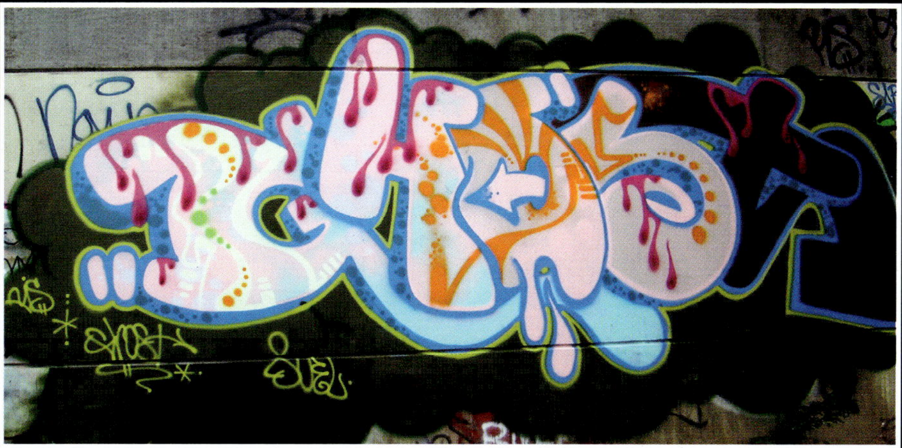

Ghost, New Jersey

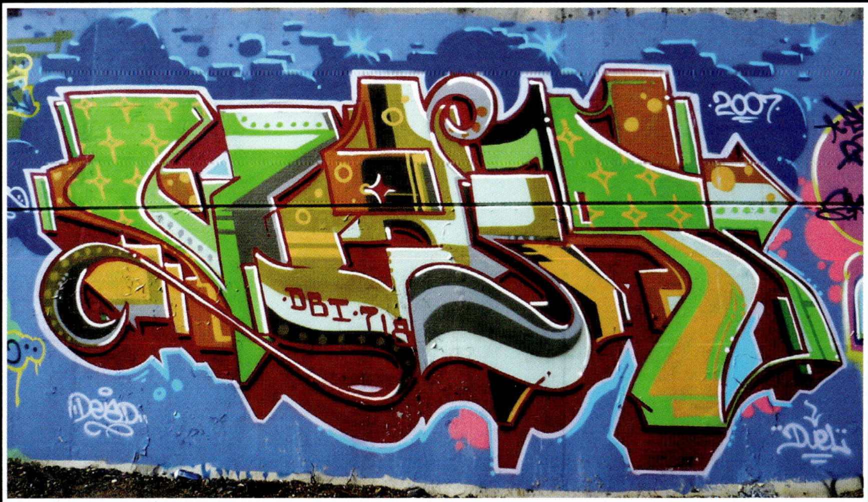


Vor, New Jersey

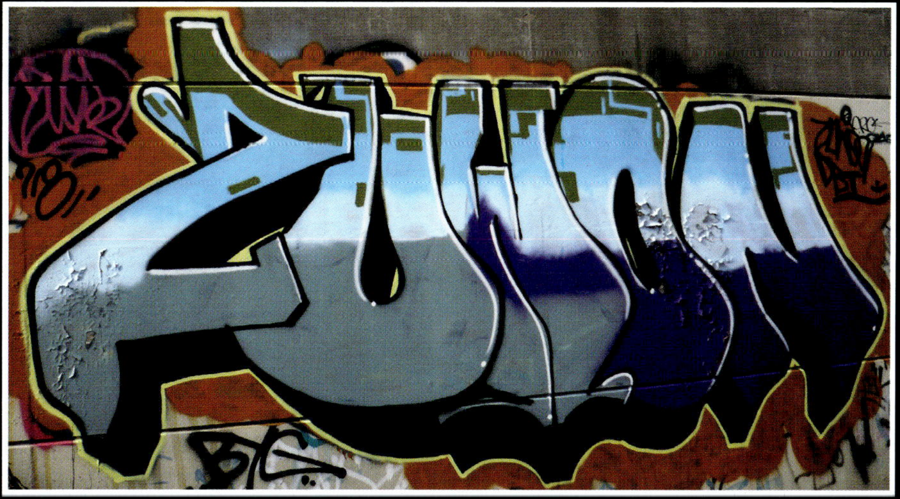

Zu, New Jersey

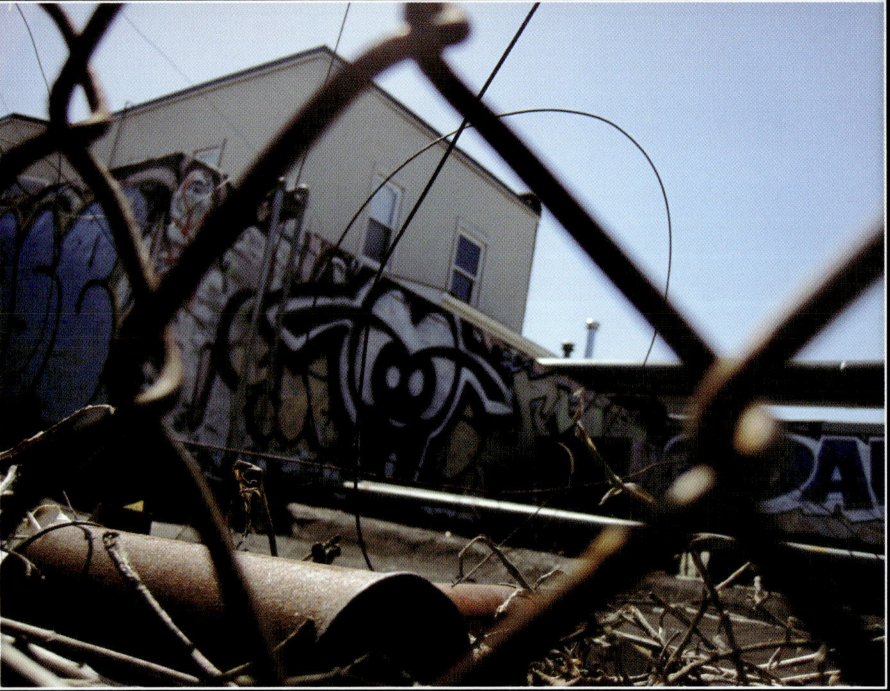

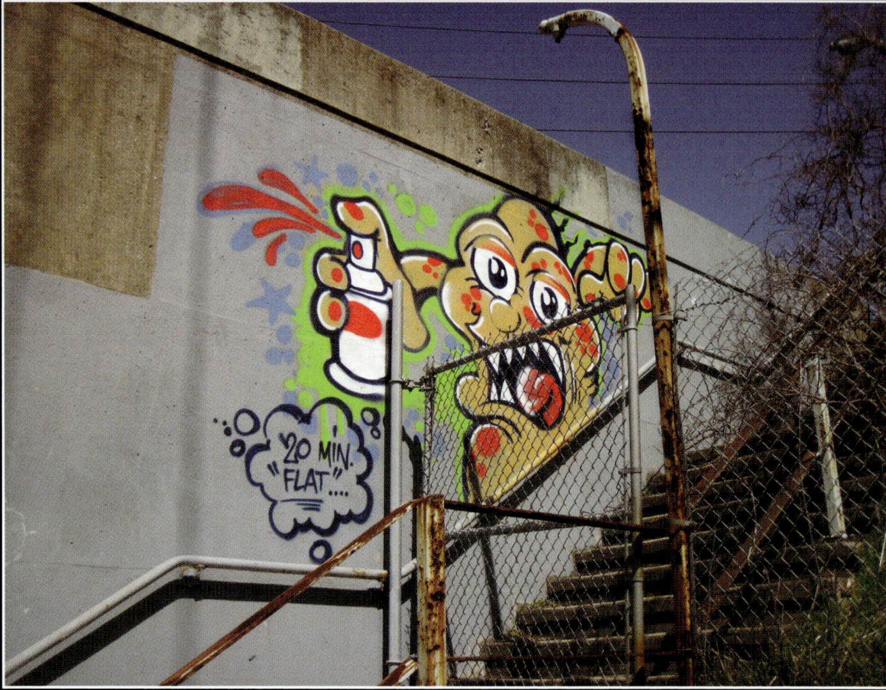
"20 MIN.
"FLAT"....

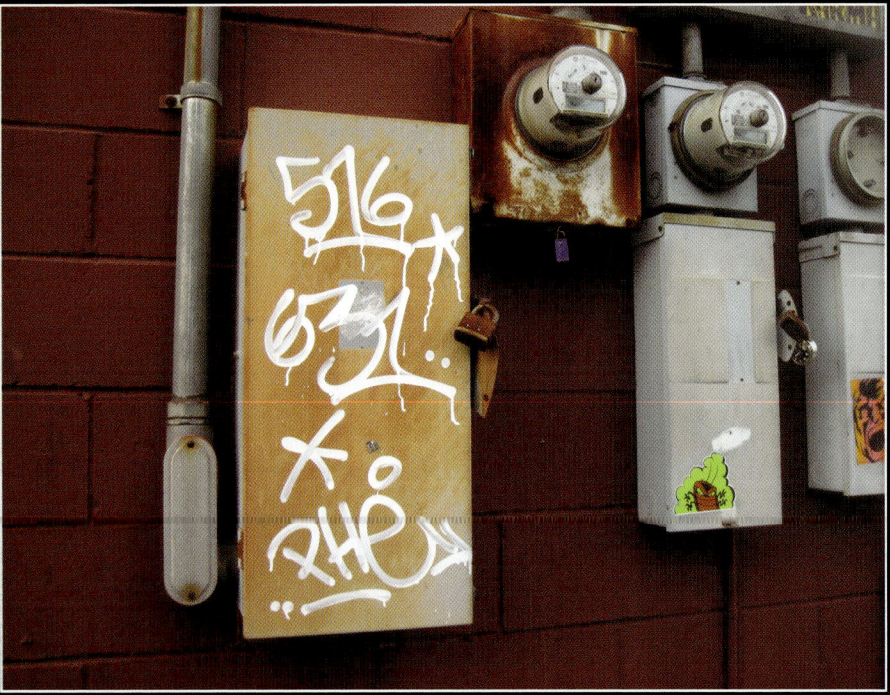

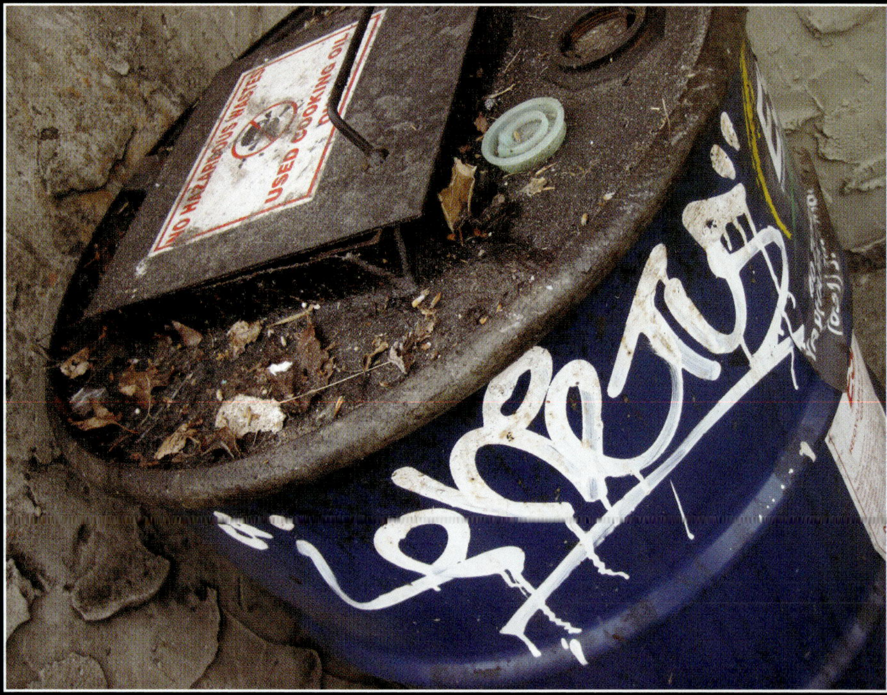

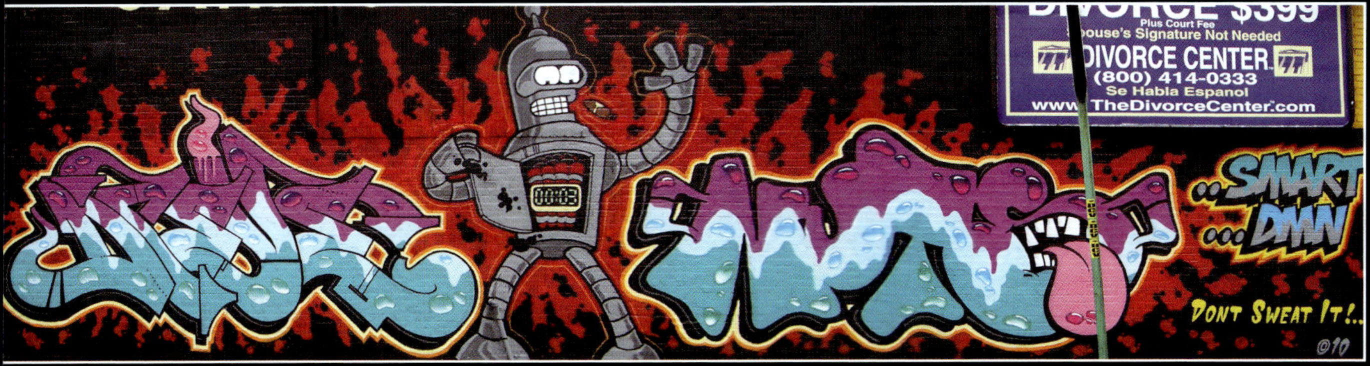
Plus Court Fee
Signature Not Needed
DIVORCE CENTER
(800) 414-0333
Se Habla Espanol
www.TheDivorceCenter.com
..SMART
...DMN
DONT SWEAT IT!..

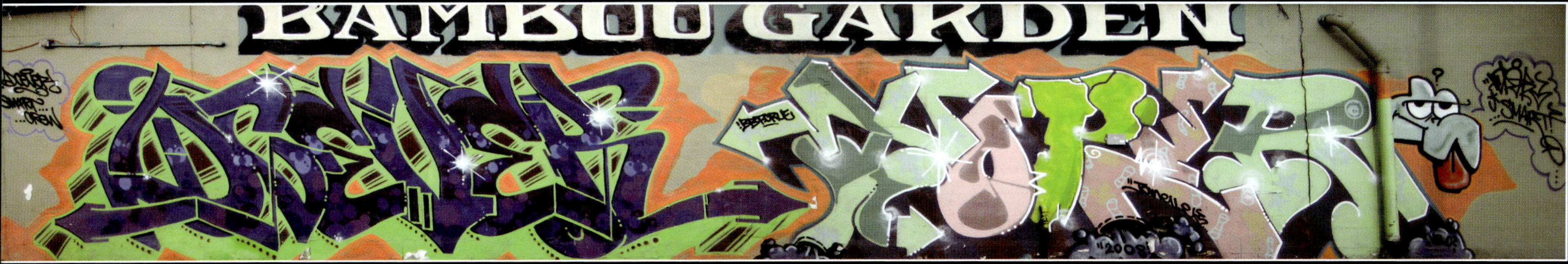
BAMBOO GARDEN

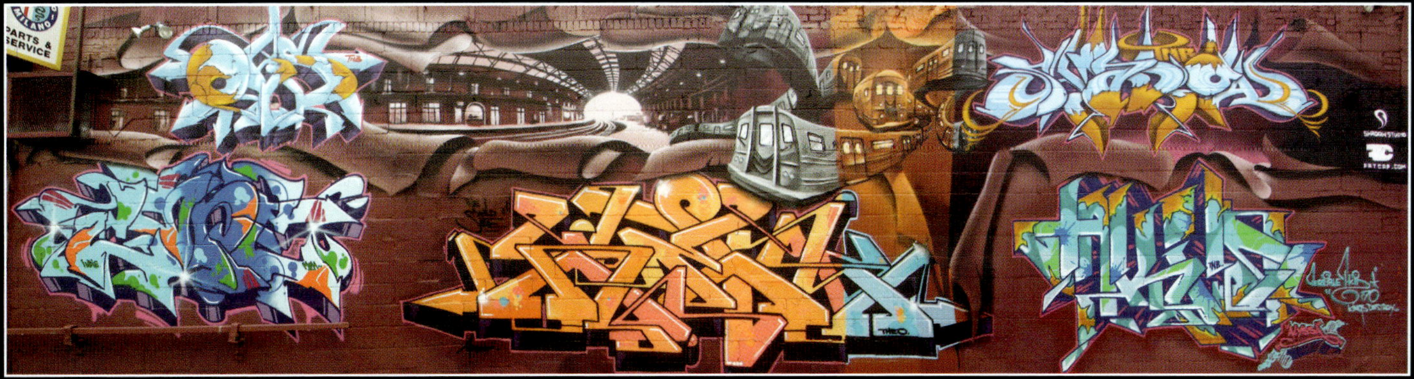
PARTS &
SERVICE

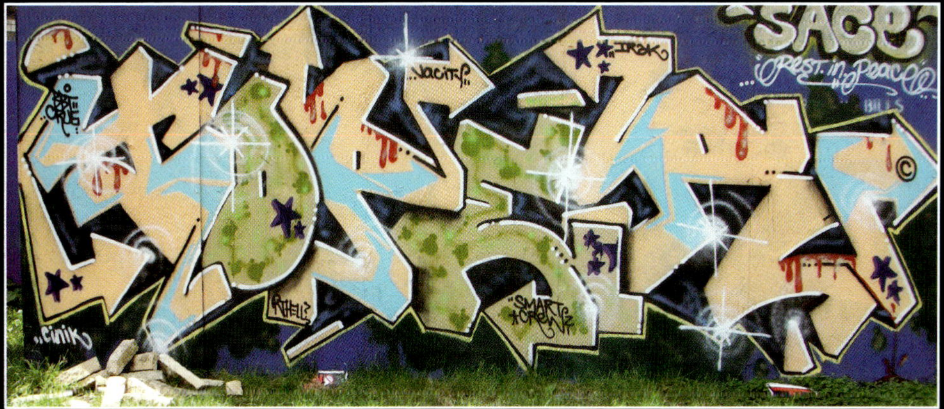
SACE
Rest in Peace

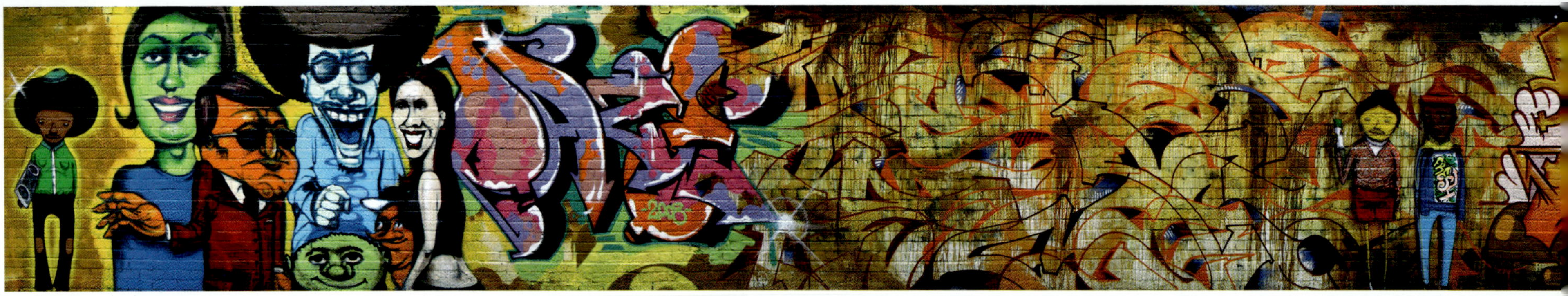

Daze, West, Brooklyn, NY

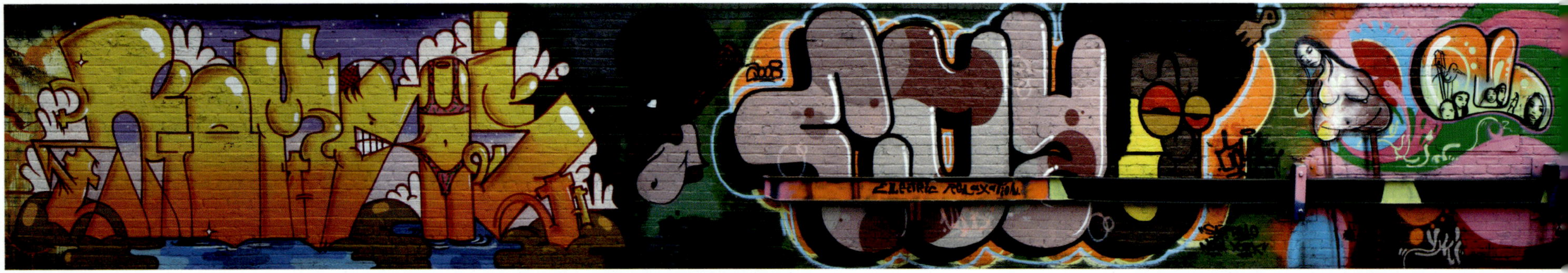

Os Gemeos, Coyo, Cern, Brooklyn, NY

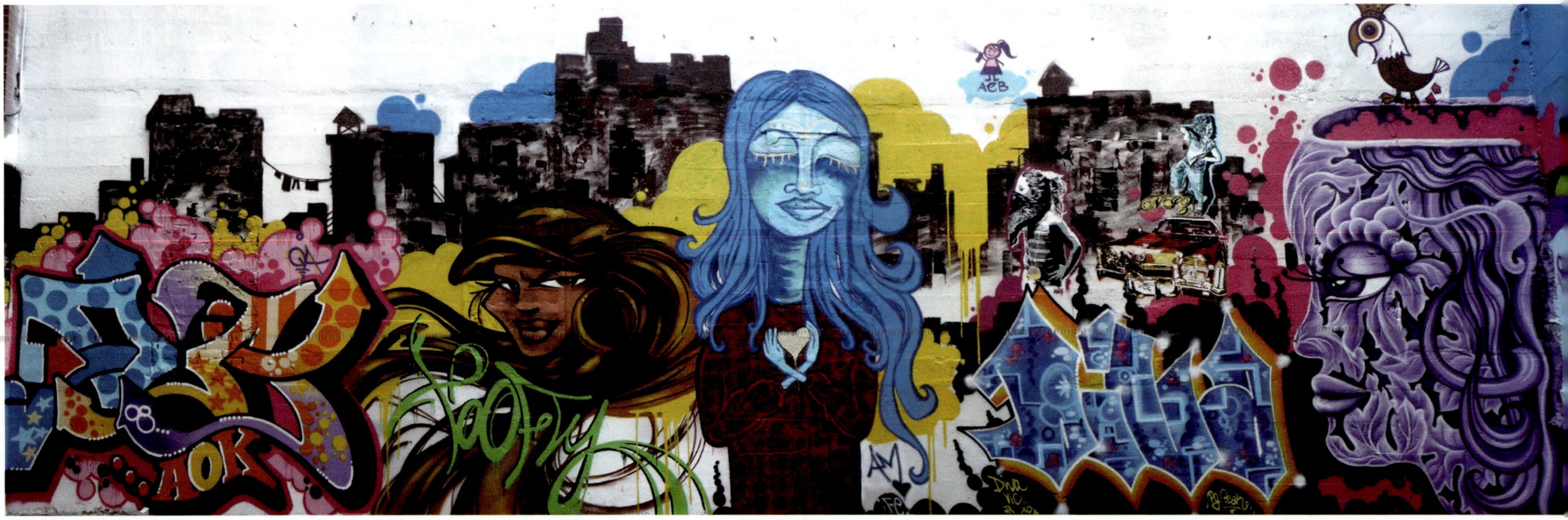

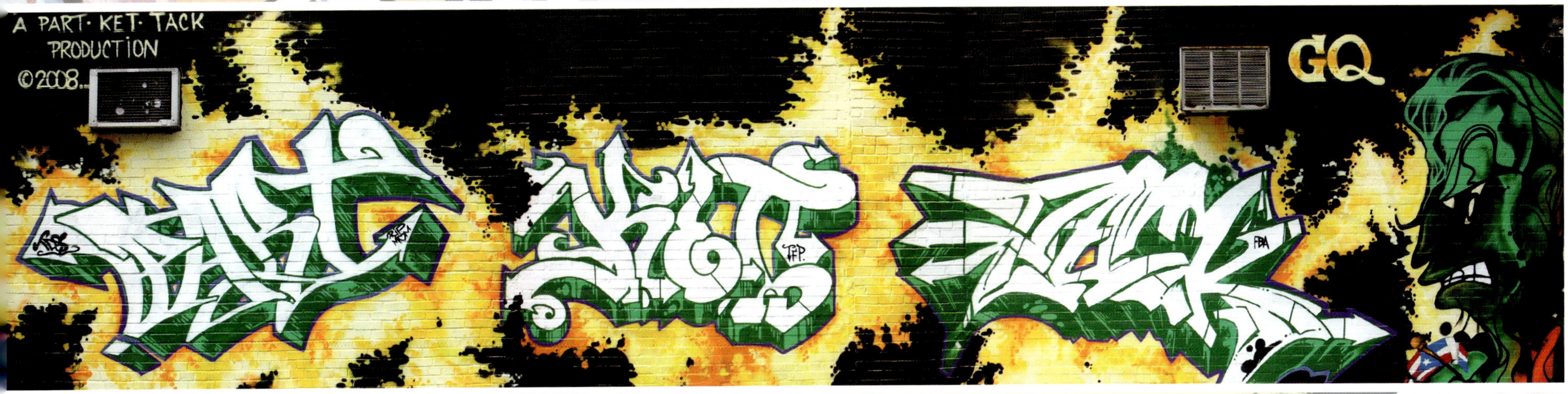

Part, Ket, Tack, Manhattan, NY

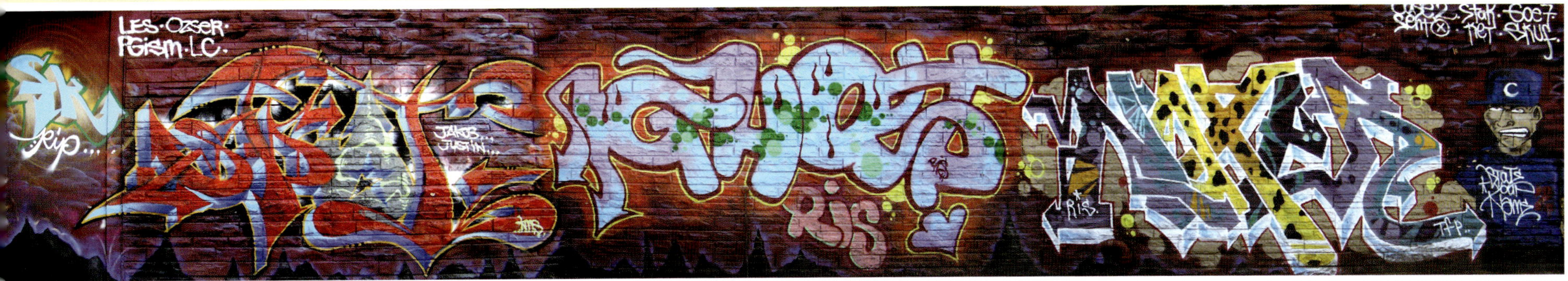

Spot, Ghost, Noxer, Brooklyn, NY

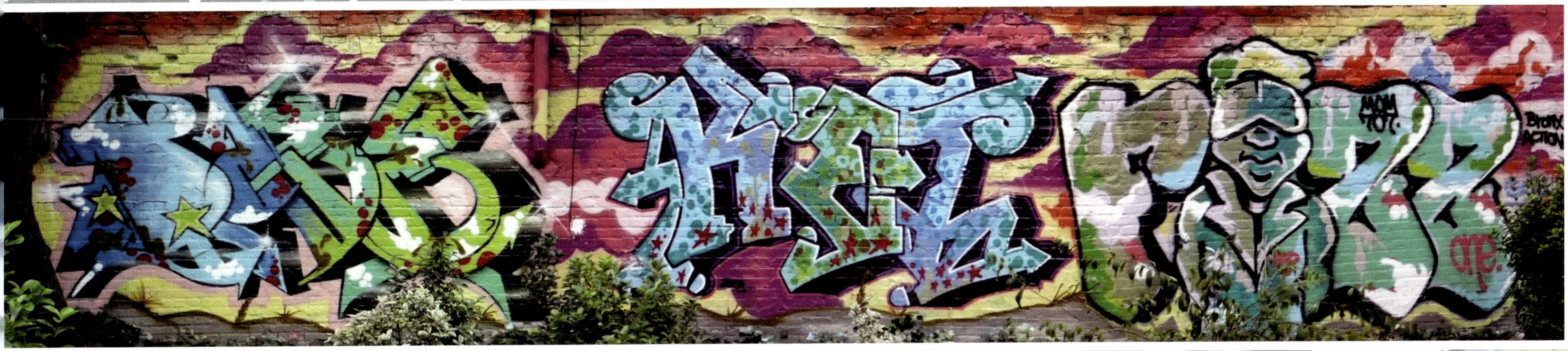
Daze, Ket, Fuzz, Manhattan, NY

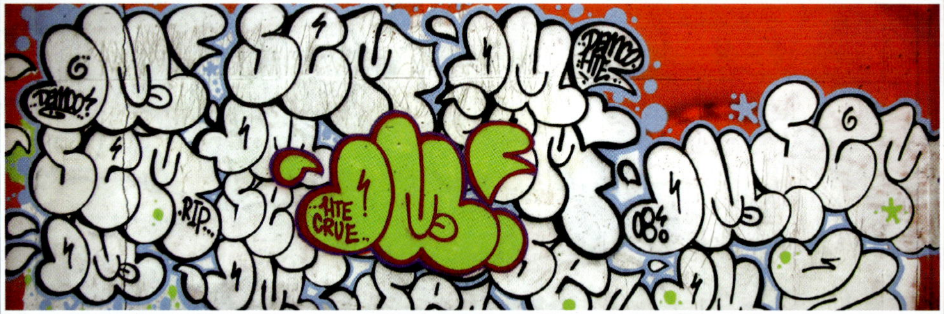

Demco, Long Island, NY

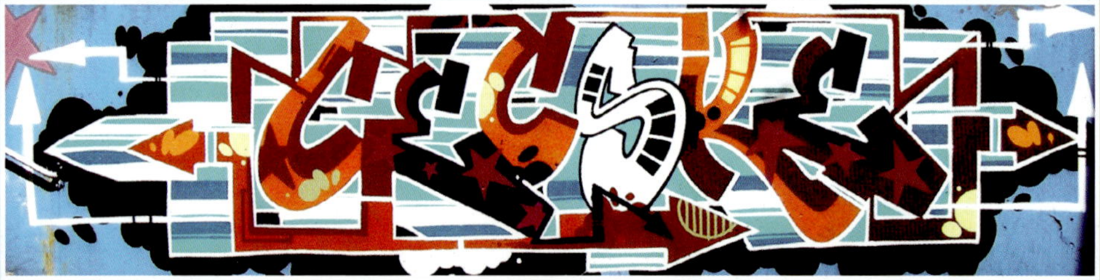

Cecster, Brooklyn, NY

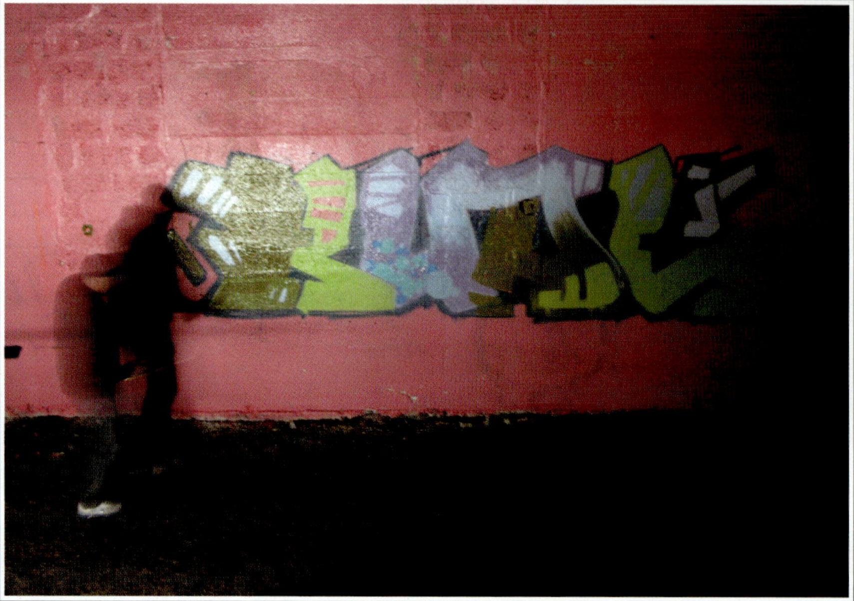

Rude, Brooklyn, NY

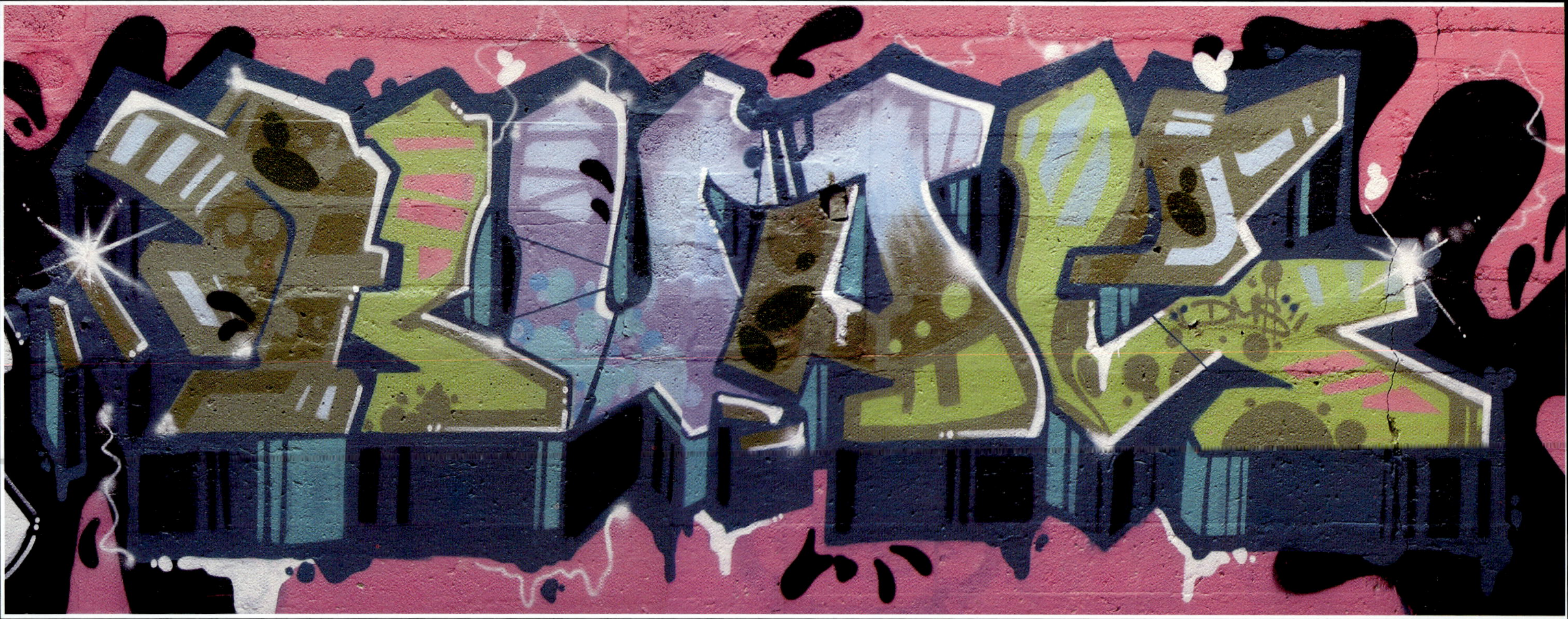

Rude, Brooklyn, NY

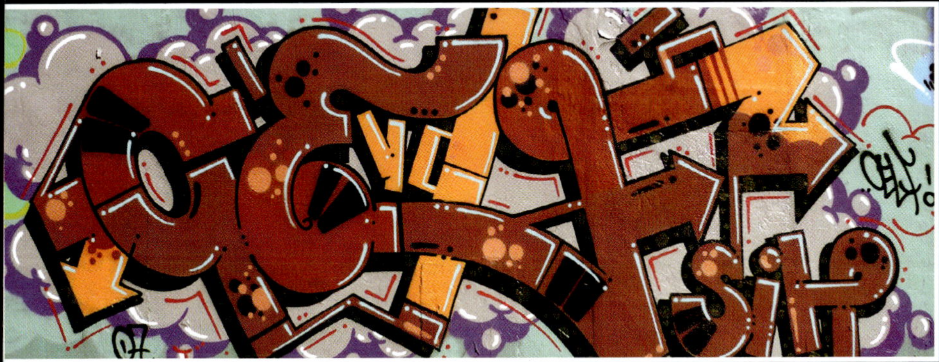

Celf, Queens, NY

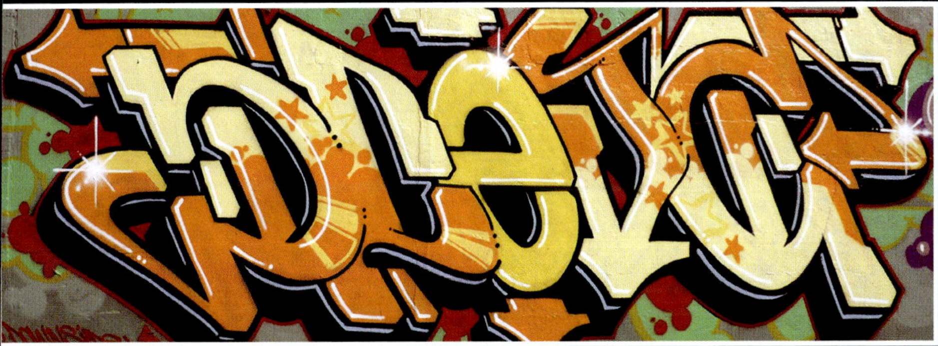

Dceve, Queens, NY

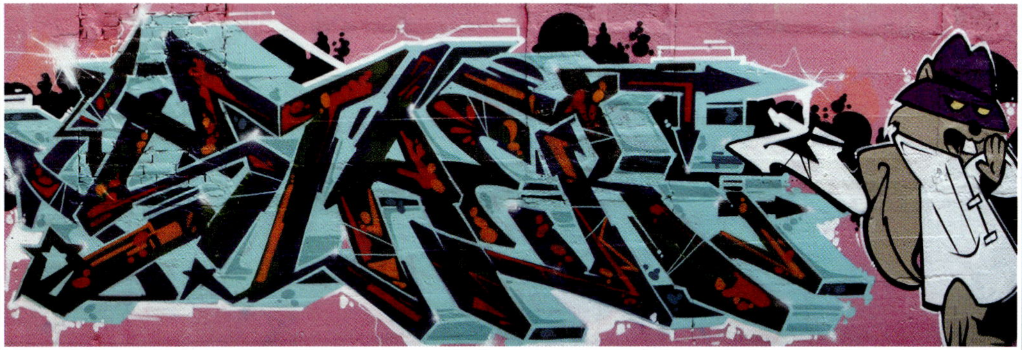

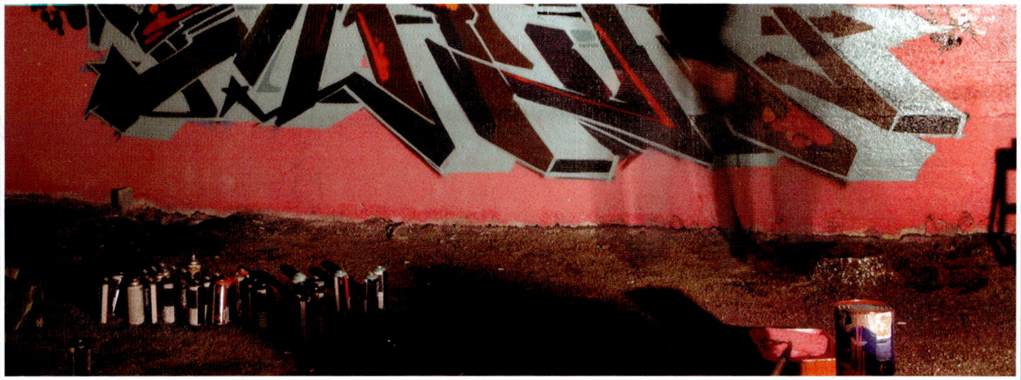

Stae2, Brooklyn, NY

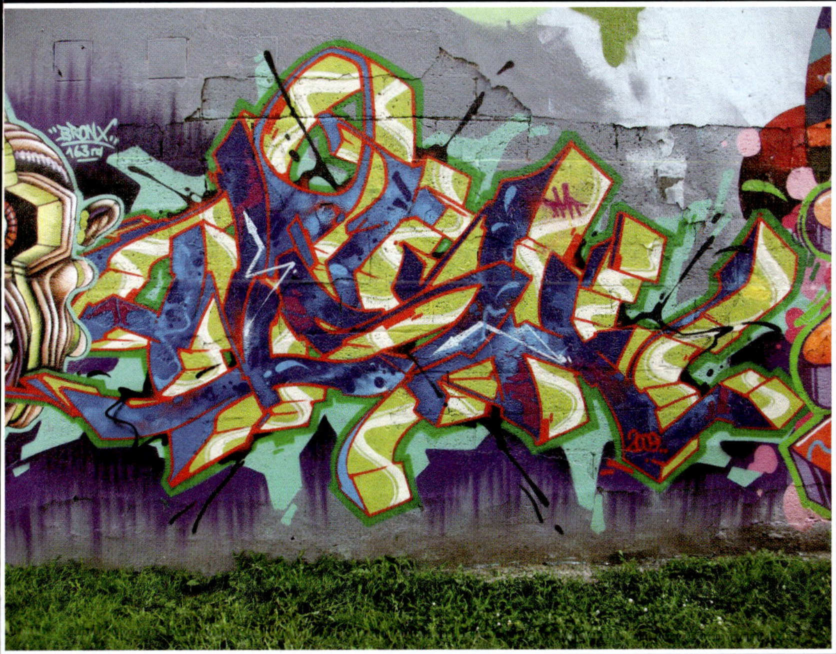

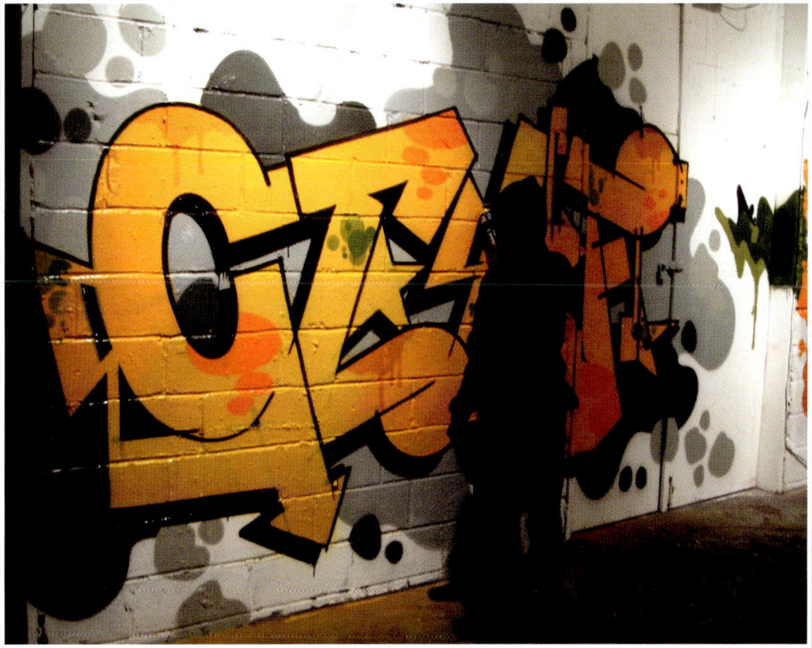

Celf, Brooklyn, NY

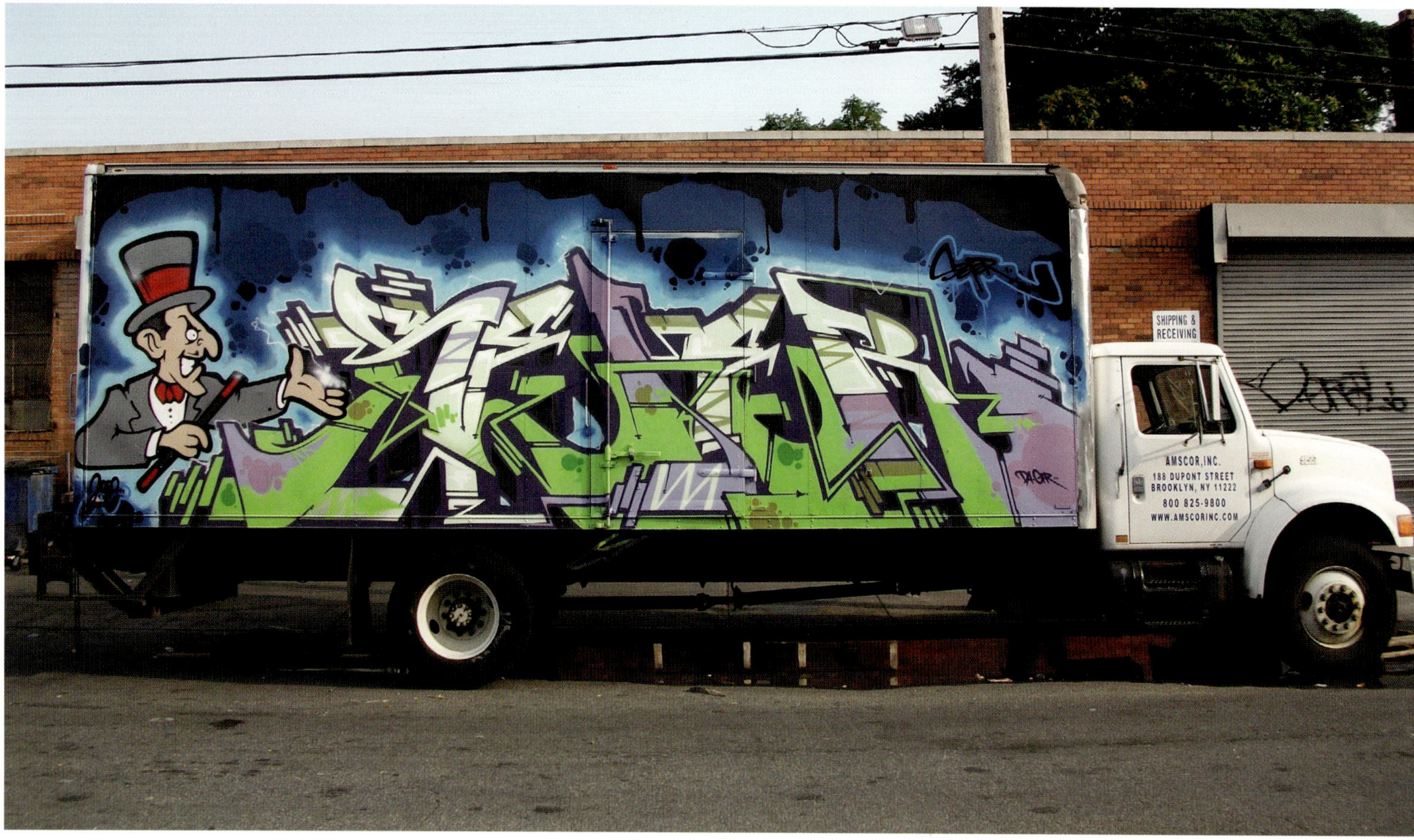


Seter, Brooklyn, NY

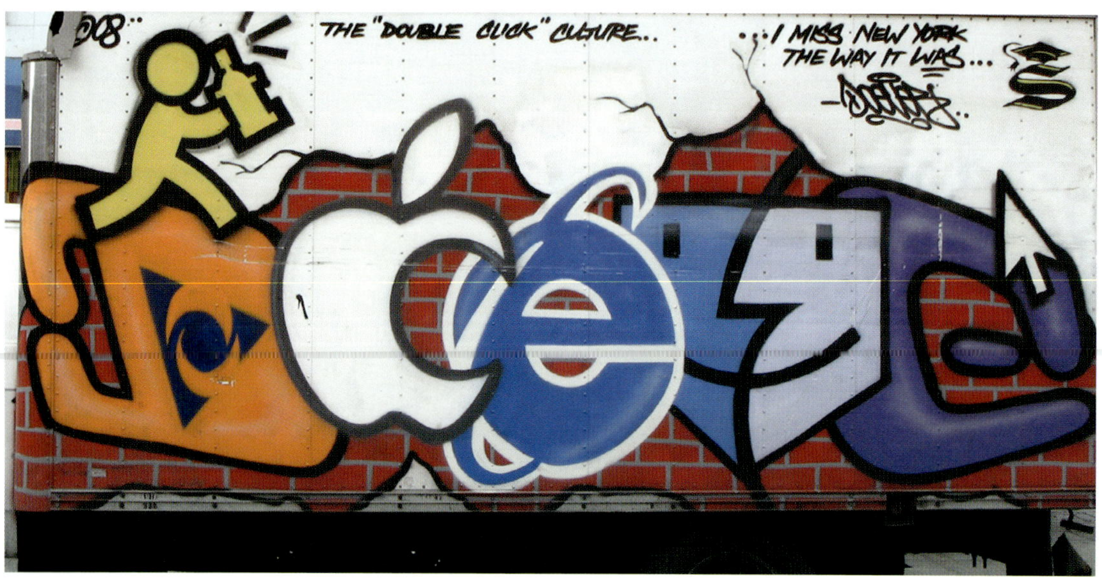


Dceve, Brooklyn, NY

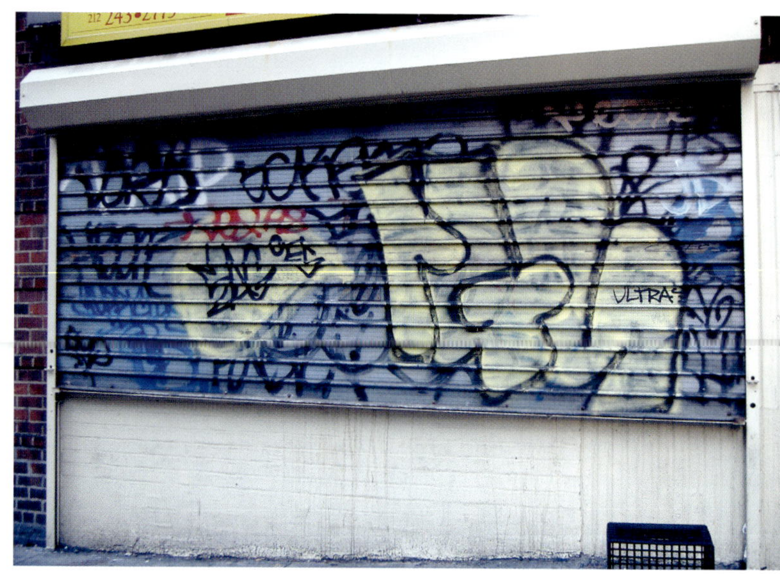

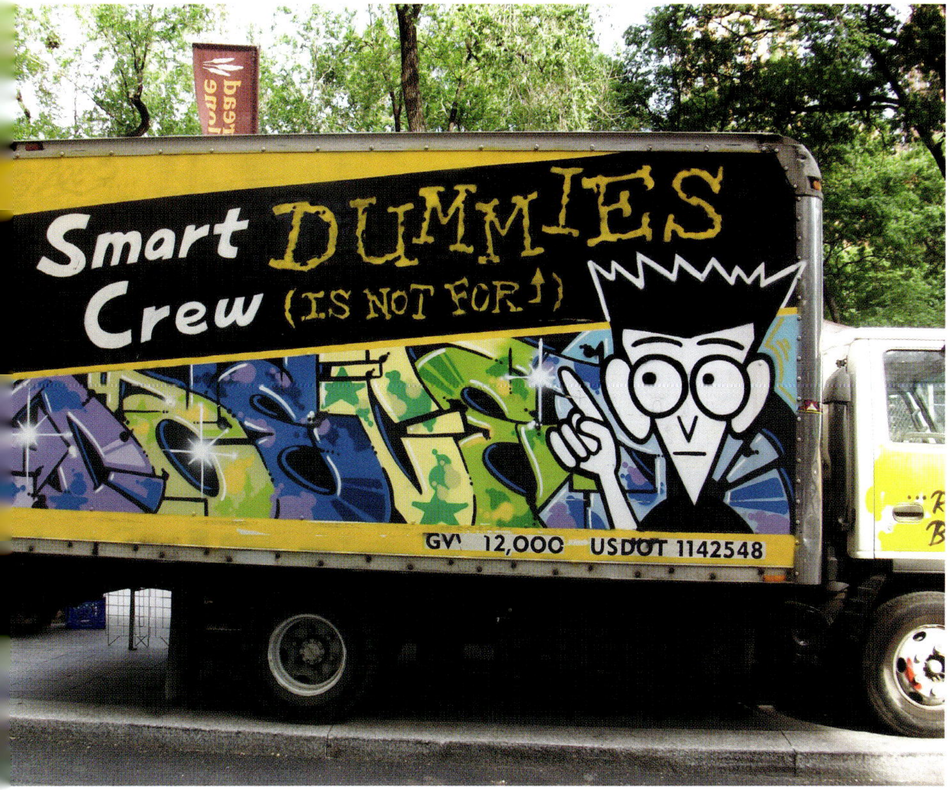


Dceve, Brooklyn, NY

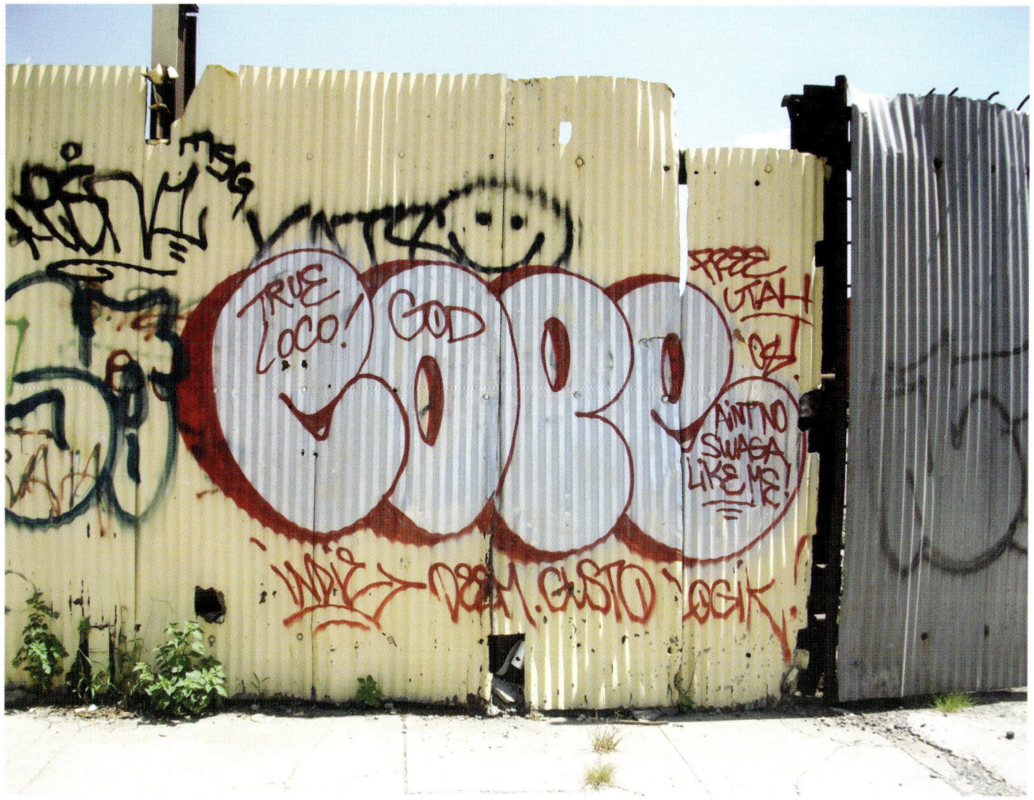


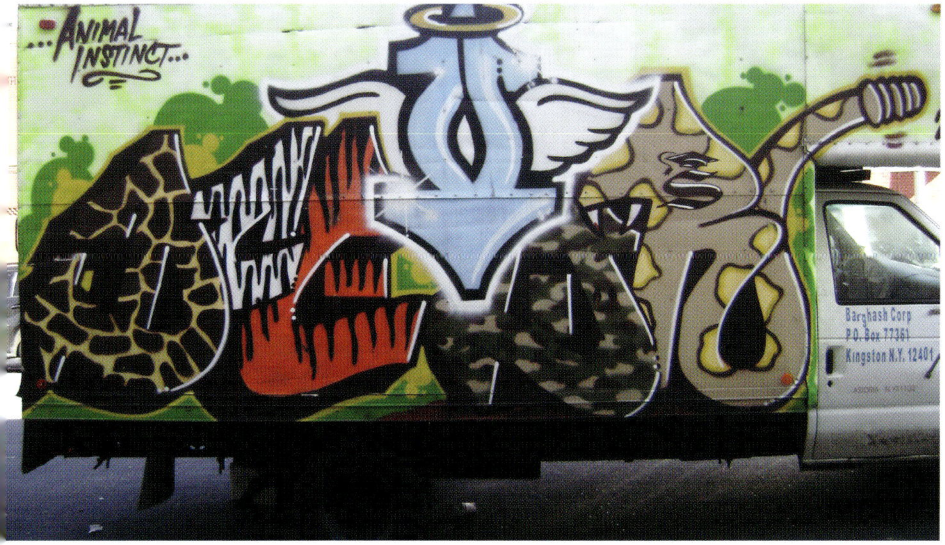


Dceve, Brooklyn, NY

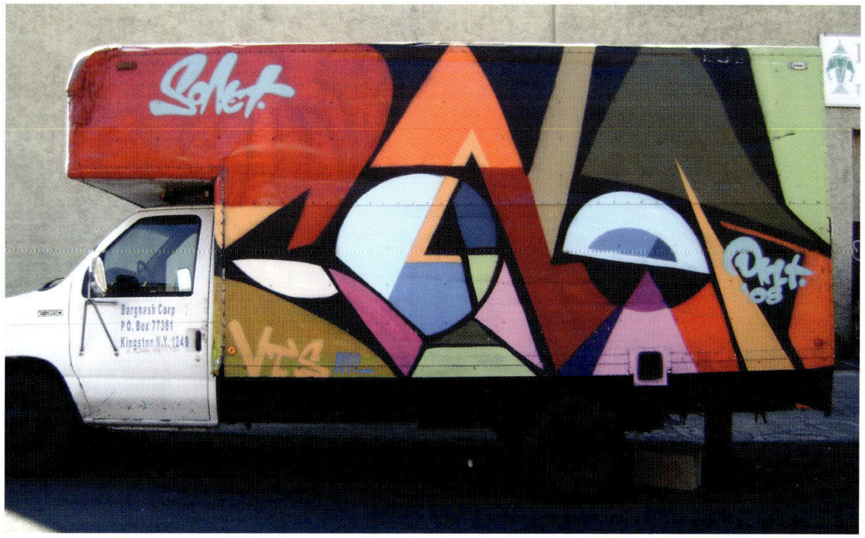


Sonet, Brooklyn, NY

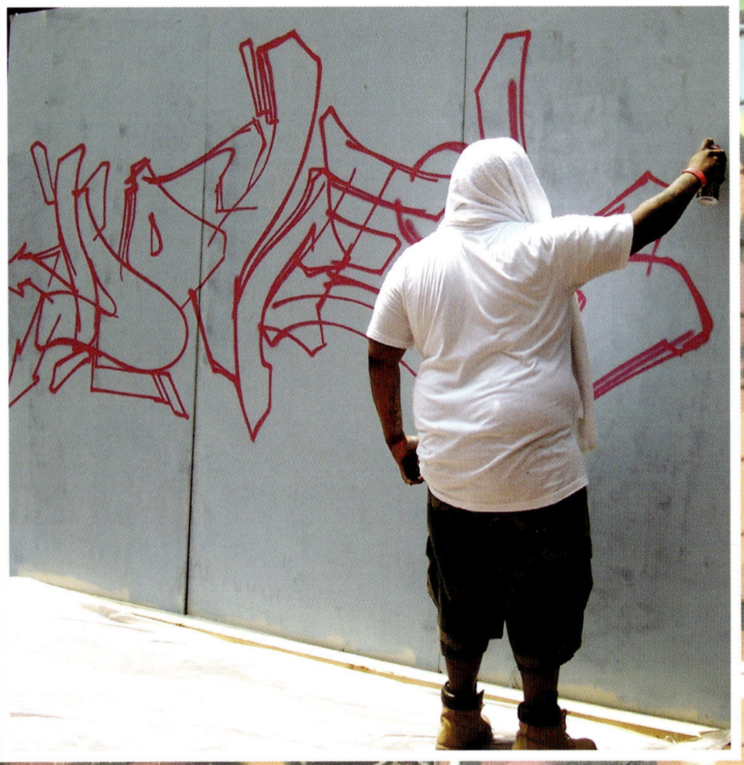

Doves - Action, Manhattan, NY

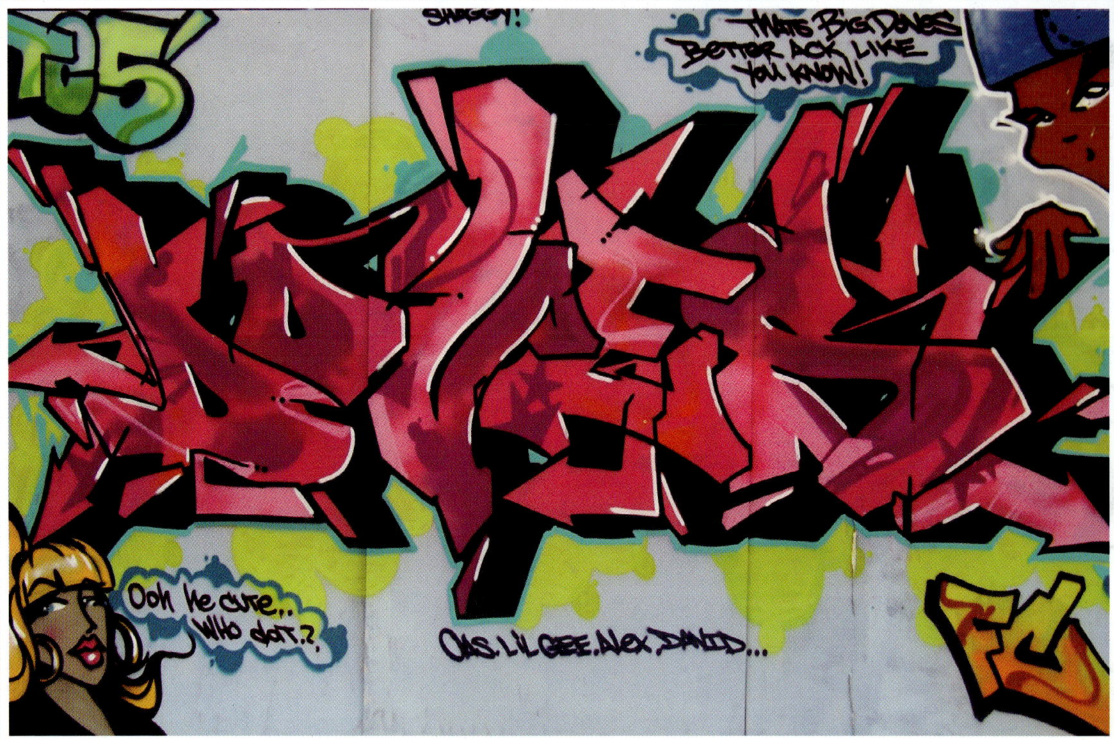


Doves, Manhattan, NY

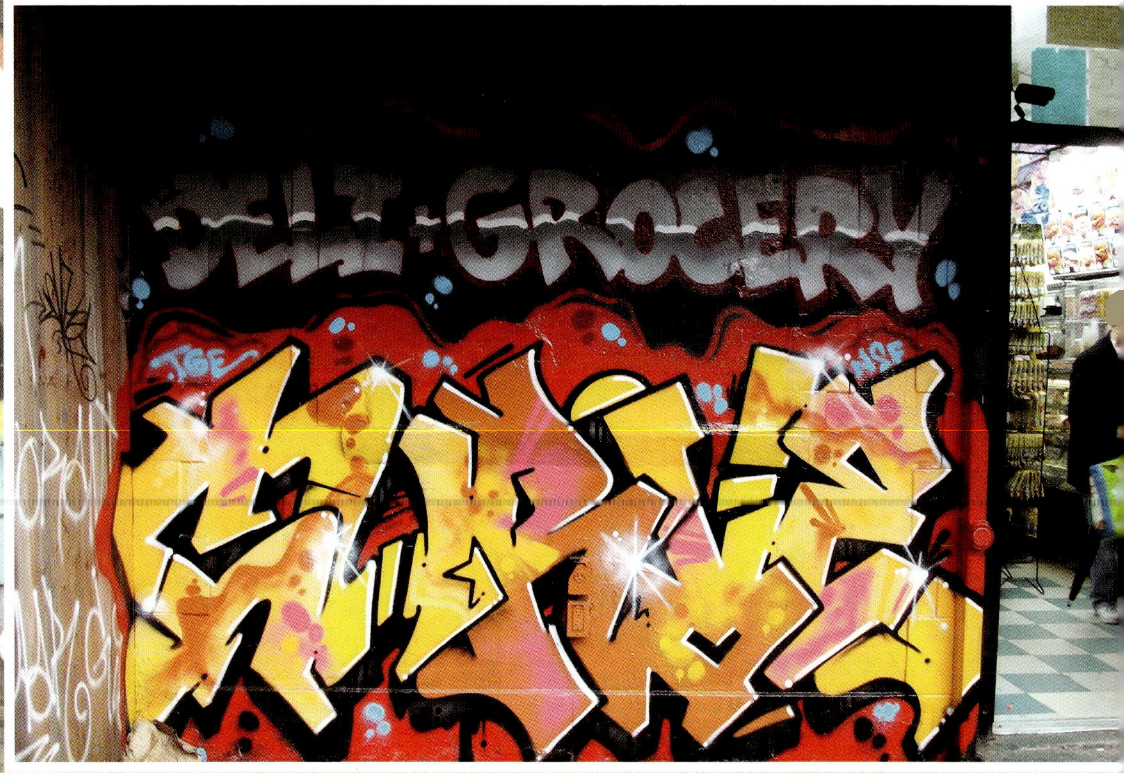

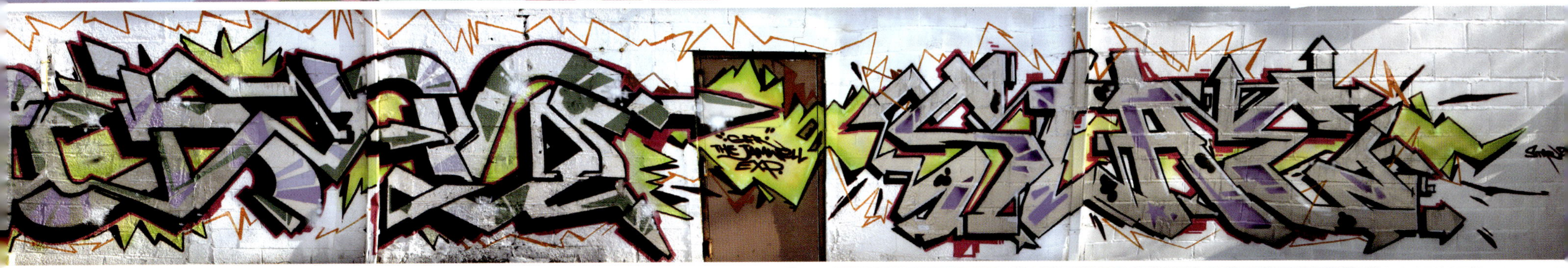

Uend, Stae2, Long Island, NY

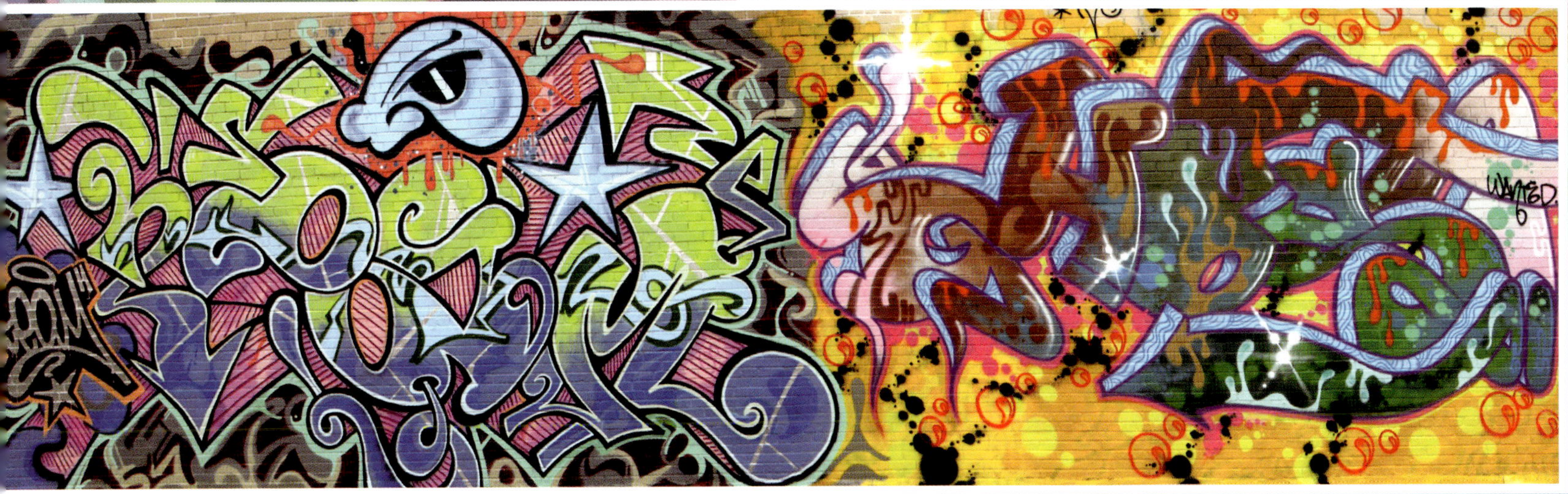

Team, Ghost, Manhattan, NY

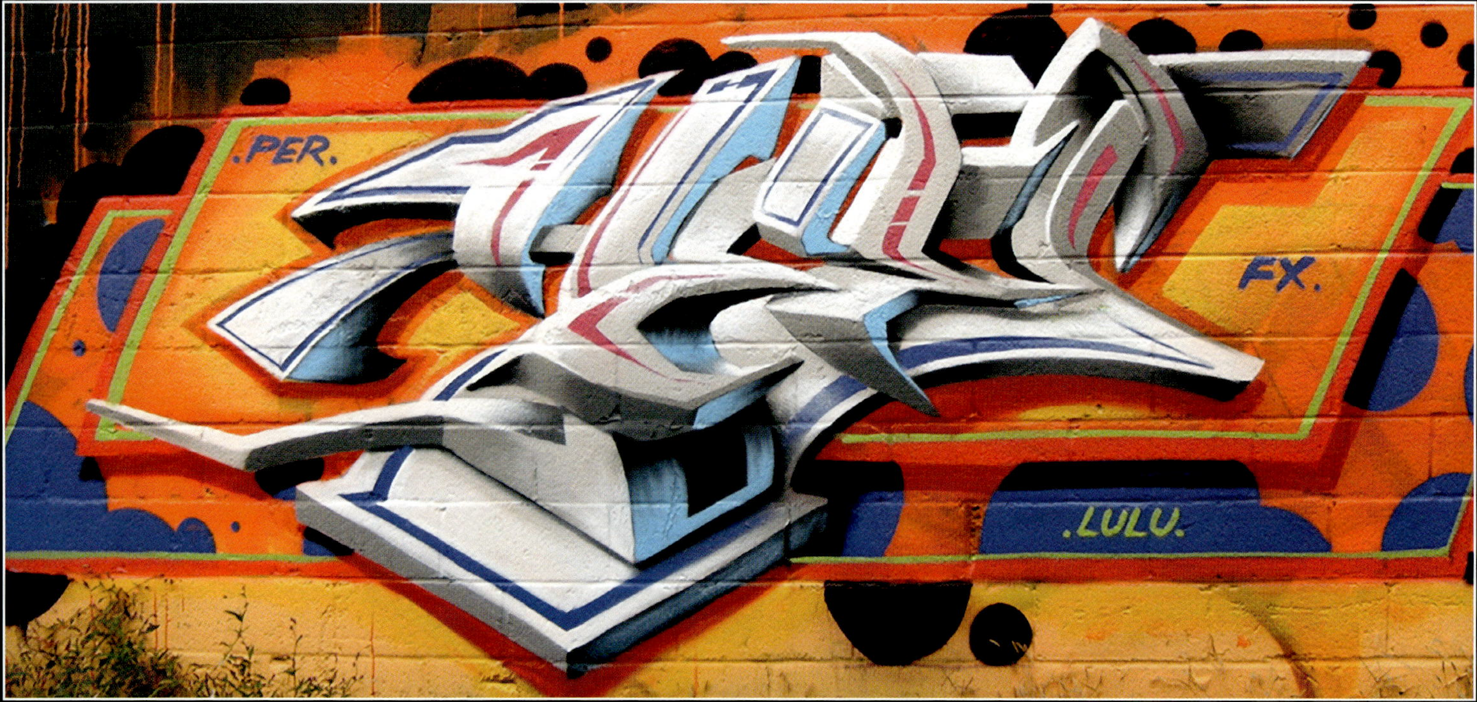


Hef, Brooklyn, NY

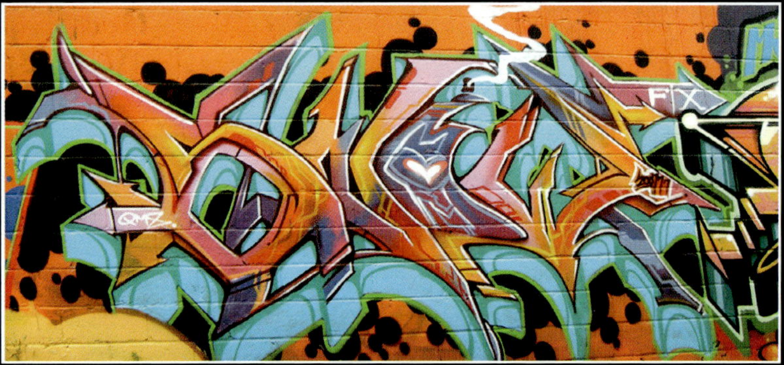


Snow, Brooklyn, NY

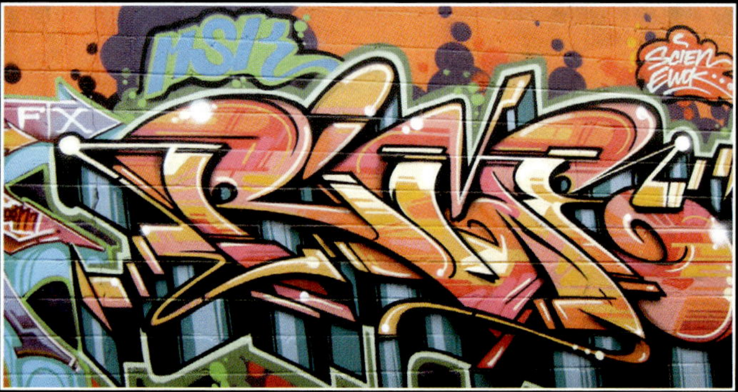


Rime, Brooklyn, NY

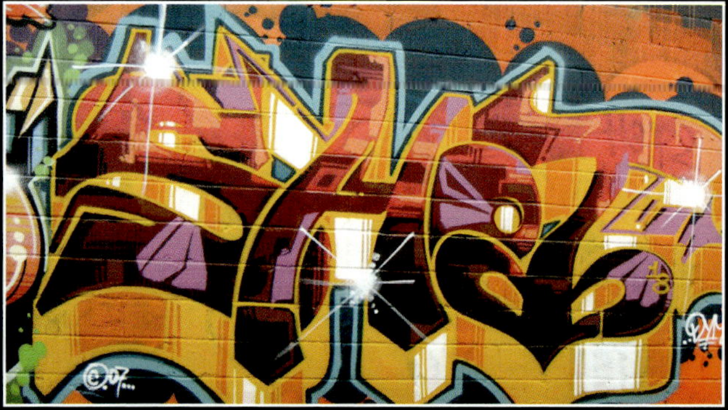

Shots, Brooklyn, NY

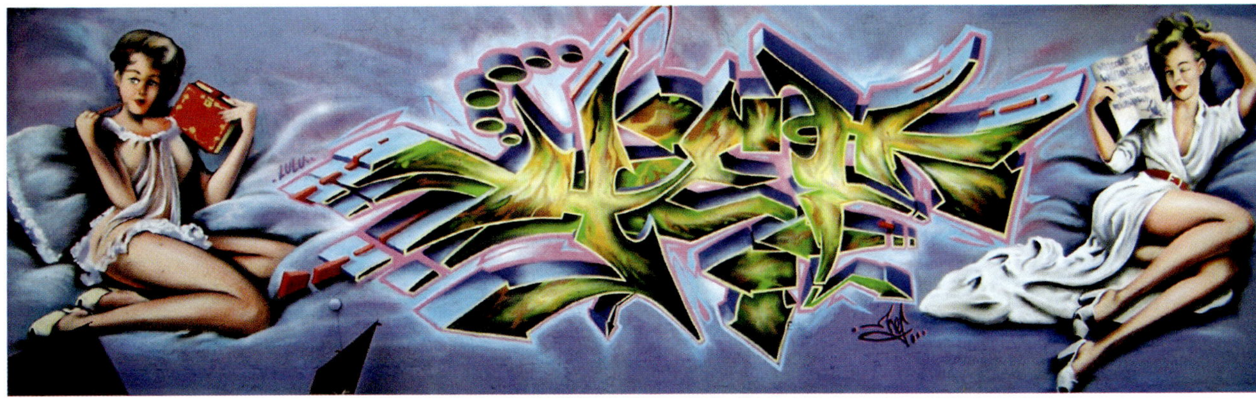

Hef, Brooklyn, NY

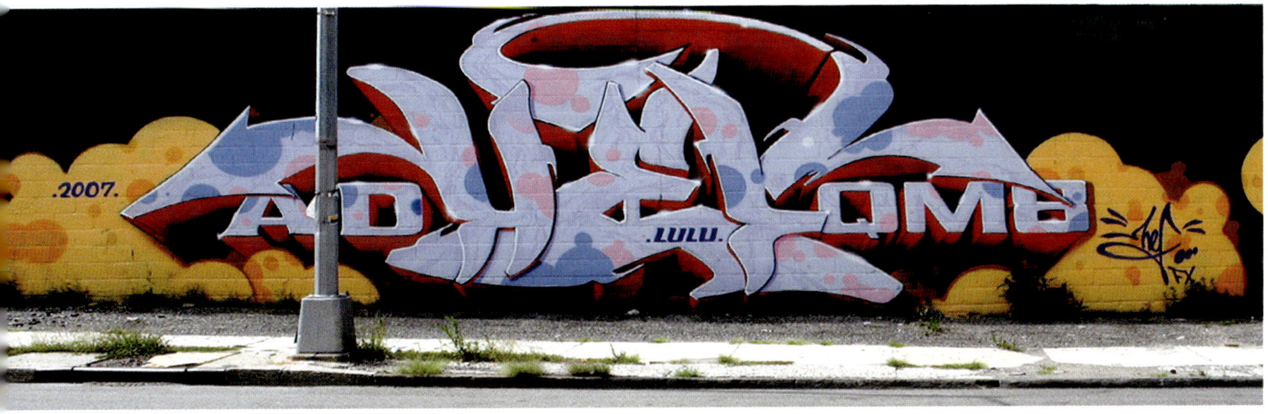


Hef, Brooklyn, NY

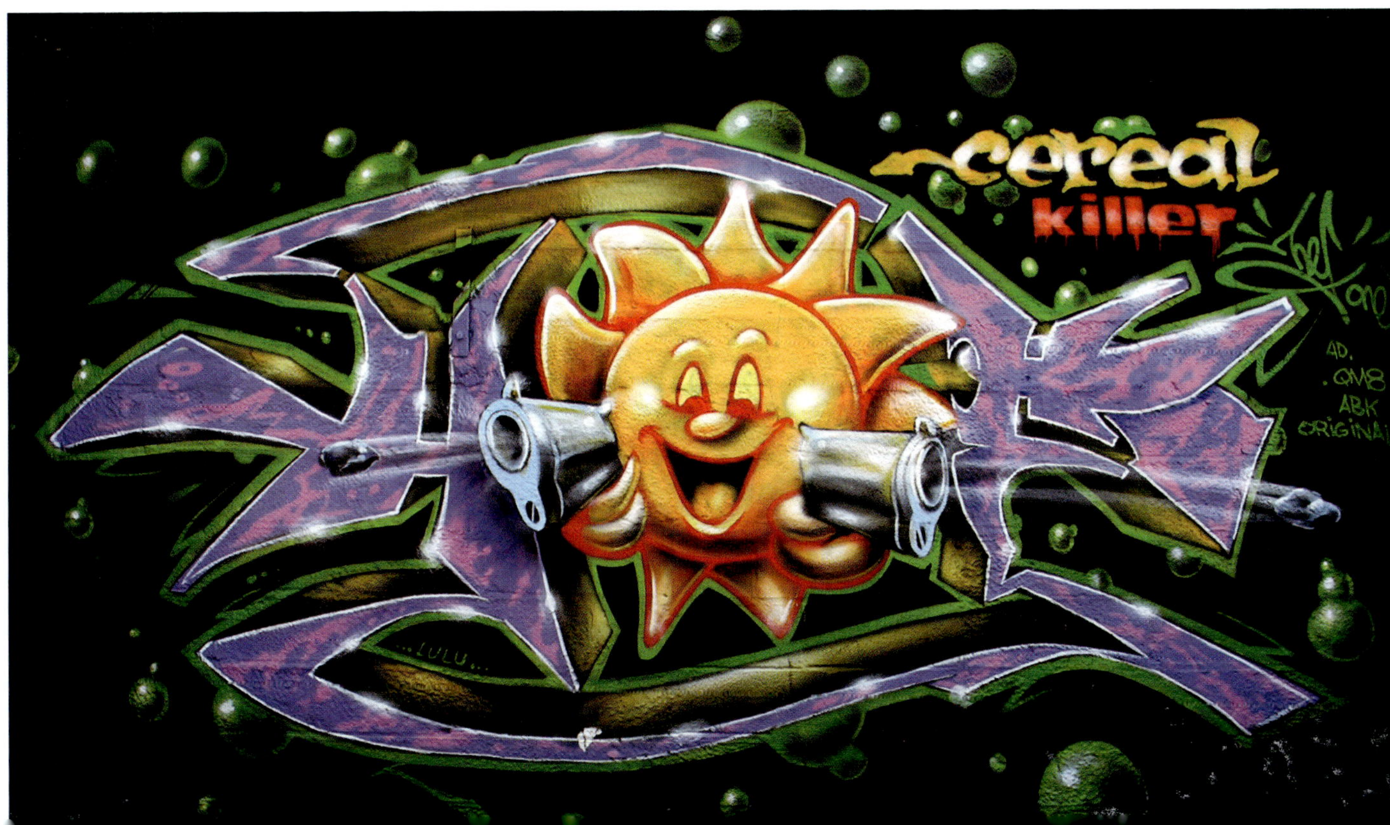


Hef, Long Island, NY

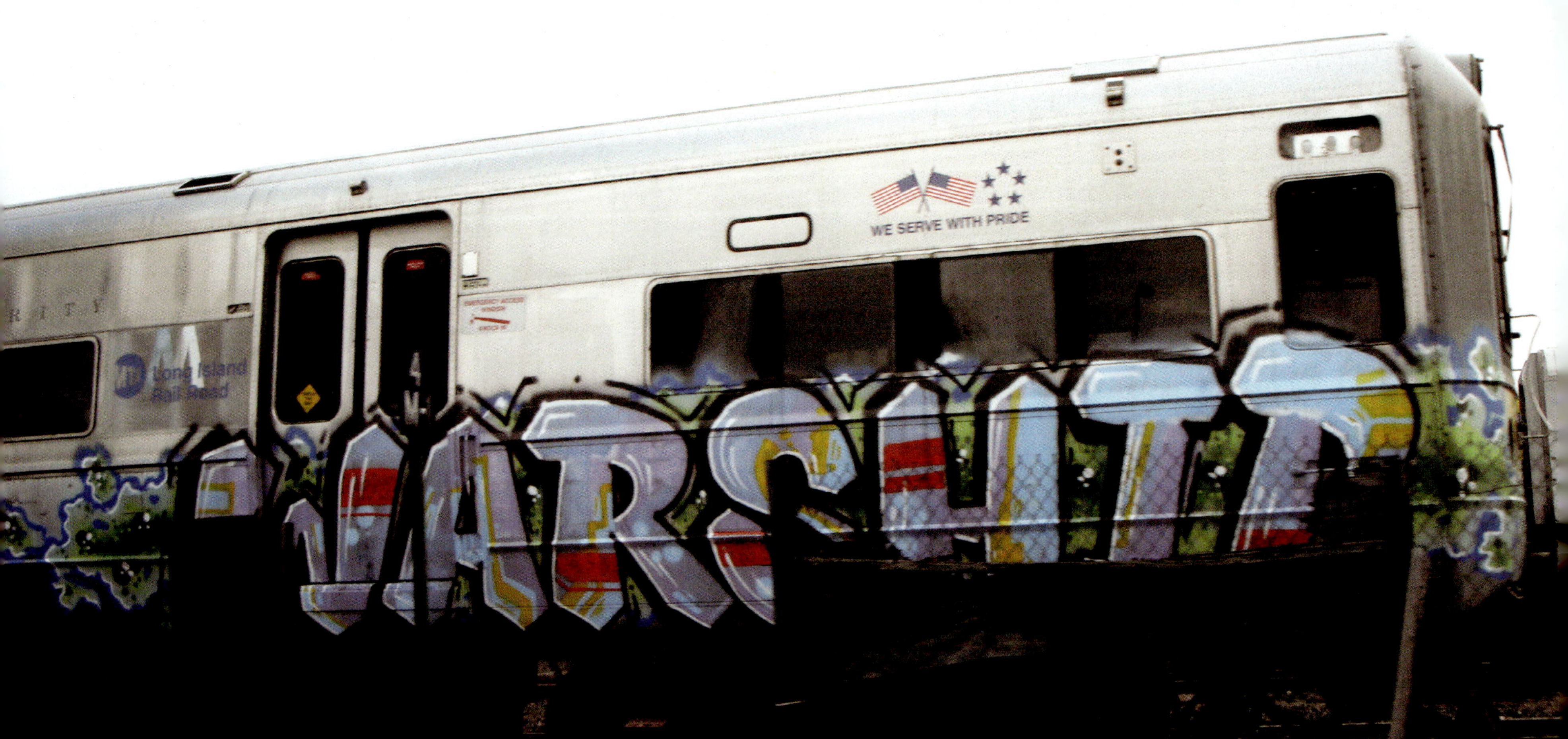


Warship (Unknown), Brooklyn, NY

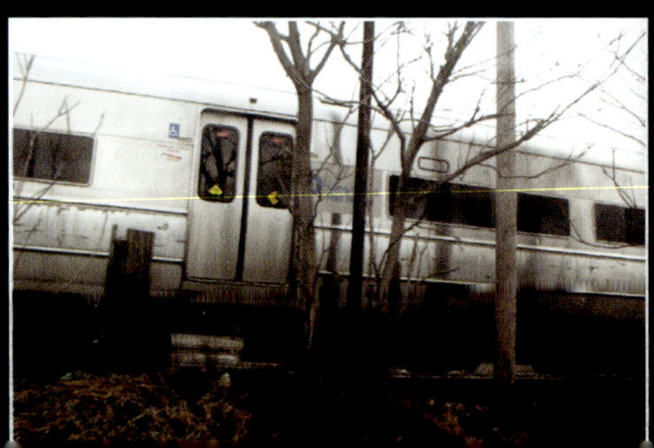

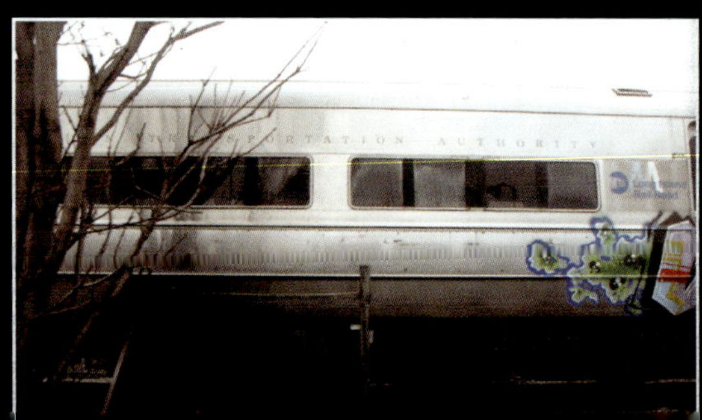

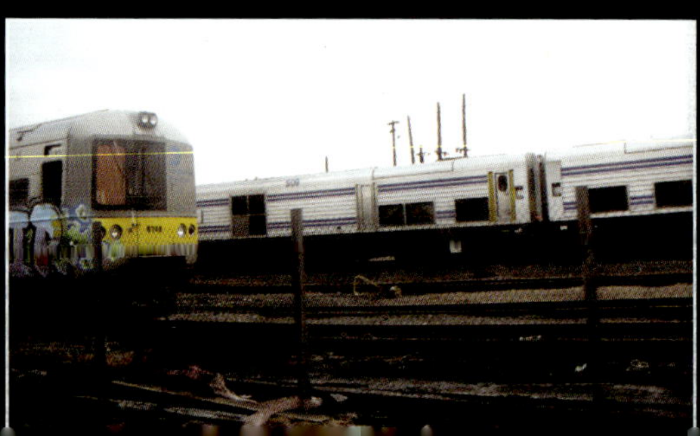

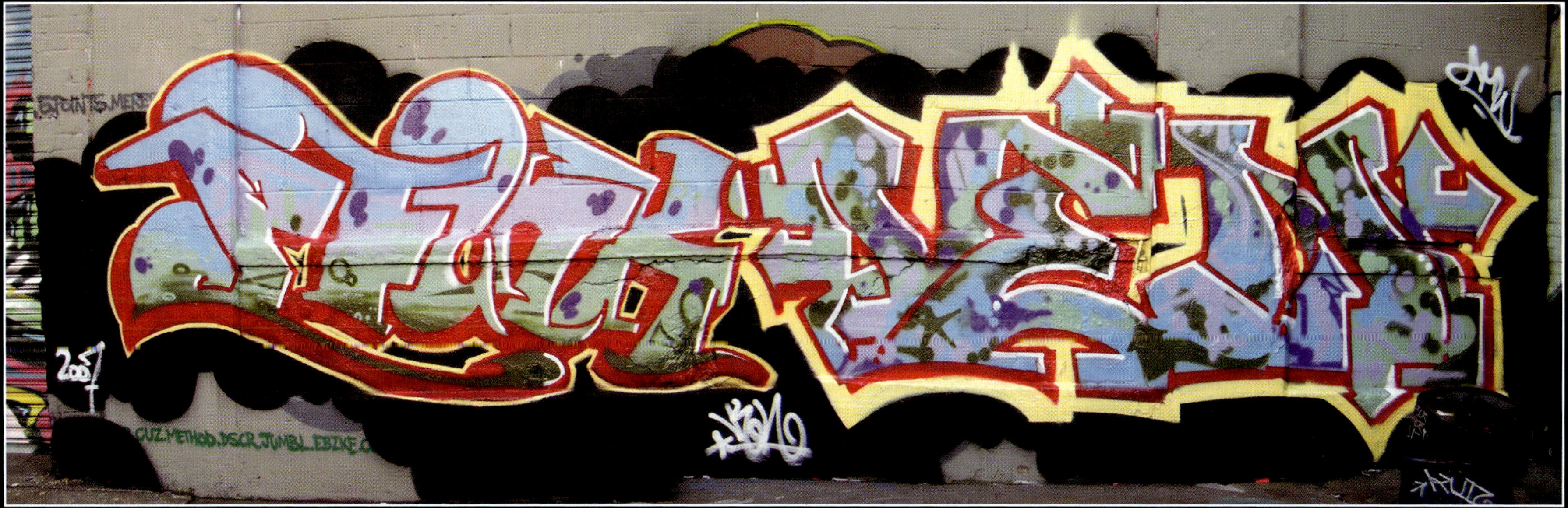


PFunk, Ven, Queens, NY, 5 Pointz

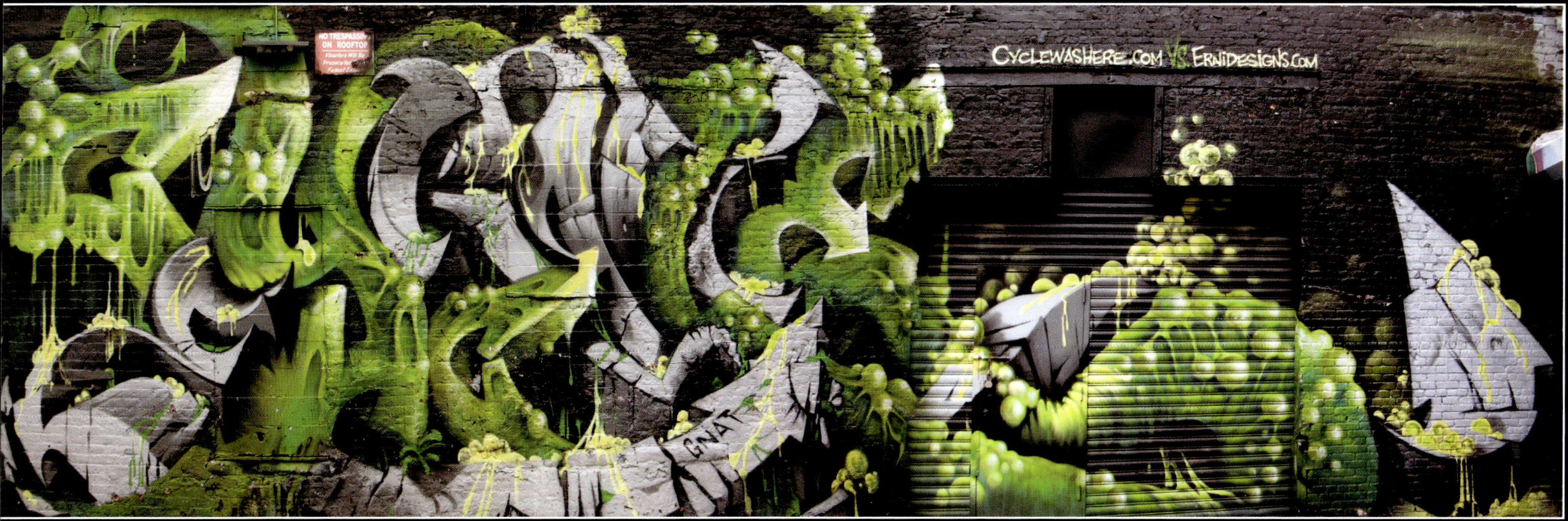


Cycle, Erni, Queens, NY, 5 Pointz

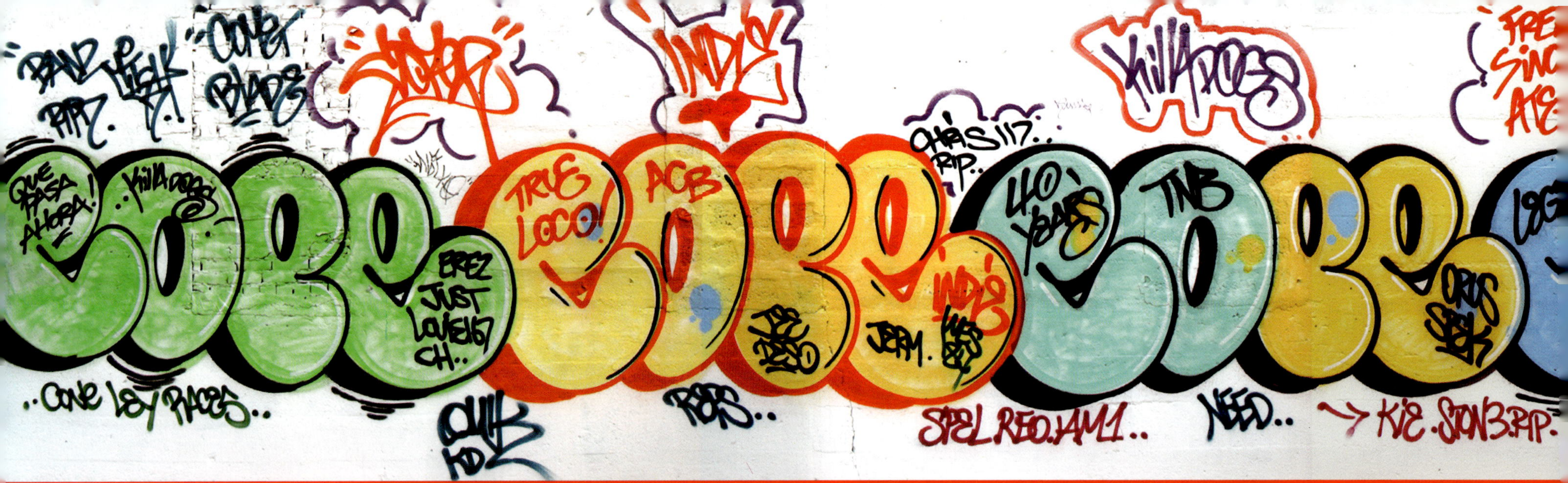

Cope2, Brooklyn, NY

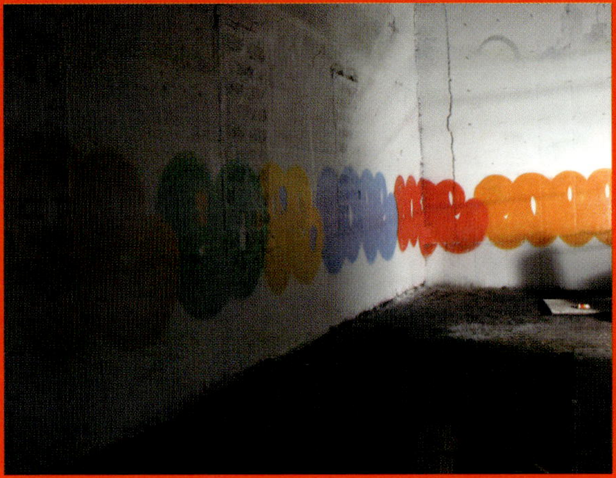

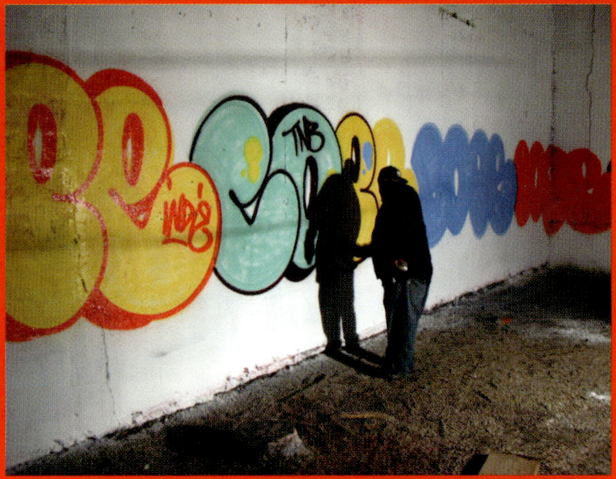

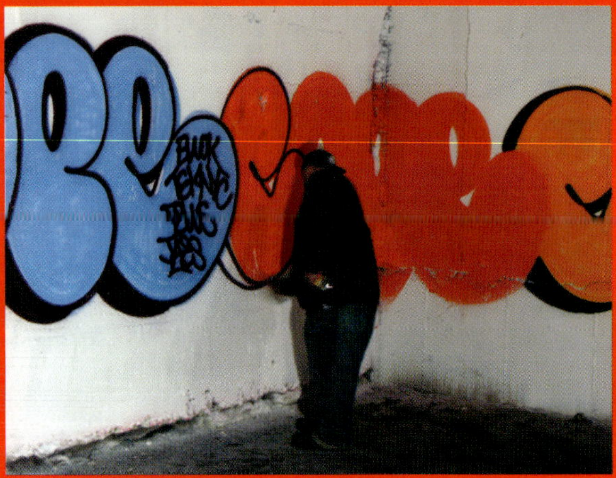

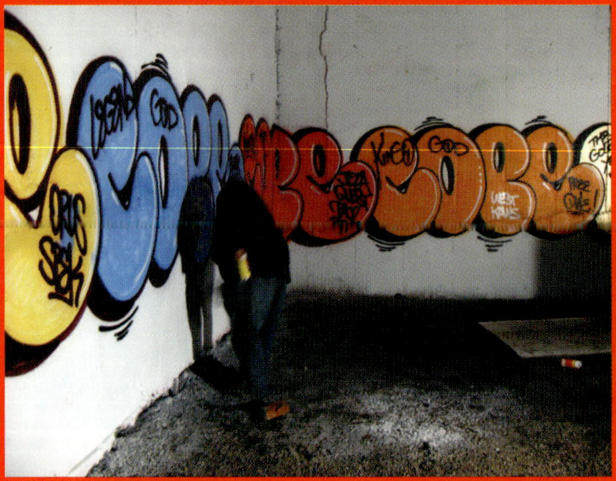

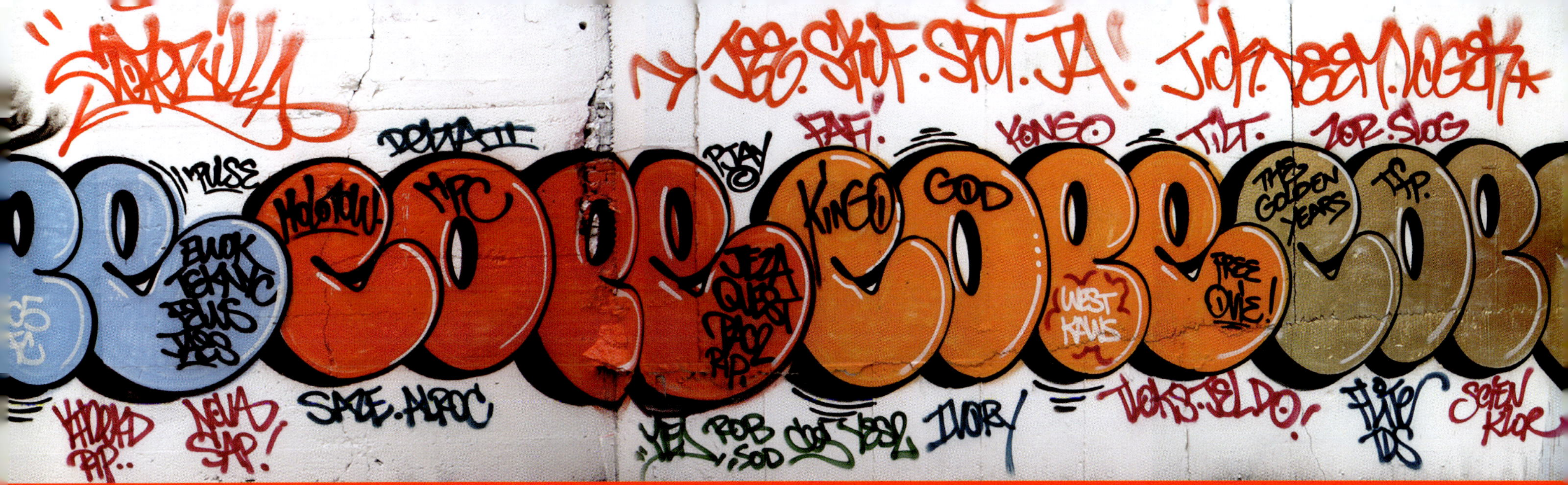

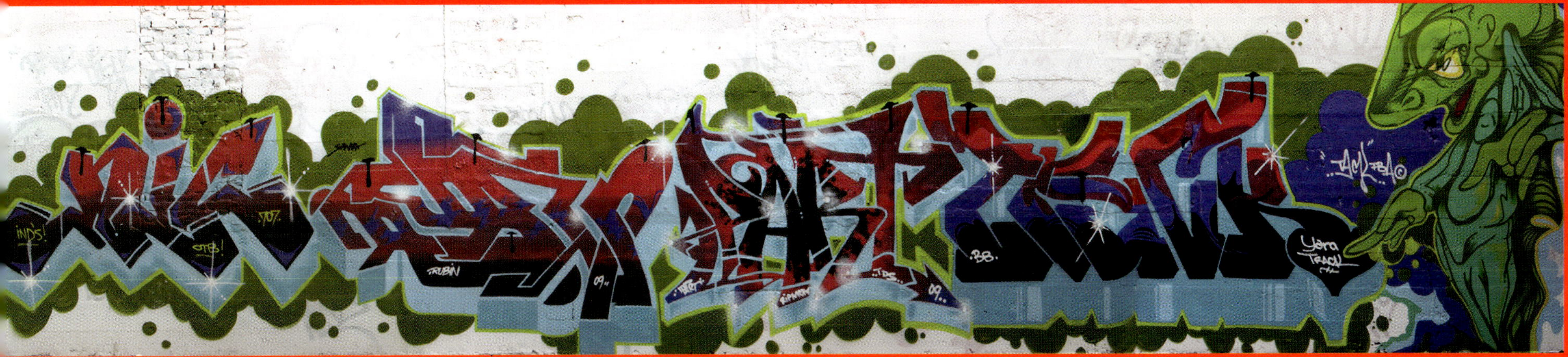

Nic707, Rubin, Part, Track, Tack FBA, Brooklyn, NY

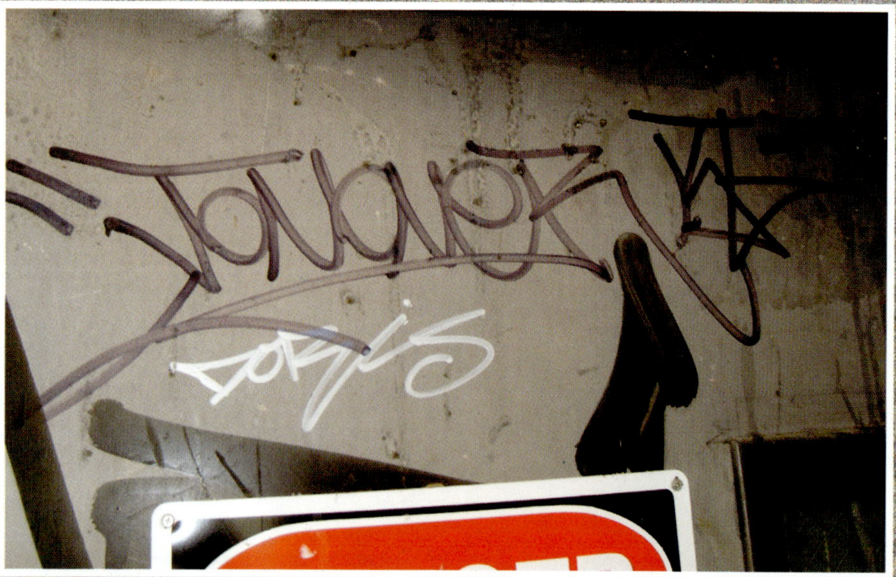

Jon156, Manhattan, NY

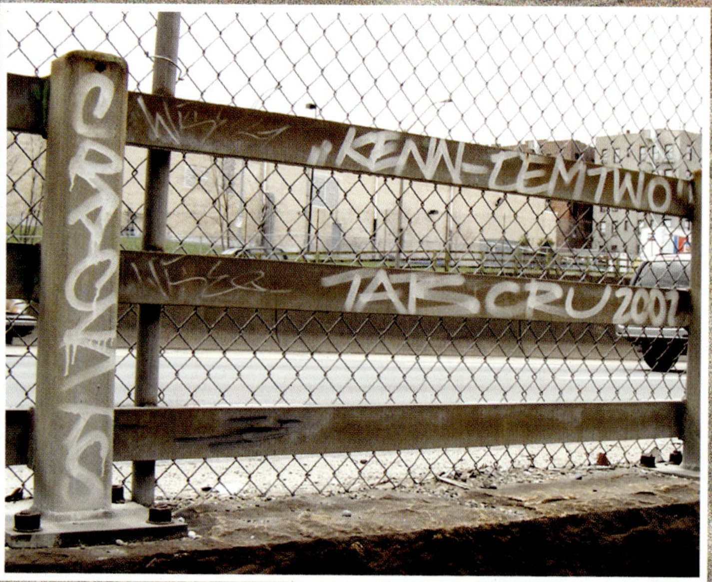

Crack TS, Bronx, NY

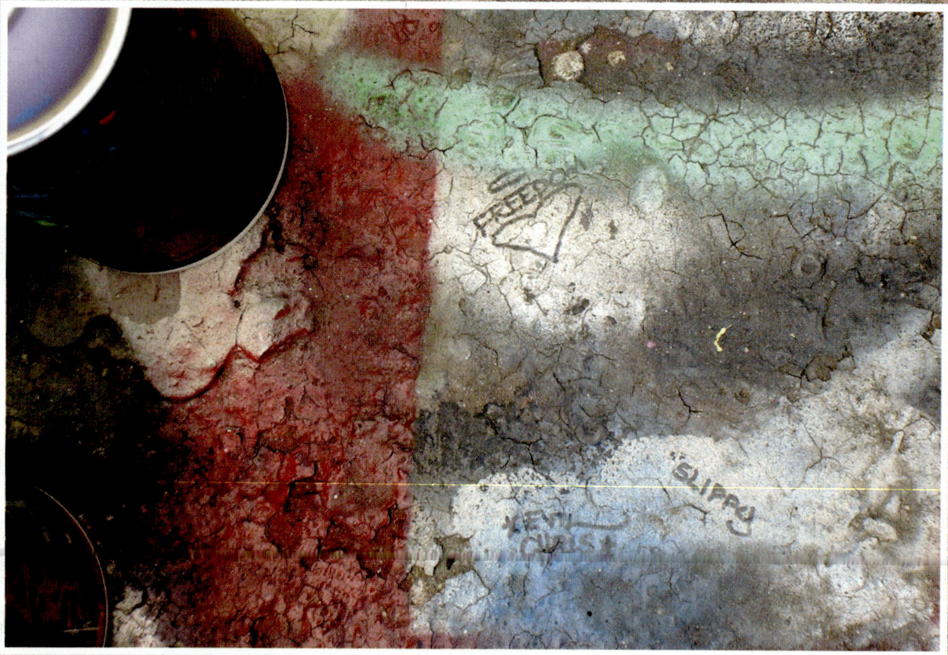

Freedom, Queens, NY

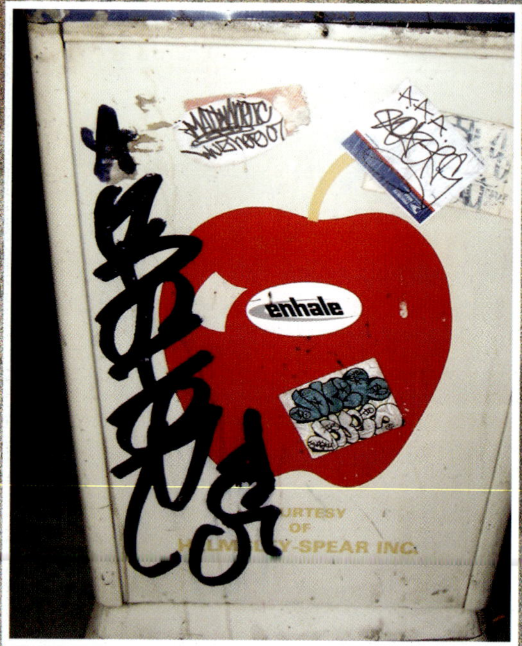


Dash TC-5, Manhattan, NY

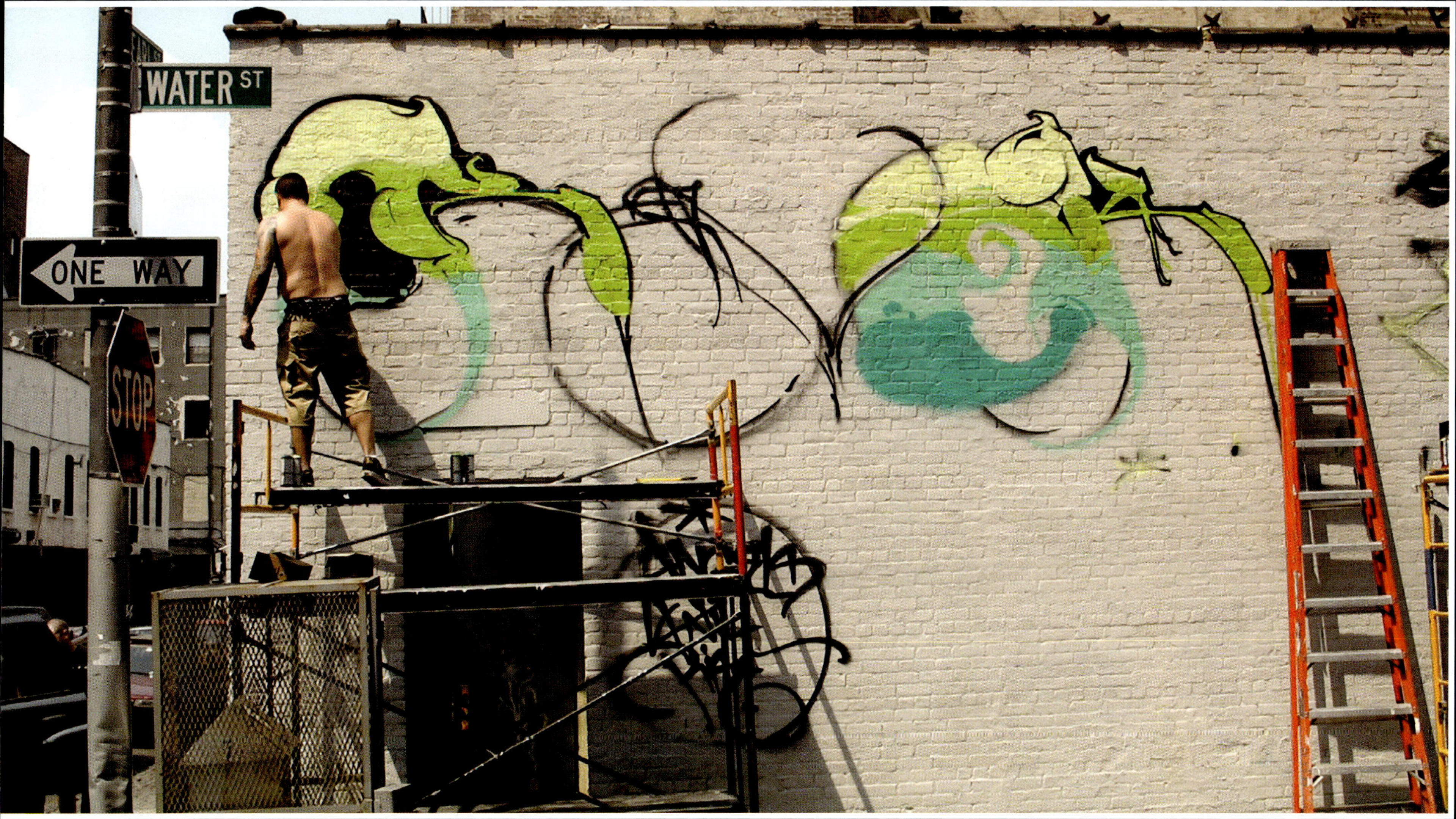


Revok – Action, Brooklyn, NY

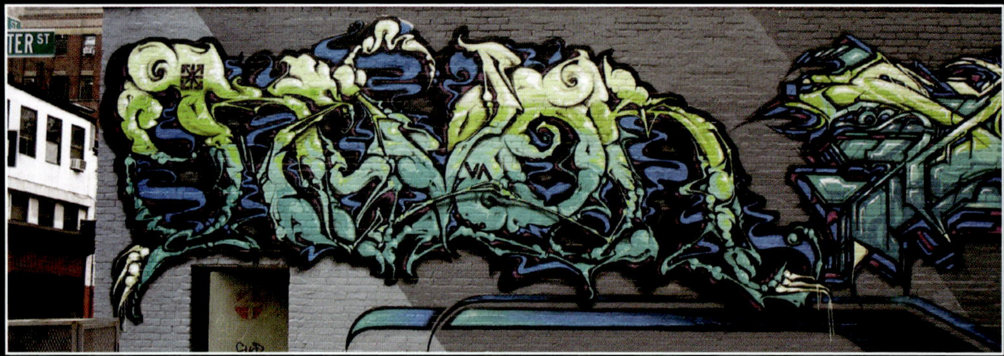


Revok, Brooklyn, NY

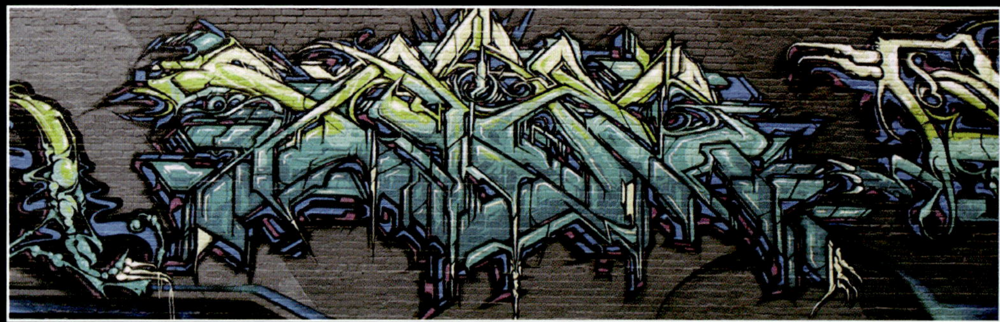

Saber, Brooklyn, NY

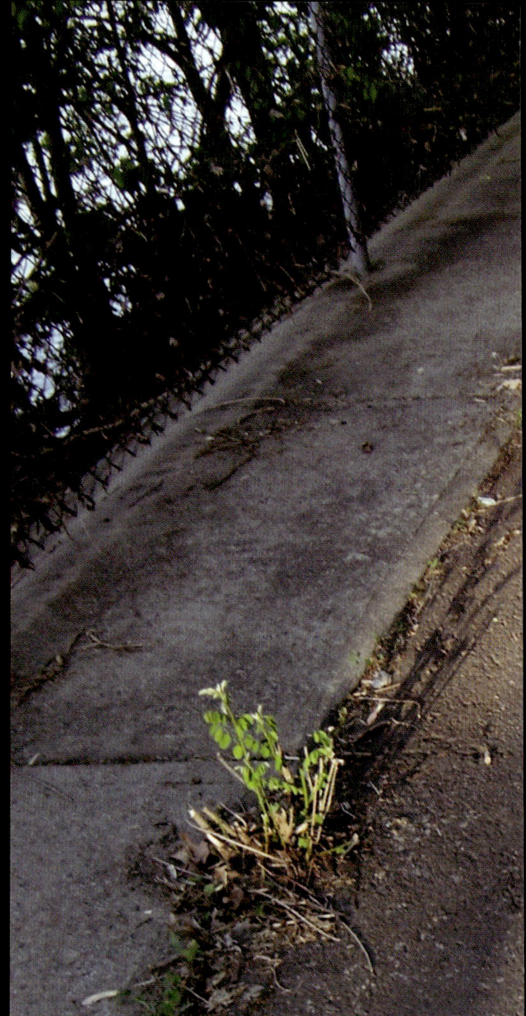

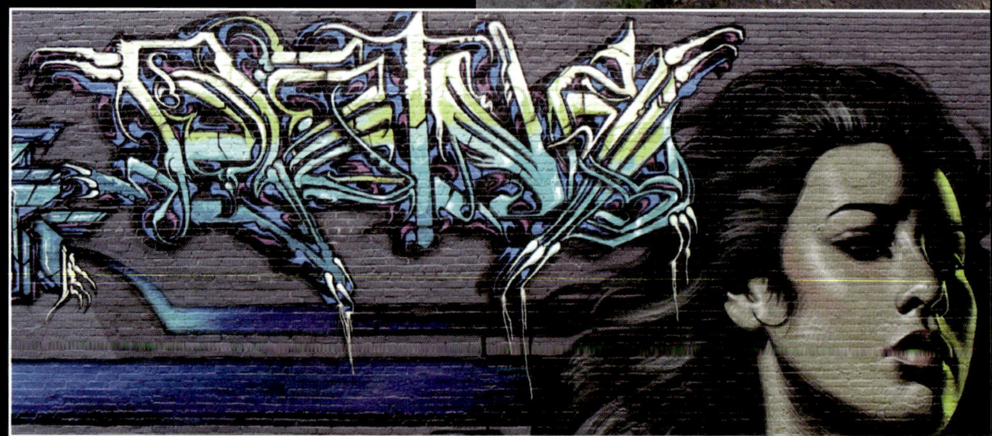

Retna, Brooklyn, NY

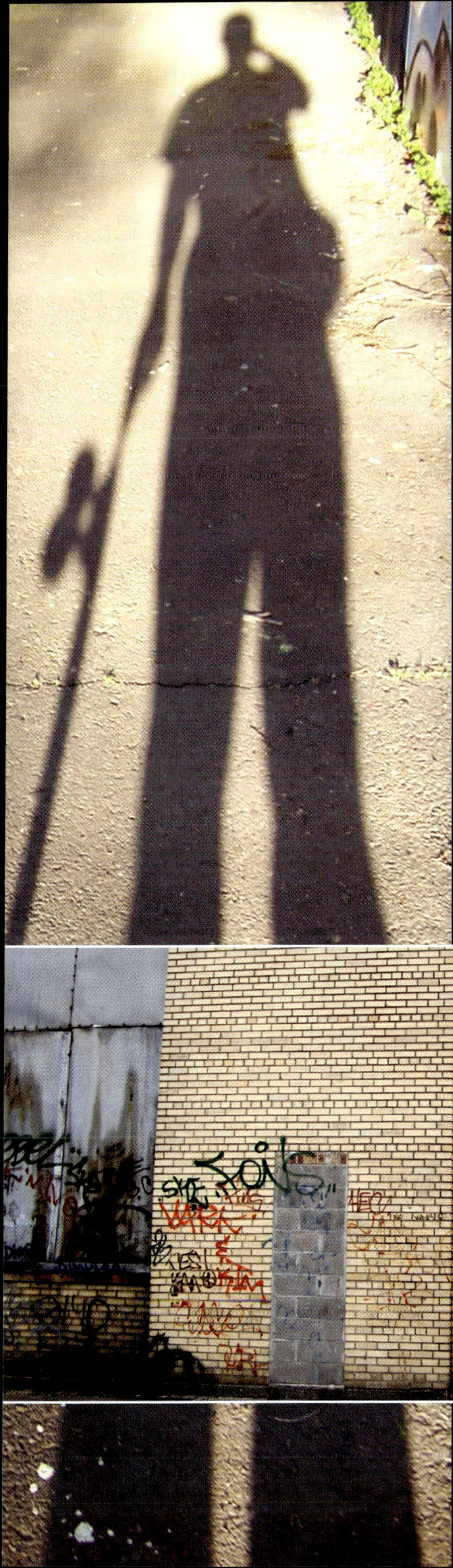

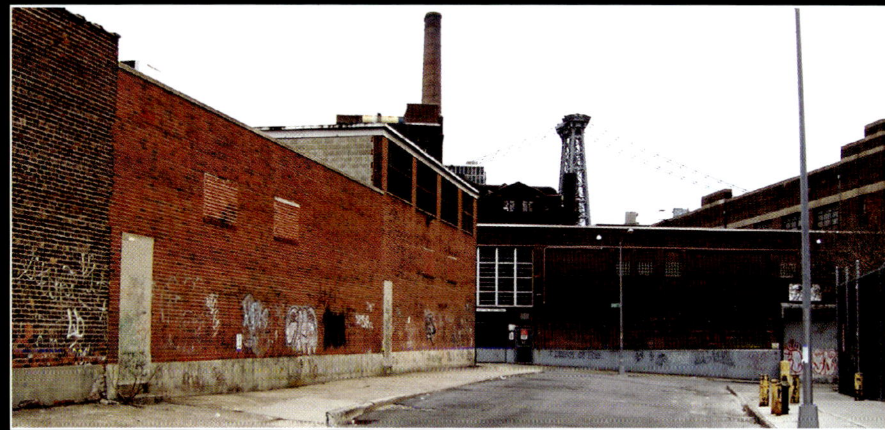

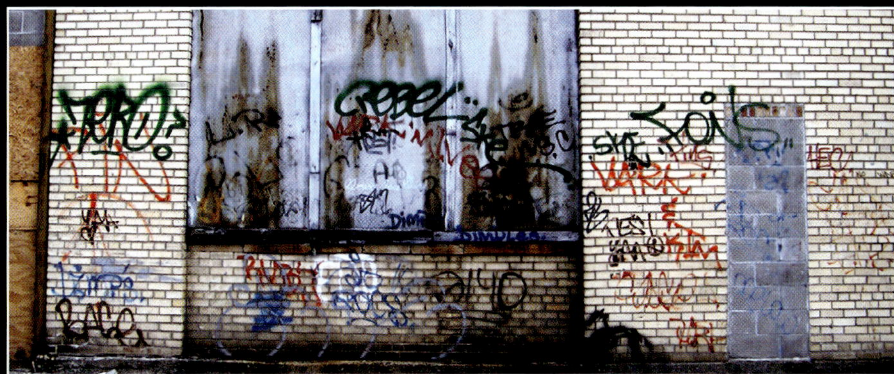

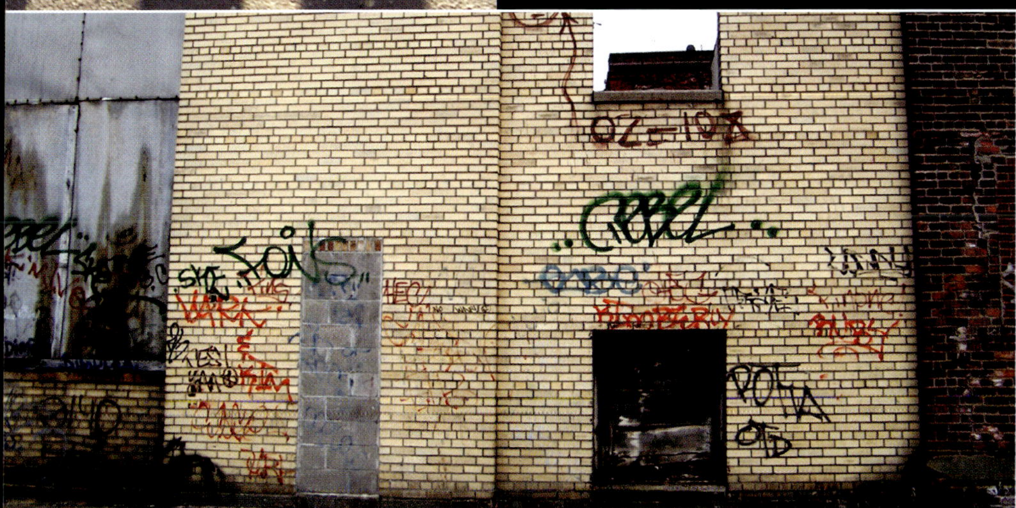

Marty, Echo, Rime, Manhattan, NY

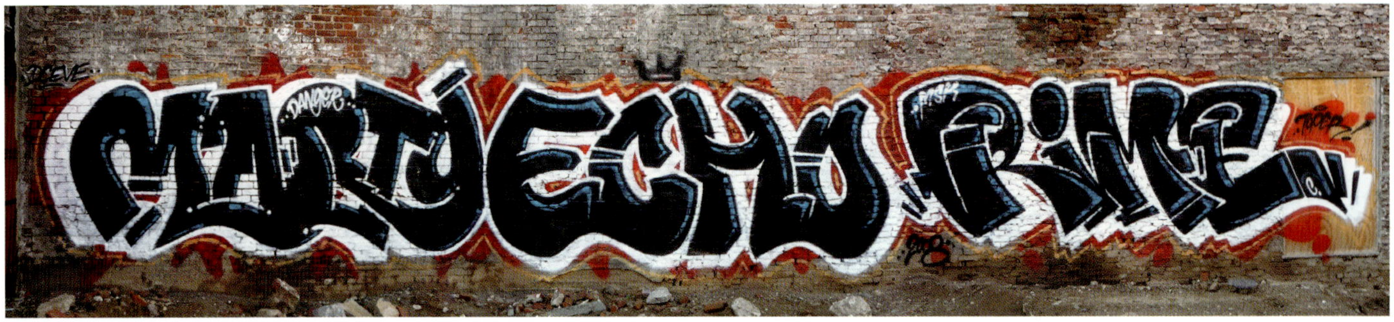

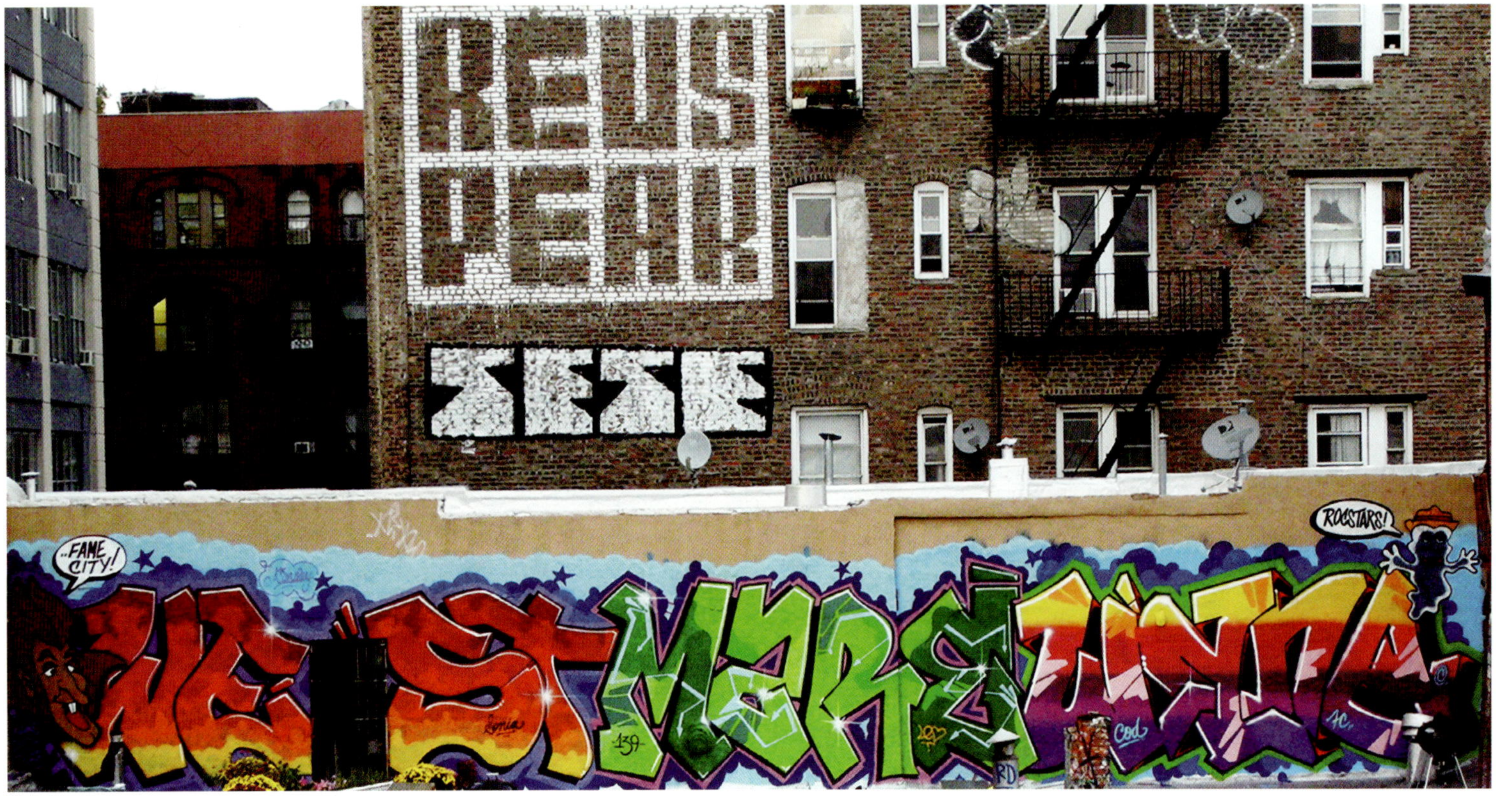


West, Mare139, Wane, Brooklyn, NY

Augor, Brooklyn, NY

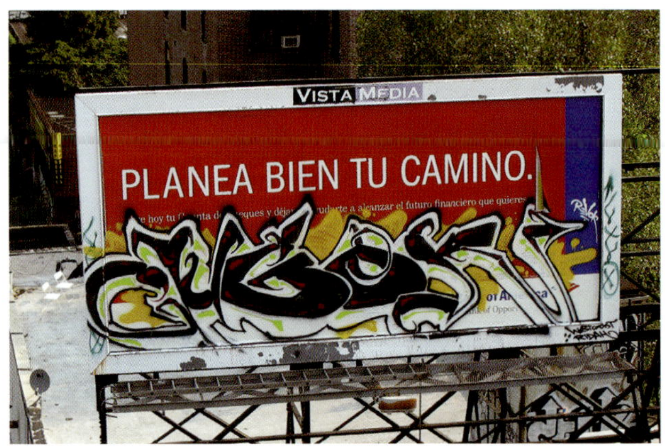

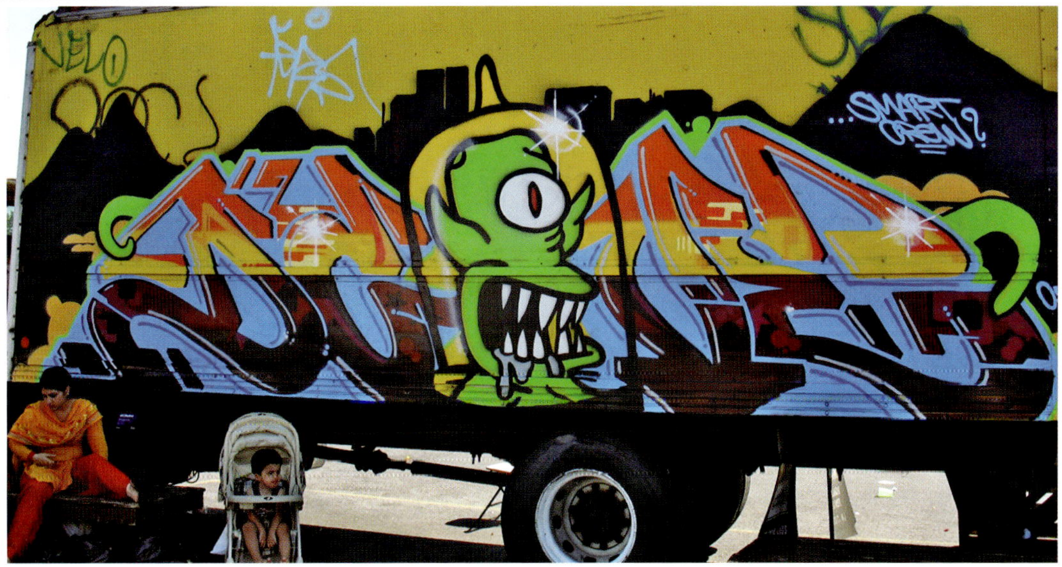


Dceve, Queens, NY

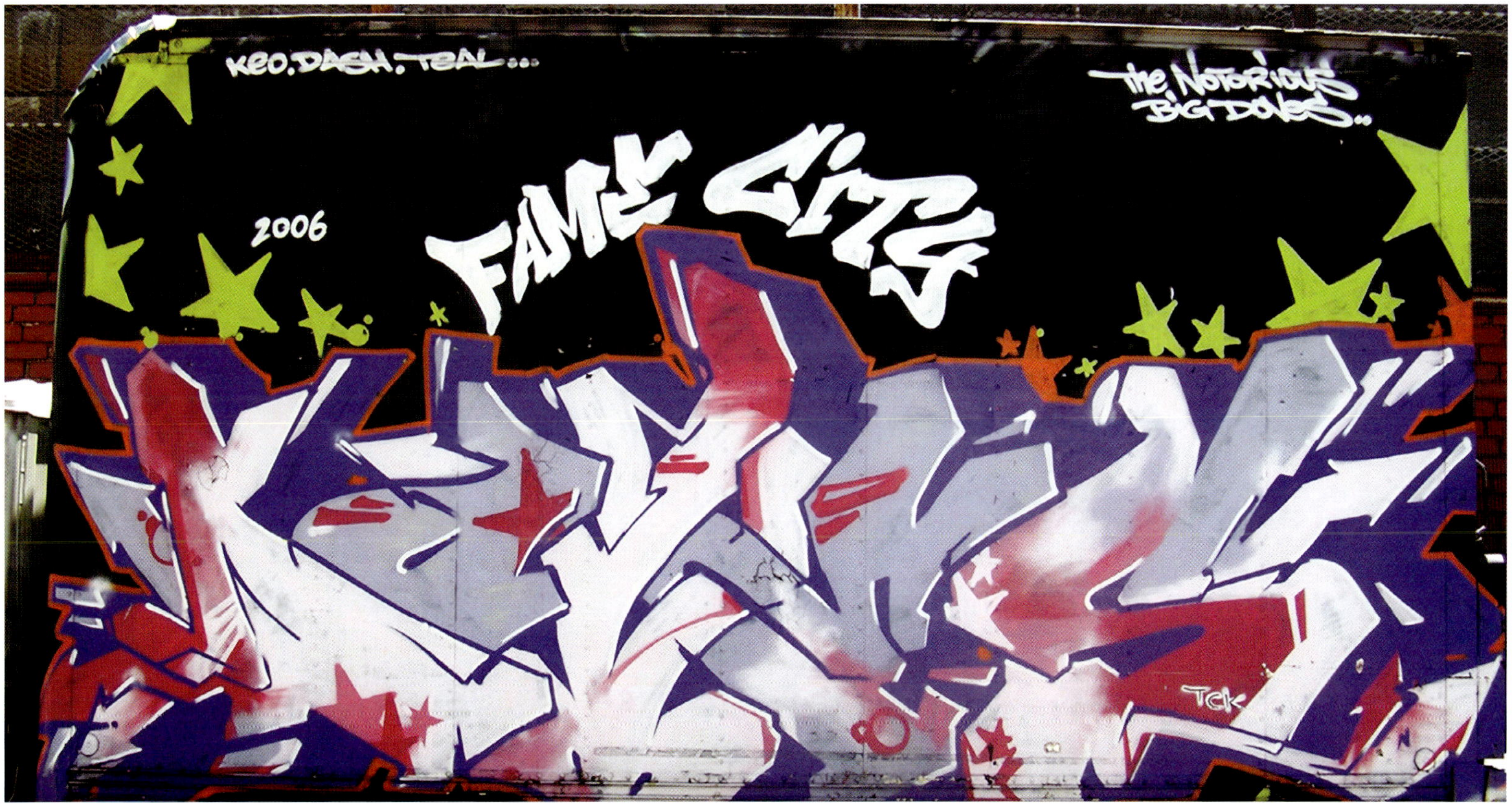


Doves, Queens, NY

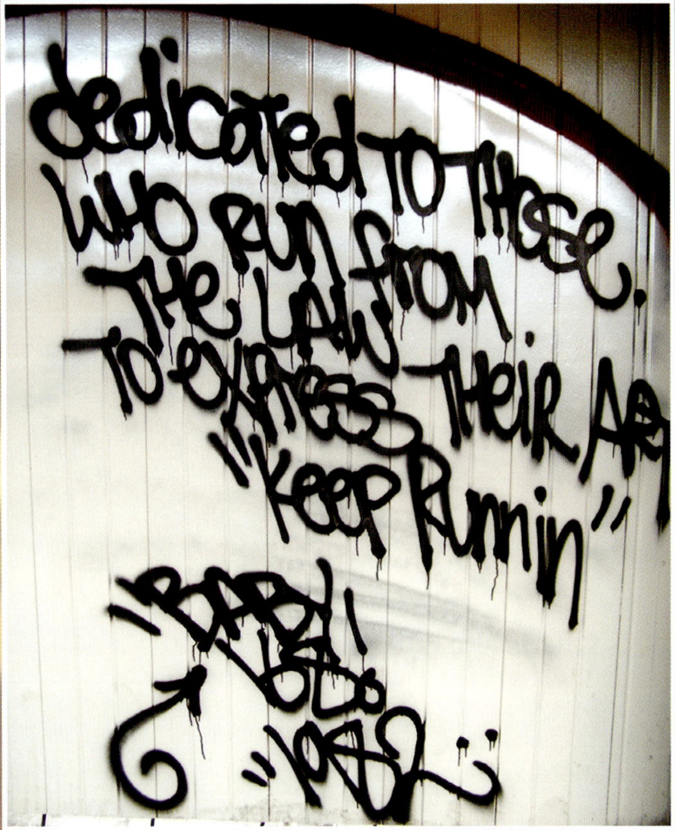


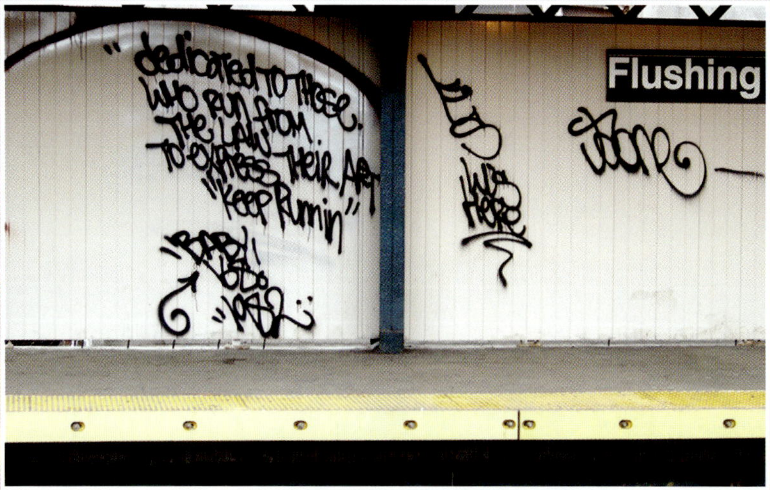


LES, Brooklyn, NY

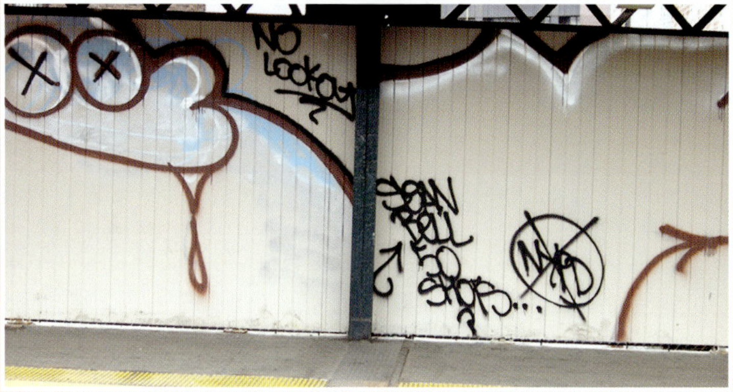

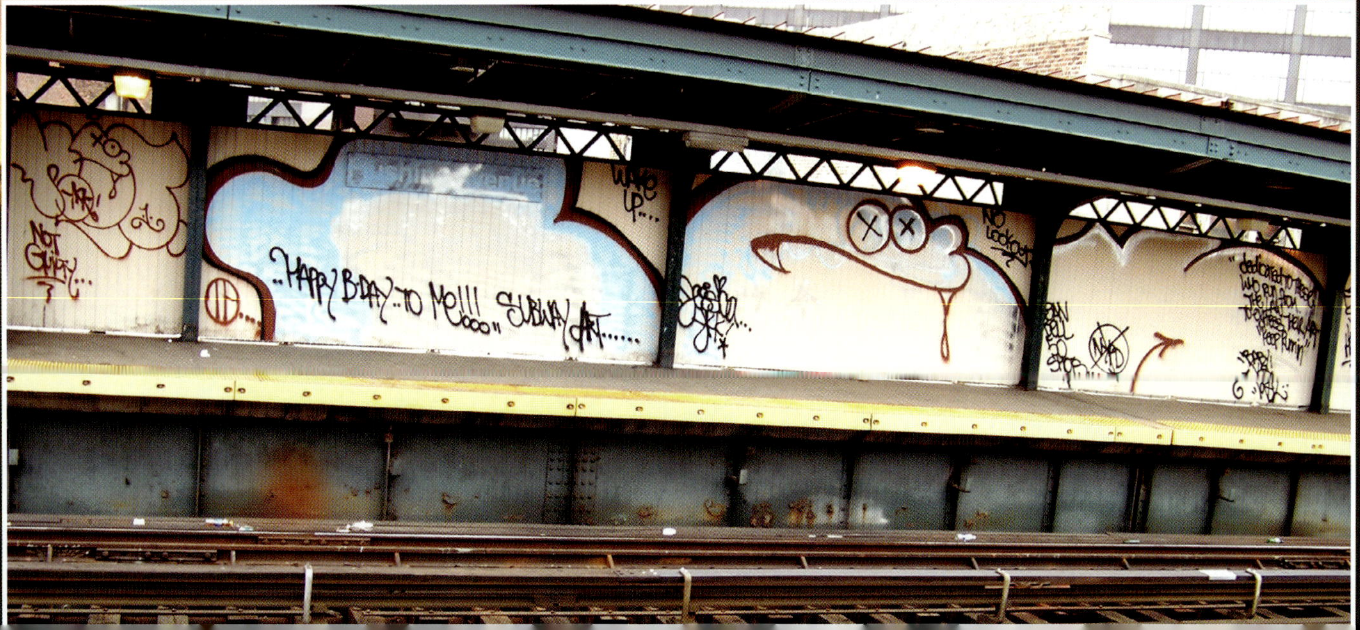

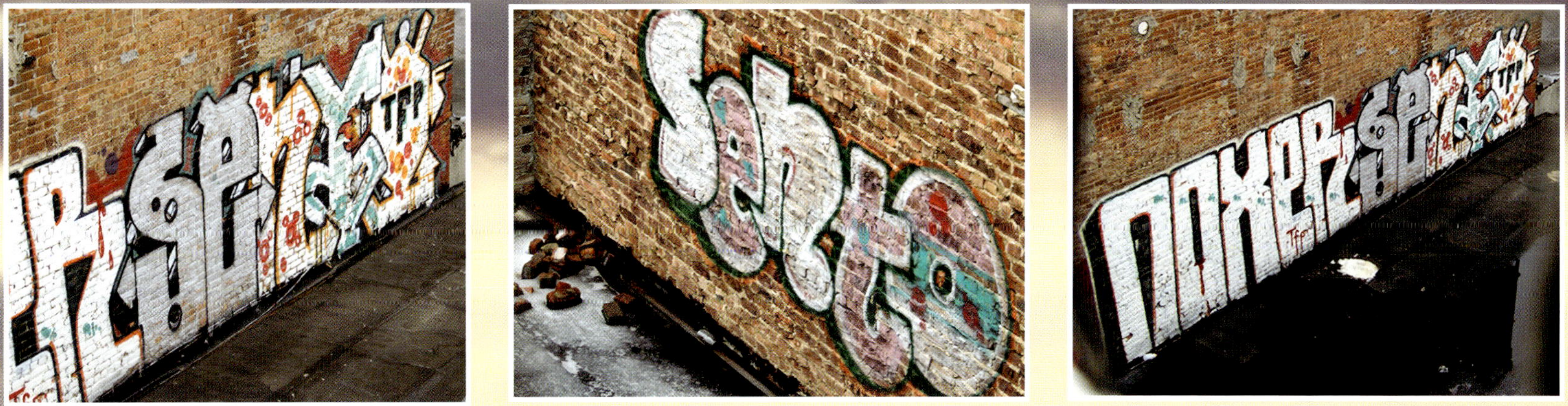

Noxer, Sento, Brooklyn, NY

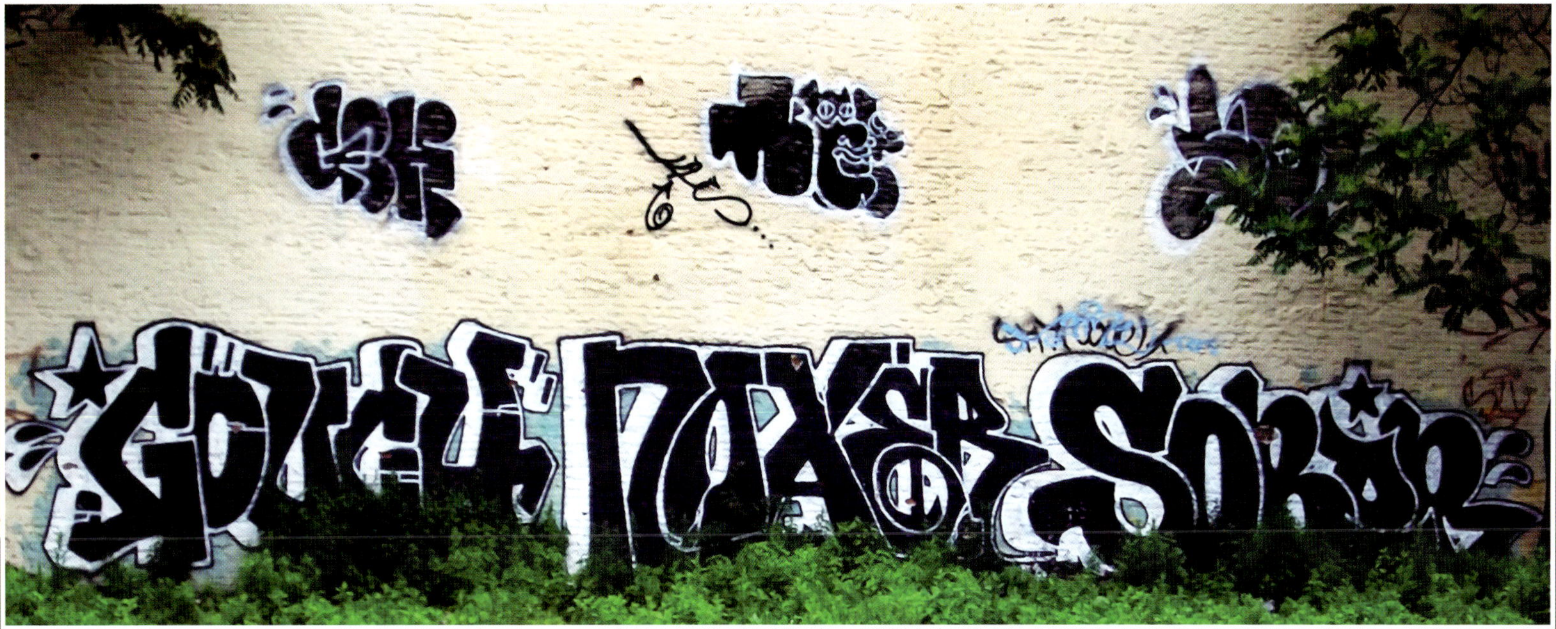

Gouch, Noxer, Sober, Brooklyn, NY

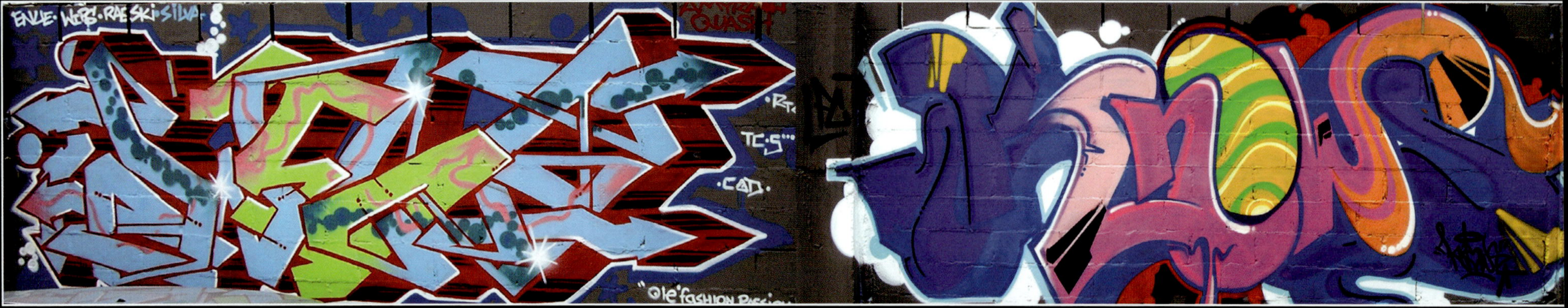

Wen, Knows, Queens, NY

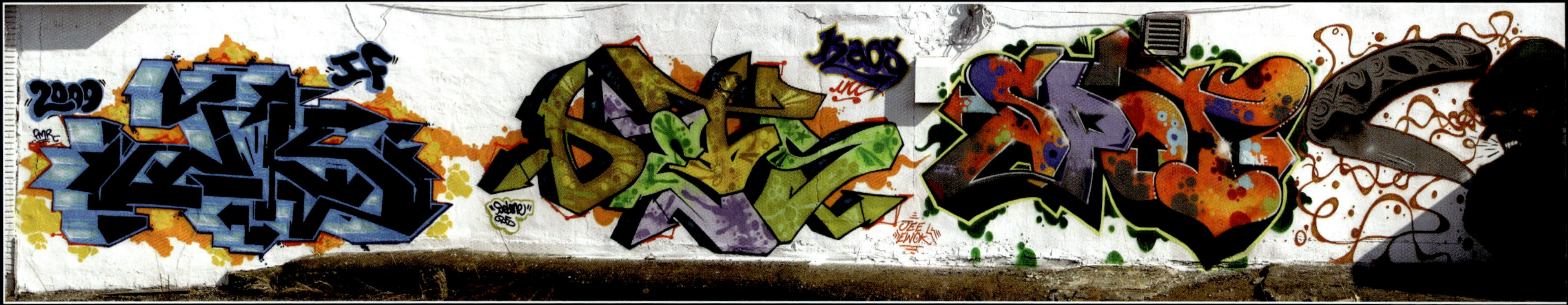

Jick, Det, Spot, Trap, Queens, NY

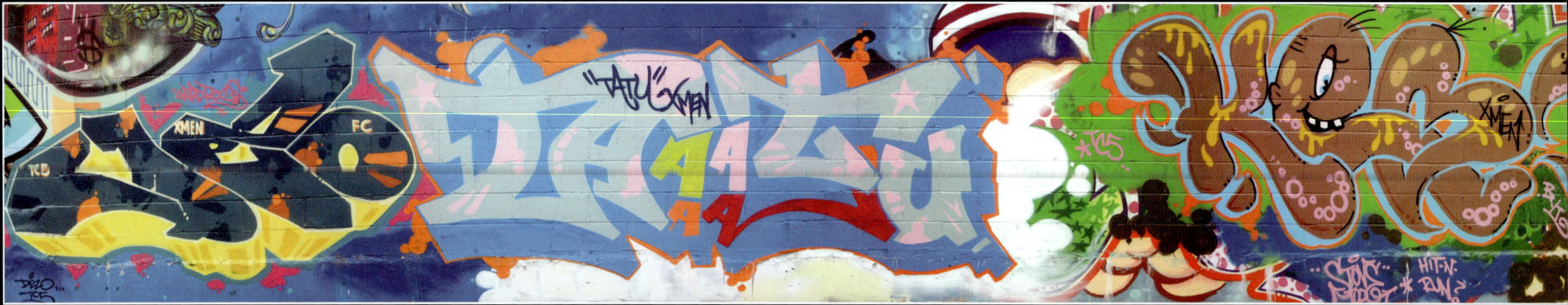

Dezo, Tatu, Keo, Brooklyn, NY

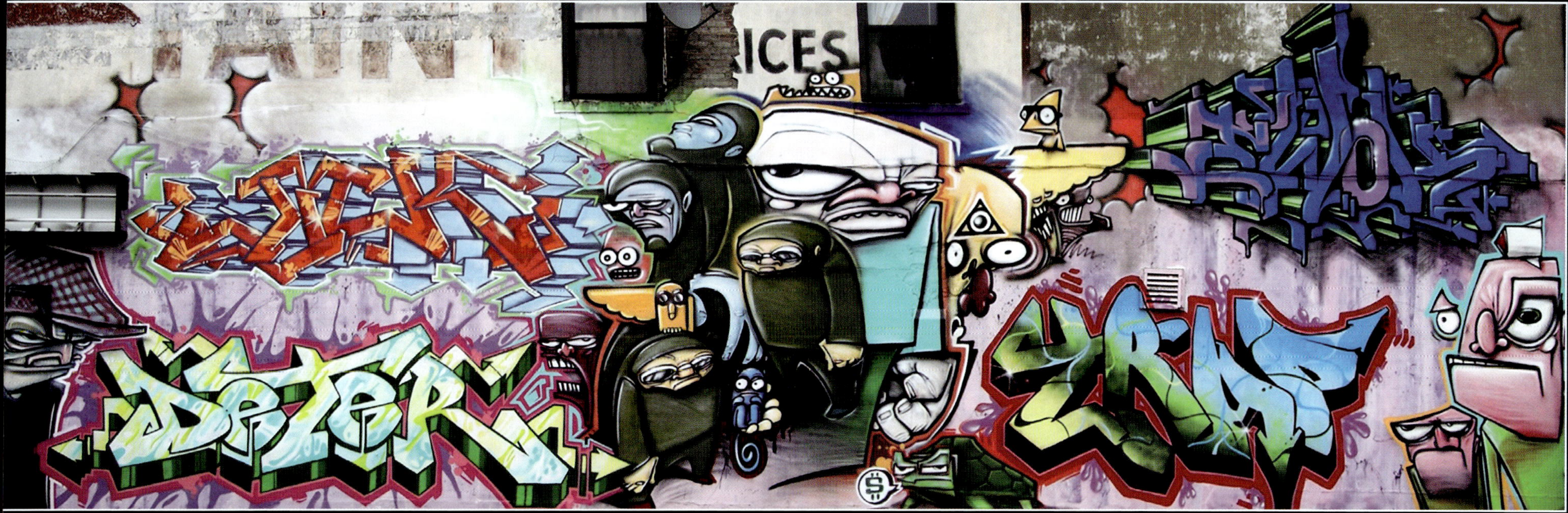


Det, Jick, Ewok, Trap, Queens, NY

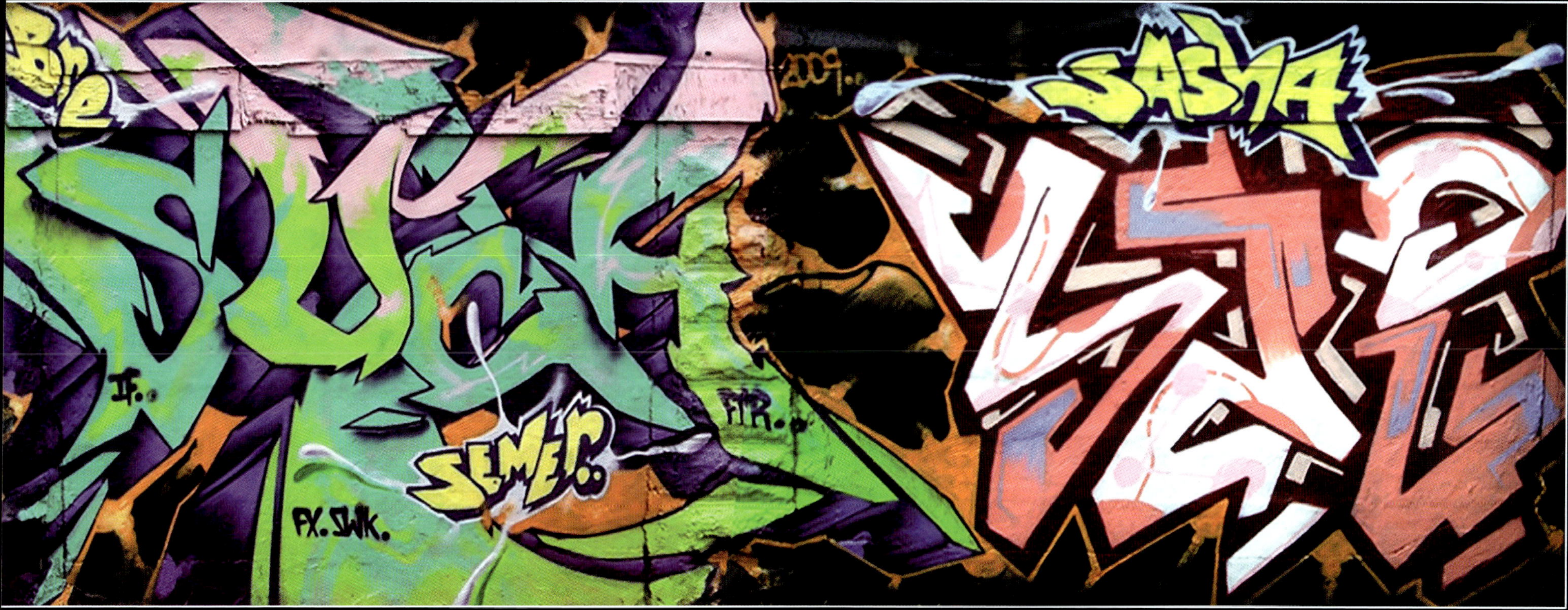


Such, Lae, Queens, NY

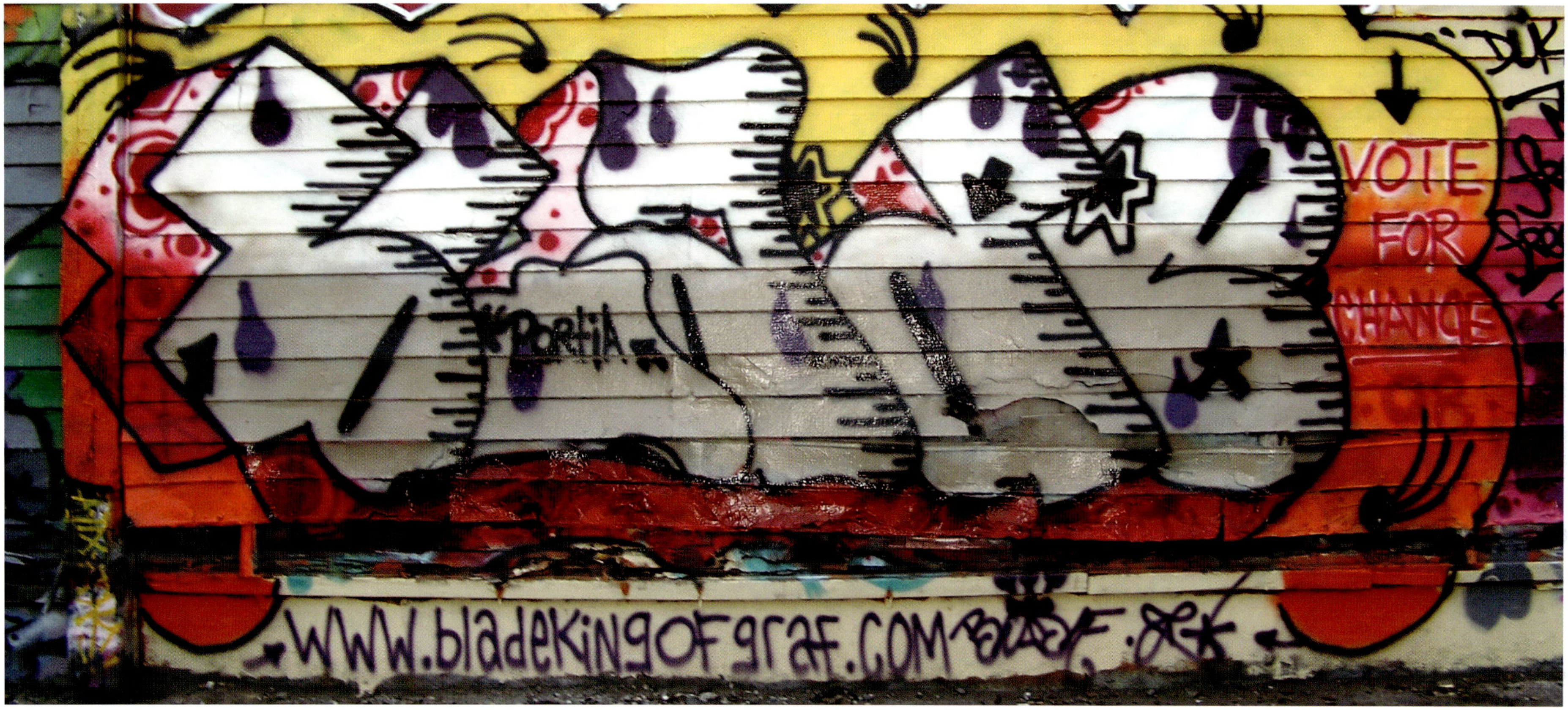


Blade, Queens, NY, 5 Pointz

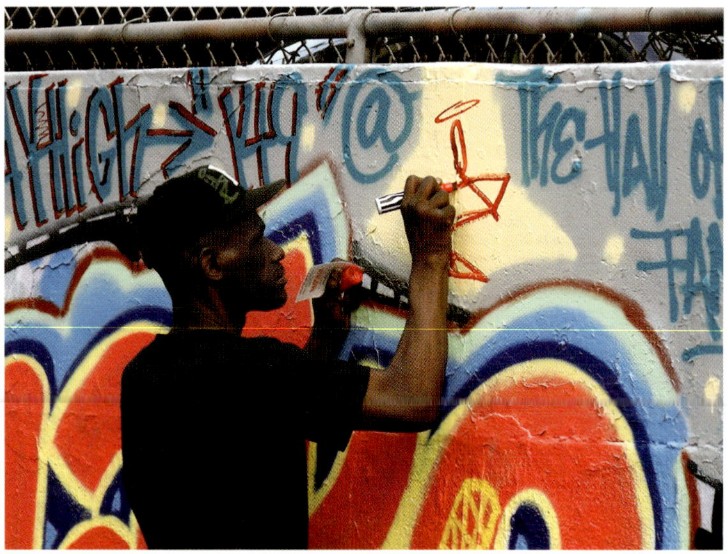

Stay High 149, Manhattan, NY

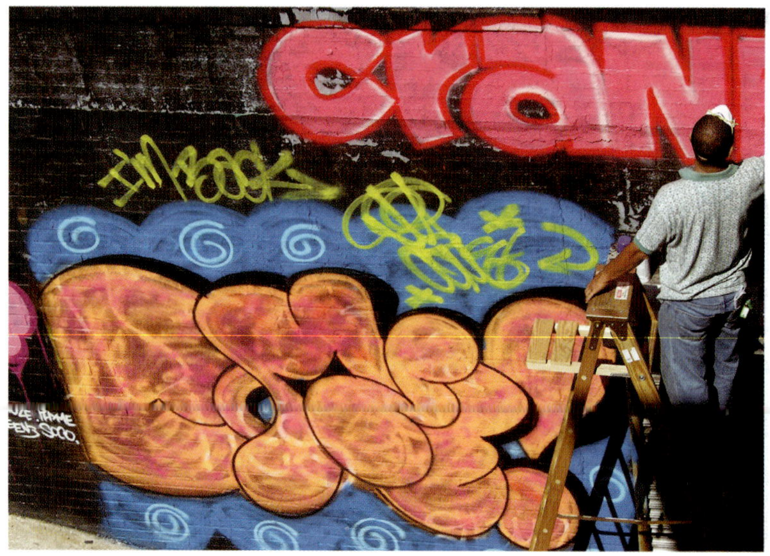

Comet, Crane, Manhattan, NY

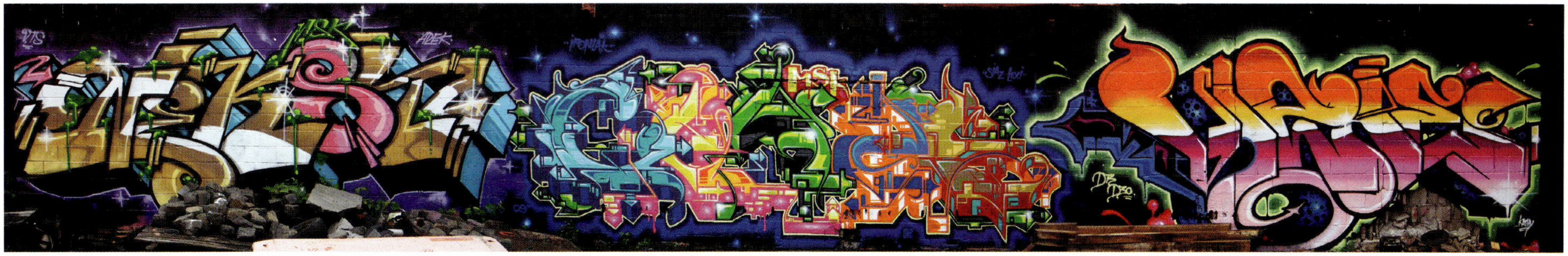

Nekst, Ceaze, Vizie, New Jersey

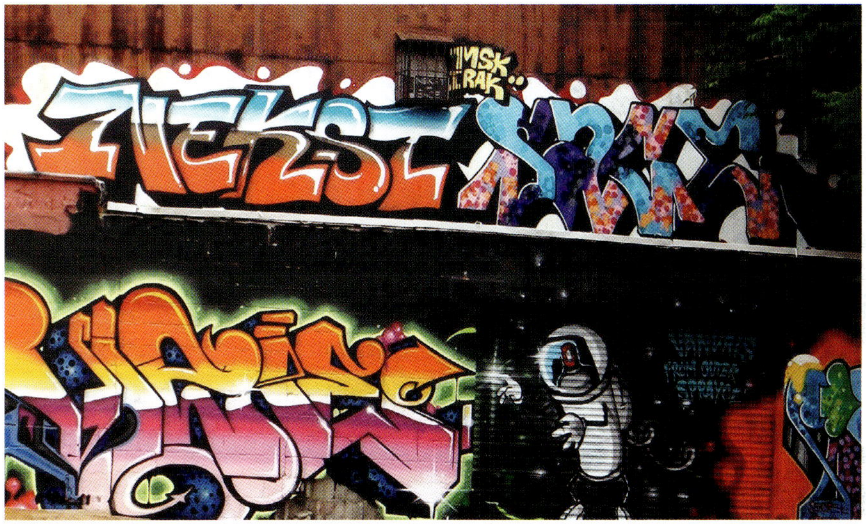

Nekst, Sace R.I.P., New Jersey

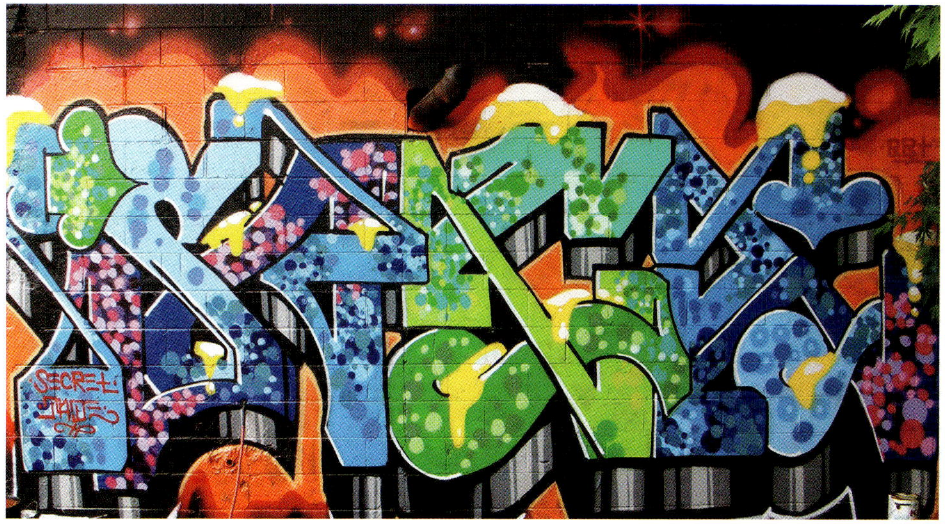

Sace R.I.P, New Jersey

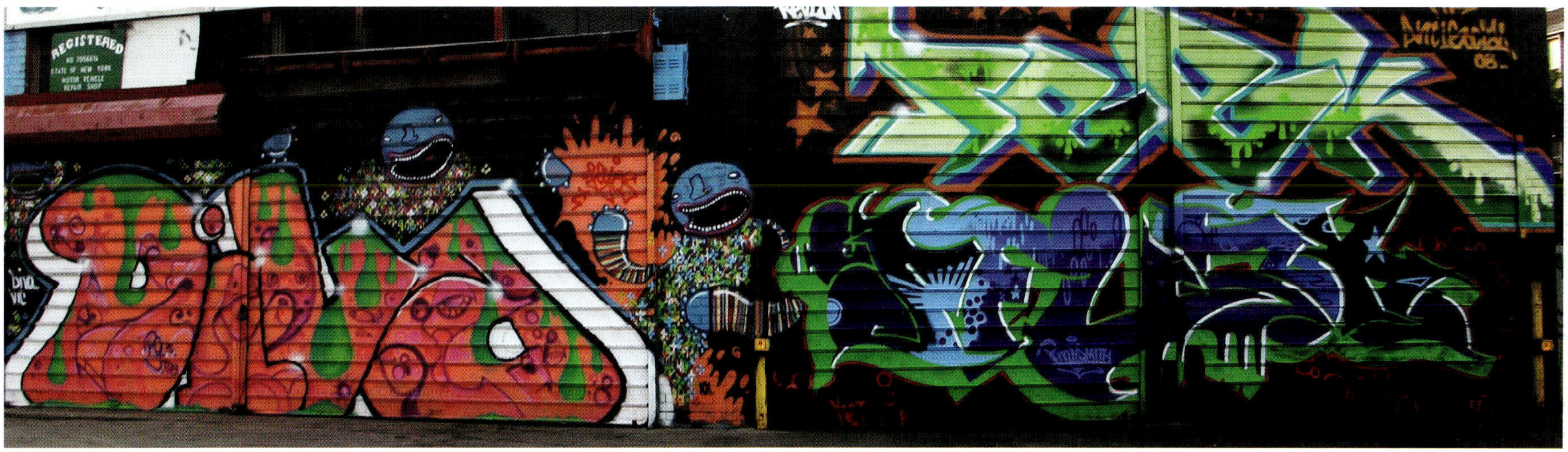


Diva, Peek, PFunk, Brooklyn, NY

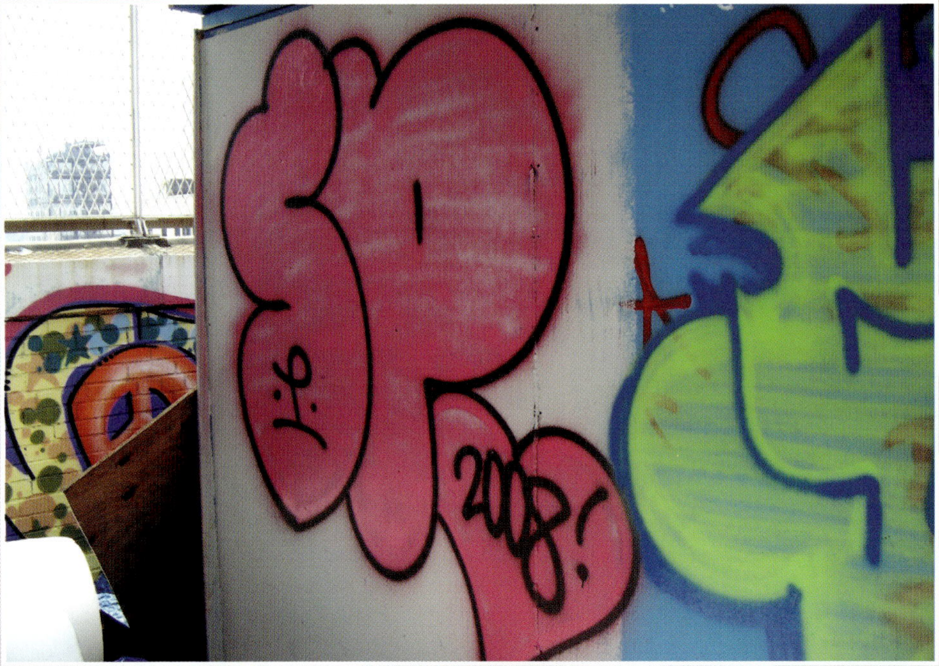

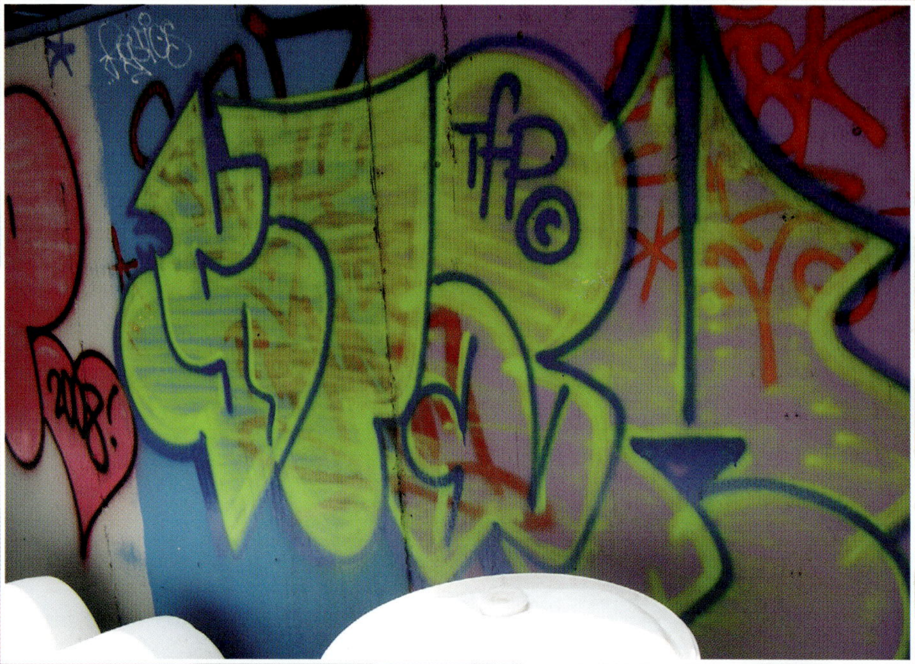

SP ONE, Stak, Manhattan, NY

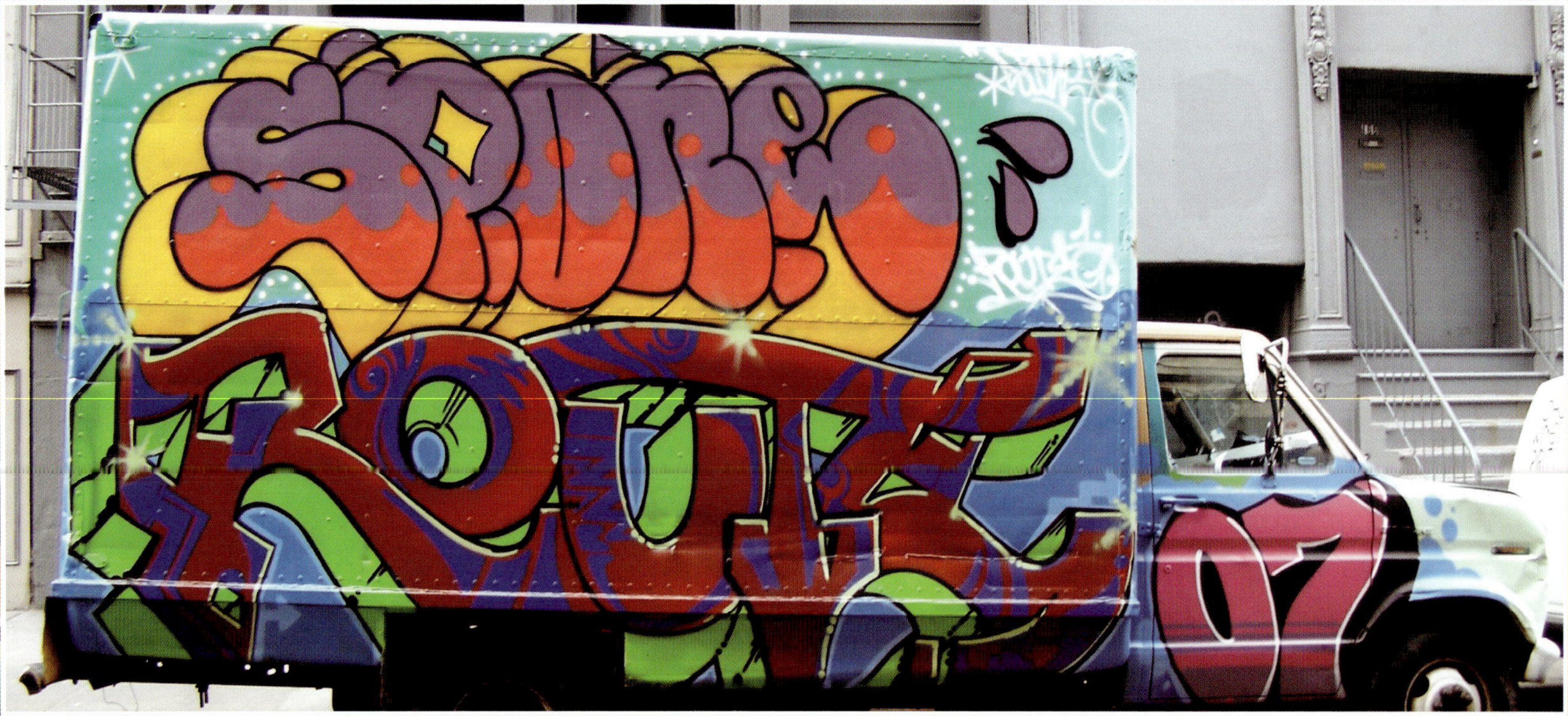

SP ONE, Route, Manhattan, NY

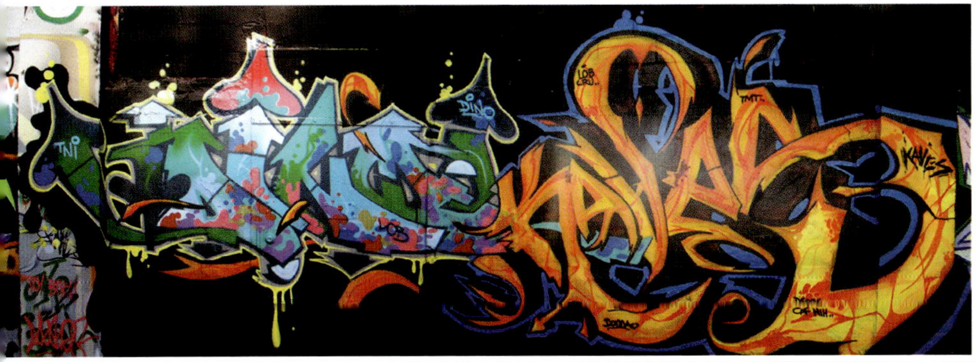

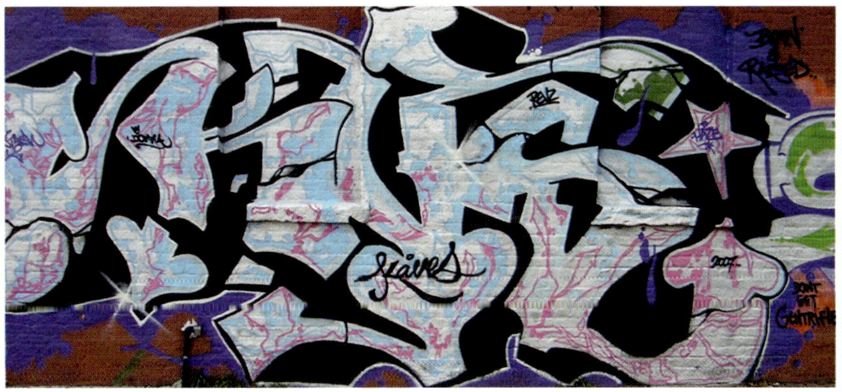

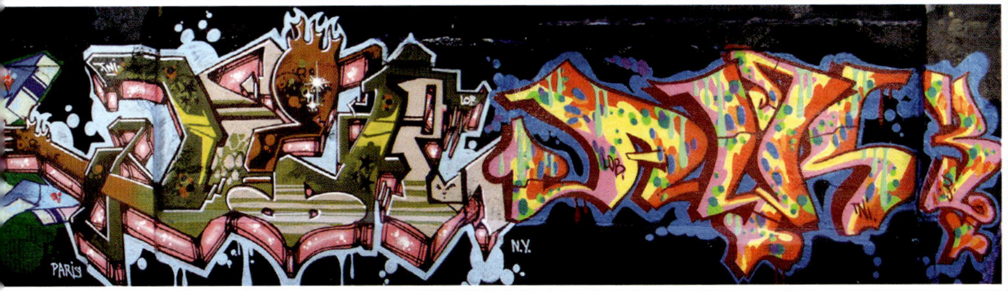

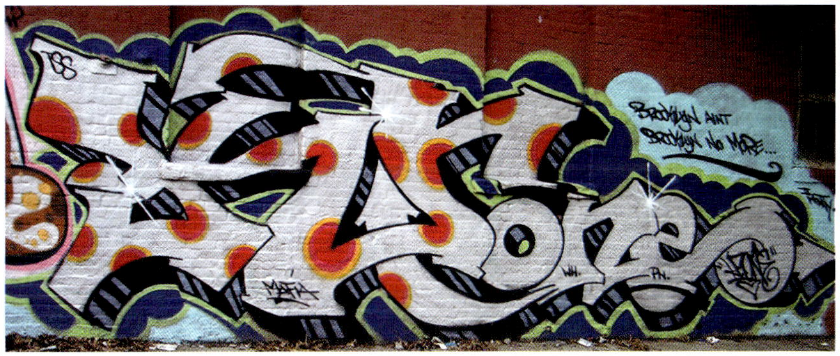

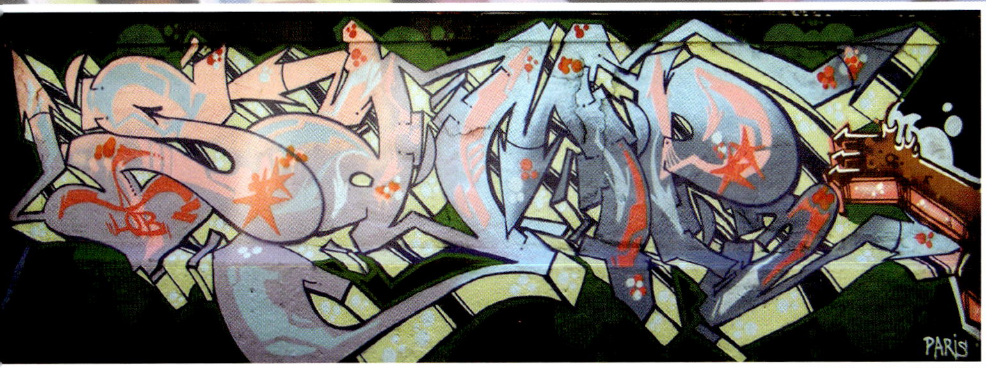

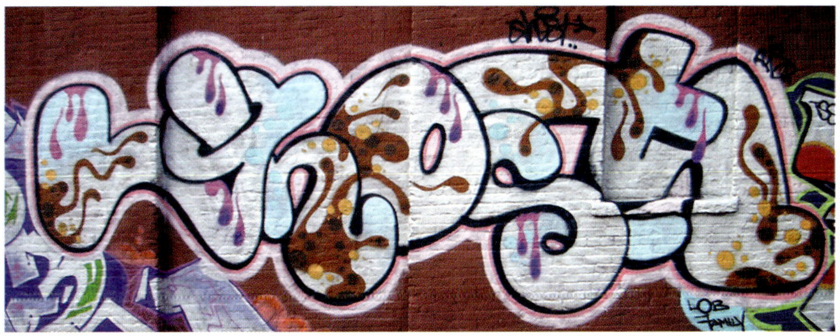

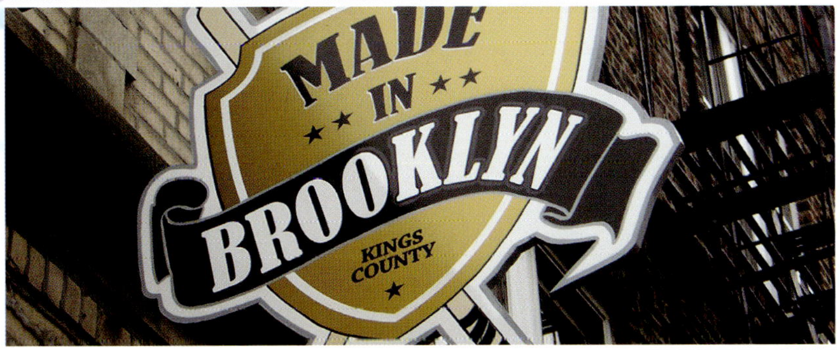
MADE
IN
BROOKLYN
KINGS COUNTY

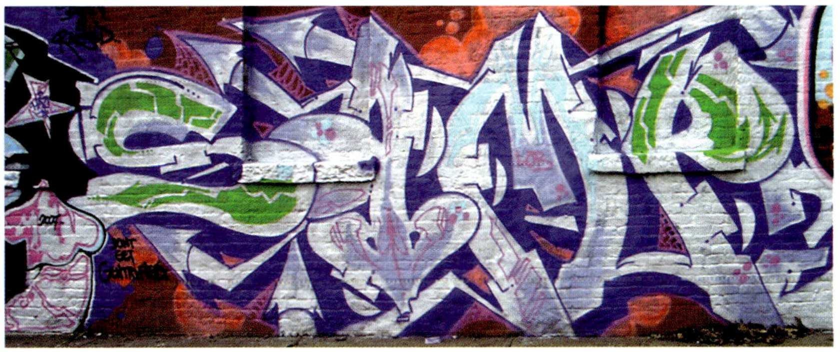

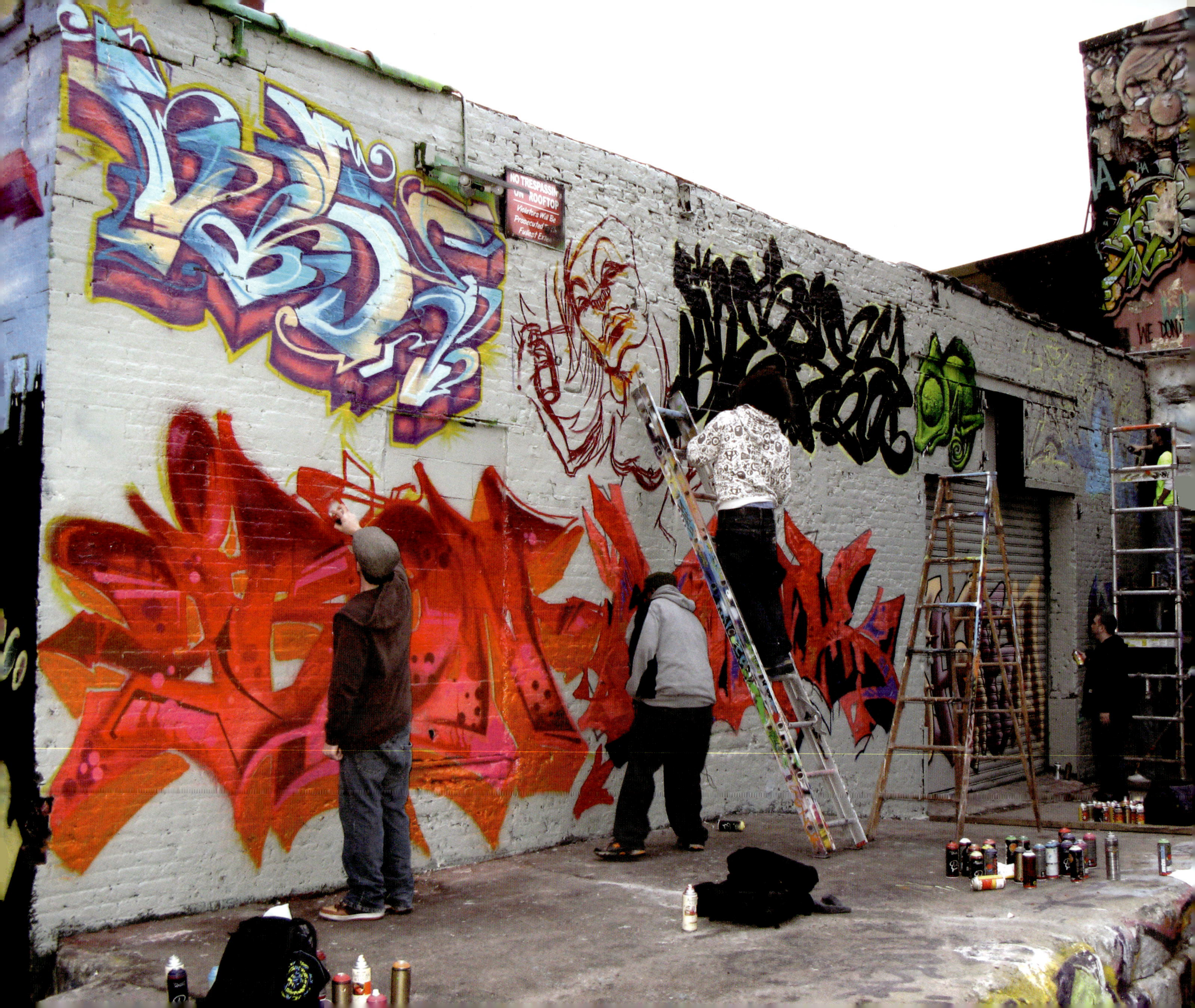
NO TRESPASSIN
ROOFTOP
Violators Will Be
Prosecuted
Fullest Ex

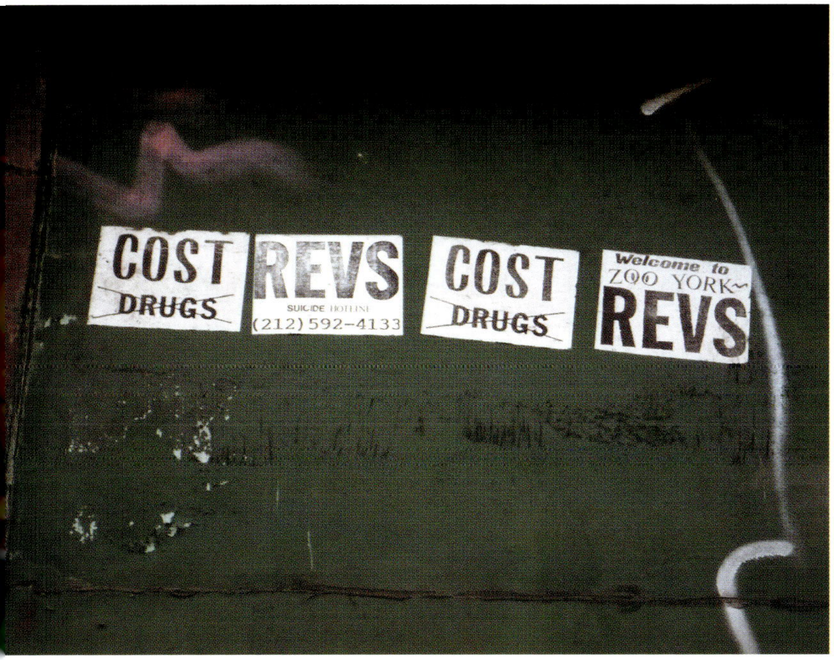


Revs, Cost, Manhattan, NY

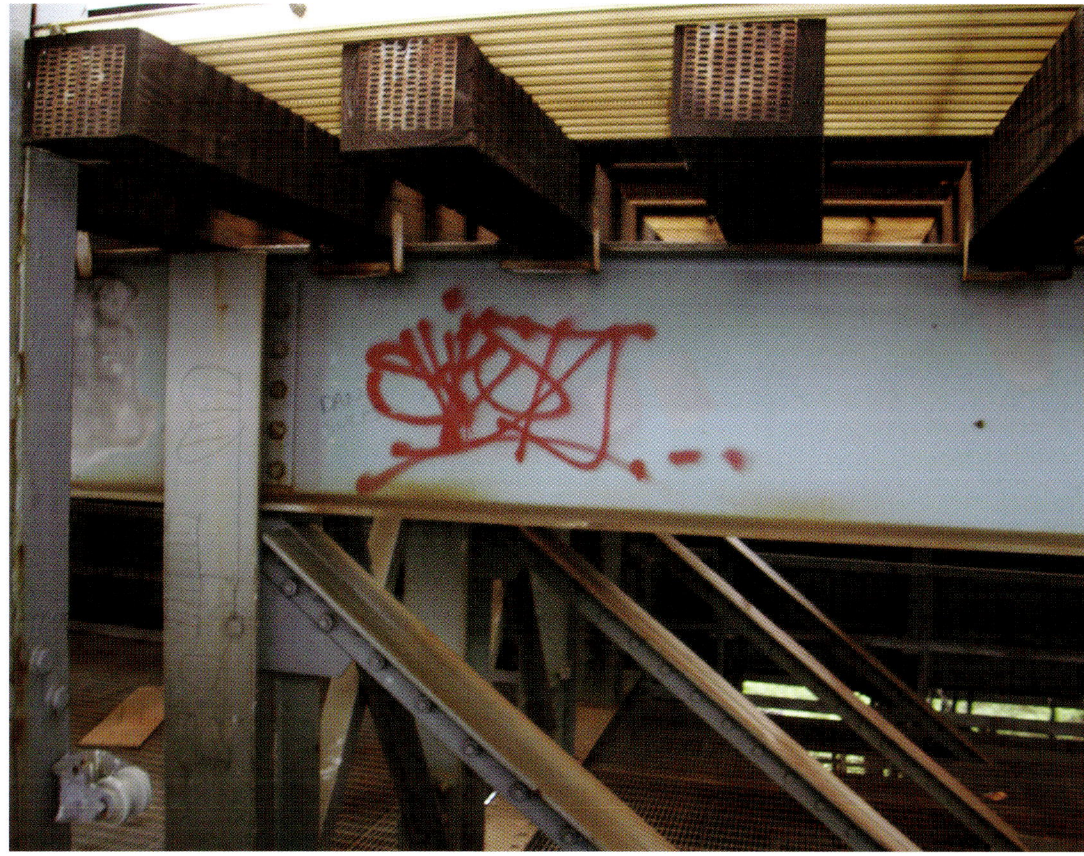

Shiesta, Manhattan, NY

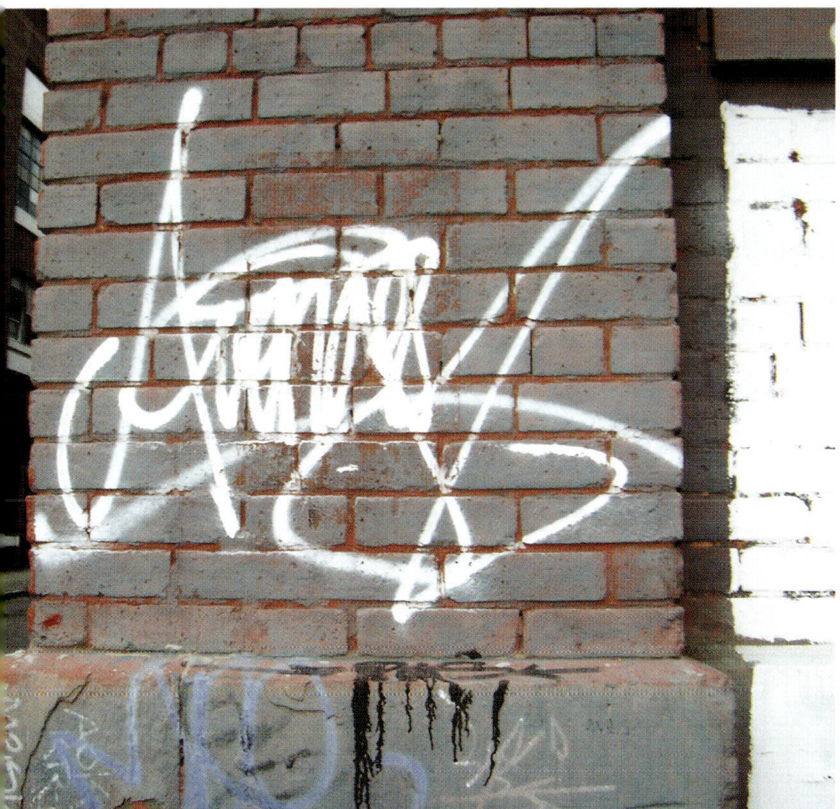

Avenger, Brooklyn, NY

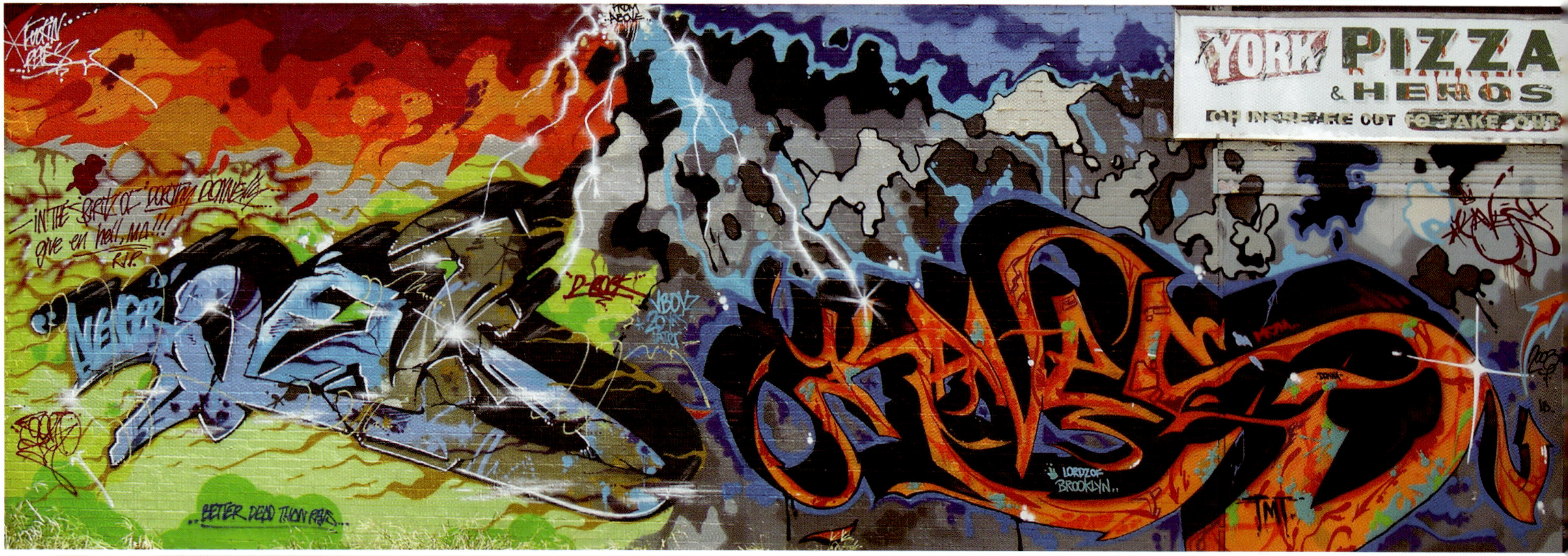

Revs, Kaves, Brooklyn, NY

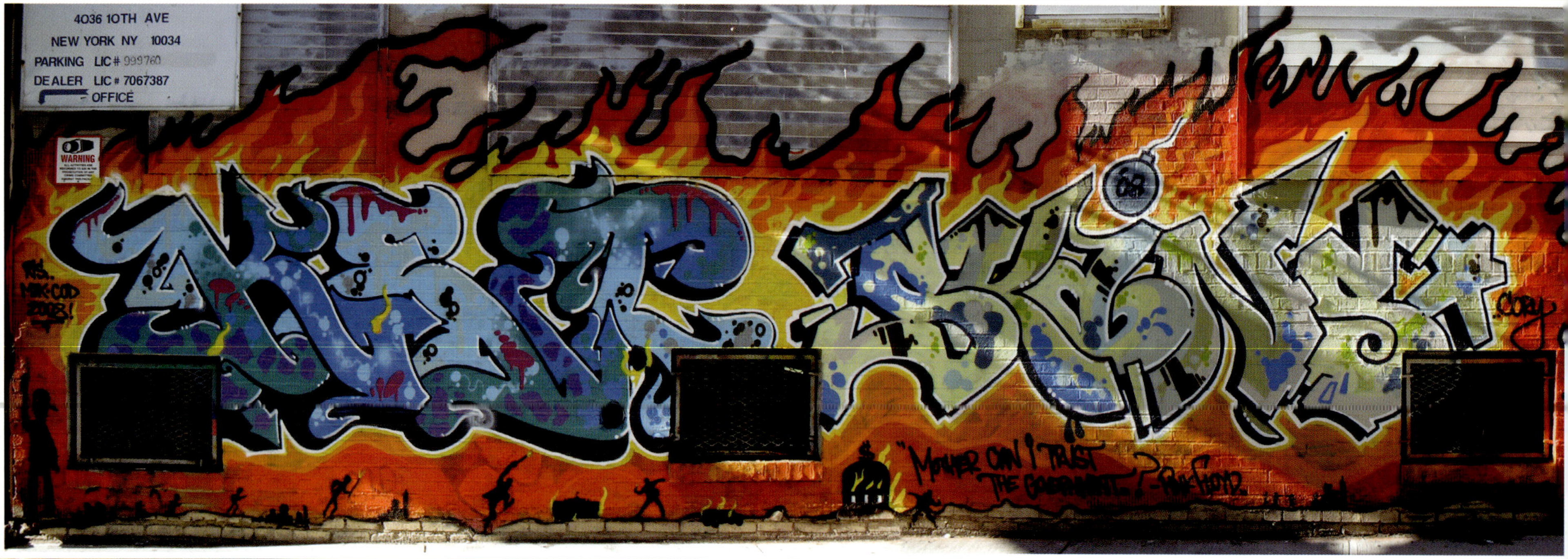

Ket, Skins, Manhattan, NY

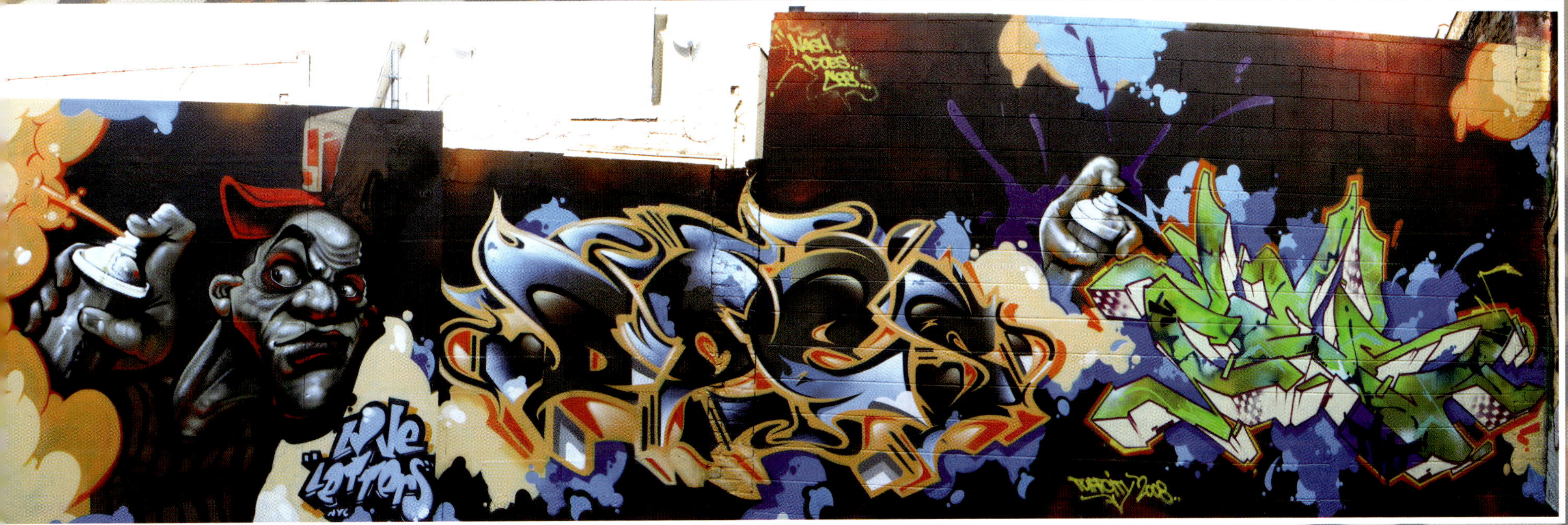

Nash, Does, Ces, Bronx, NY, Tuff City

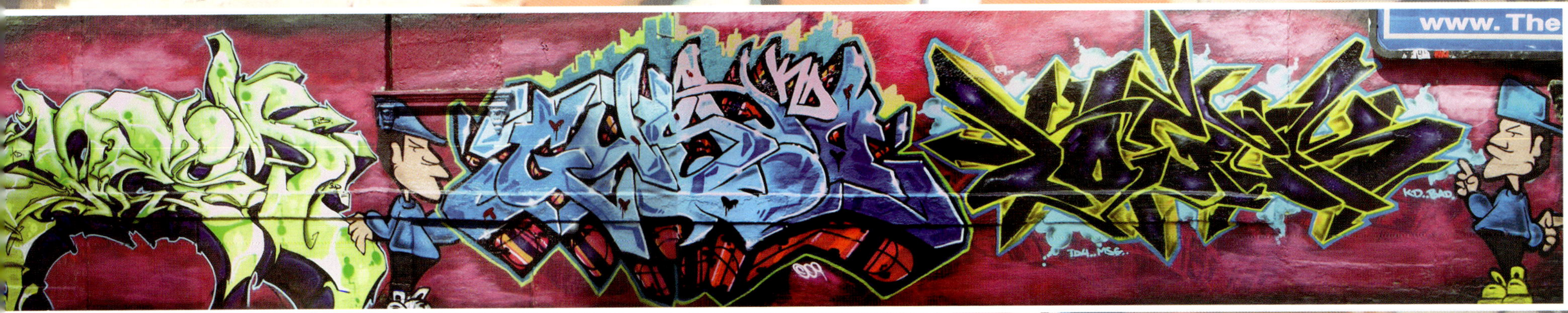


Deem, Gusto, Bronx, NY

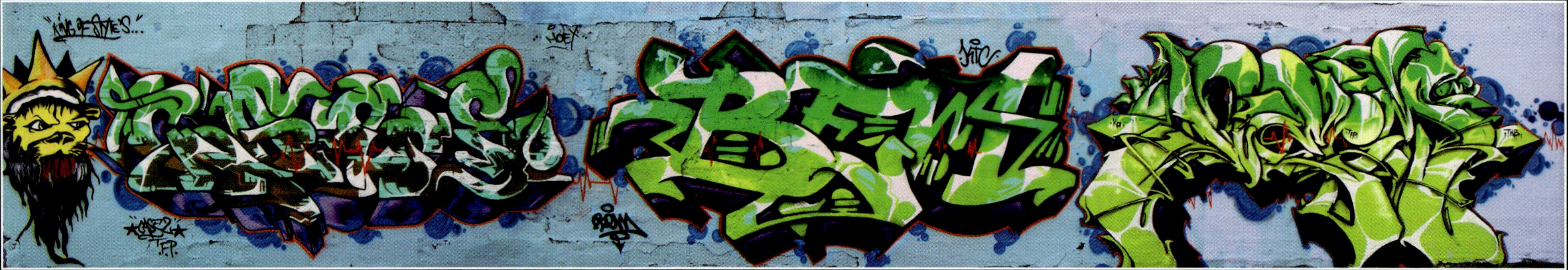

Case2, Bem, Des, Pure TFP, Bronx, NY

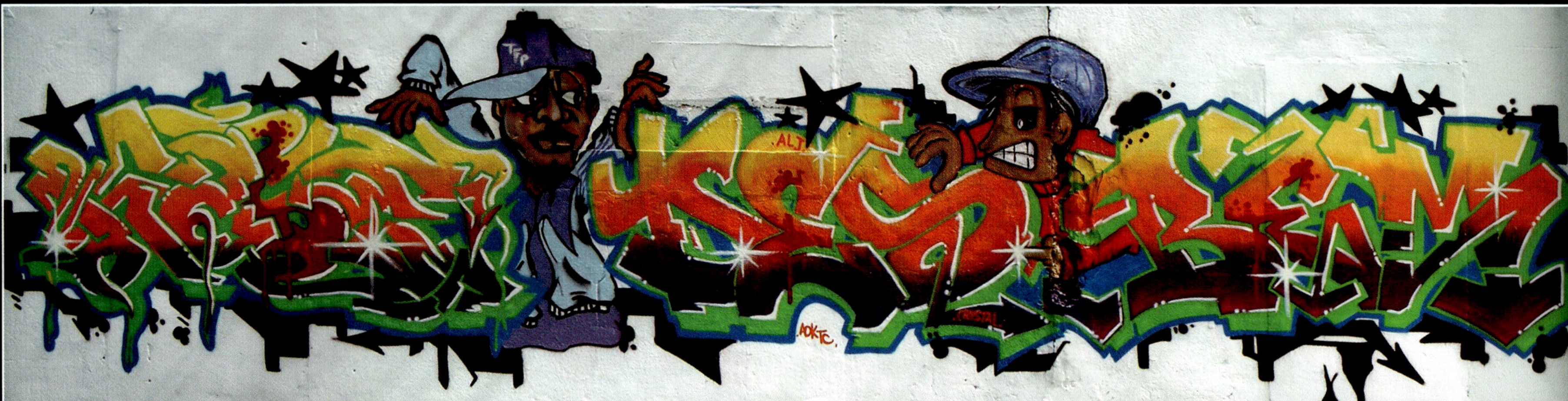

Case2, Des, Bem, Bronx, NY

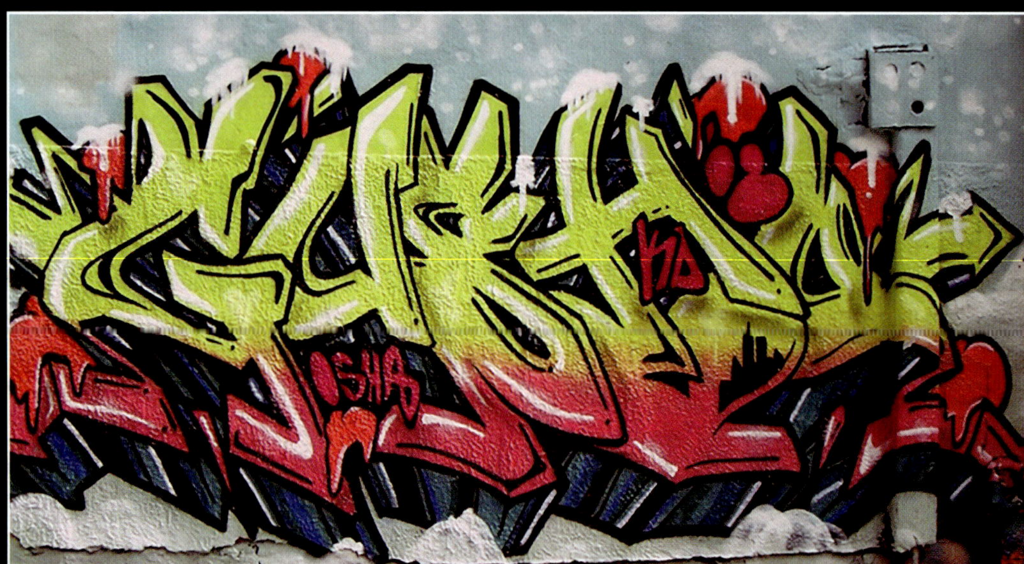

Gusto, Bronx, NY

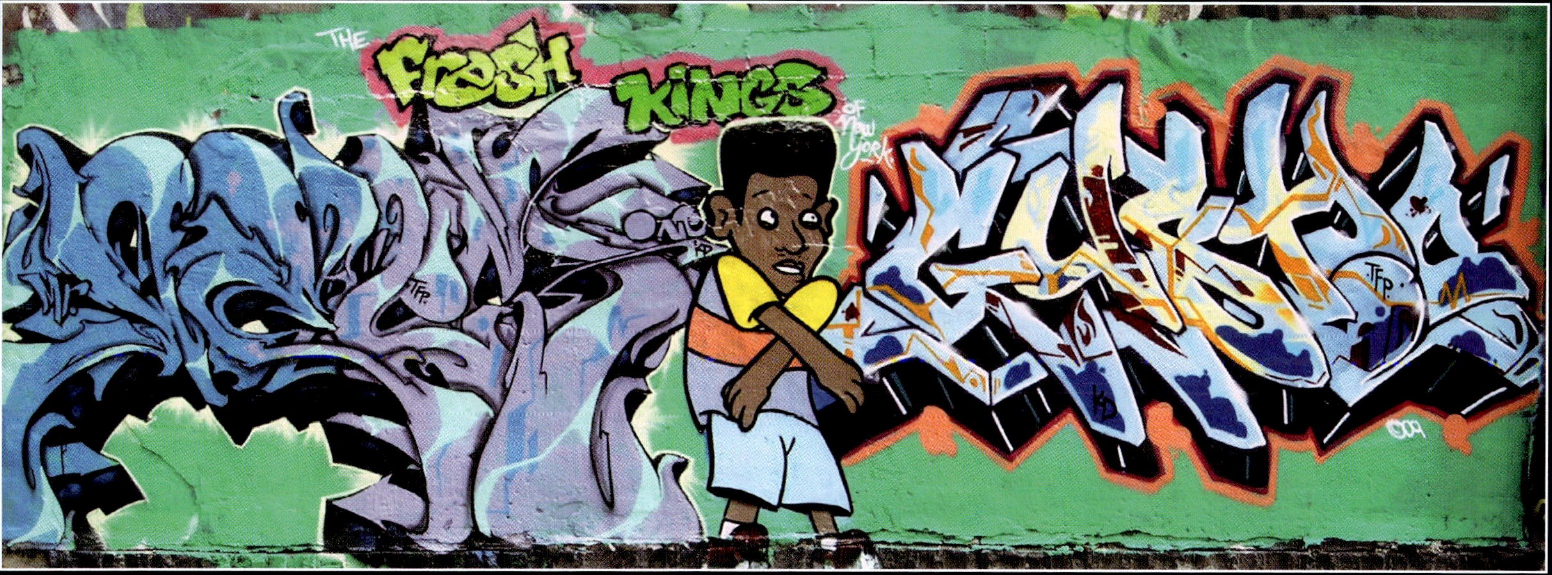


Deem, Gusto, Bronx, NY

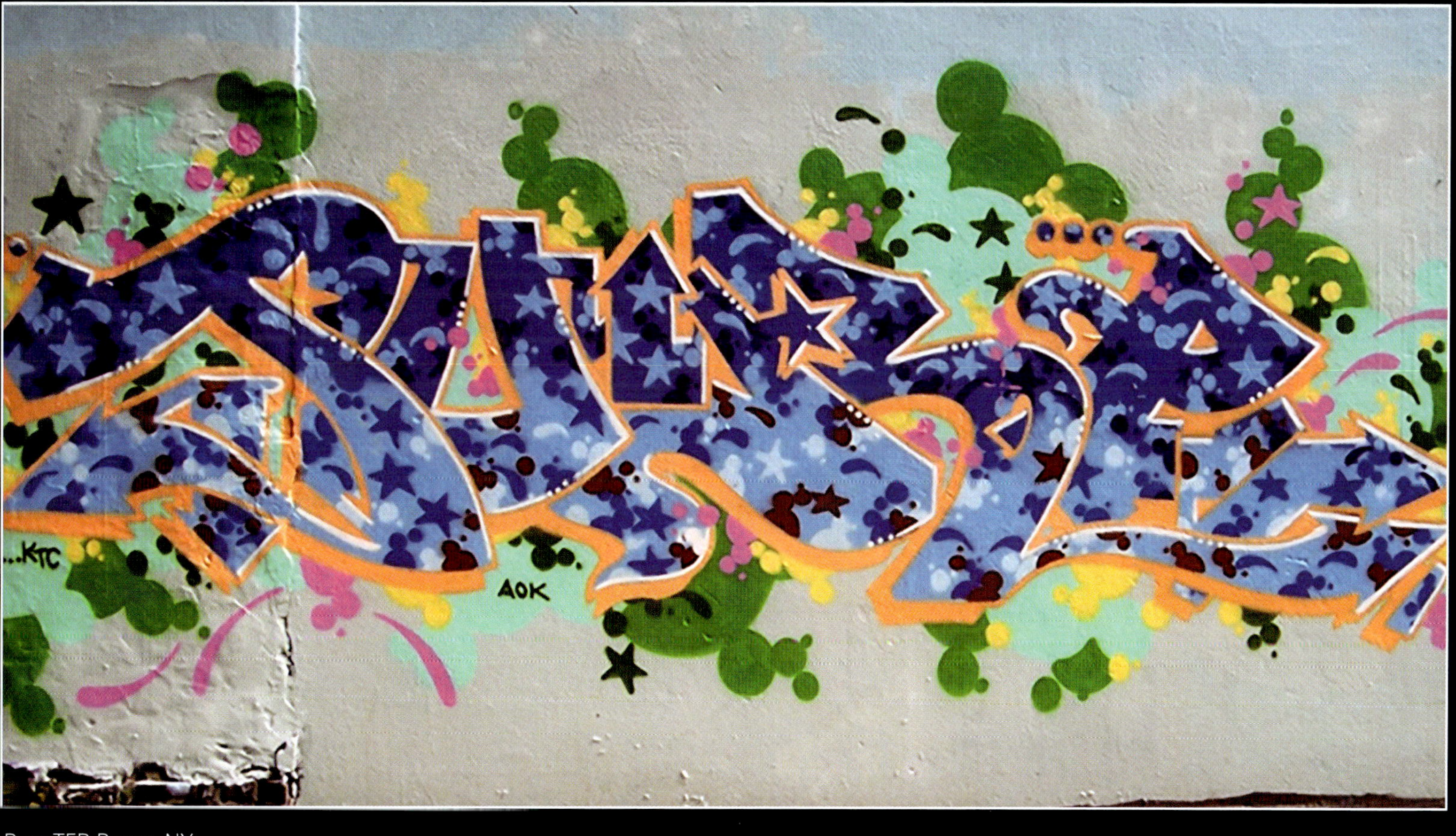


Pure TFP, Bronx, NY

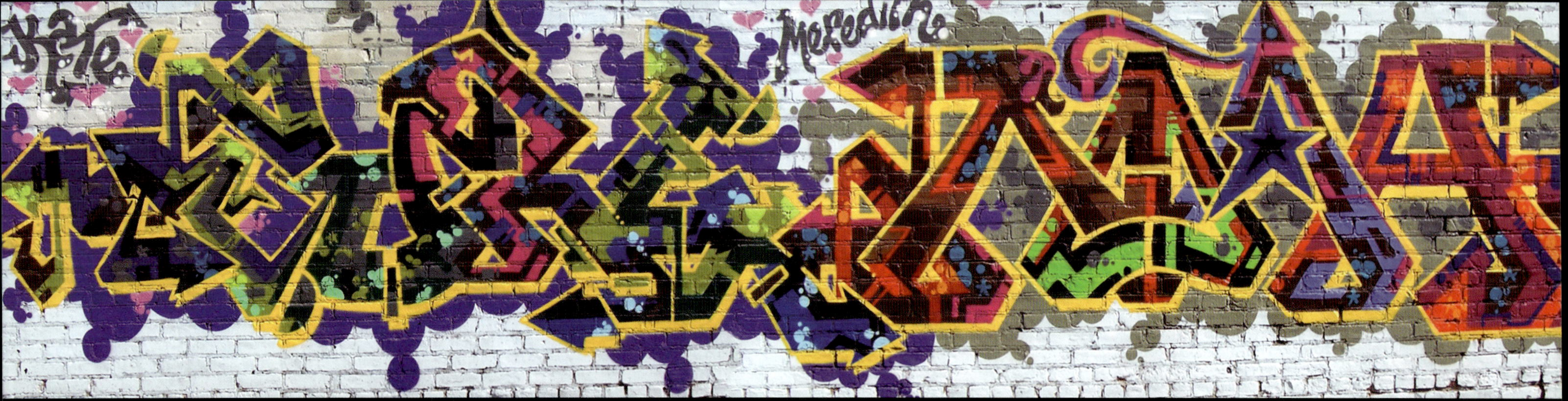

Pure, Noah, Bronx, NY

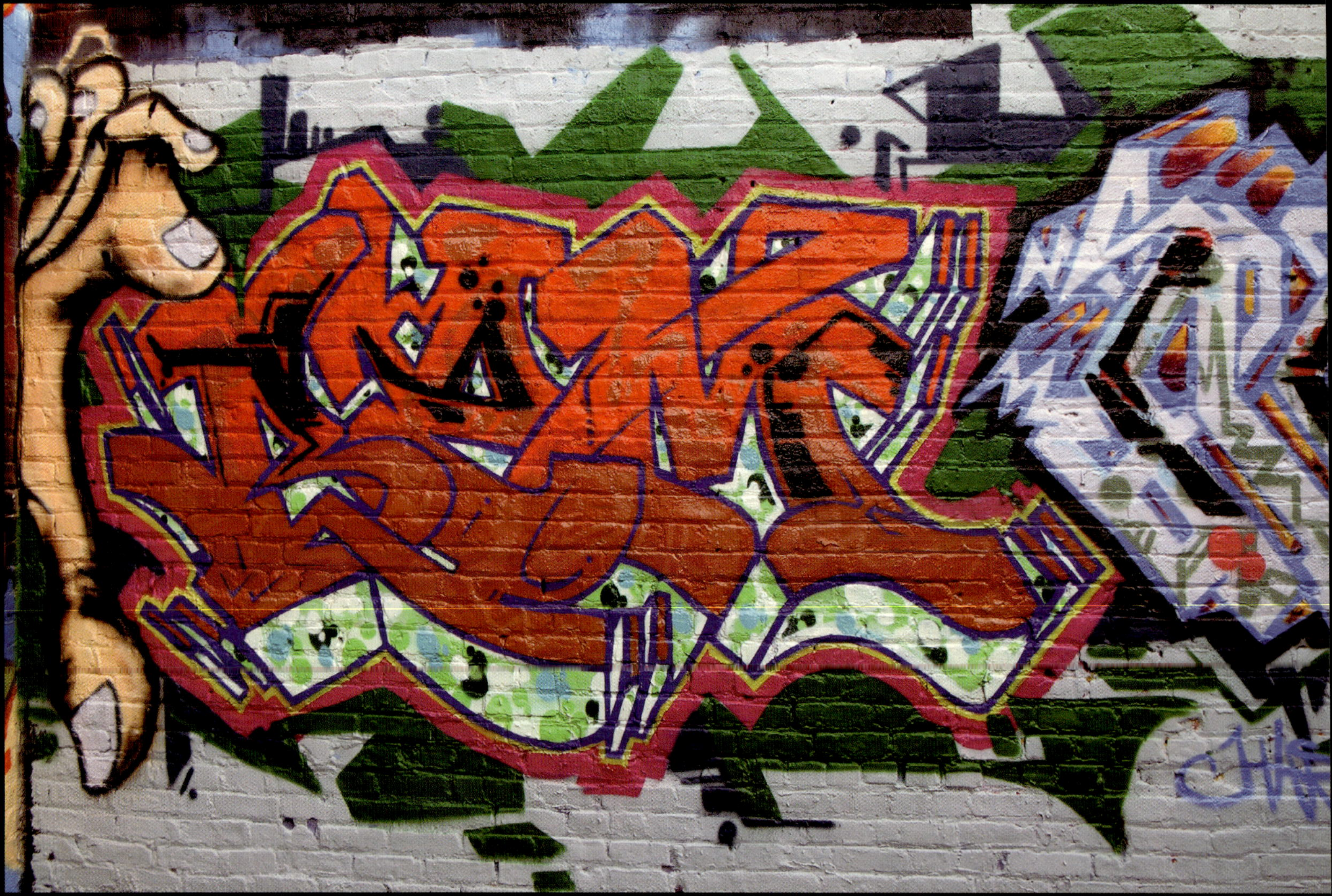

Bem, Moet, Case 2, Bronx, NY, Tuff City

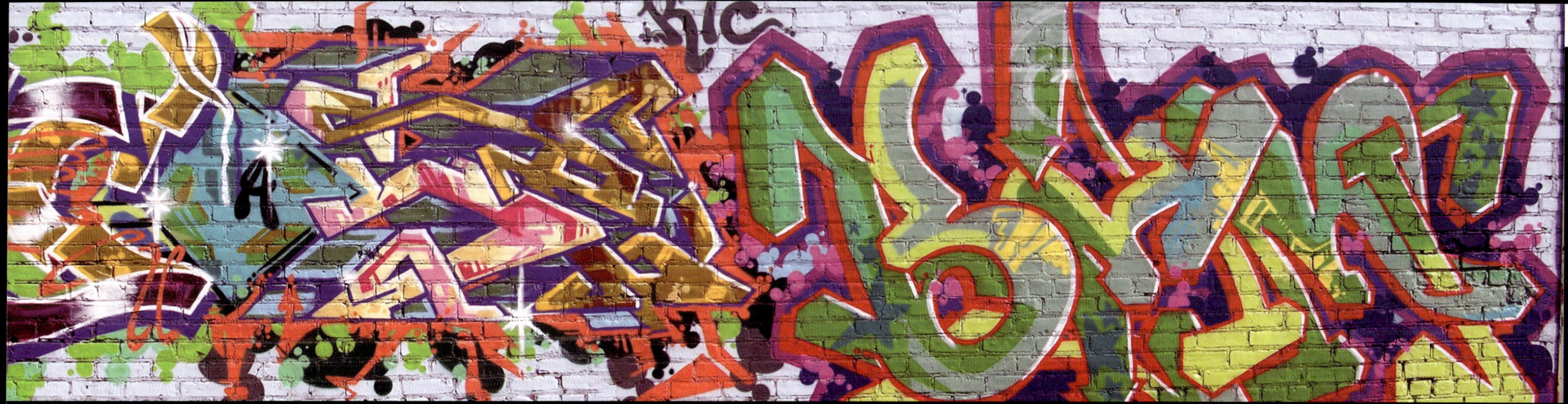

Case2, Bem, Bronx, NY

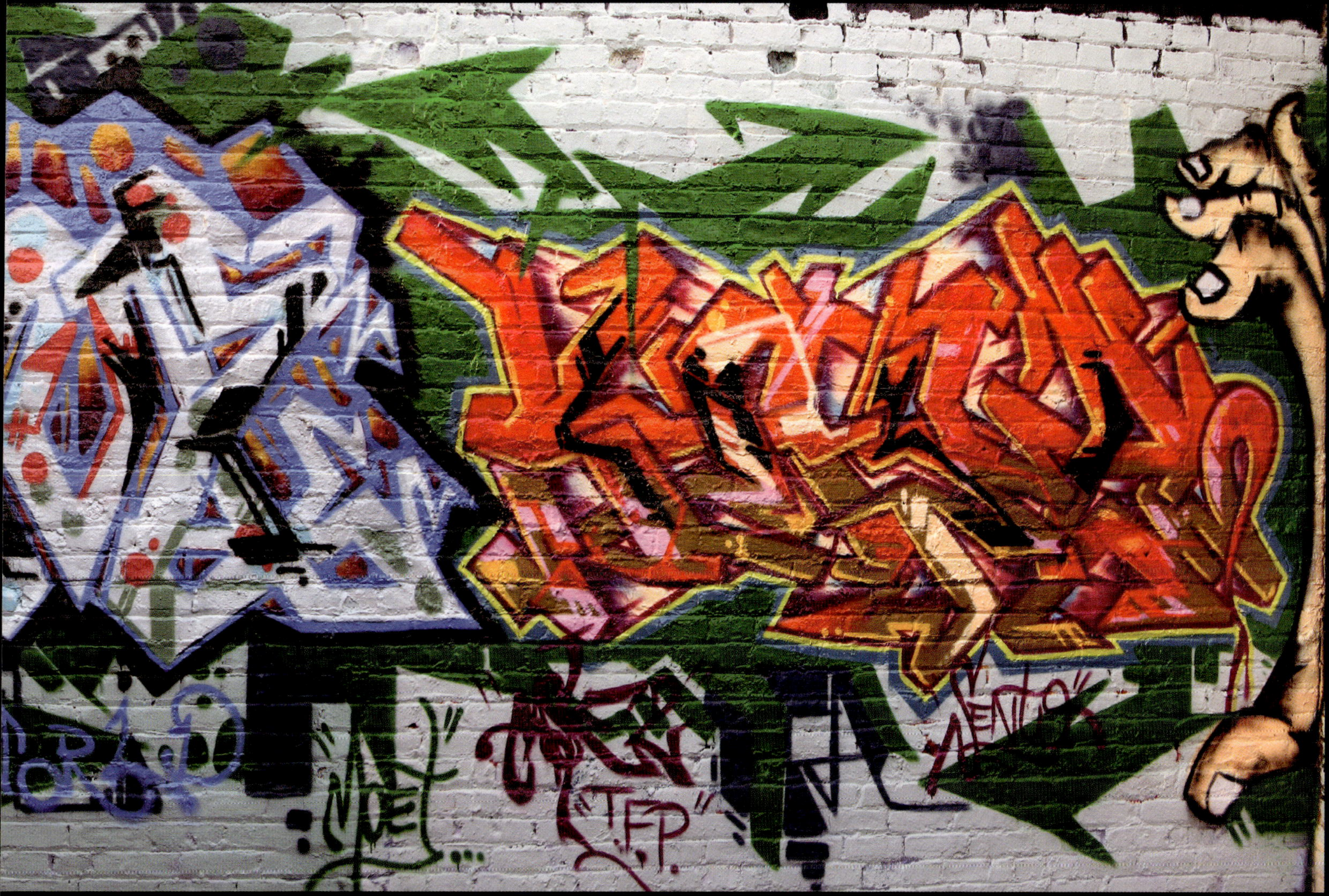

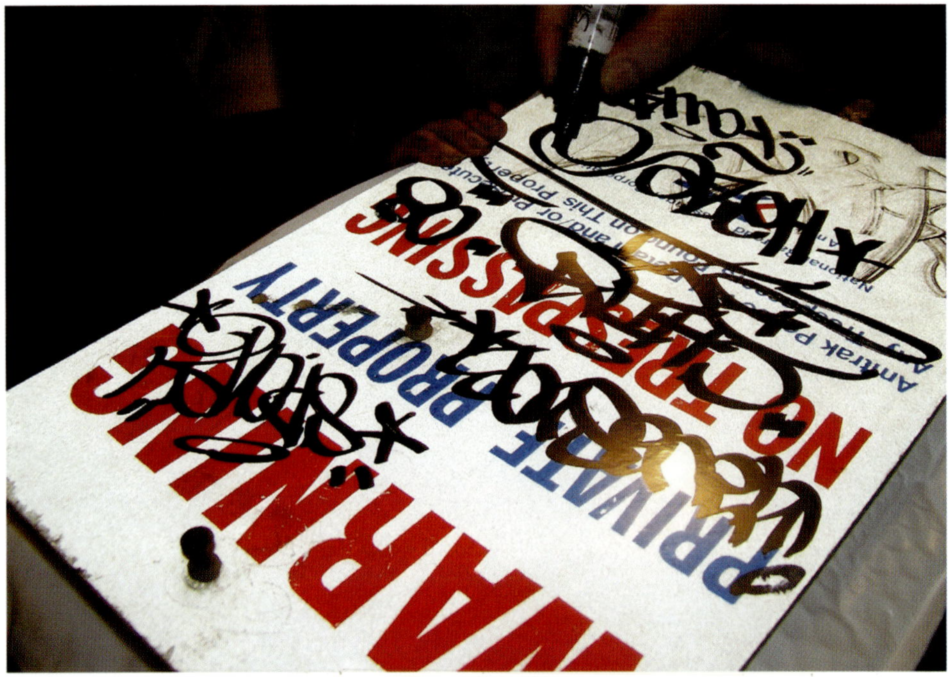

Haze, Manhattan, NY

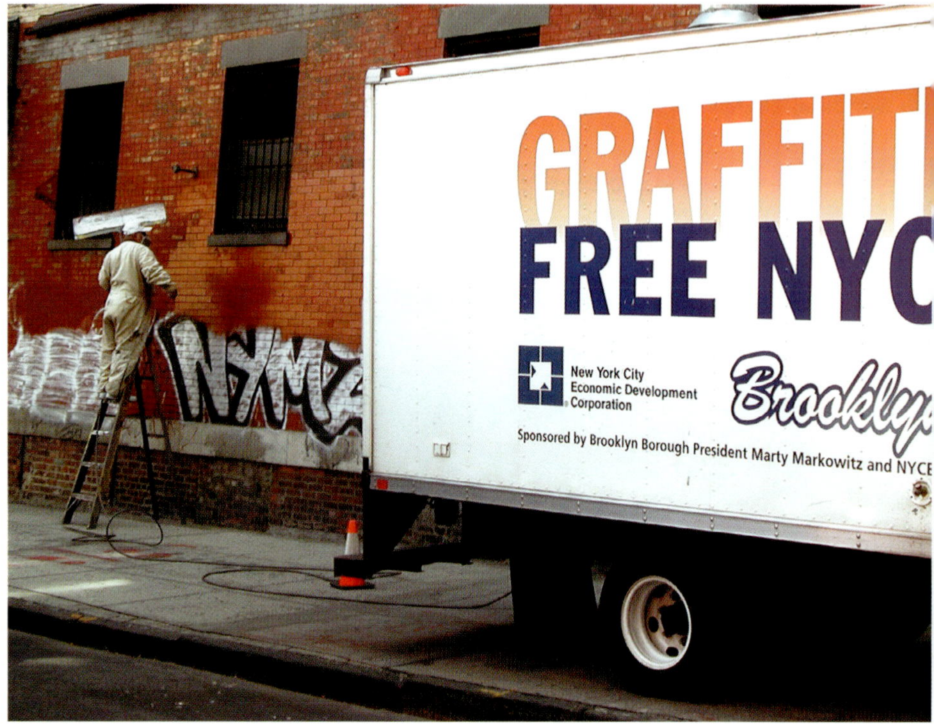

Graffiti Free NYC

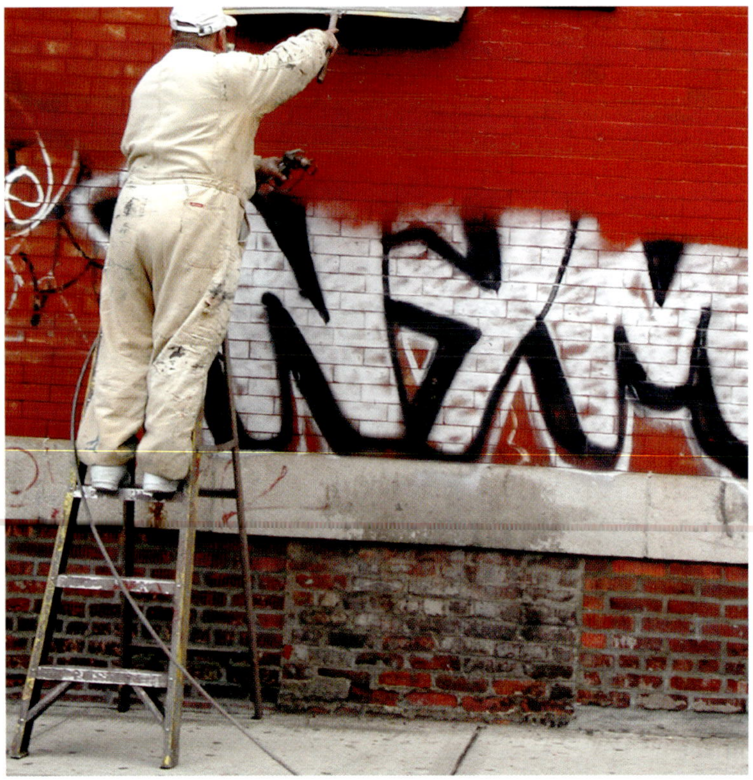
Graffiti Free NYC

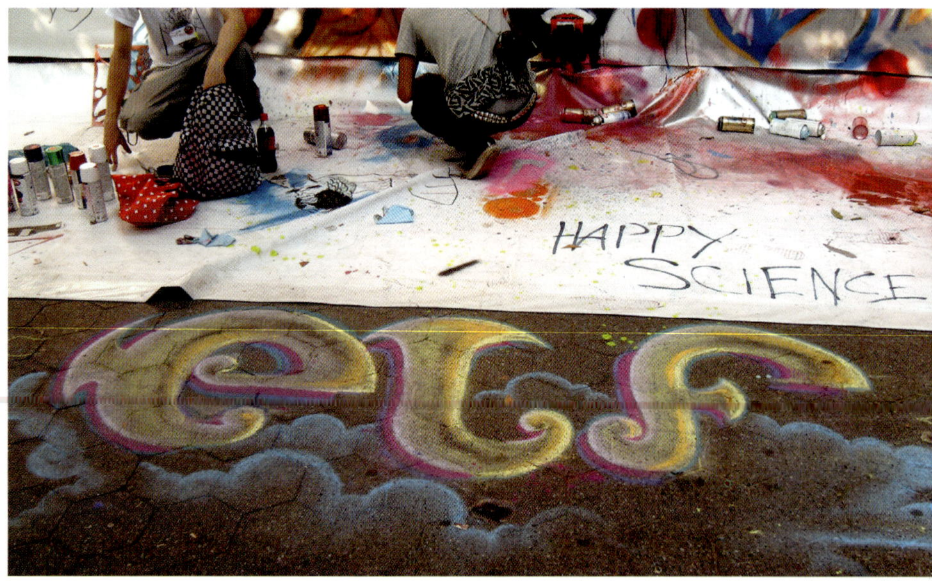

Elf MPC R.I.P. (Spar), Manhattan, NY

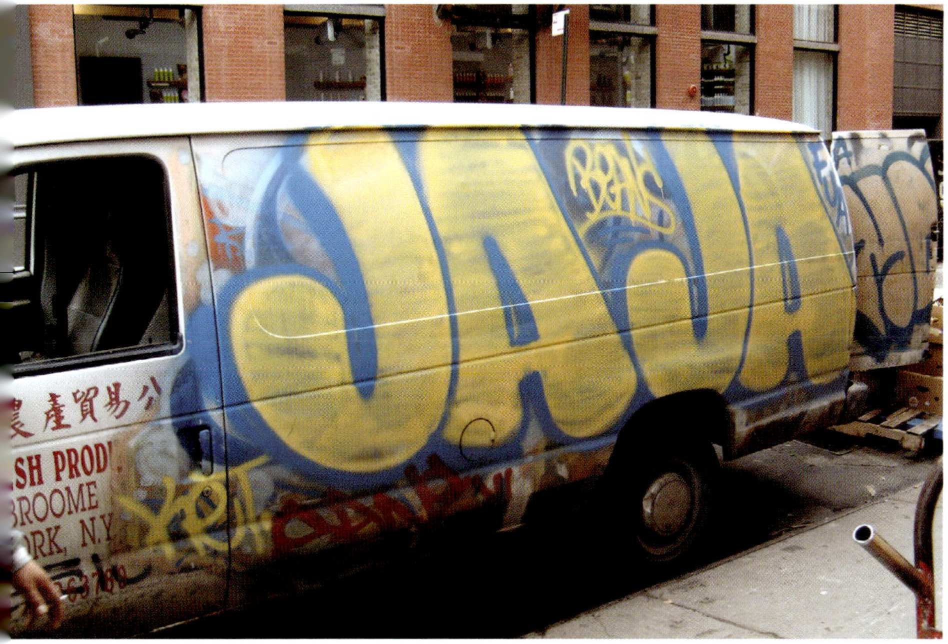

JA, Manhattan, NY

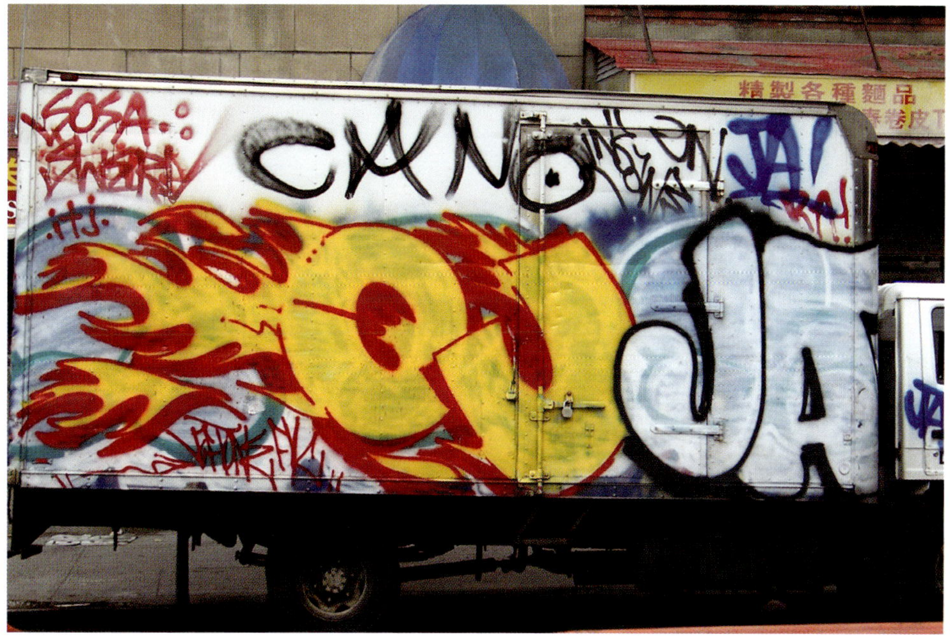

JA, OJ, Manhattan, NY

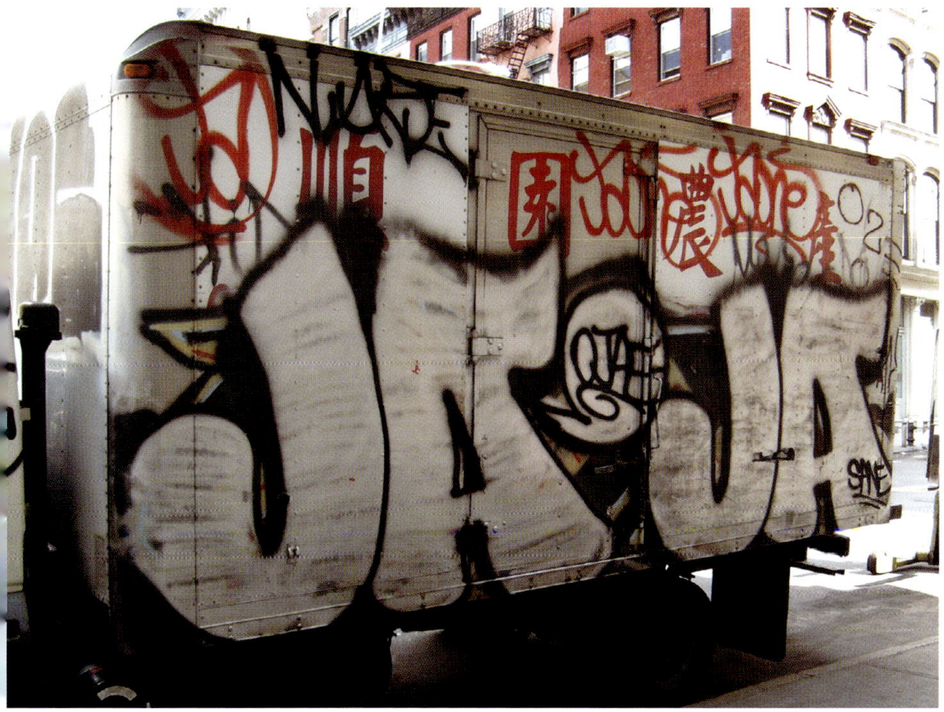

JA, OJ, Manhattan, NY

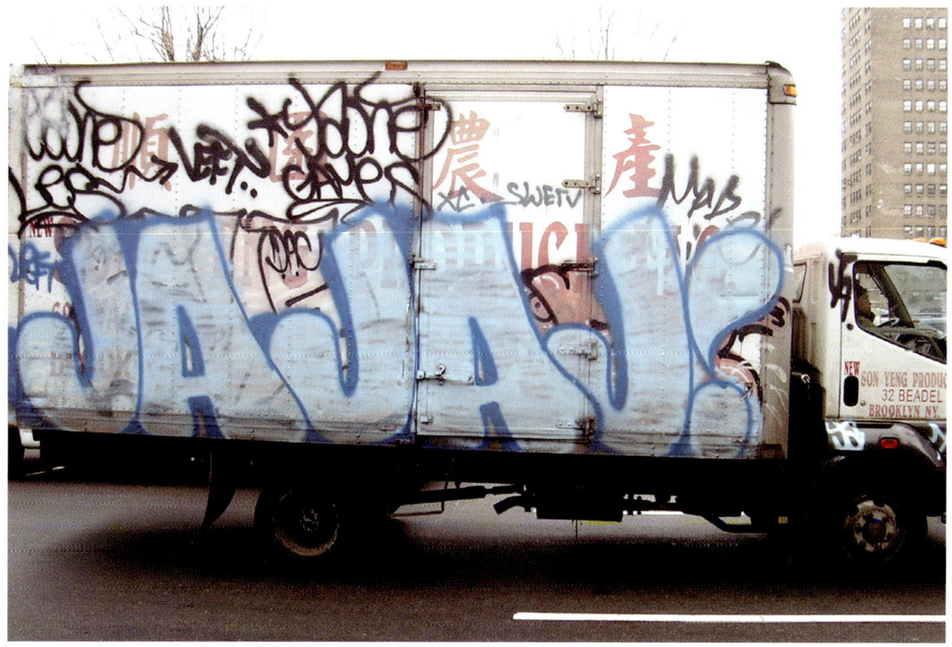

JA, Manhattan, NY

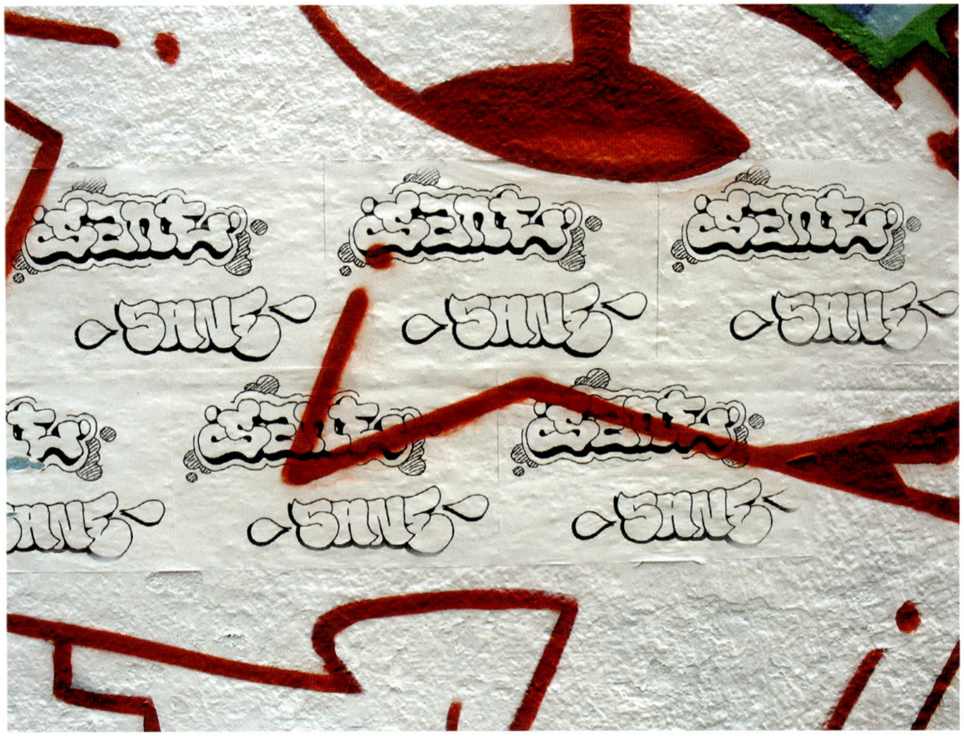

Smith, Brooklyn, NY

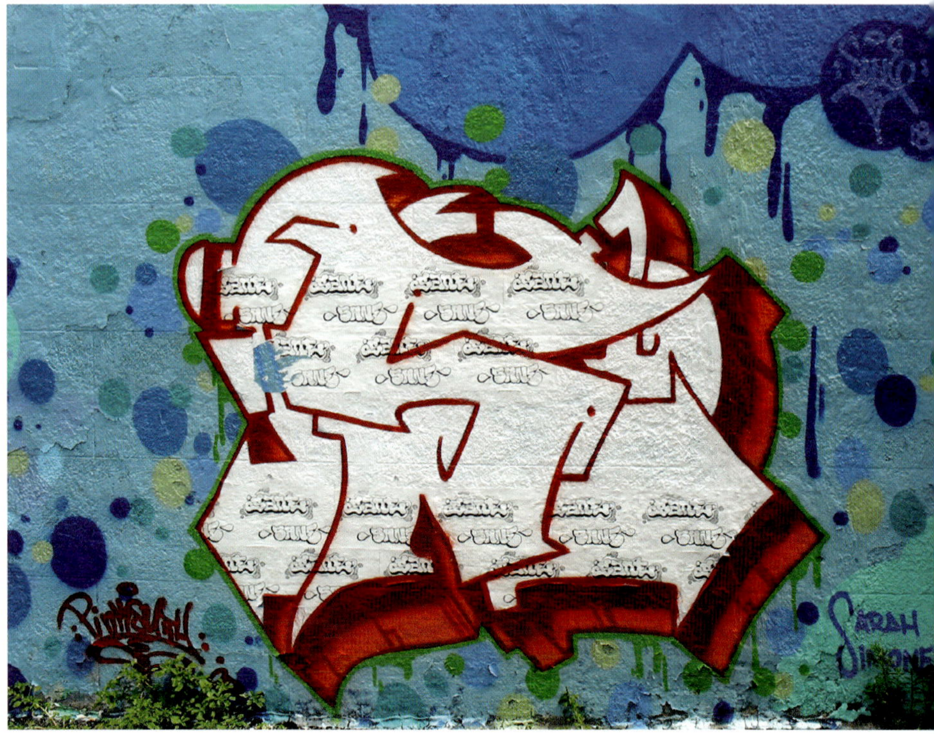

Smith, Brooklyn, NY

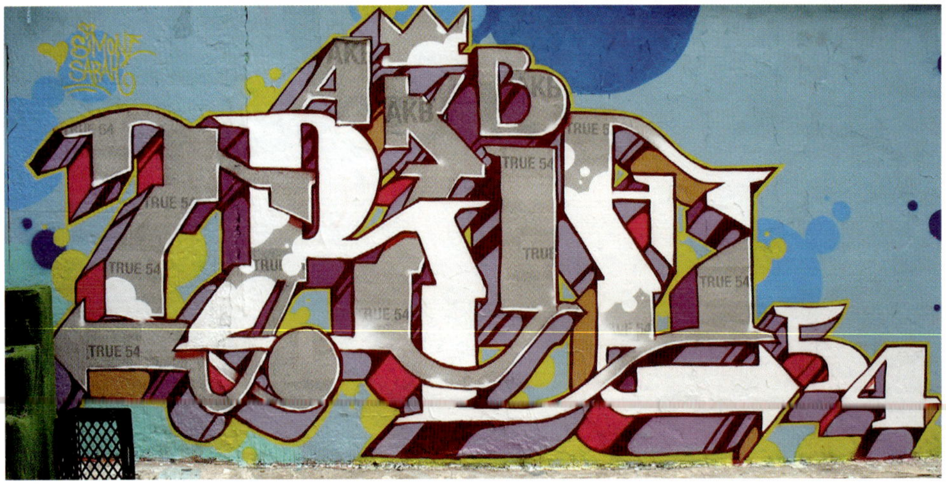

True54, Brooklyn, NY

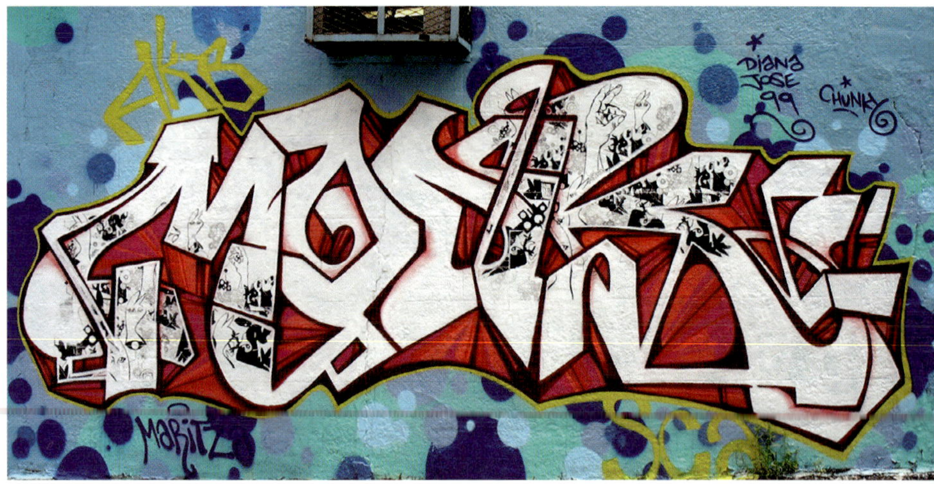

Monk, Brooklyn, NY

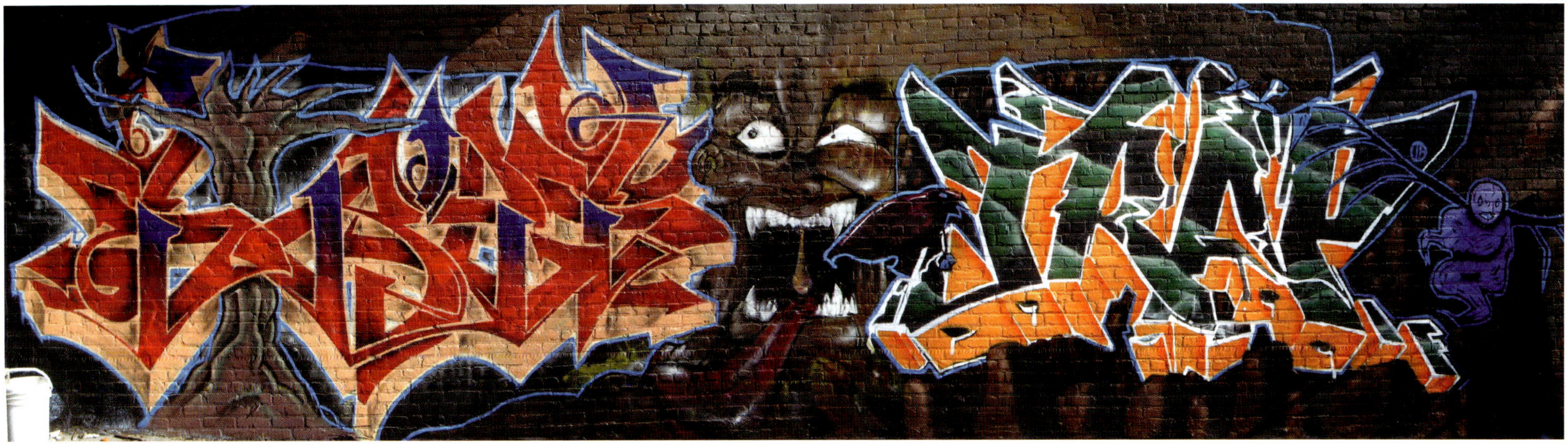

Stres, Trap, Queens, NY

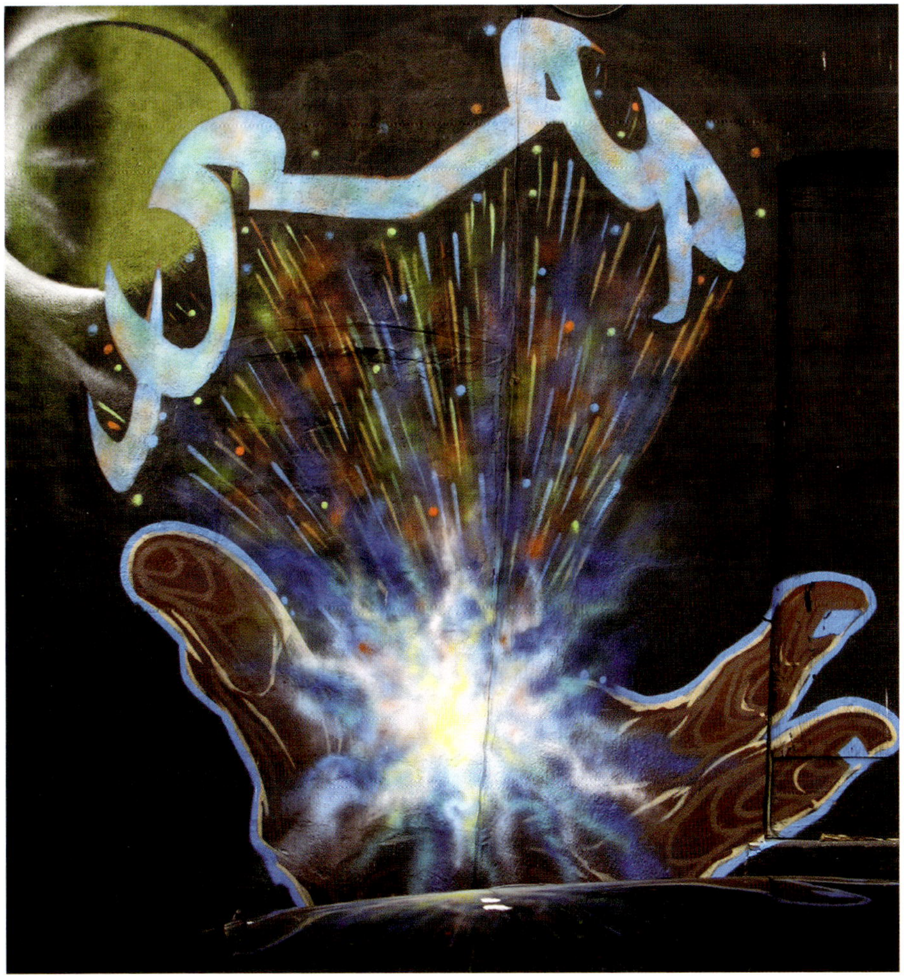

Trap, Queens, NY

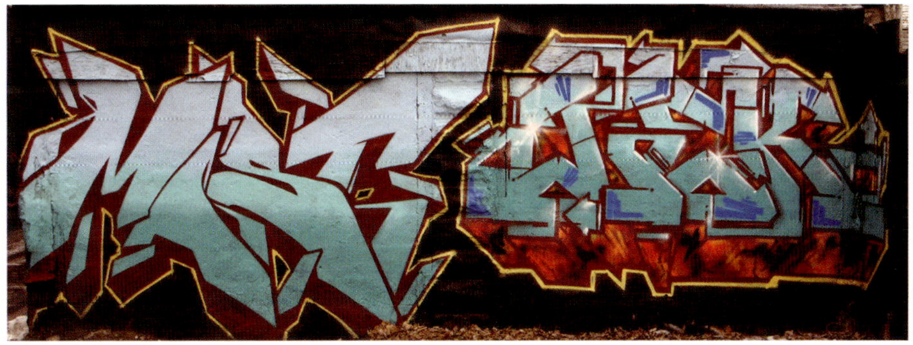

Mast, Jick, Queens, NY

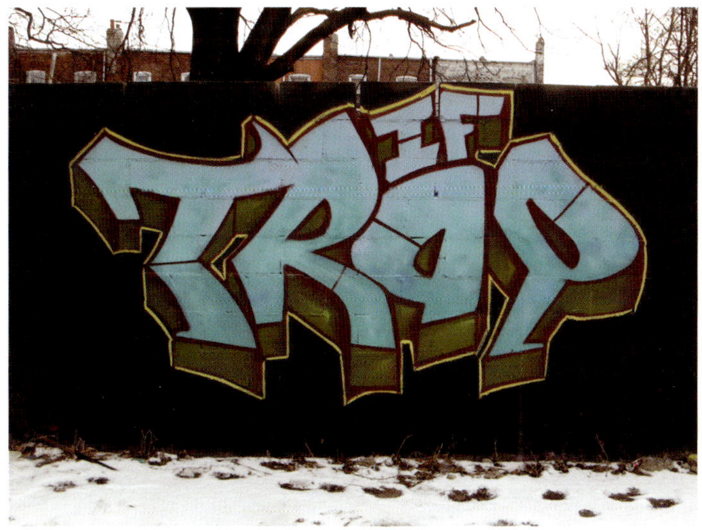

Trap, Queens, NY

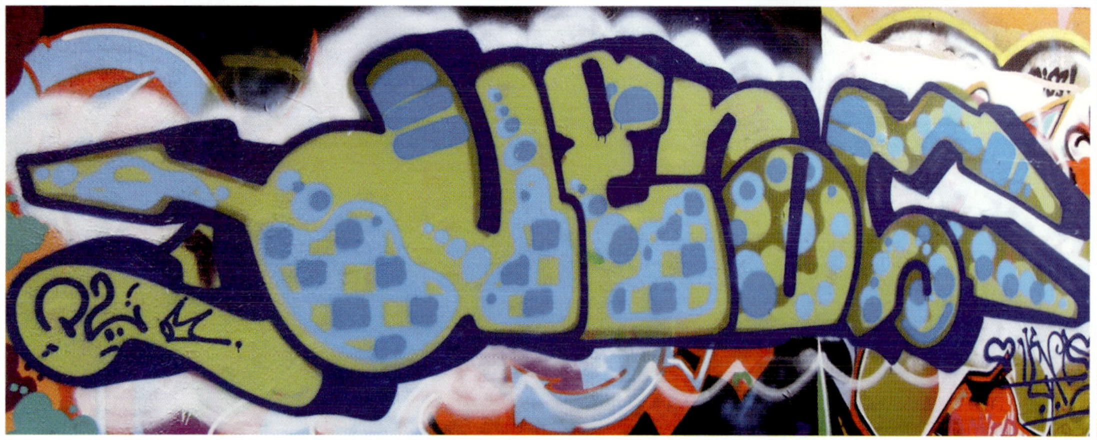

Uend, New Jersey

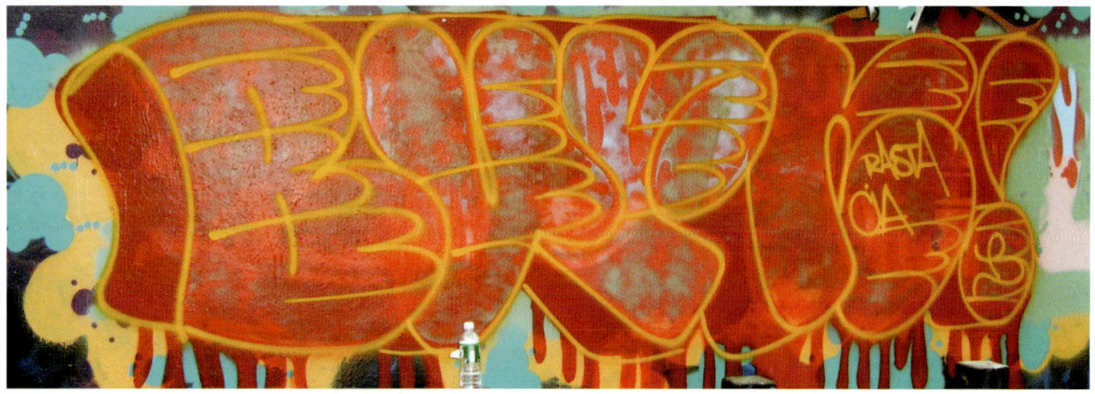

Burn, New Jersey

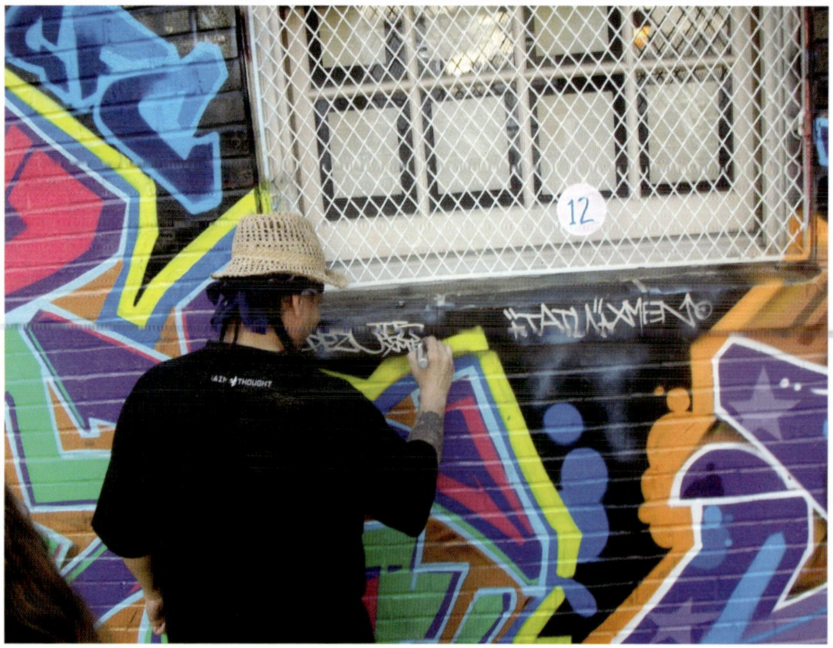

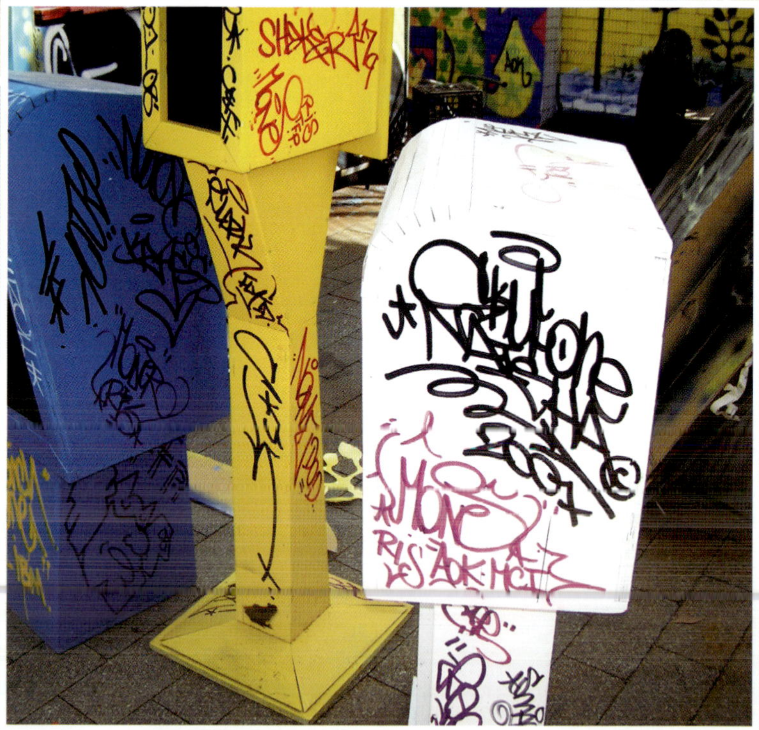

Spot, Klass, Shaker, Mone, Skuf, Noxer, Clark, Manhattan, NY

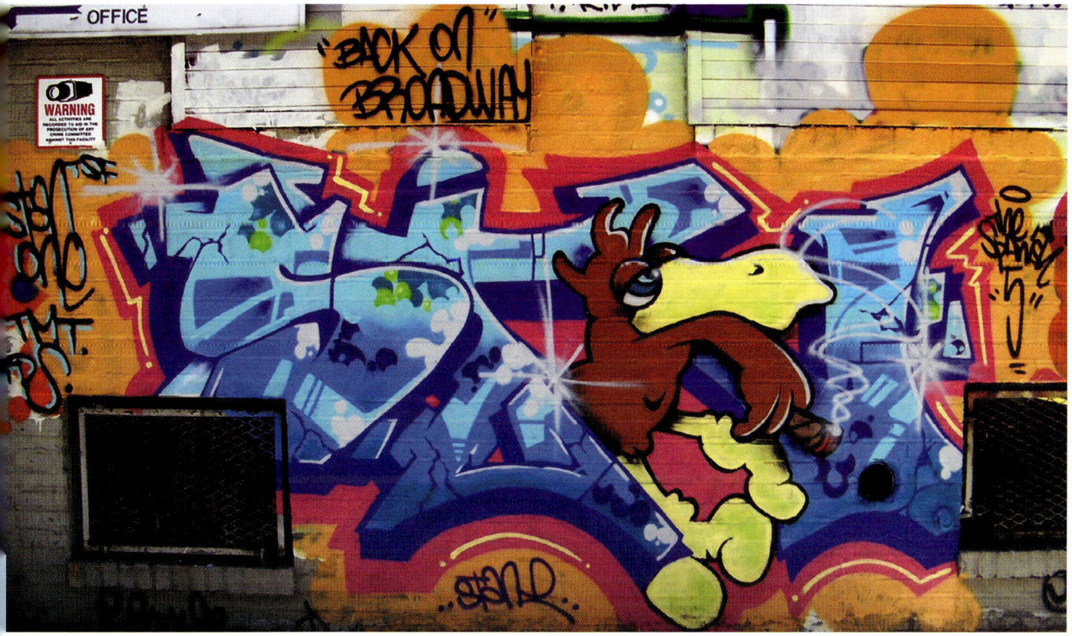

Stan, Manhattan, NY

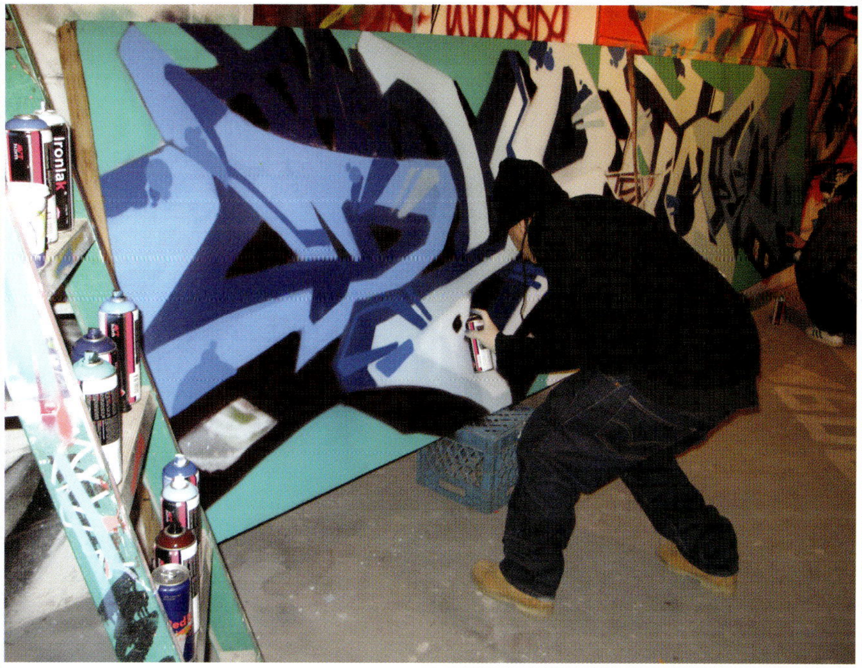


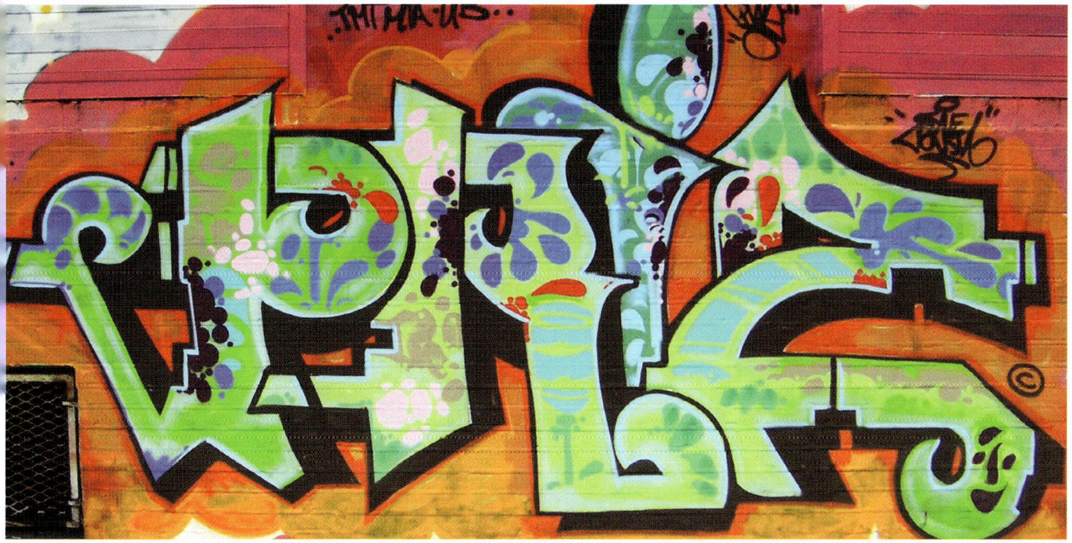
Priz, Manhattan, NY

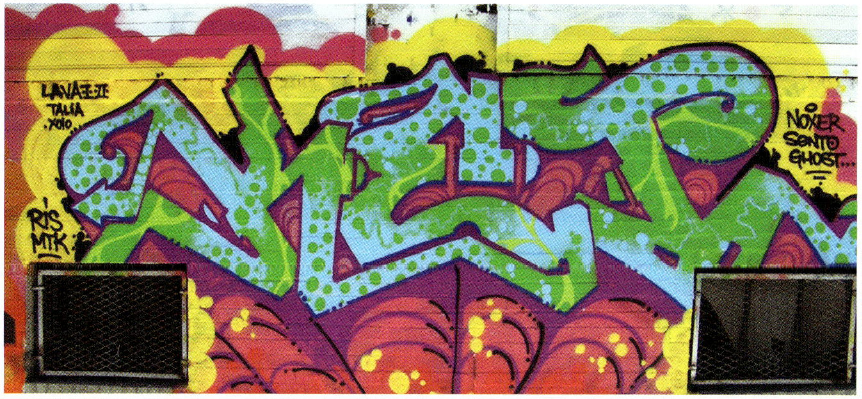
Ket, Manhattan, NY

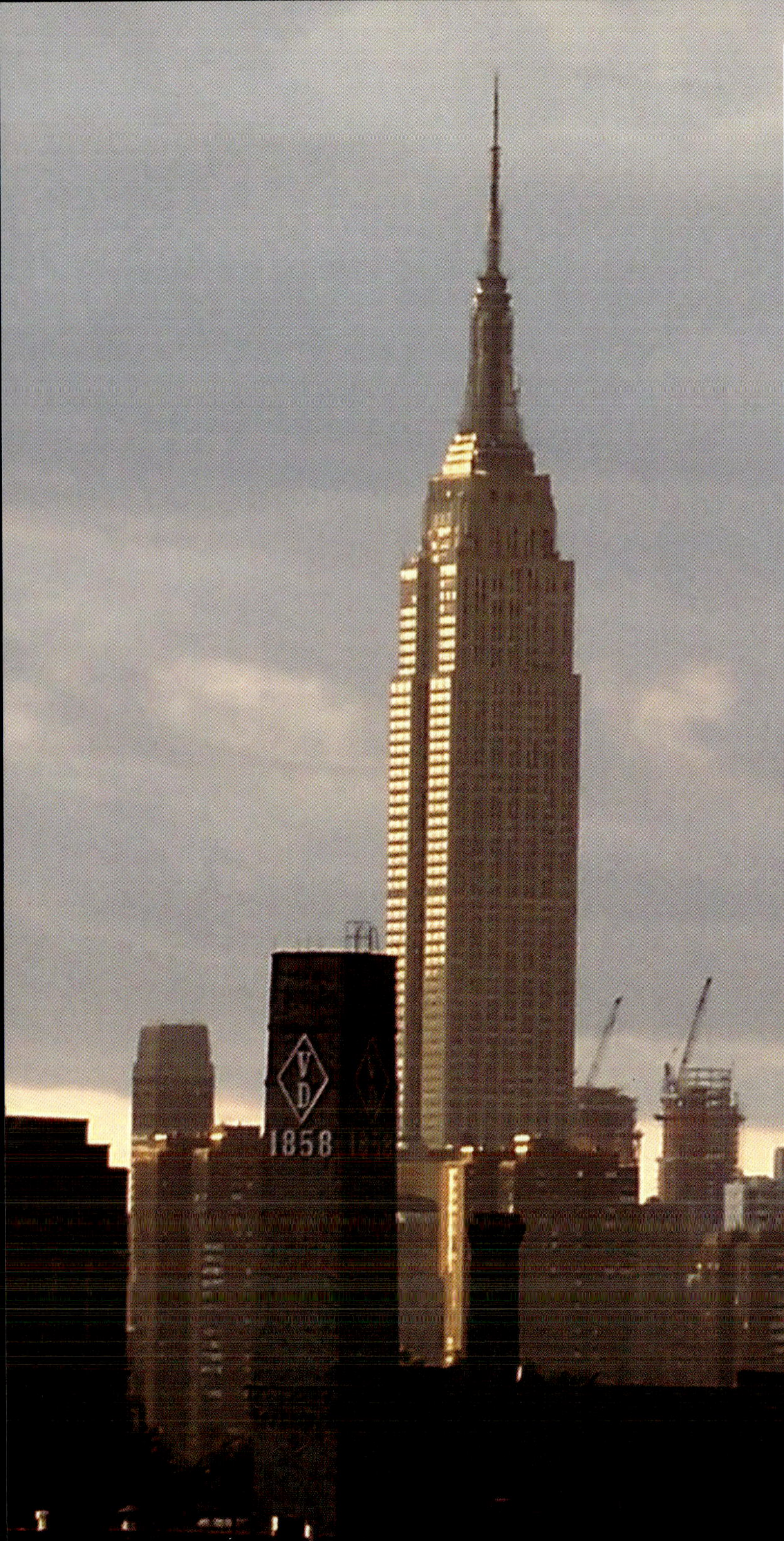


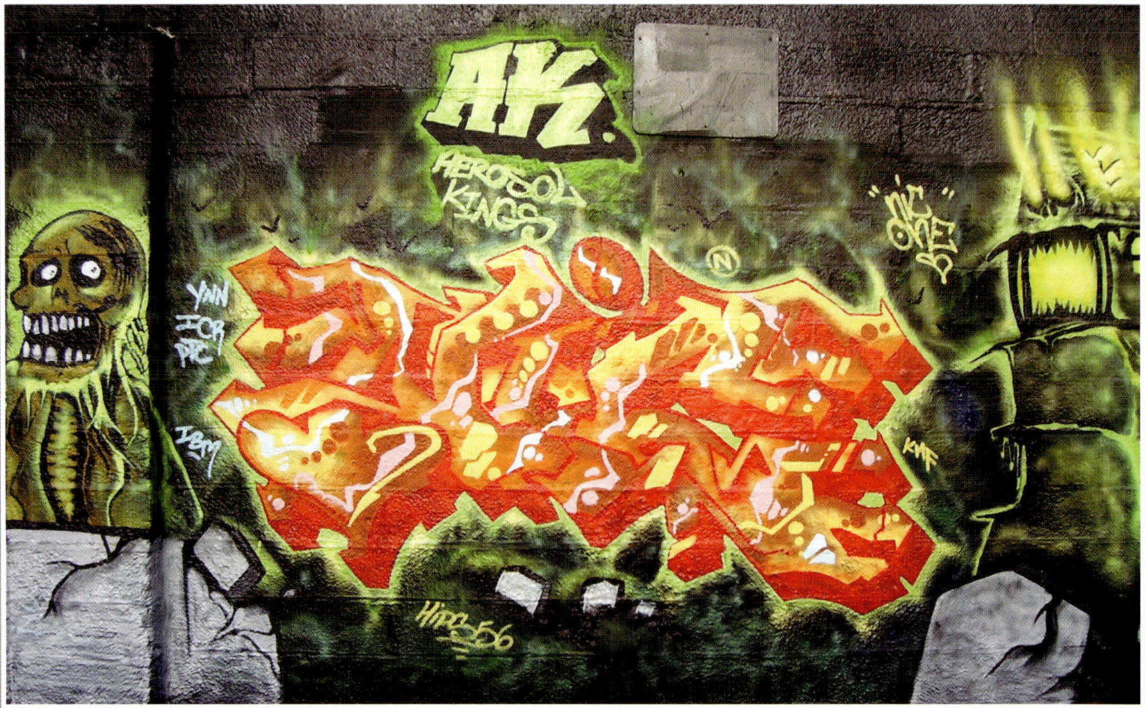


Nic1, Long Island, NY

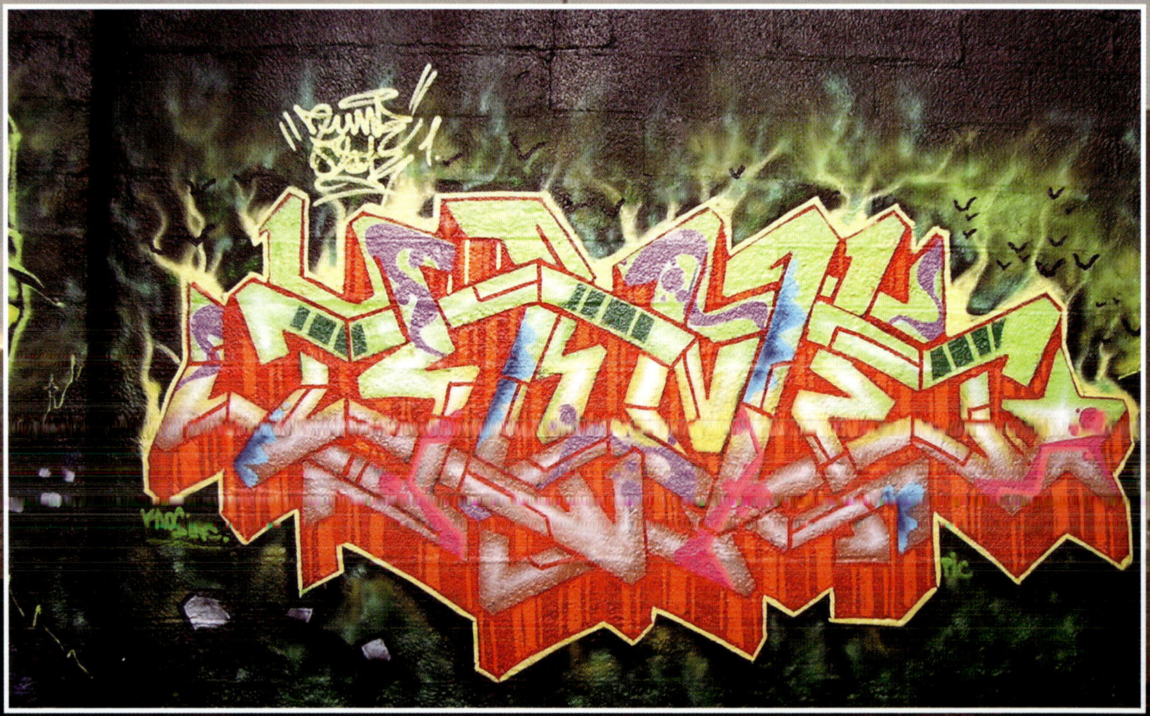

Fume, Long Island, NY

Goal, Long Island, NY

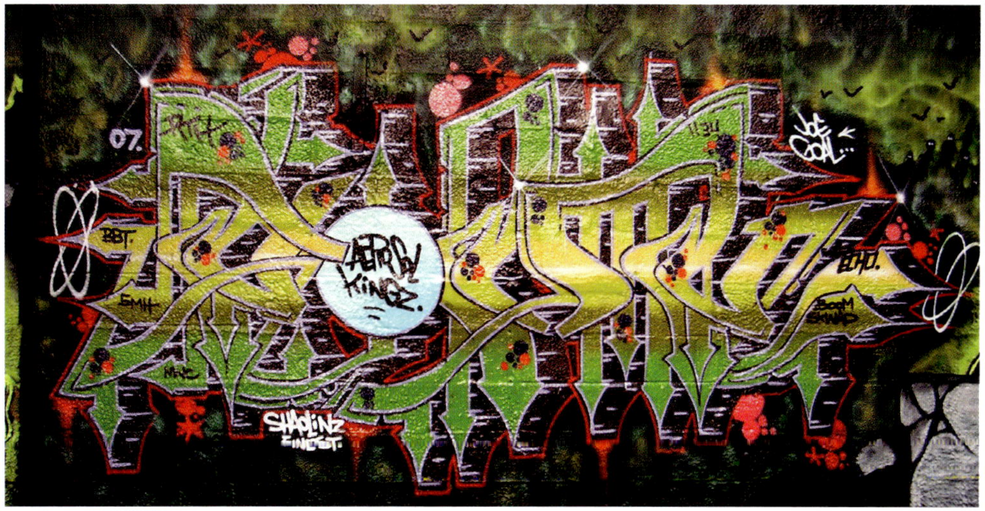

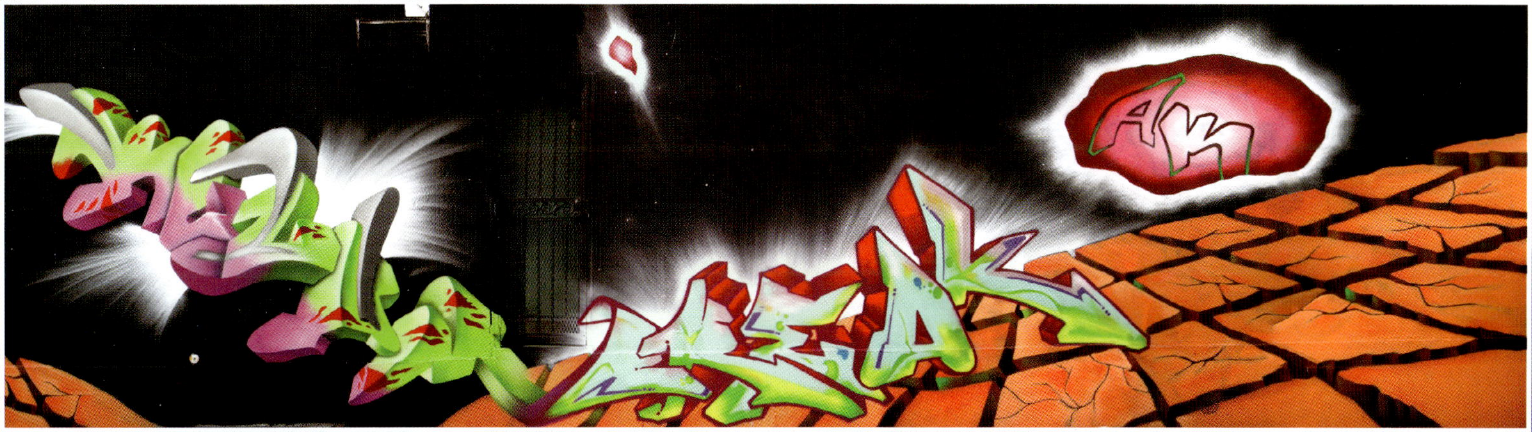

Kezam, Break, Brooklyn, NY

Ros, Long Island, NY

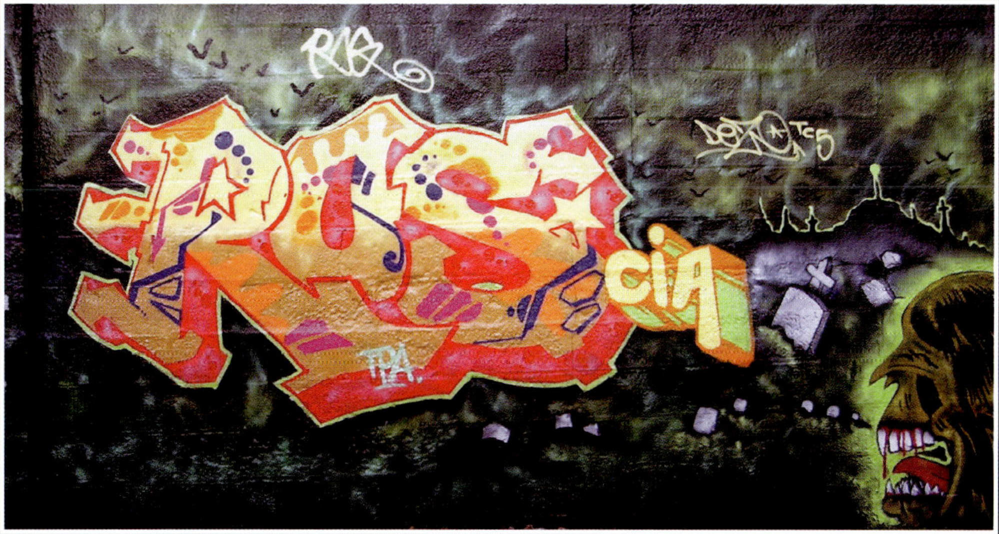

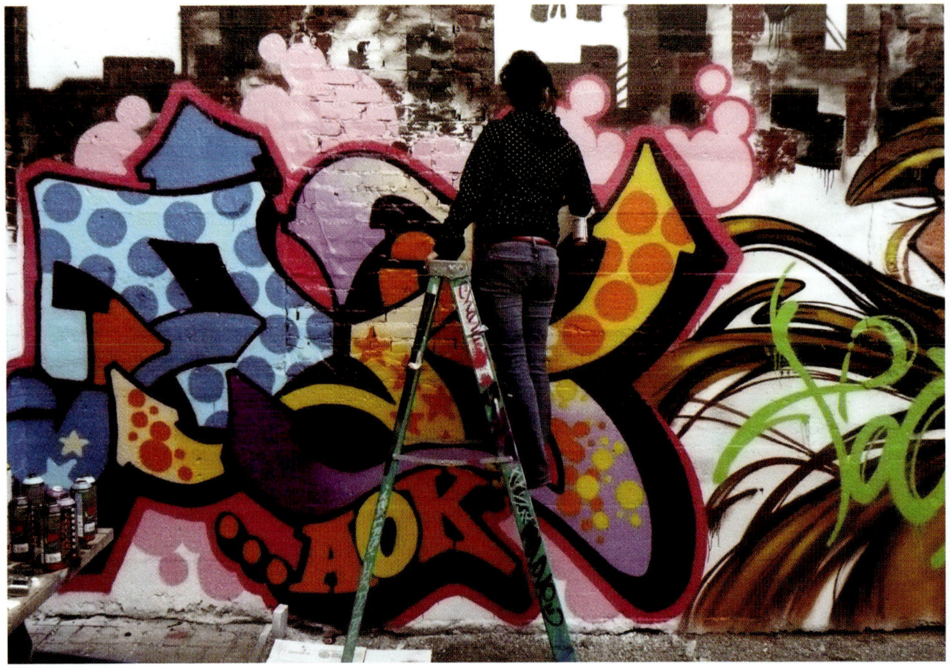


QA, Brooklyn, NY

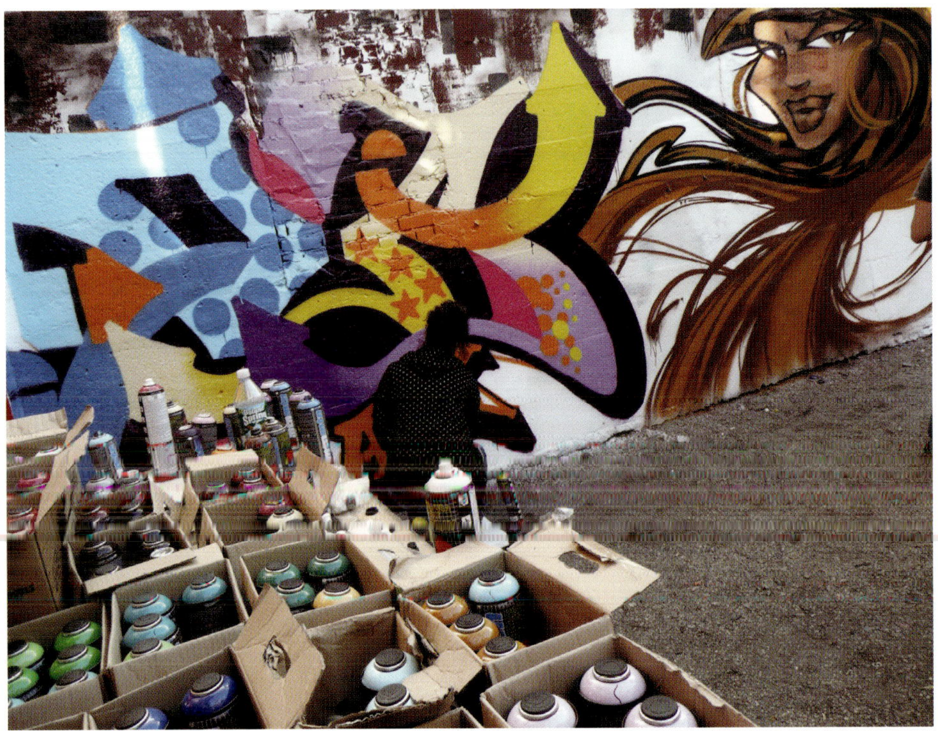

QA, Brooklyn, NY

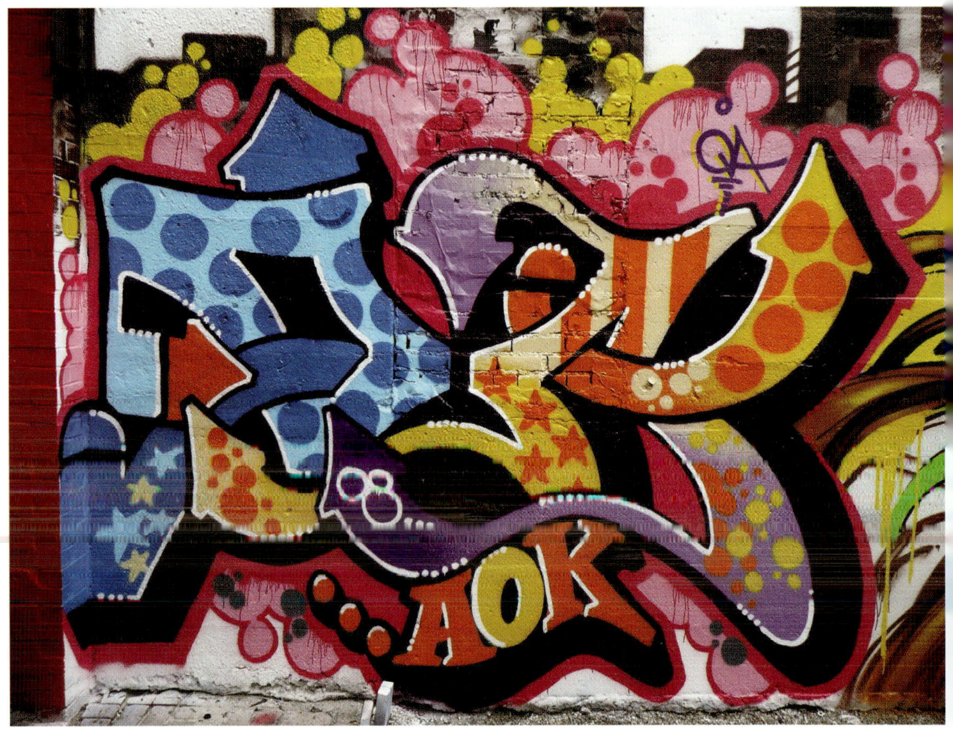


QA, Brooklyn, NY

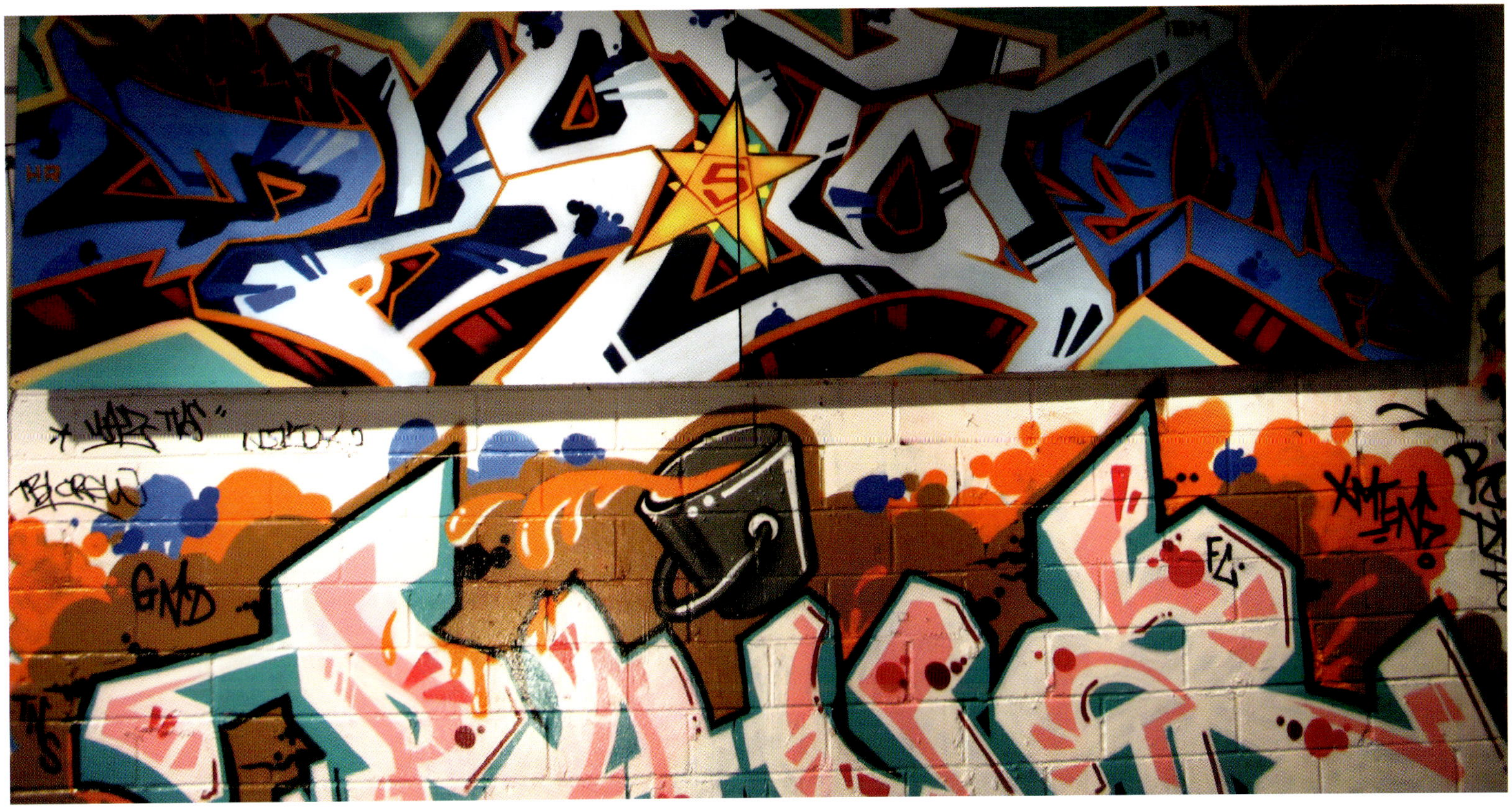

Dezo, Totem, Brooklyn, NY

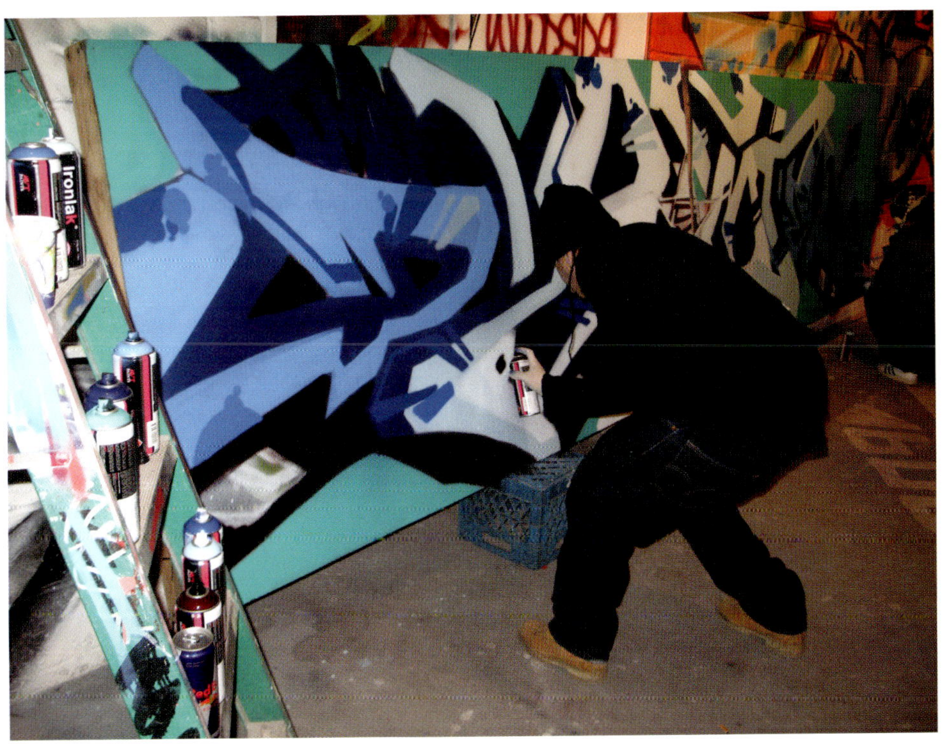


Dezo, Totem, Brooklyn, NY

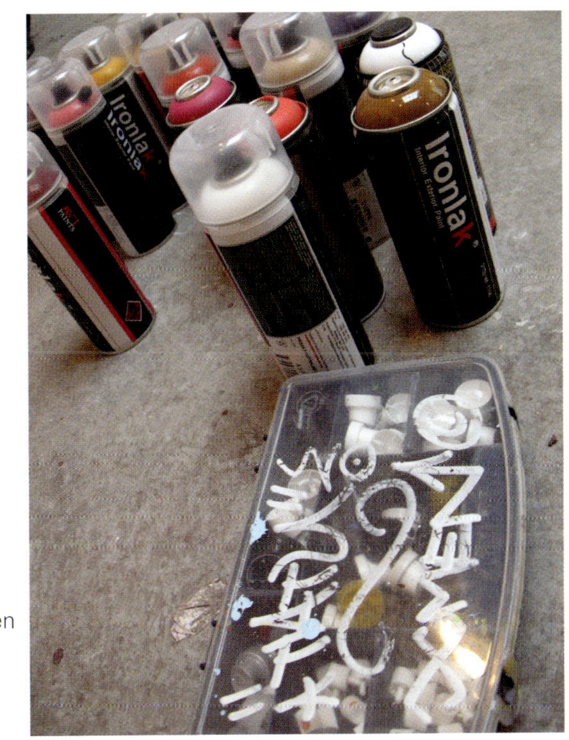


Tatu X-Men

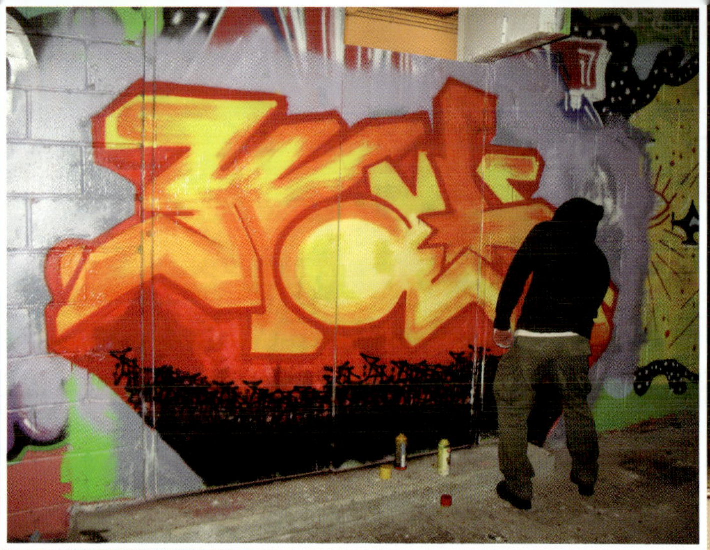

Wak, Brooklyn, NY

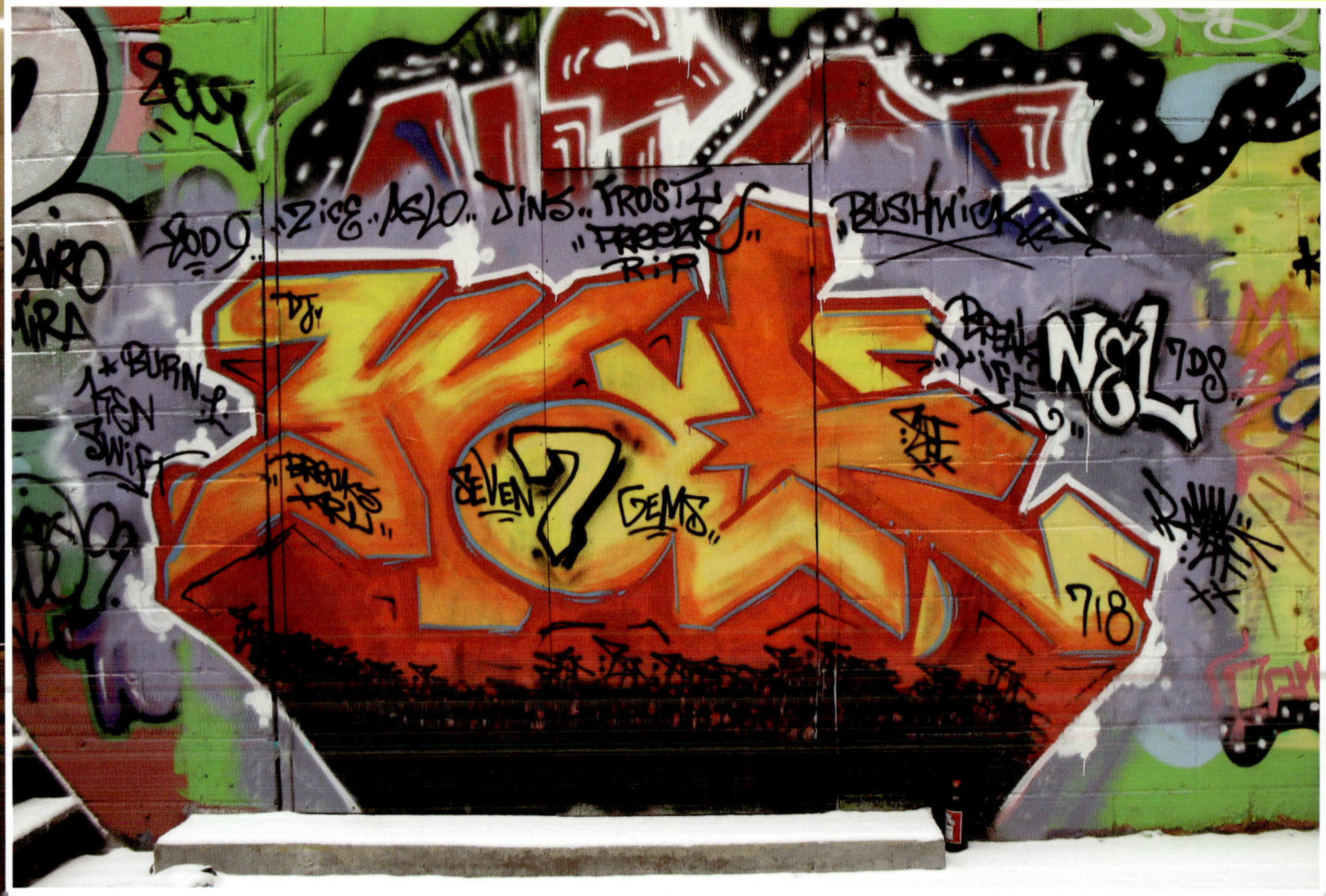

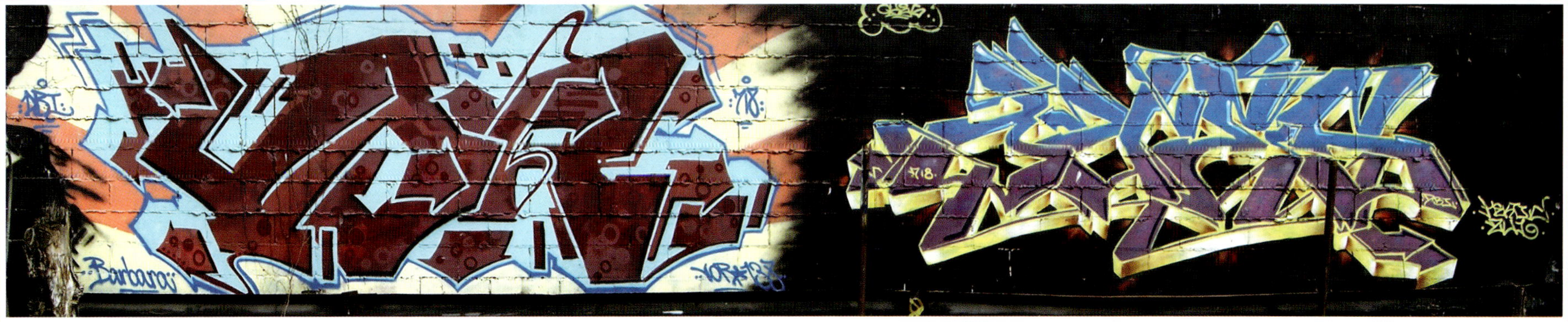

Vor, Ques, Queens, NY

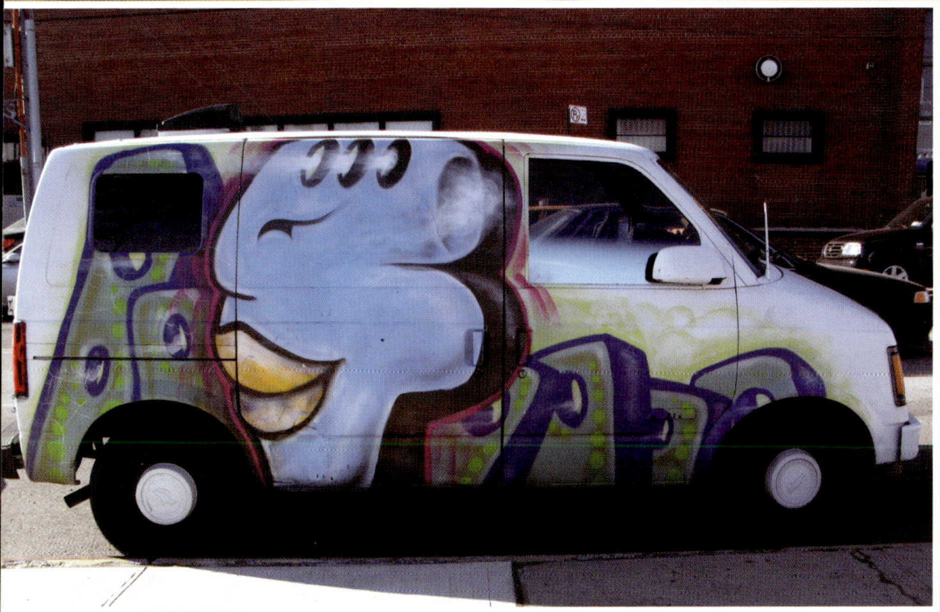

Free5, Queens, NY

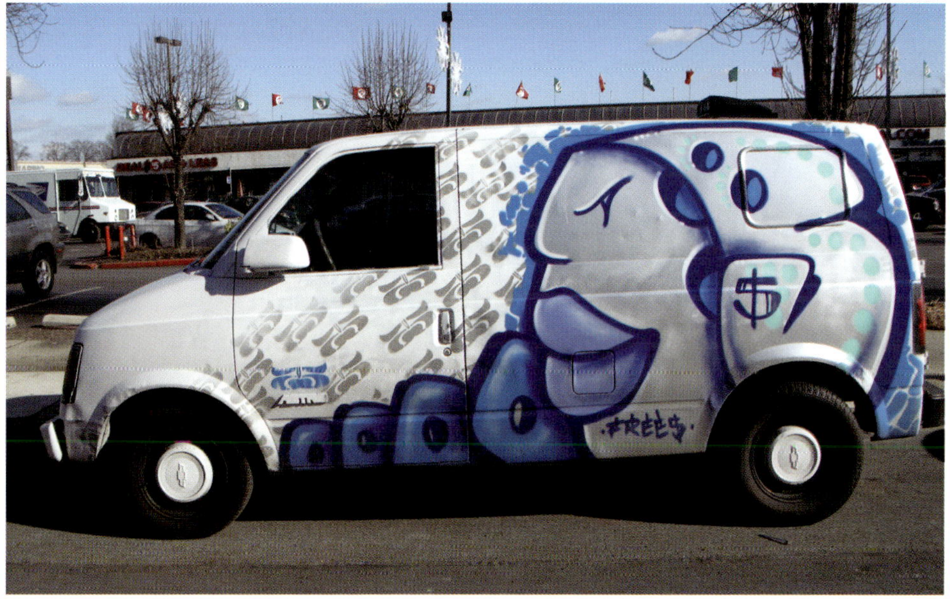

Free5, Queens, NY

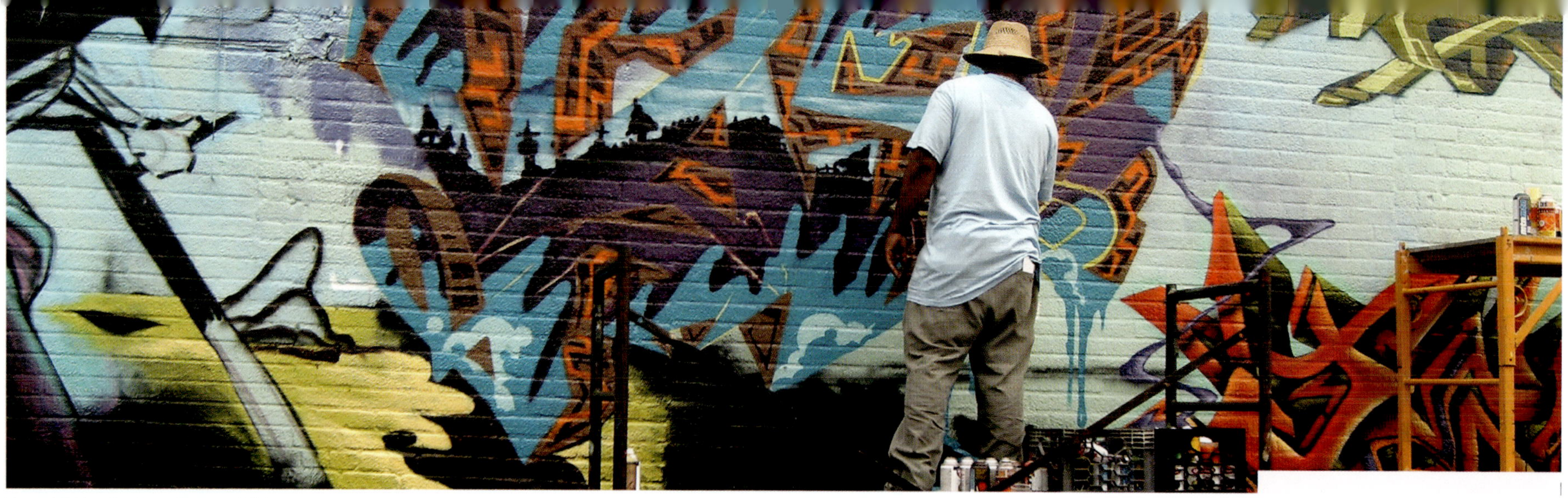

Vase UW – Action, Bronx, NY

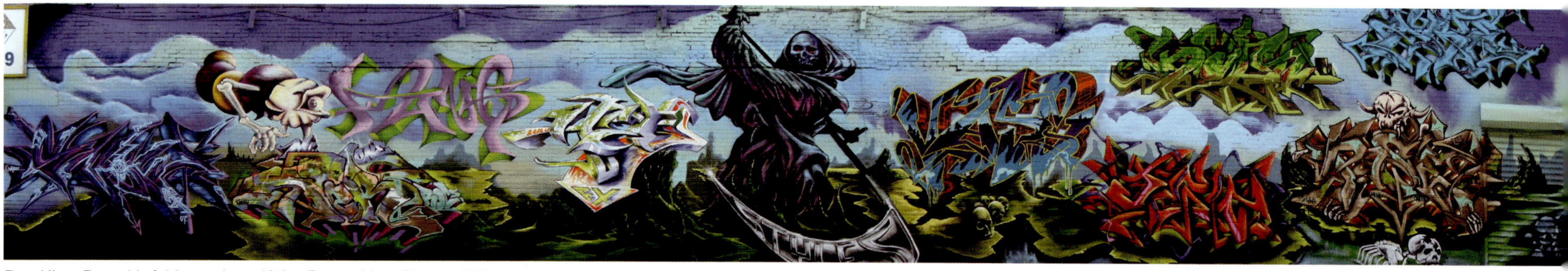

Per, King Bee, Hef, Vase, Jew, Kais, Pase, Abe, Bronx, NY,

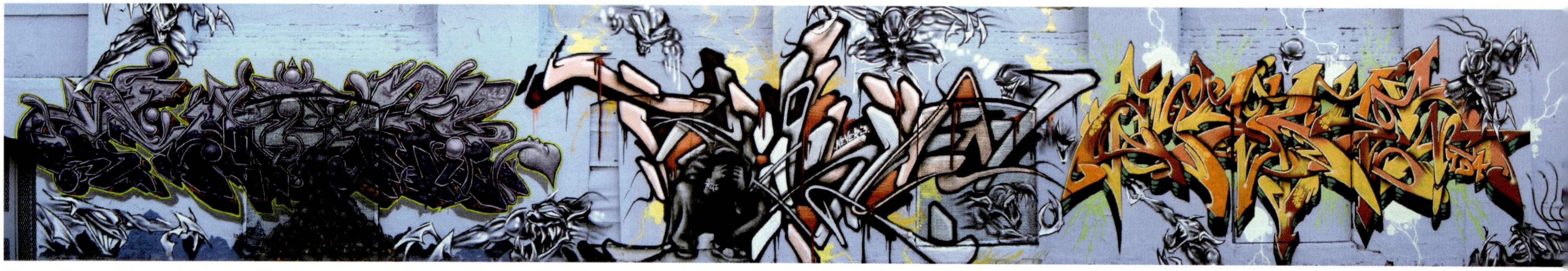

Haze, Never, Meres, Queens, NY

Seter, Sebs, FSN, Meres, Zymer, Vik, Zimad, Bronx, N

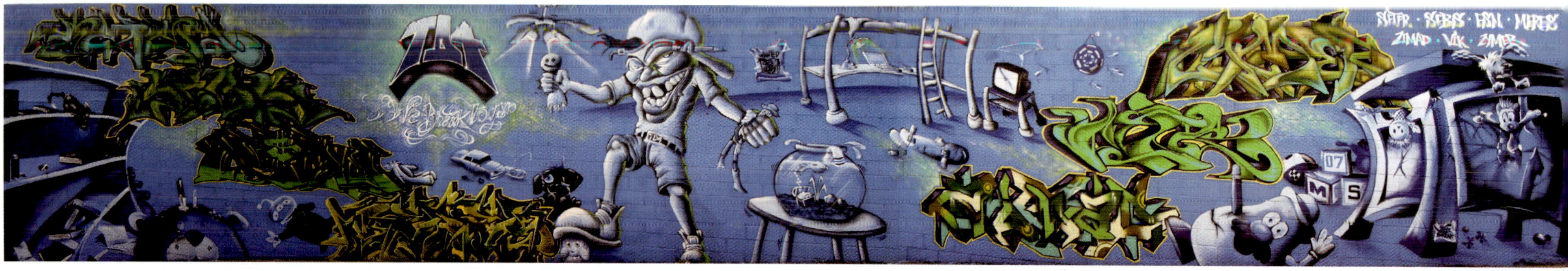

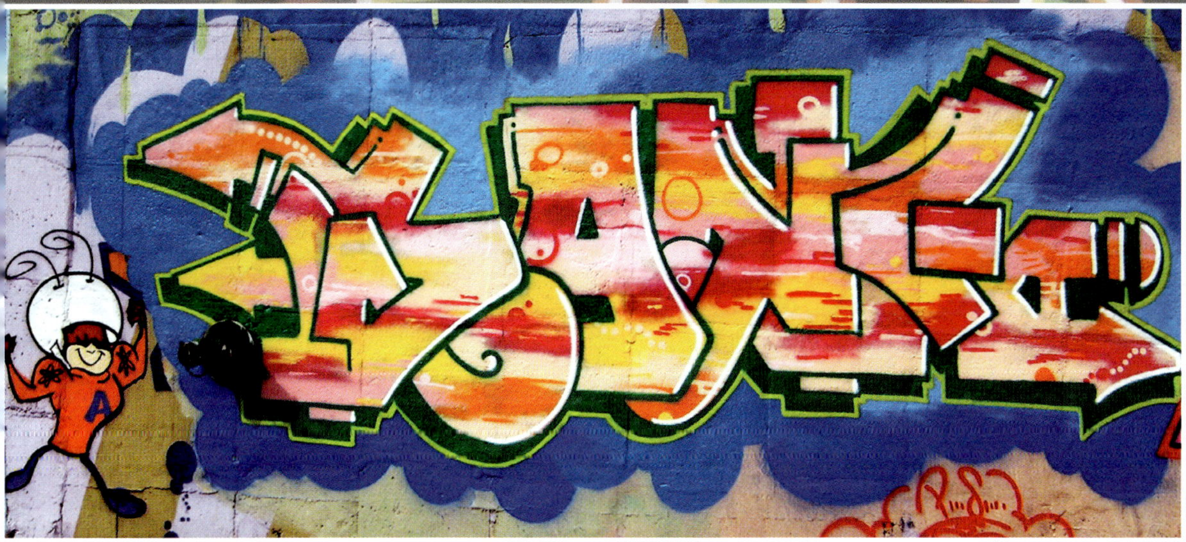

Sane (Smith, Queens, NY

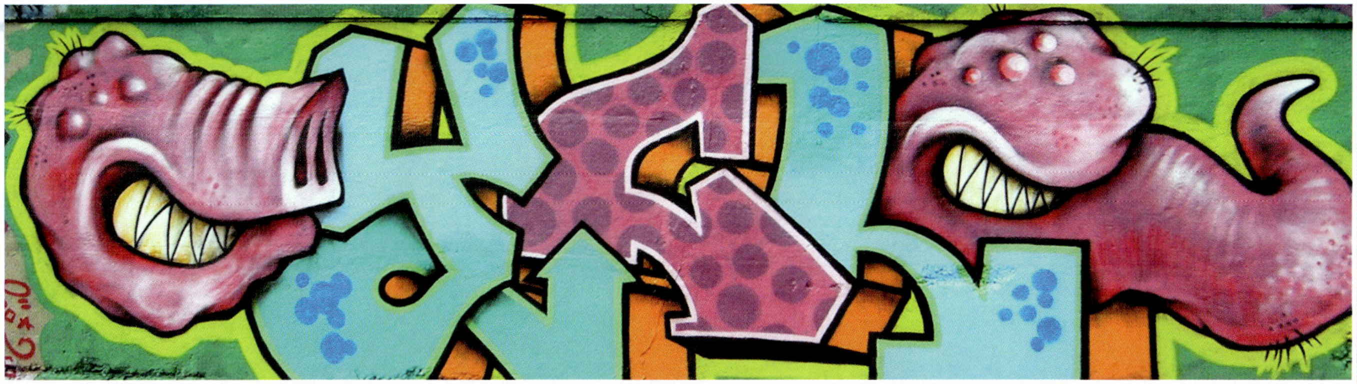

Cycle, Queens, NY

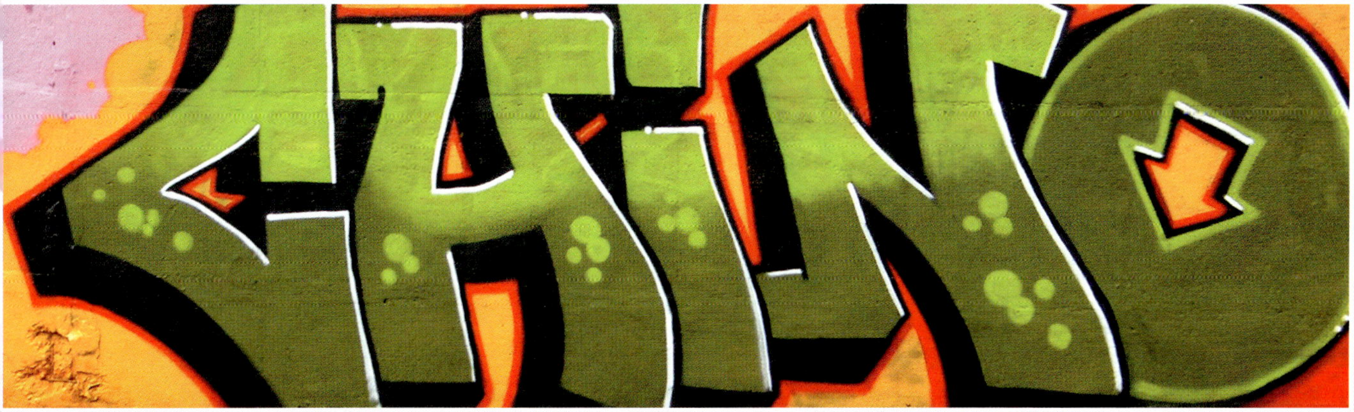

Chino, Queens, NY

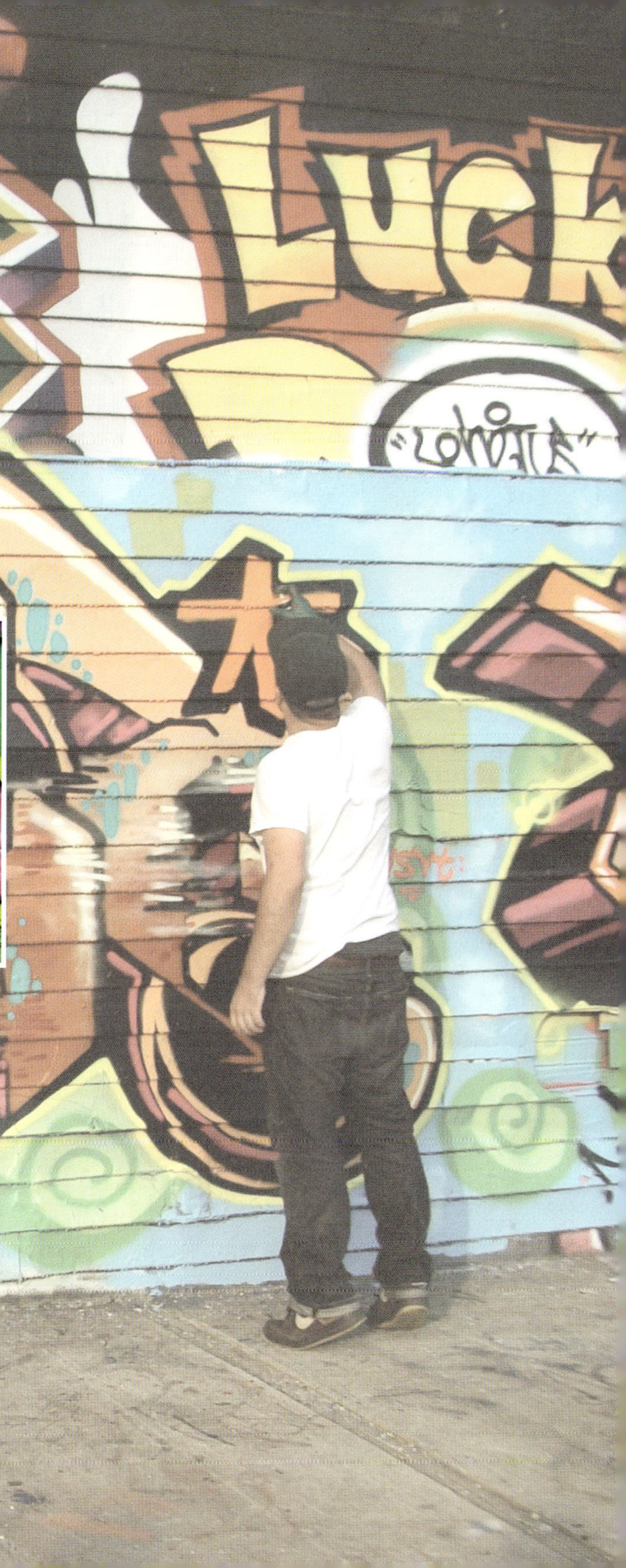

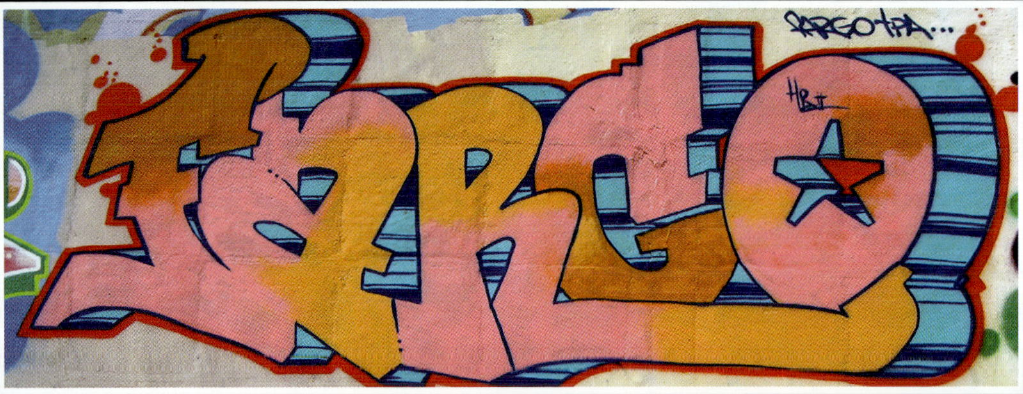

Fargo, Queens, NY

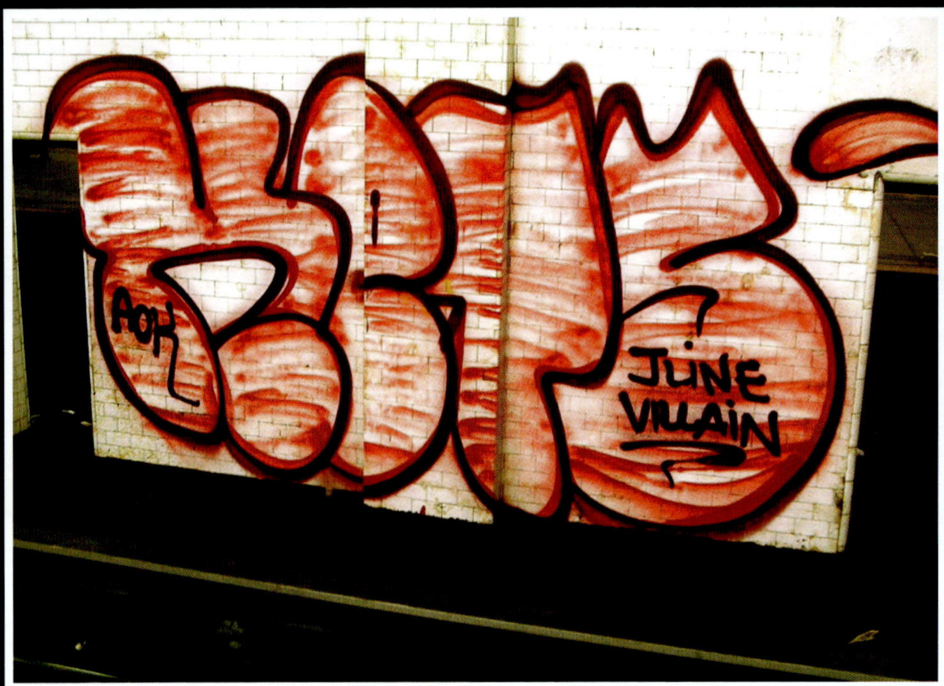


Ket, Manhattan, NY

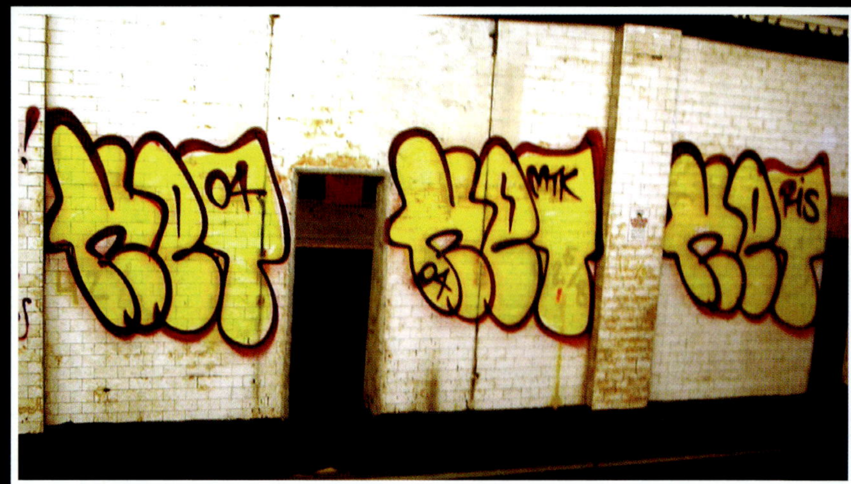

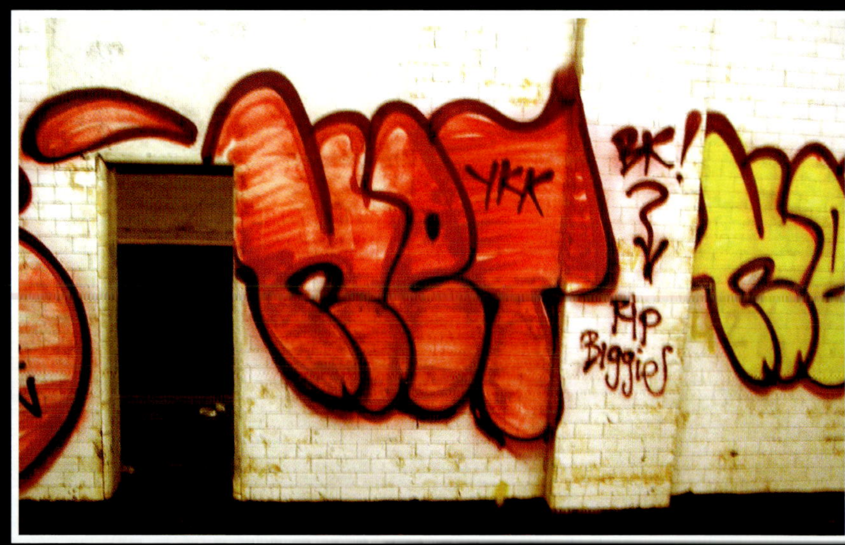

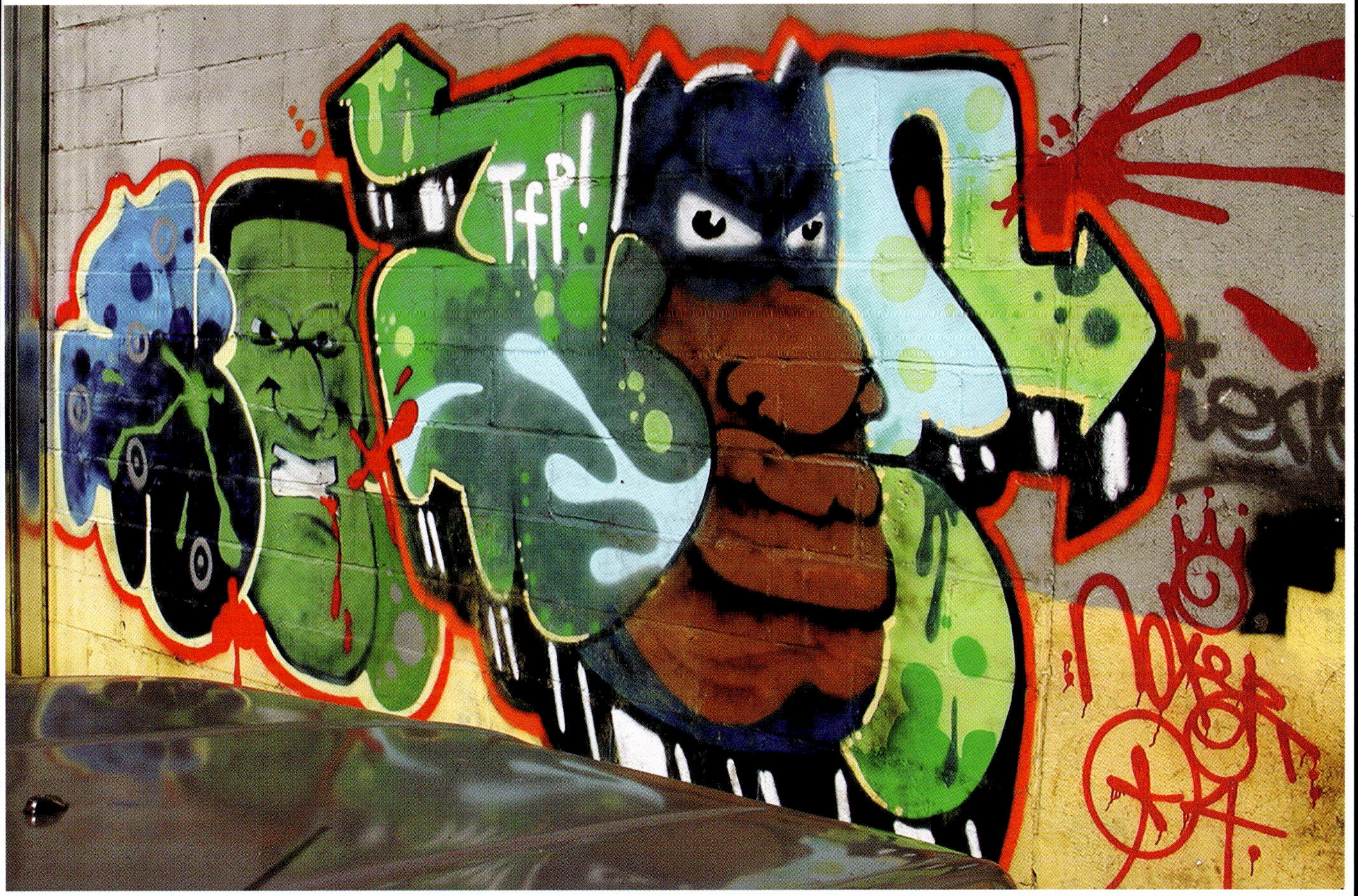

Noxer, Brooklyn, NY

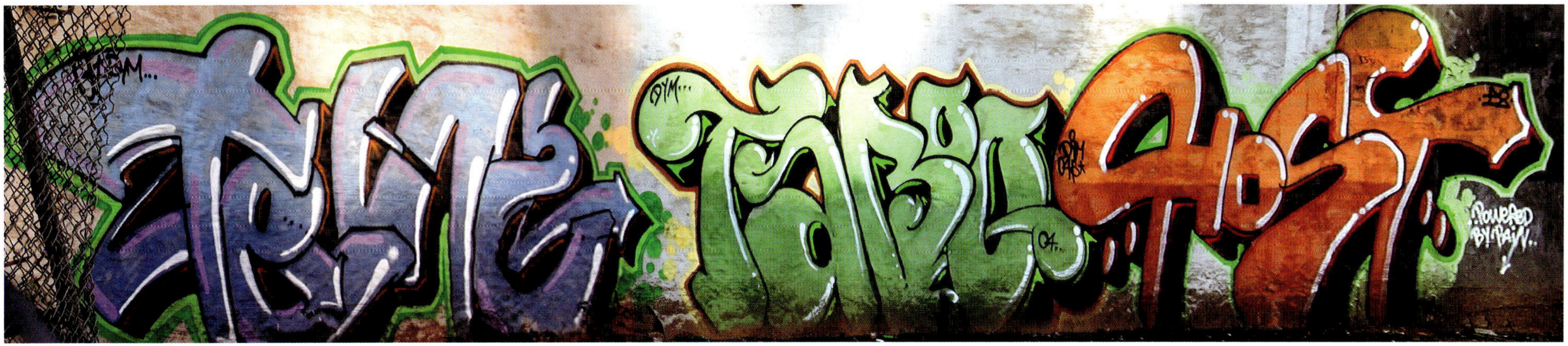

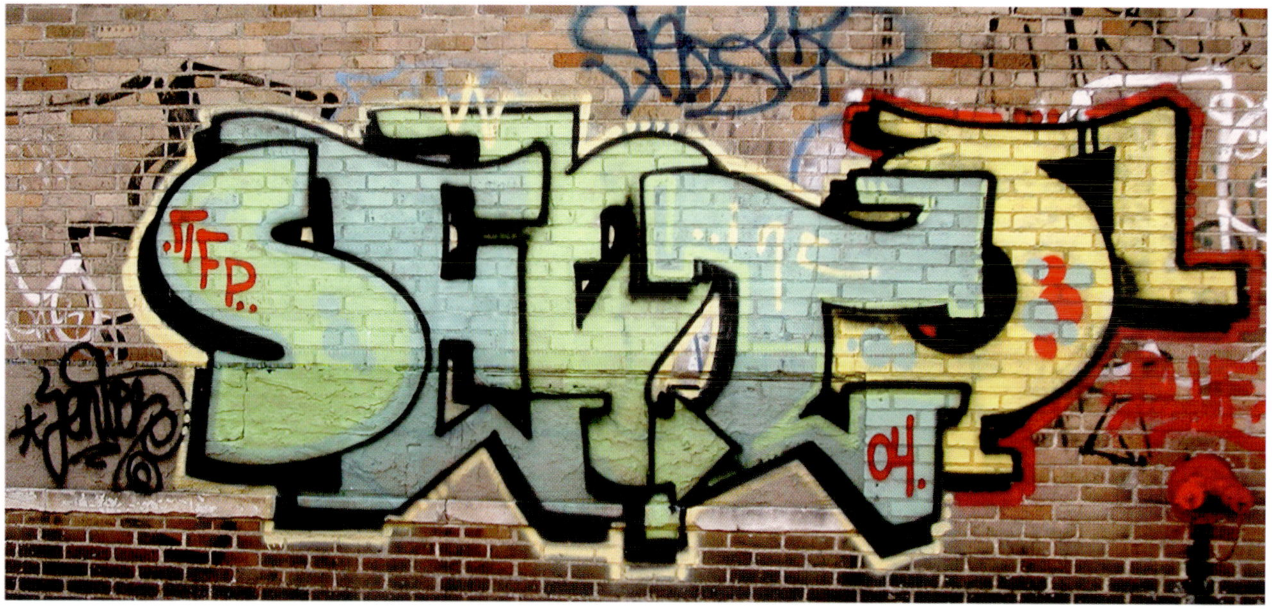

Sento, Bronx, NY

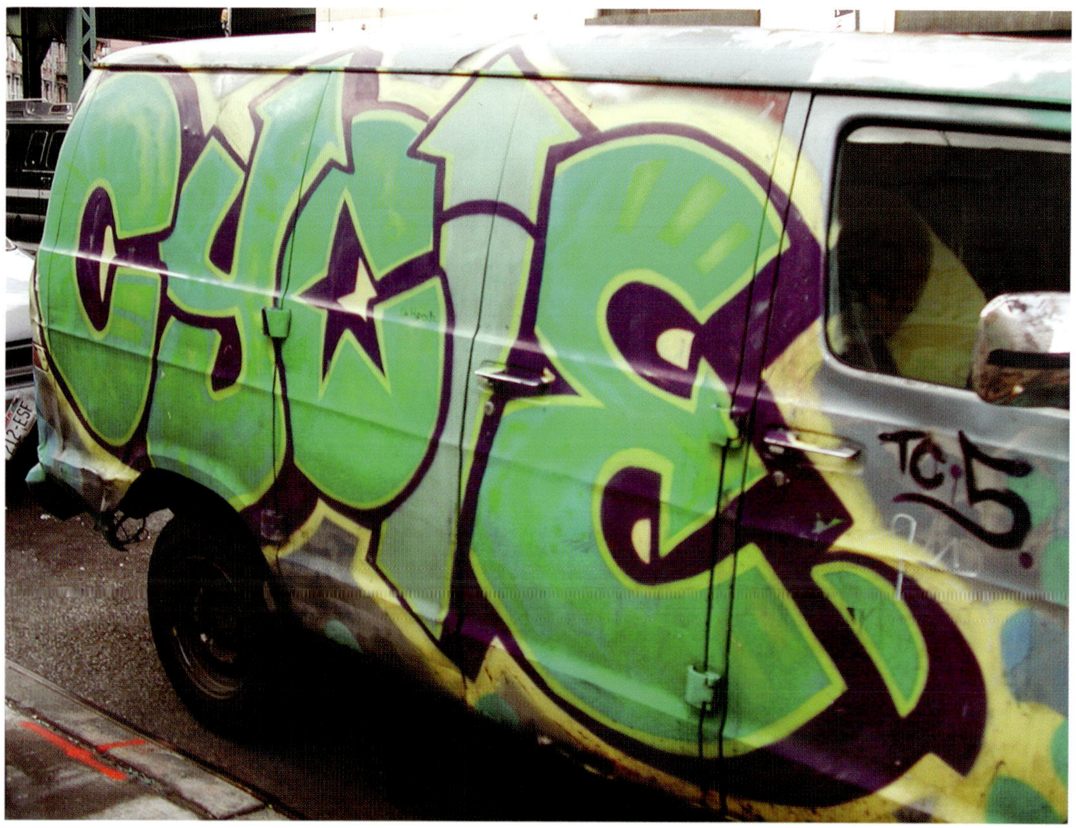

Cycle, Brooklyn, NY

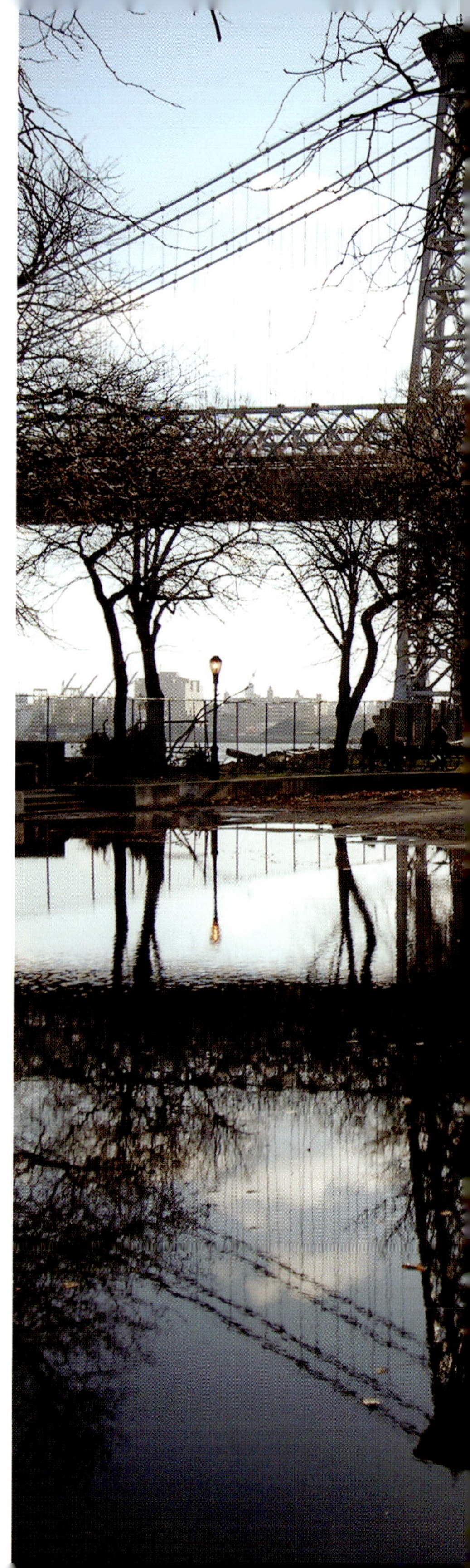

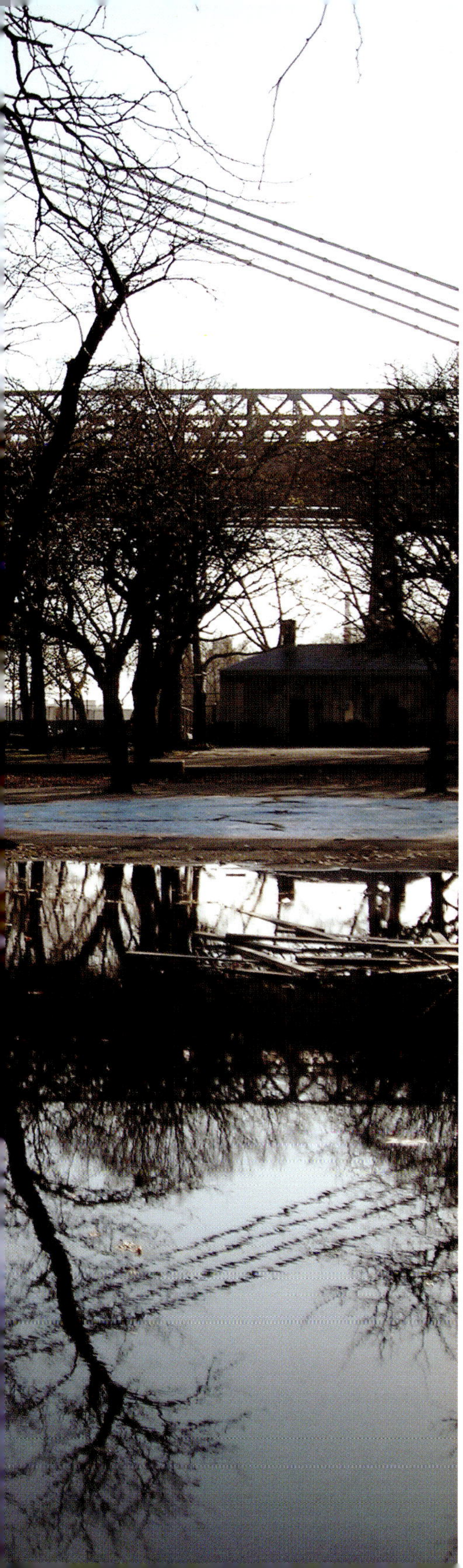

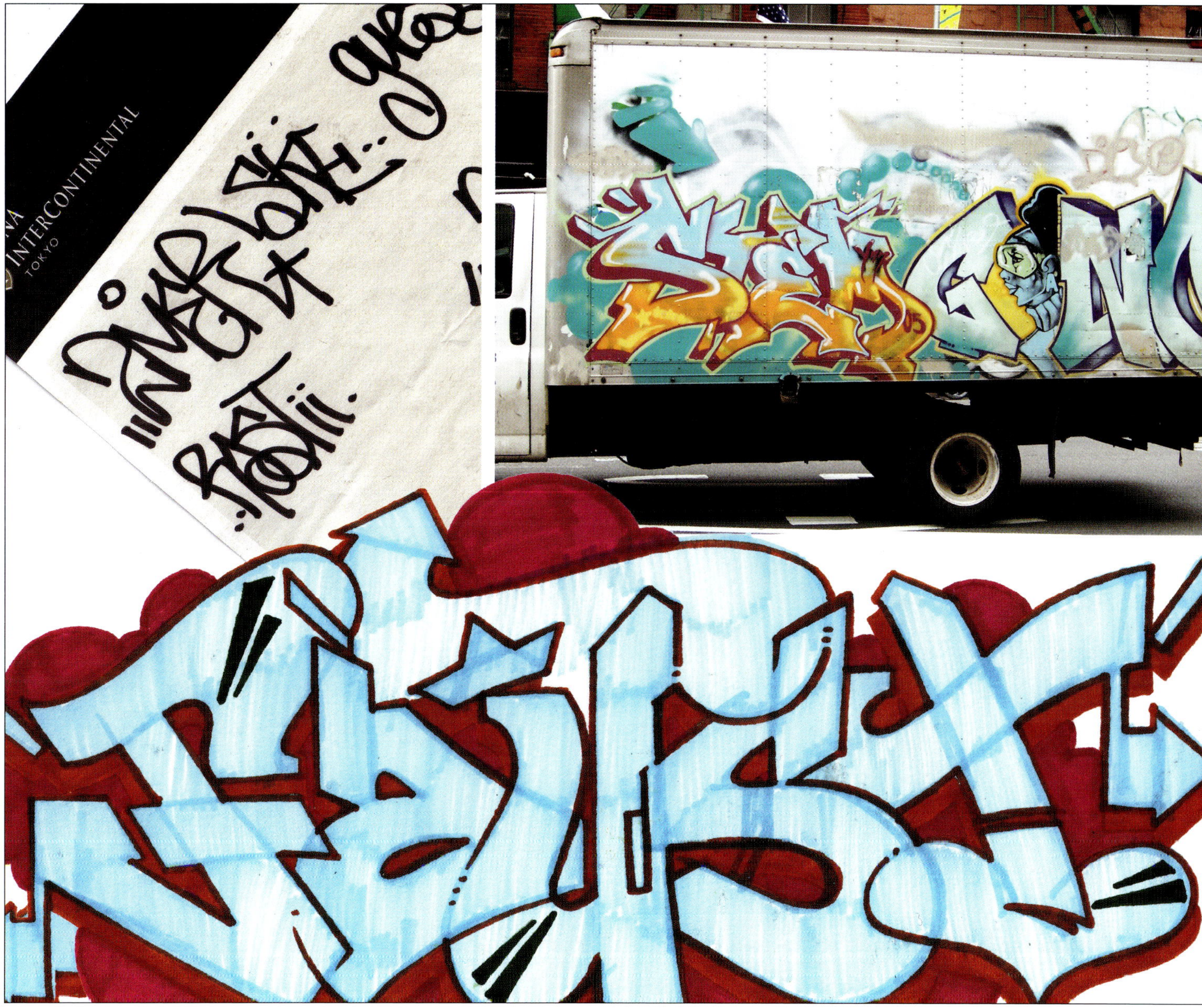


Top left: 2mer, Guess, 2008; top right: Stem, Gano, Manhattan, NY; bottom: Faust, 2006

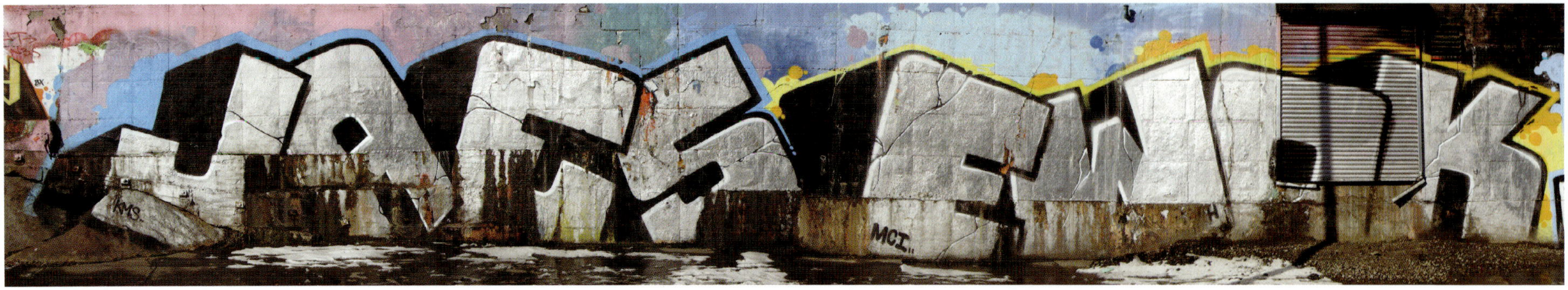

Jaes, Ewok, Bronx, NY

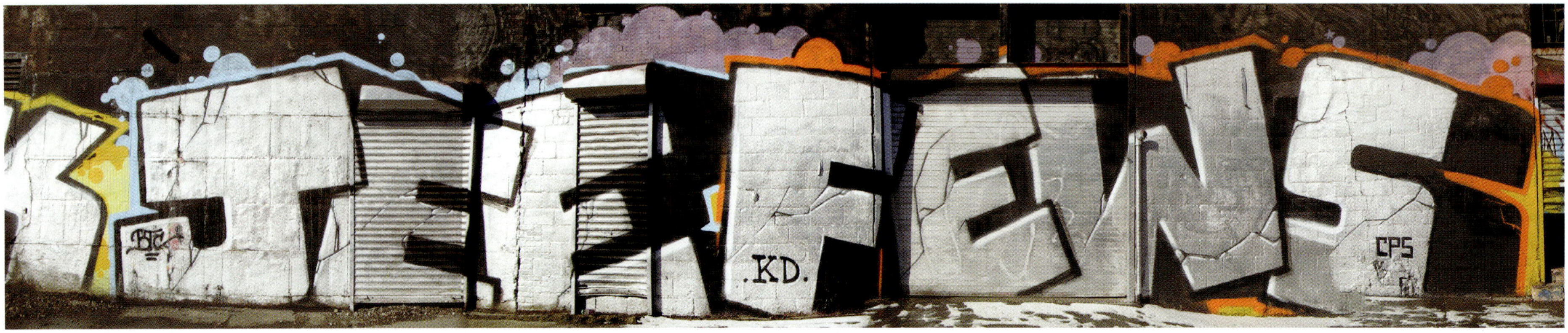

Jee, Fews, Bronx, NY

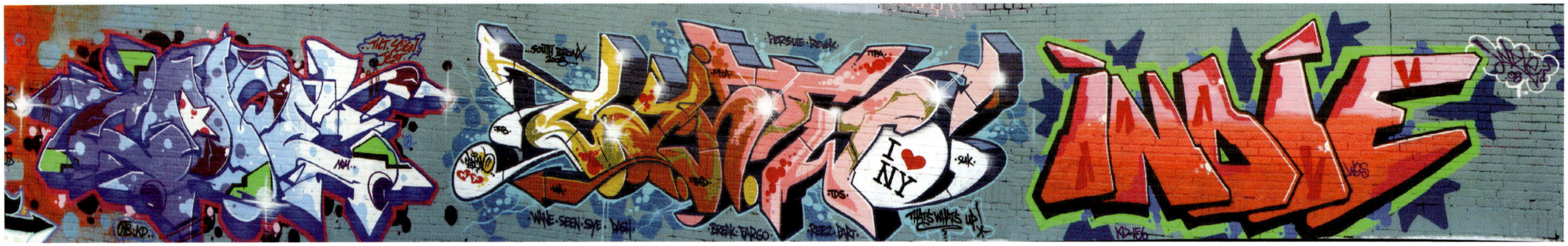
Cope2, Can2, Indie, Bronx, NY

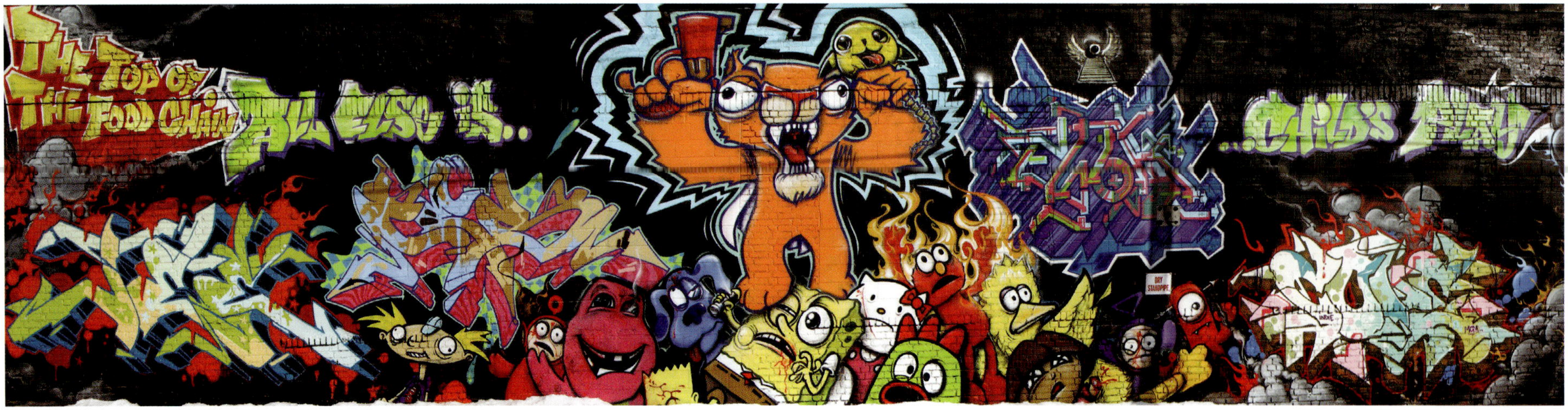
Jee, Ces, Ewok, Cope2, Bronx, NY

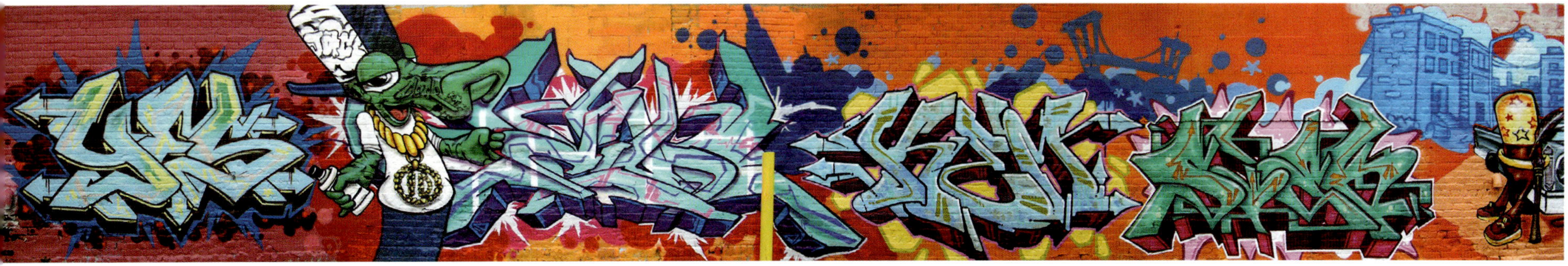

’es, Clark, Kem, Siek, Bronx, NY

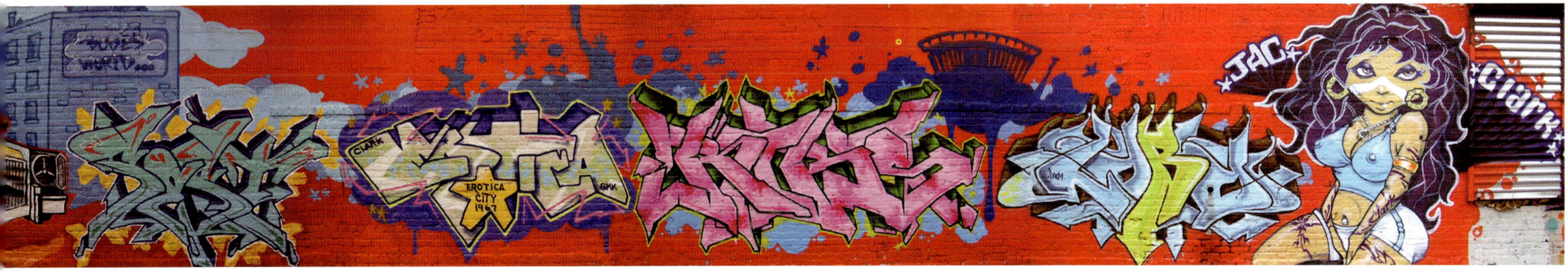


Sest, Erotica, Ribs, Lobo, Bronx, NY

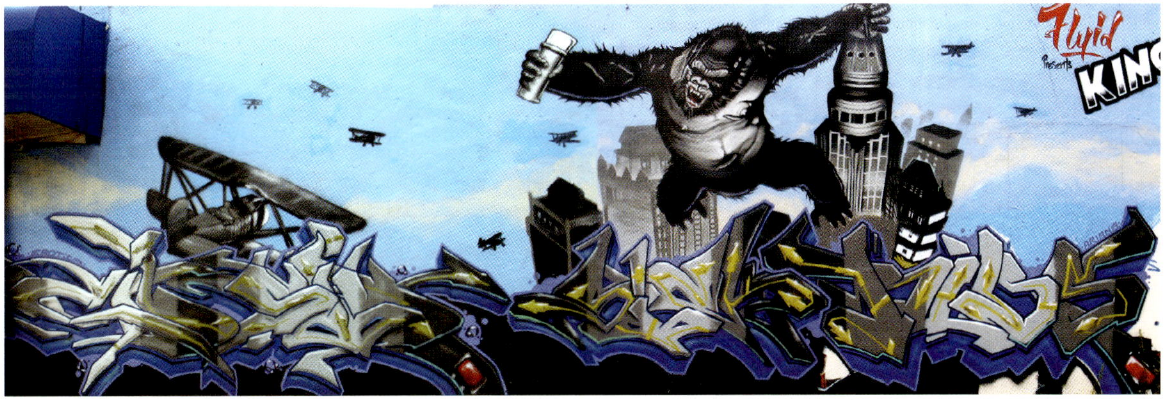


Clark, Sest, Siek, Ribs, Queens, NY

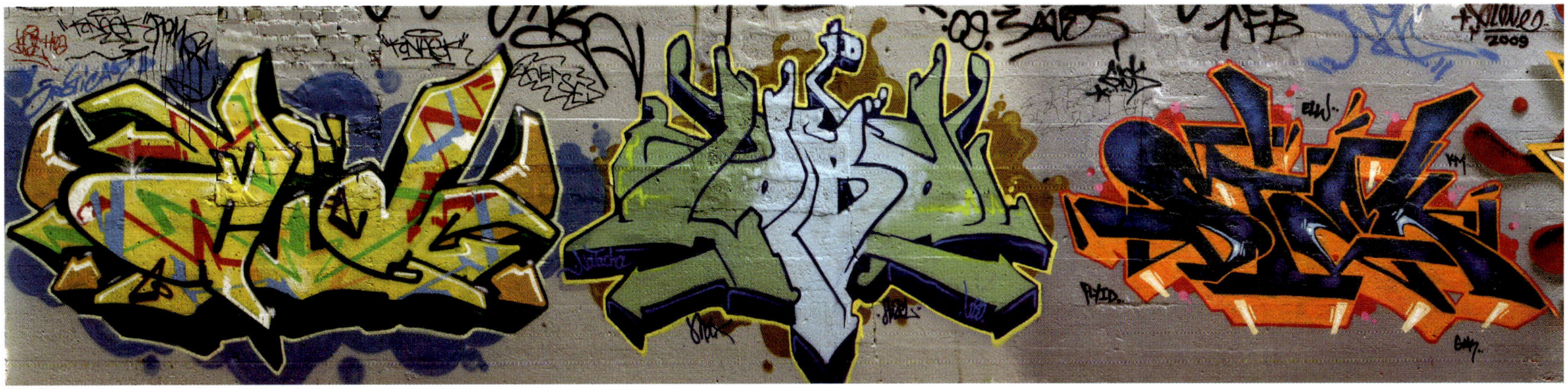


Clark, Lobo, Siek, Brooklyn, NY

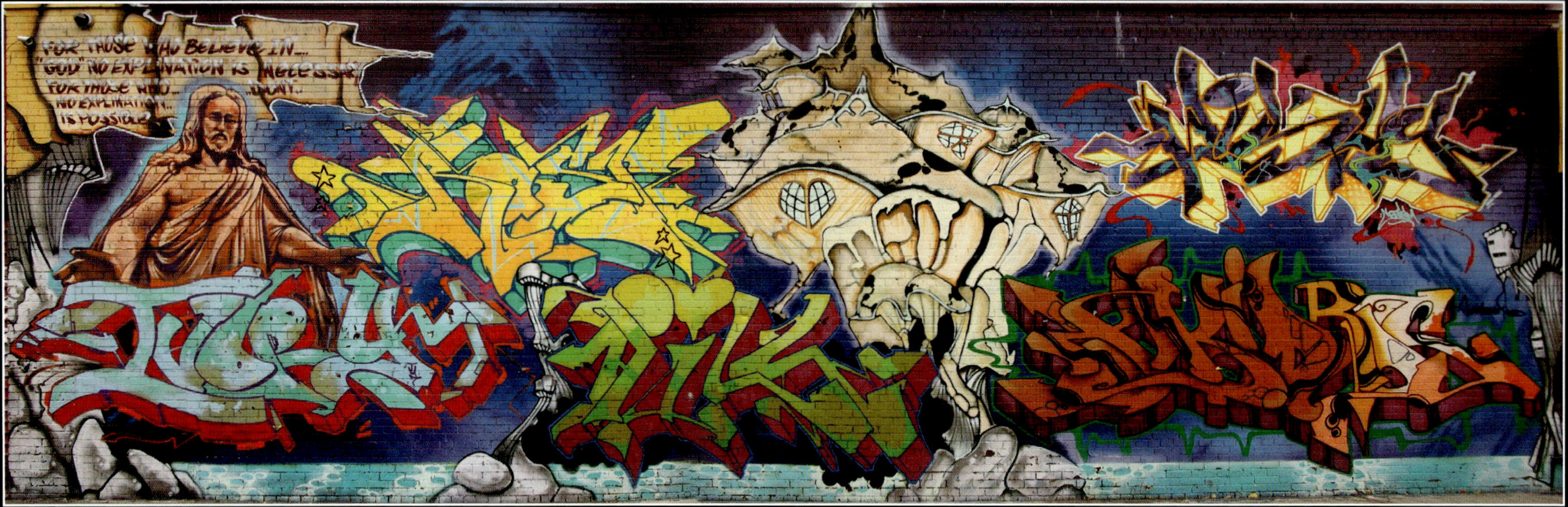


Ivory, Rasp (Yes2), Tich (Pill), T-Kid, Wishy (Ces), Manhattan, NY

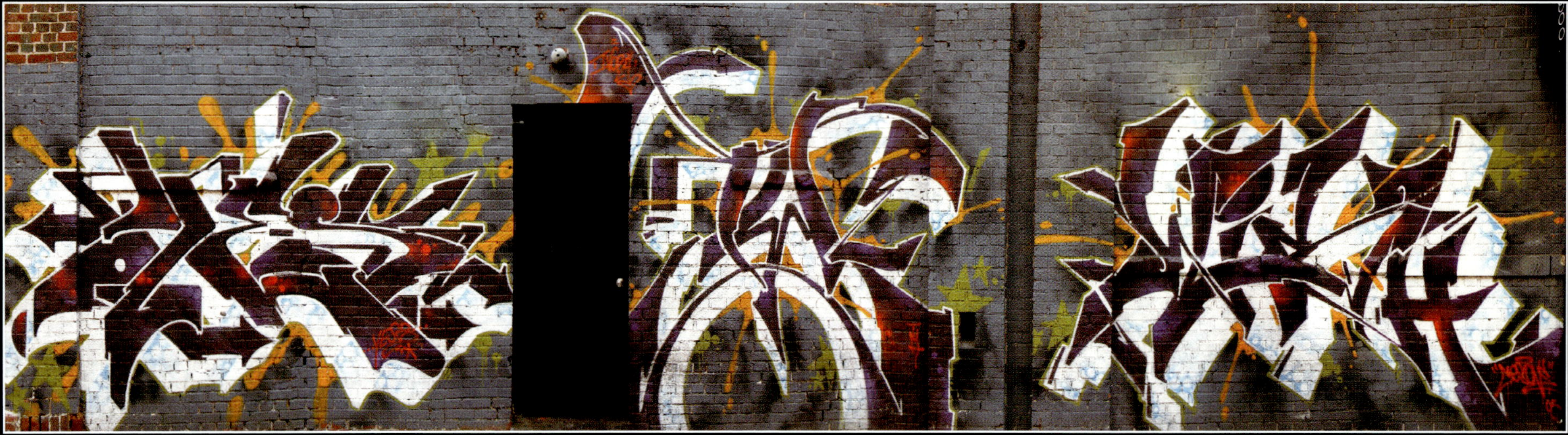

Yes2, Ivory, Wish (Ces), Manhattan, NY

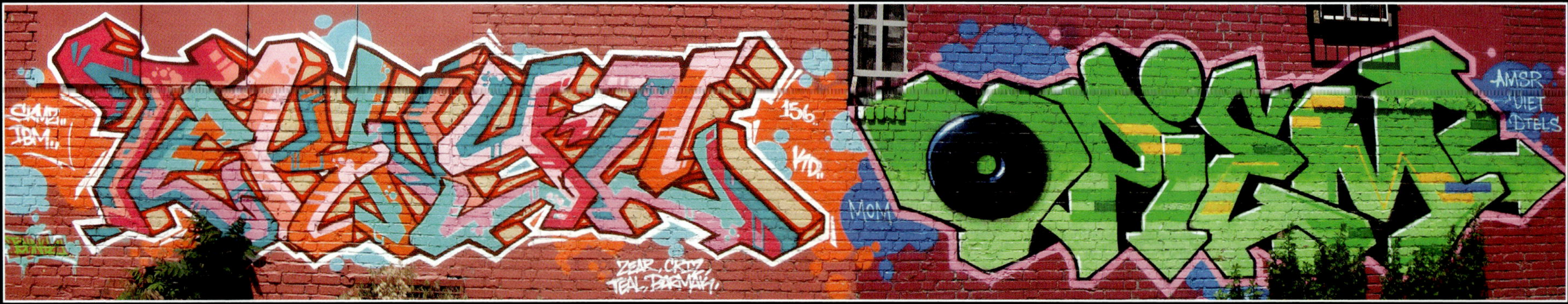


Teknyc, Opiem, Bronx, NY

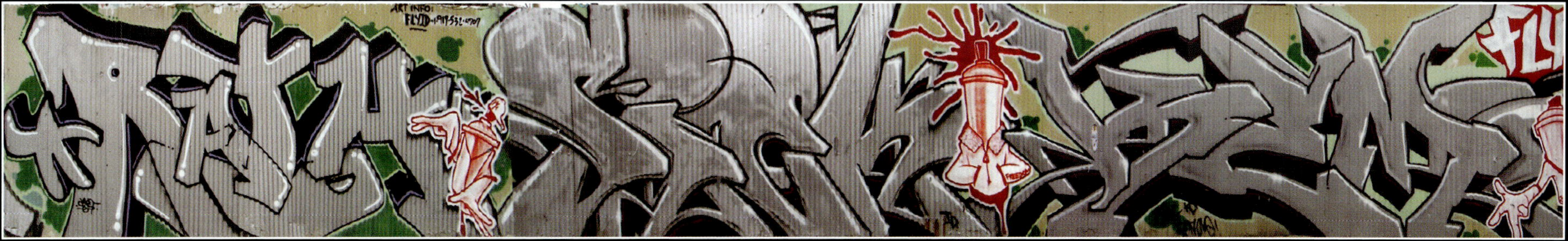

Rath, Siek, Kem, Clark, Ribs, Sen2, Per, Erotica, Kems, Themo, Leia (not pictured: Ewok, Jew), Bronx, NY

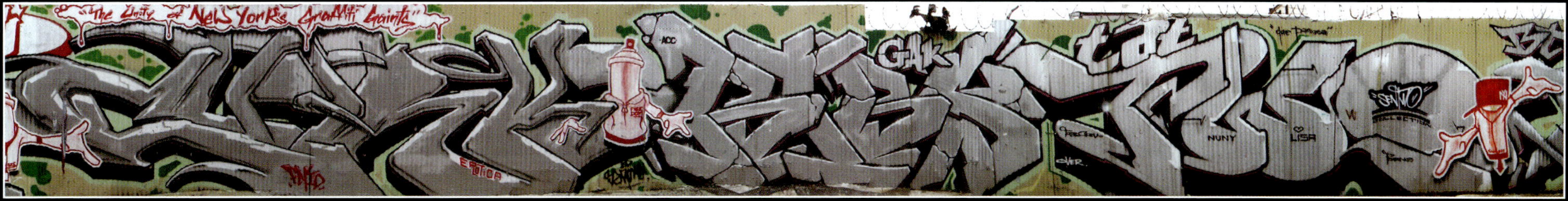


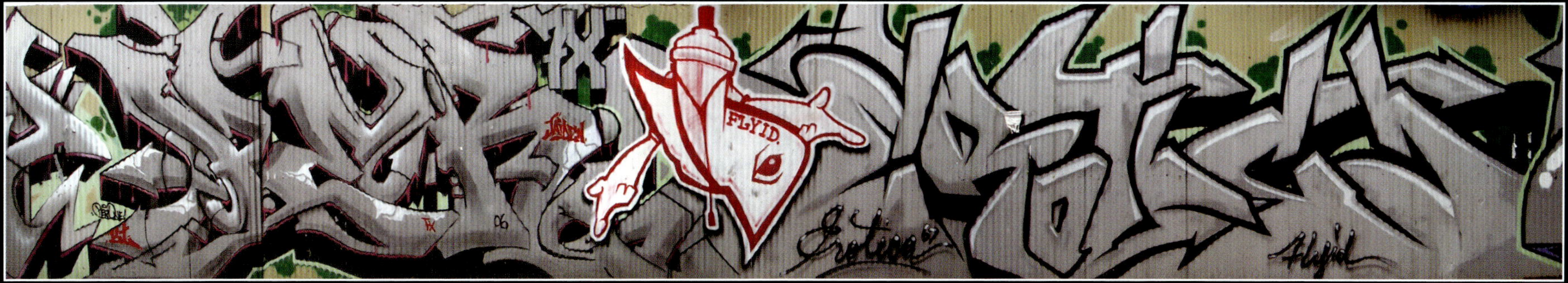


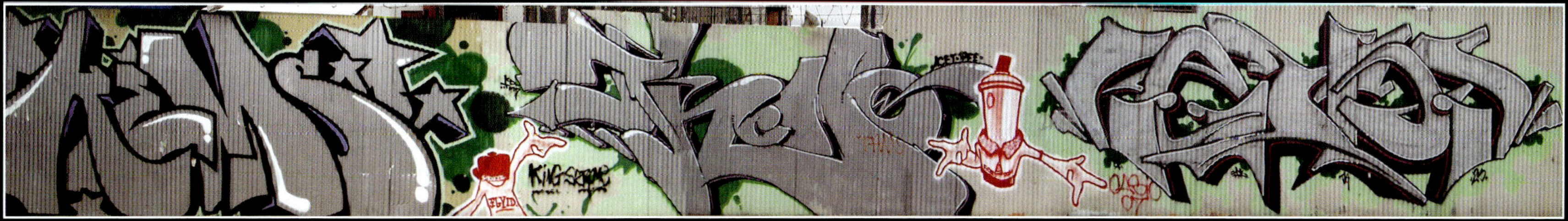

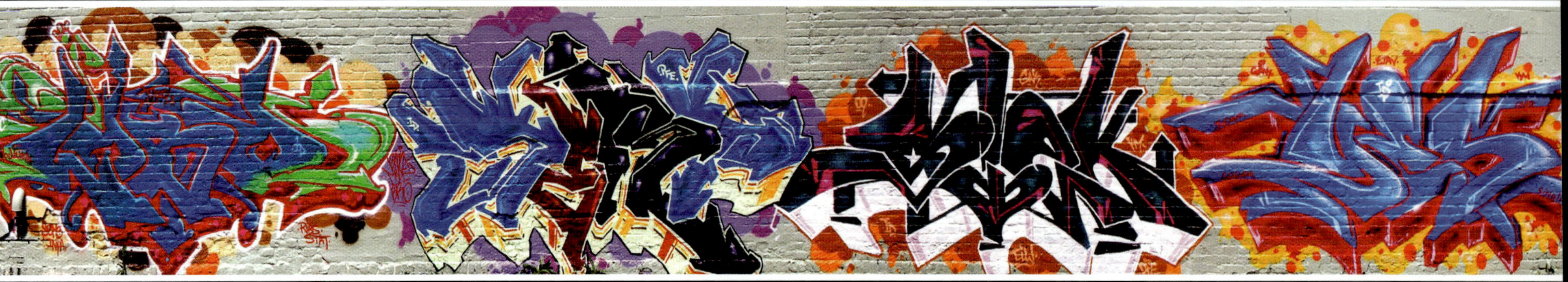

Lobo, Serp, Siek, Yes, Bronx, NY

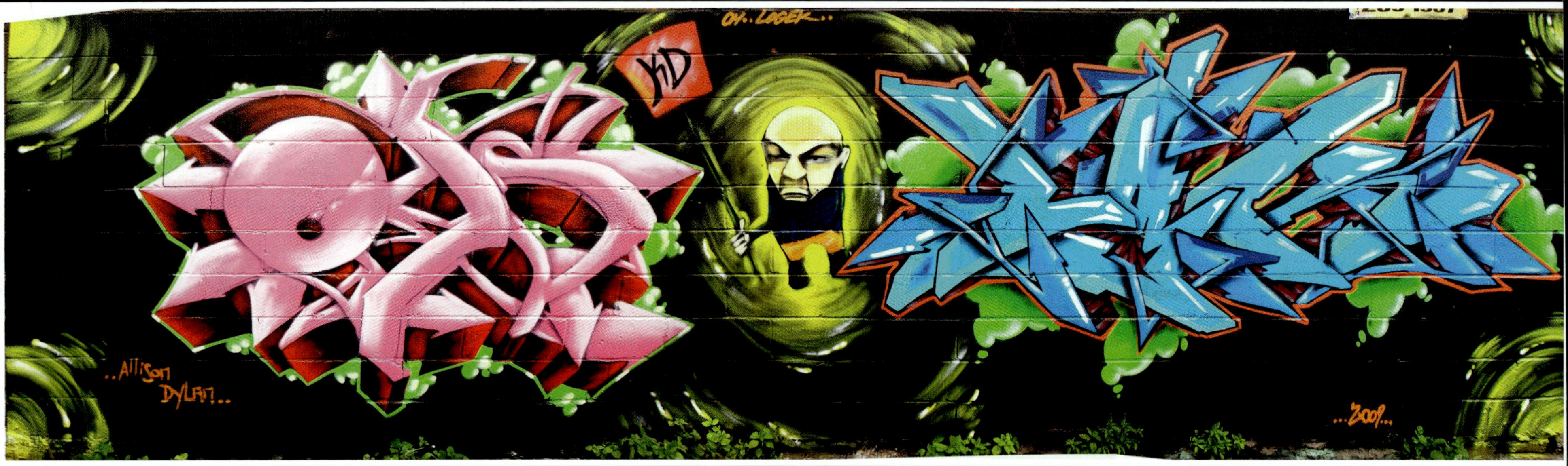


Oh, Logek, Bronx, NY

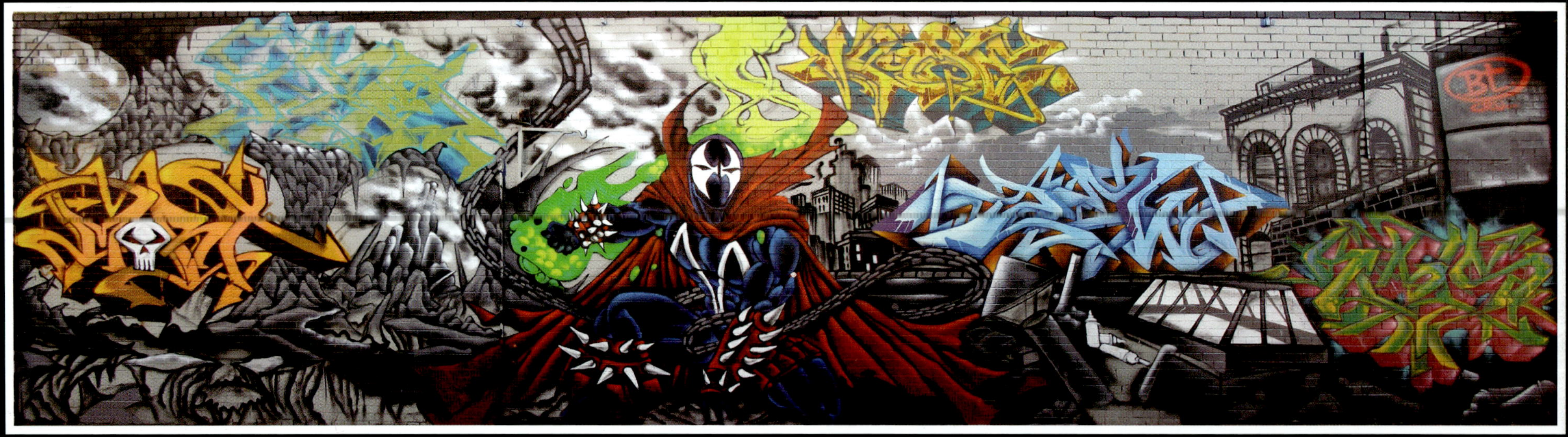

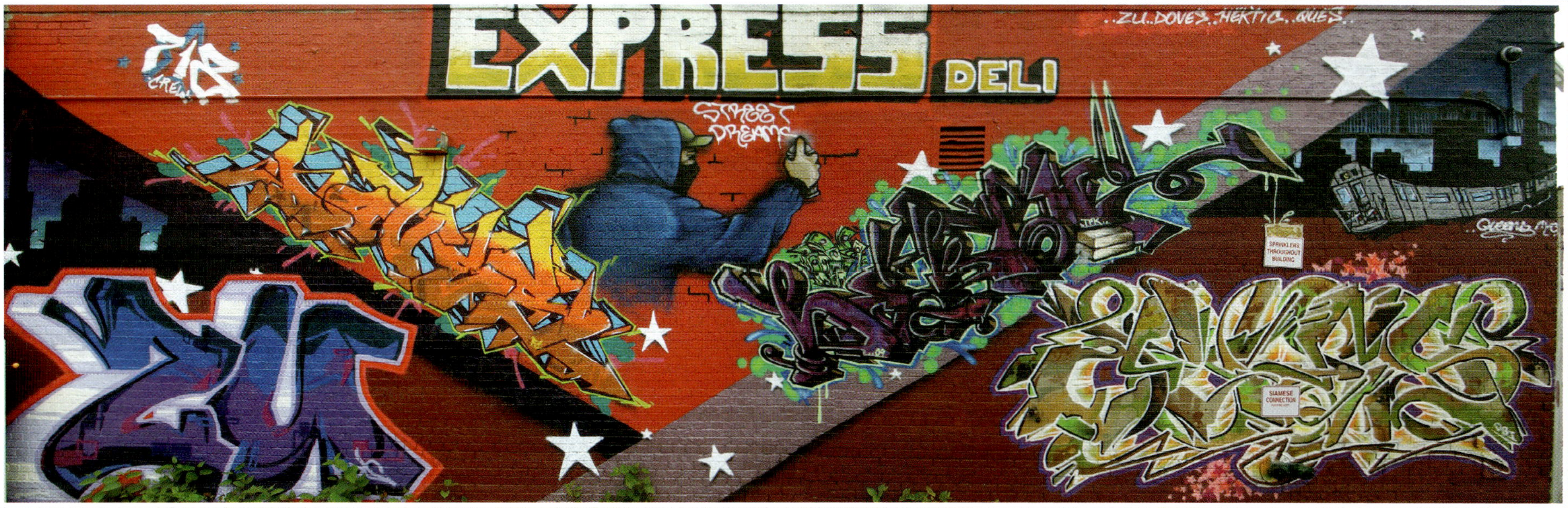


Zu, Doves, Hektic, Ques, Queens, NY

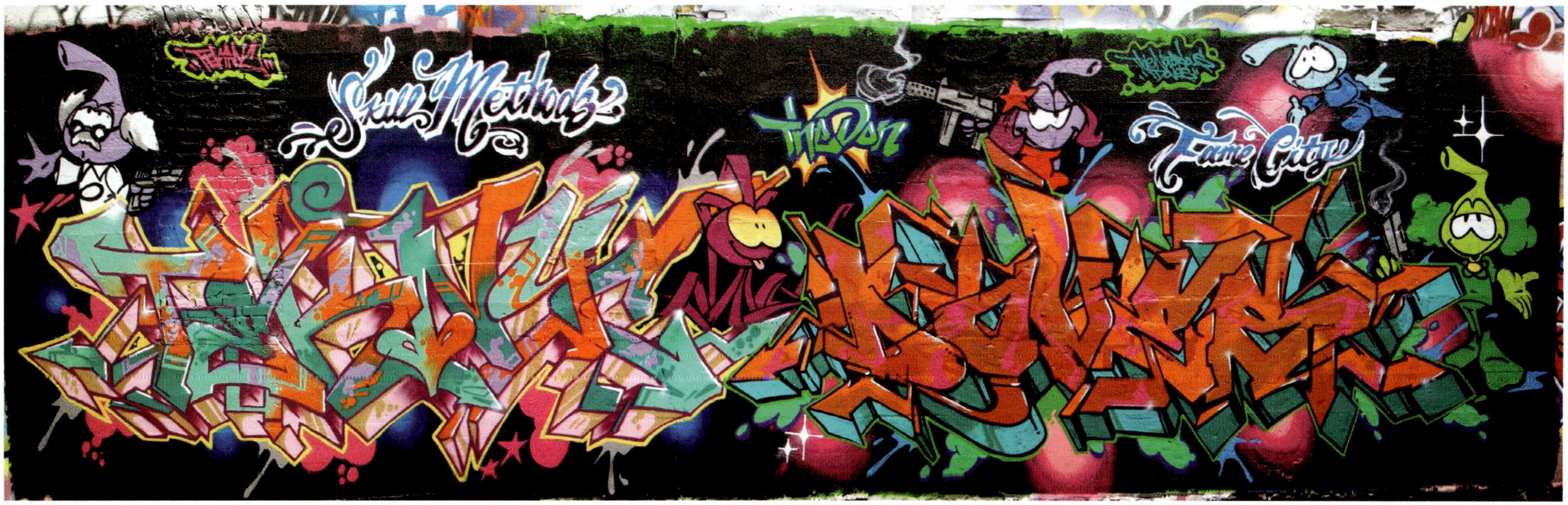


Teknyc, Doves, Brooklyn, NY

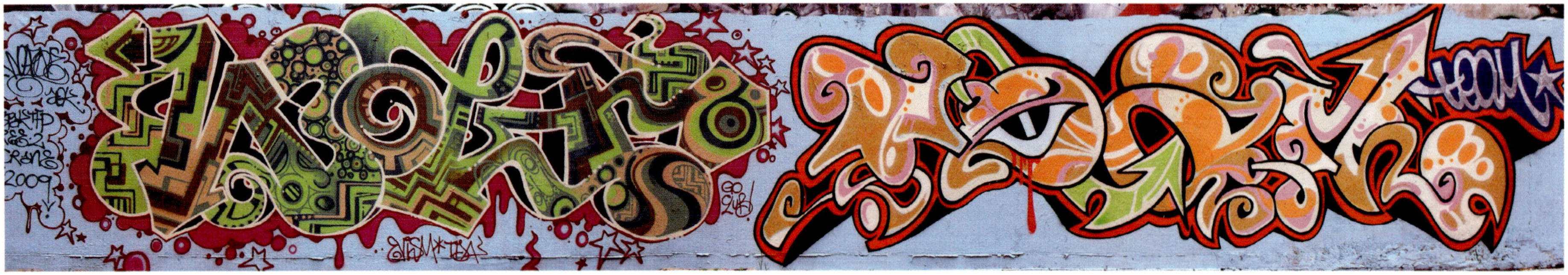

Team, Wolf, Manhattan, NY

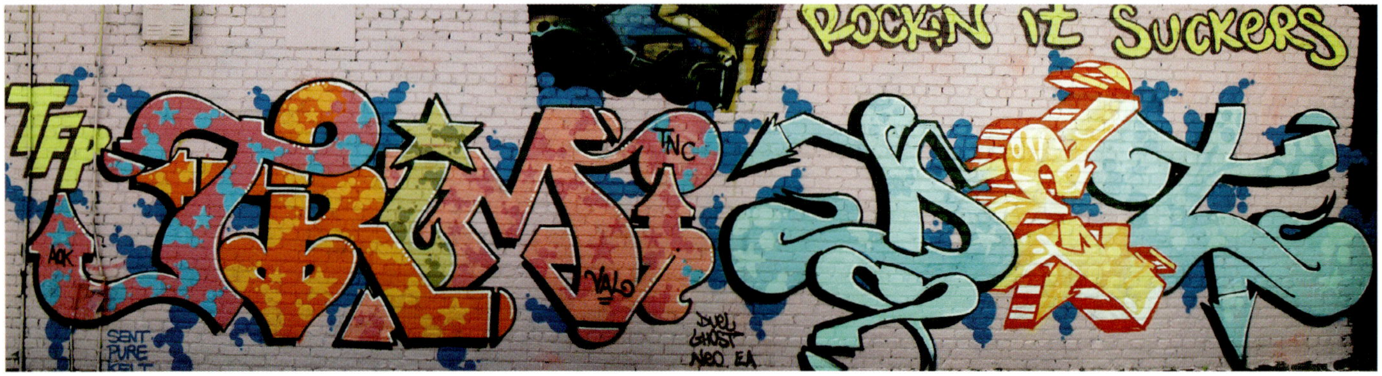


Trim (Noah), Det, Queens, NY

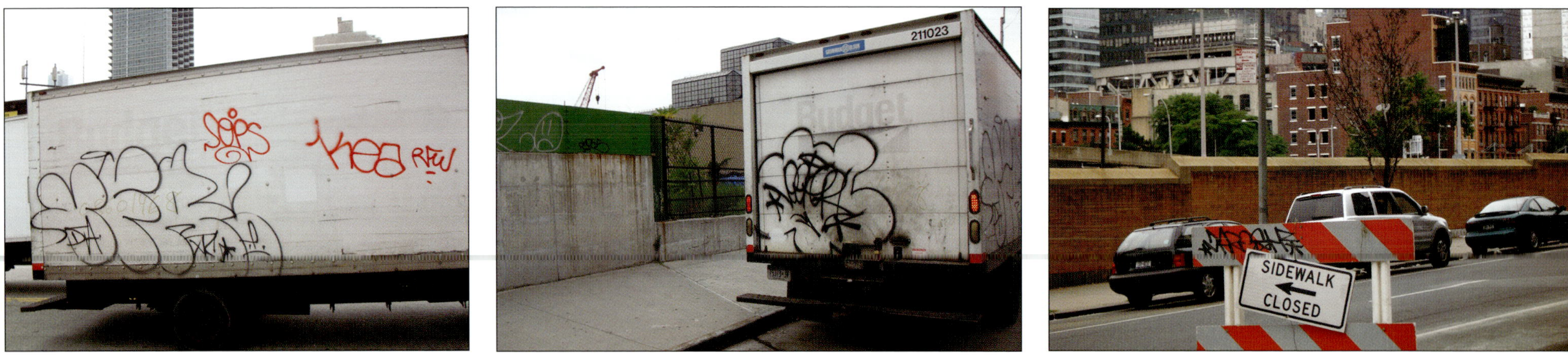


VFR, Manhattan, NY

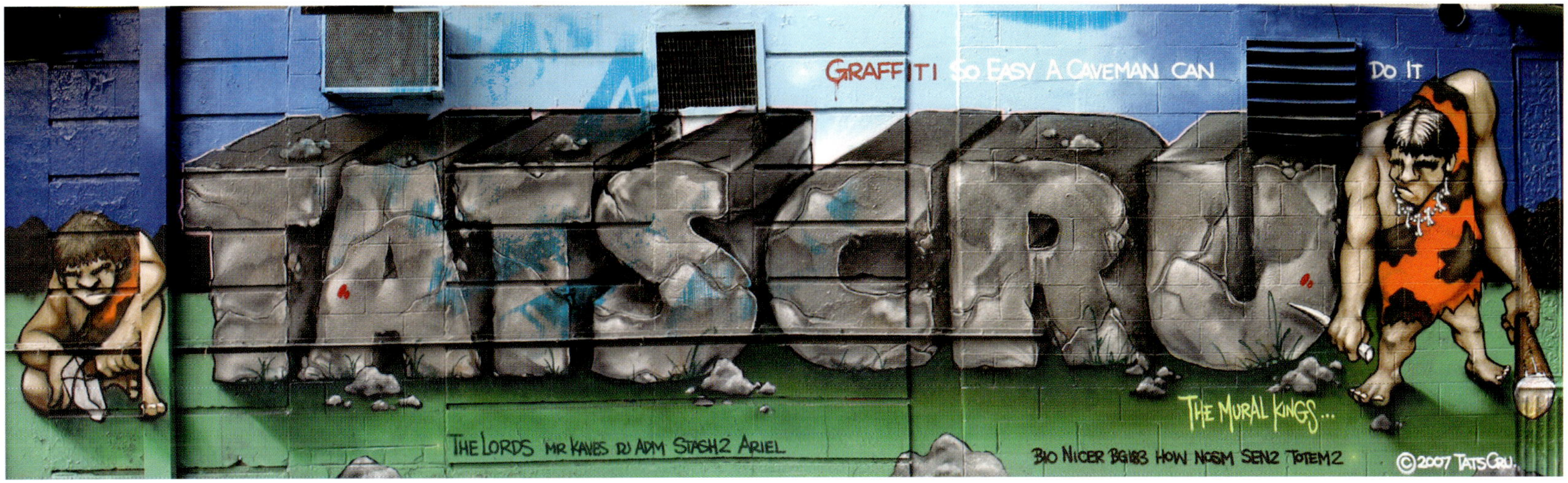


Tats Cru, Manhattan, NY

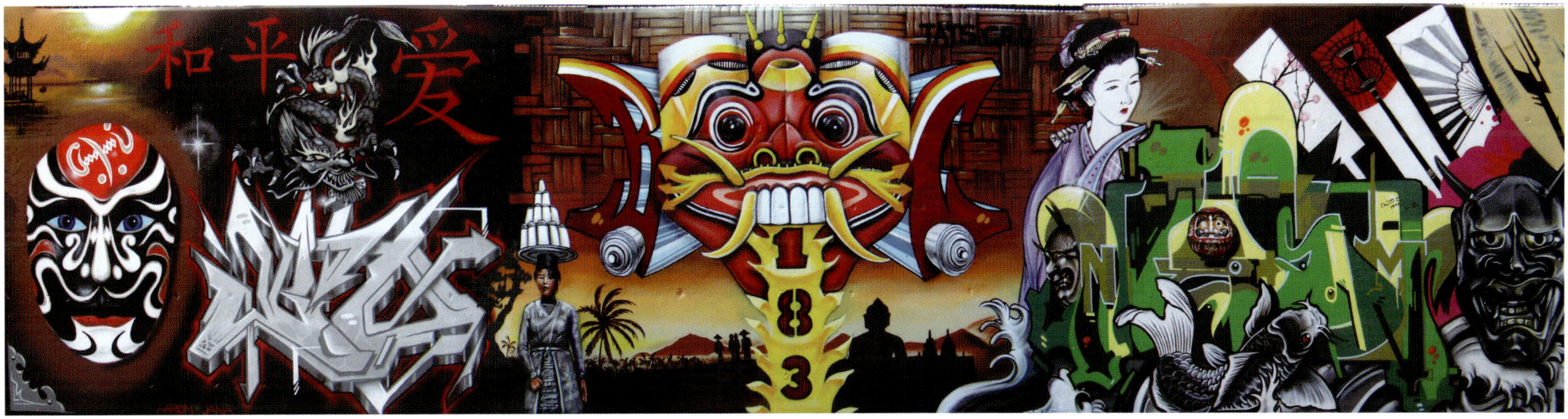


Bio, BG183, Nosm, Manhattan, NY

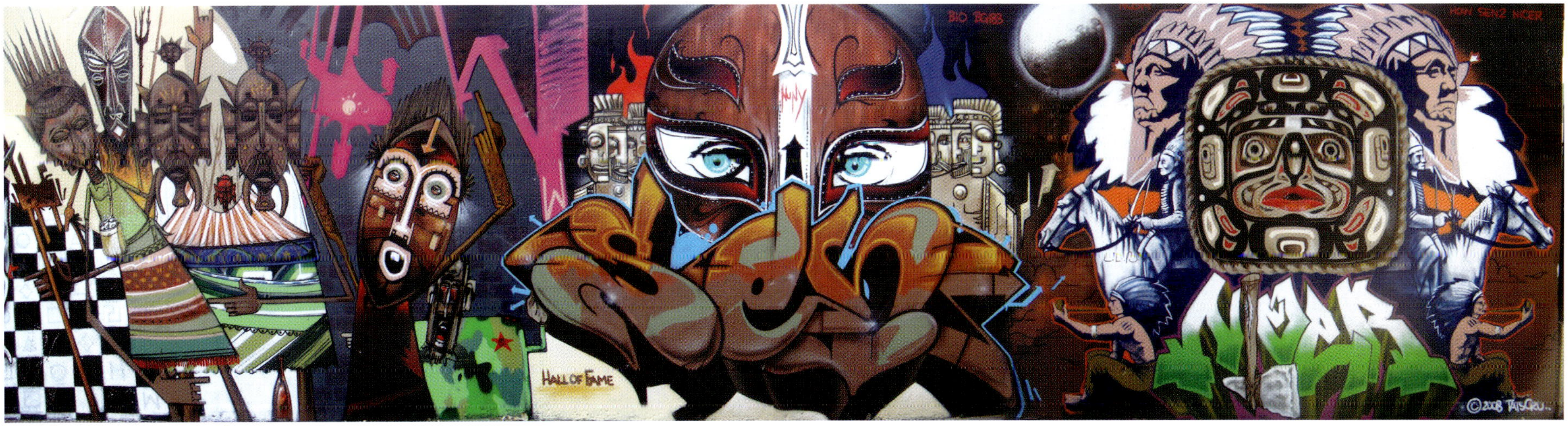


Sen2, Nicer, Manhattan, NY

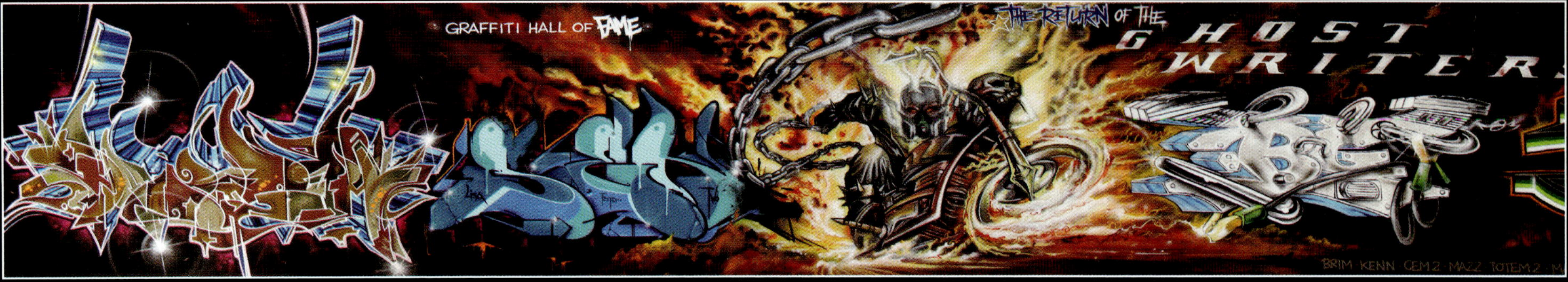


Nosm, Sen2, BG183, Manhattan, NY

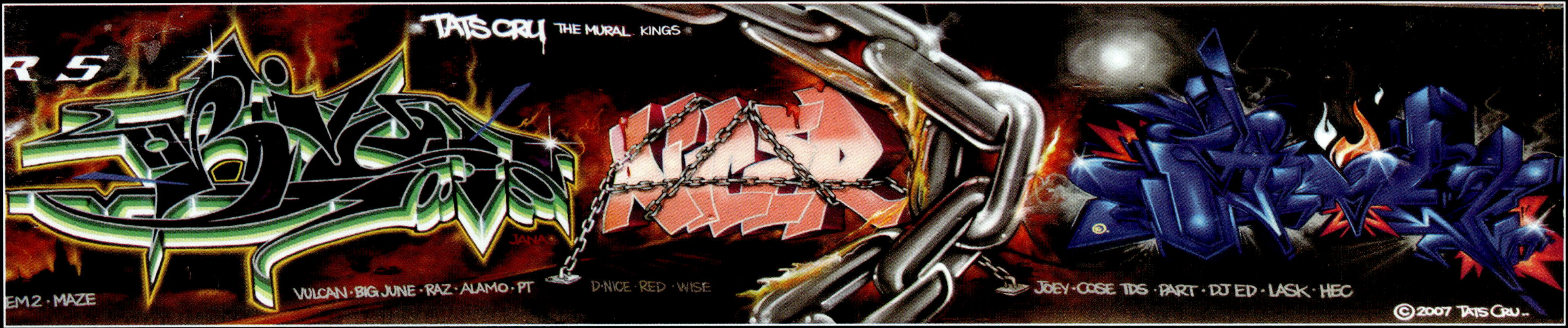


Bio, Nicer, How, Manhattan, NY

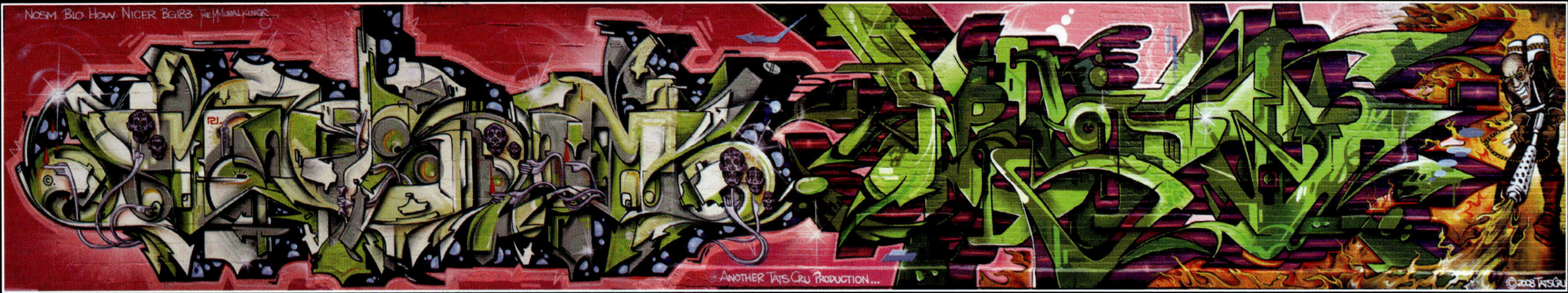


Nosm vs. Bio, Manhattan, NY

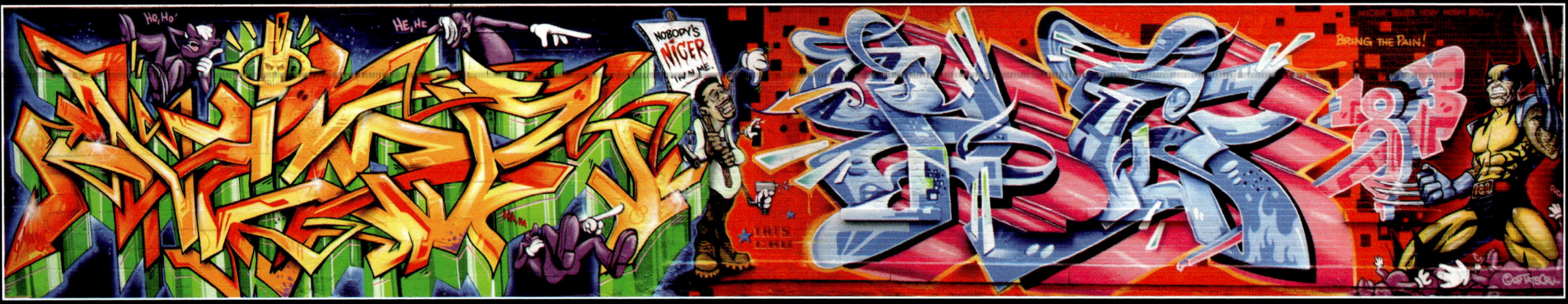


Nicer vs. BG183, Manhattan, NY

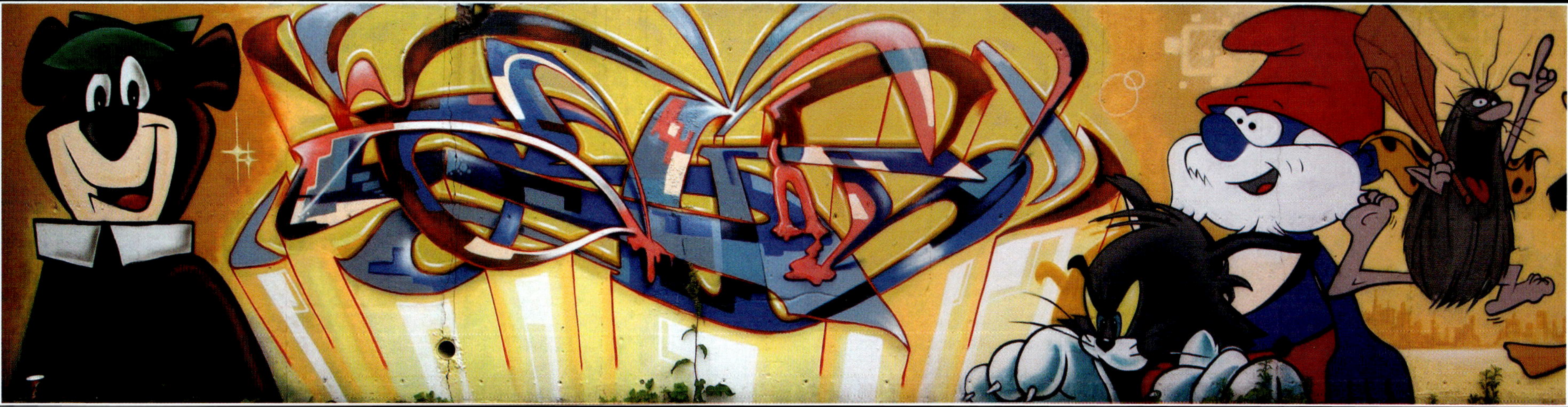

BG183, Bronx, NY

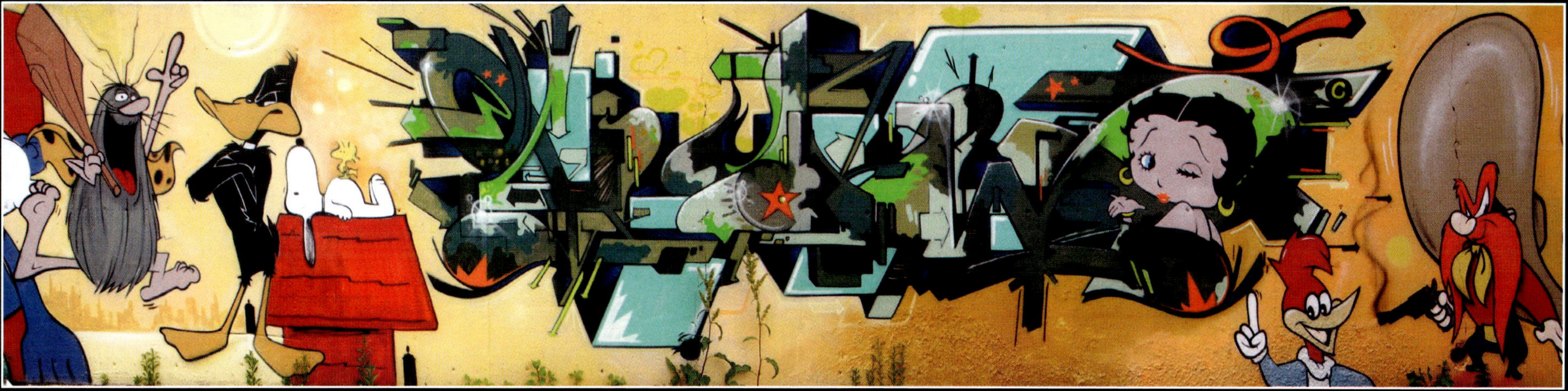

How, Bronx, NY

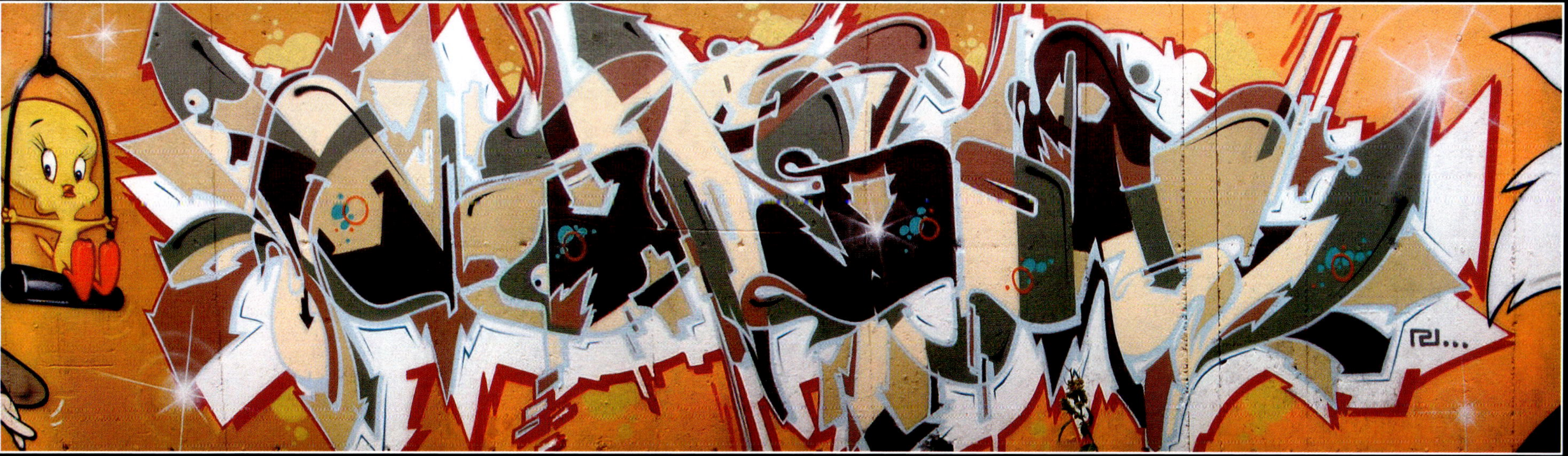

Nosm, Bronx, NY

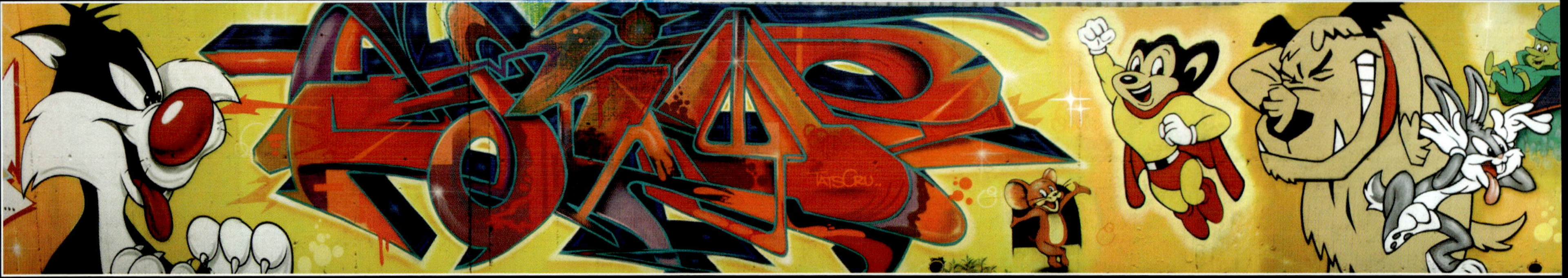

Bio, Bronx, NY

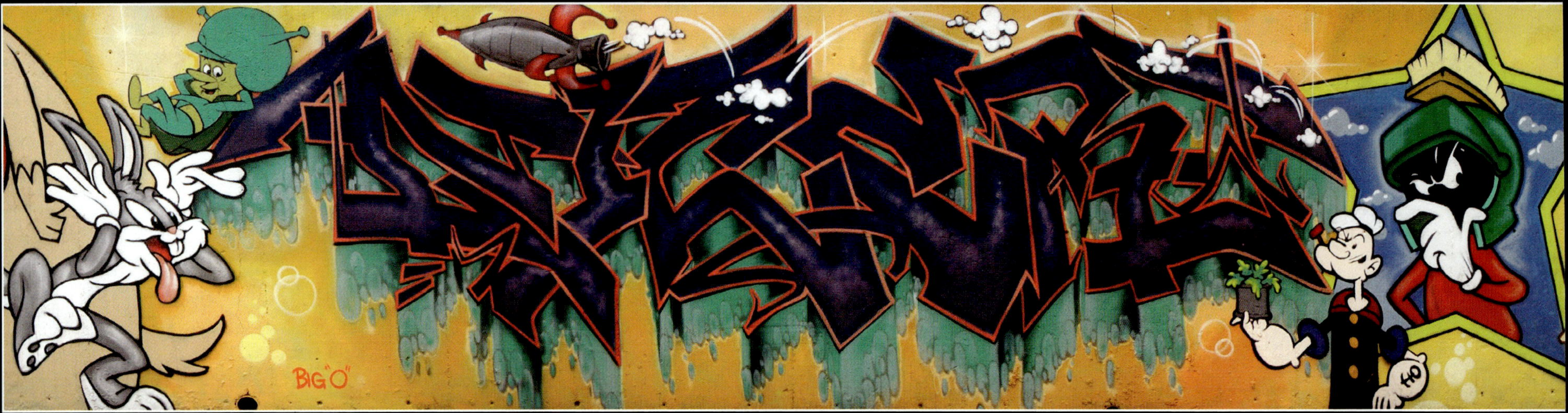

Nicer, Bronx, NY

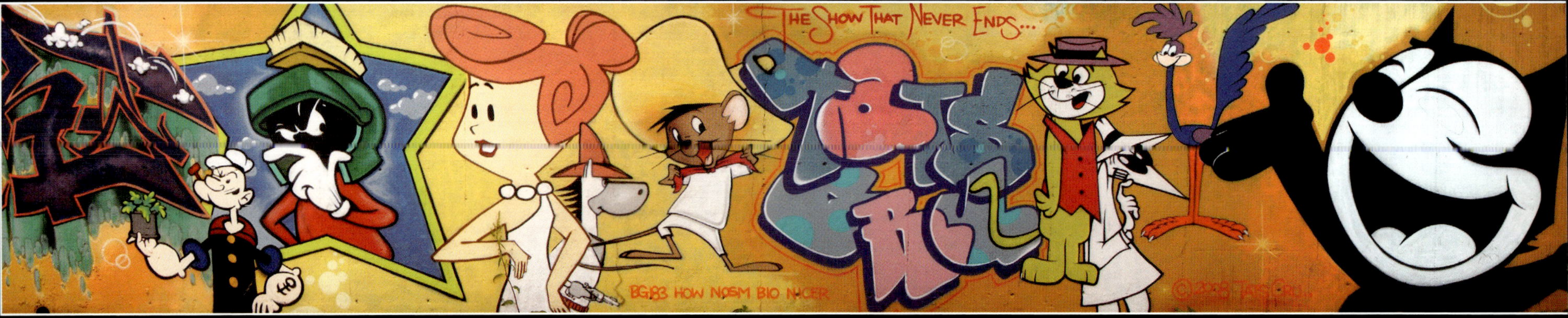

Tats Cru, Bronx, NY

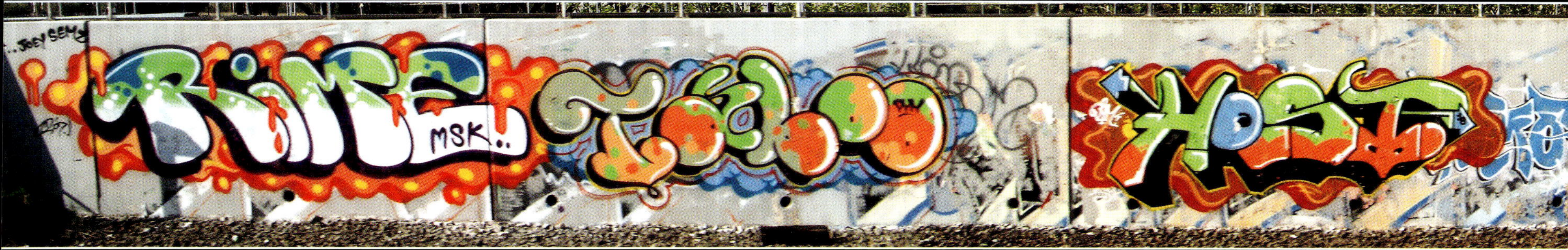

Rime, Taboo, Host, New Jersey

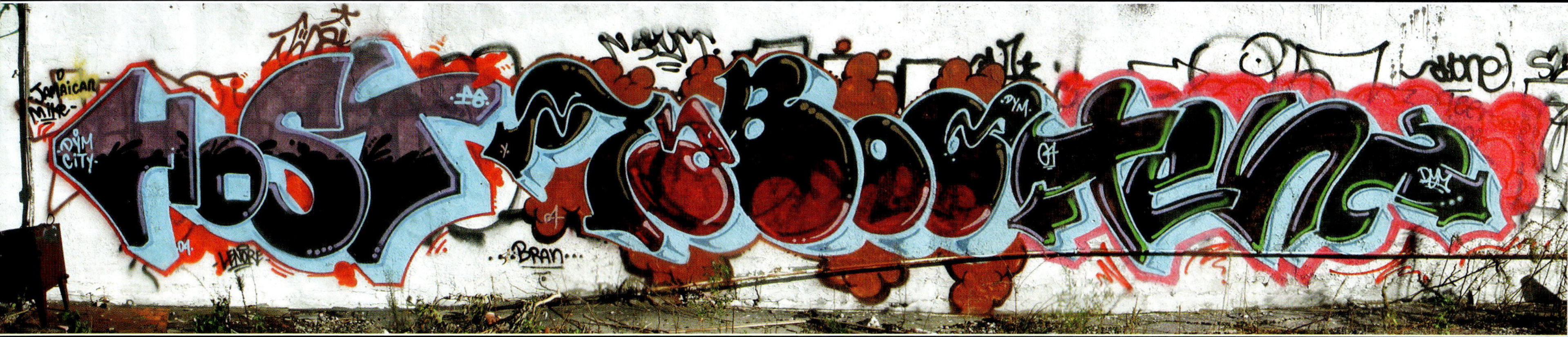

Host, Taboo, Tenz, Manhattan, NY

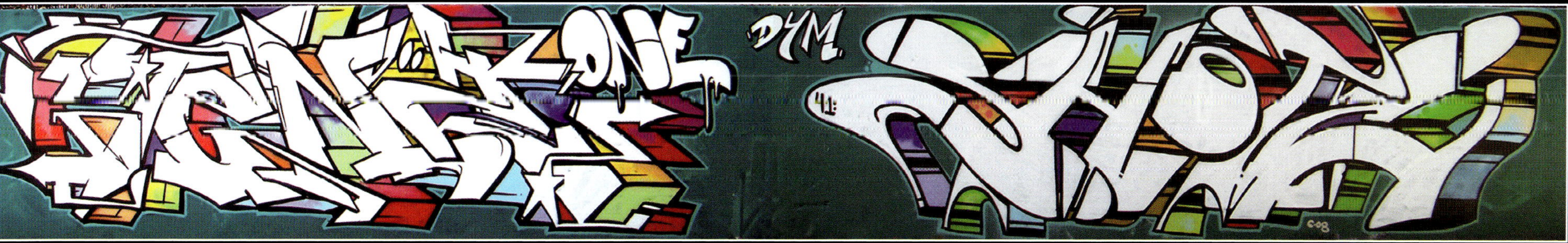

Tenz, Shot, Brooklyn, NY

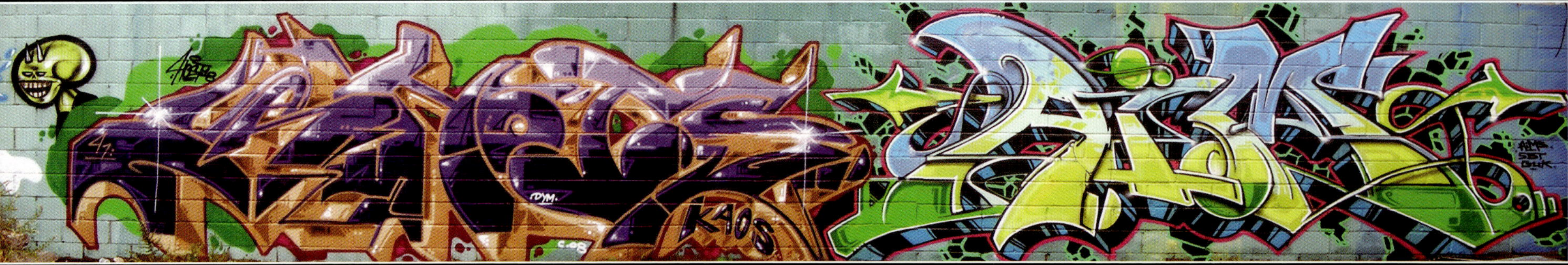

Shots, Aim, Brooklyn, NY

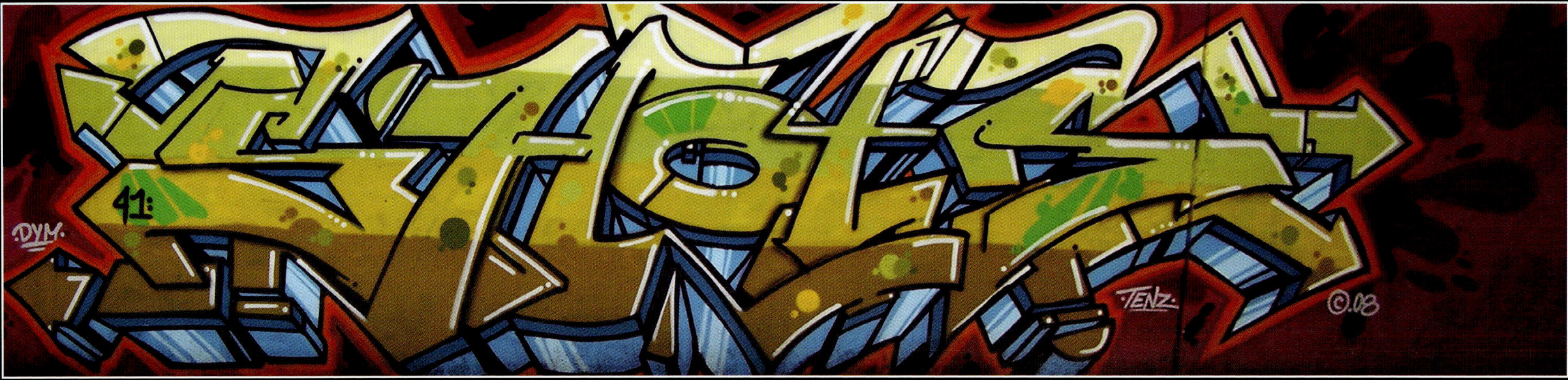

Shots, Brooklyn, NY

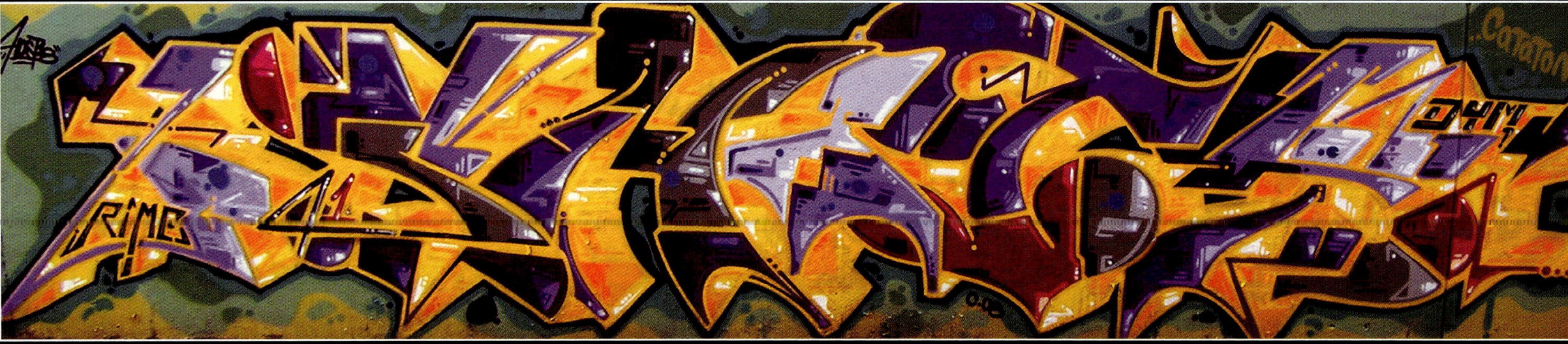

Shots, Brooklyn, NY

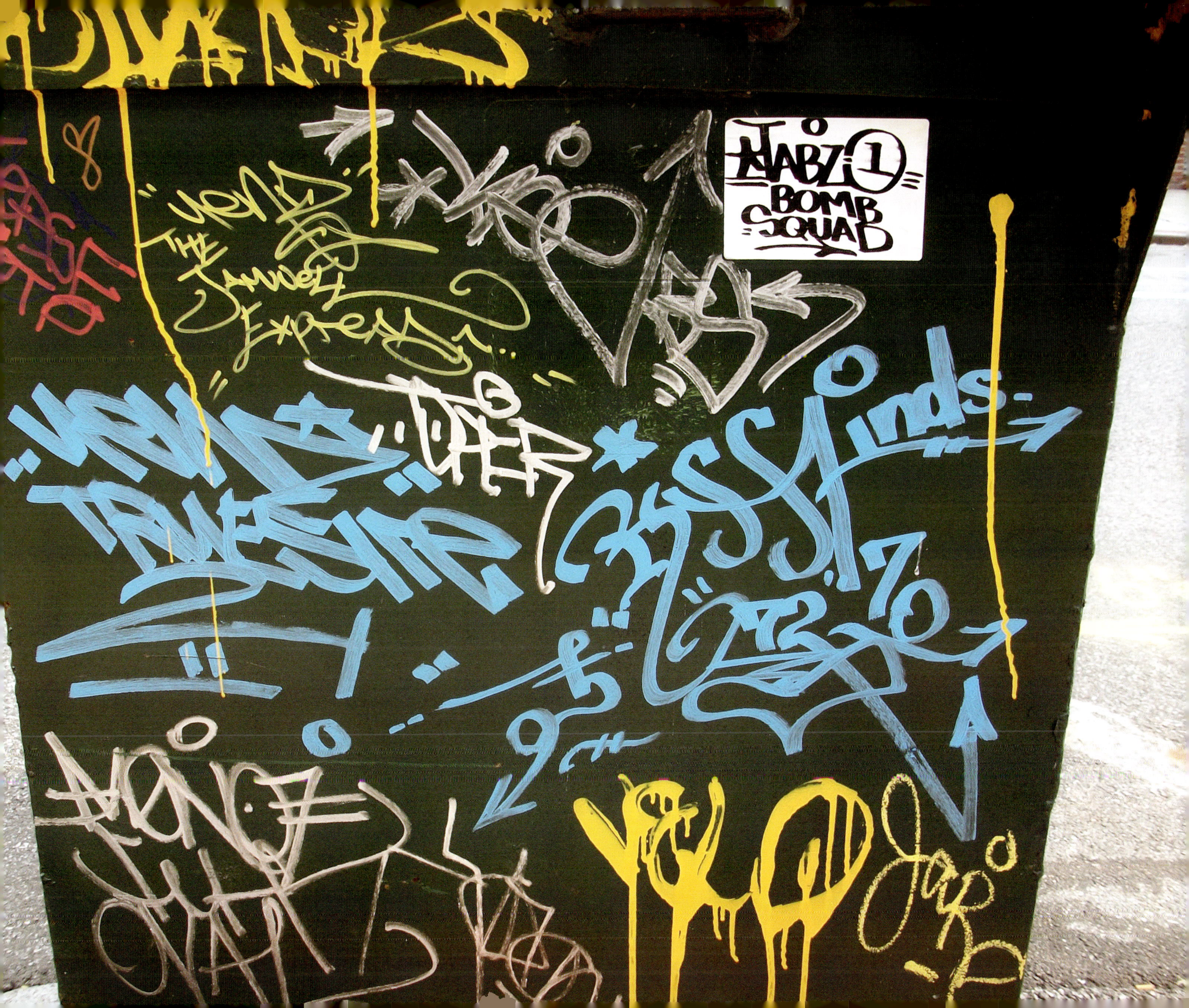
BOMB
SQUAD

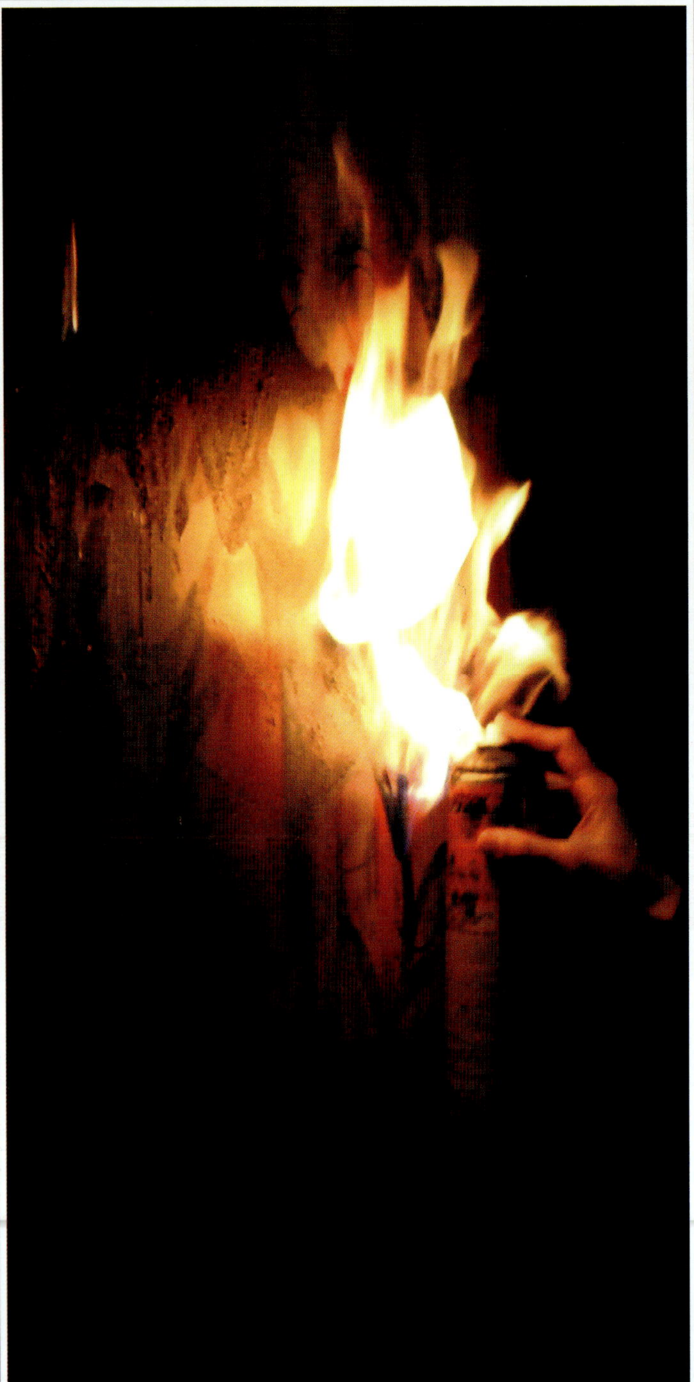

Net, Brooklyn, NY

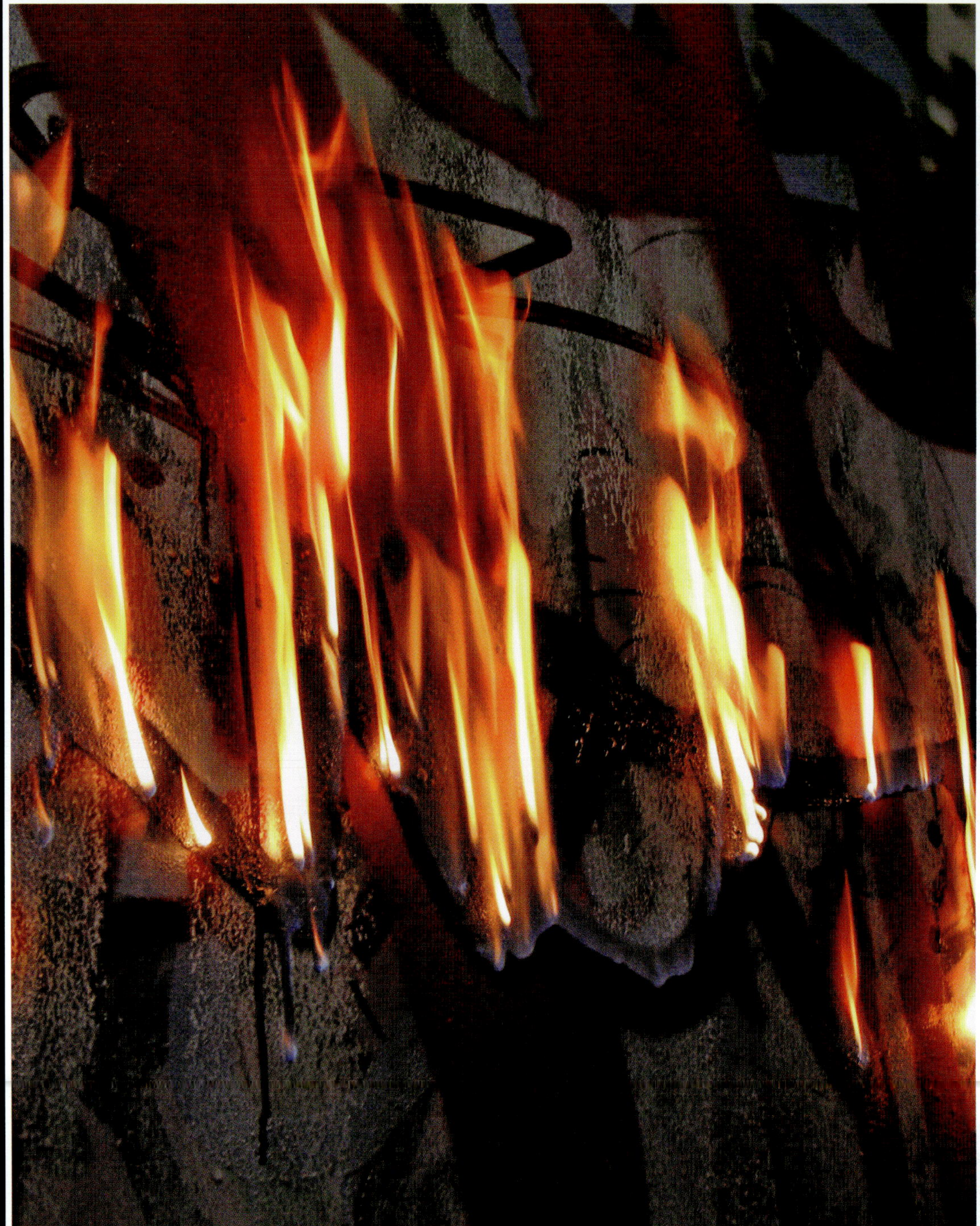

Net, Brooklyn, NY

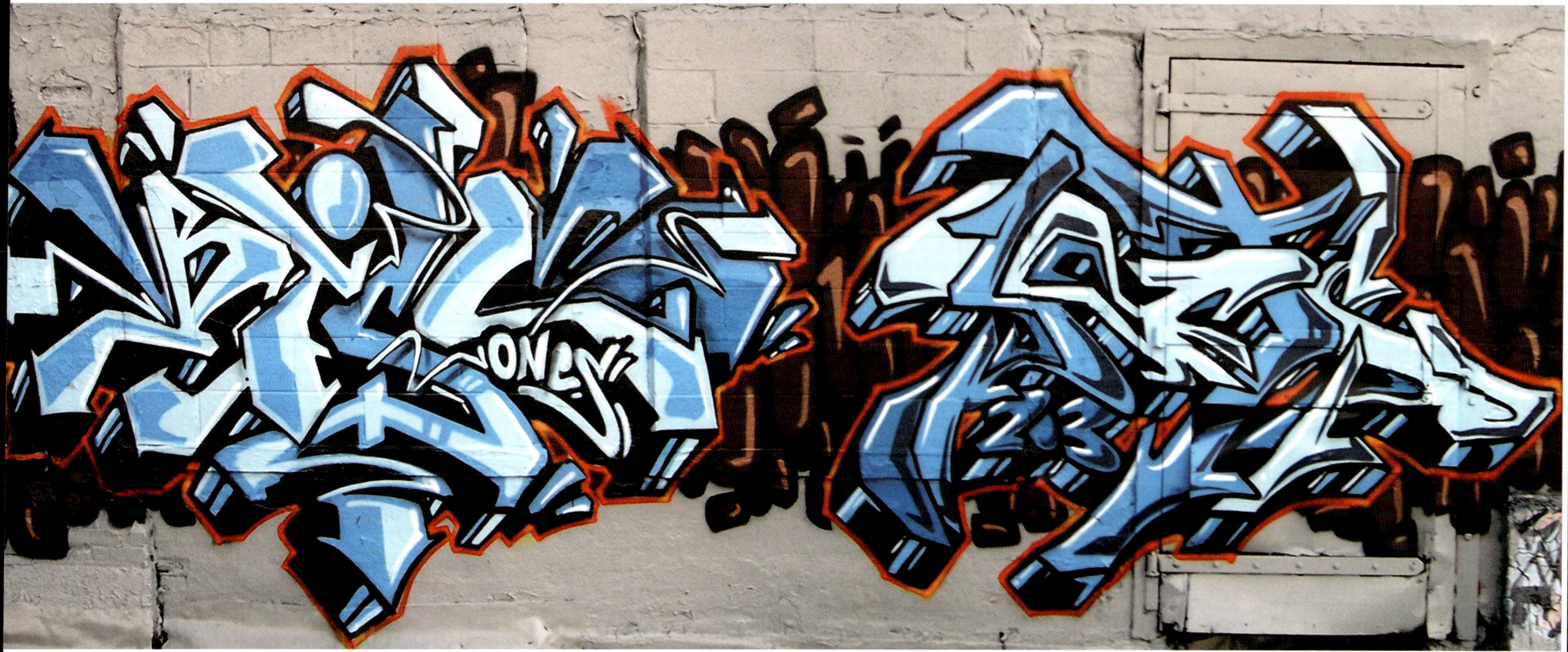

Bisc, Jats, Queens, NY, 5 Pointz

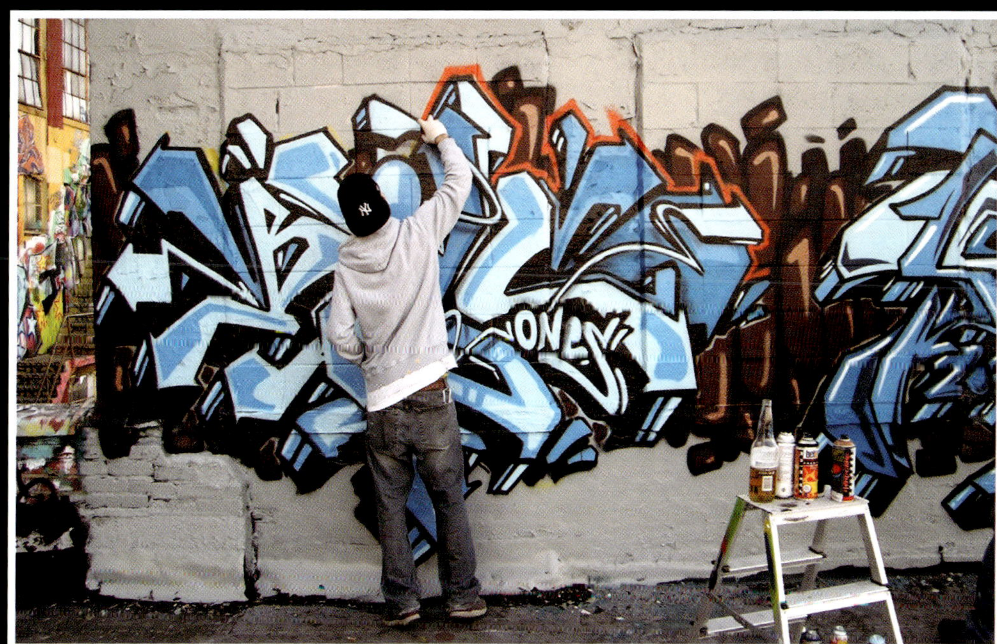

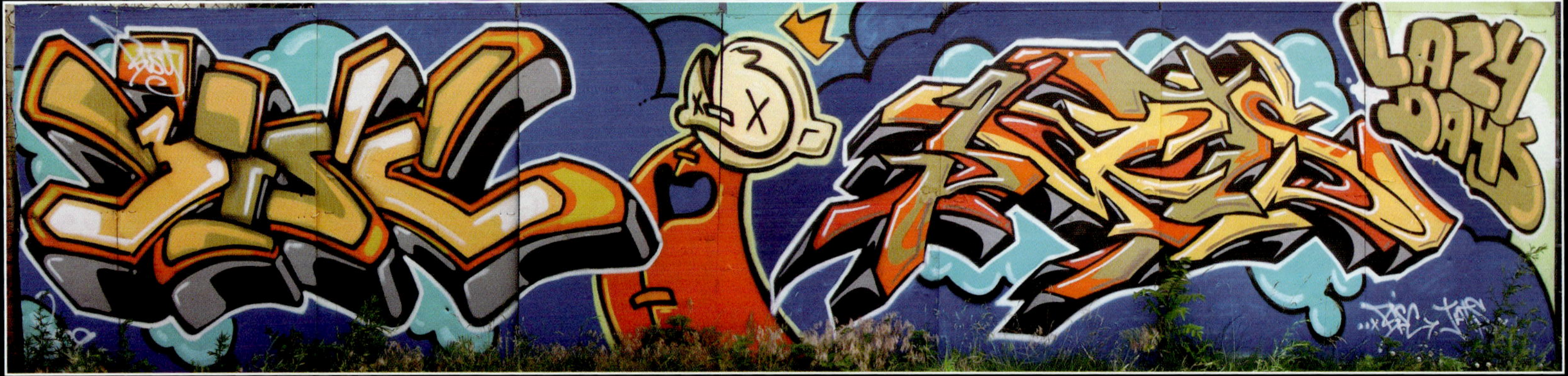


Bisc, Jats, Brooklyn, NY

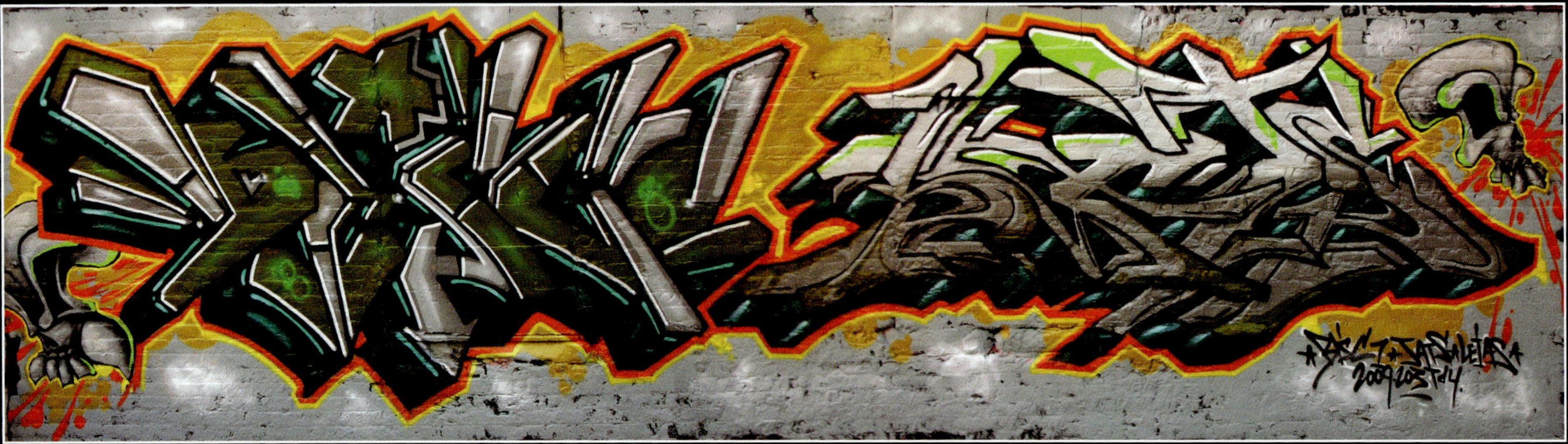

Bisc, Jats, Queens, NY, 5 Pointz

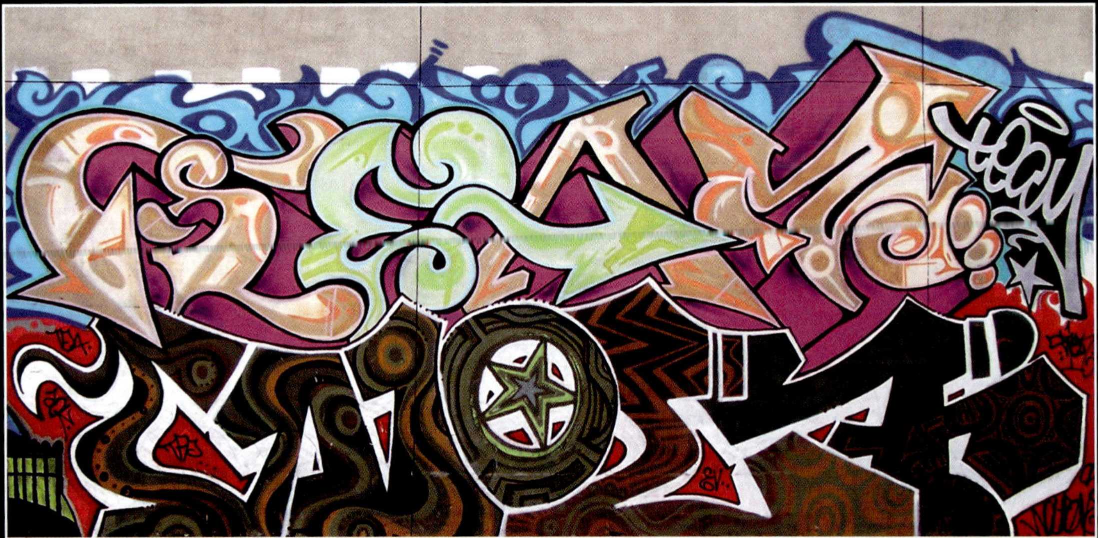

Team, Wolf, Manhattan, NY

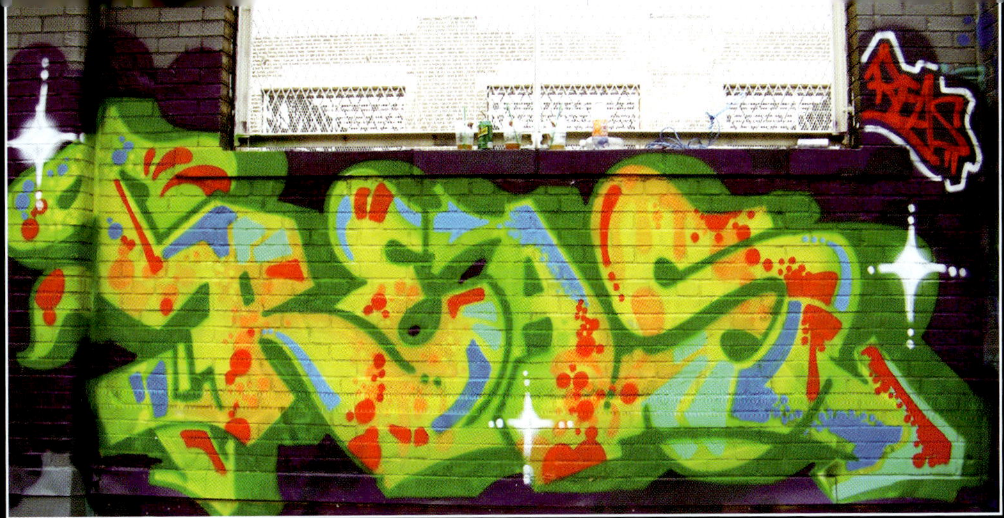

Reas, Manhattan, NY

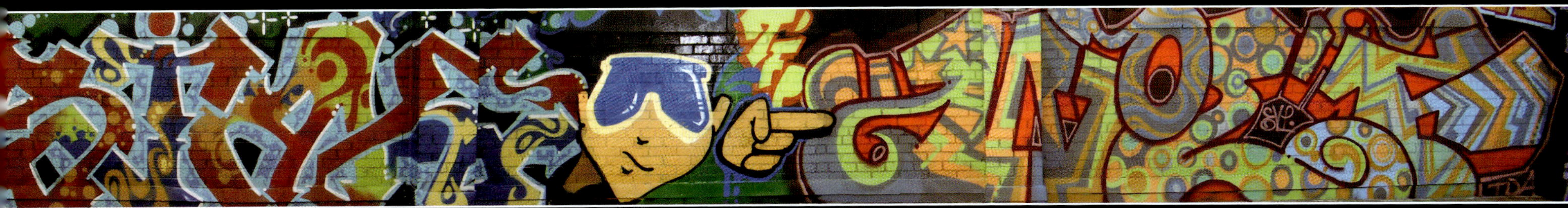

Stak, Wolf, Manhattan, NY

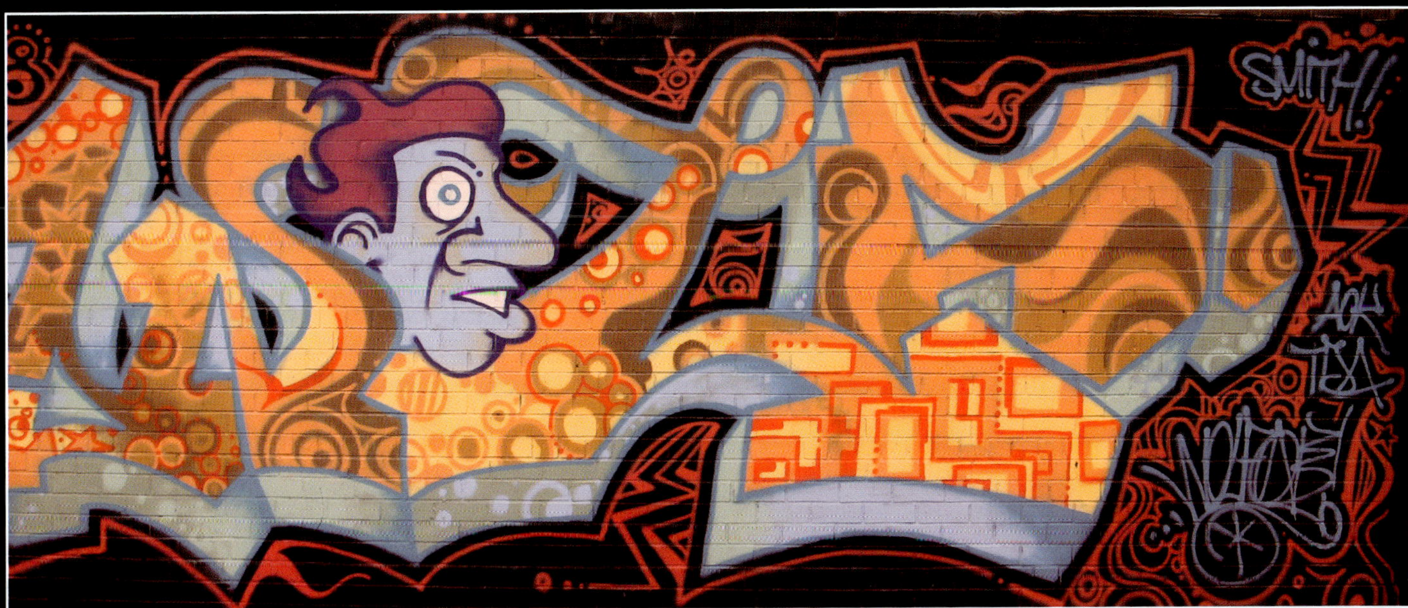


Wolf, Brooklyn, NY

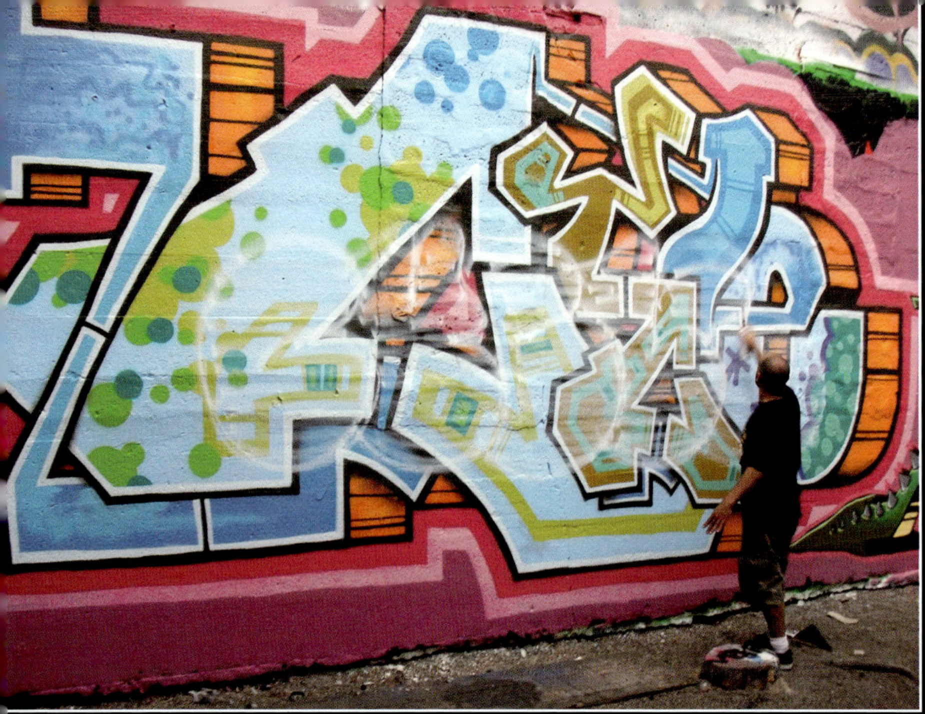

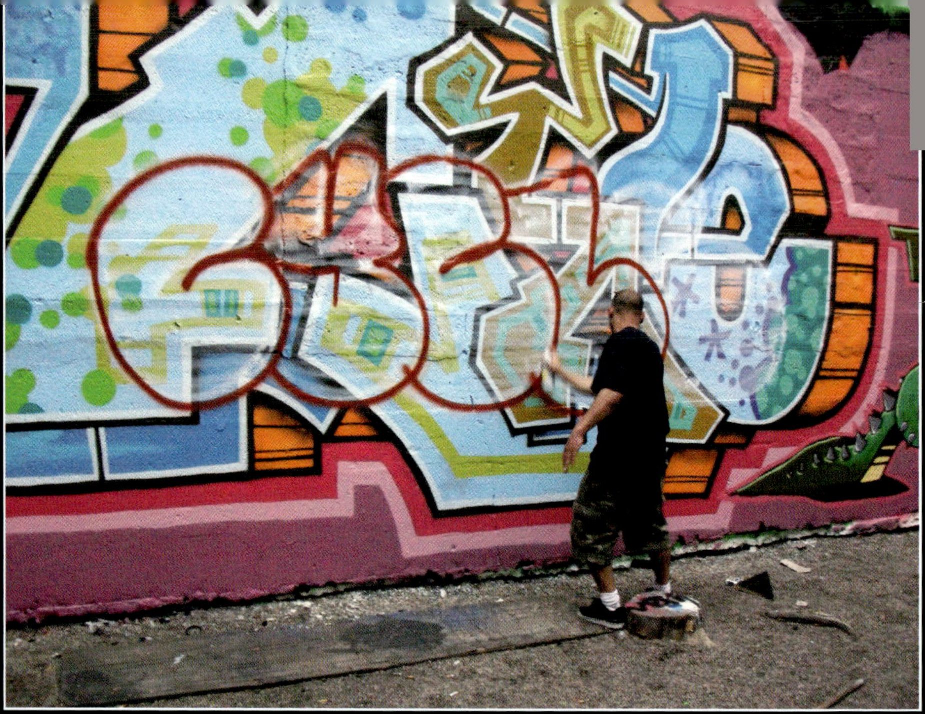

Cycle, Brooklyn, NY

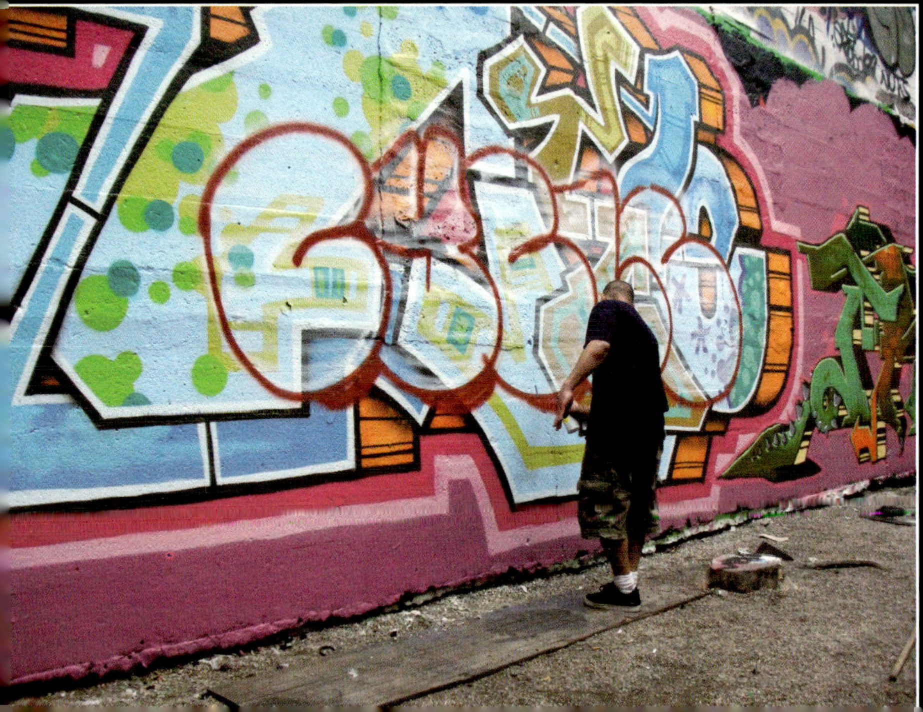

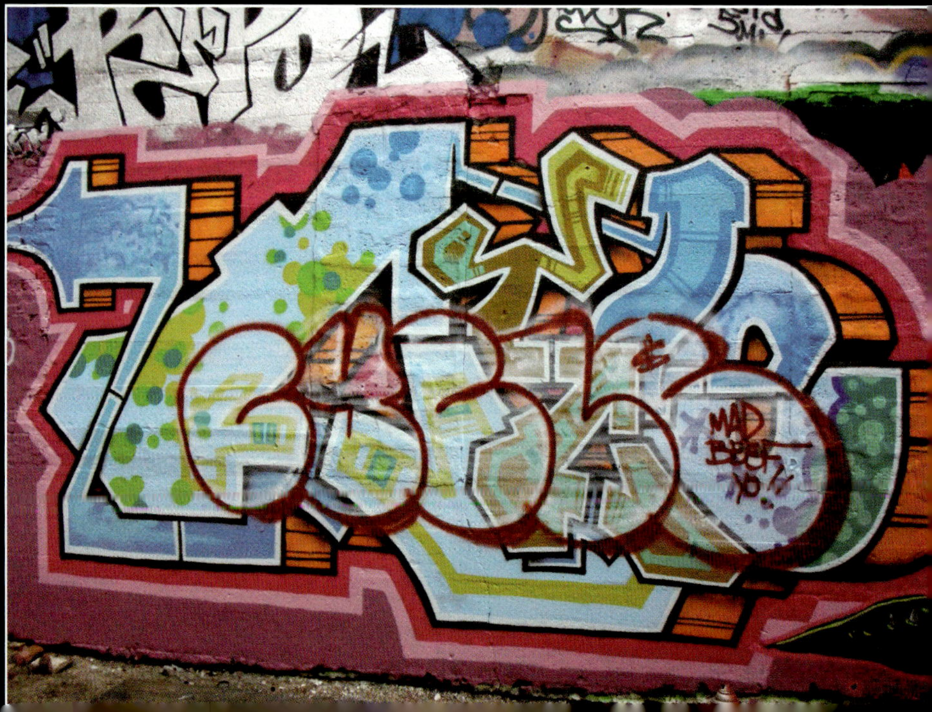

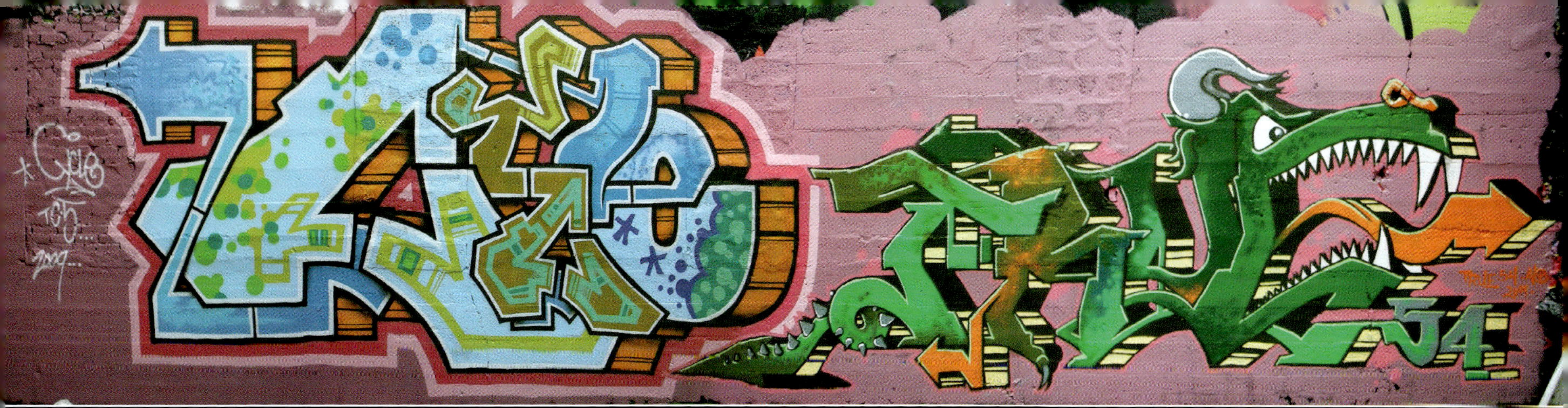

Cycle, True54, Brooklyn, NY

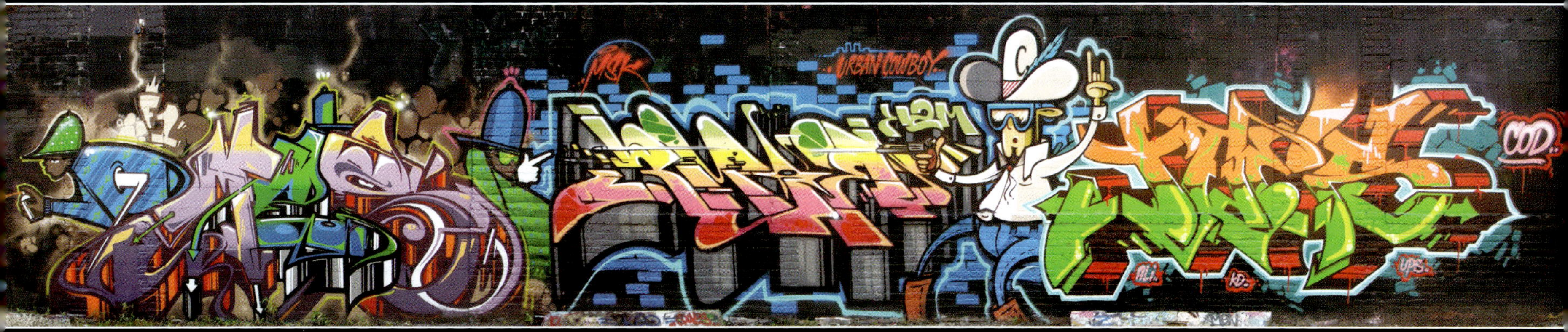


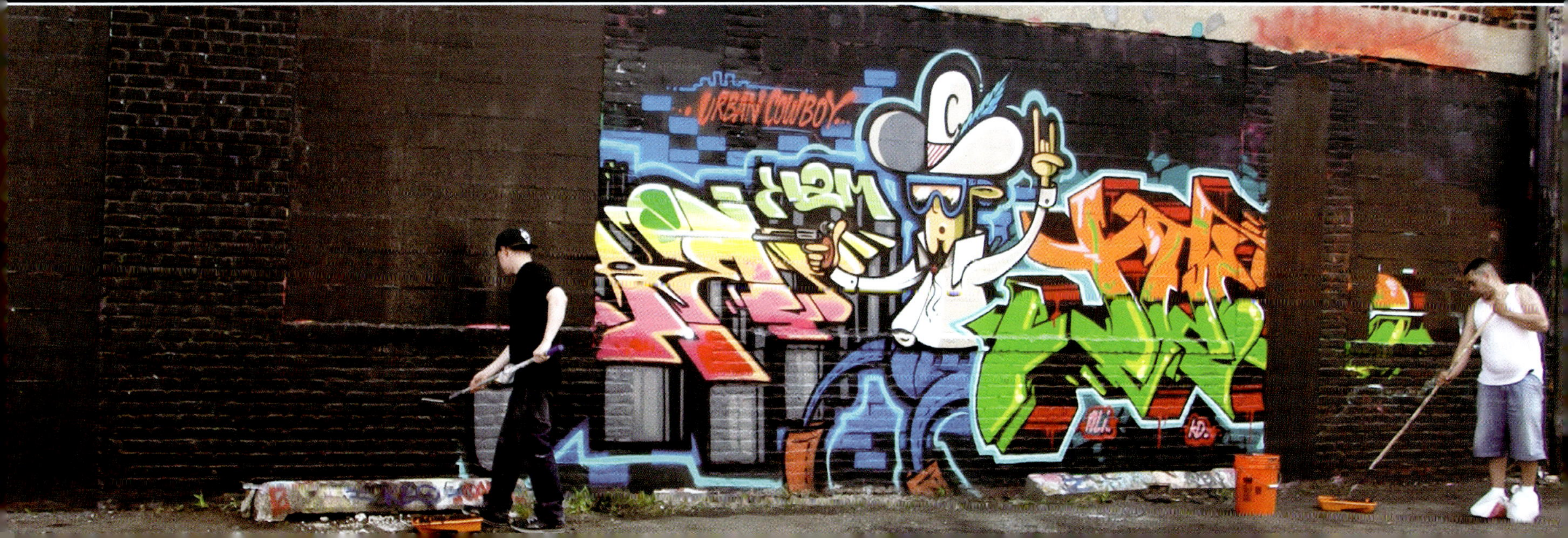

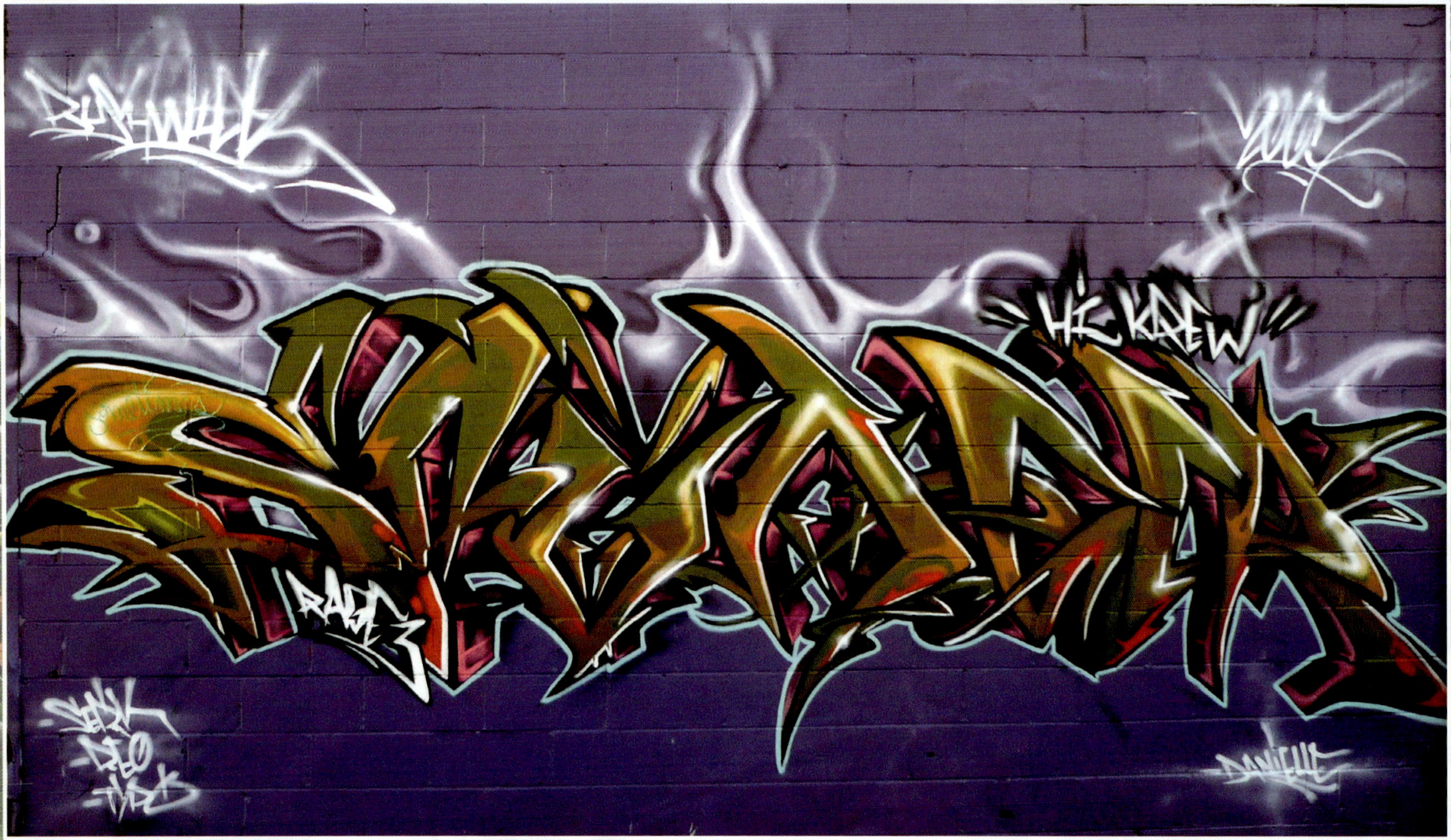

Savager, Brooklyn, NY

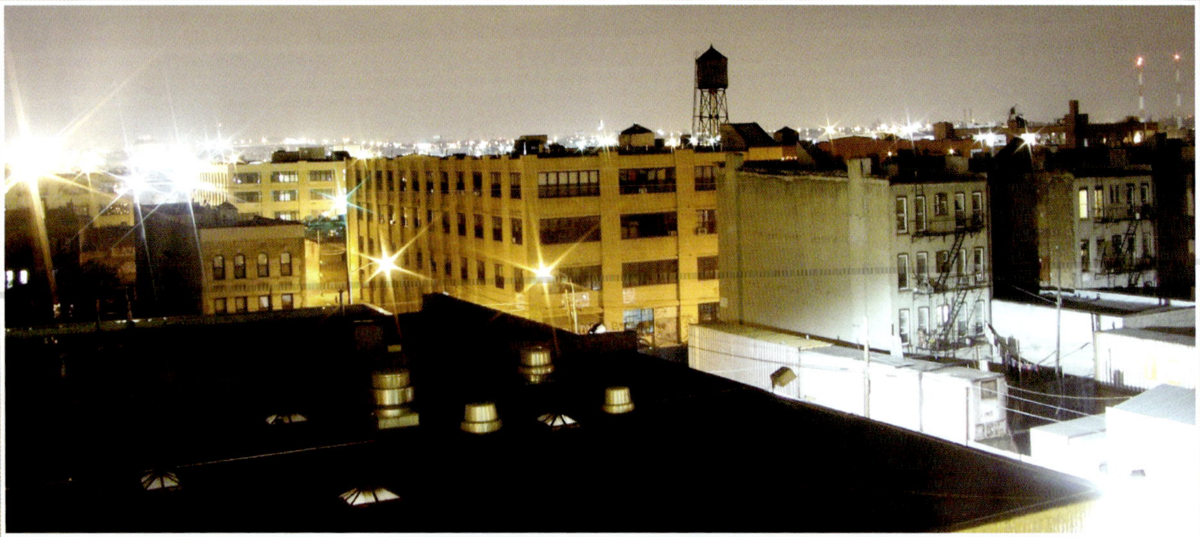
Bushwick, Brooklyn

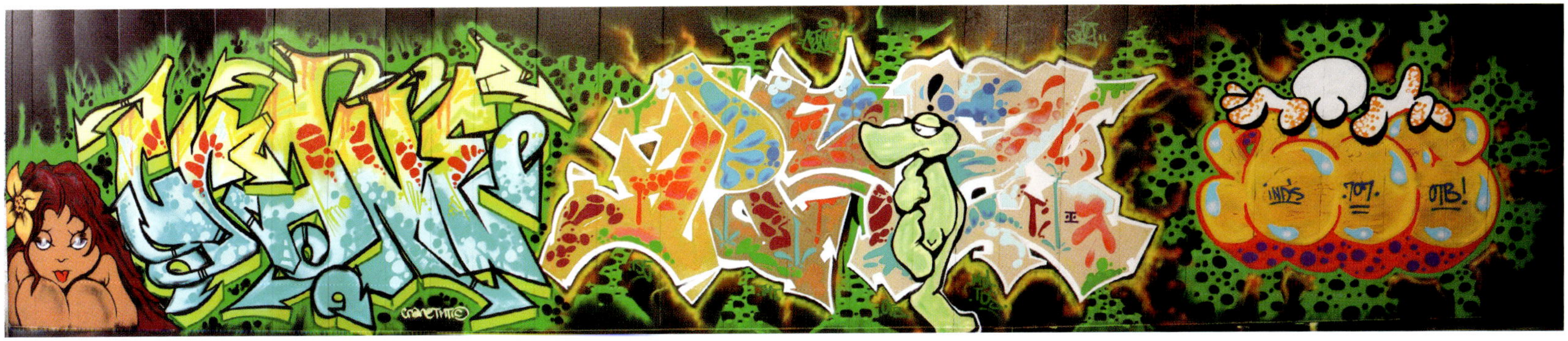

Crane, Priz, Nic707, Manhattan, NY

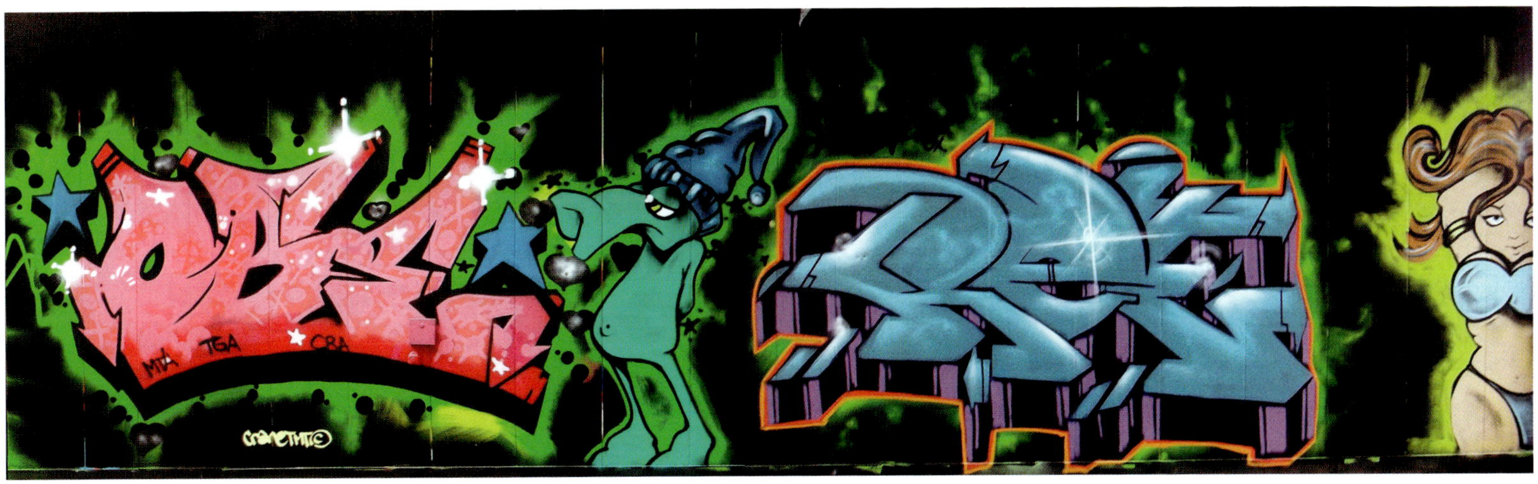

Obe, Ree, Manhattan, NY

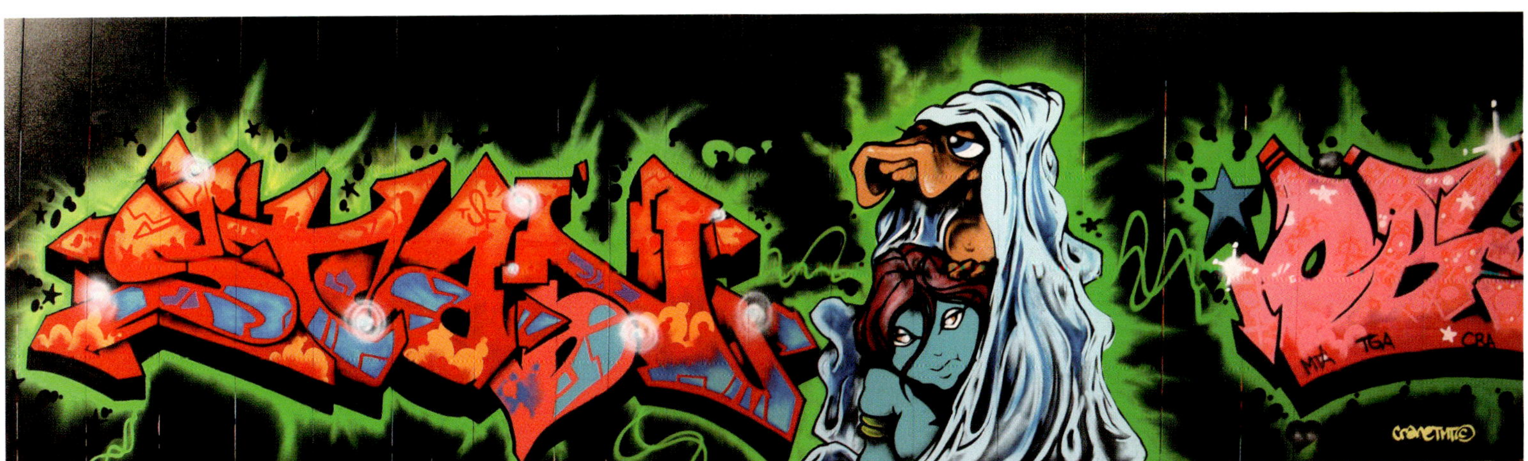

Stan, Manhattan, NY

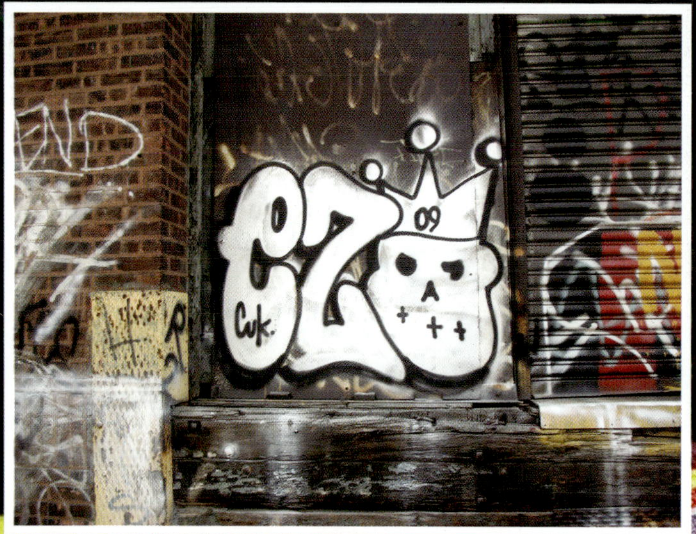

Ezo, Brooklyn, NY

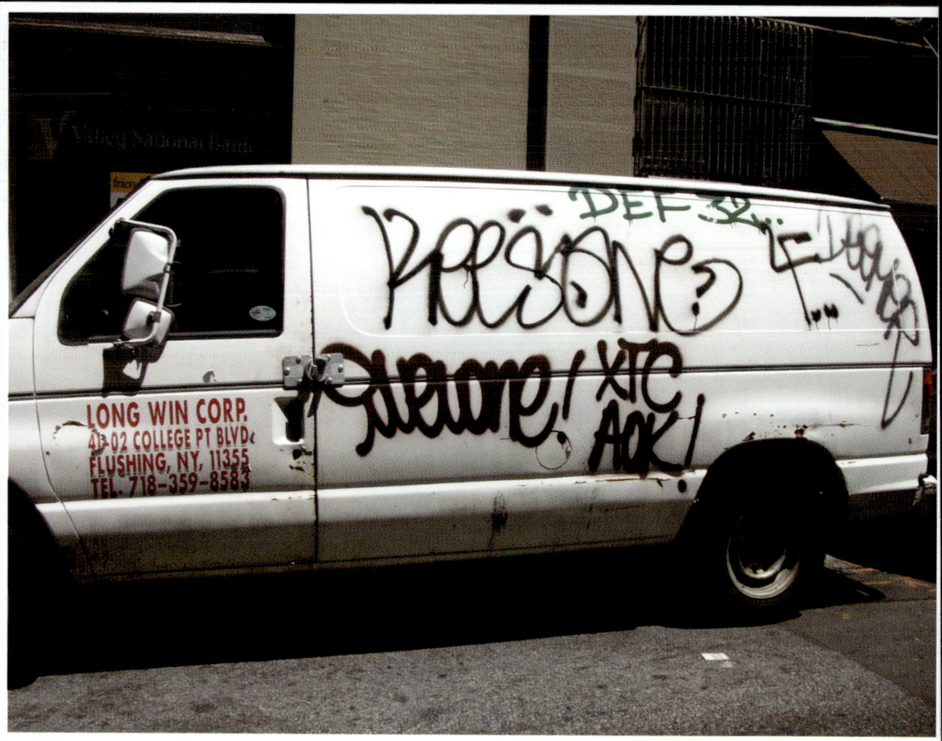


Duel, Manhattan, NY

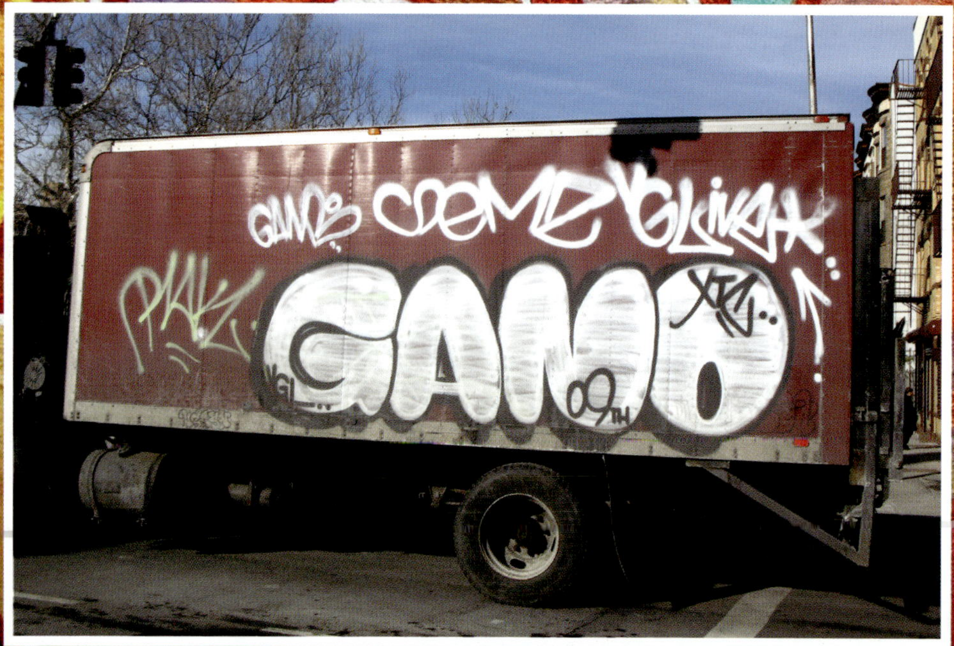

Gano, Brooklyn, NY

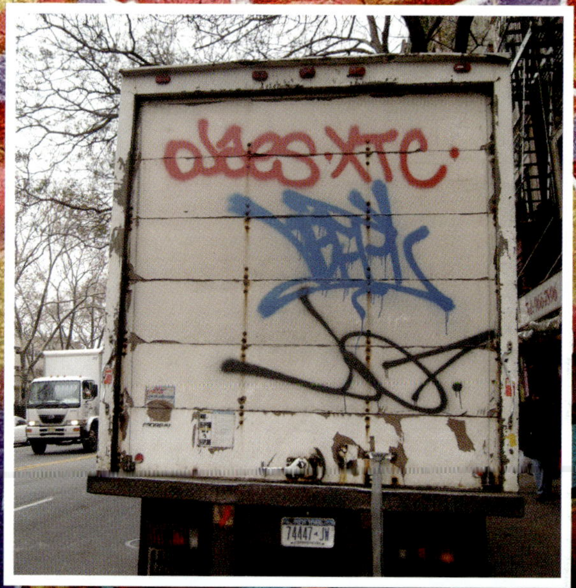

Ojaes, Left, Cost, Manhattan, NY

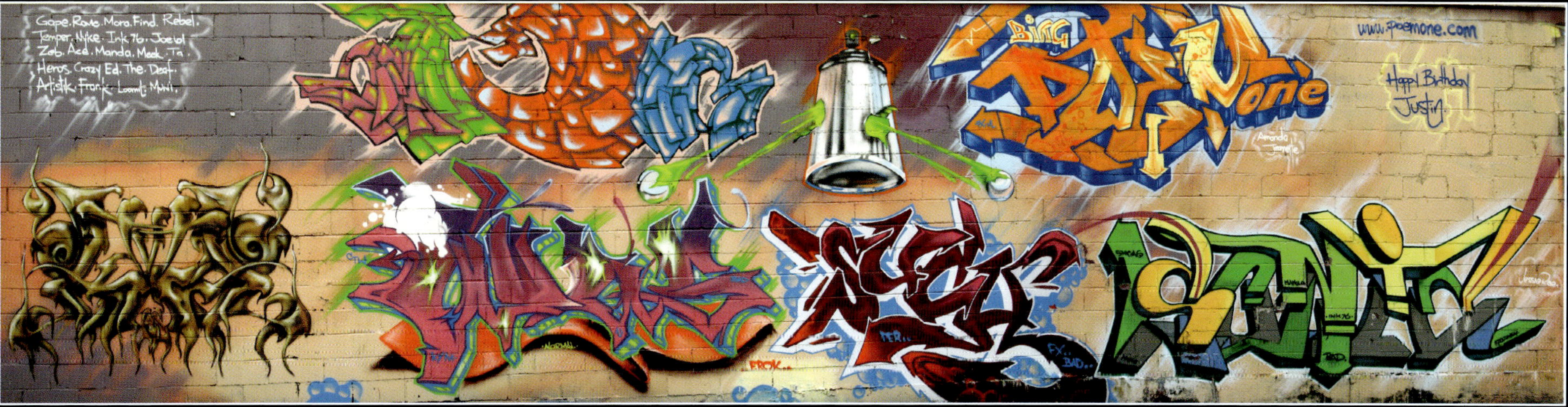


KA, Unkown, Poem, Such, Sonic, Unkown, Queens, NY

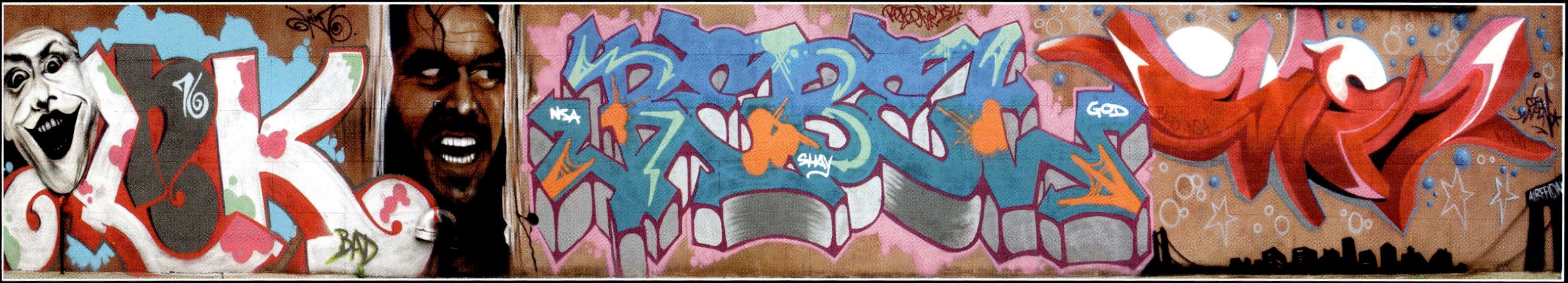

Rebel, Ink76, Sien, Brooklyn, NY

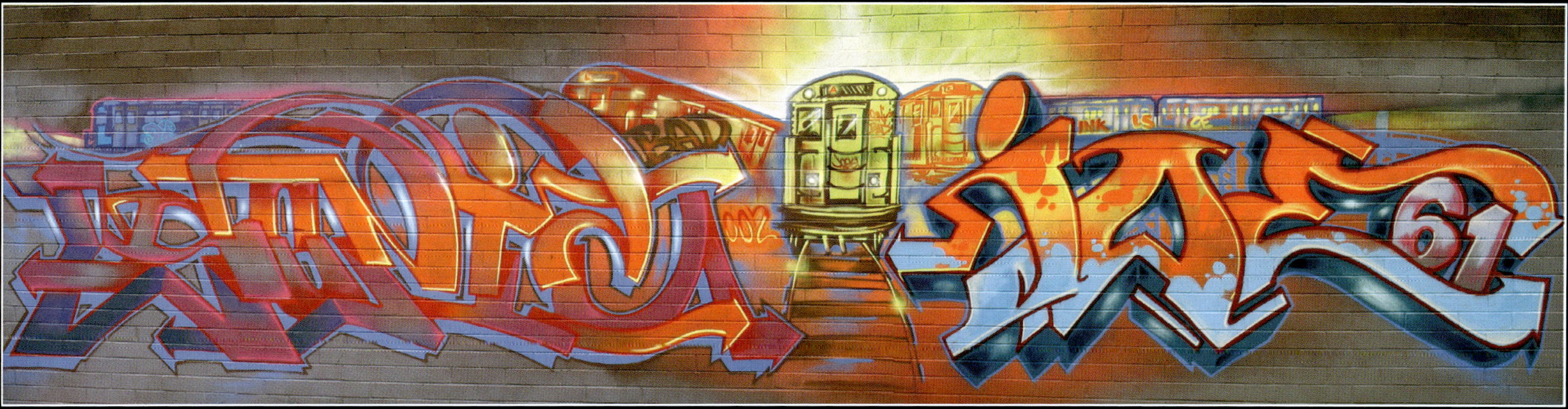

Sonic, Joe61, Brooklyn, NY

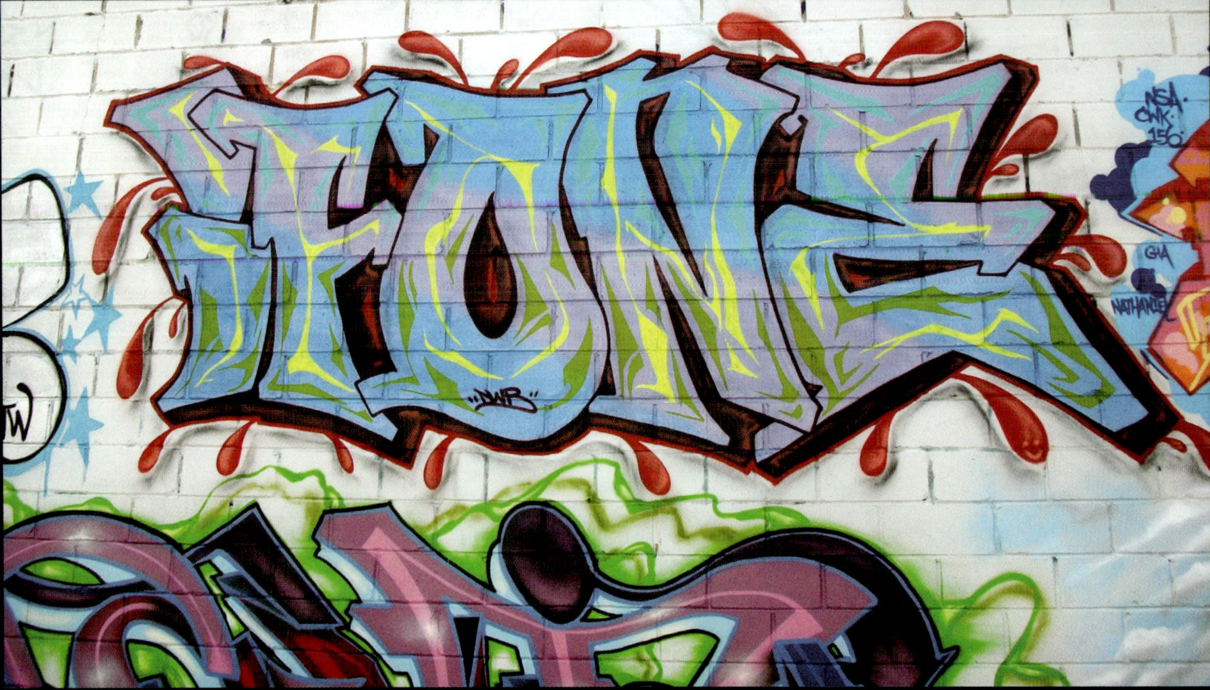

IF One, Brooklyn, NY

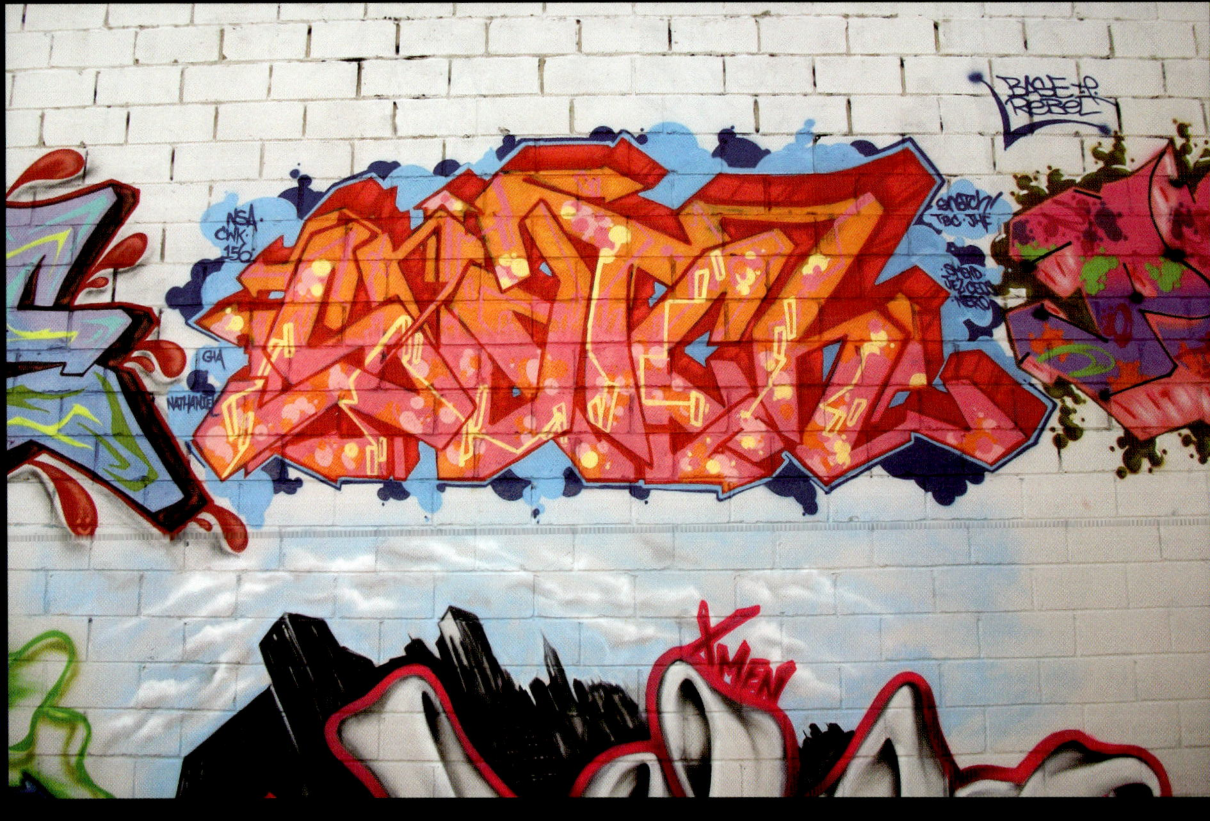

Snatch, Brooklyn, NY

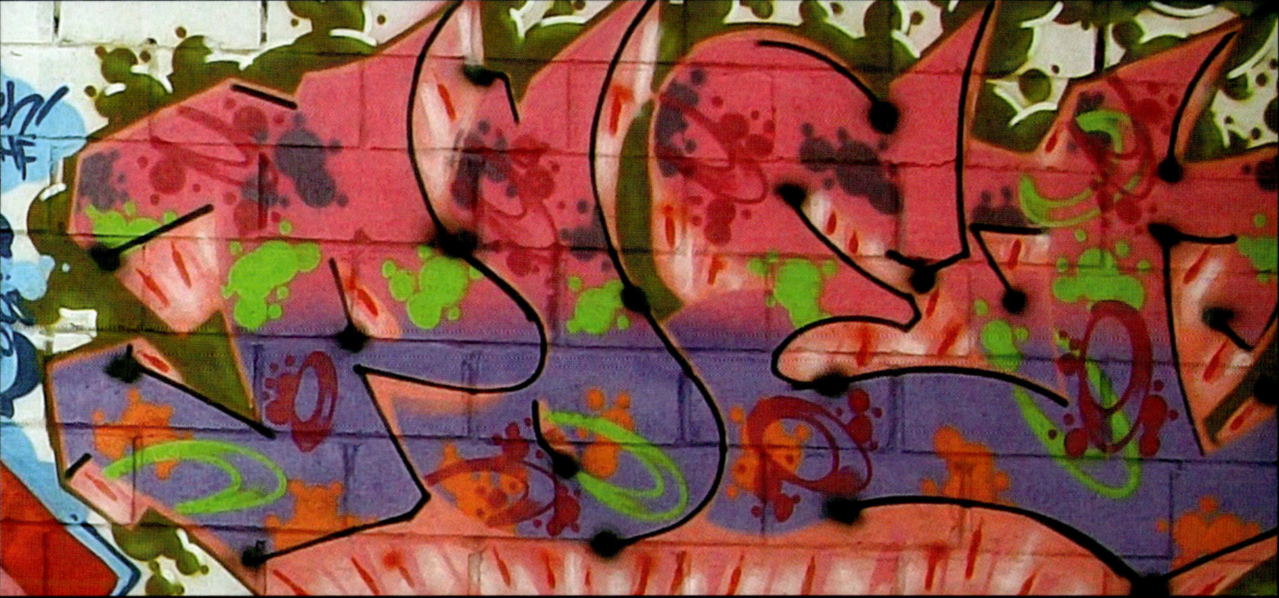

Poet, Brooklyn, NY

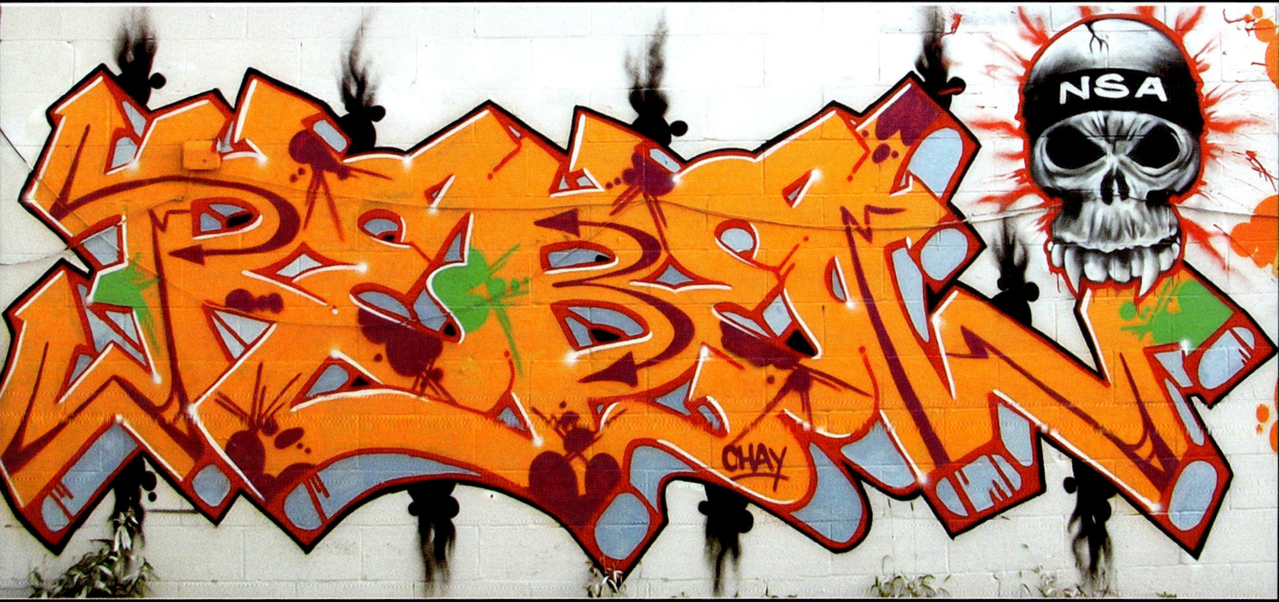


Rebel, Brooklyn, NY

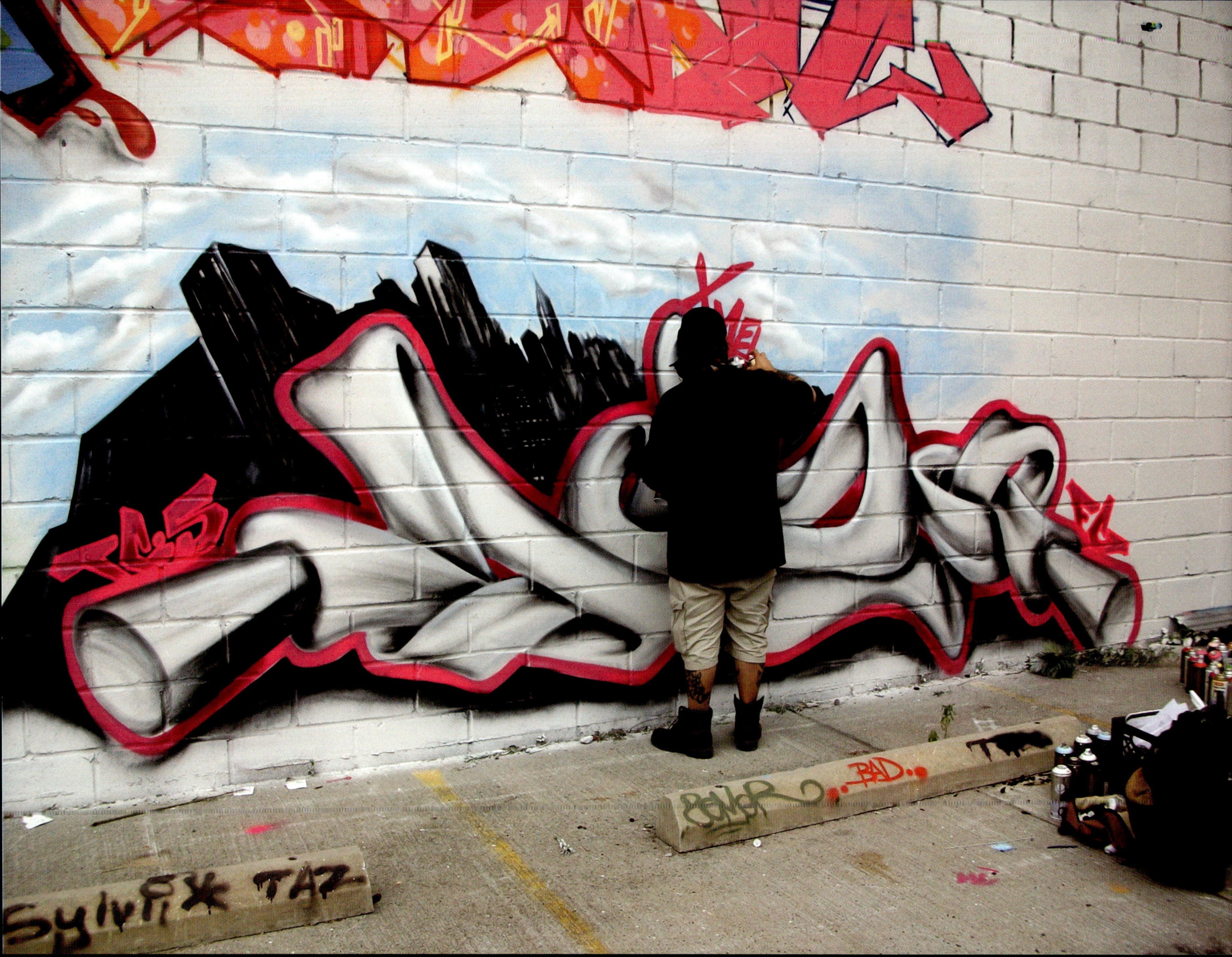

Dezo, Brooklyn, NY

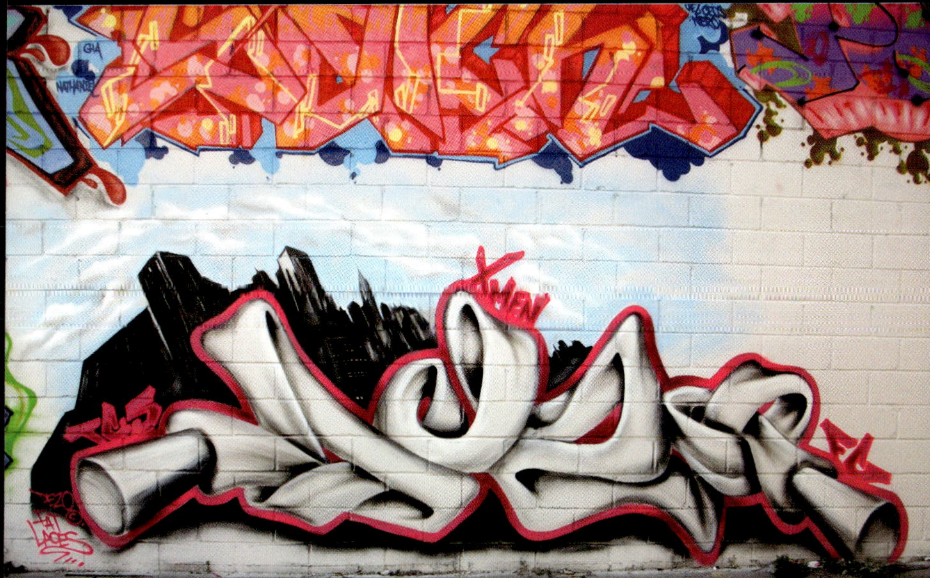

Dezo, Brooklyn, NY

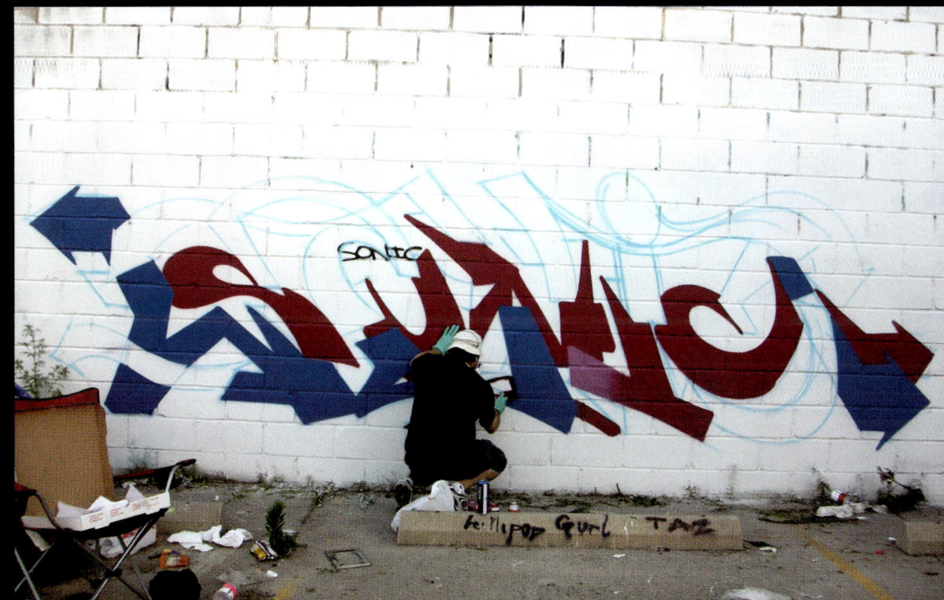

Sonic, Brooklyn, NY

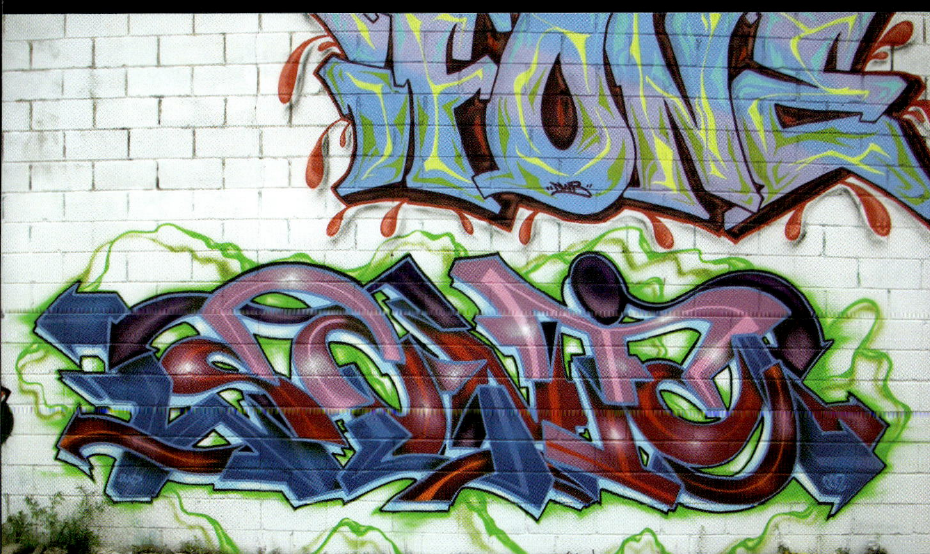

Sonic, Brooklyn, NY

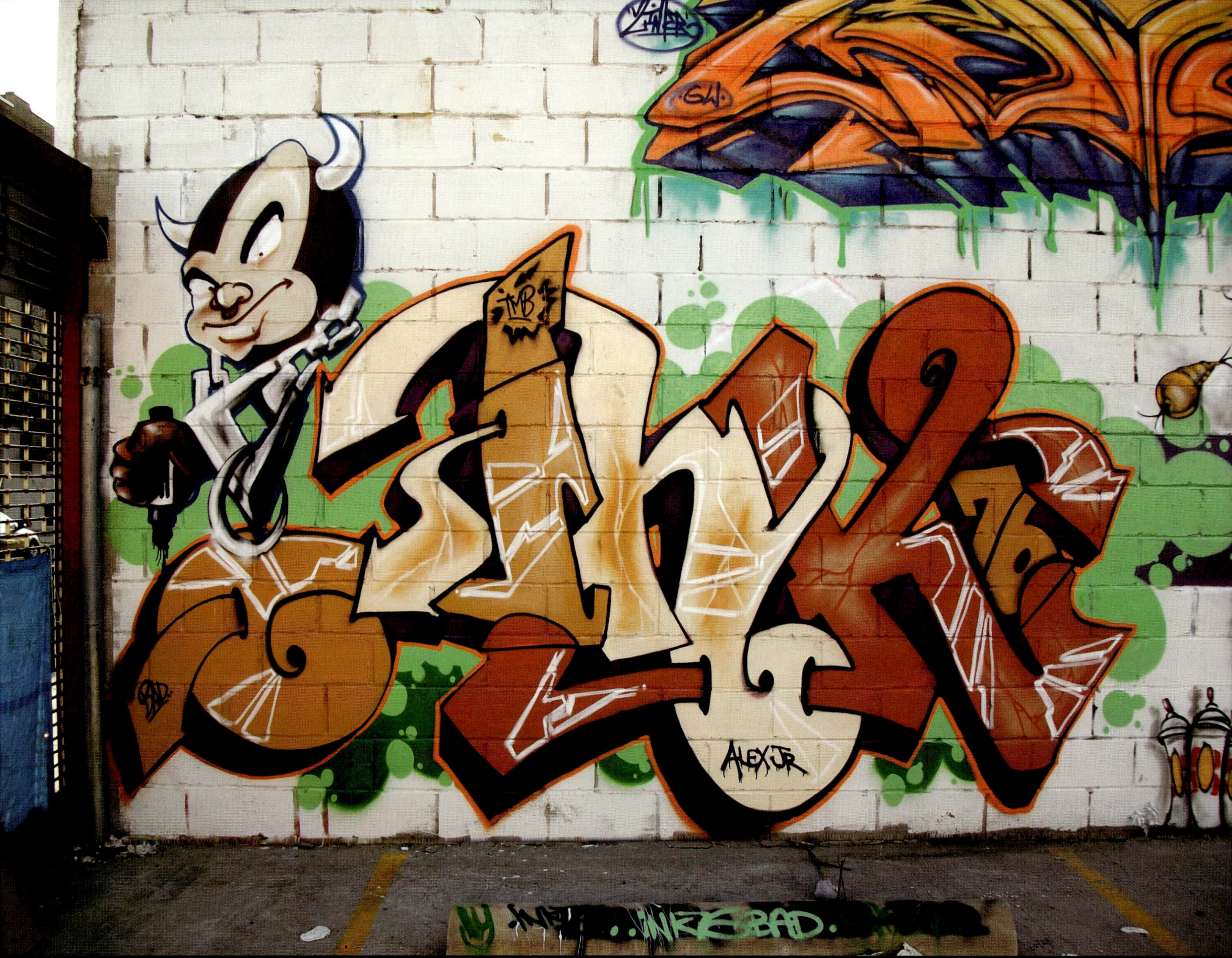


Ink76, Brooklyn, NY

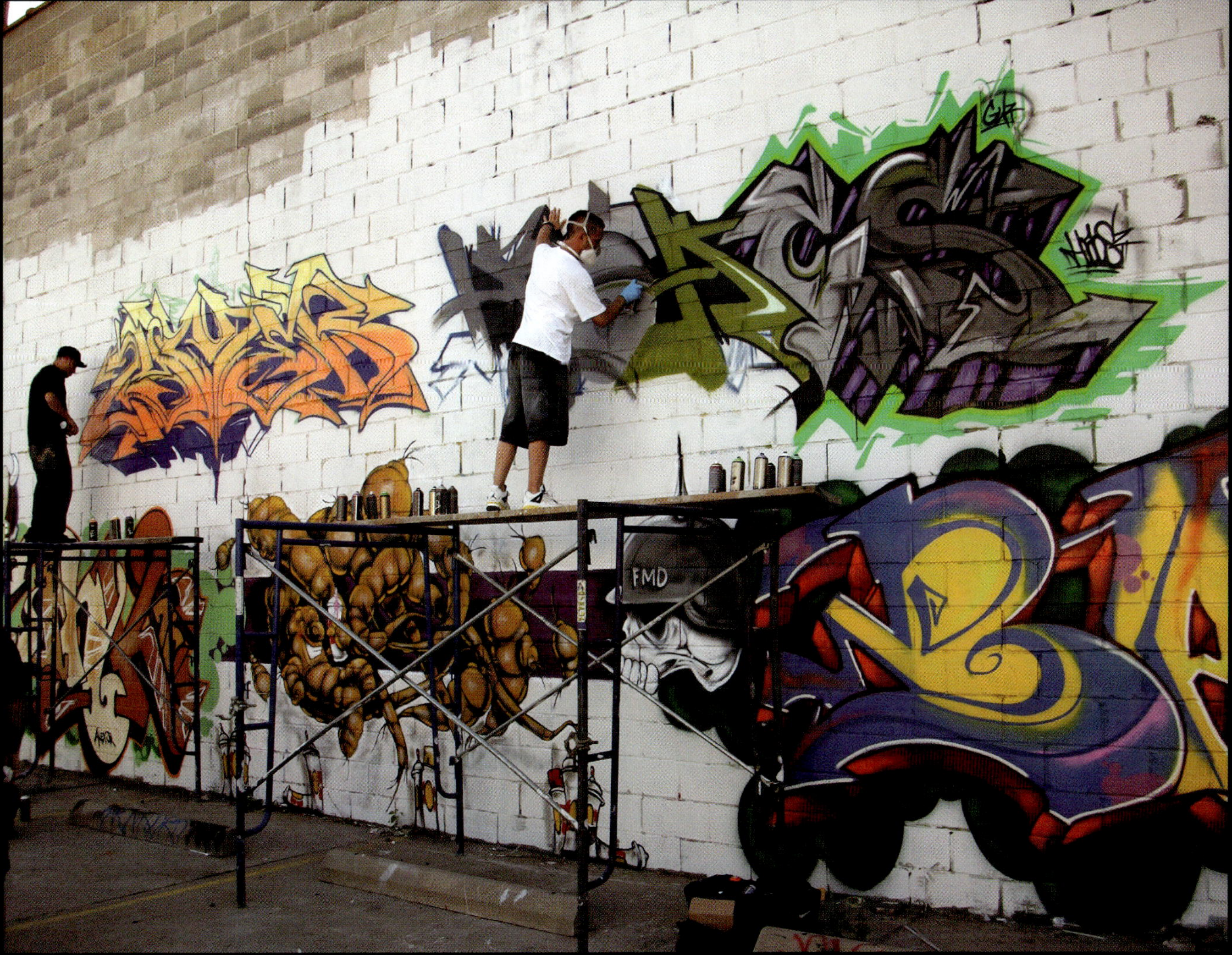


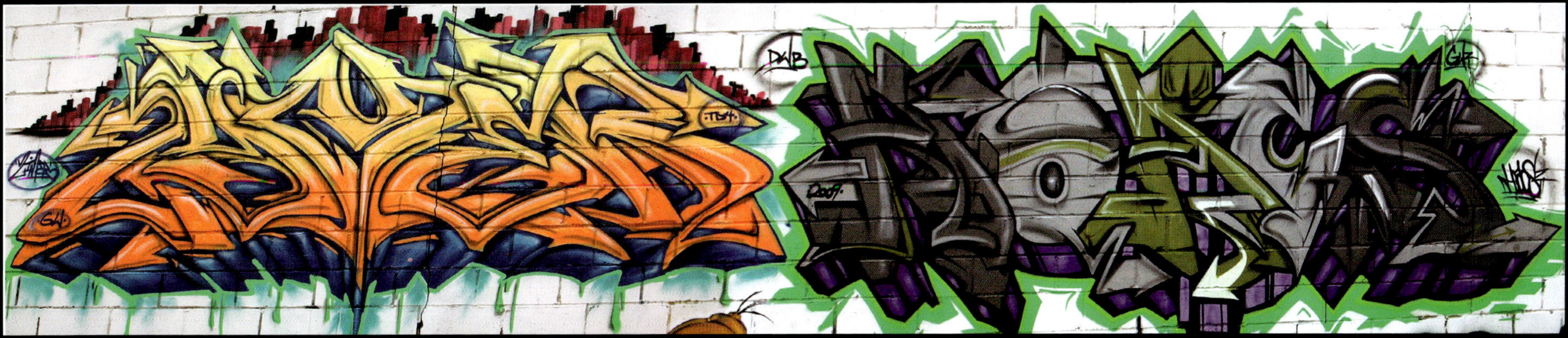

Zymer, Hoacs, Brooklyn, NY

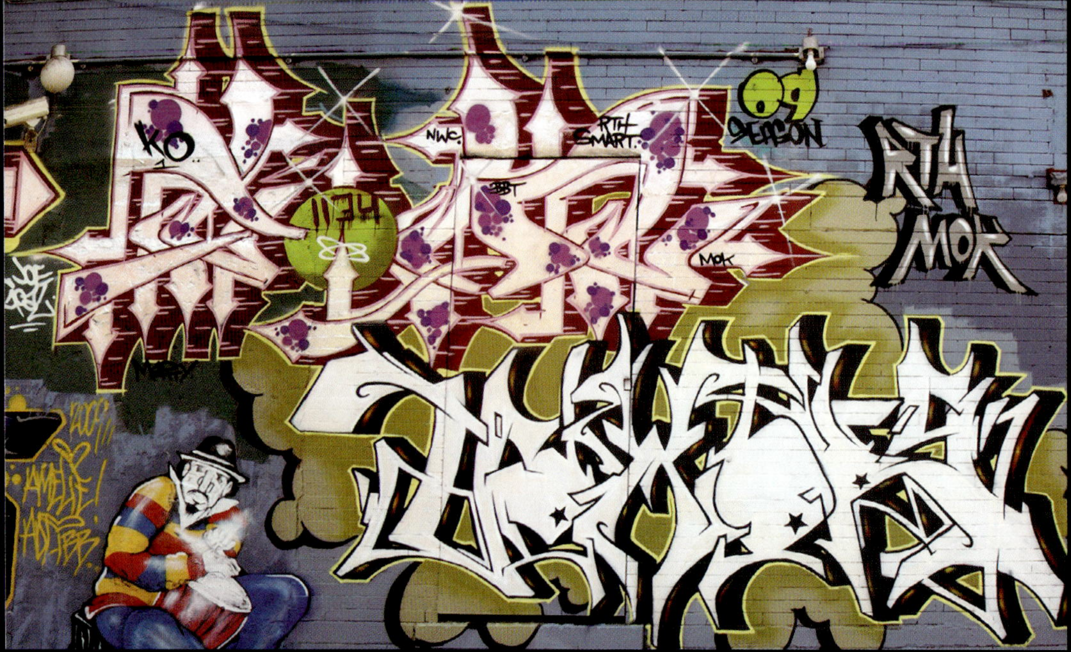

Goal, Vexor, Brooklyn, NY

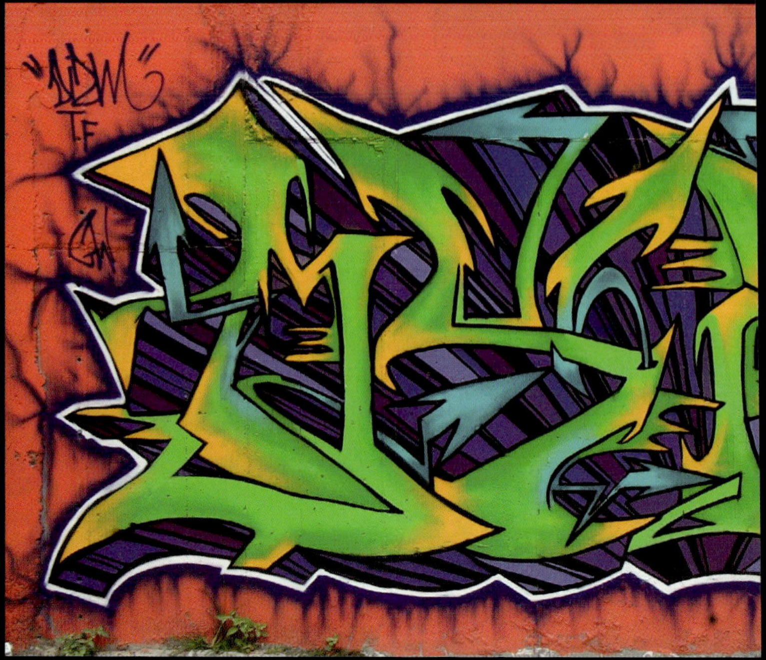

Dizm, Brooklyn, NY

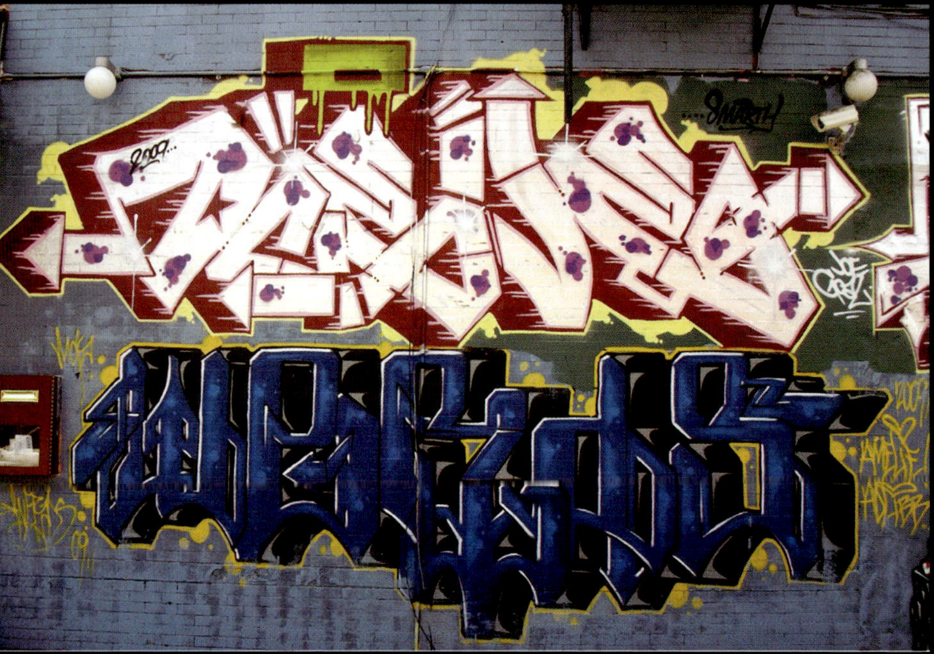

Oceve, Werds, Brooklyn, NY

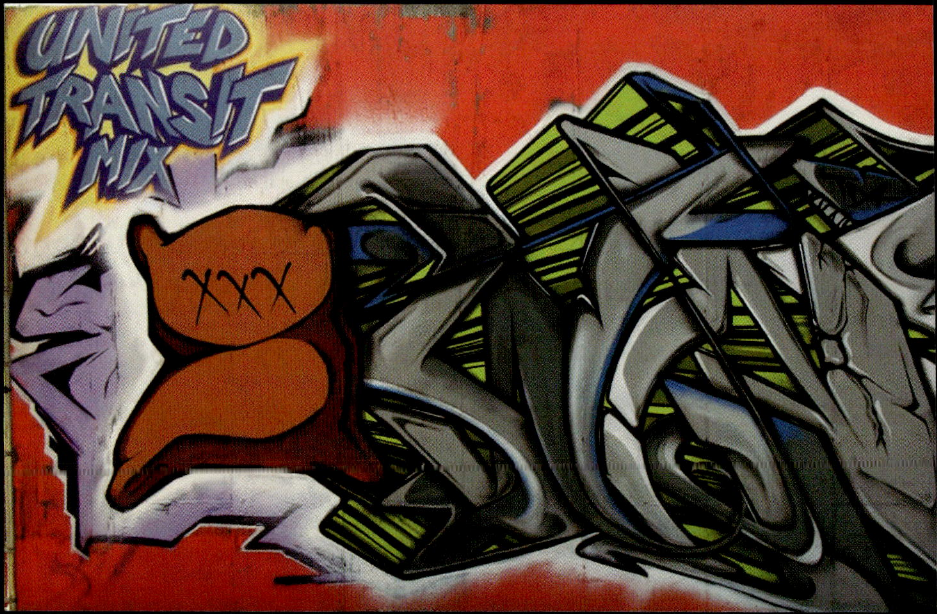


Owns, Meres, Then, Brooklyn, NY

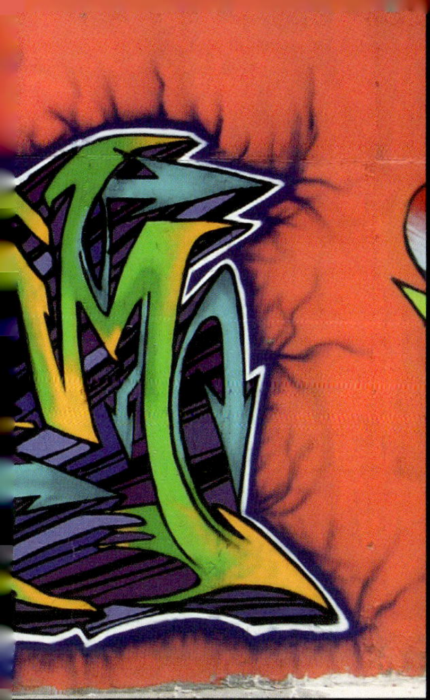

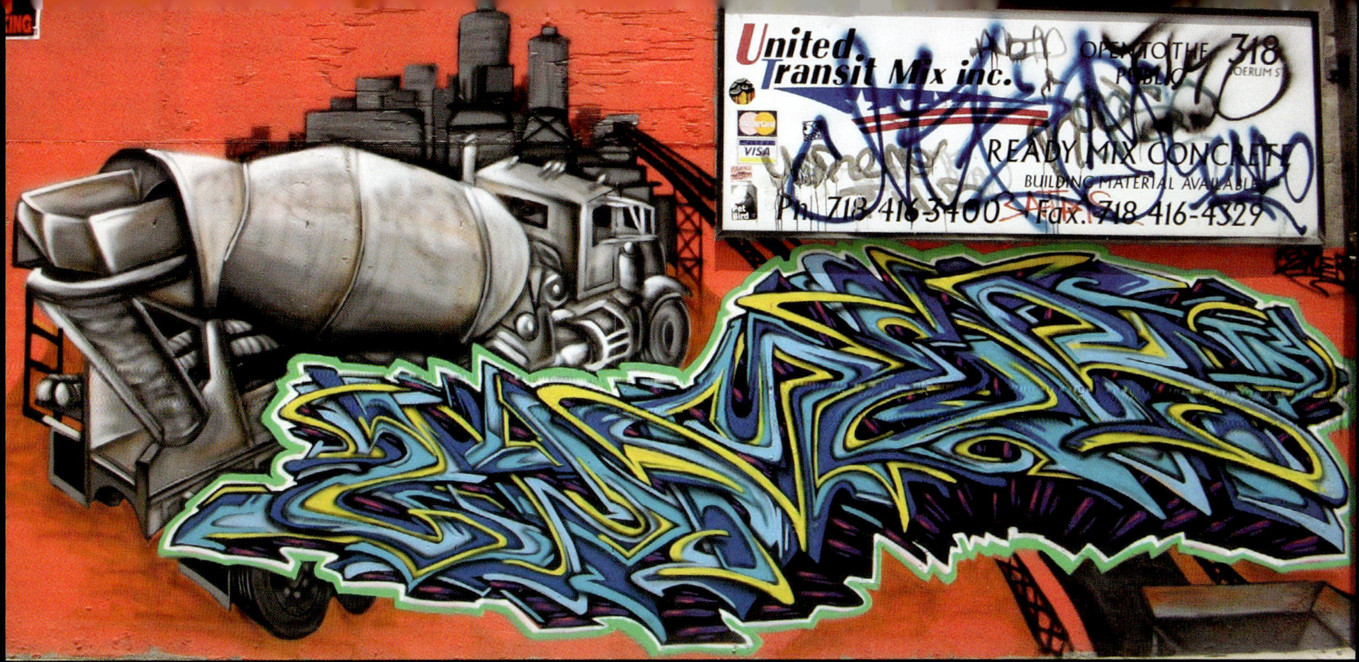


Zymer, Brooklyn, NY

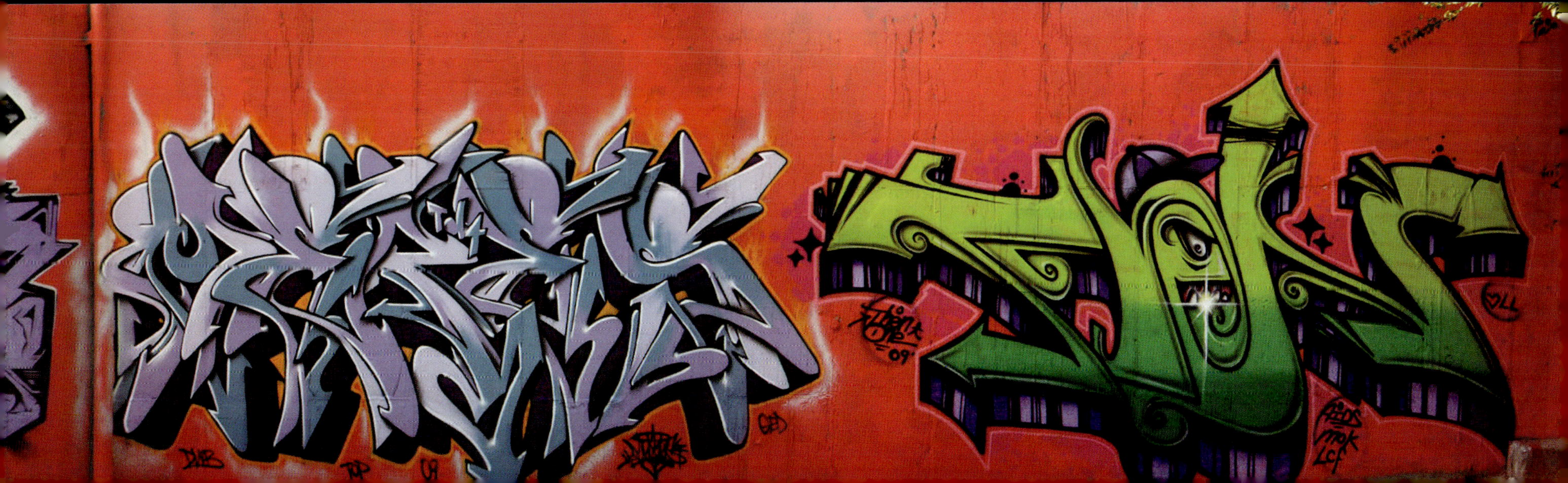

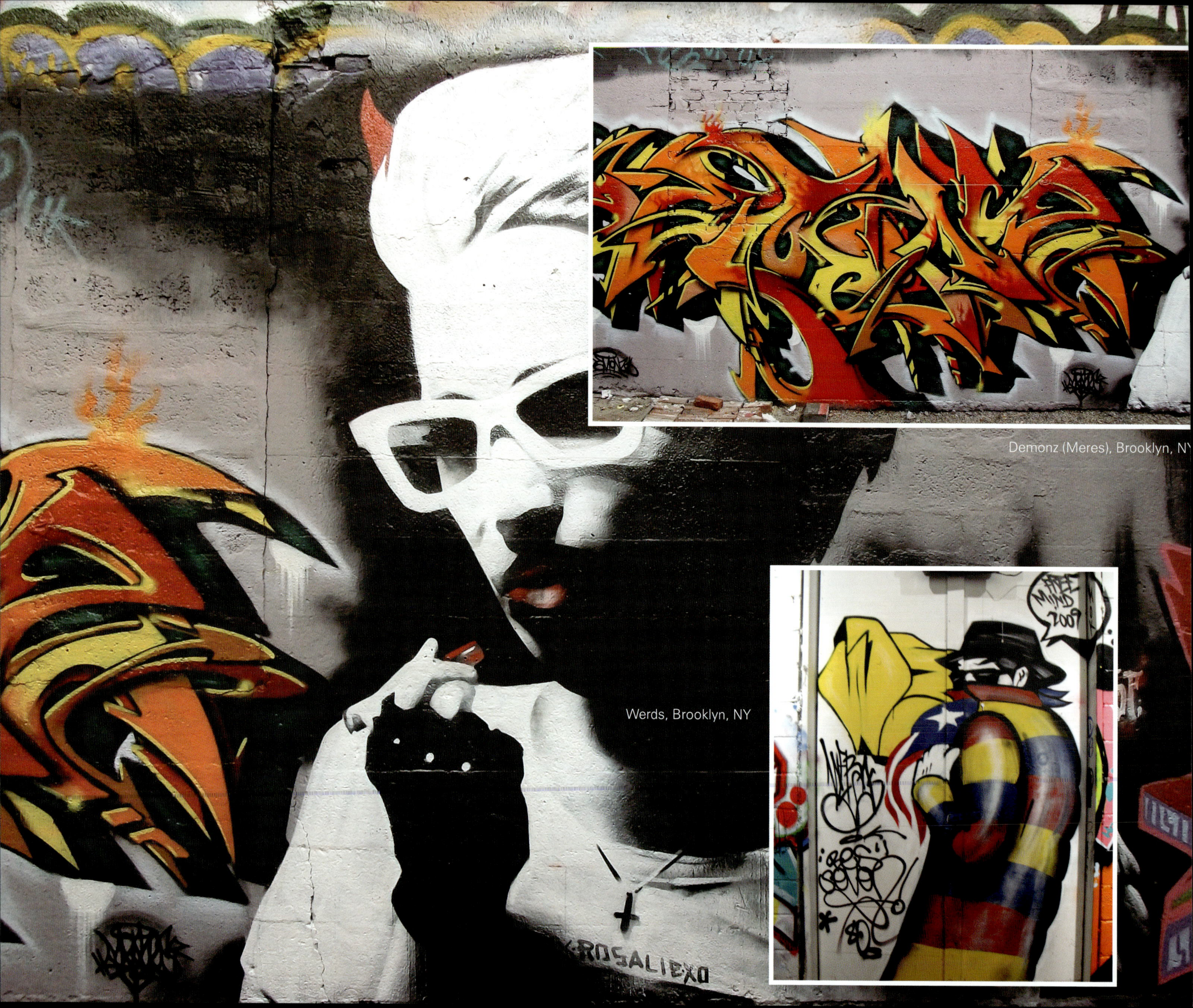


Demonz (Meres), Brooklyn, NY

Werds, Brooklyn, NY

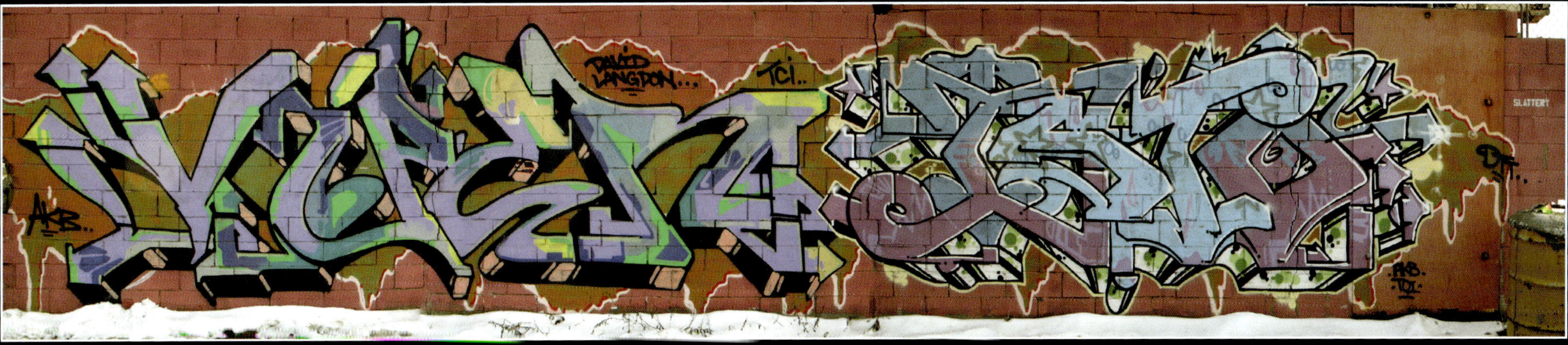

Viper, Isto, Brooklyn, NY

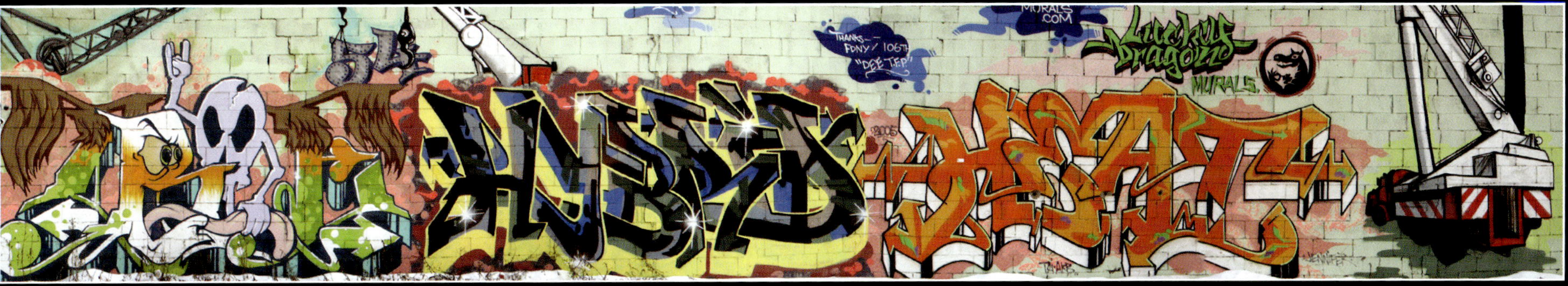

True54, Hybrid, Heat, Brooklyn, NY

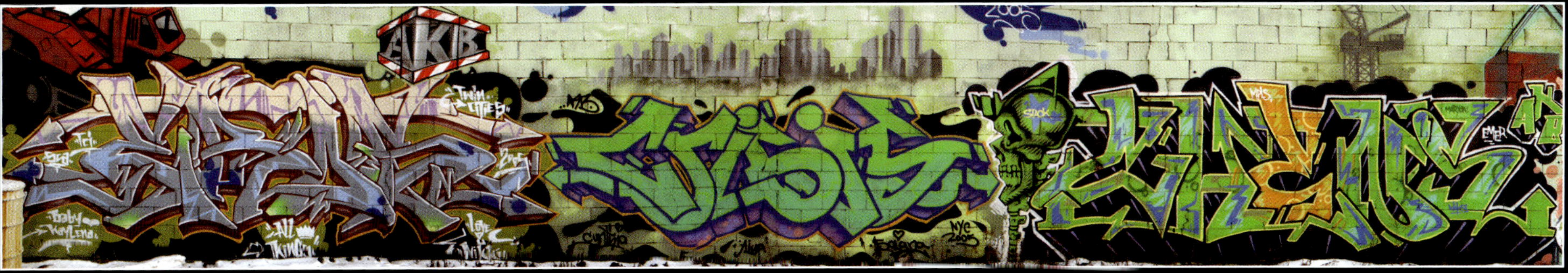

Eros, Crisis, Chens, Brooklyn, NY

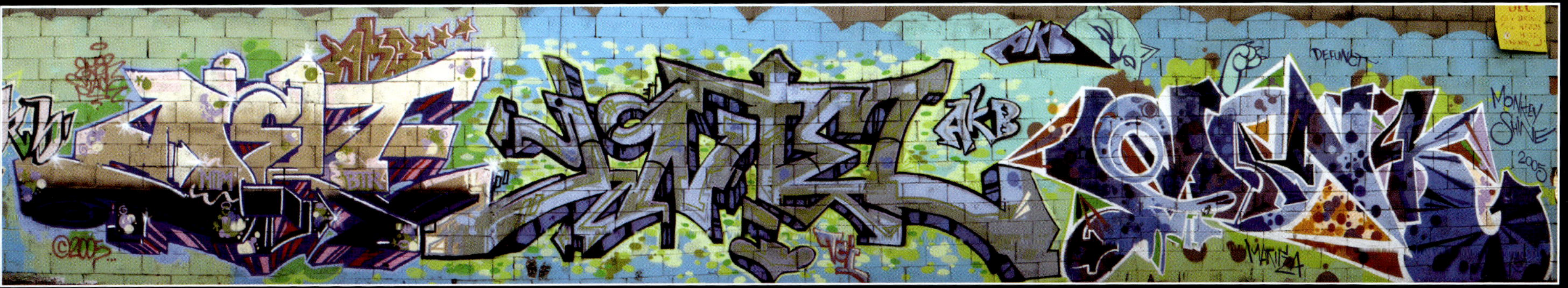

Delt, Intel, Monk, Brooklyn, NY

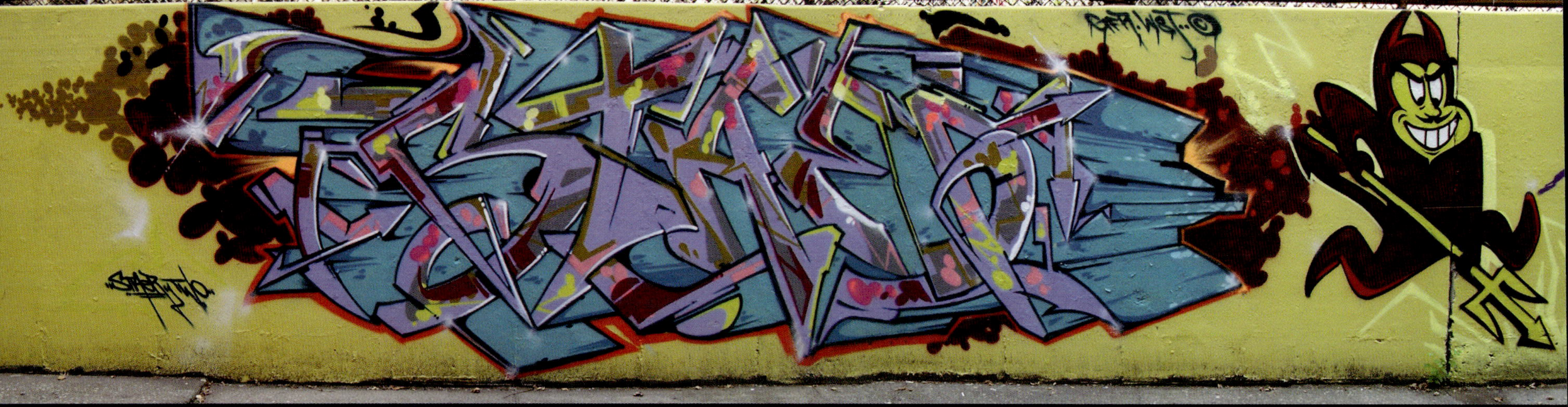

Stae2, Brooklyn, NY

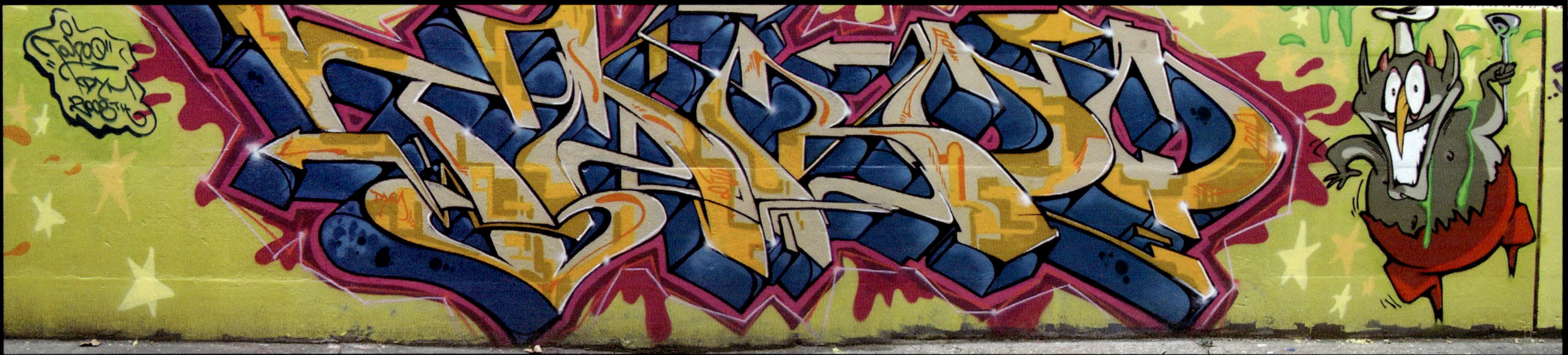

Taboo, Brooklyn, NY

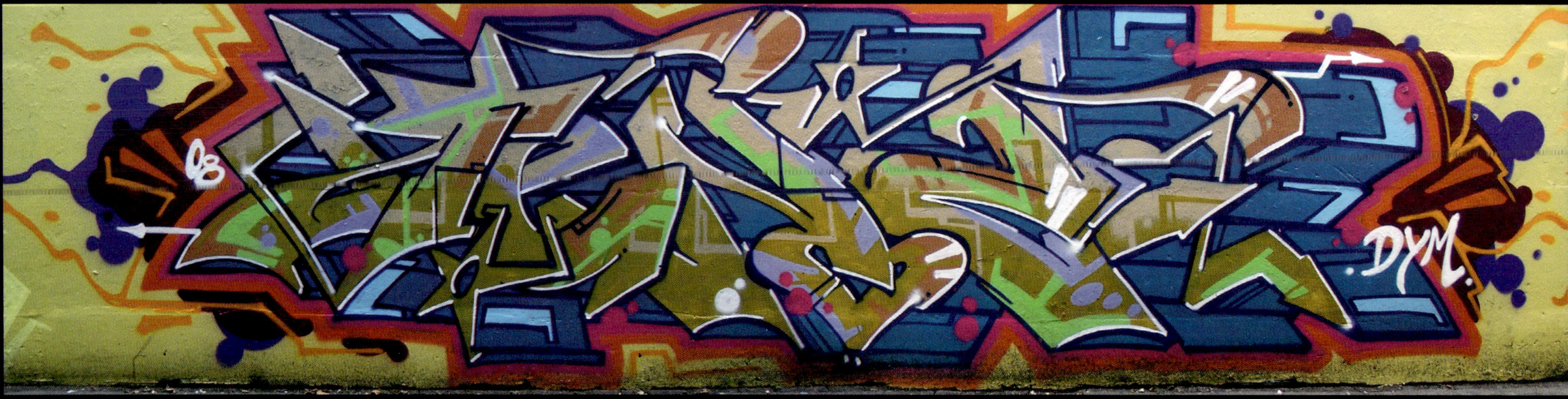


Tenz, Brooklyn, NY

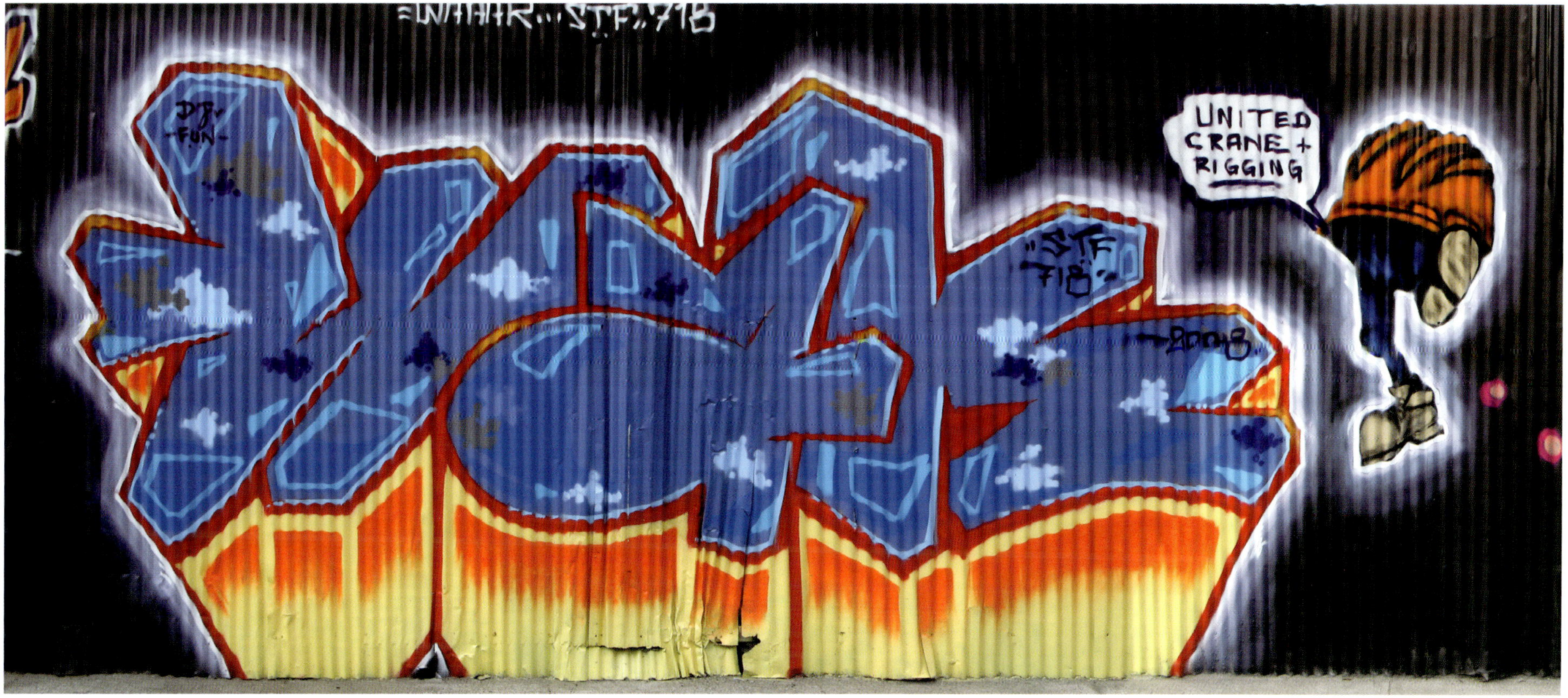


Wak, Queens, NY

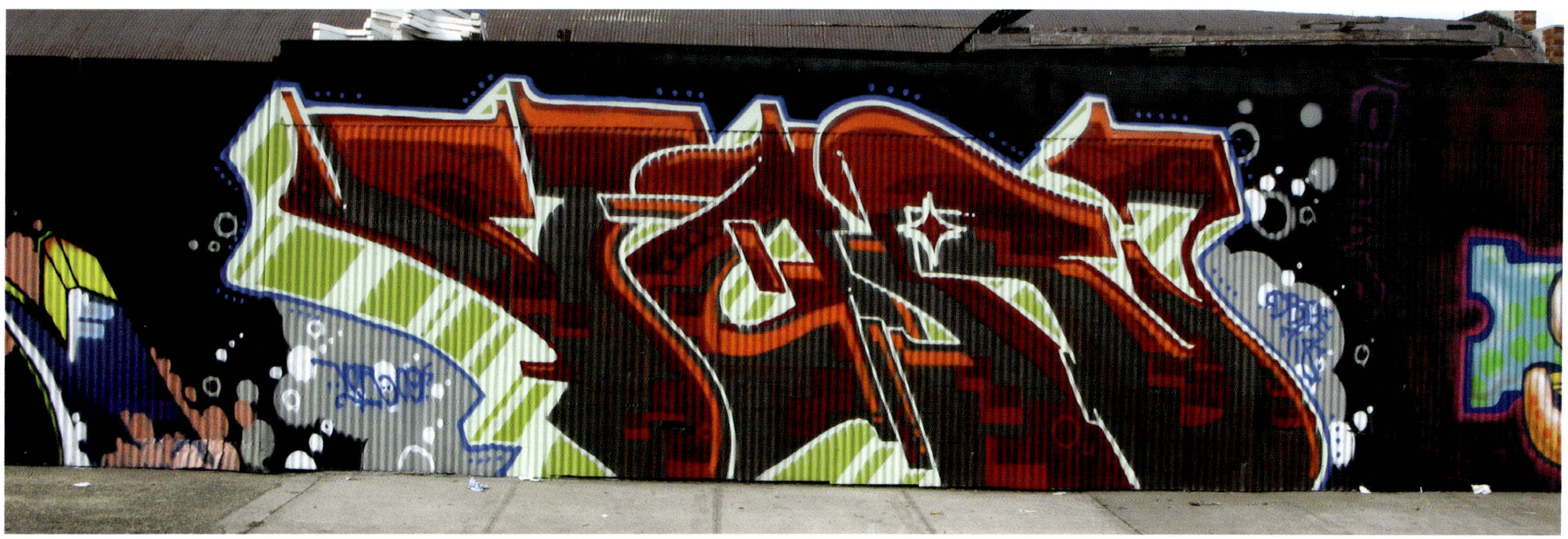

Vor, Queens, NY

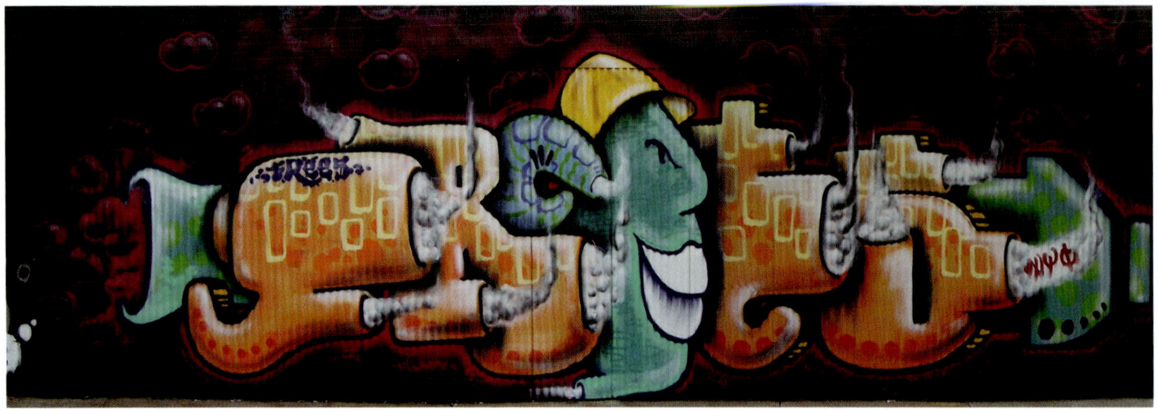

Free5, Queens, NY

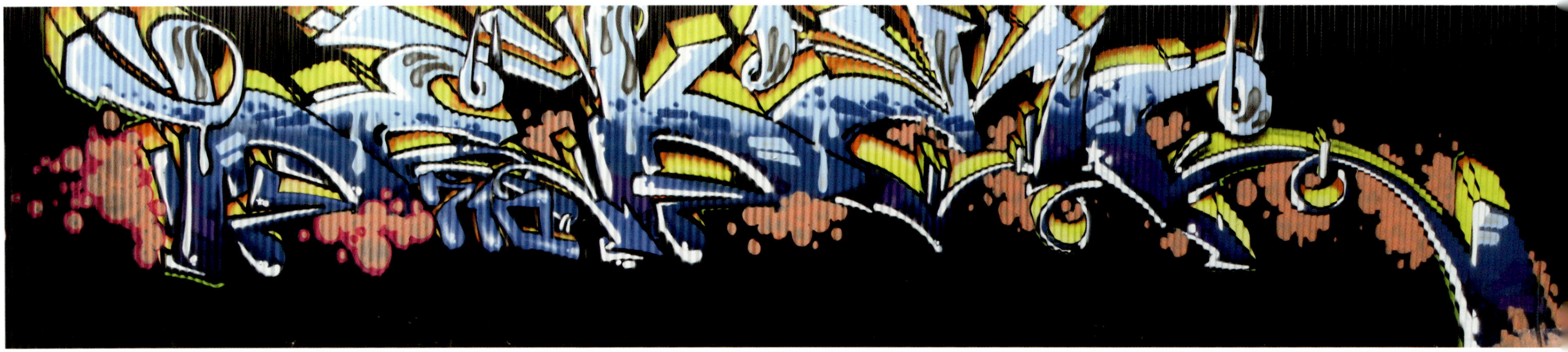

Hektic, Queens, NY

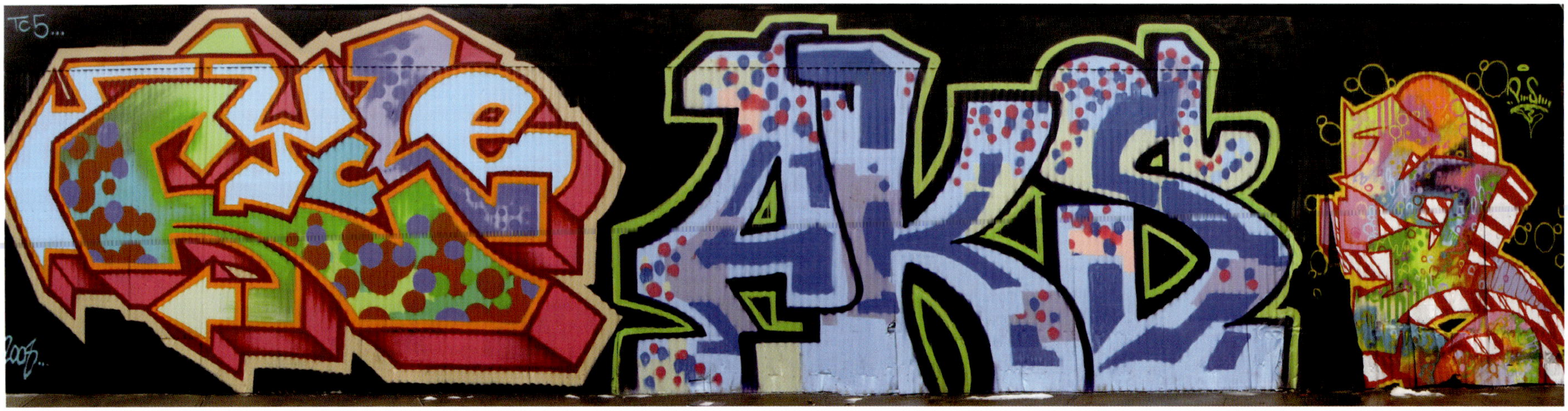

Cycle, AKS, Smith, Queens, NY

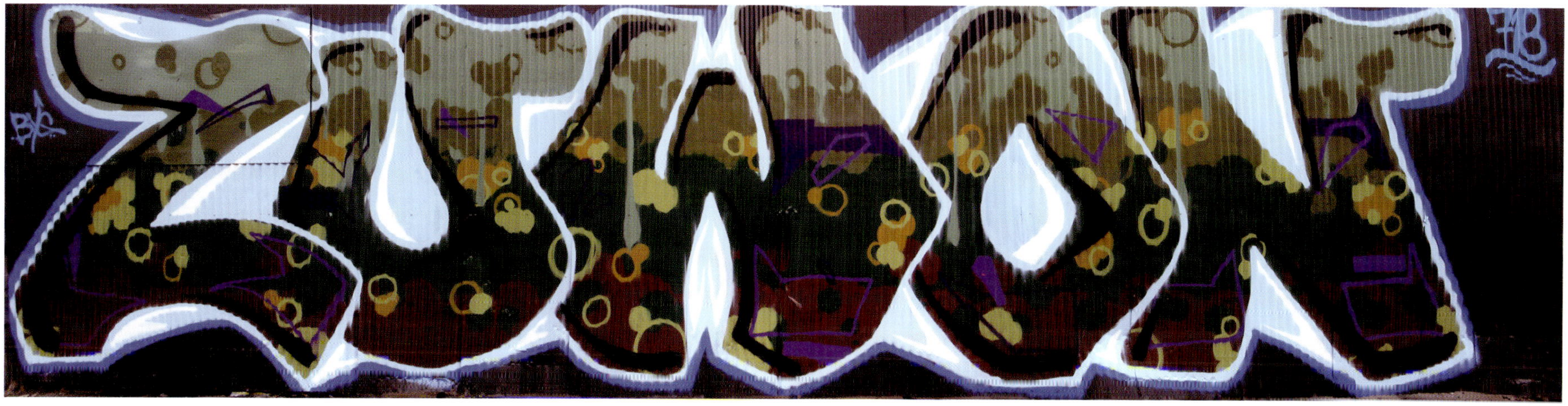

Zu, Queens, NY

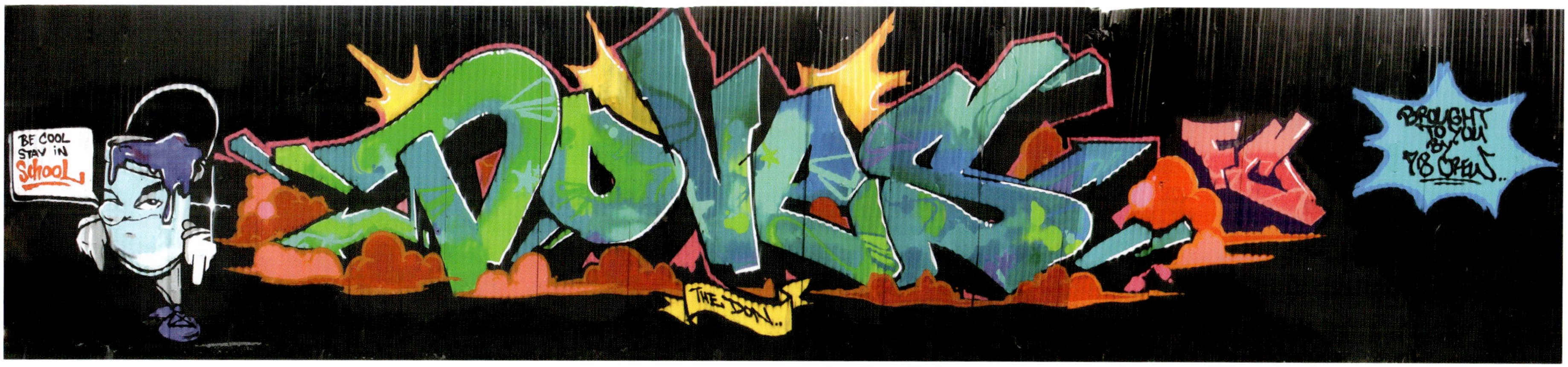


Doves, Queens, NY

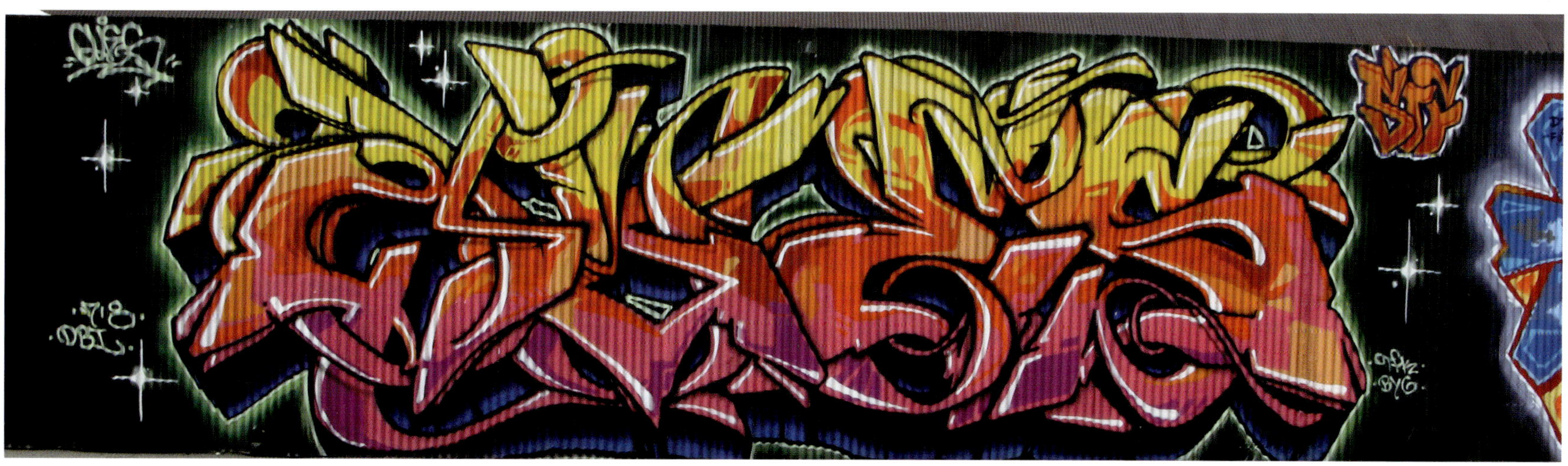

Ques, Queens, NY

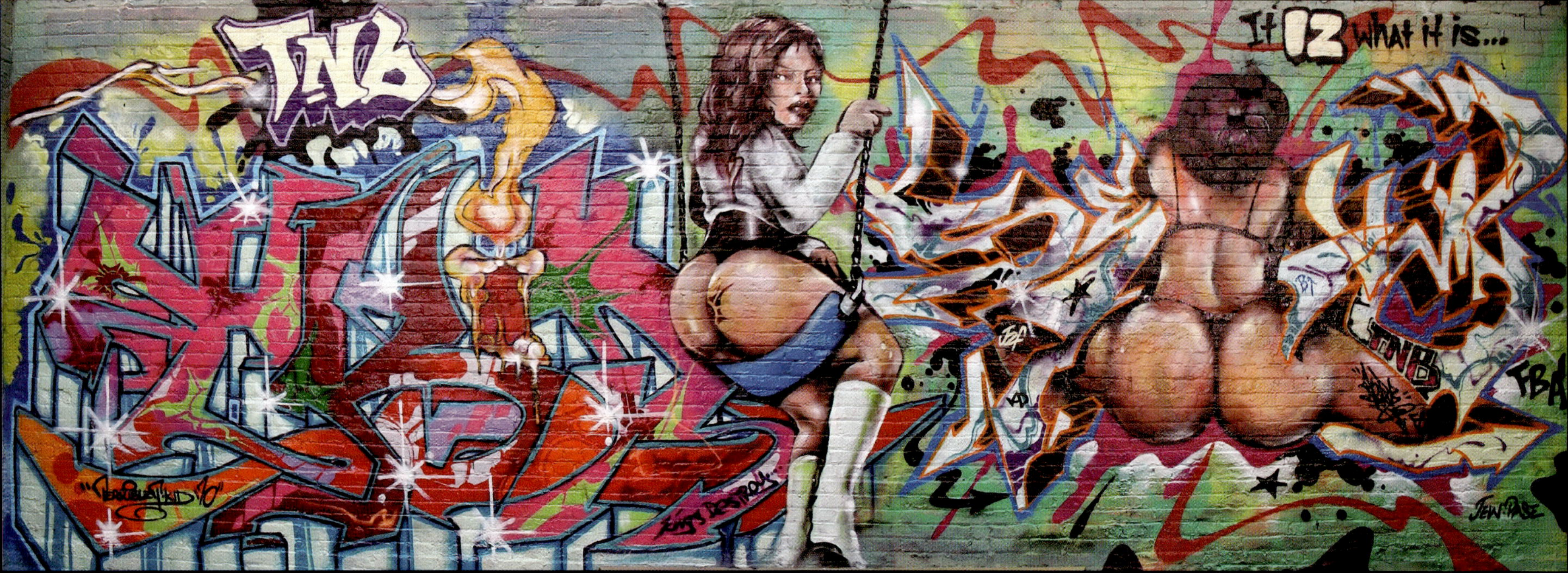

T-Kid, Serve, Bronx, NY, Tuff City

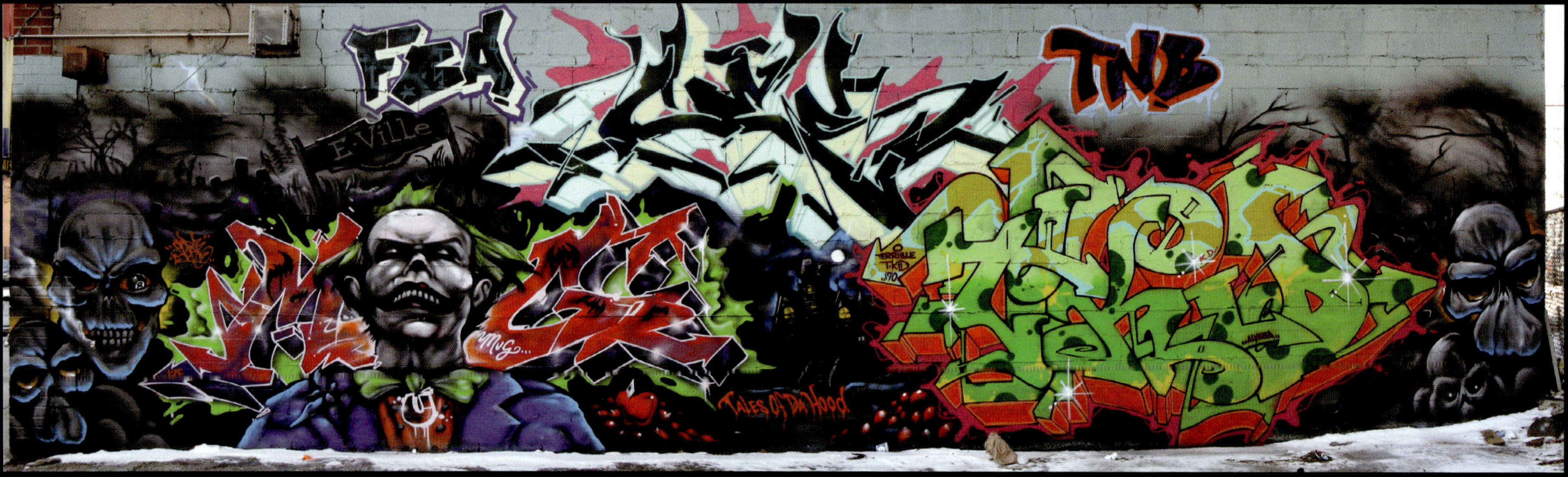

T-Kid, Ces, Serve, Bronx, NY

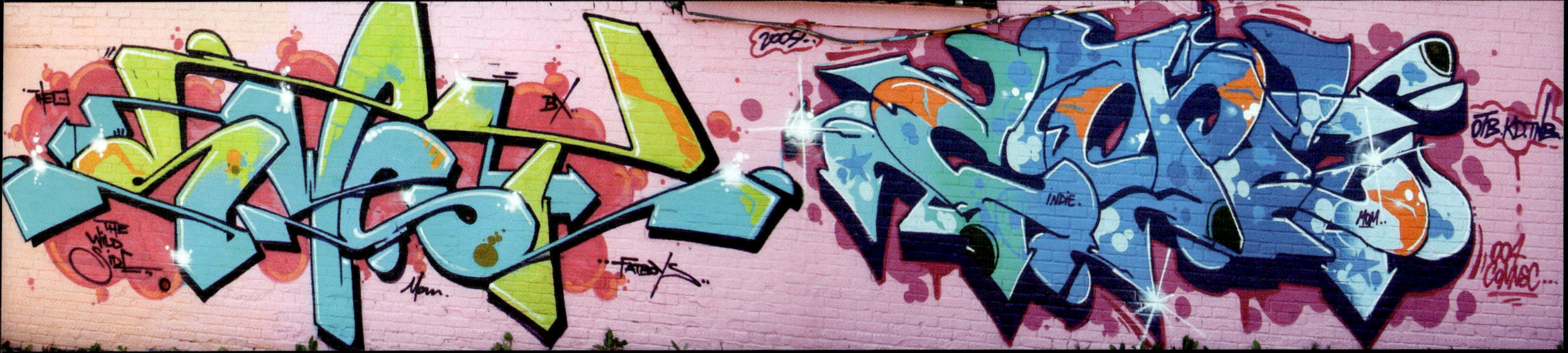

Swet, Cope2, Bronx, NY

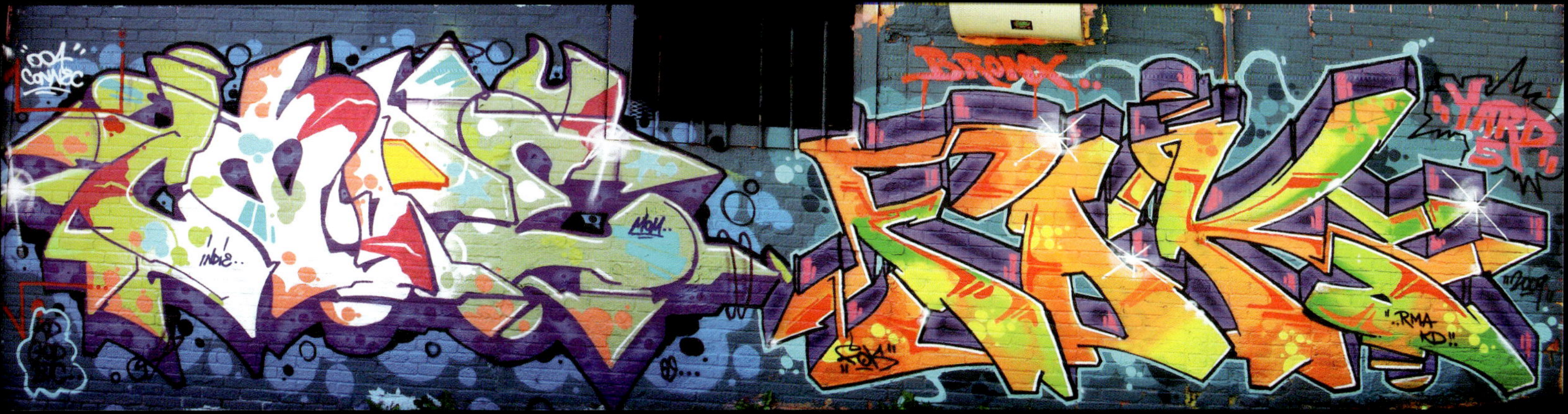

Cope2, Fok, Bronx, NY

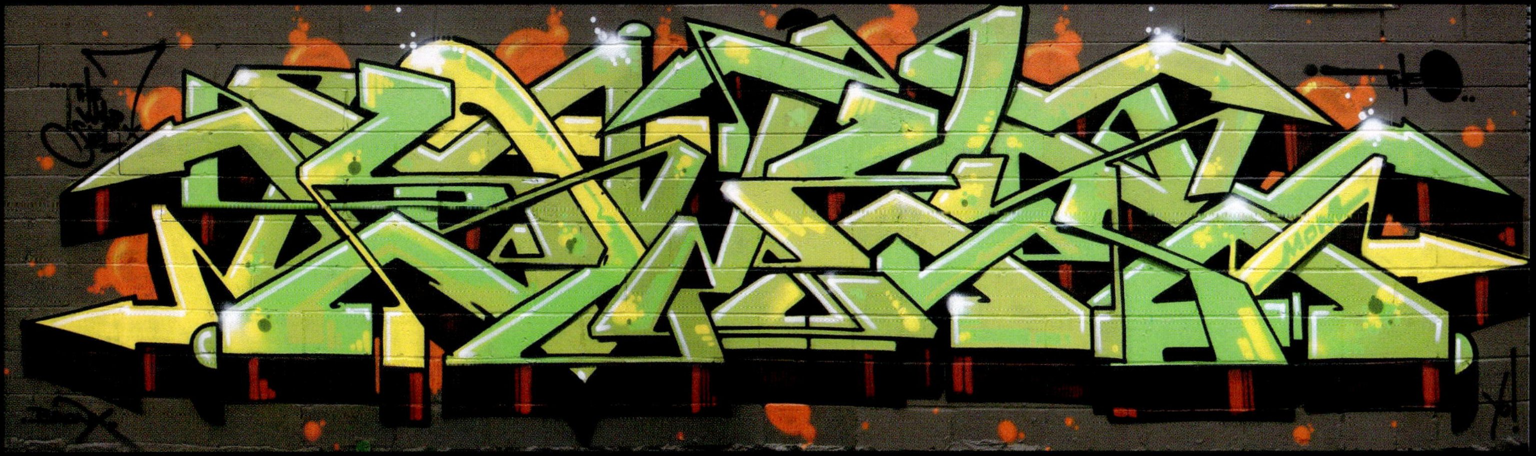

Swet, Bronx, NY

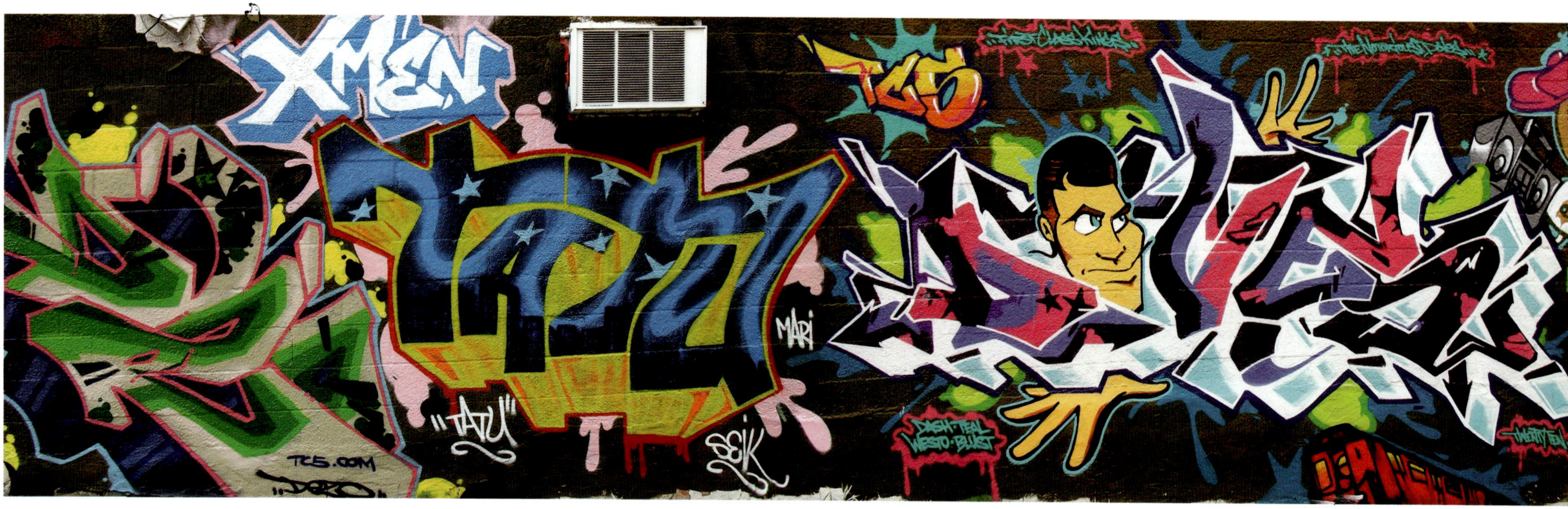

Dezo, Tatu, Doves, Queens, NY

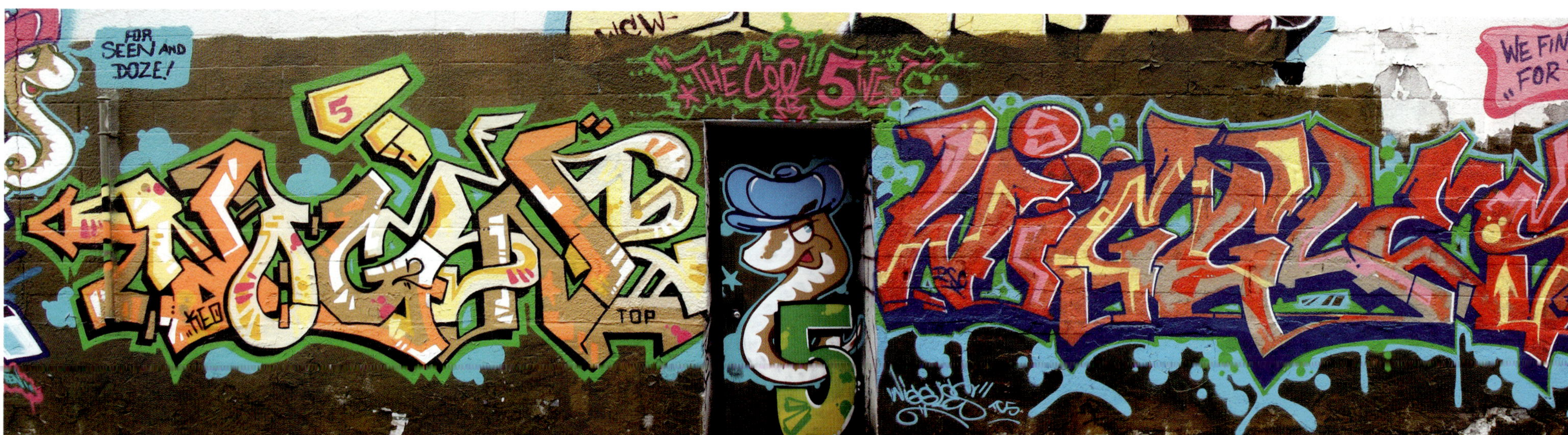

Noggin (Keo), Wiggles, Queens, NY

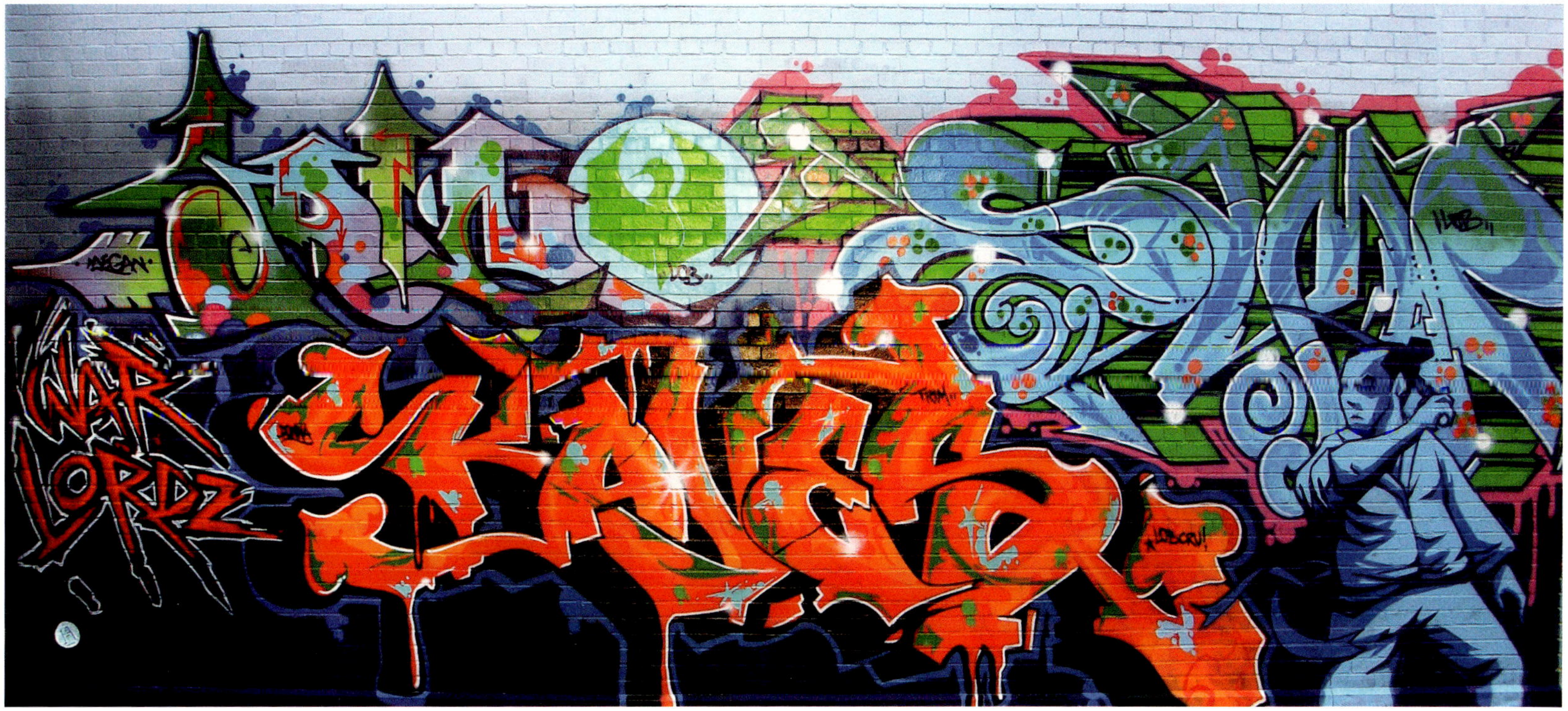


Dino, Kaves, Samp, Manhattan, NY

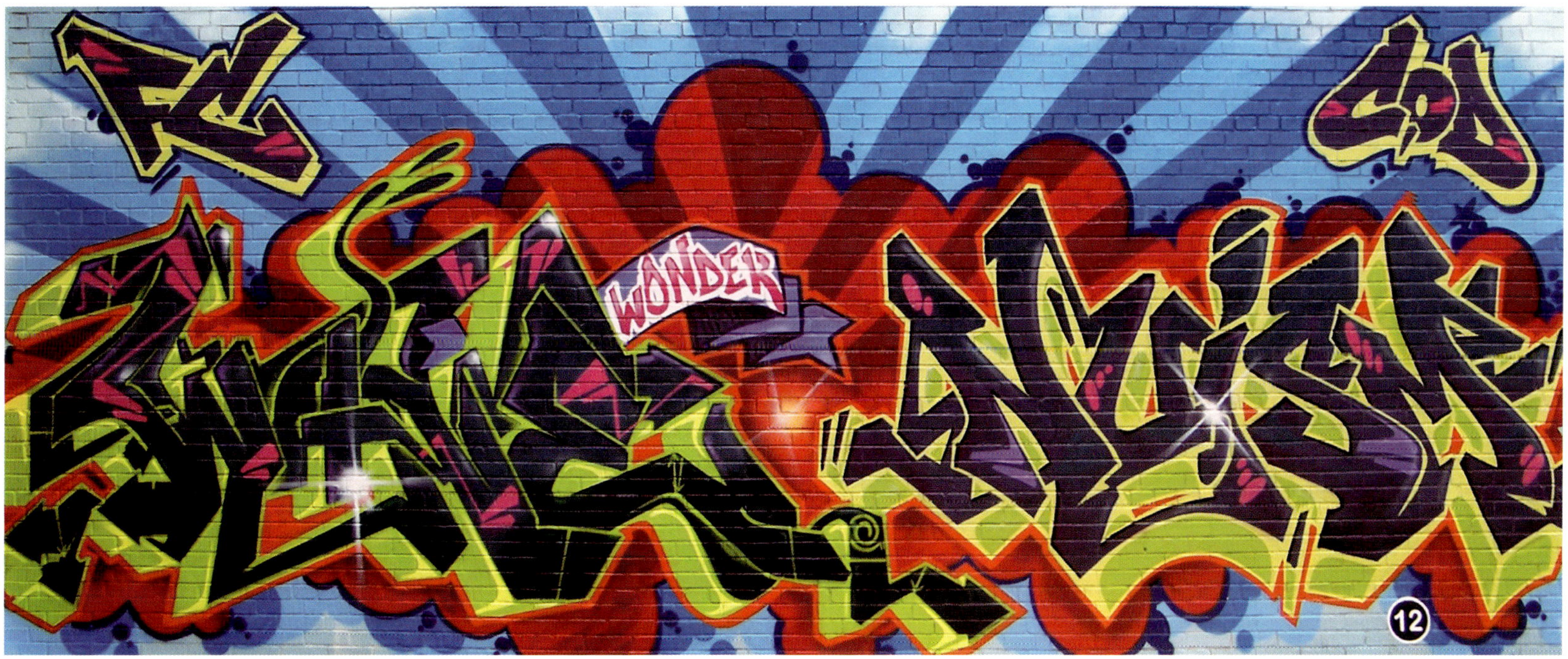


Wano, Enuo, Manhattan, NY

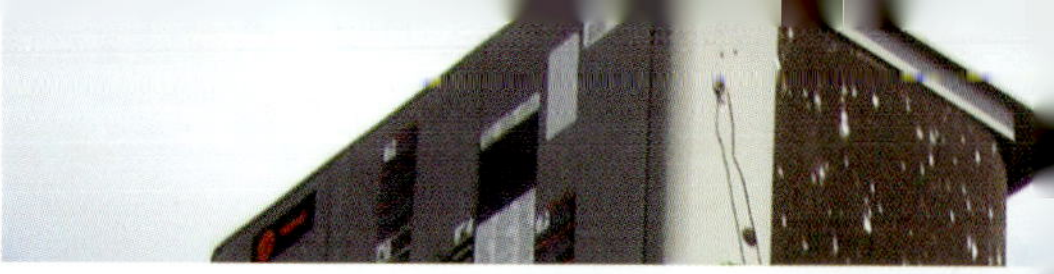

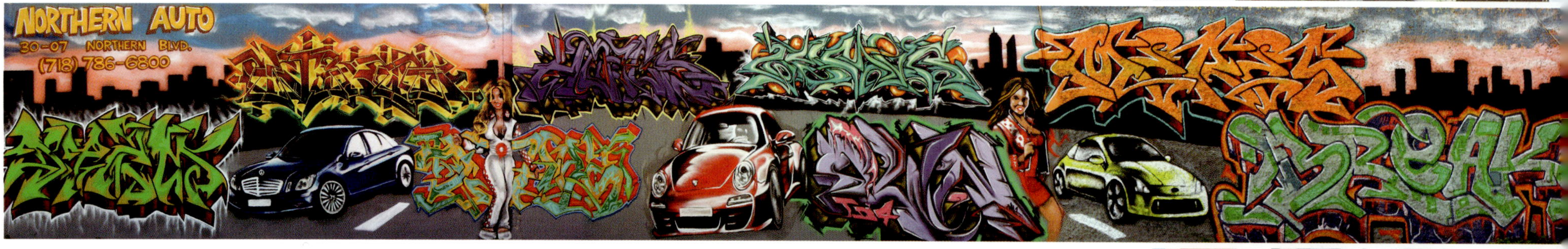


Dizm, Stres, Topaz, Hoacs, Zymer, Owns, Meres, Break, Queens, NY

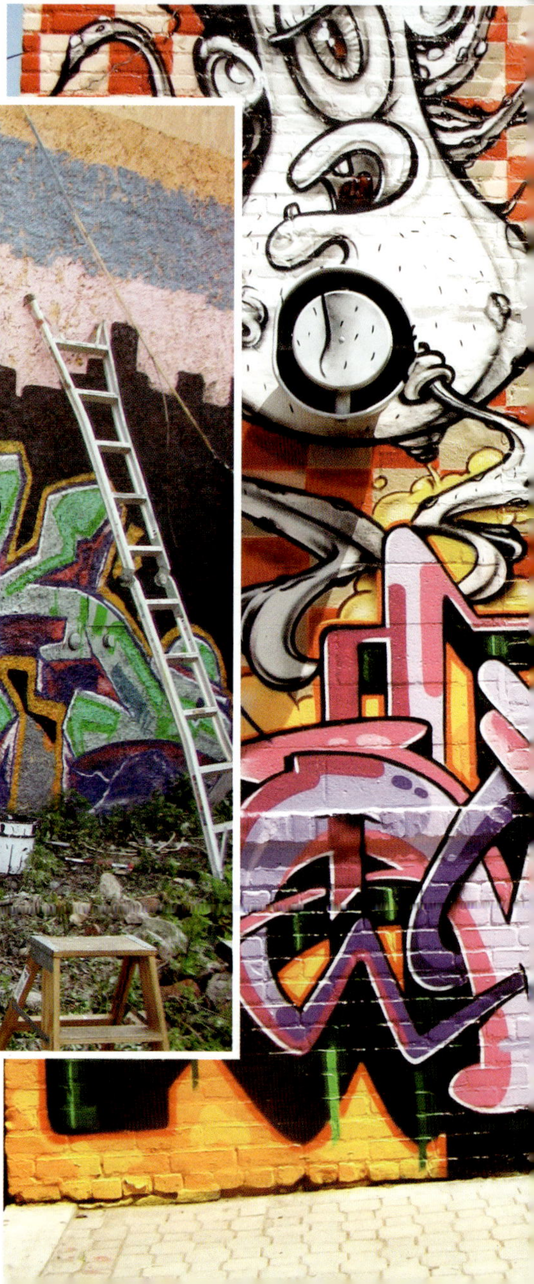

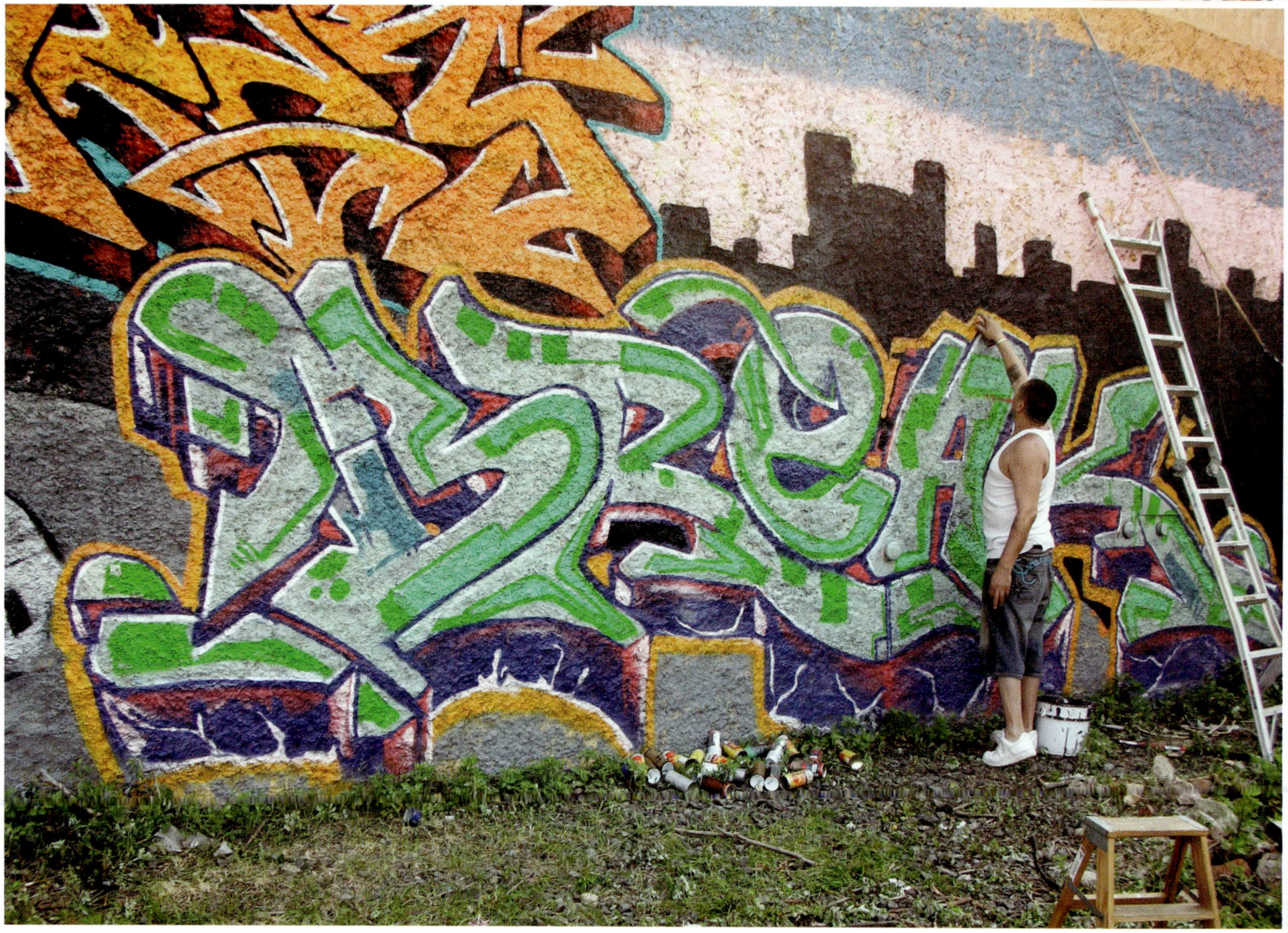

Break – Action, Queens, NY

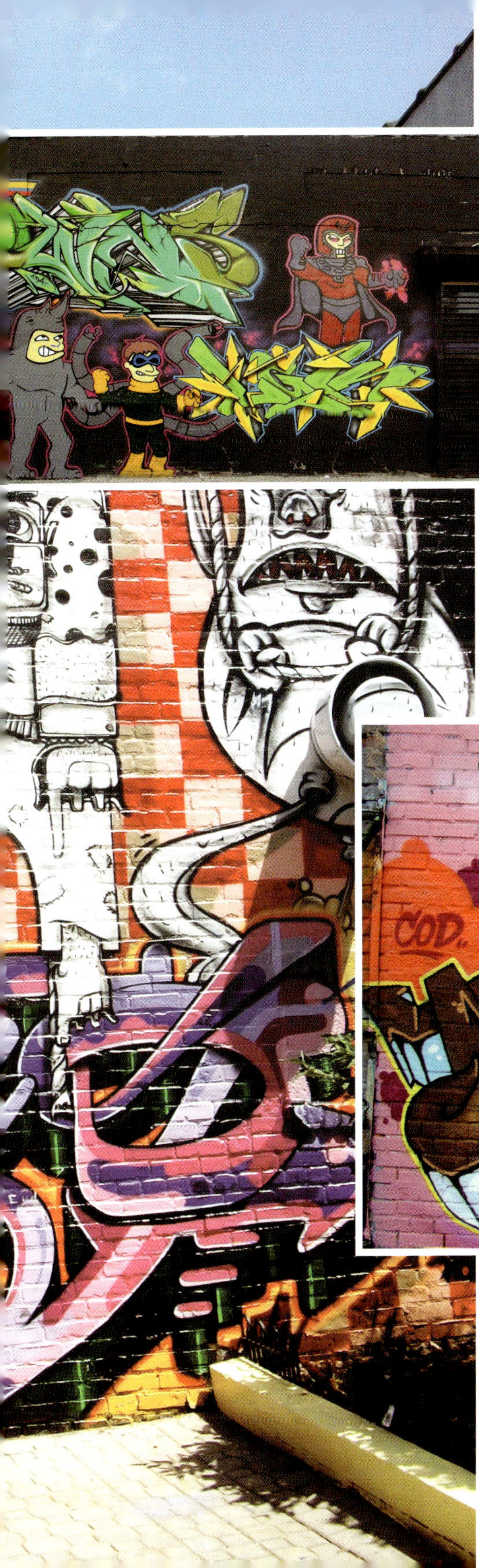

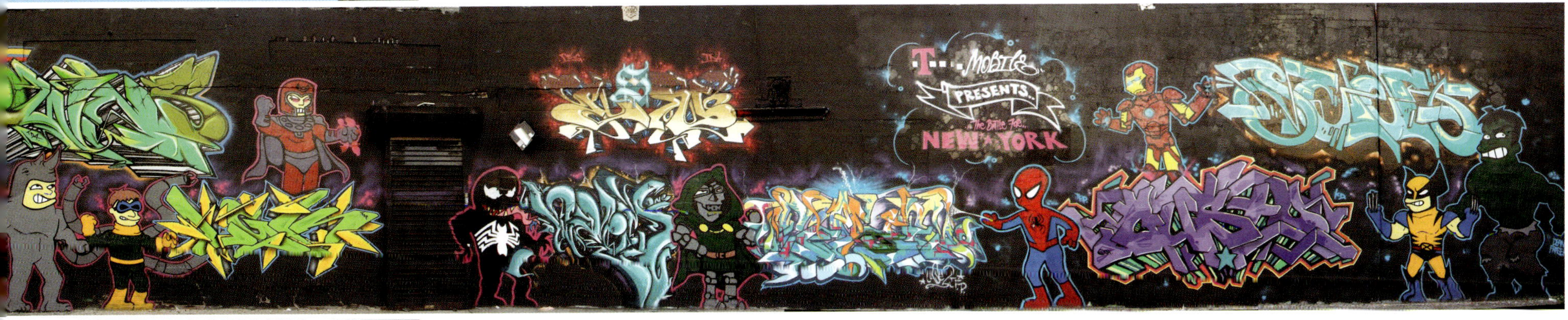


Owns, Logek, ESN, Deem, Case2, Gusto, Seter, Queens, NY

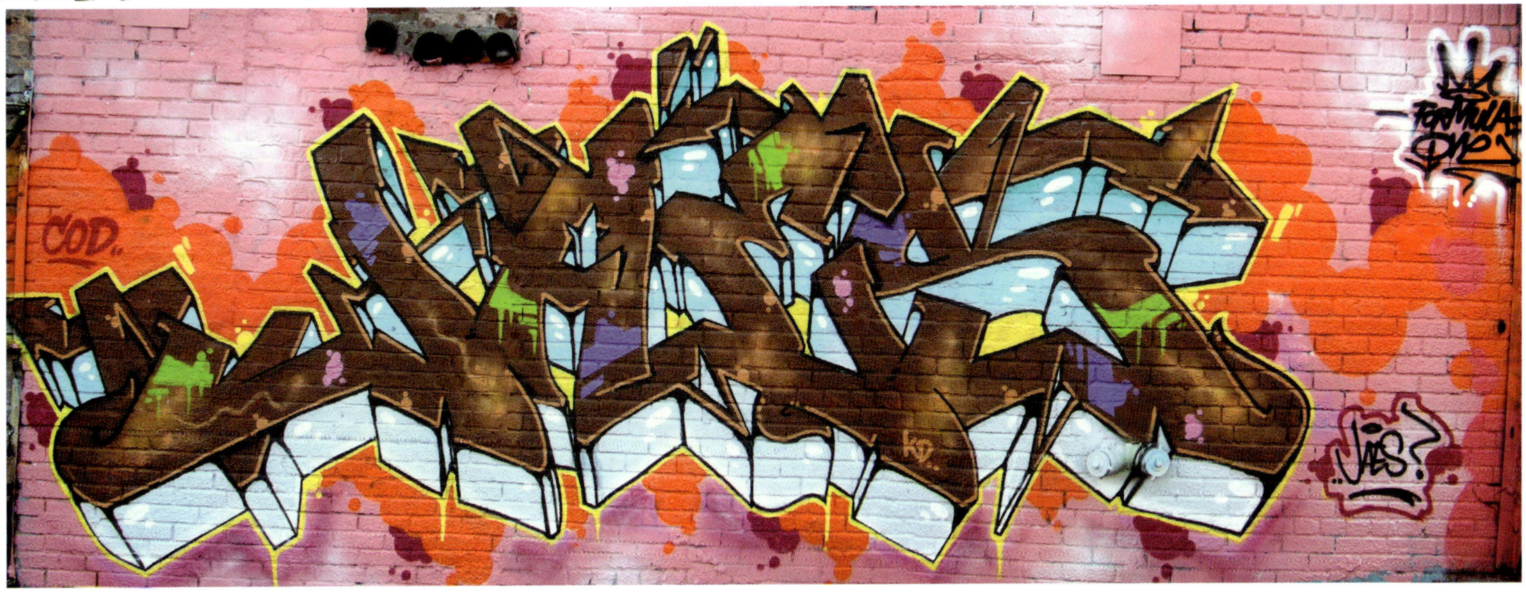


Jaes, Bronx, NY

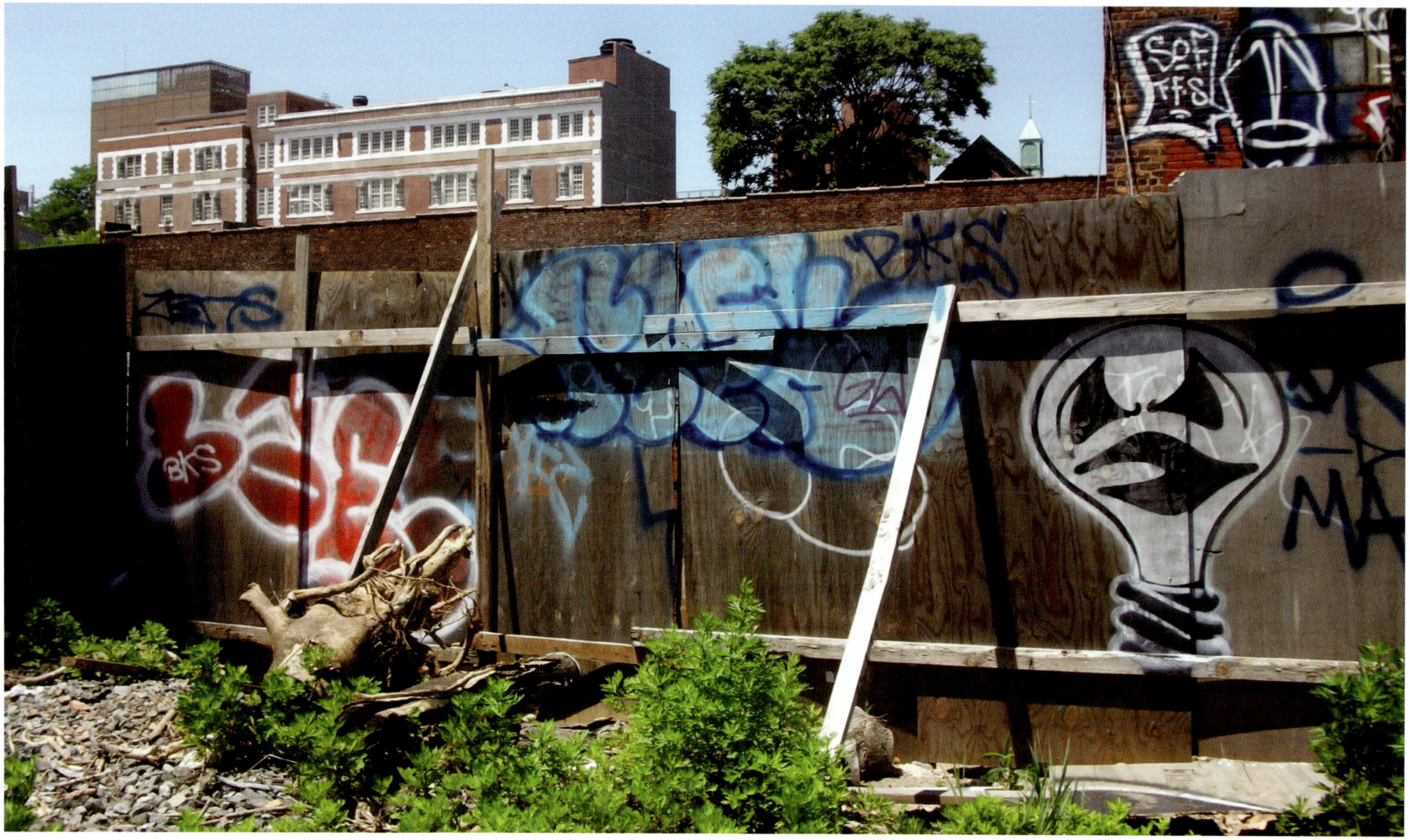

Lae, Reek, Meres, Queens, NY

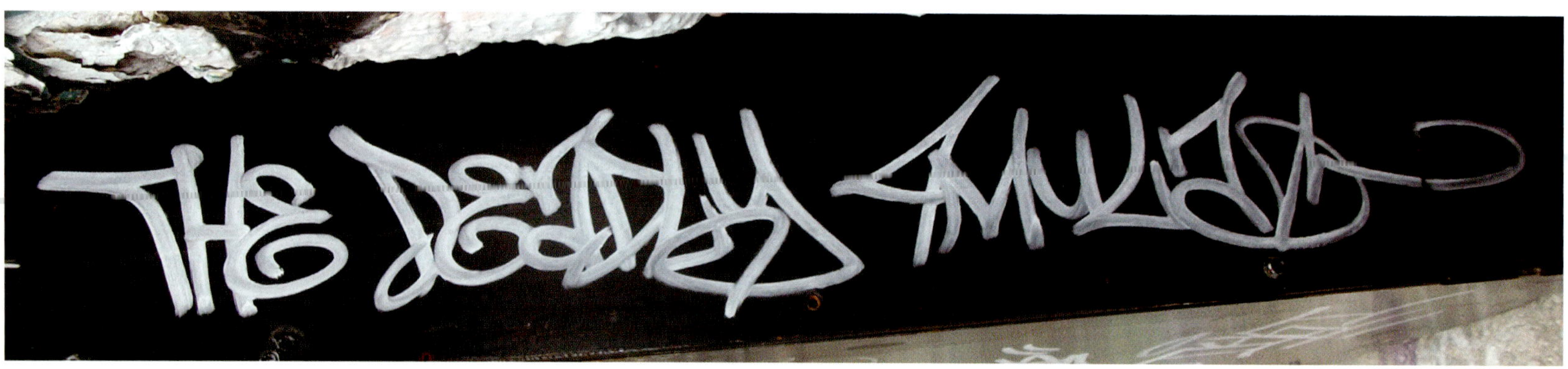

The Deadly 4Mula

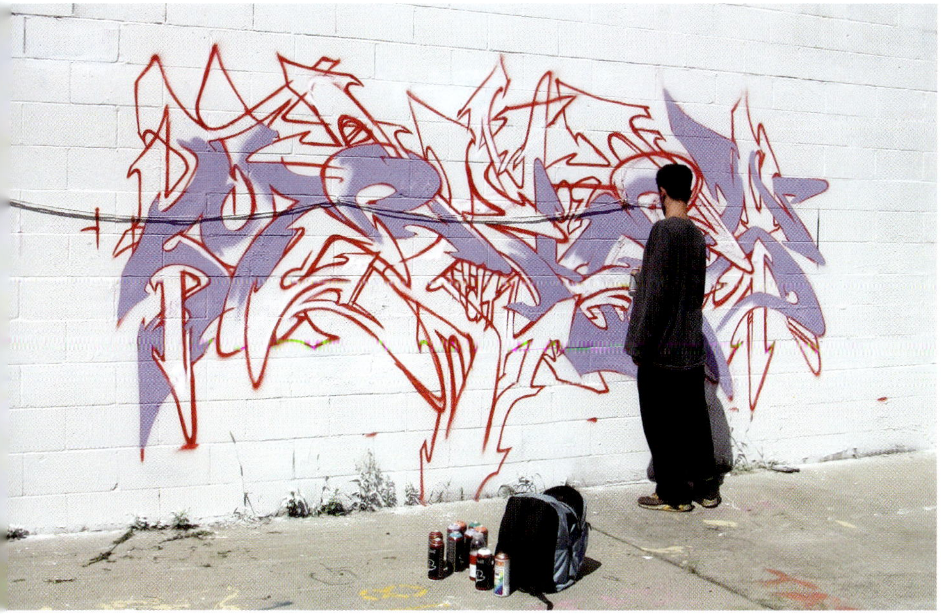

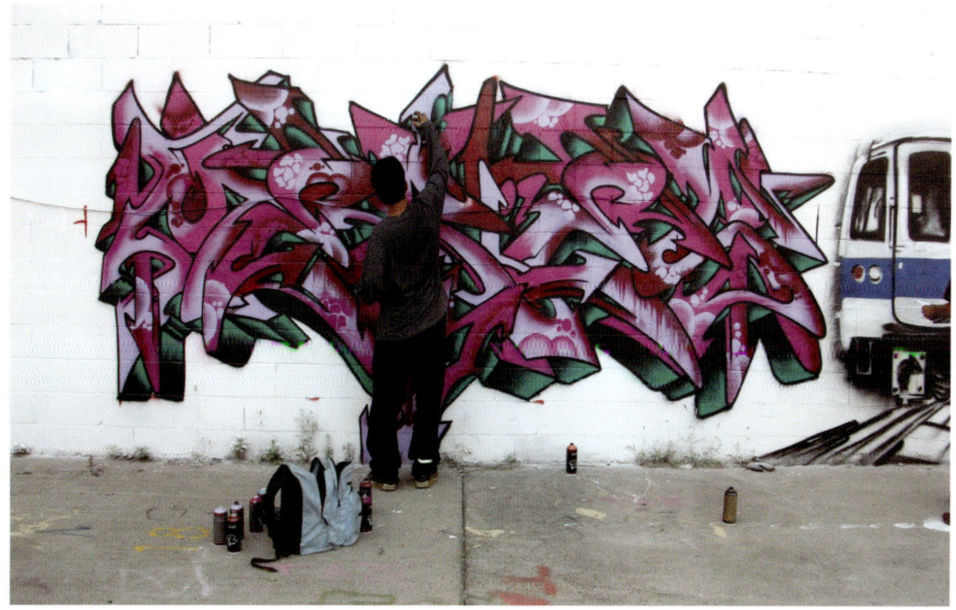

Meres, Brooklyn, NY

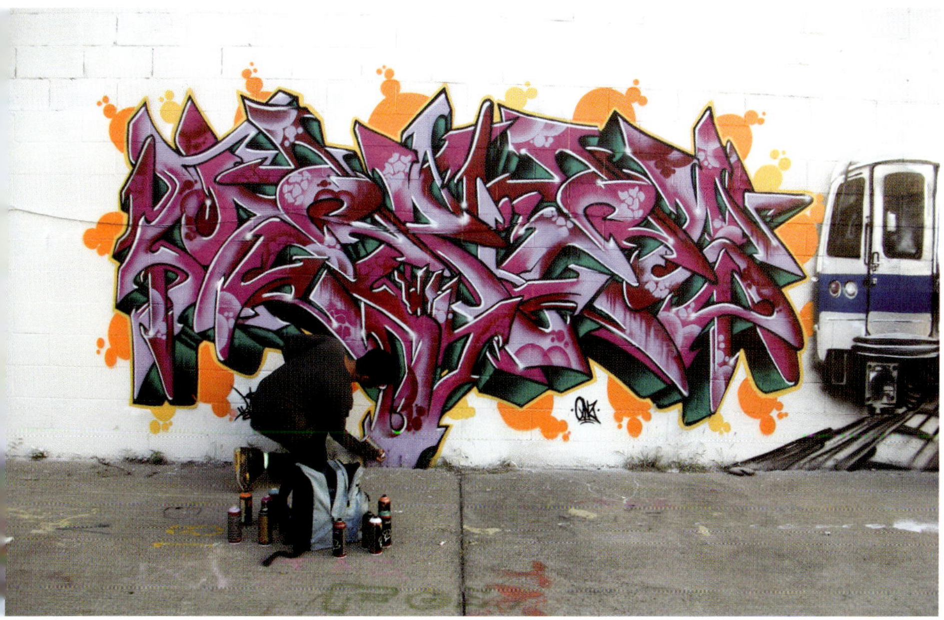

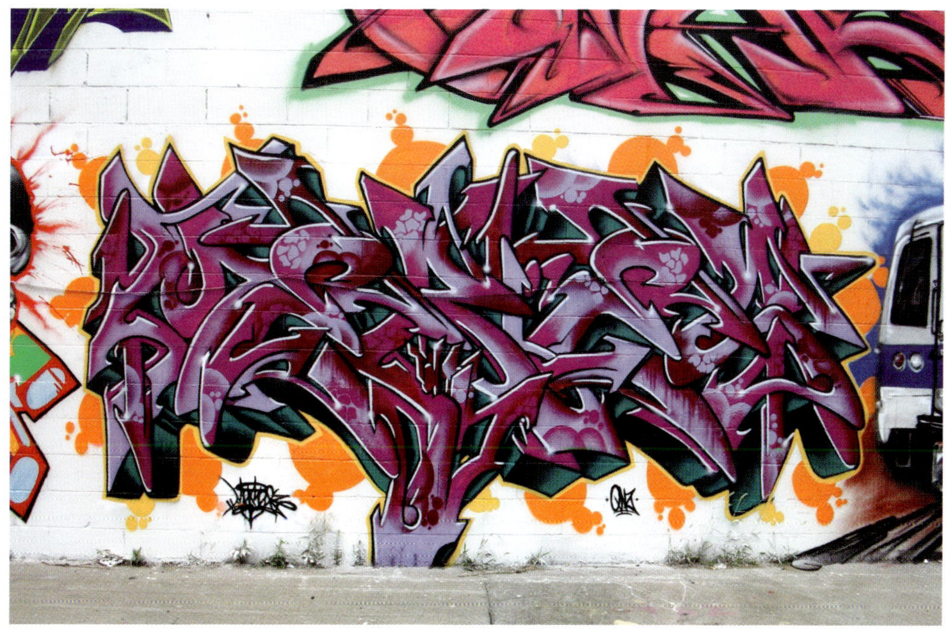

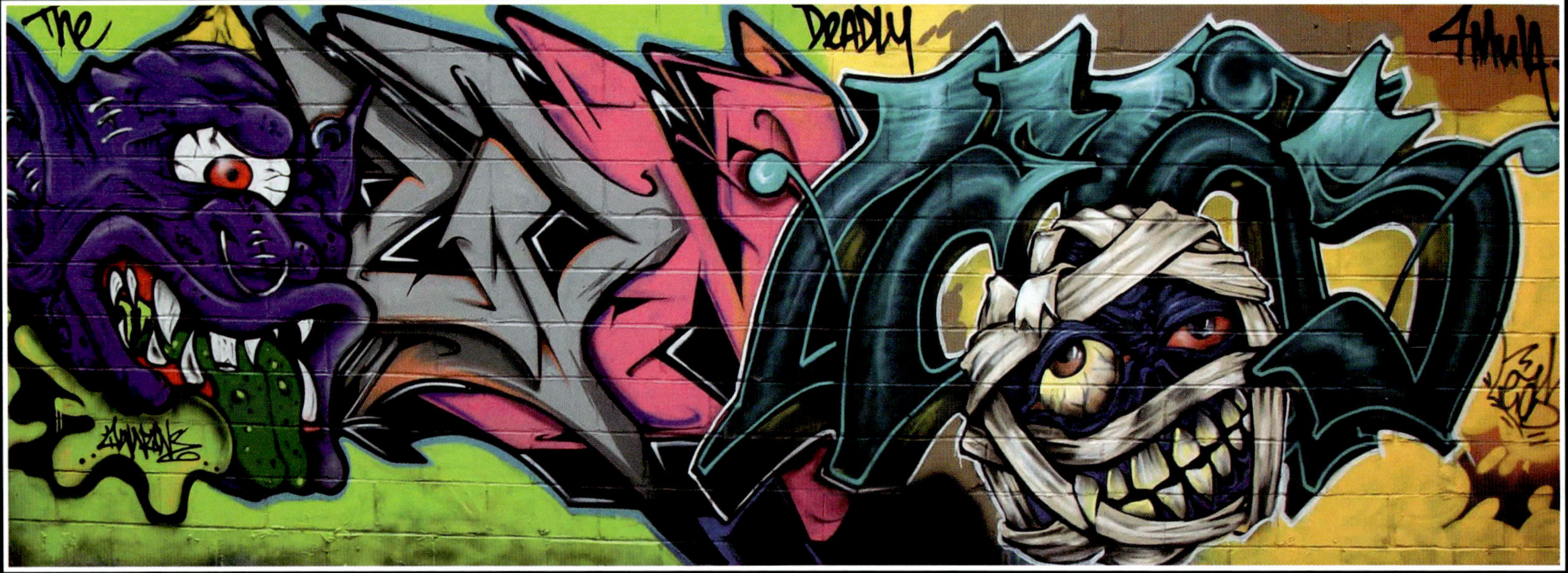


Own, Leia, Queens, NY, 5 Pointz

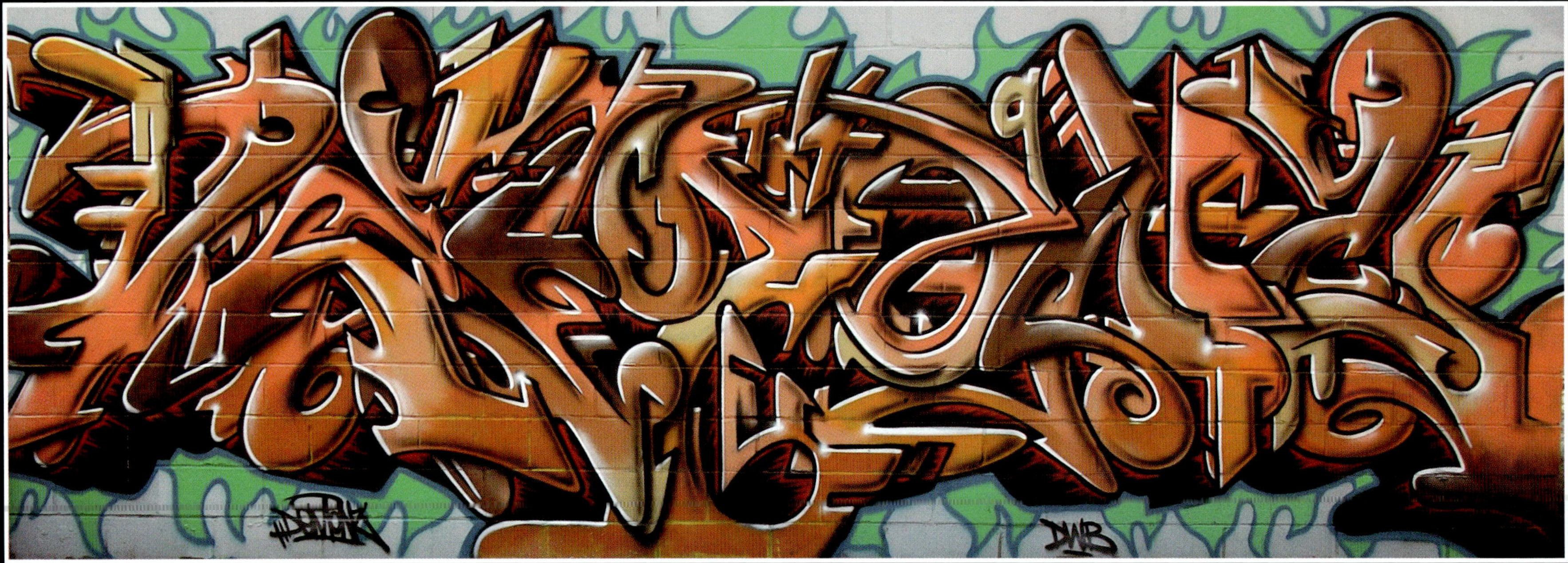

Meres, Queens, NY, 5 Pointz

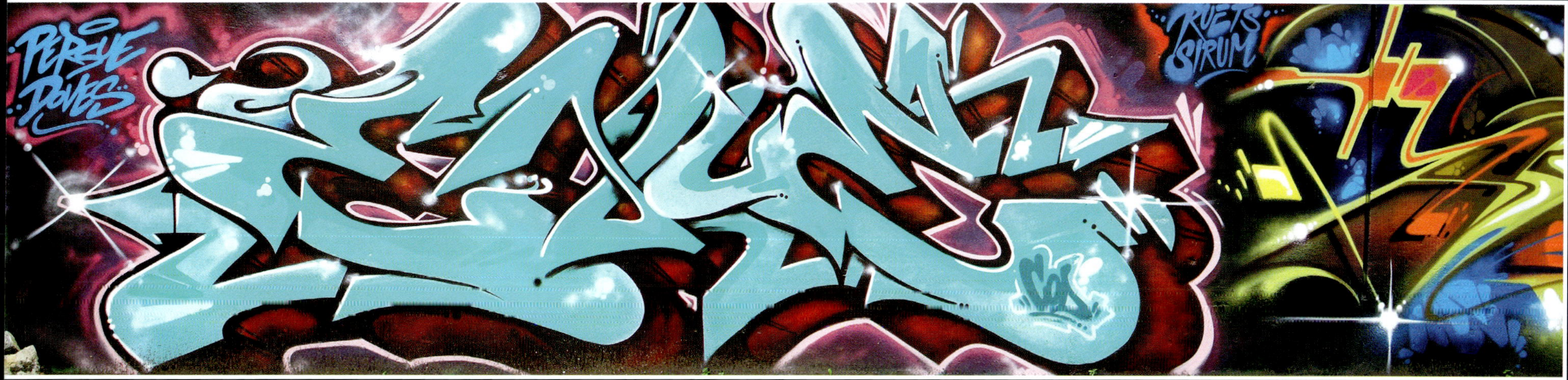

Enue Brooklyn, NY

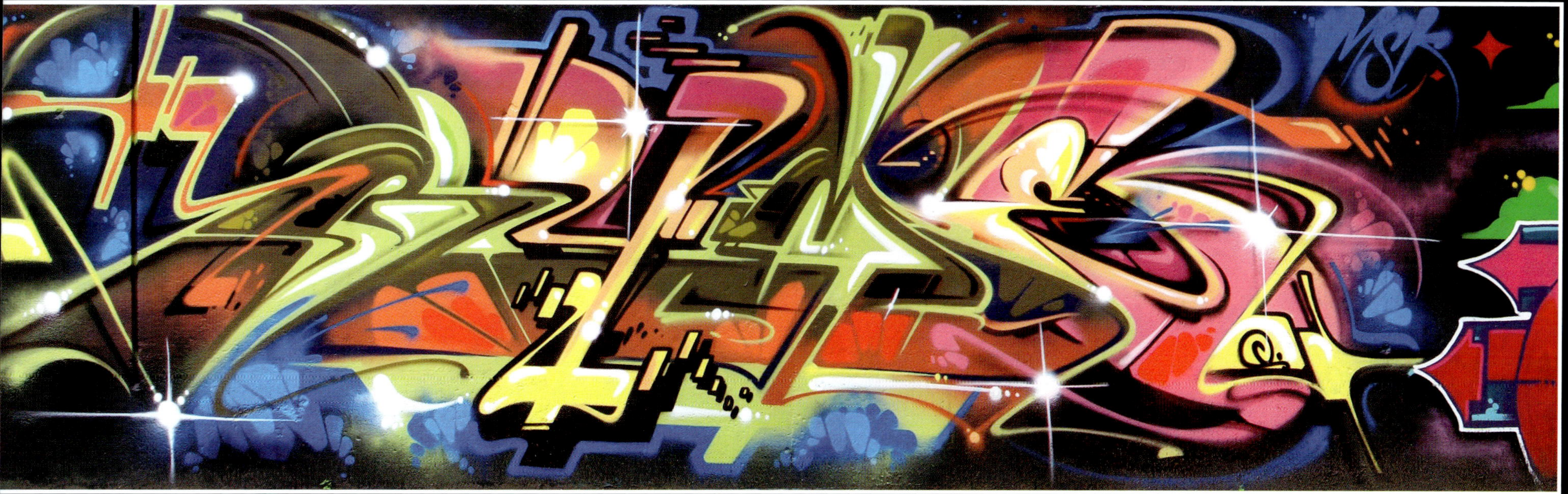

Rime, Brooklyn, NY

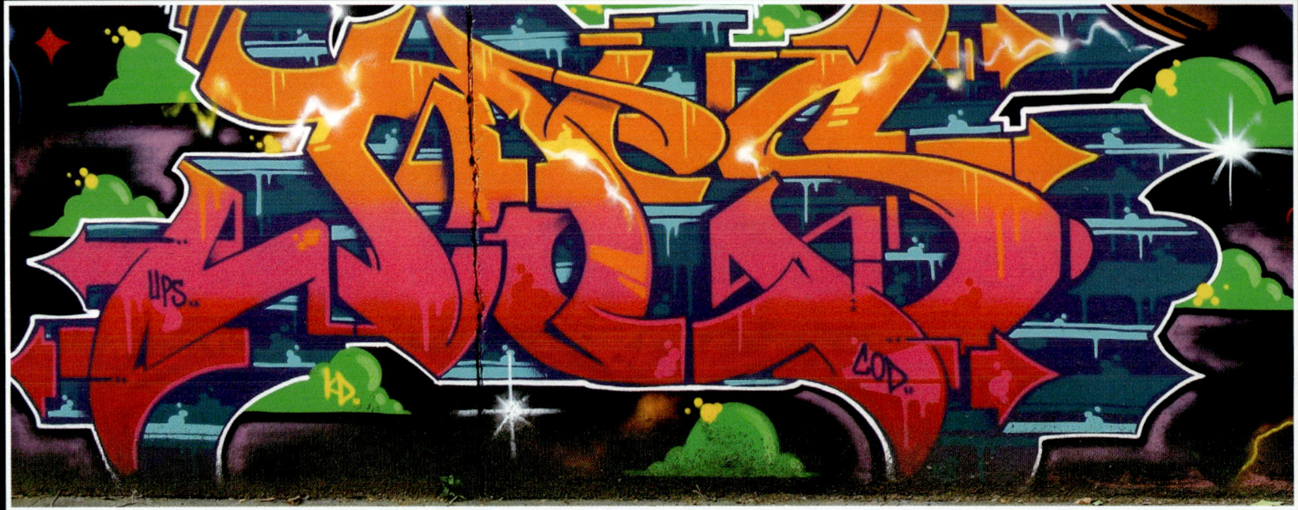

Jaes, Brooklyn, NY

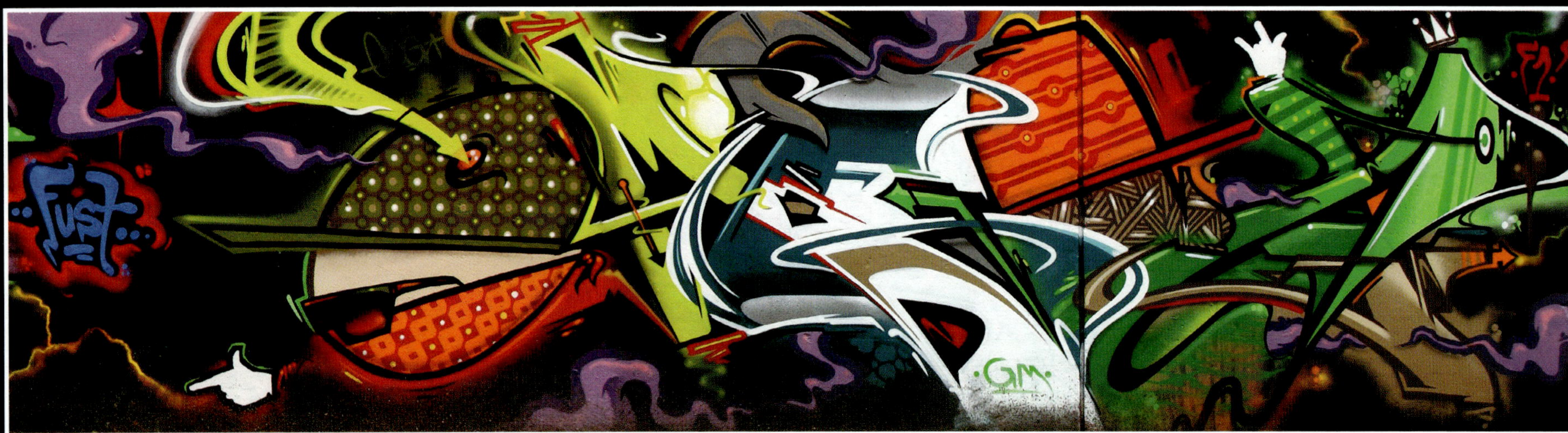

Vans the Omaga, Brooklyn, NY

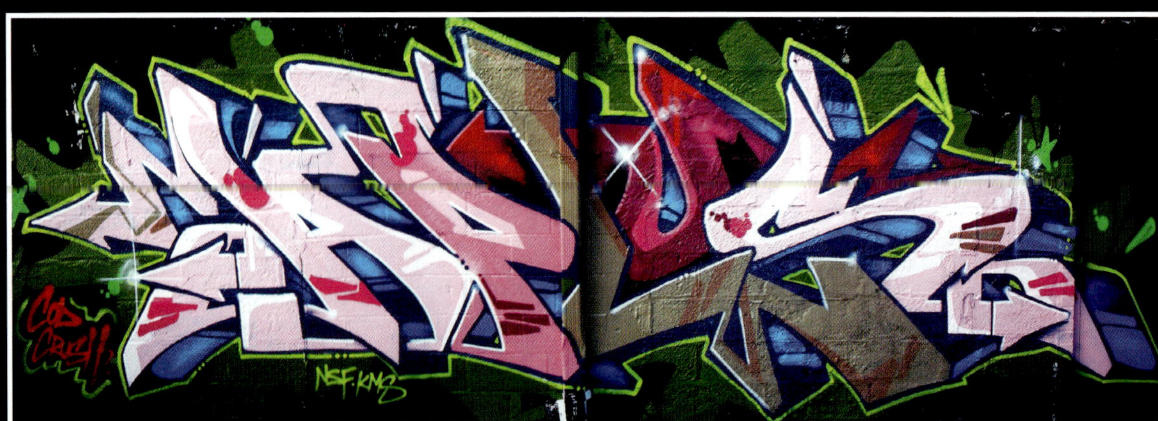

Aplus (Enue), Long Island, NY

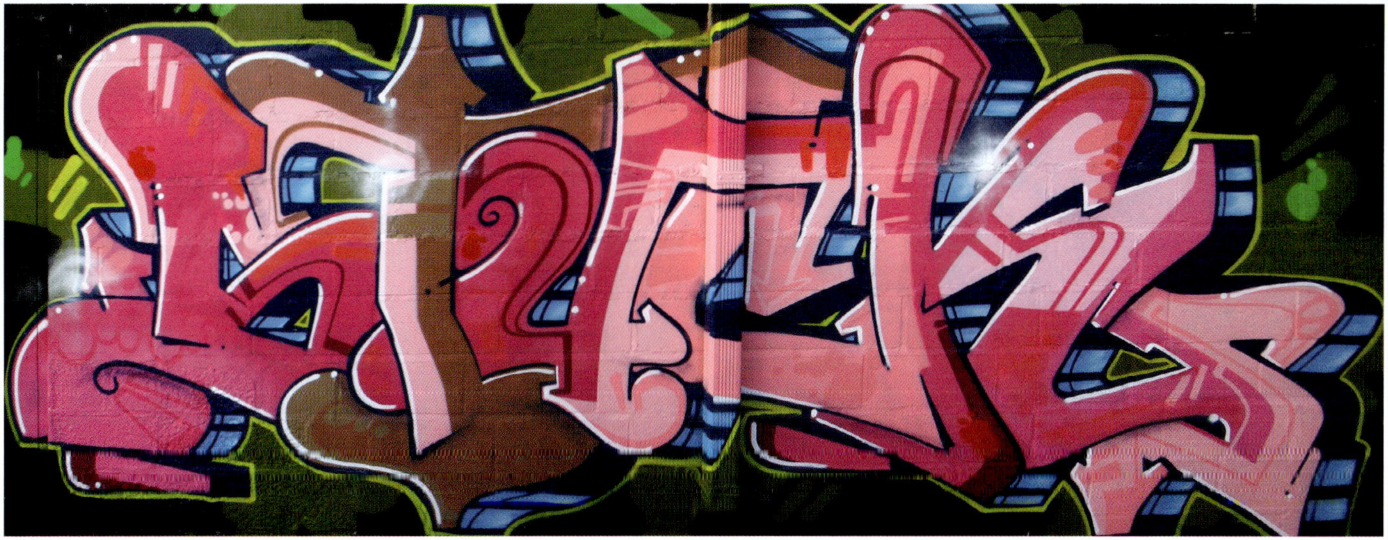

Sluck (Arek), Long Island, NY

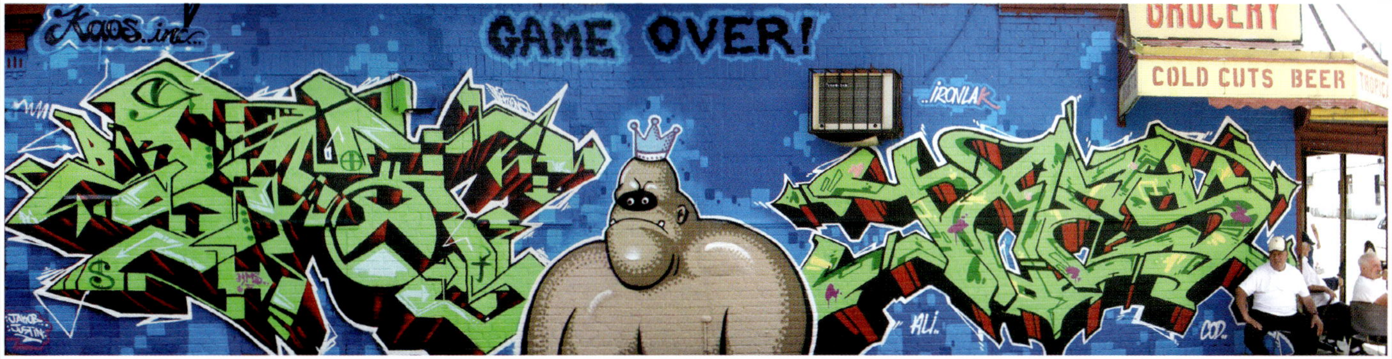


Spot, Jaes, Brooklyn, NY

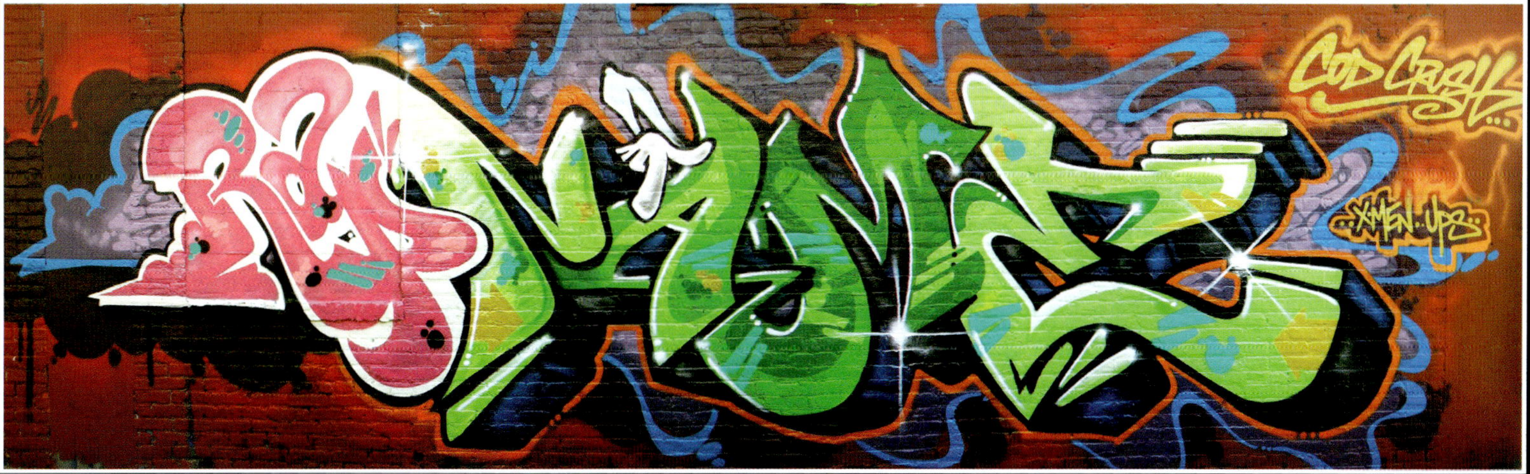

Rap Name (Enue), New Jersey

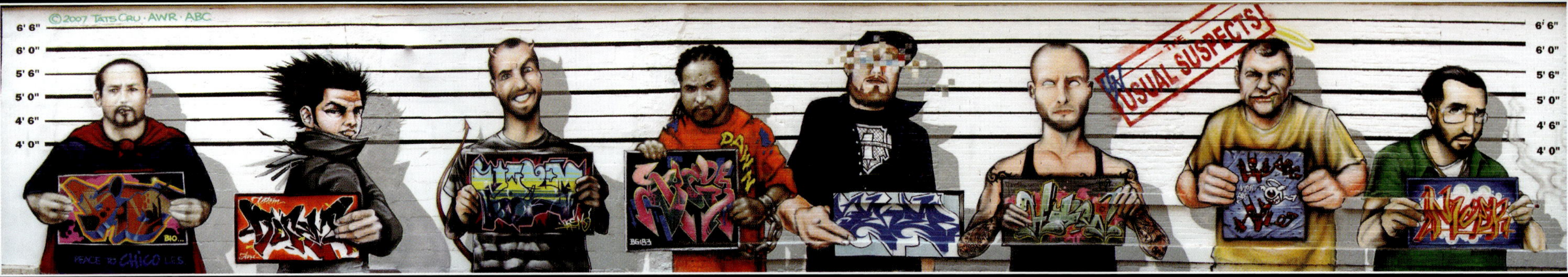


Tats Cru, Manhattan, NY

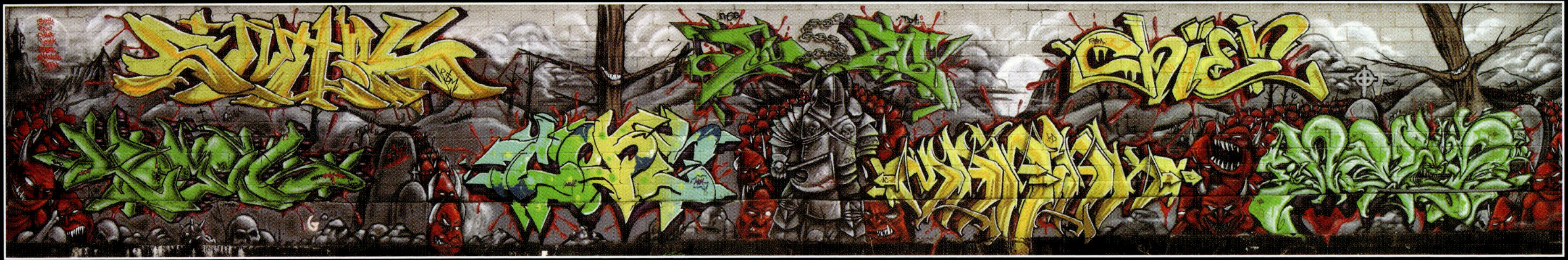

Smik, ESN, Chief, Logek, Cope, Maniak, Deem, Bronx, NY

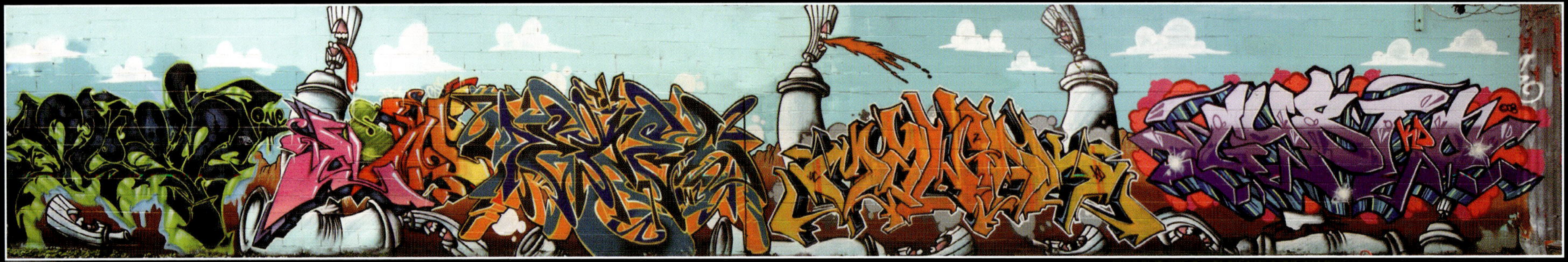

Deem, ESN, Meres, Maniak, Gusto, Bronx, NY

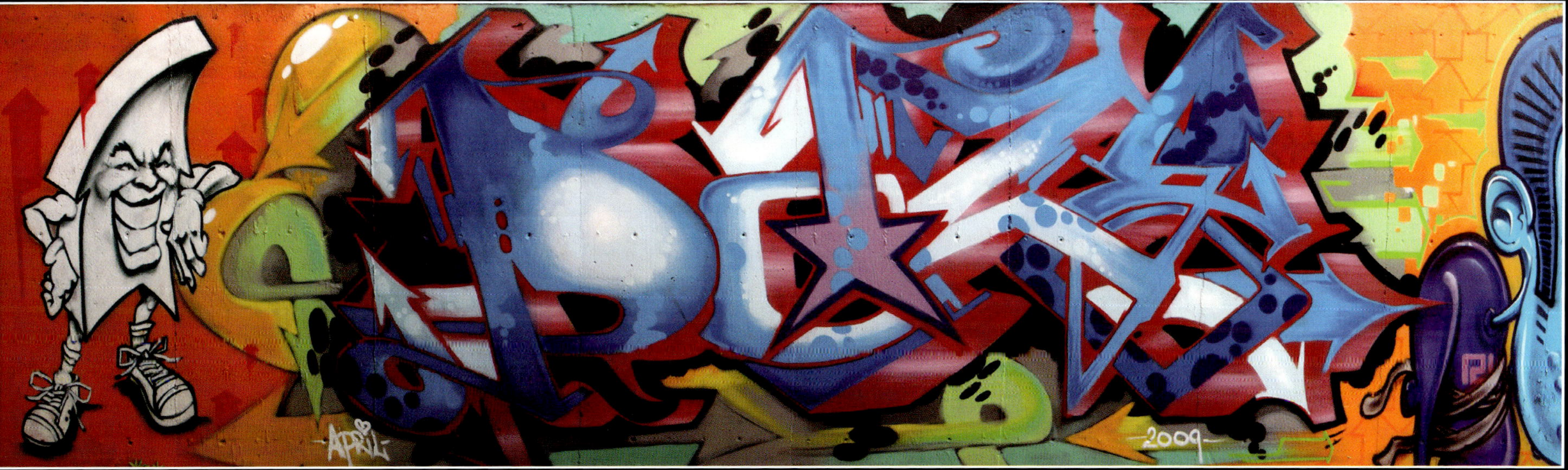


Daze, Bronx, NY

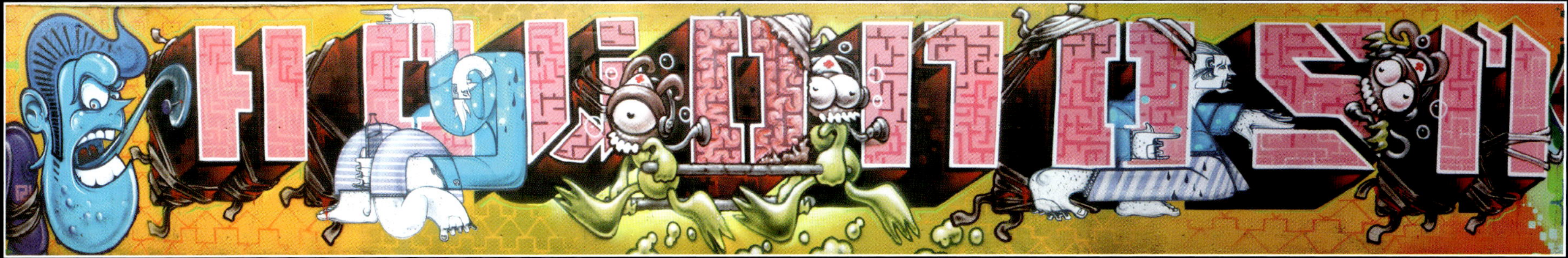

How, Nosm, Bronx, NY

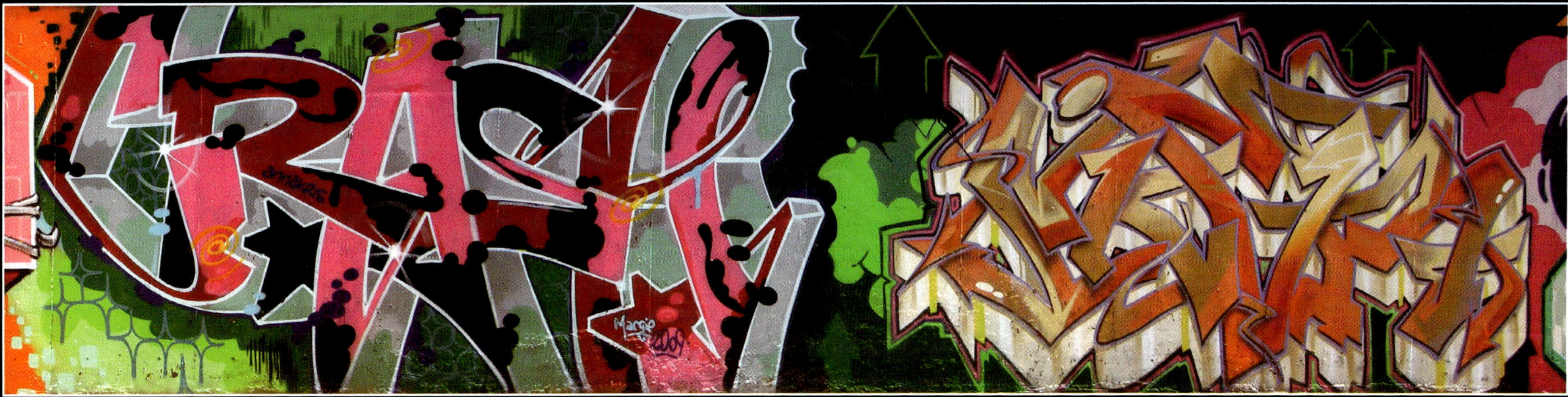

Crash, Nicer, Bronx, NY

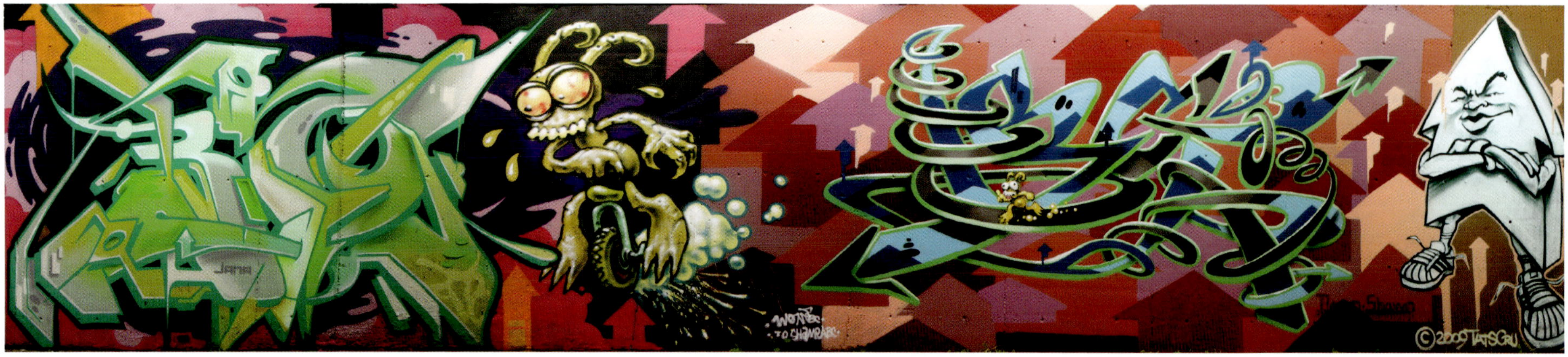

Bio, BG183, Won ABC, Bronx, NY

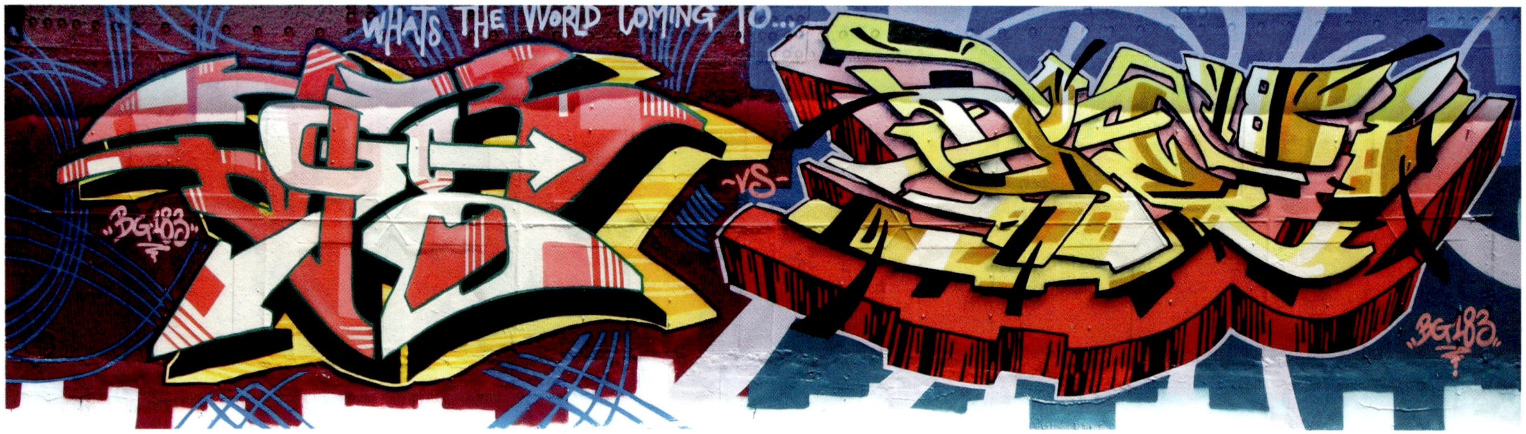


BG183, Bronx, NY

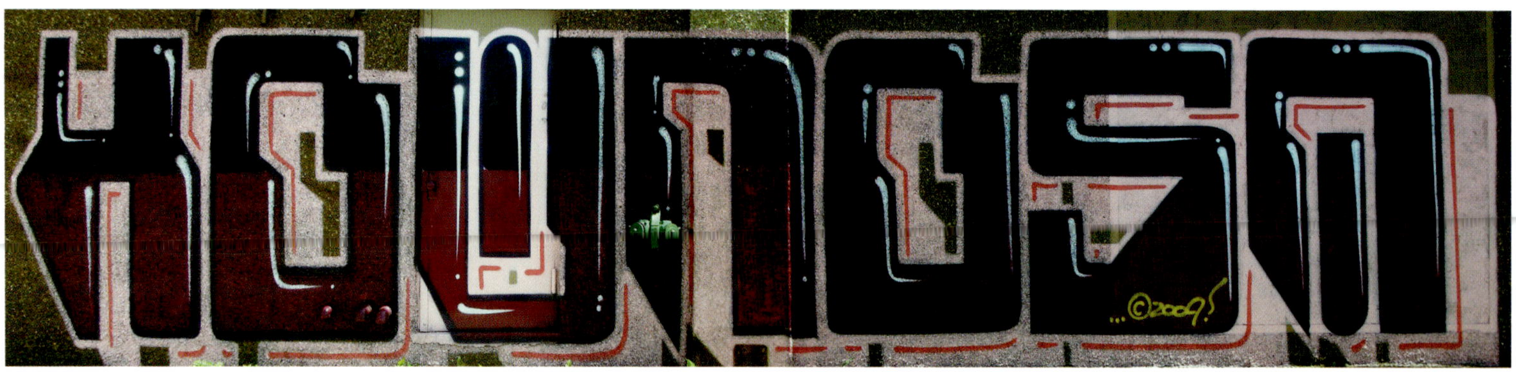

How, Nosm, Bronx, NY

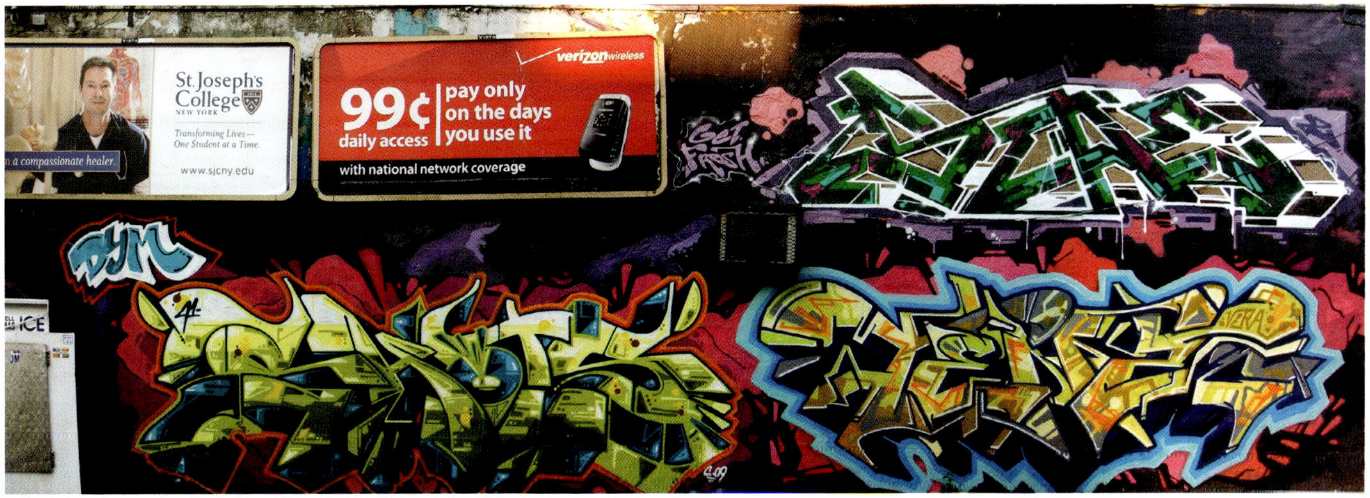


Stae2, Shots, Tenz, Brooklyn, NY

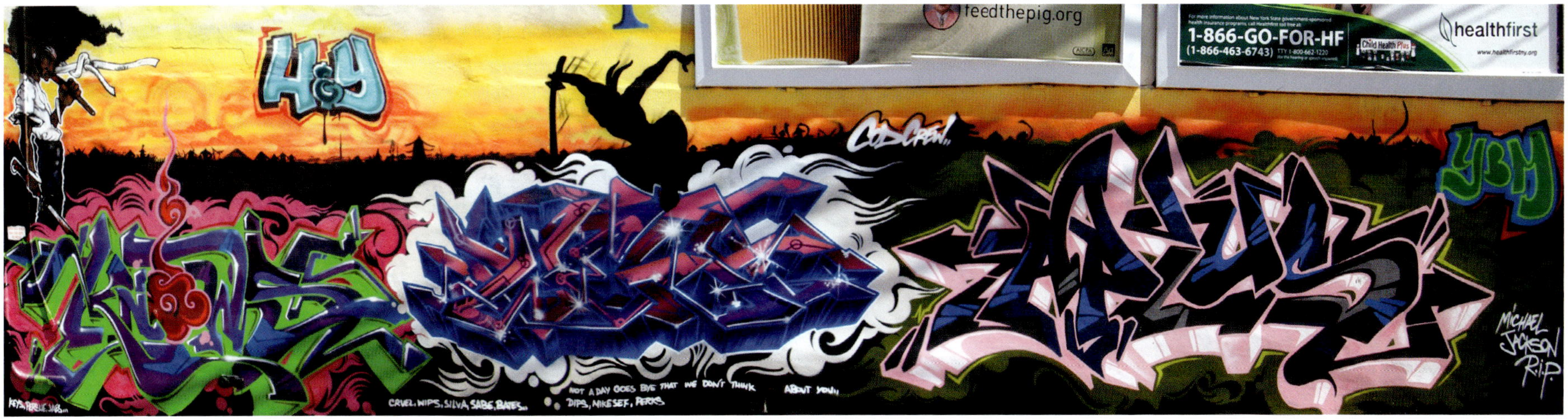


Knows, Wen, Aplus, Bronx, NY

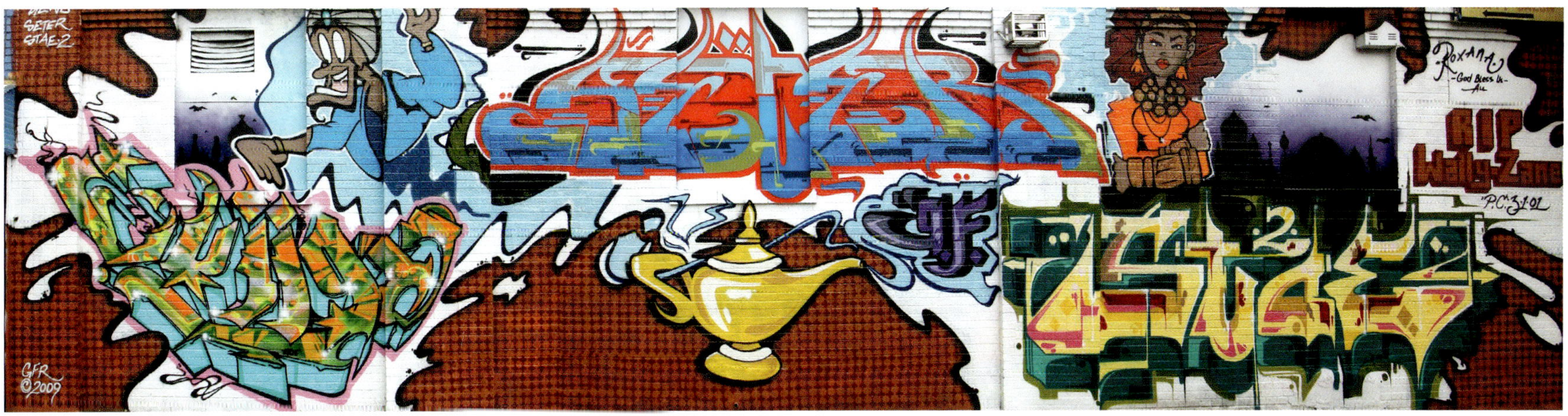


Uend, Seter, Stae2, Queens, NY

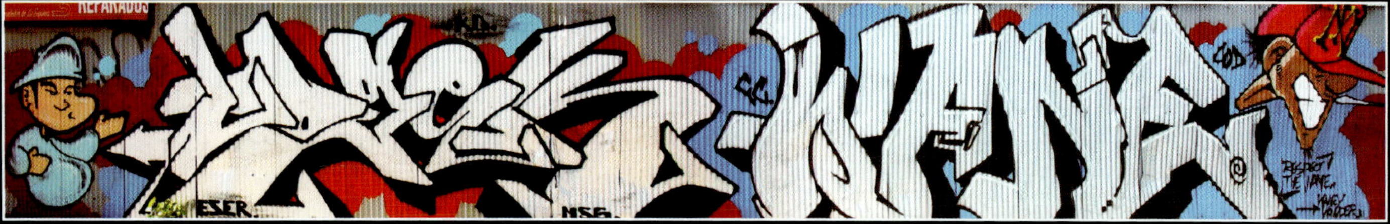

Logek, Wane, Bronx, NY

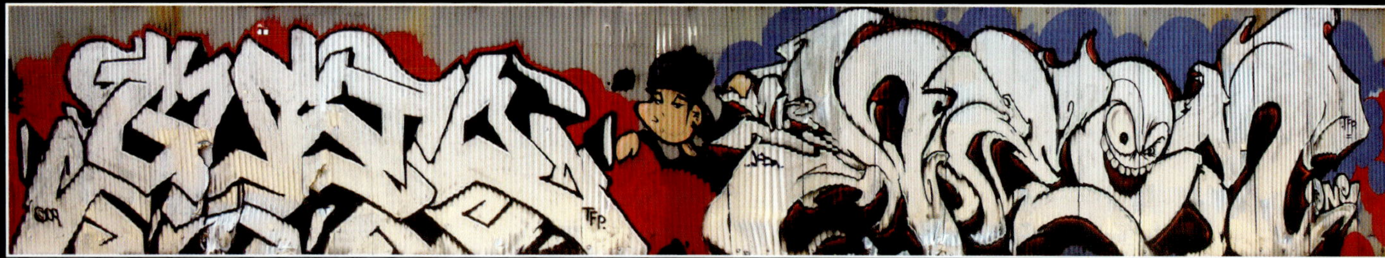

Gusto, Deem, Bronx, NY

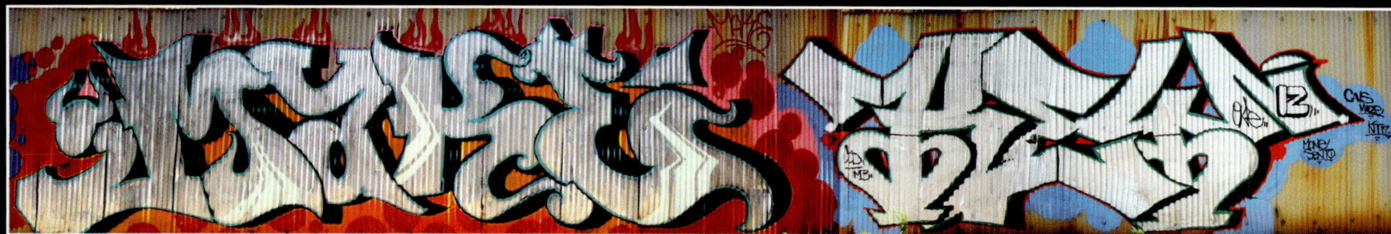

Make, Key, Bronx, NY

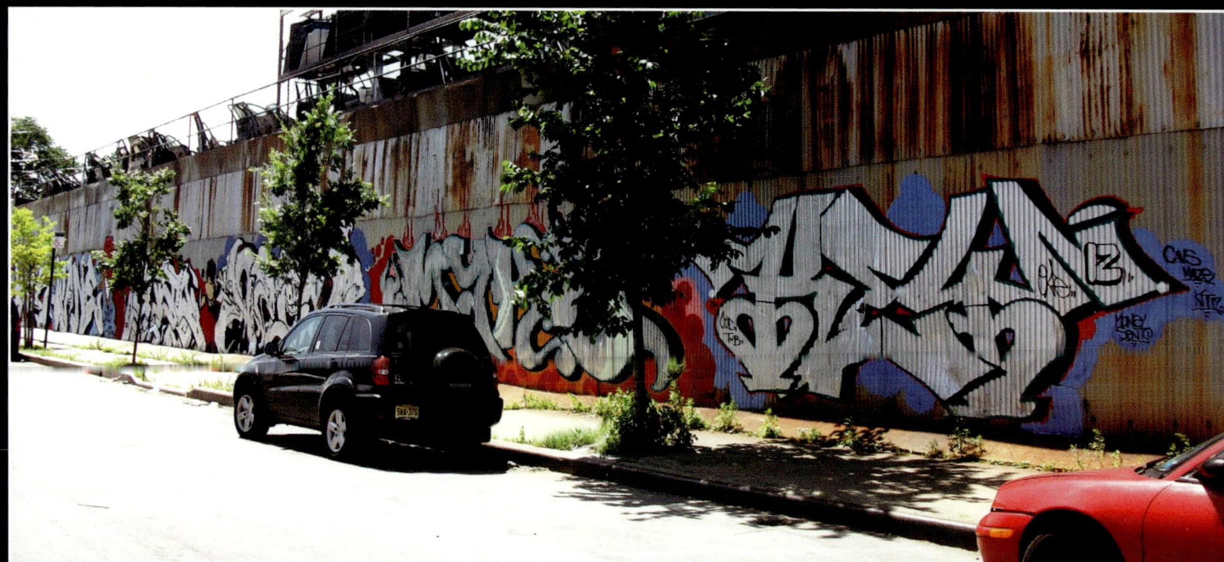

Hunts Point, The Bronx

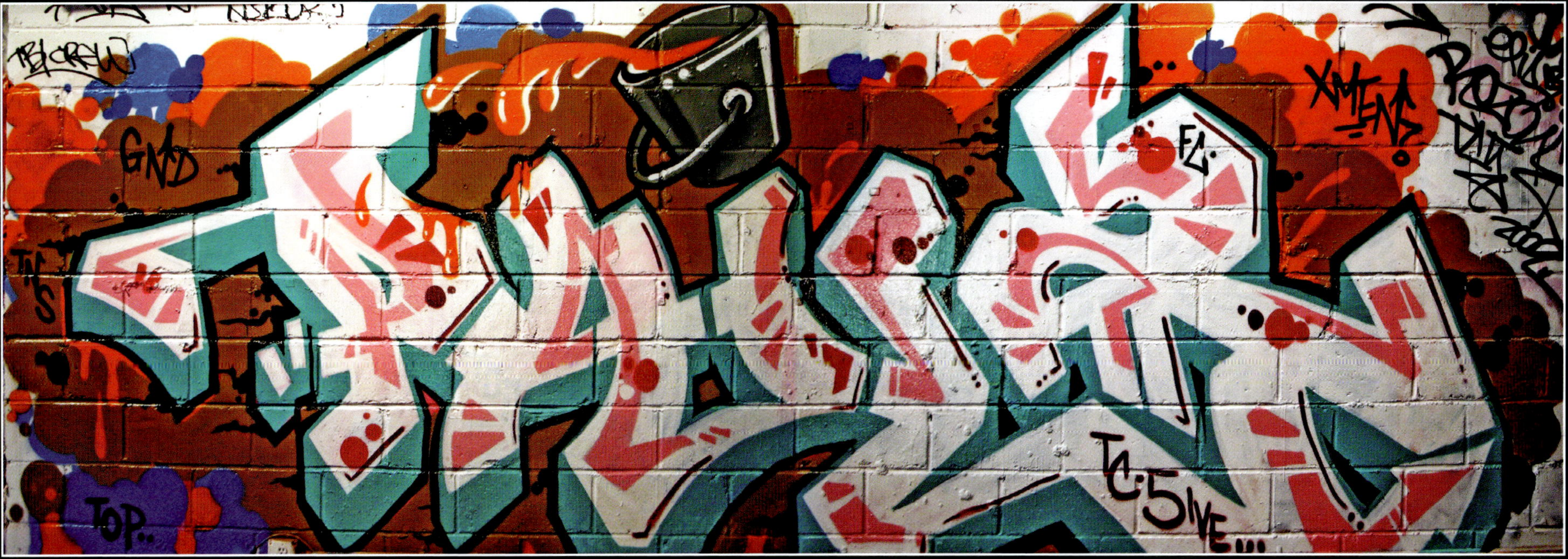

Pail2 (Keo), Brooklyn, NY

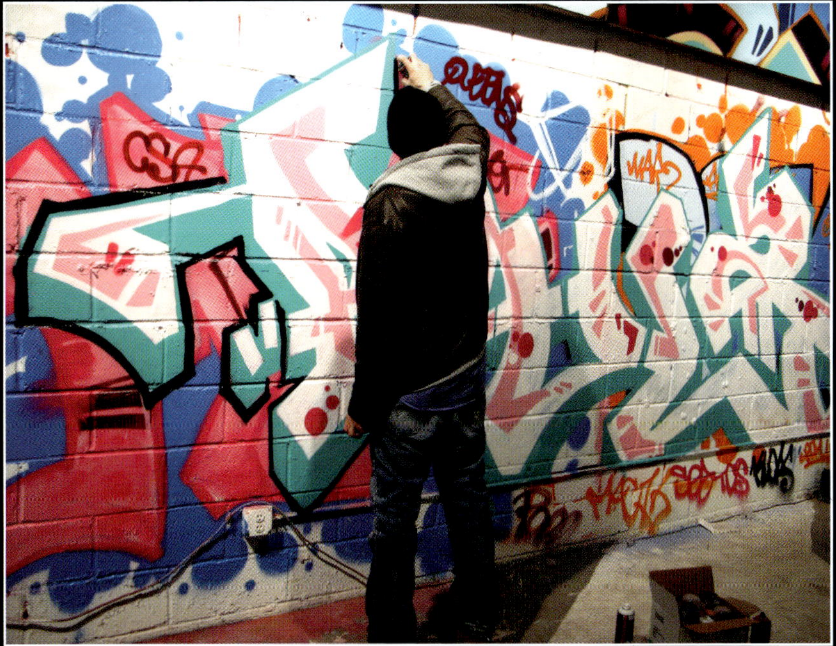

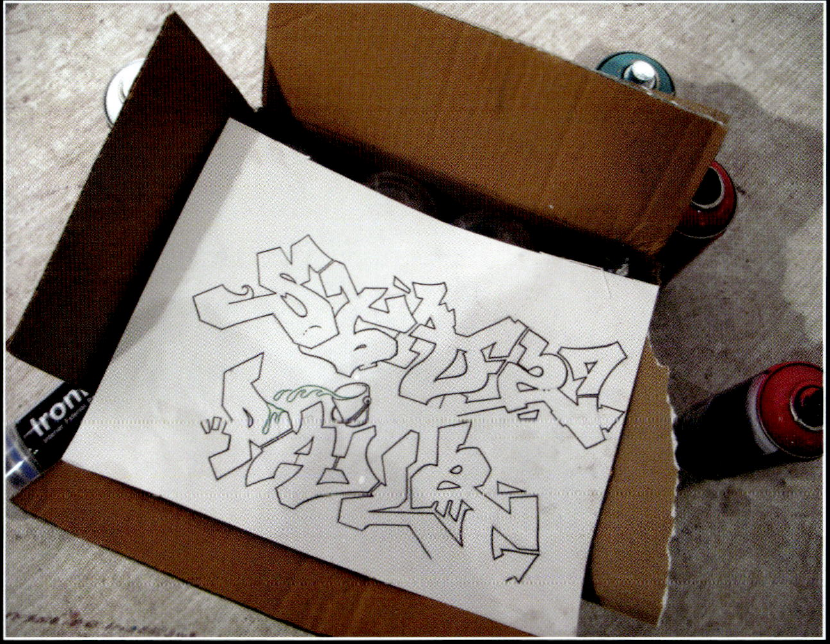

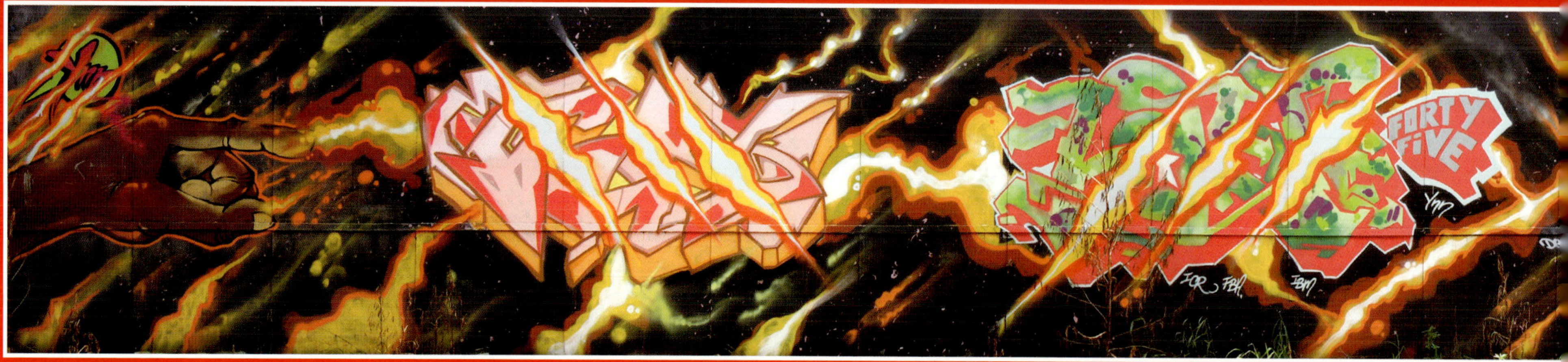


YNN Crew, Brooklyn, NY

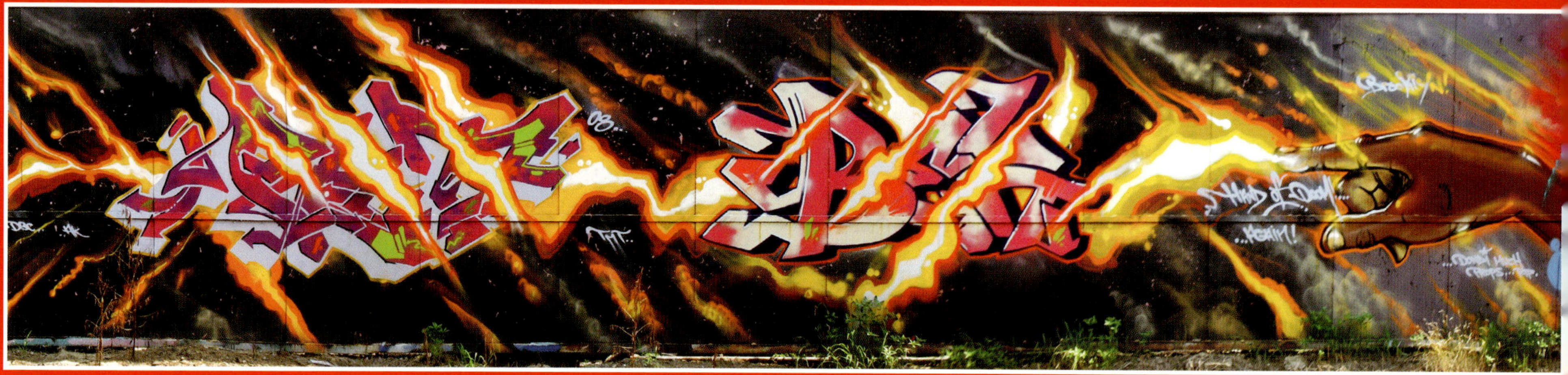

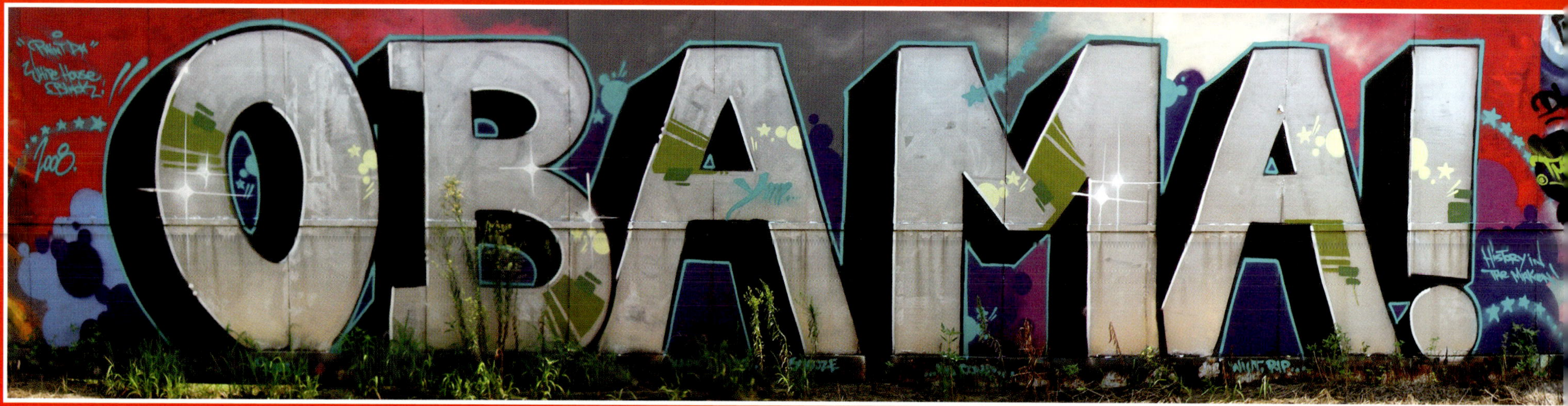

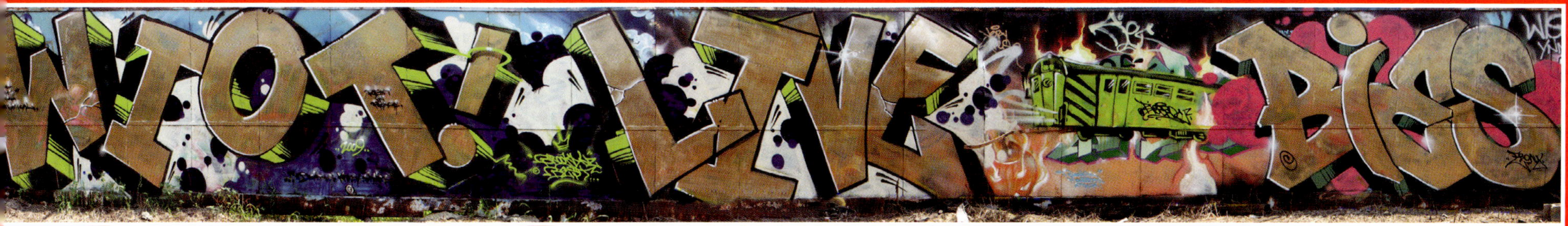

YNN Crew, Brooklyn, NY

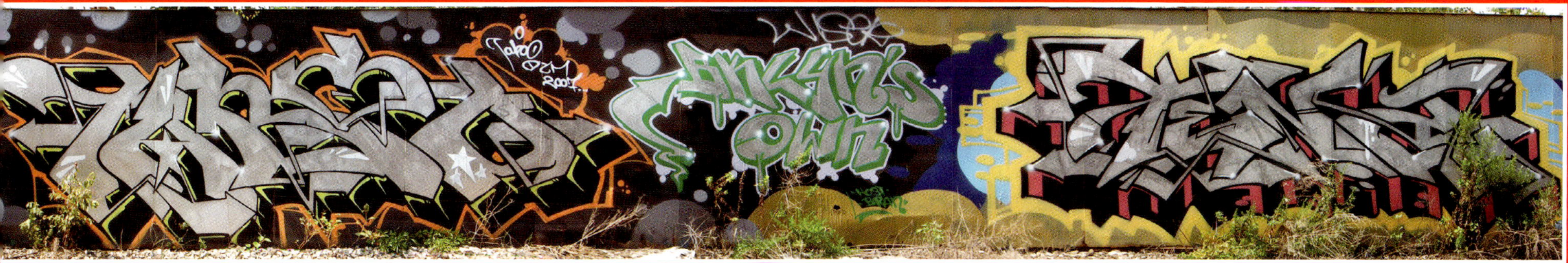

Taboo, Tenz, Brooklyn, NY

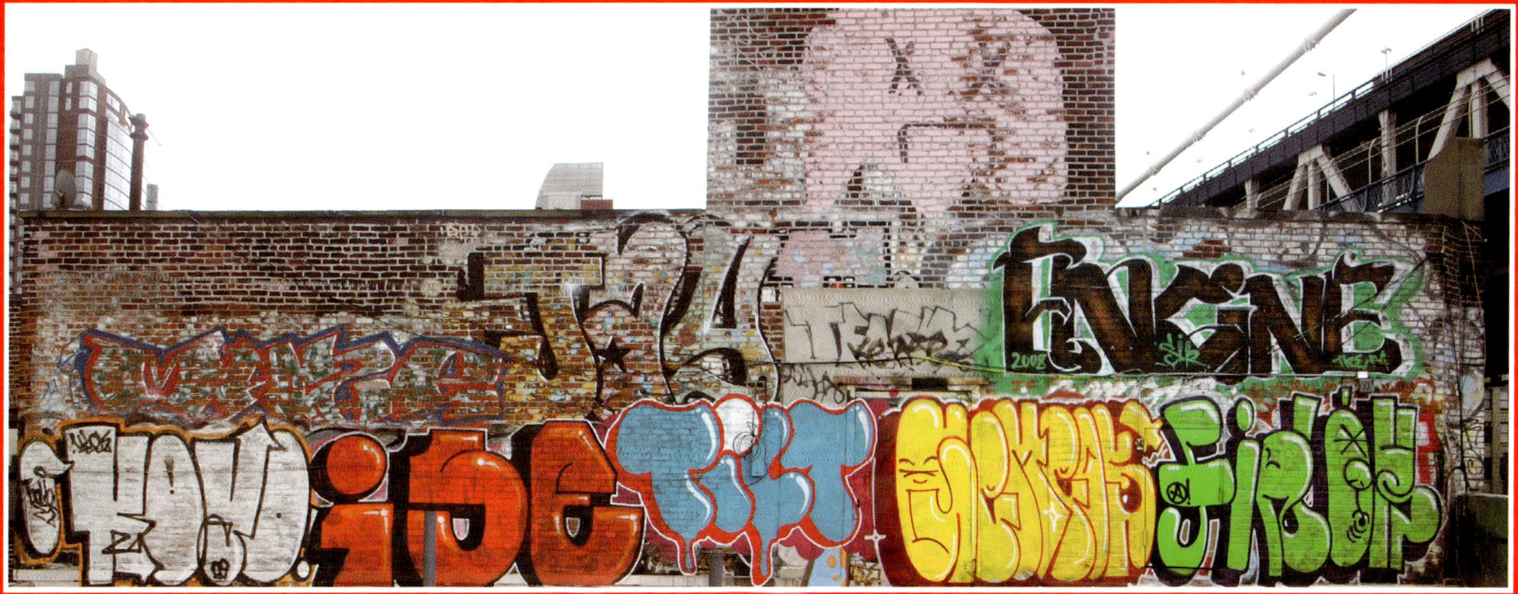

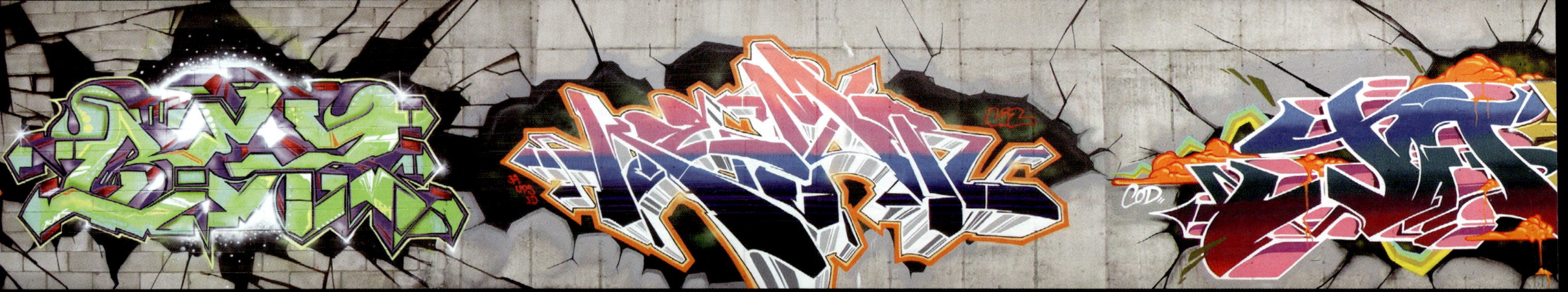

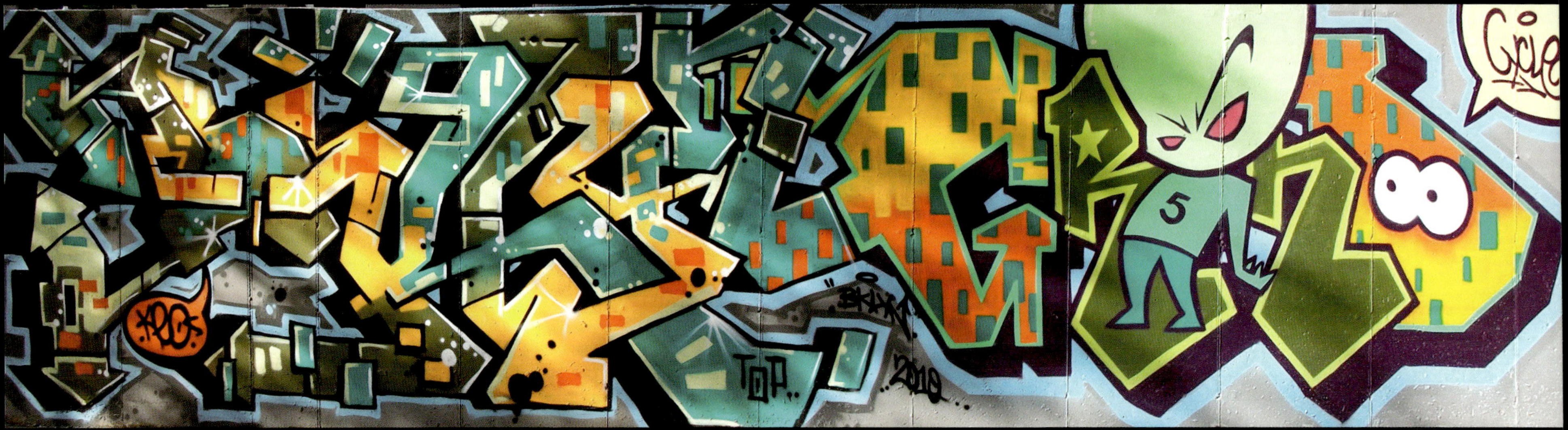
TOP.
2010

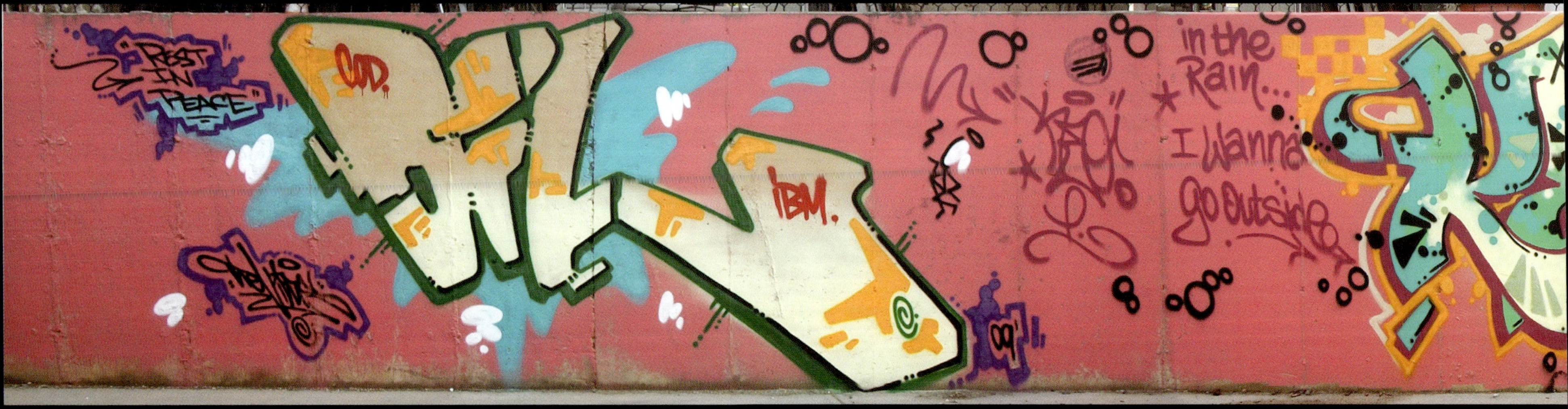
REST IN PEACE
COD.
IBM.
in the Rain...
I wanna go outside

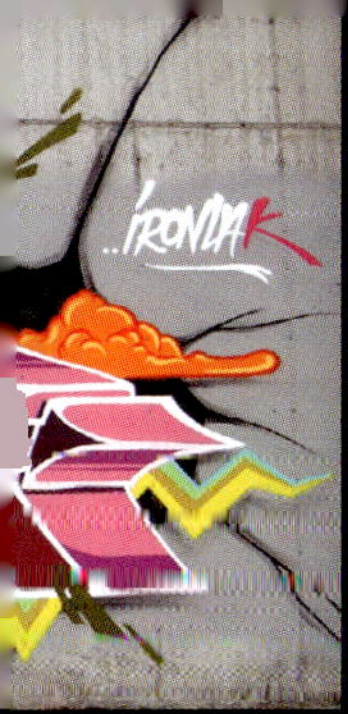

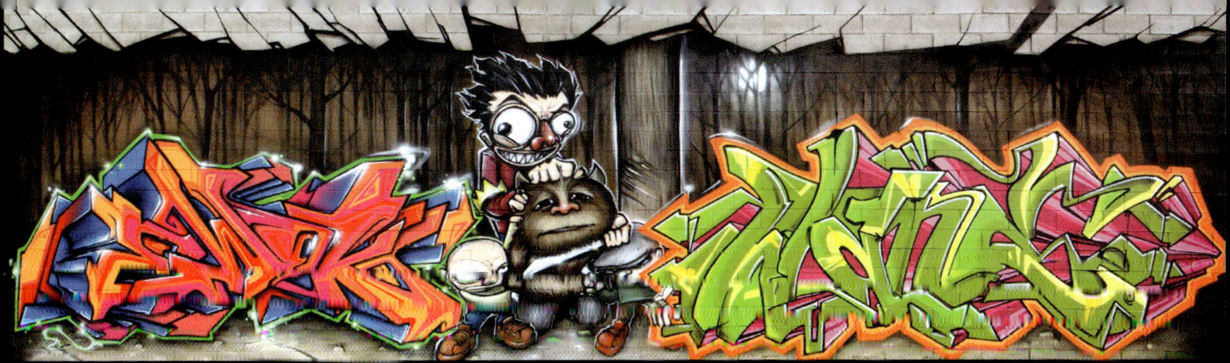

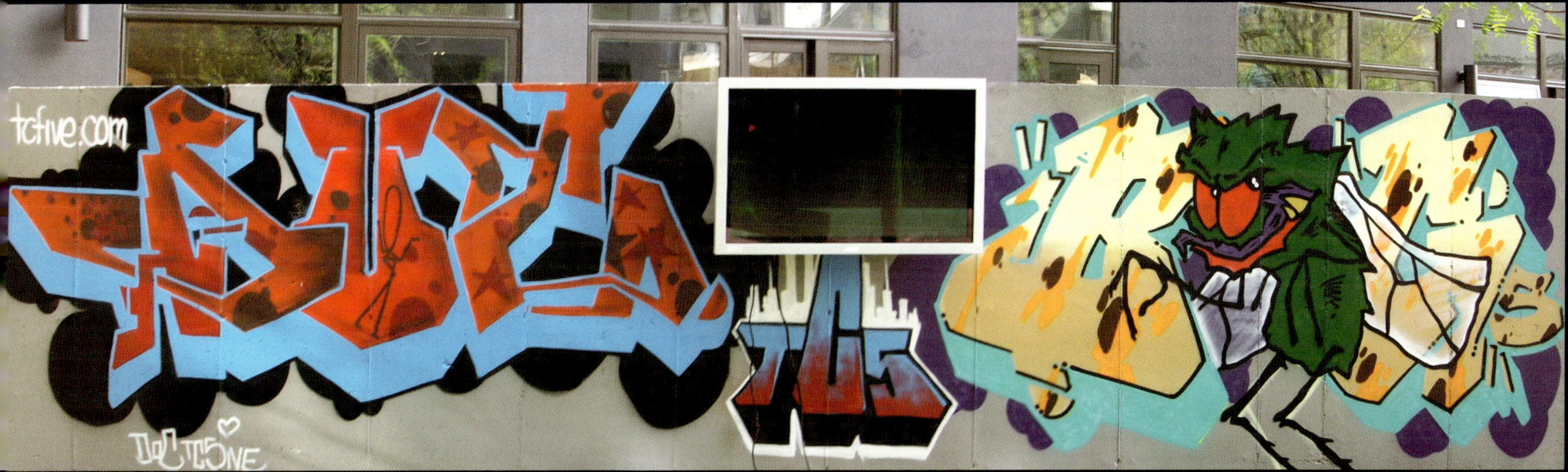
tcfive.com

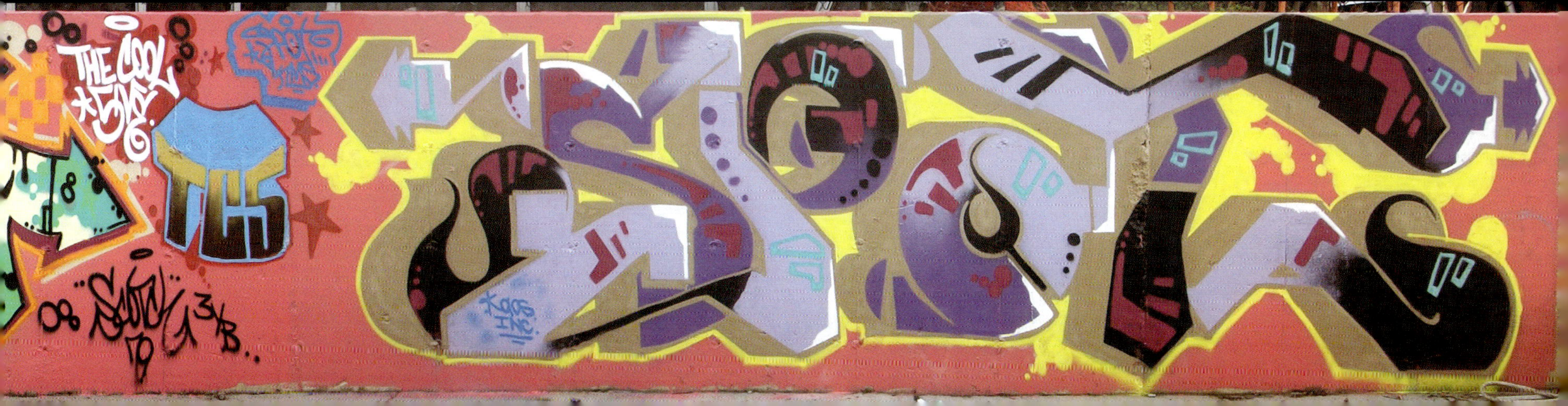
THE COOL

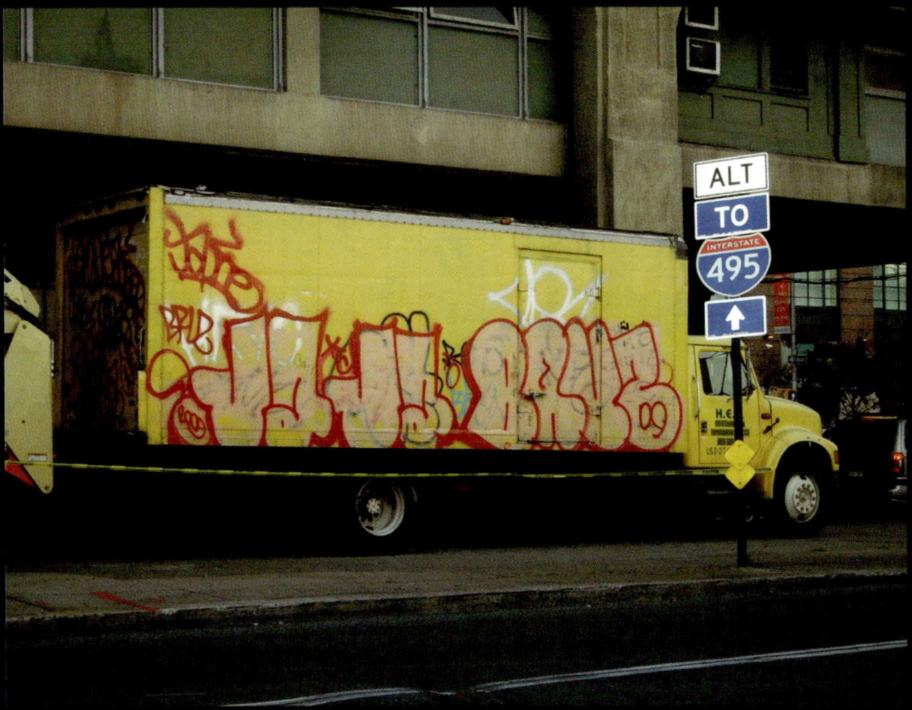
ALT
TO
INTERSTATE
495
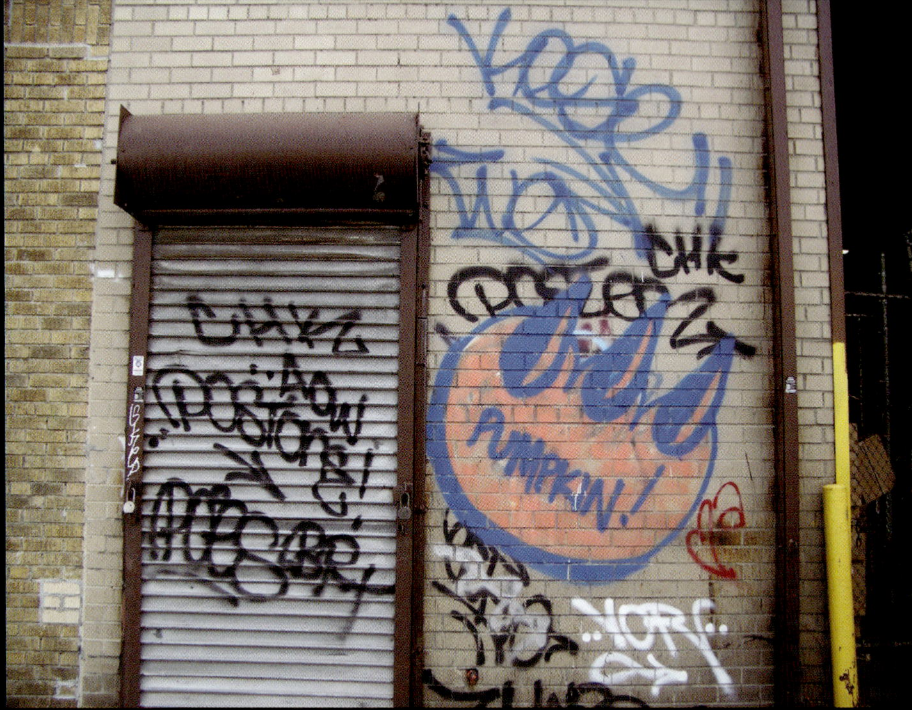
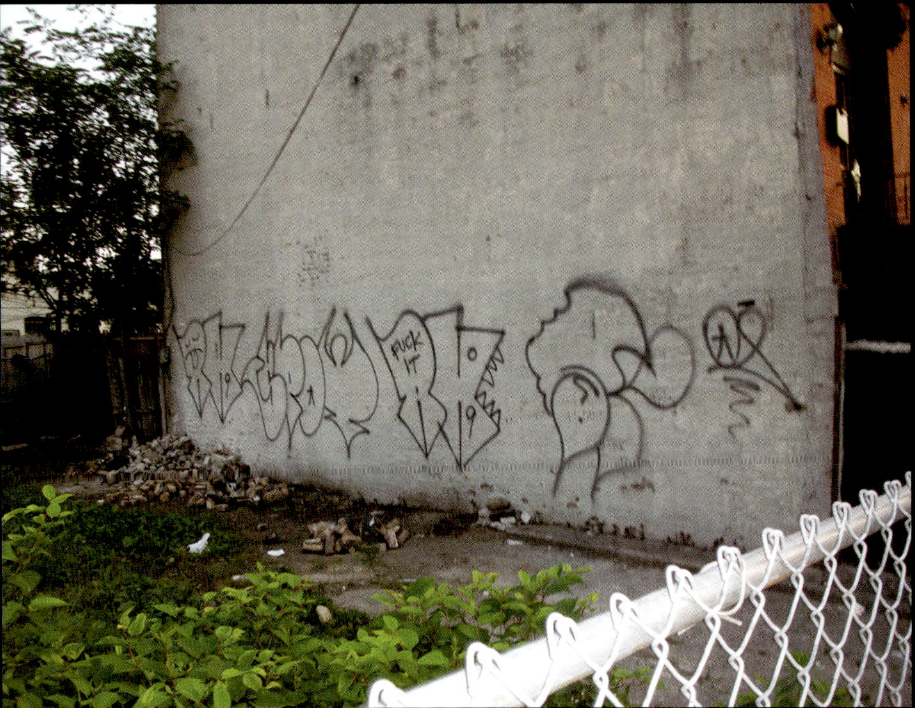
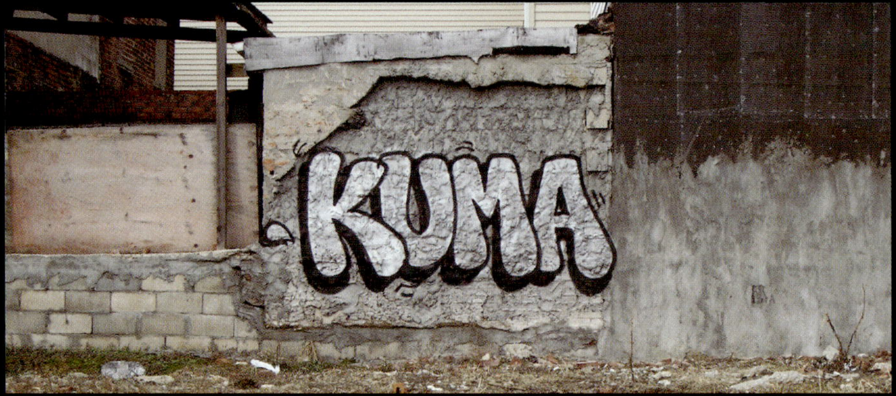
KUMA
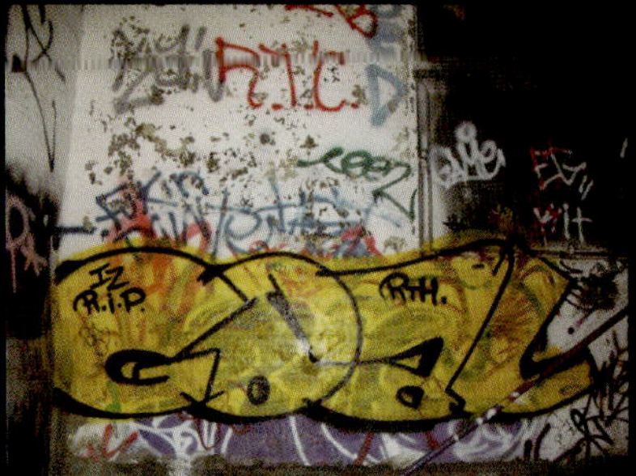
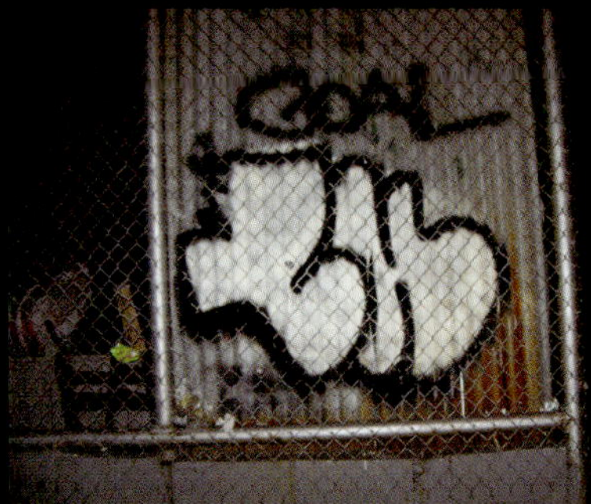

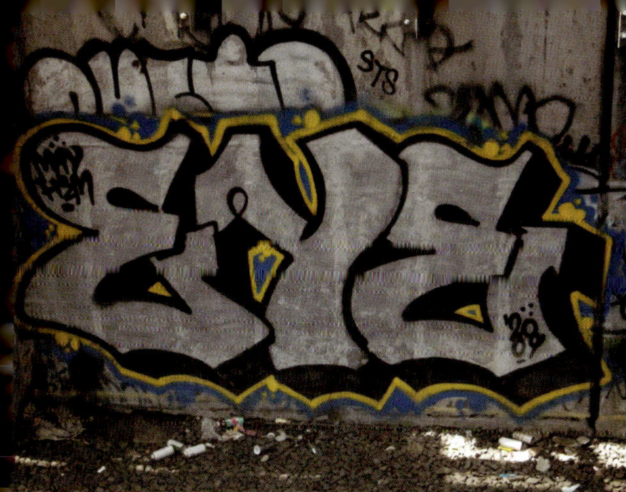

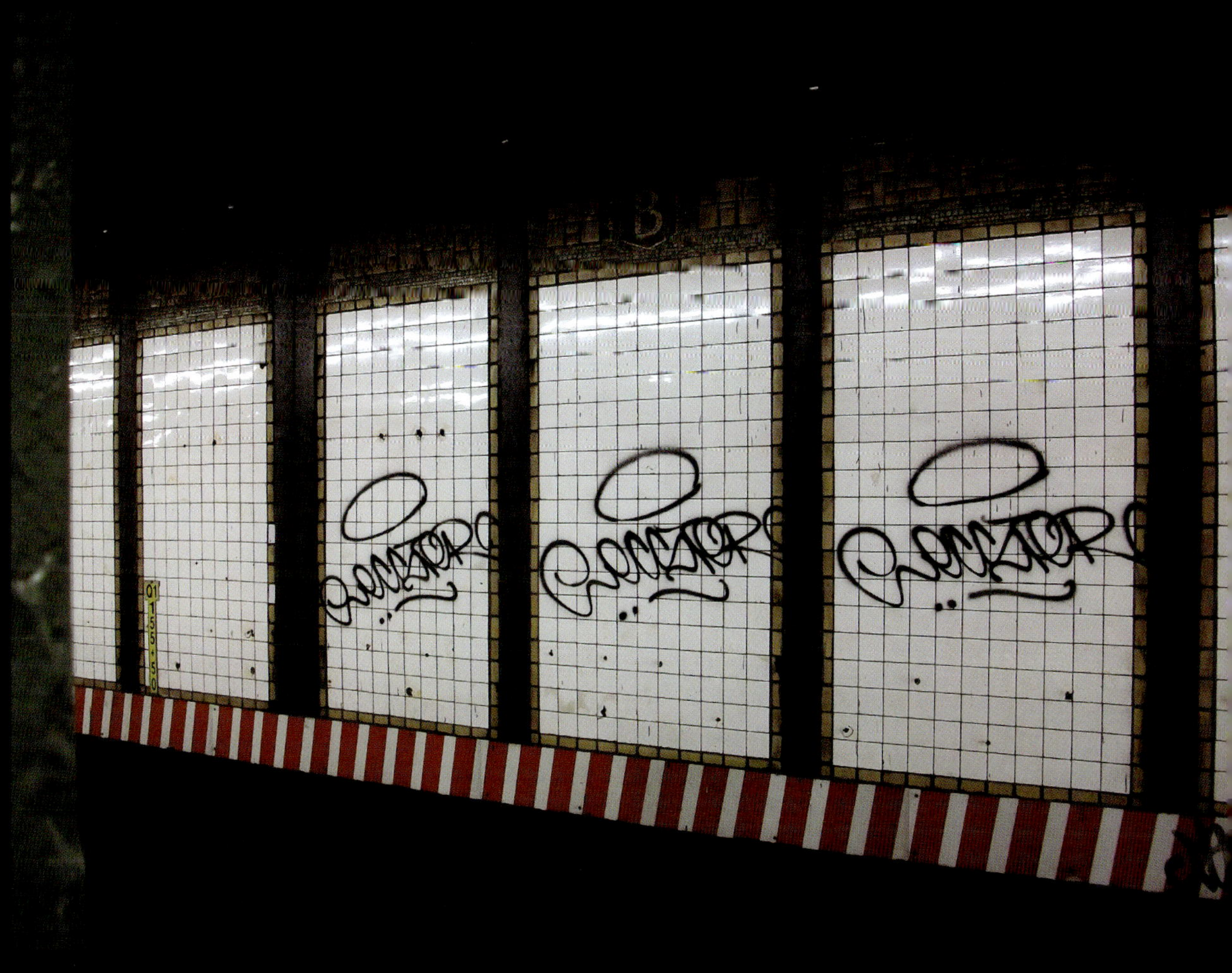

PBS
FUCK YOU

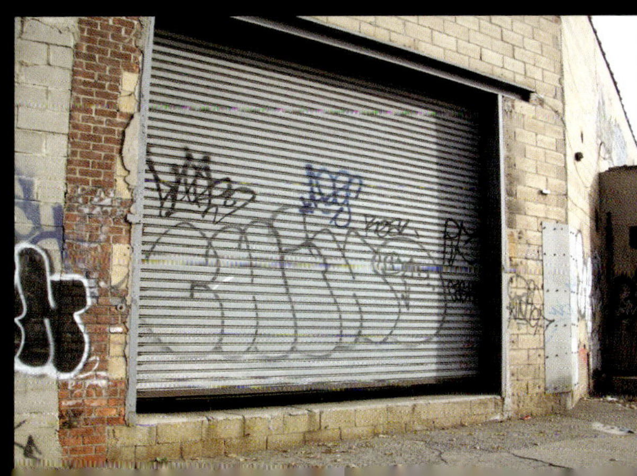

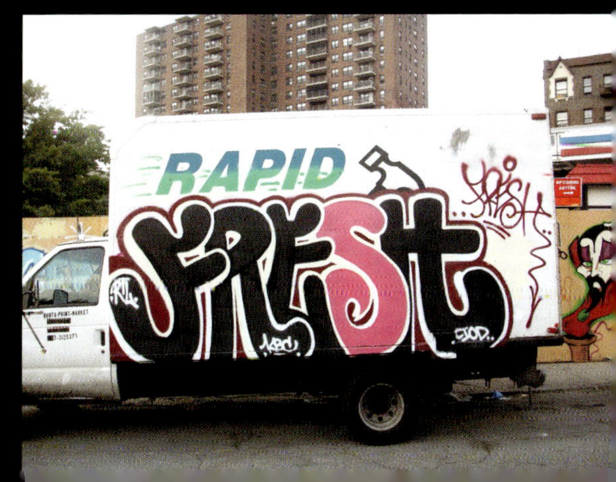
RAPID

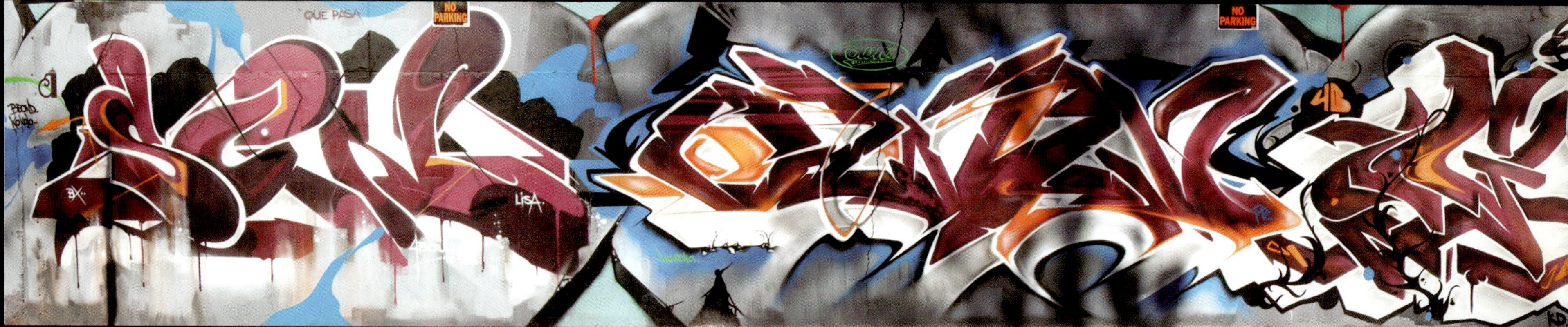
QUE PASA
NO PARKING
NO PARKING

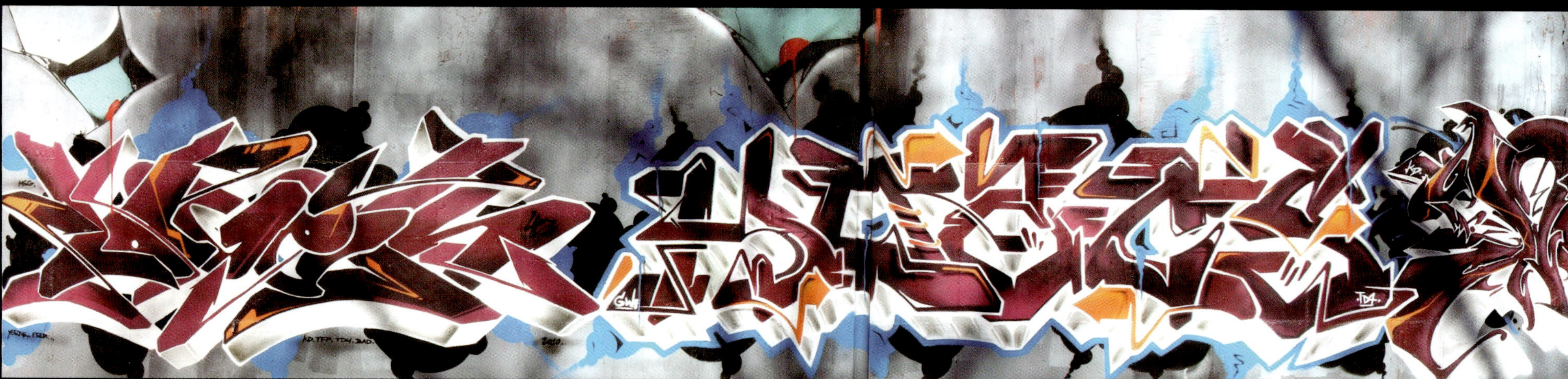

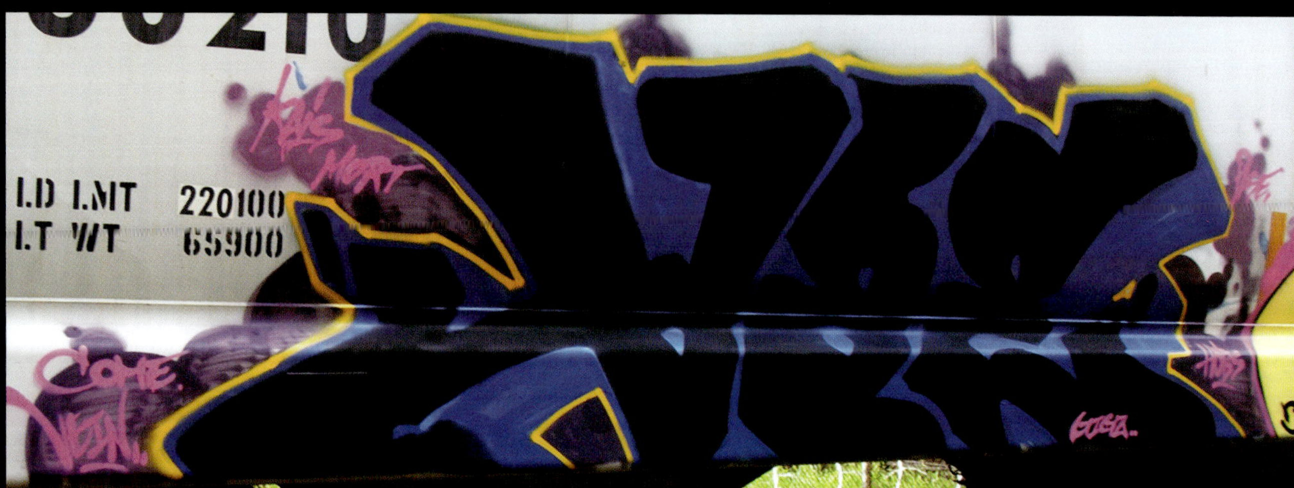
LD LMT 220100
LT WT 65900

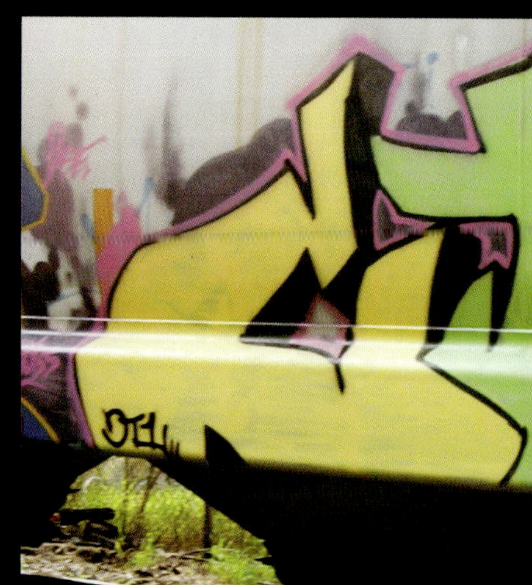

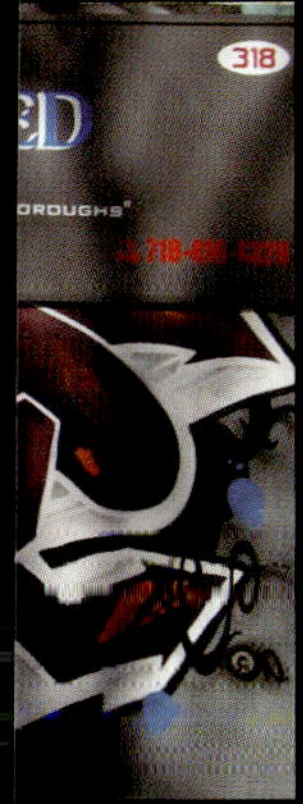

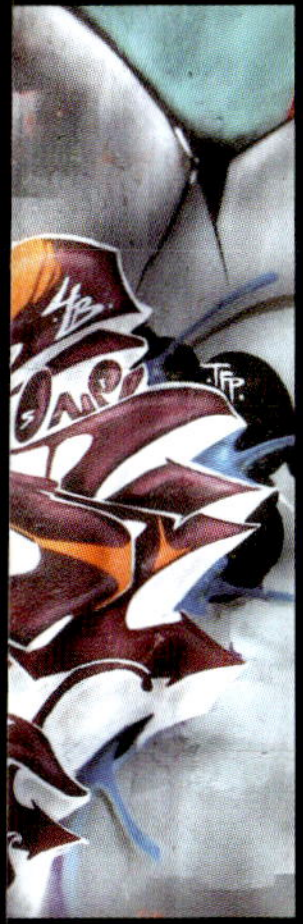

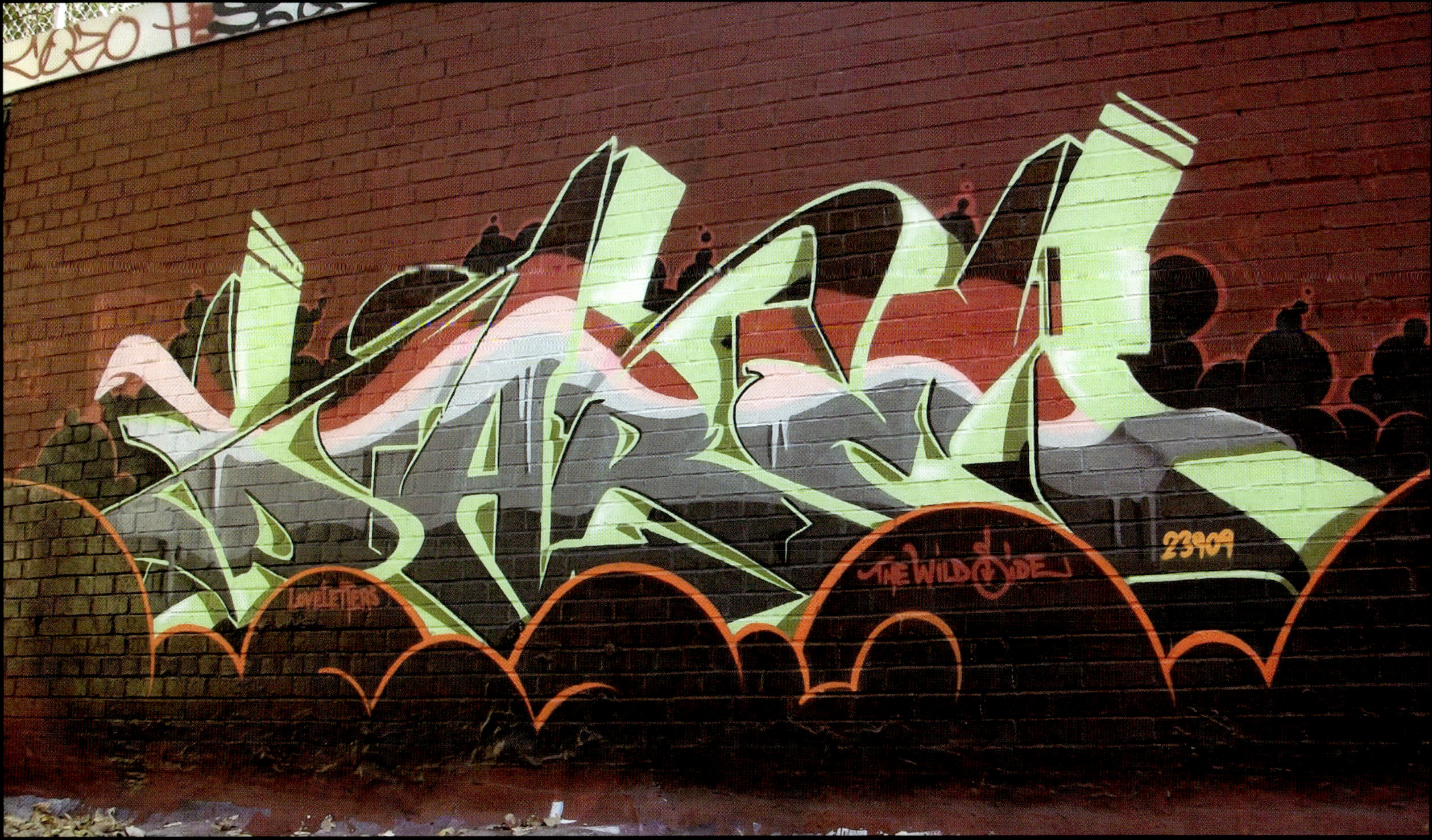
LOVELETTERS
23909

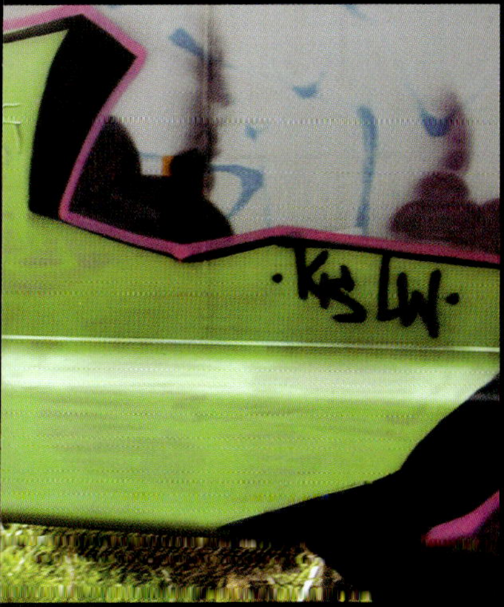

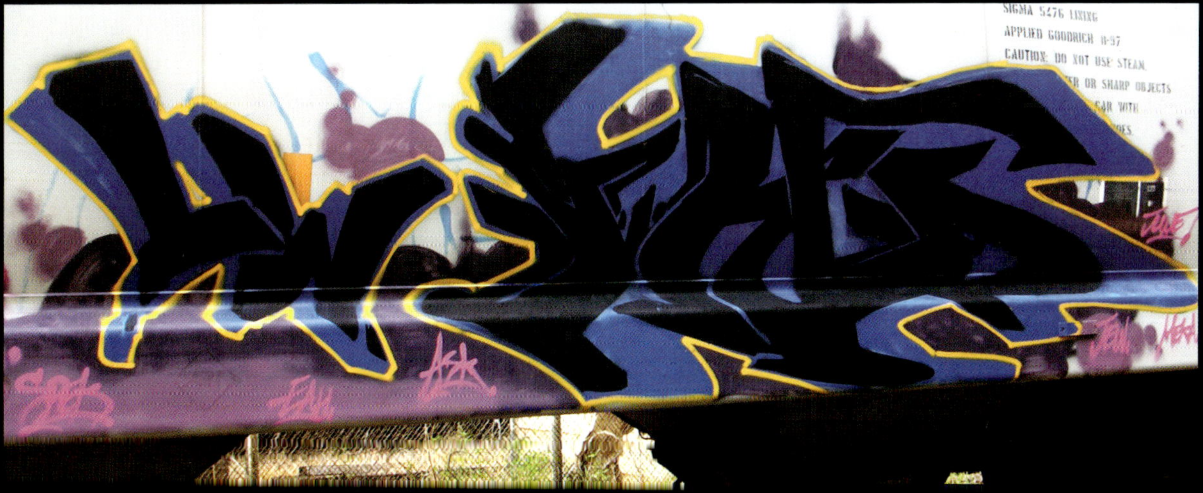

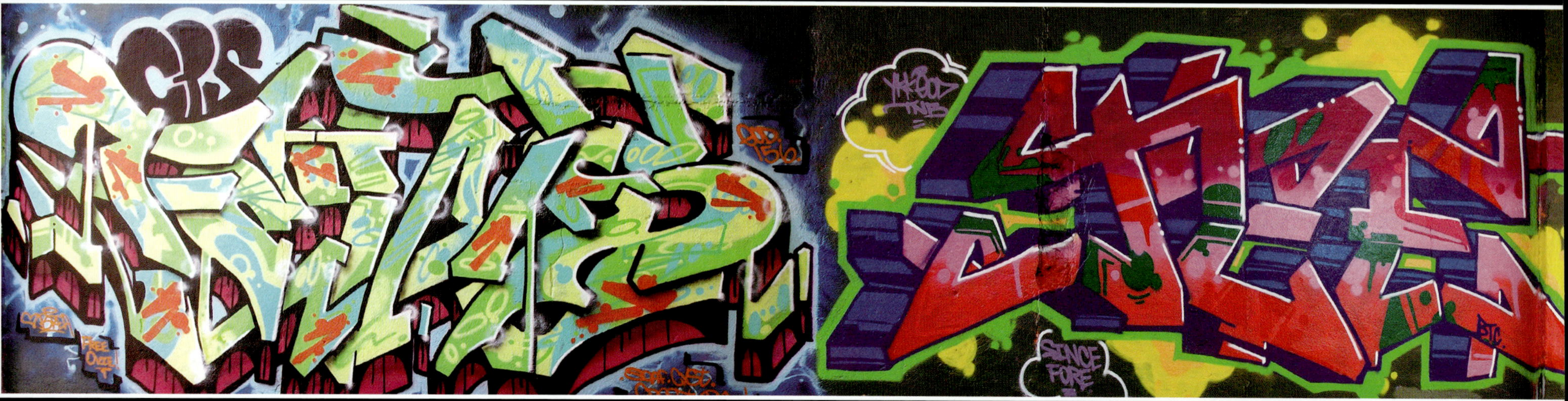

Fews, Jee, Bronx, NY

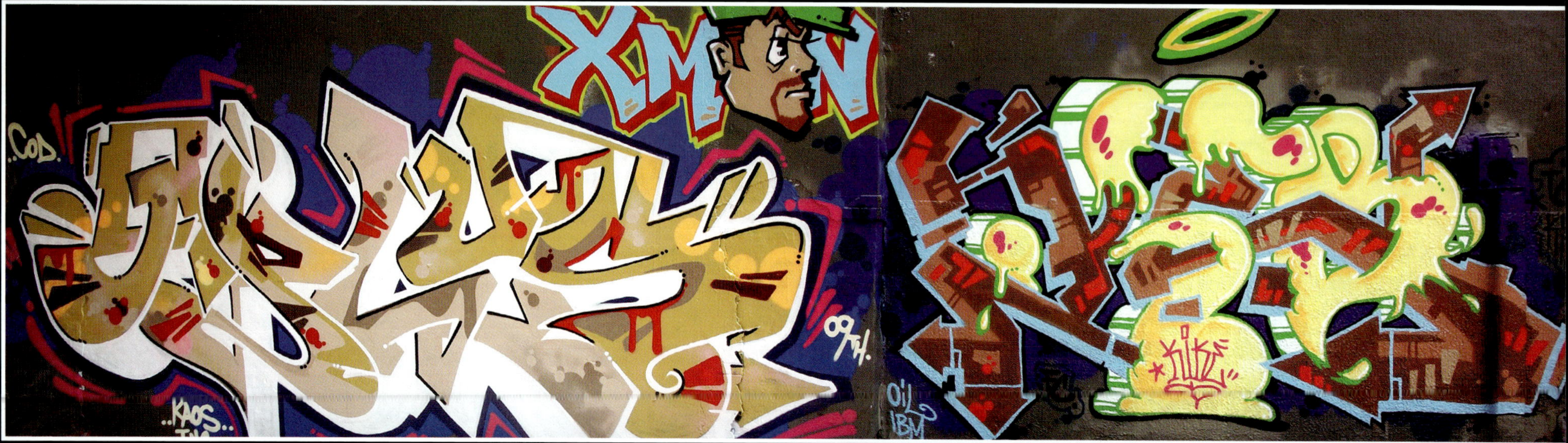

Aplus (Enue), Keo, Bronx, NY

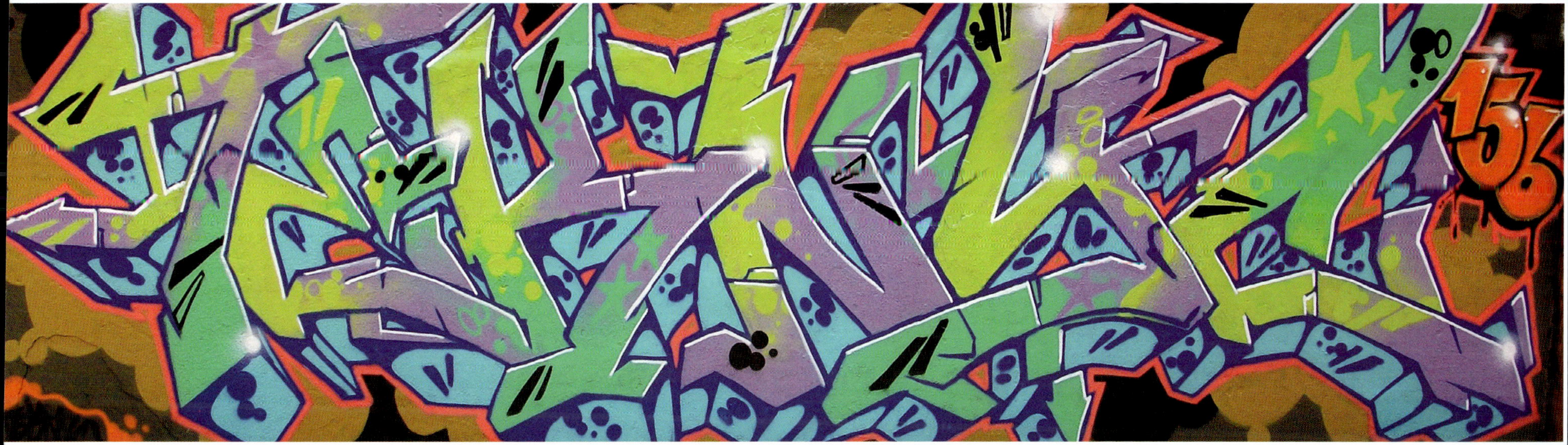

Teknyc, Bronx, NY

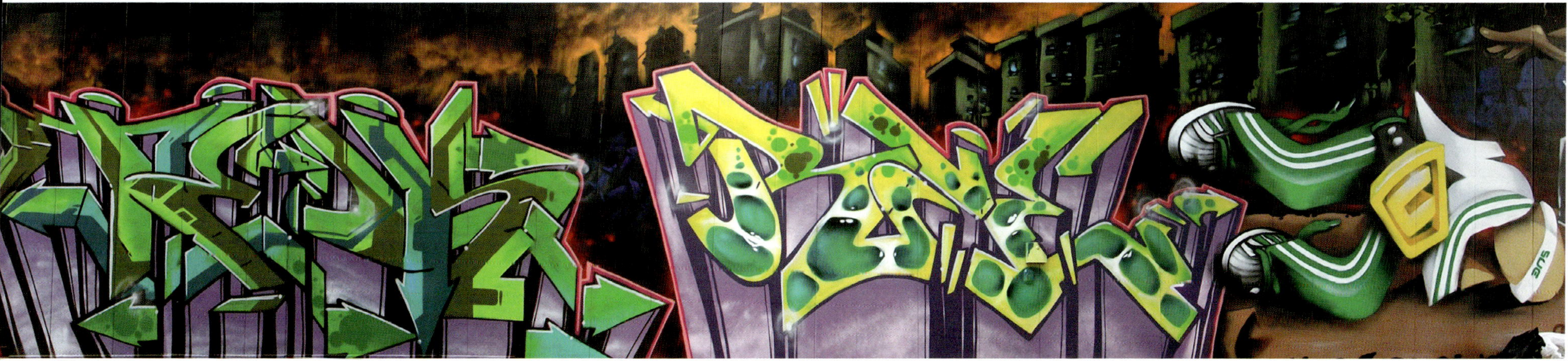

Teck, Ree, Manhattan, NY

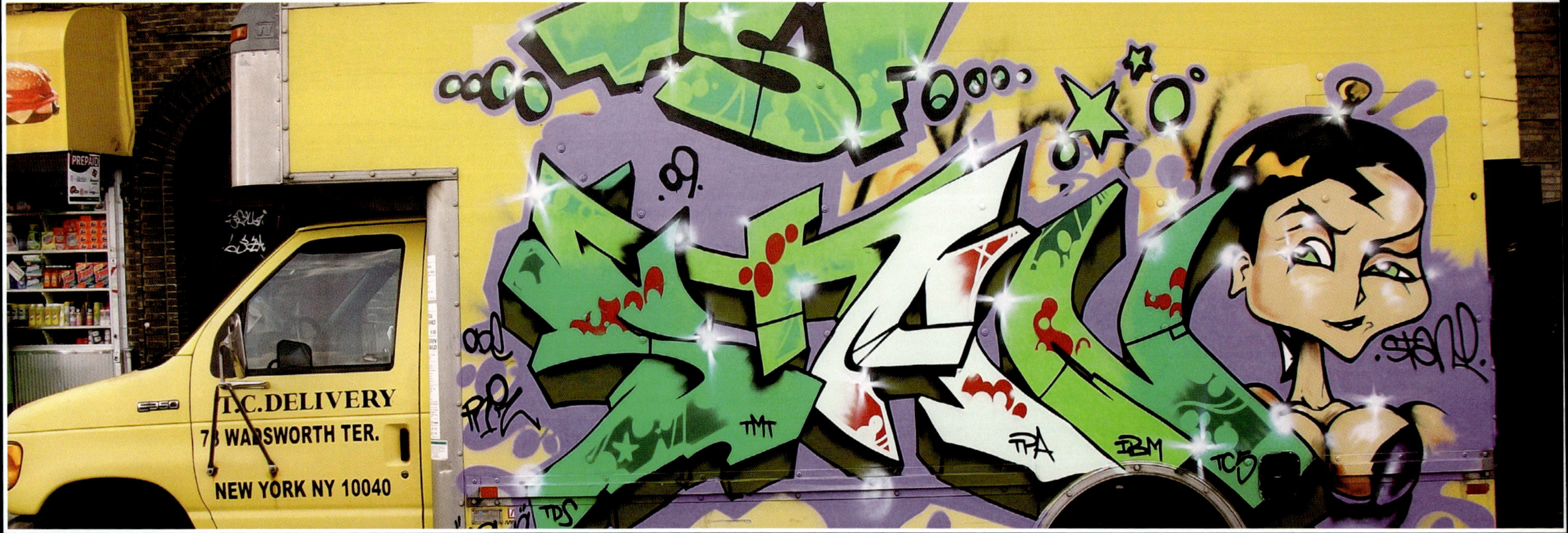


Stan, Manhattan, NY

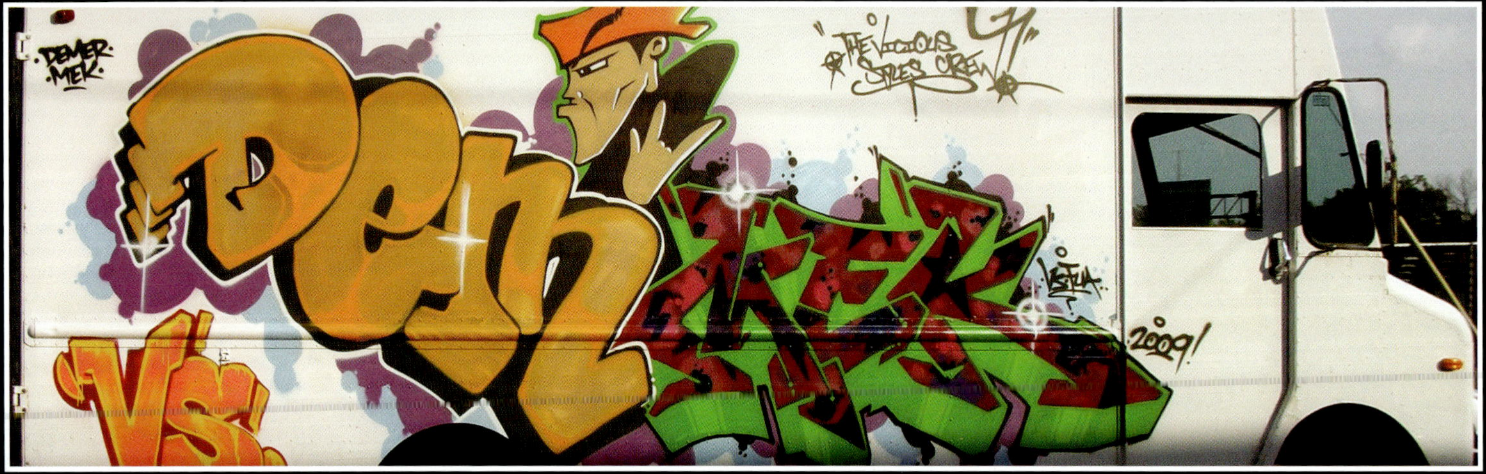


Demer, Mek, New jersey

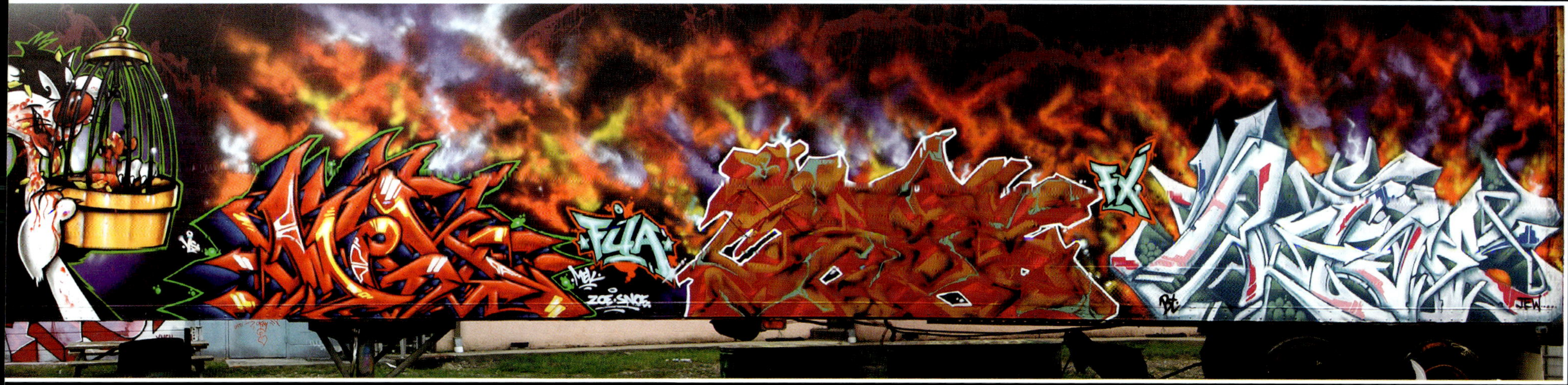

Mek, Abe, Pase, New Jersey

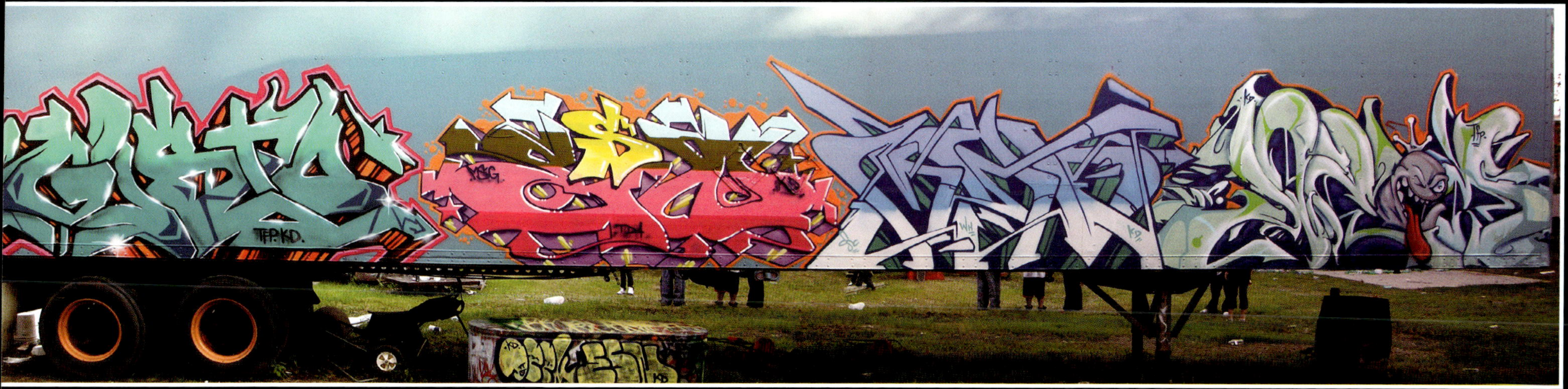

Gusto, ESN, Mad, Deem, New Jersey

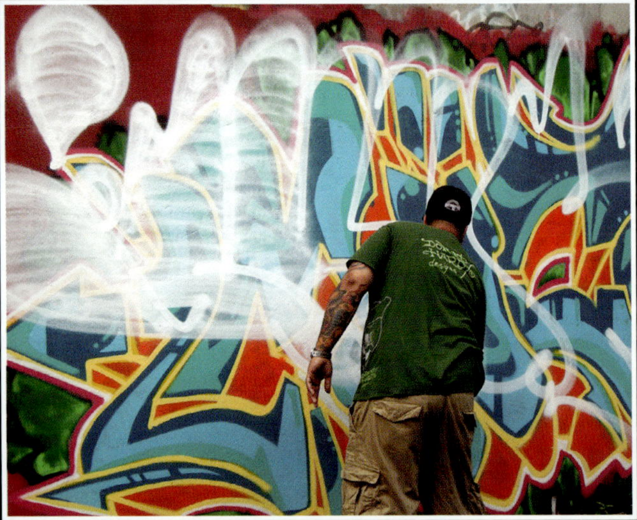

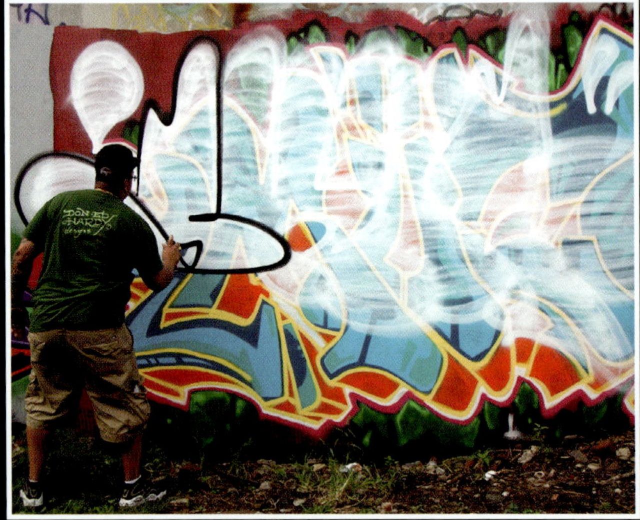

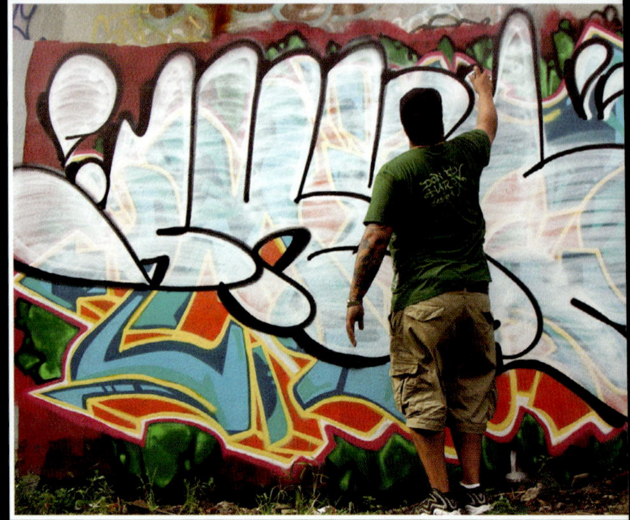

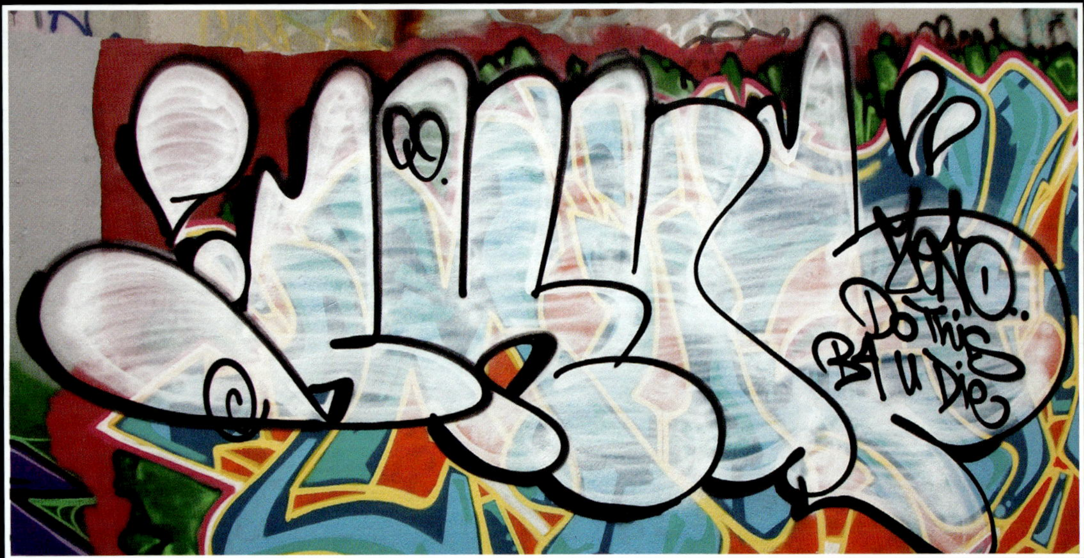
Do This
B4 U Die

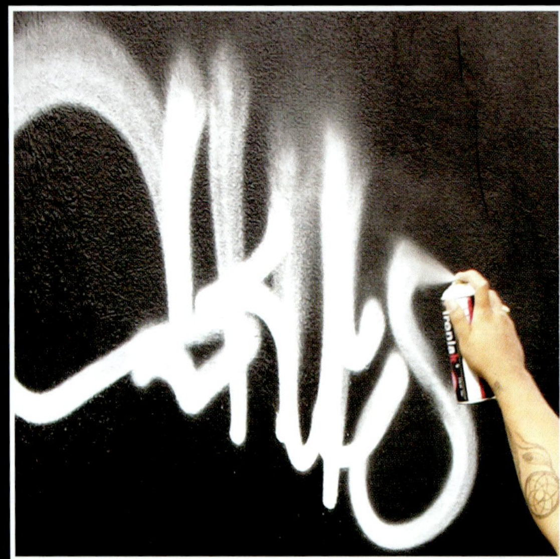

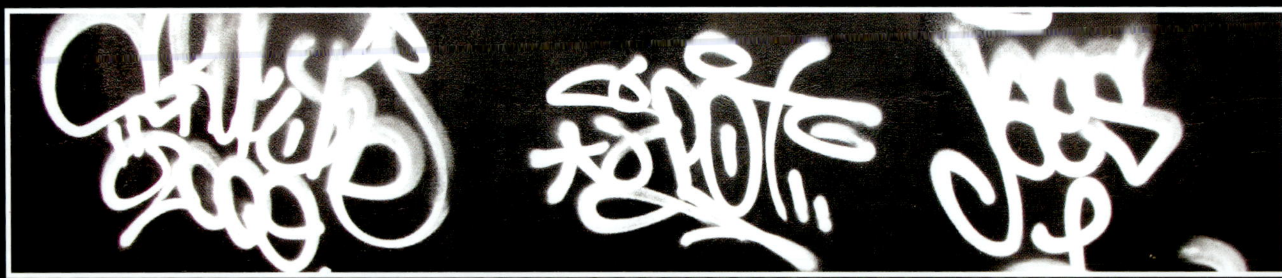

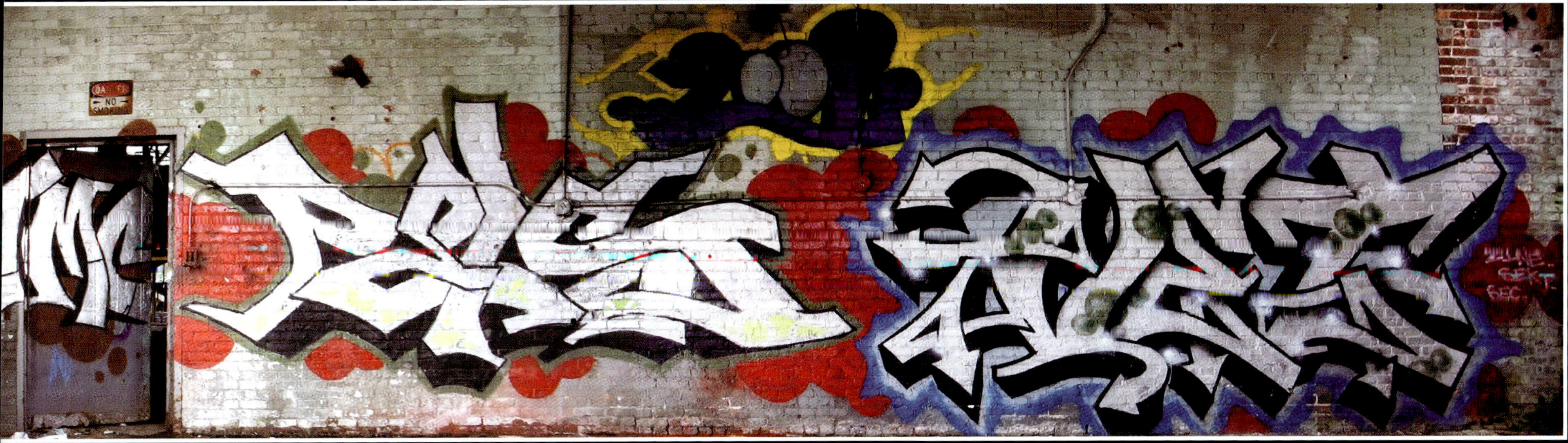

Pels, Vet, Secret Location

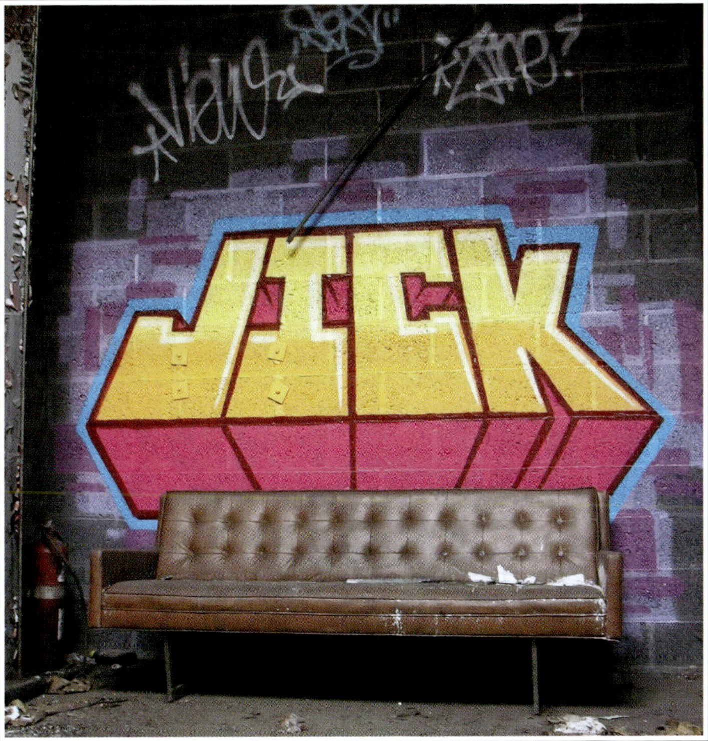

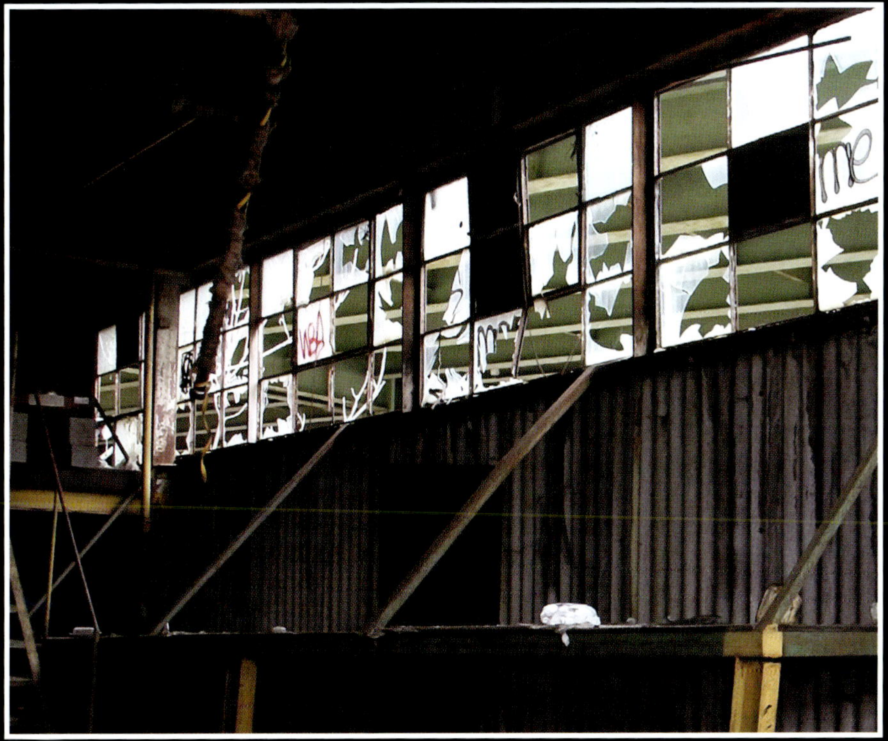

Jick, Secret Location

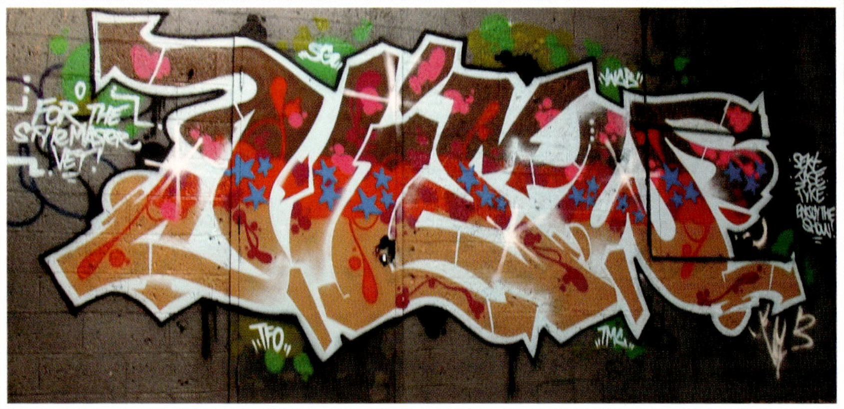

Jick, Secret Location

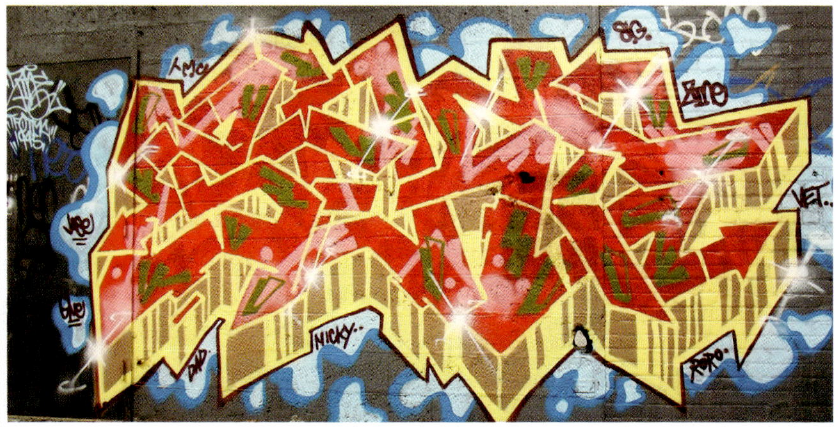

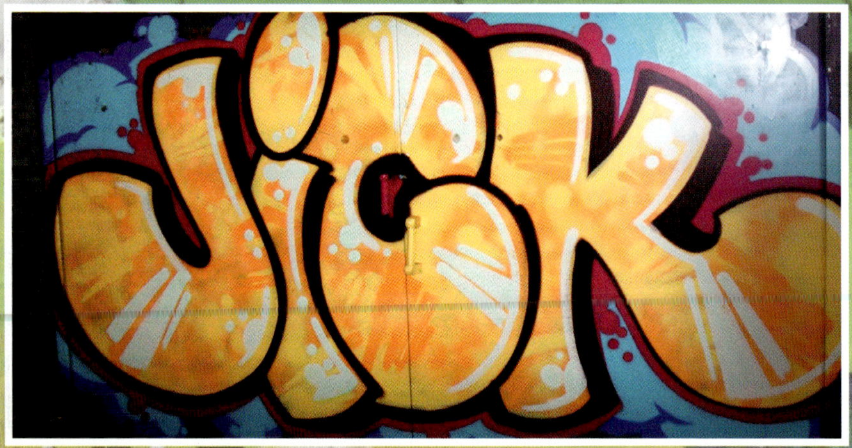

Jick, Secret Location

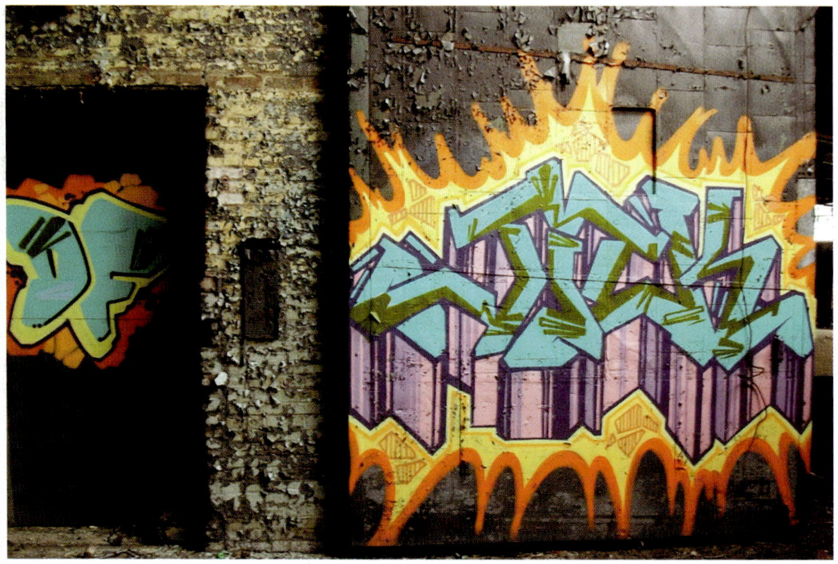

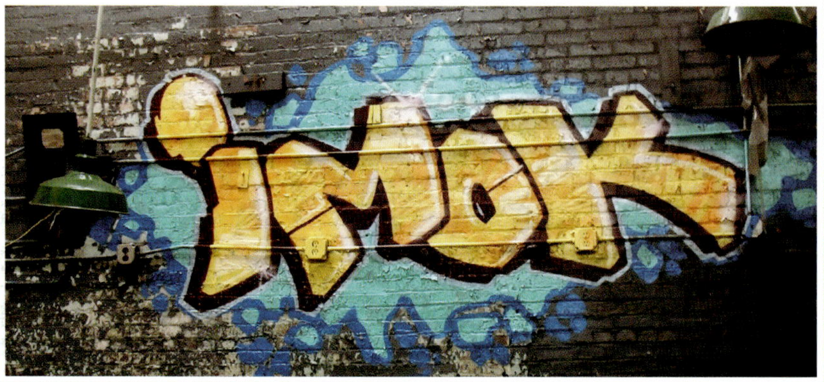

View, Secret Location

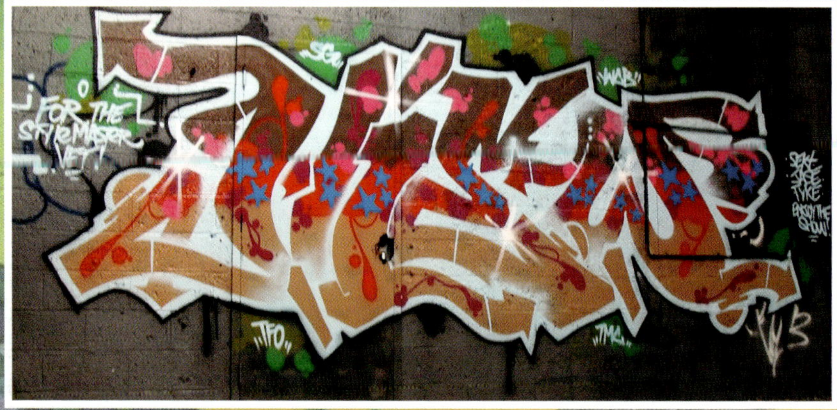

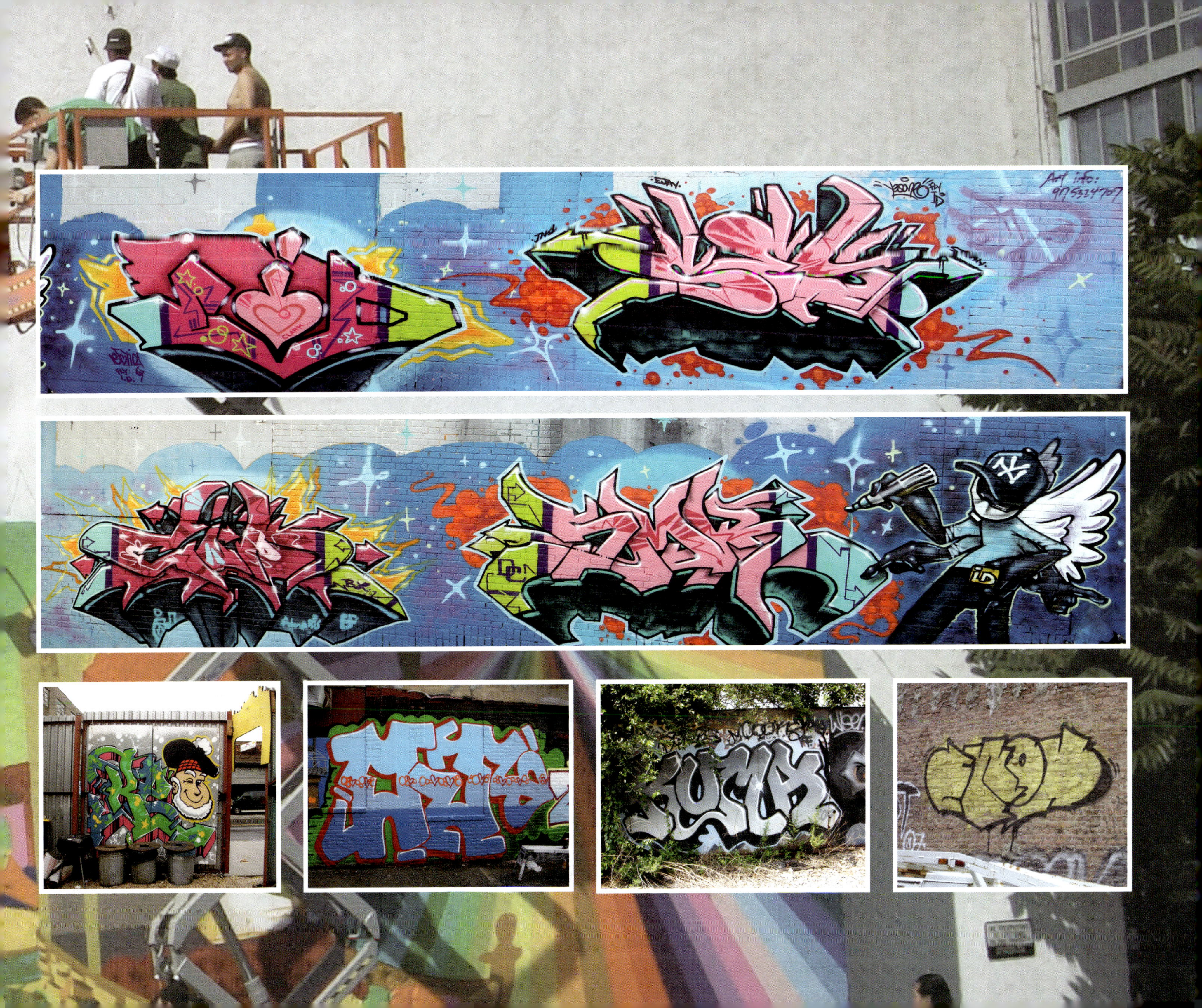

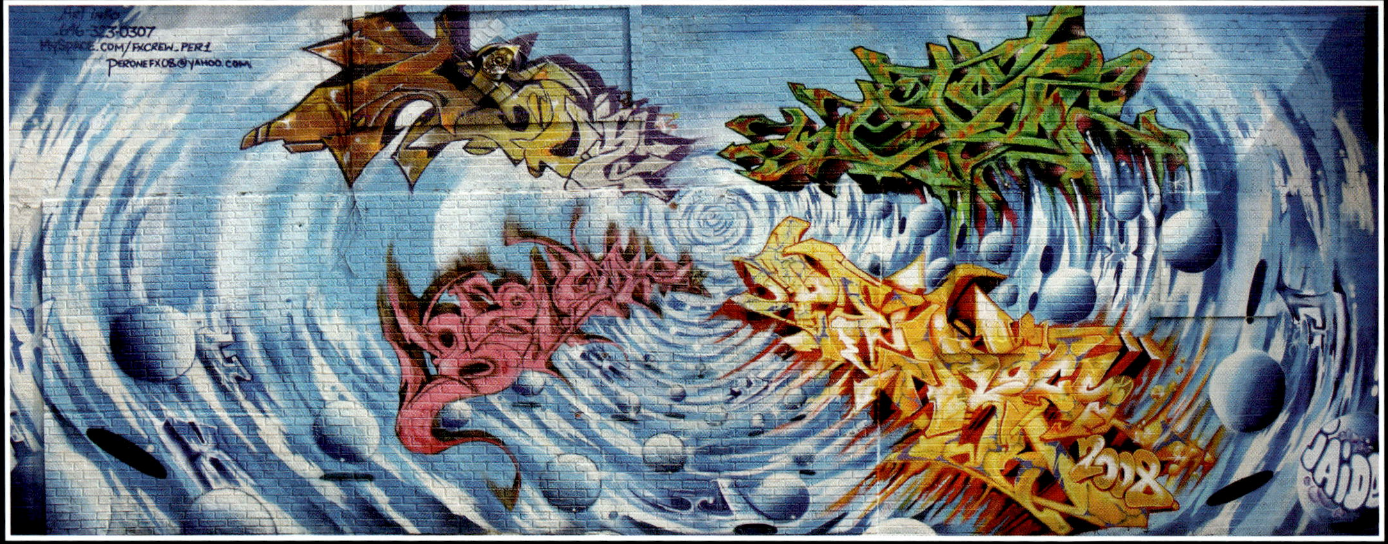


Such, Kais, Muse, Per, Bronx, NY

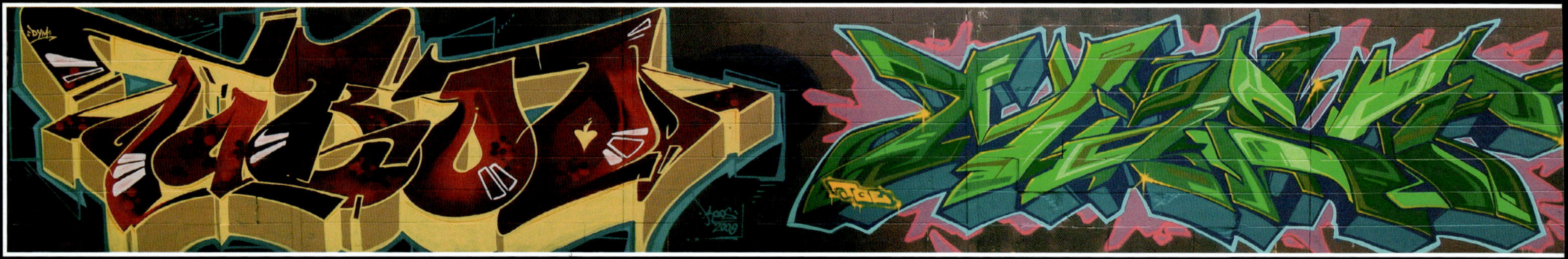

Taboo, Mast, Brooklyn, NY

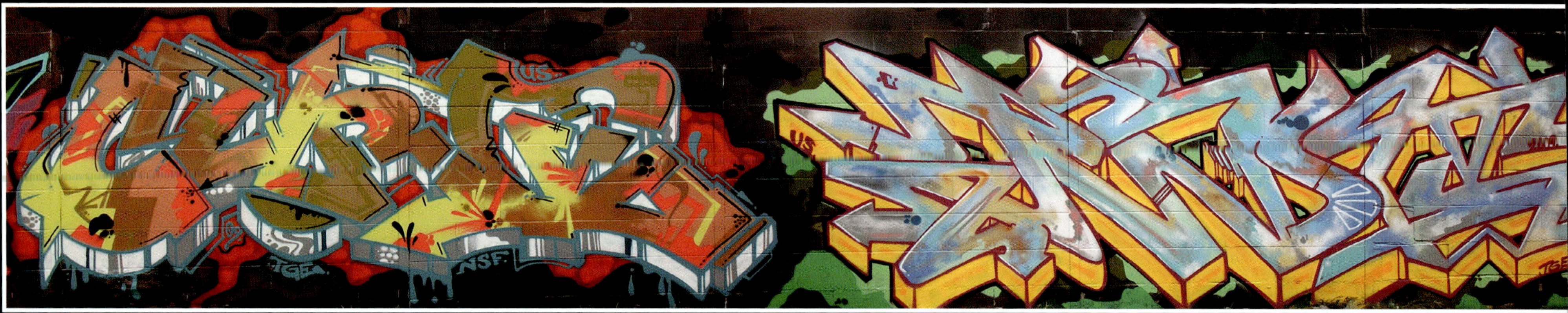

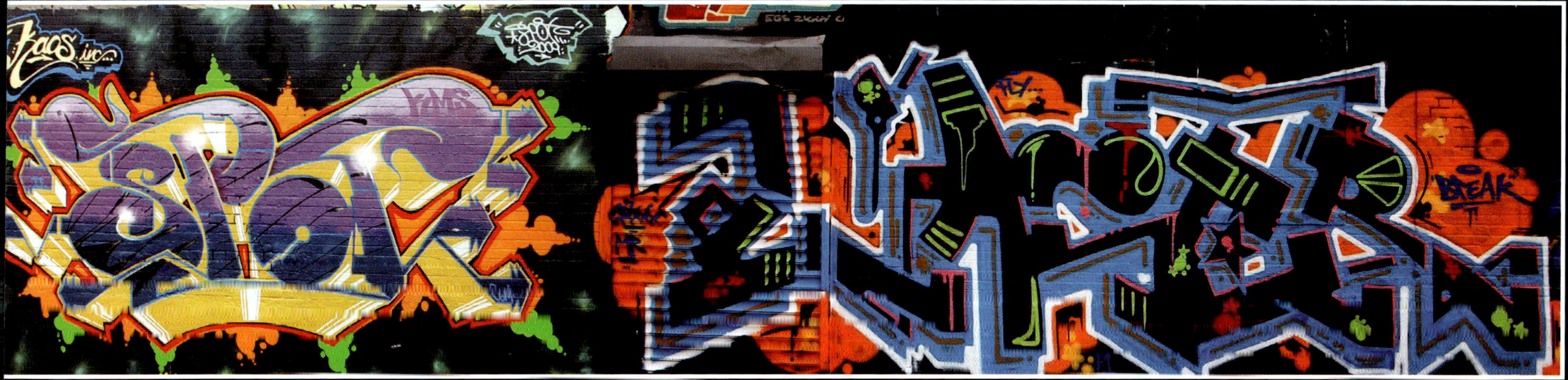

Spot, Laser (Take2), Bronx, NY

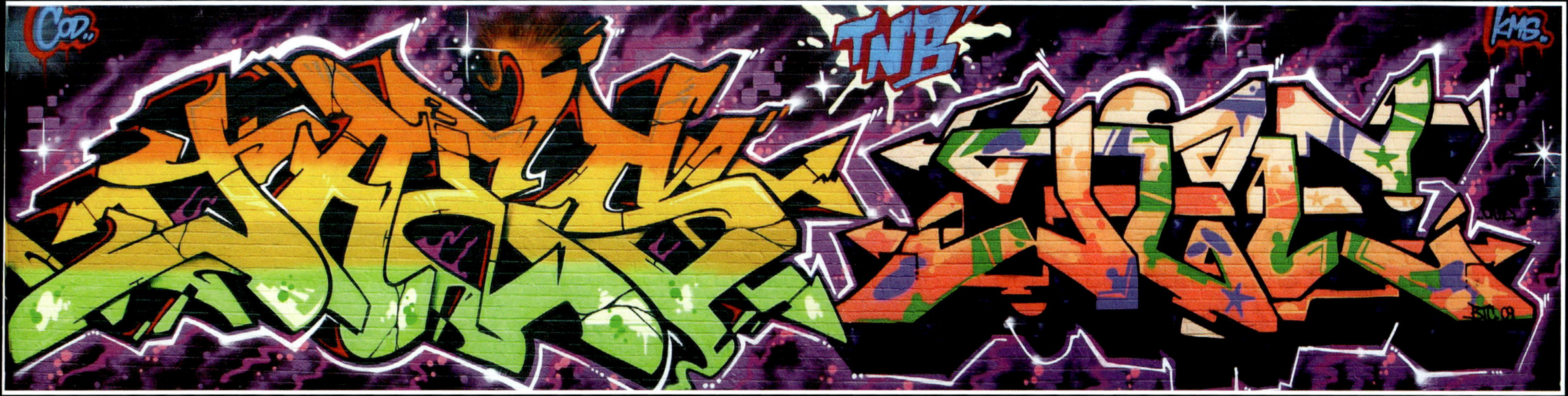

Jaes, Jee, Bronx, NY

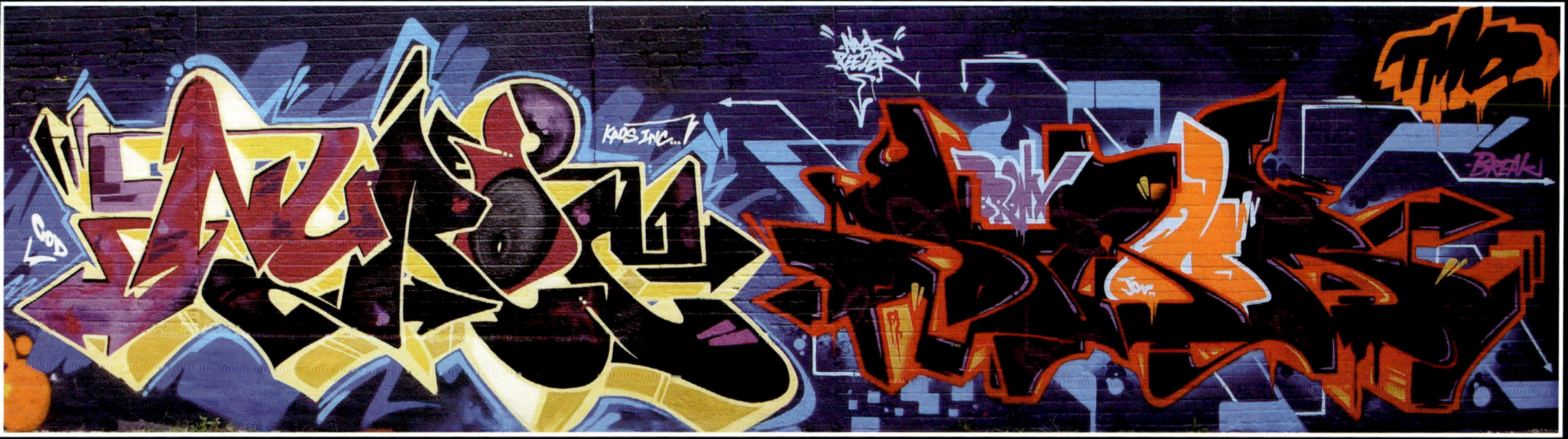

Nuroc (Enue), Sirum, Bronx, NY

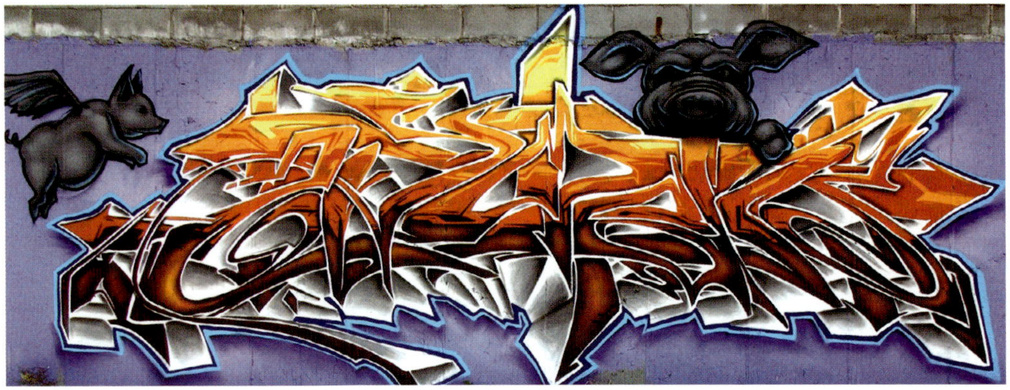

Zymer, Brooklyn, NY

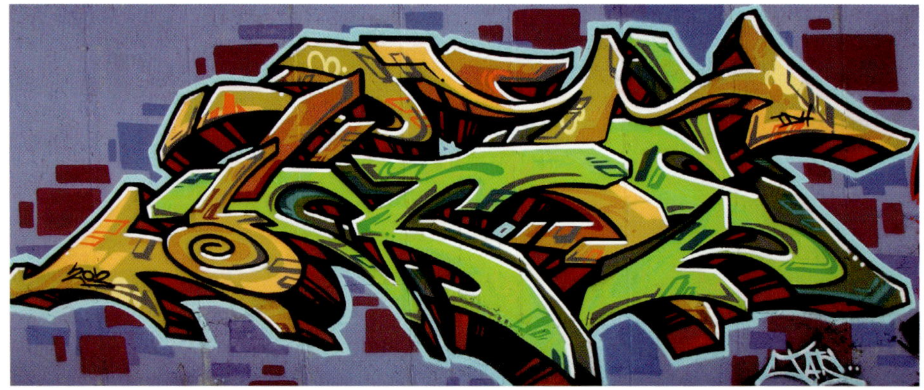

Jats, Brooklyn, NY

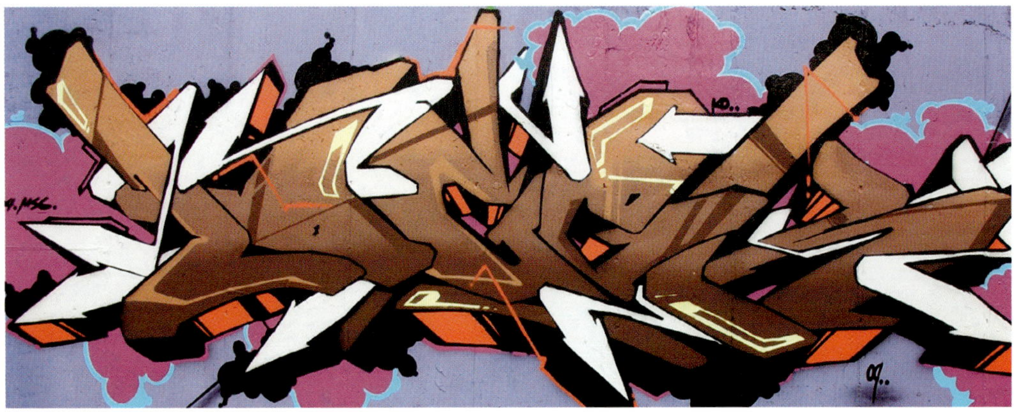

Logek, Brooklyn, NY

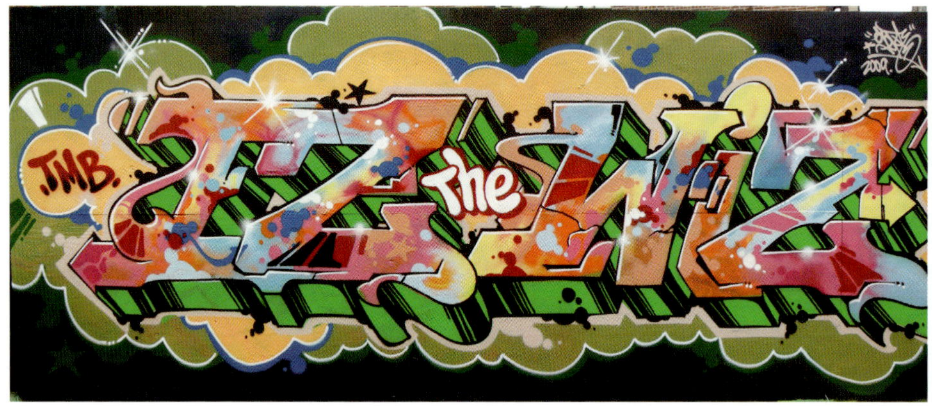


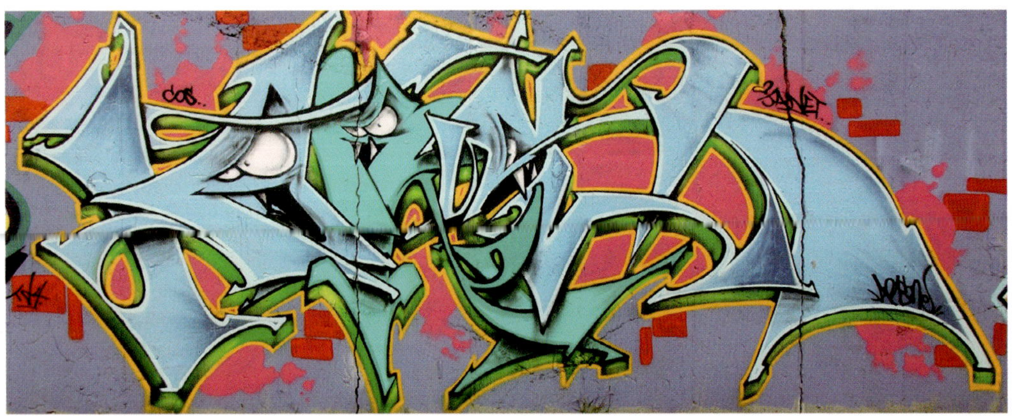

ARS, Brooklyn, NY

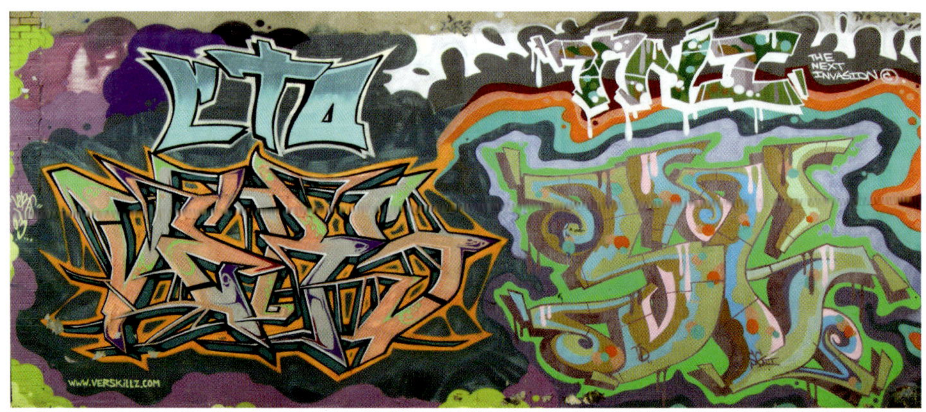

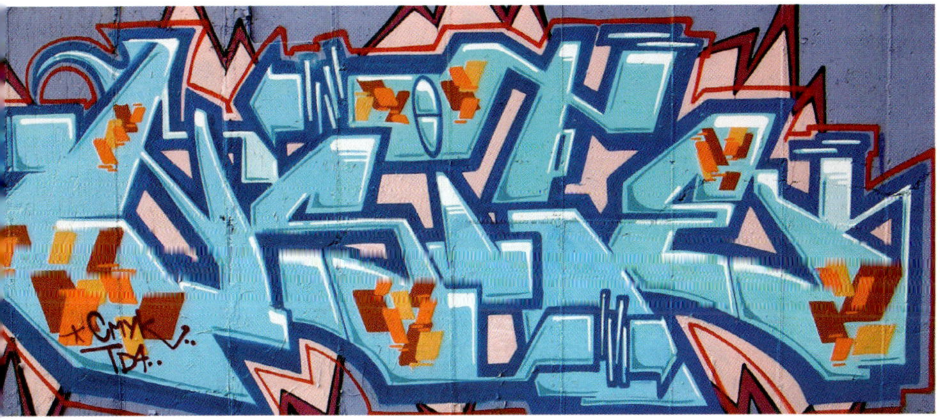

Nsite, Brooklyn, NY

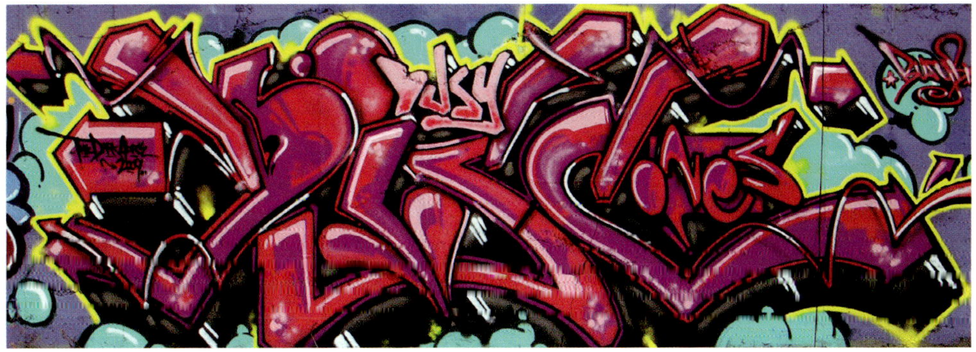

Bisc, Brooklyn, NY

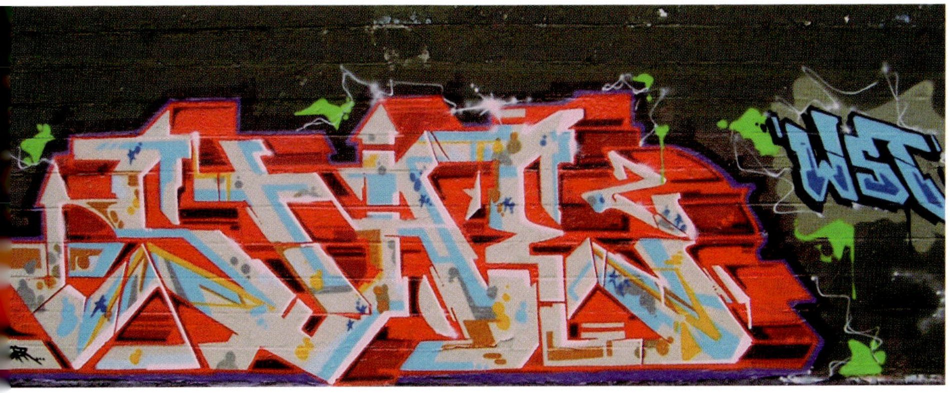

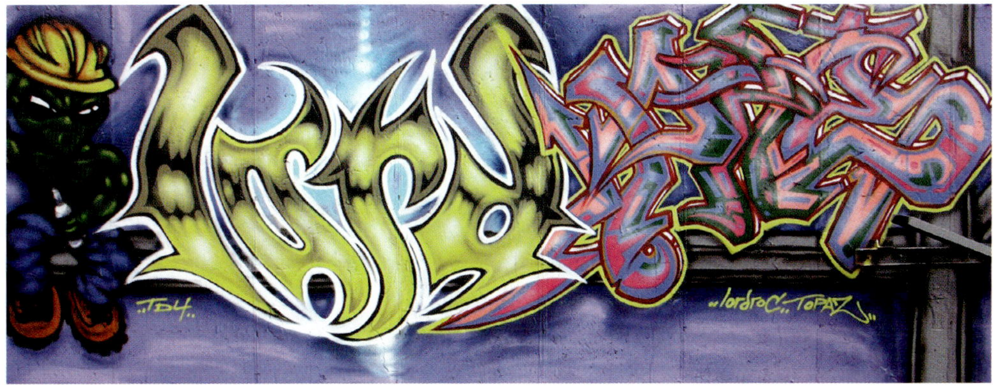

Lord Roc, Brooklyn, NY

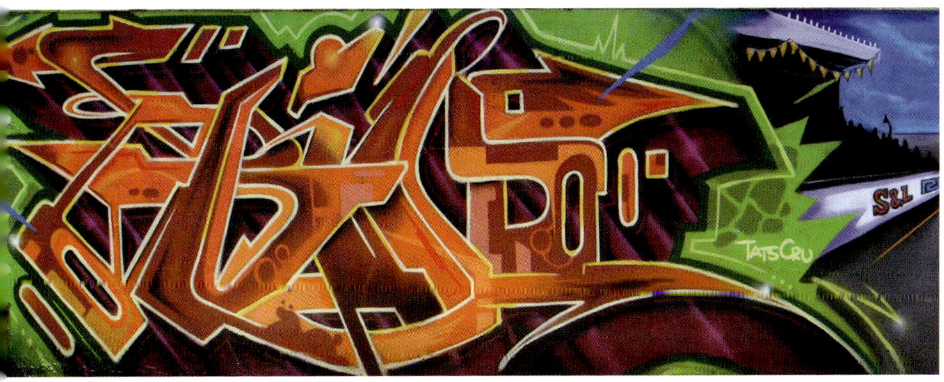

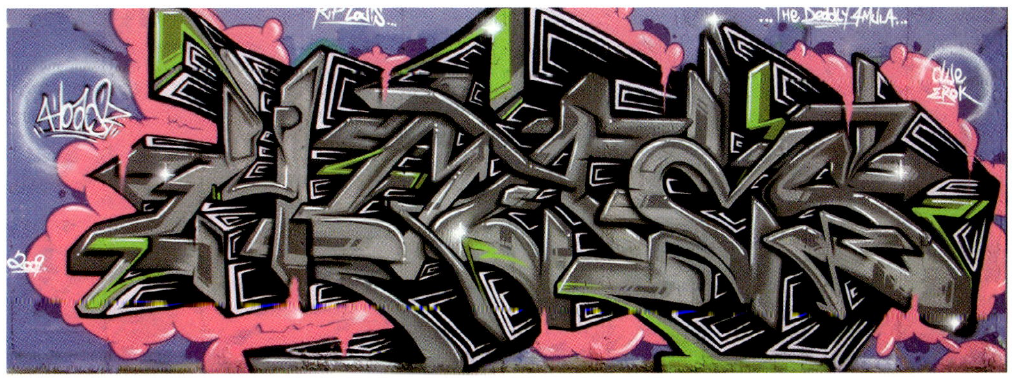

Hoacs, Brooklyn, NY

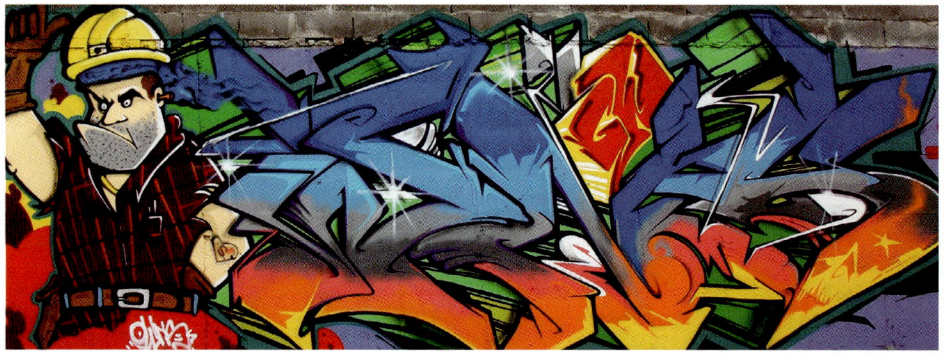

Owns, Brooklyn, NY

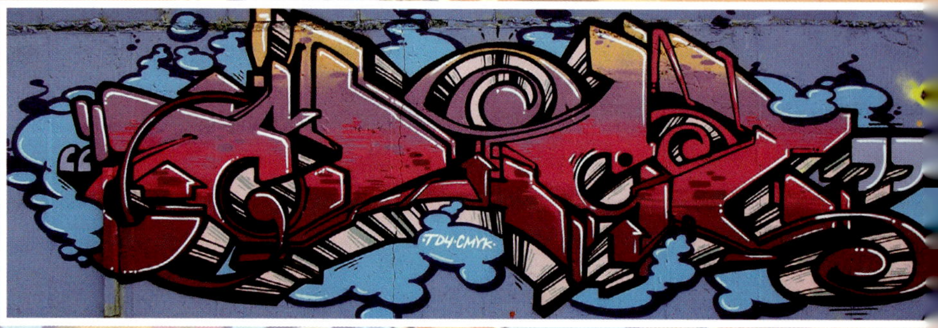

Elet, Brooklyn, NY

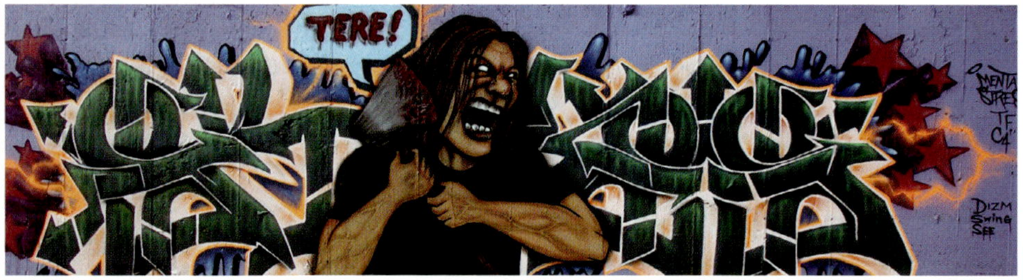


Stres, Brooklyn, NY

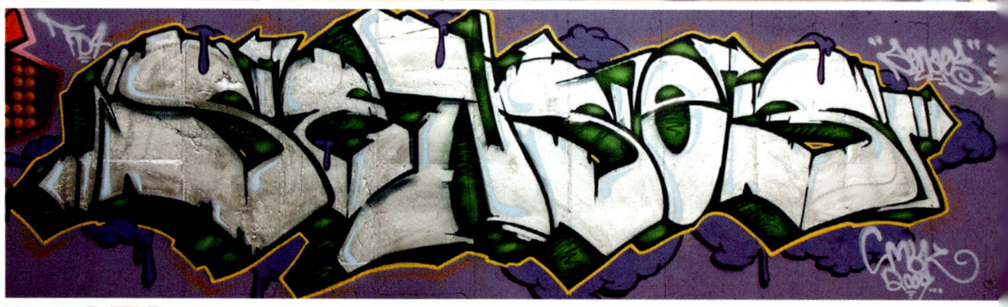

Sense2, Brooklyn, NY

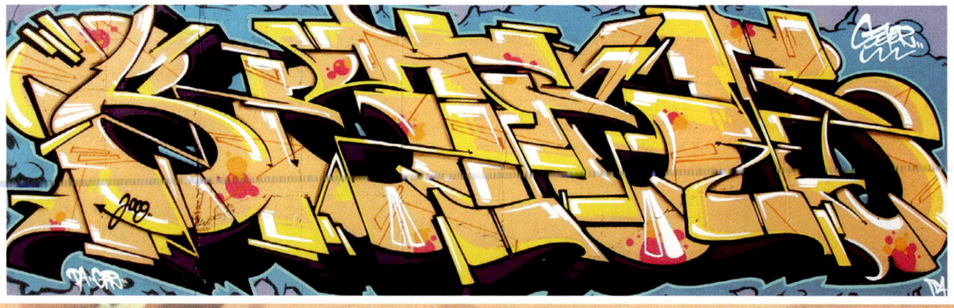

Seter, Brooklyn, NY

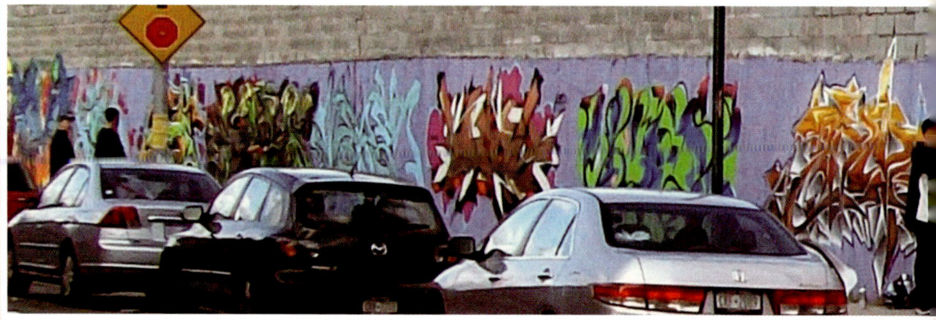

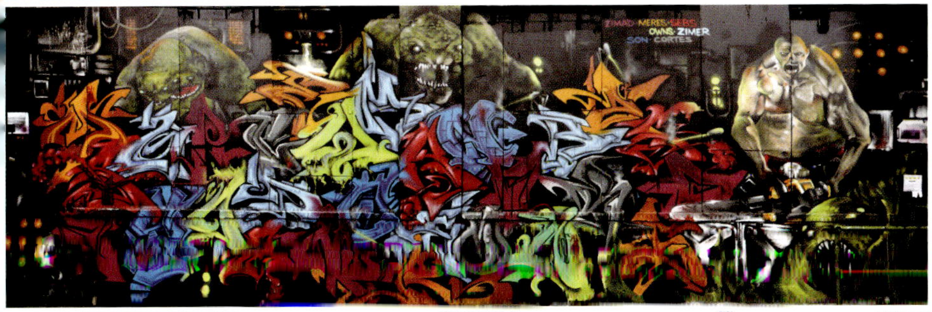

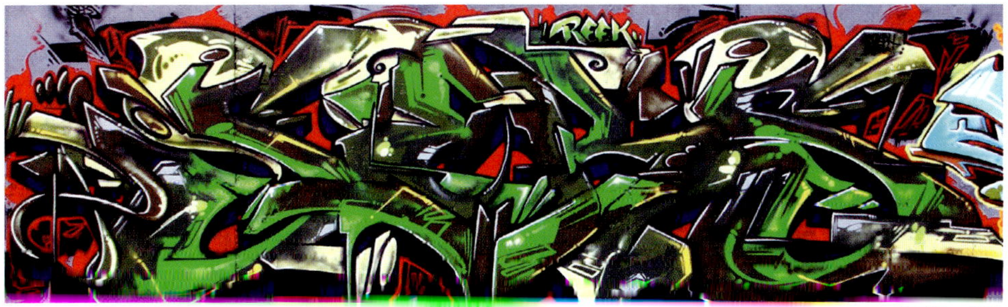

Sobs, Brooklyn, NY

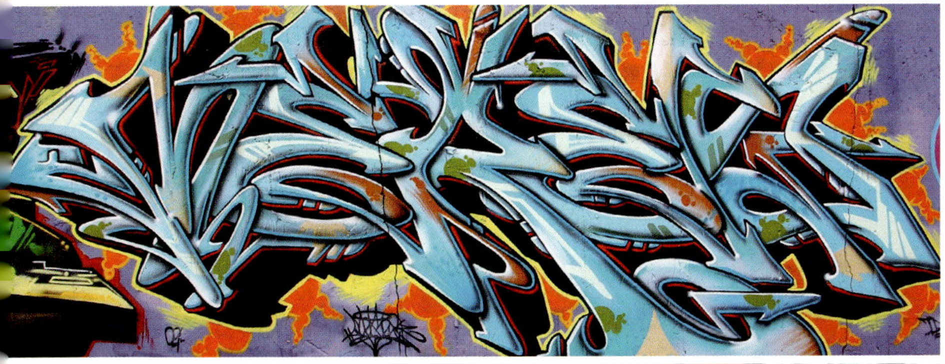

Meres, Brooklyn, NY

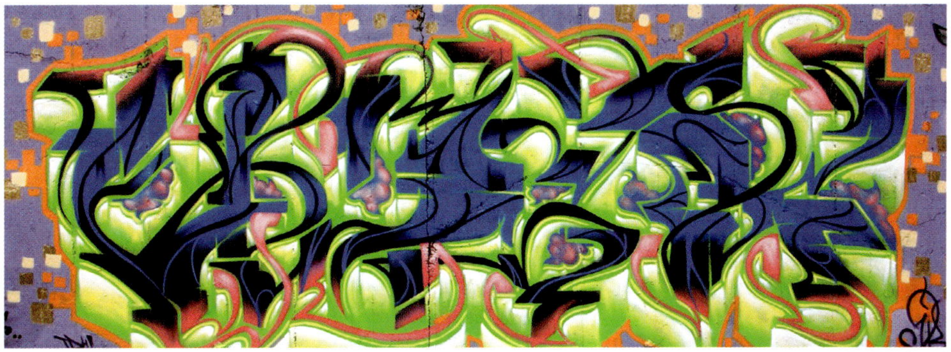

Vik, Brooklyn, NY

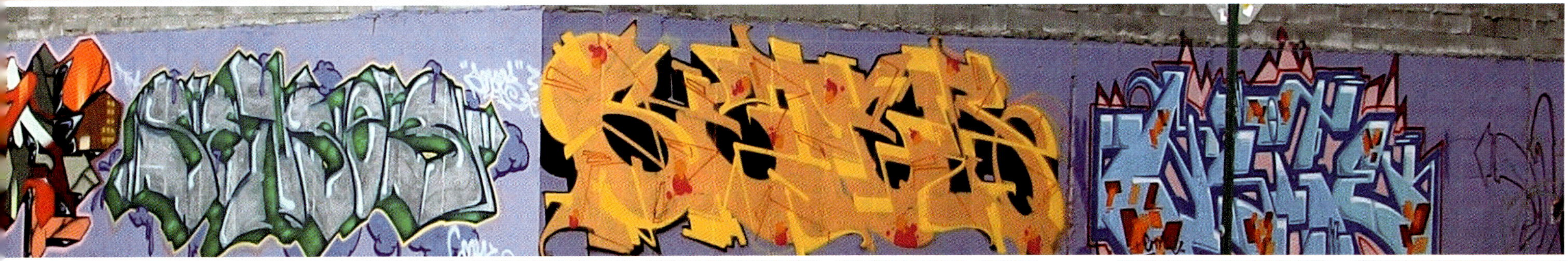

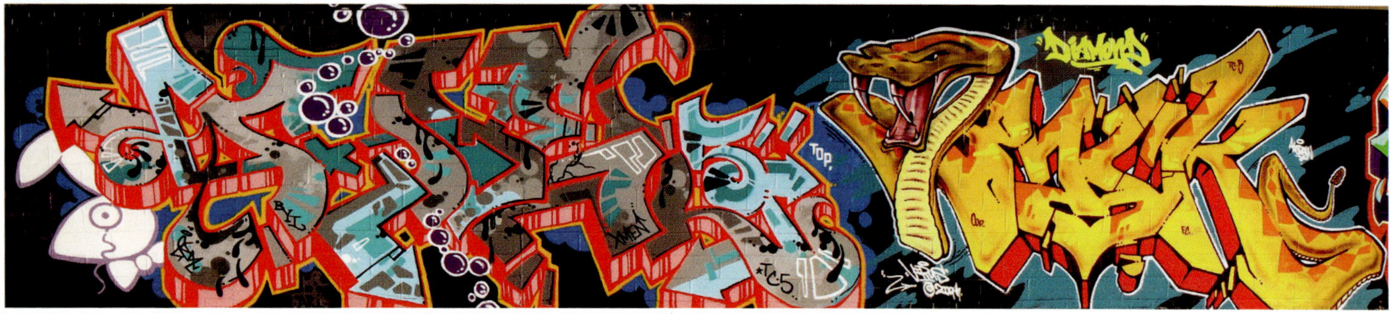

Diamond Back (Virus), Queens, NY

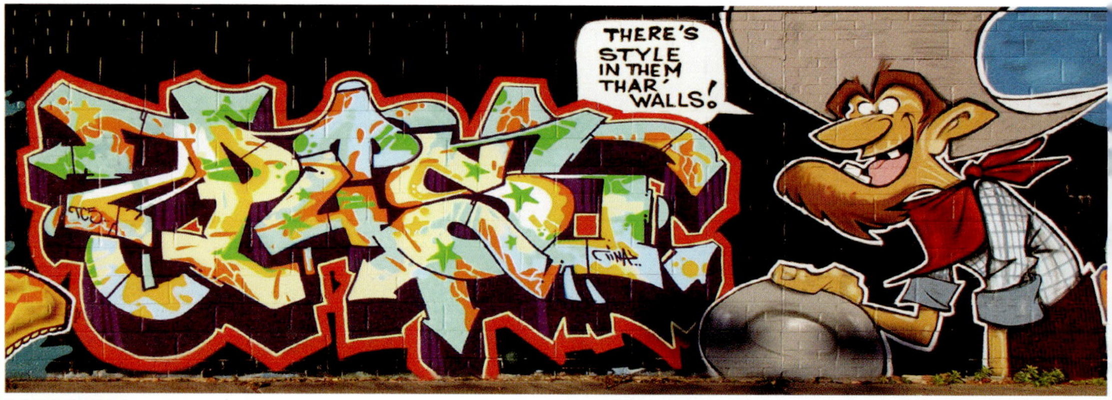


Dontay, Queens, NY

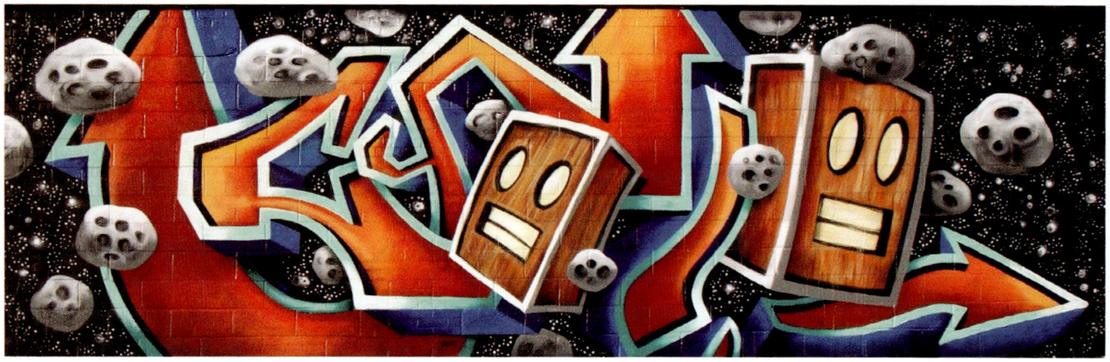

Cycle, Queens, NY

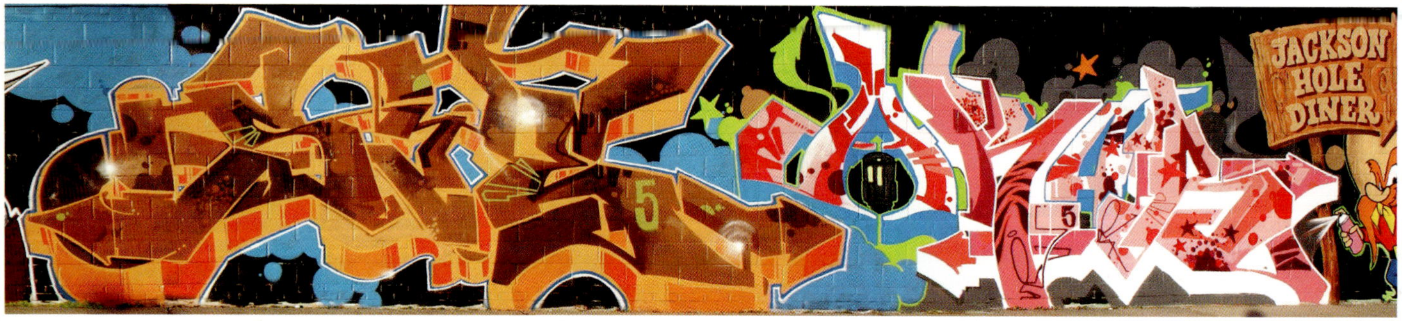


Sye, Doc, Queens, NY

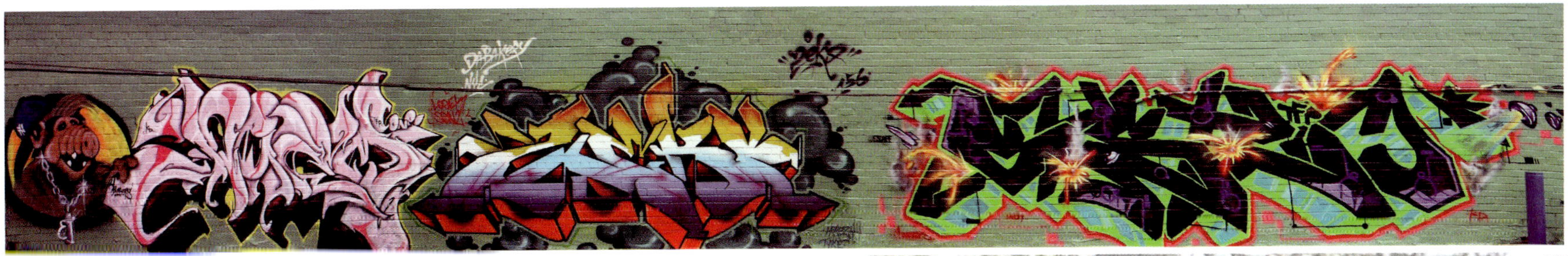

Dueno, Zek, Gusto, Bronx, NY

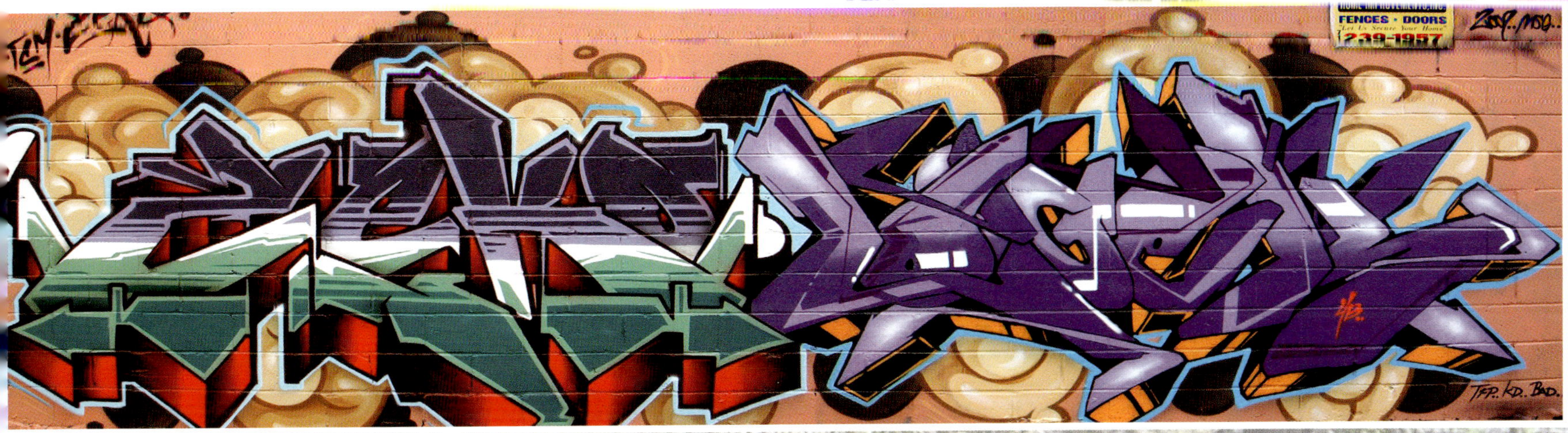


Zek, Logek, Bronx, NY

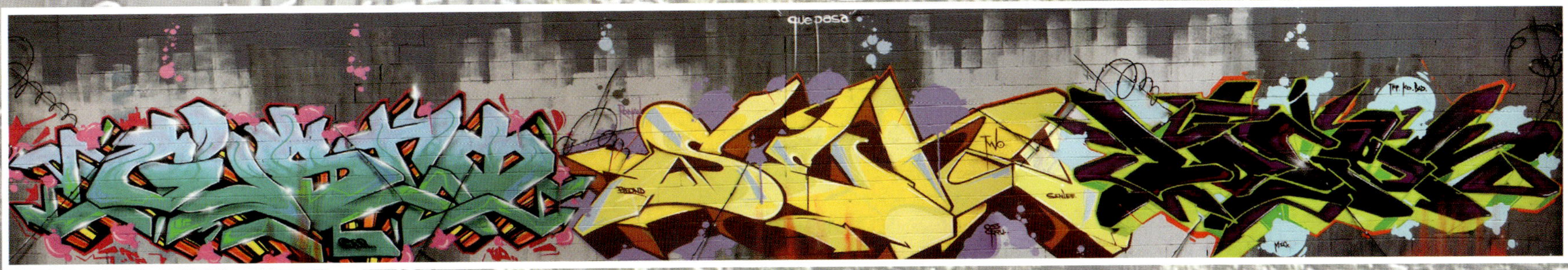

Gusto, Sen2, Logek, Bronx, NY

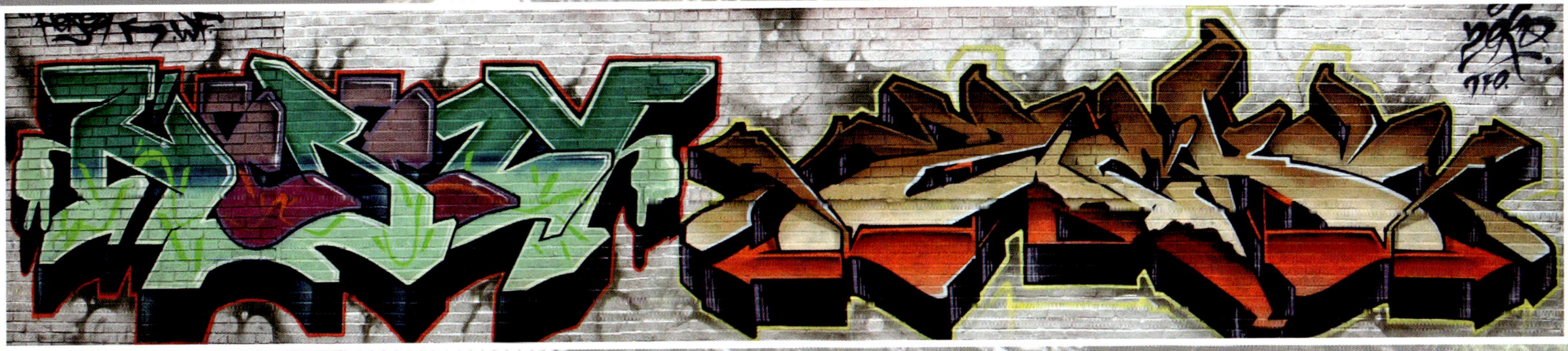

Herezy, Zek, Bronx, NY

# Black Book

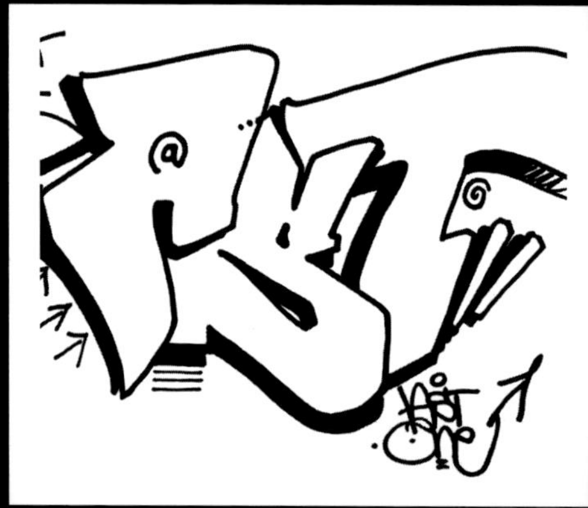

Ast

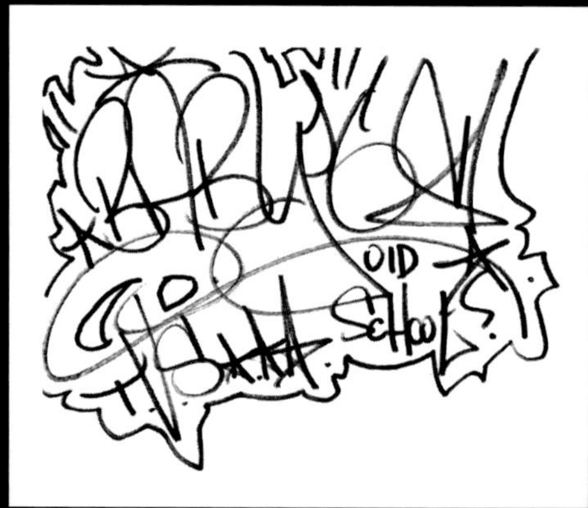

Baby168

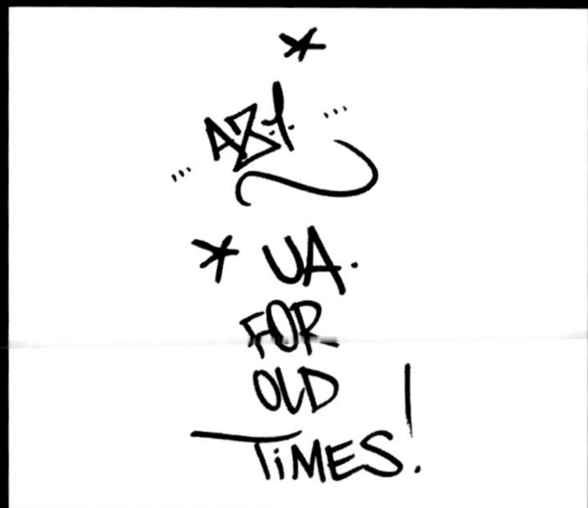


Az

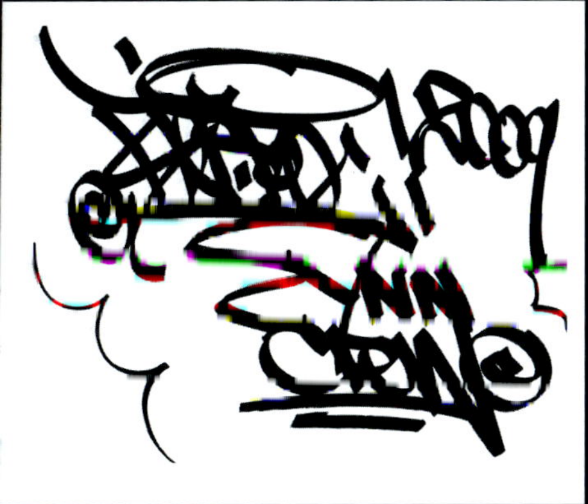
Bies

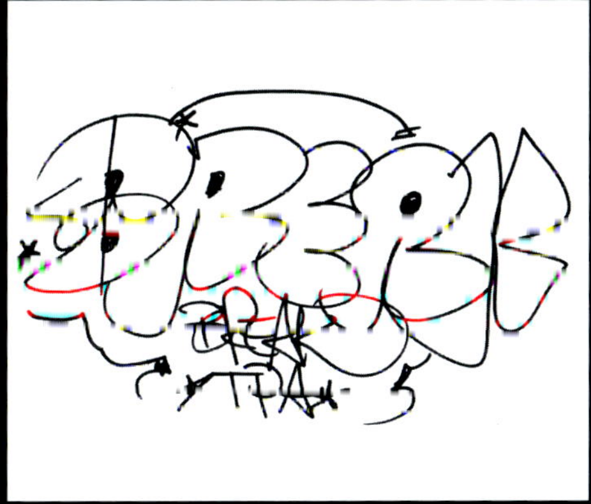
Break

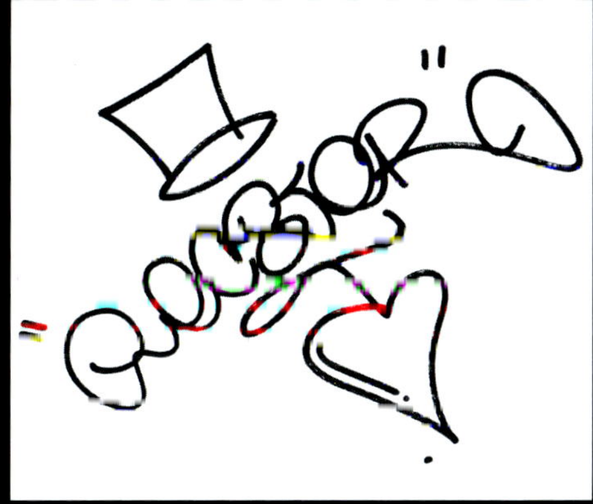
Cecs

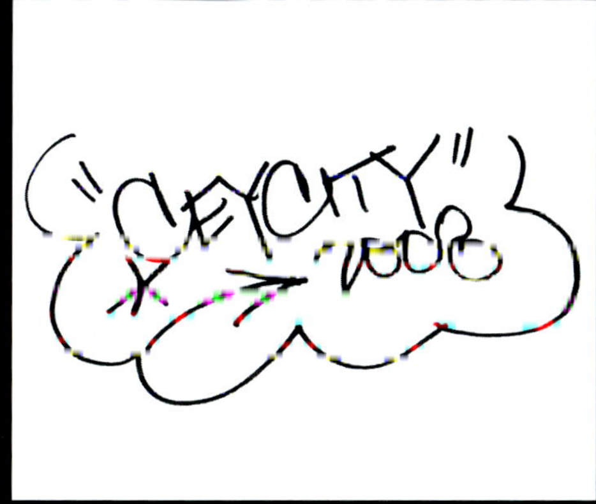
Cey

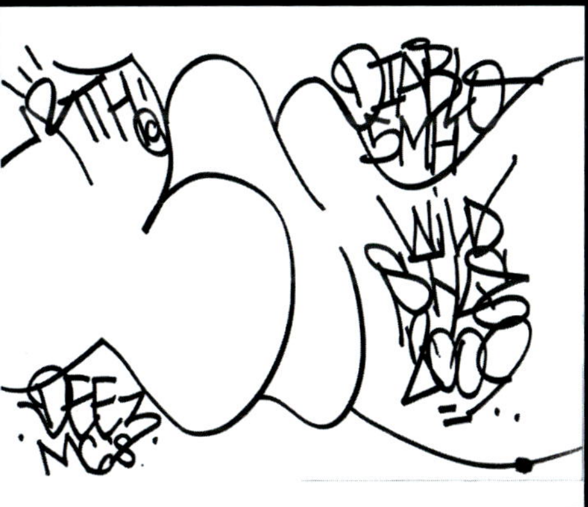
Ch

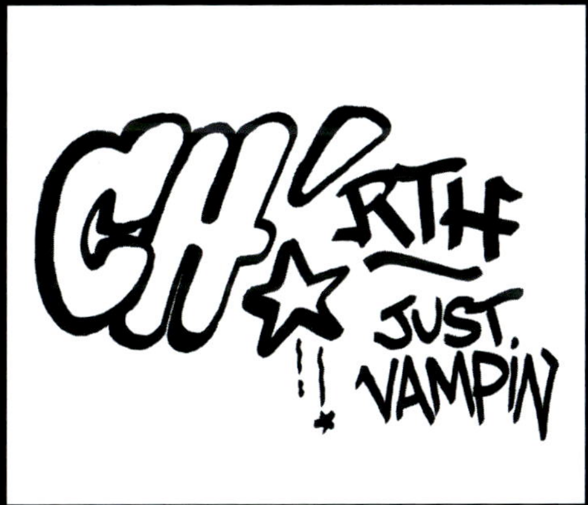

Ch

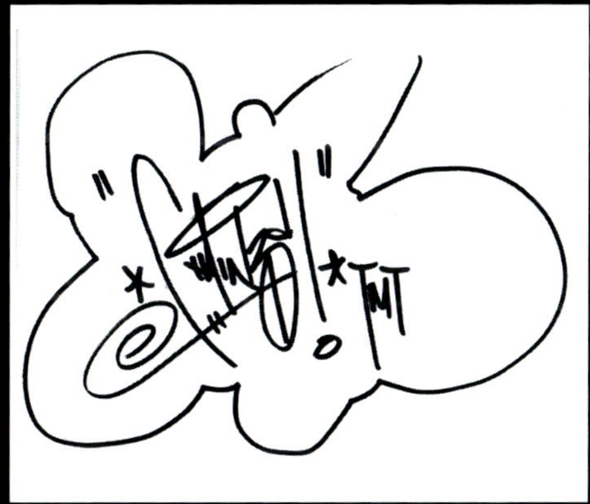
Chain

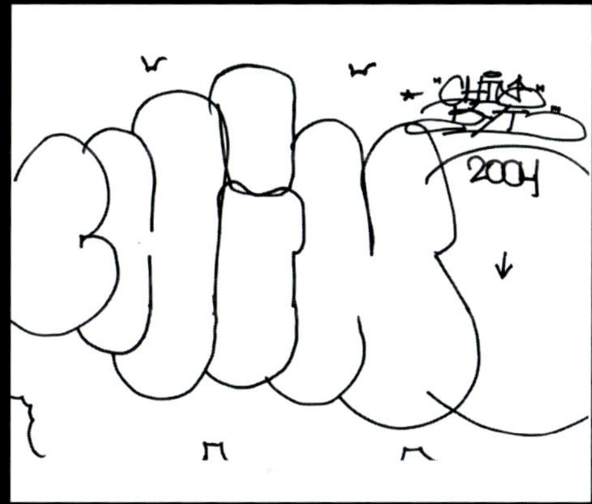

Chino

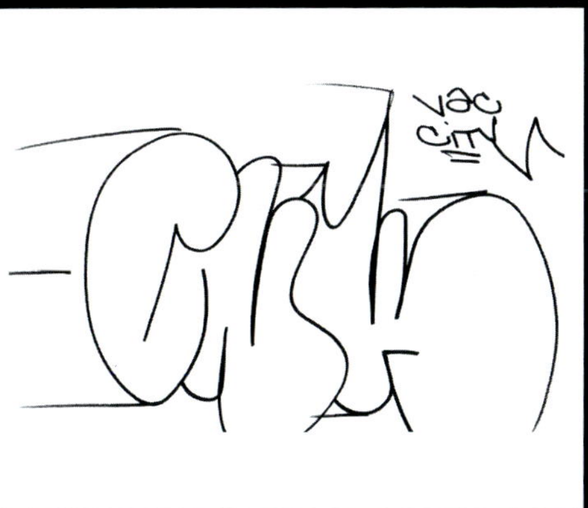
Cinik

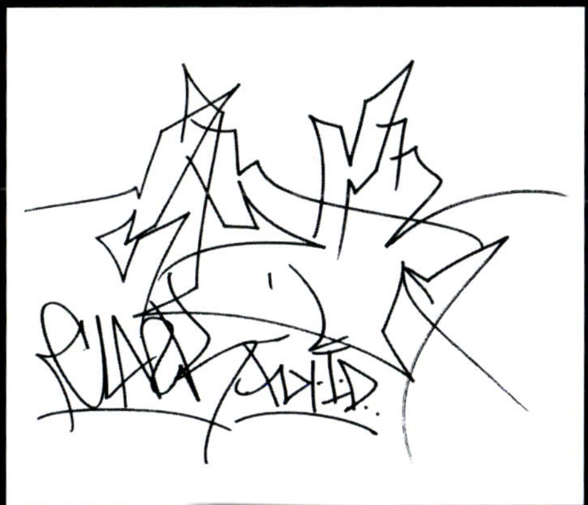
Clark

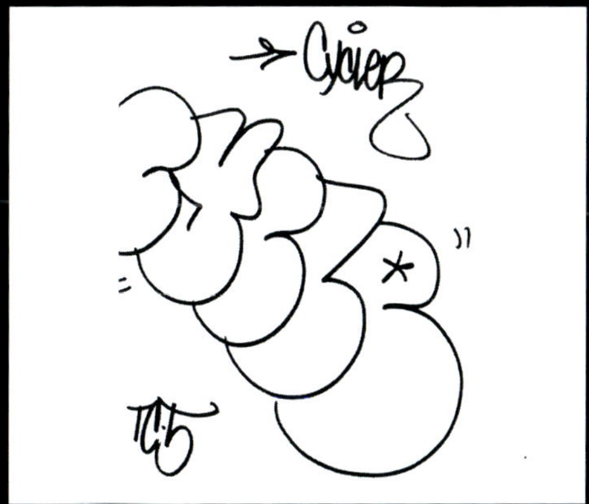
Cycle

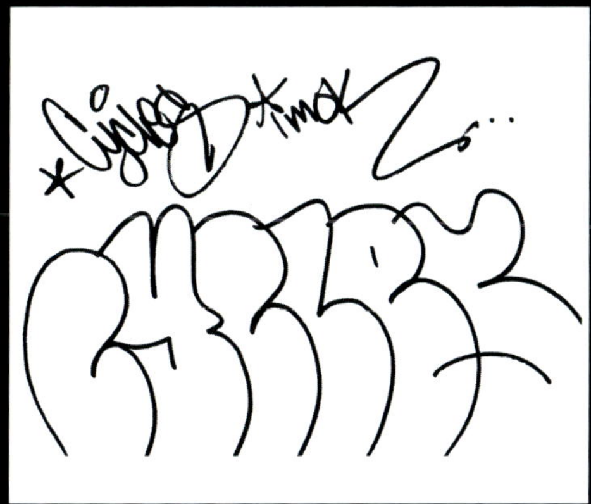
Cyclo

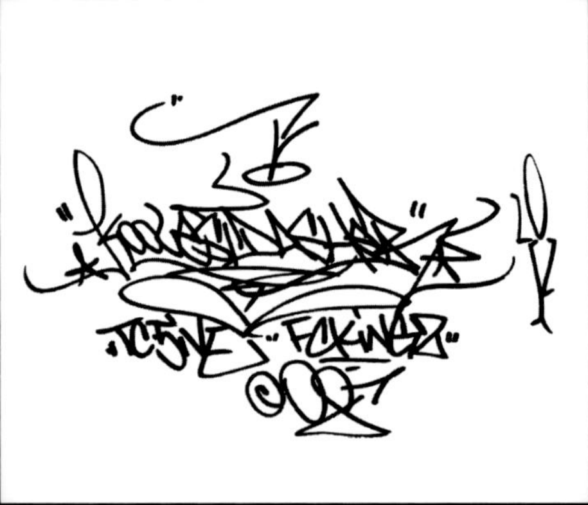

Dash

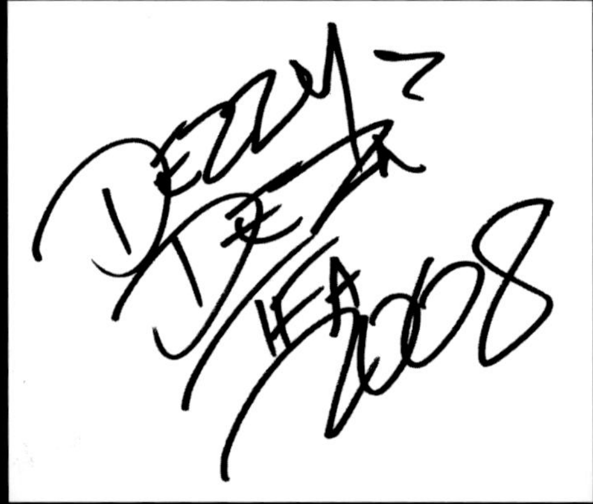


Dez

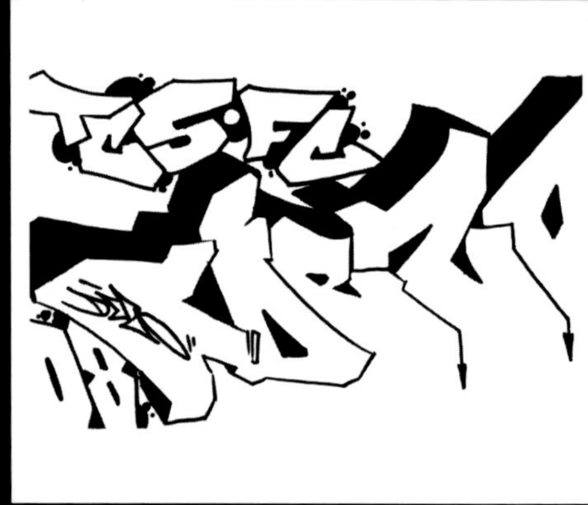

Dezo

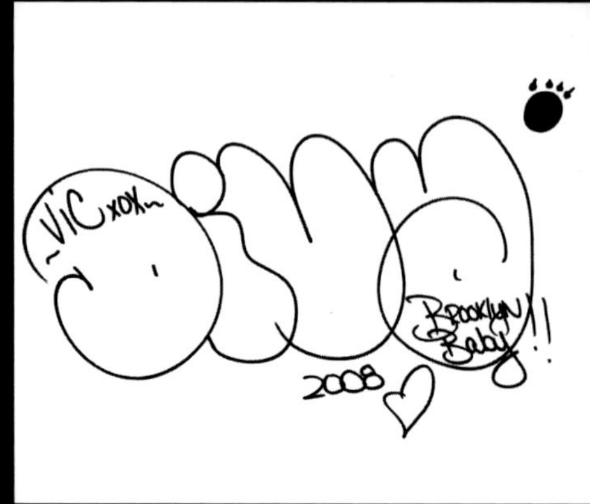


Diva

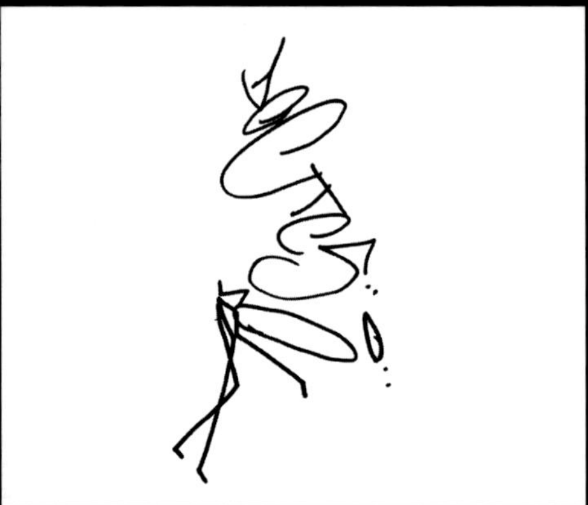

Doc

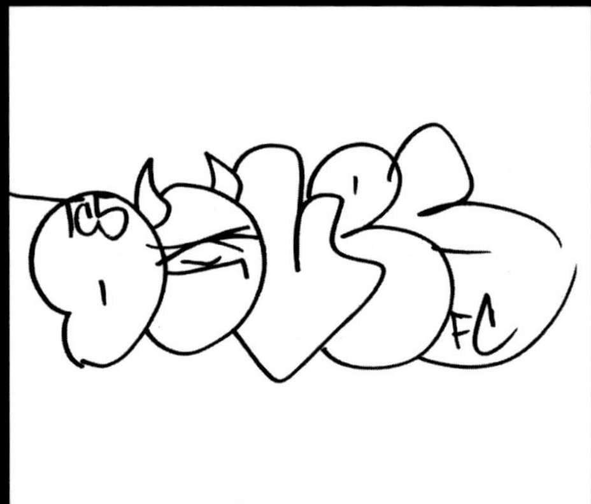

Doves

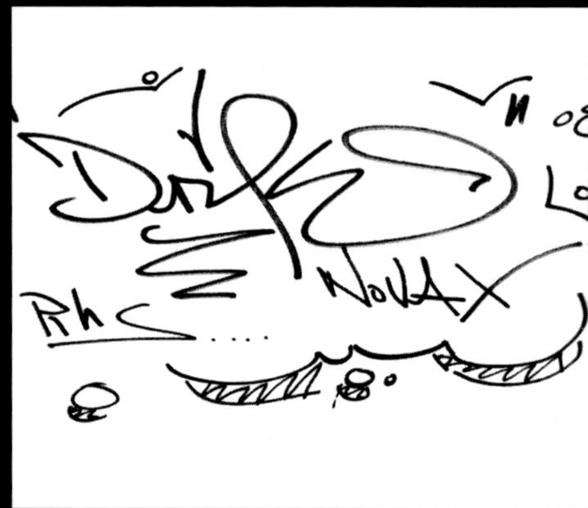

Drik

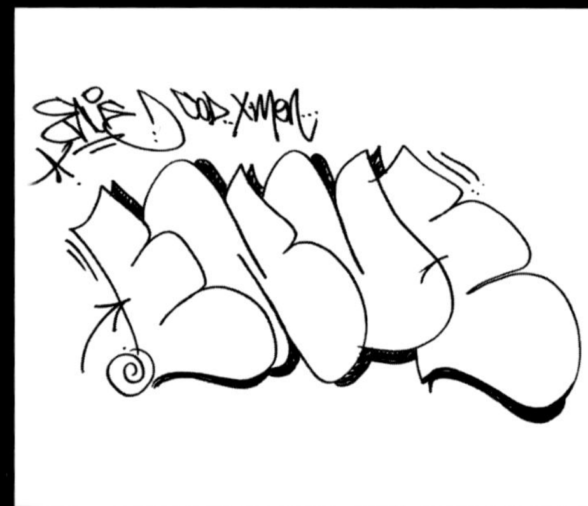

Enue

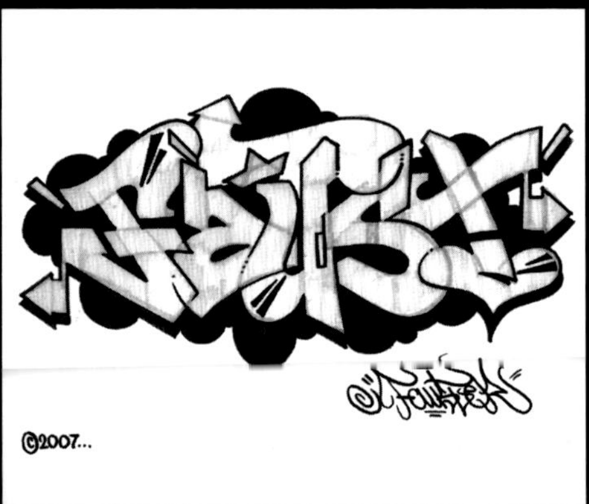


Faust

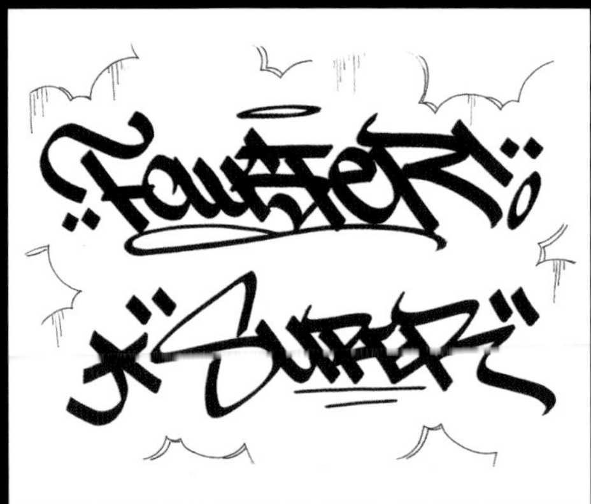

Faust

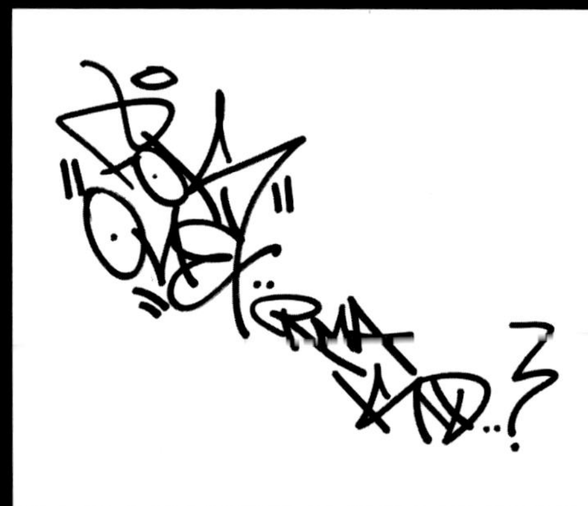

Fok

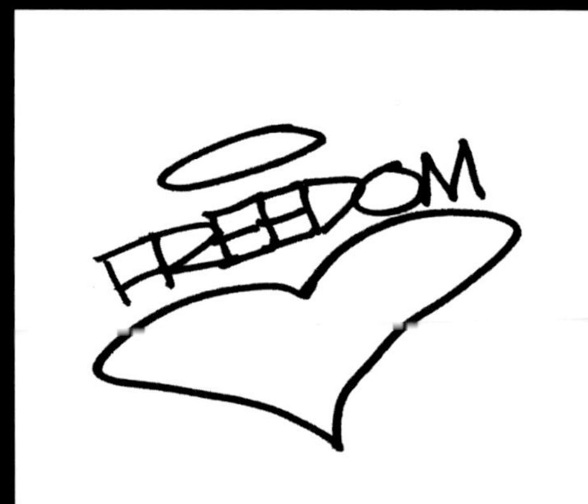


Freedom

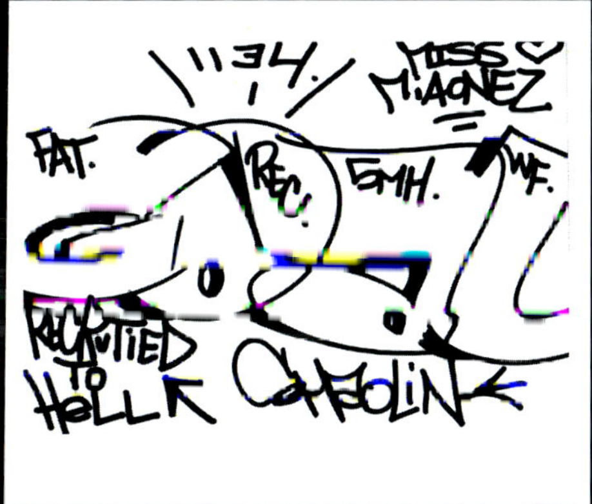

Goal

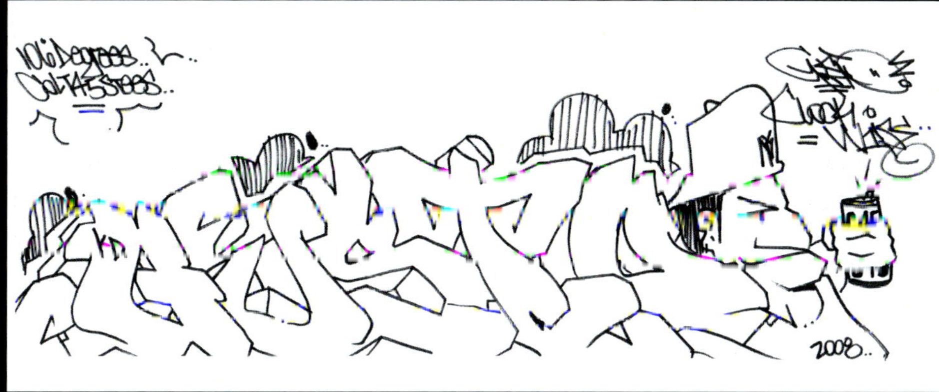

Gusto

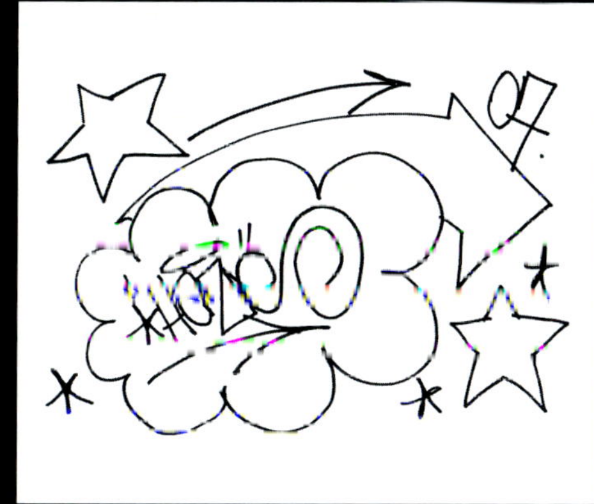

Haze

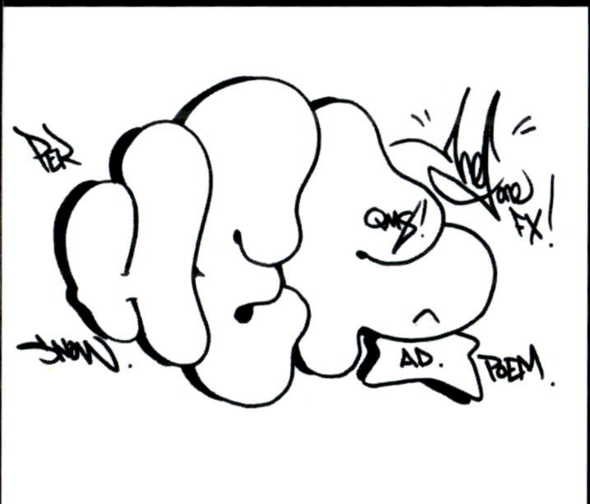

Hef

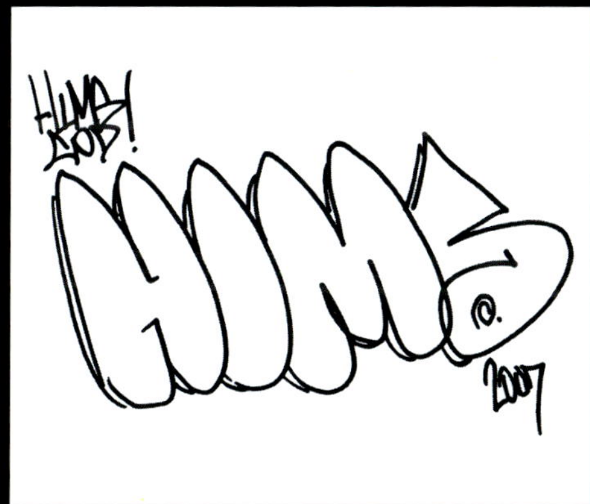

Hims

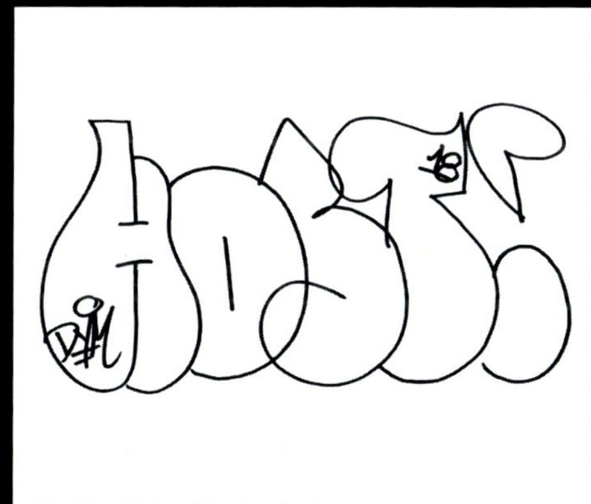

Host

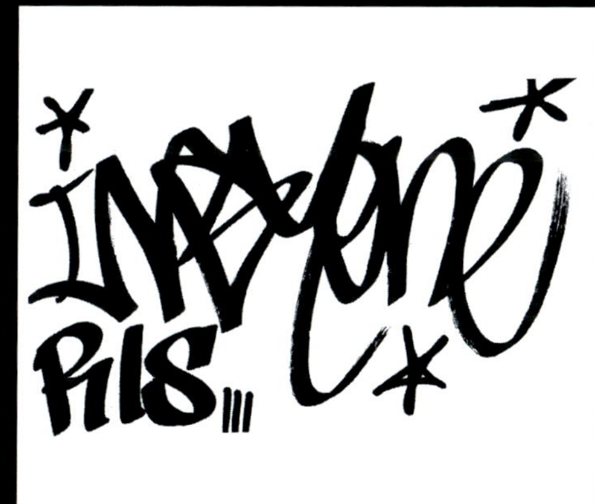

Ingy

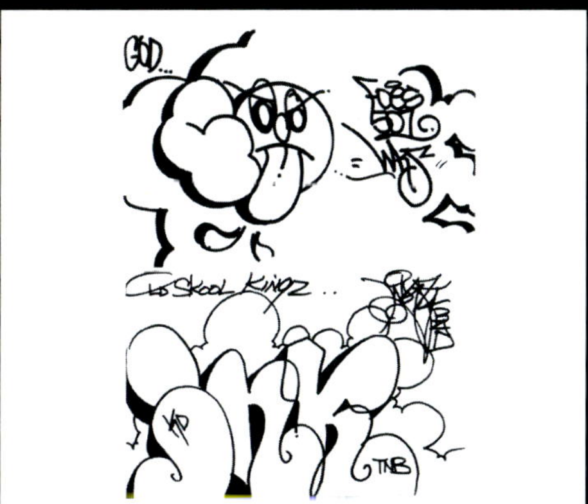

Ink76

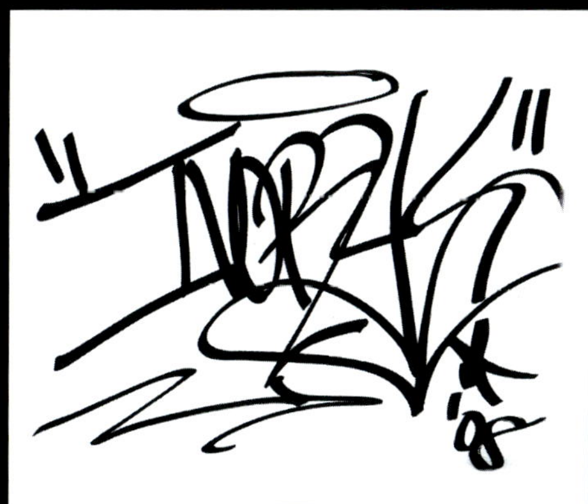

Ivory

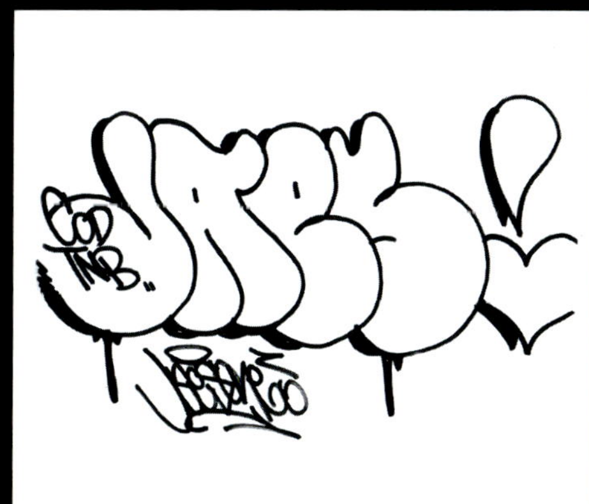

Jaes

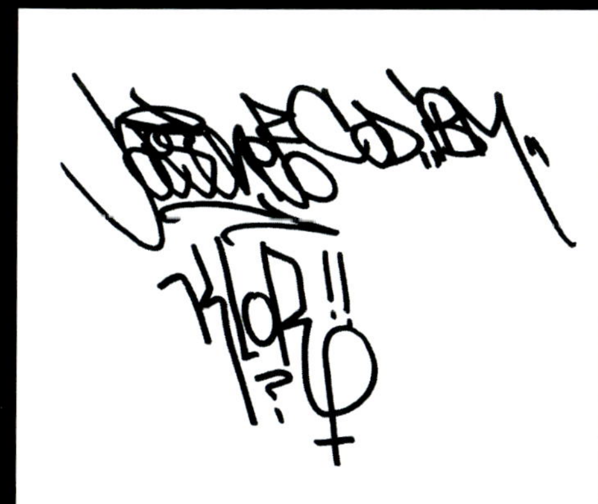

Jaes

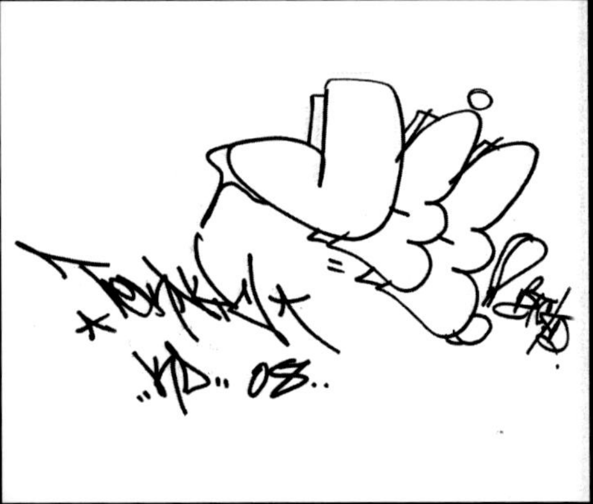

Jee

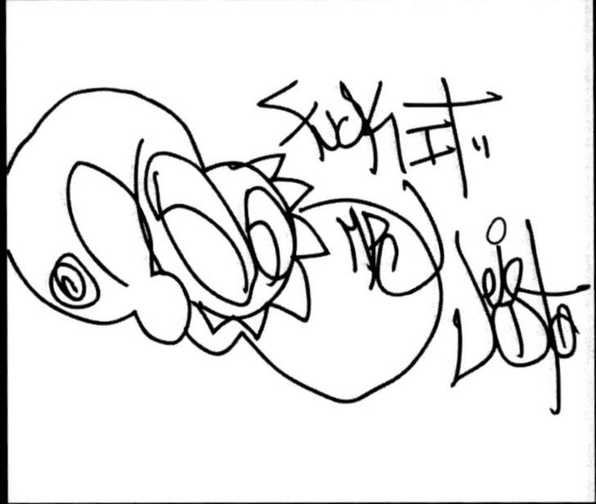

Jest

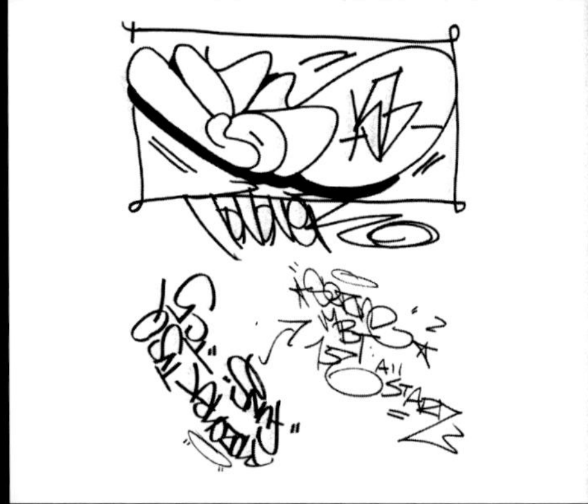

Jon156

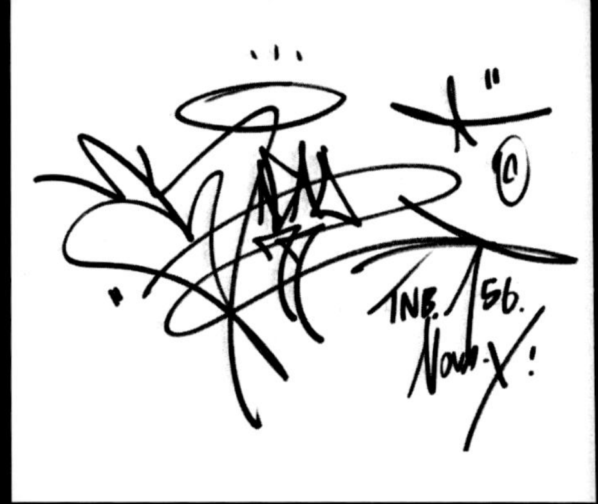

Kacao

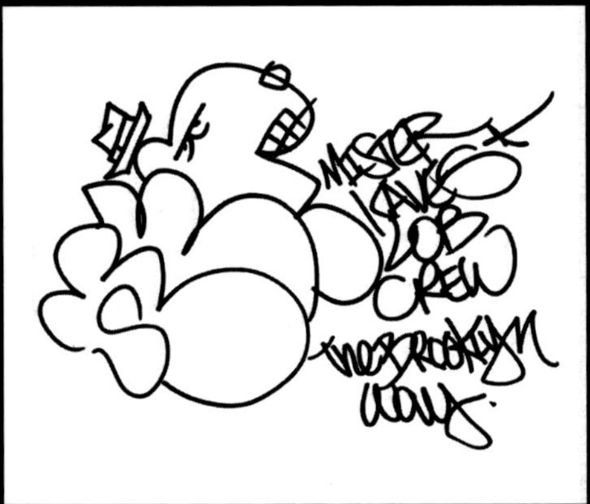

Kaves

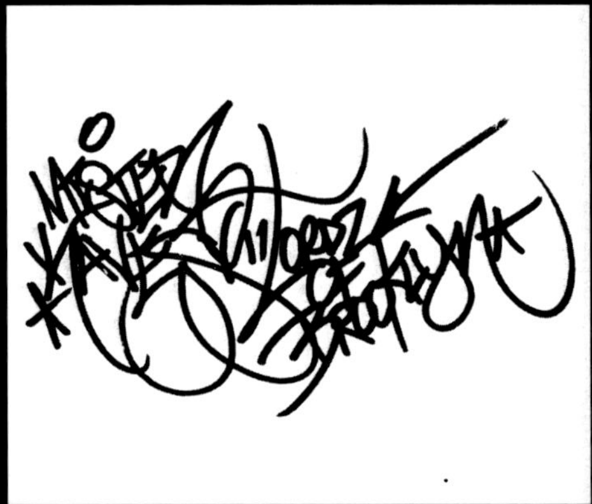

Kaves

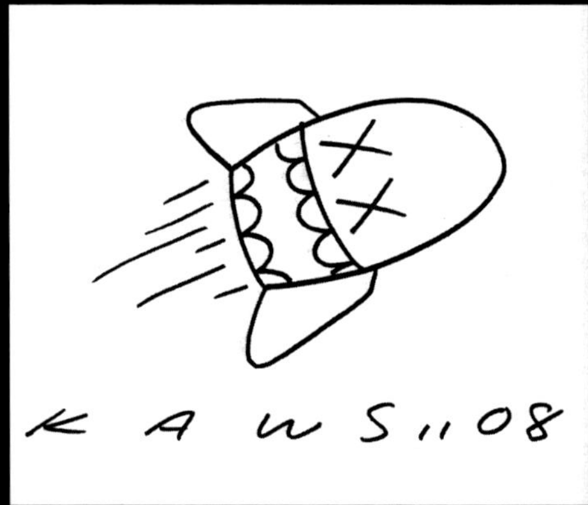


Kaws

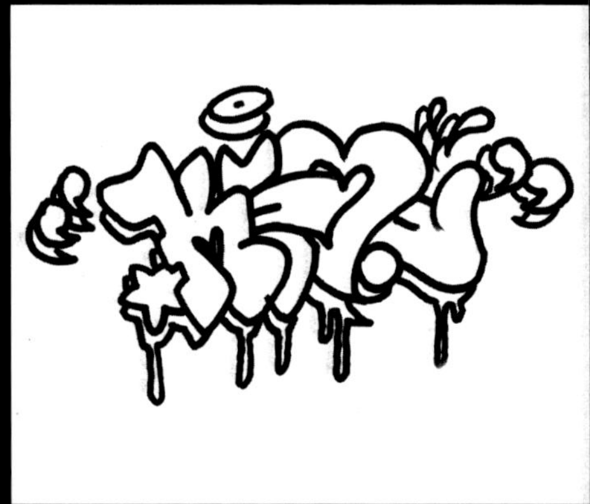

Keo

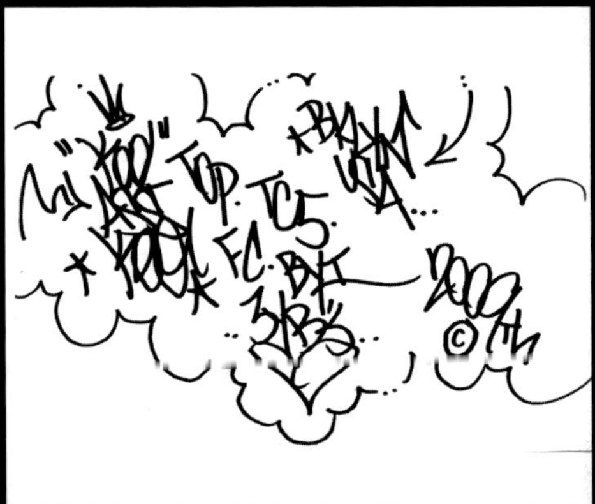

Keo

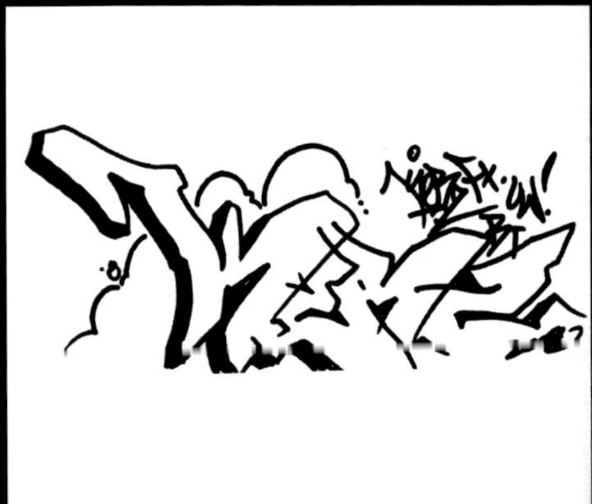

Kerz

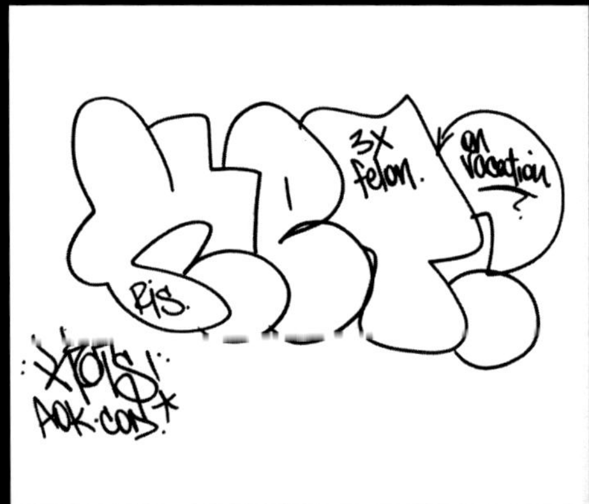


Ket

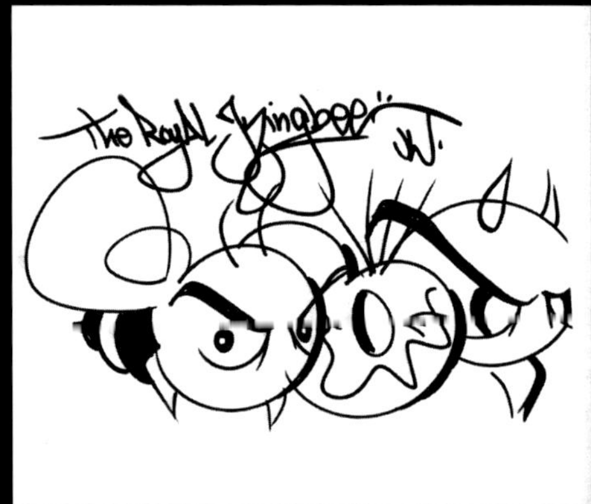


King Bee

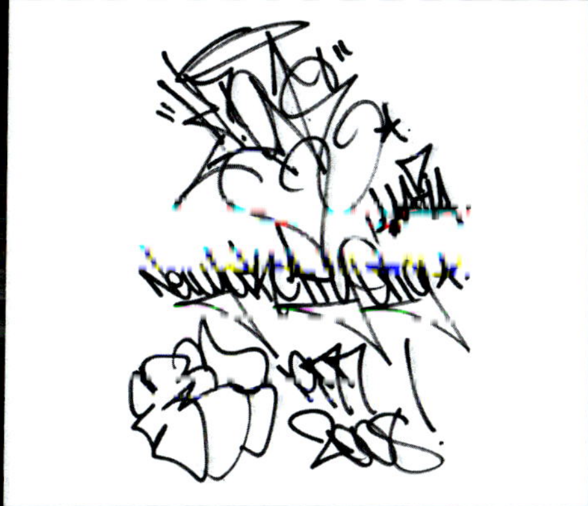

KR

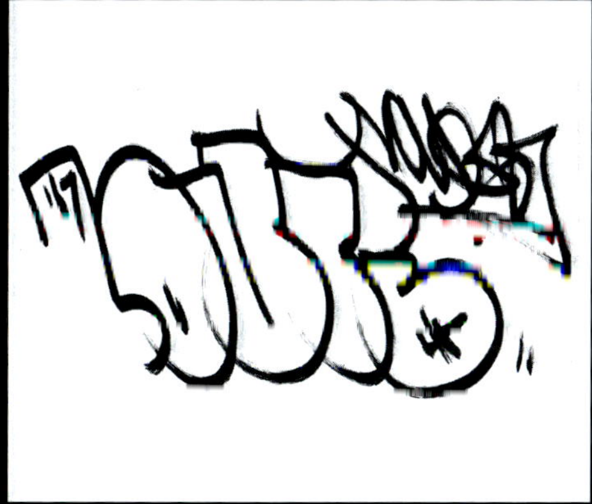

Louie167

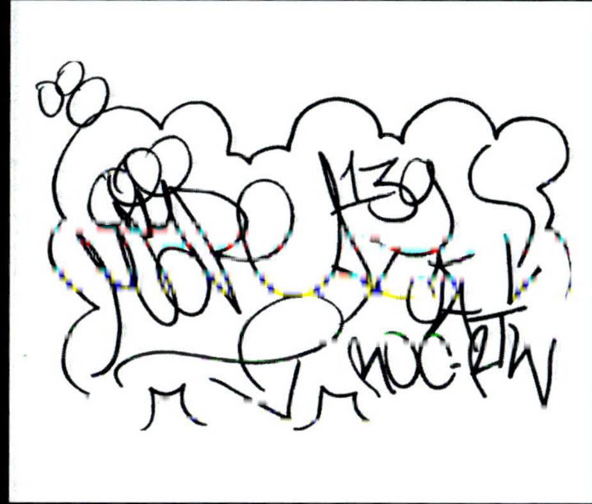

Mare139

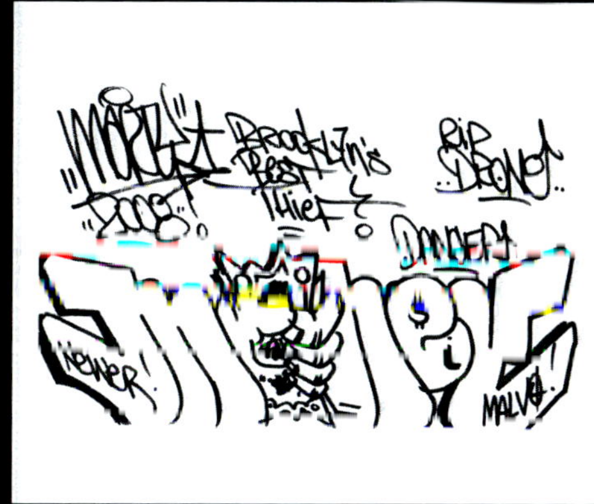

Marty

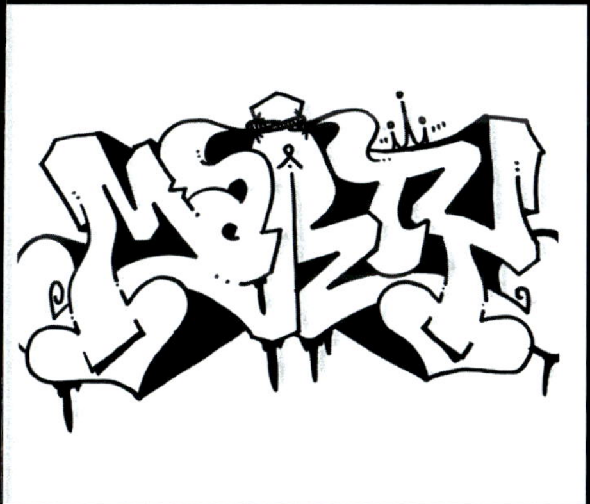

Marty

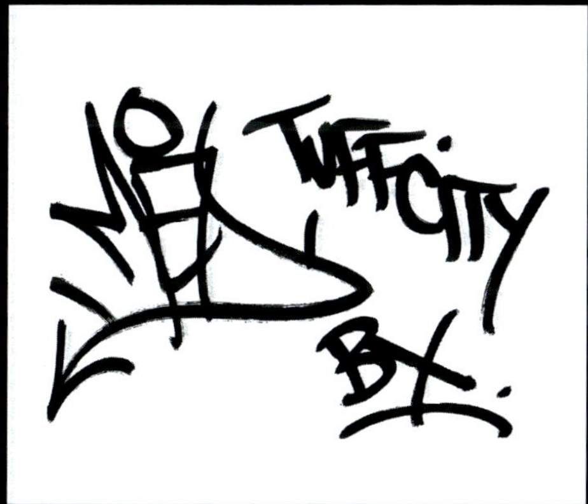


Med

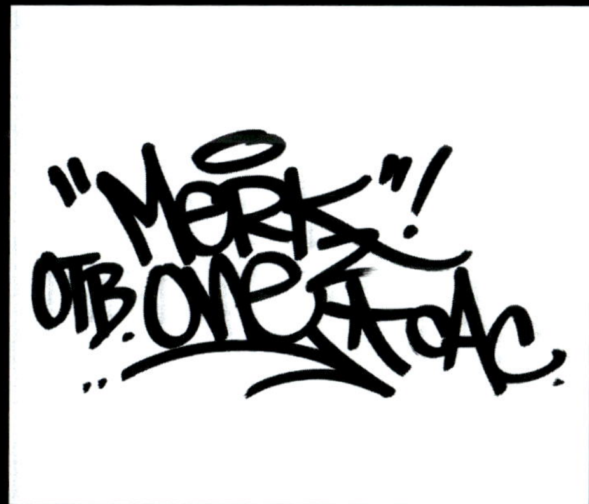


Merk

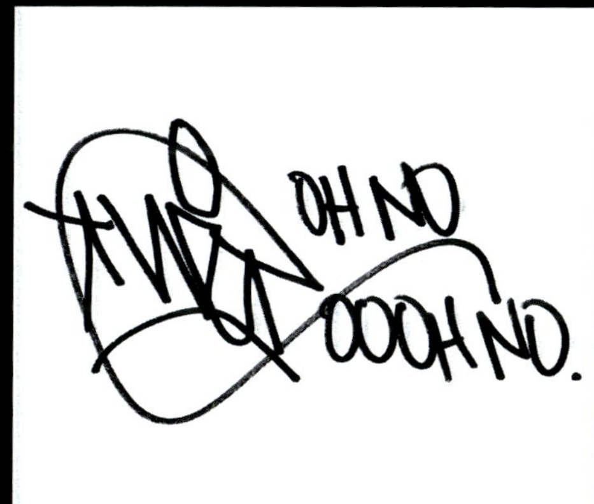


Net

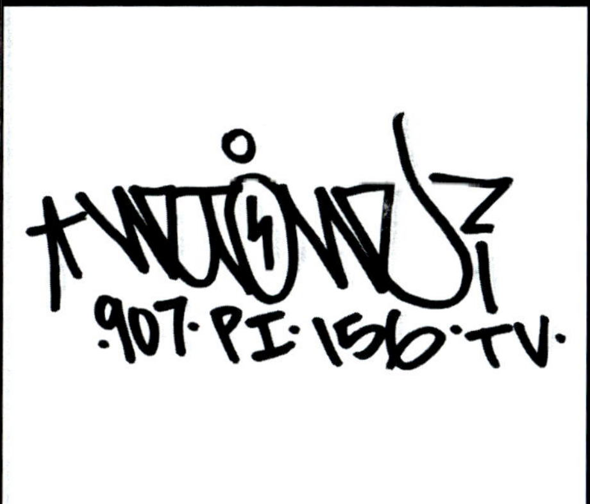


Net

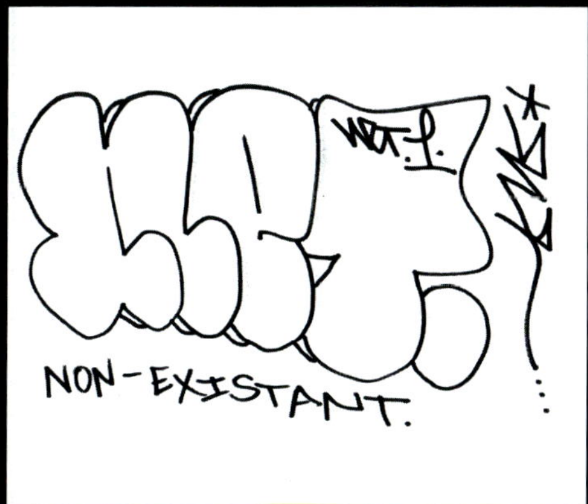


Net

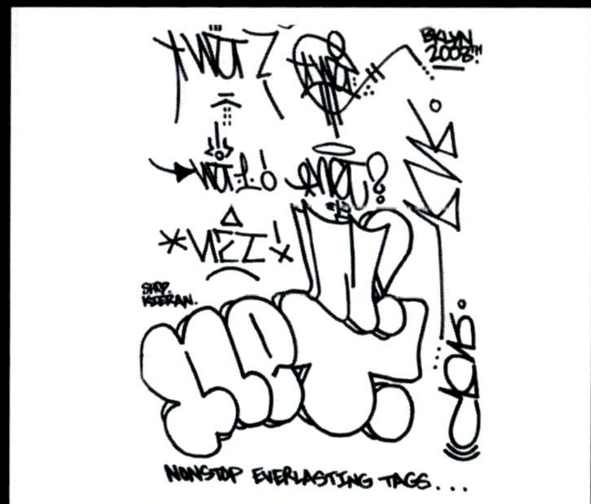


Net

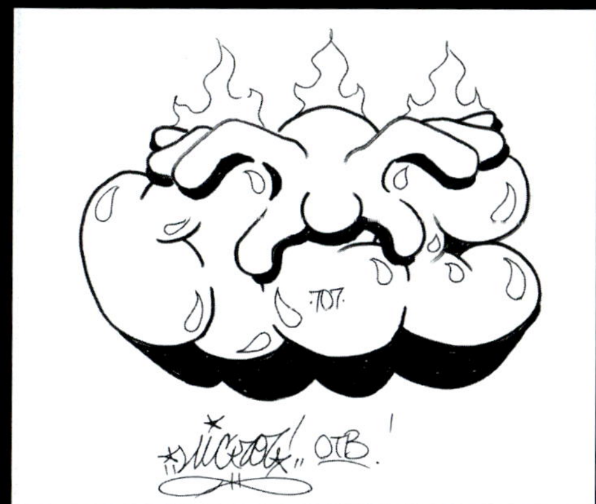


Nic707

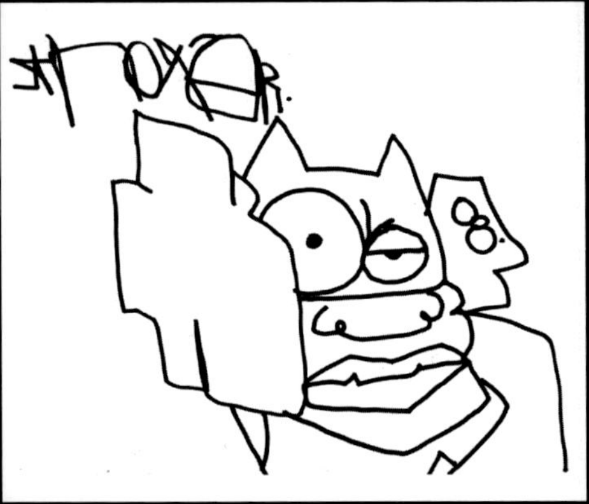

Noxer

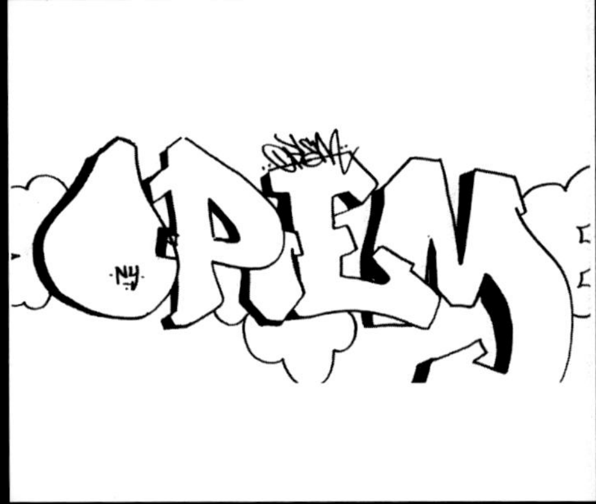


Opiem

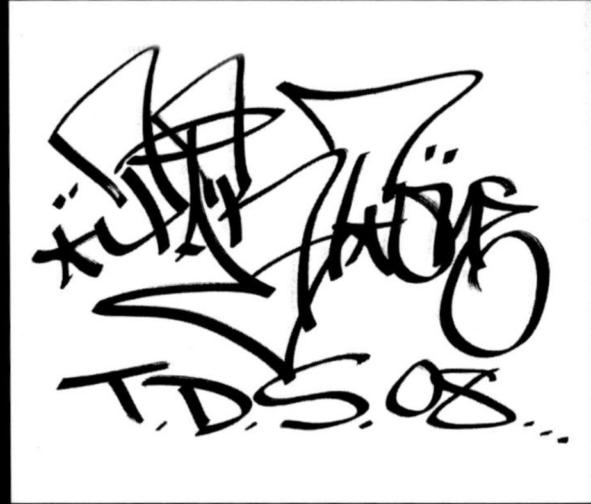


Part

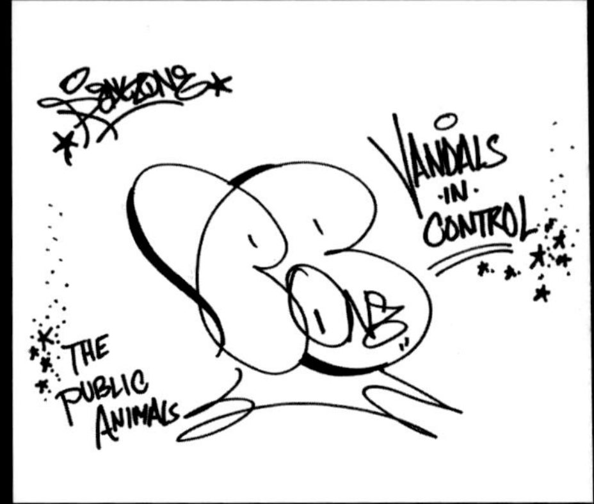


Peek

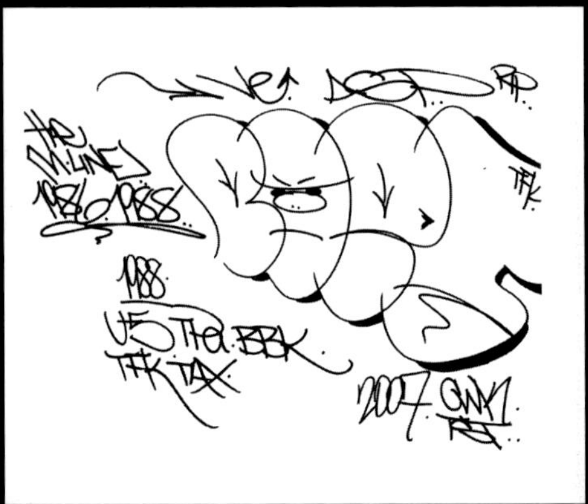

Poet

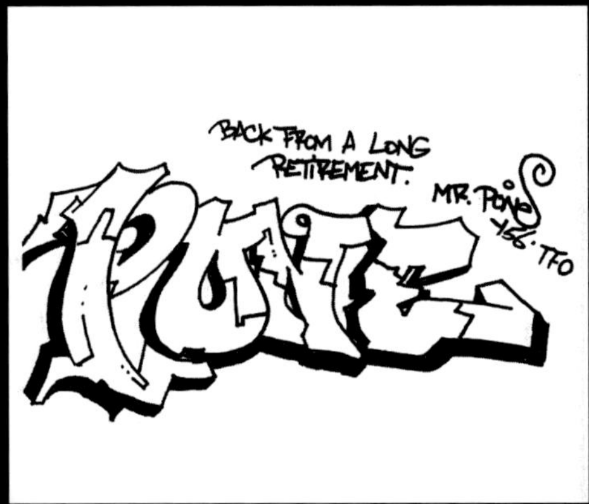


Pone

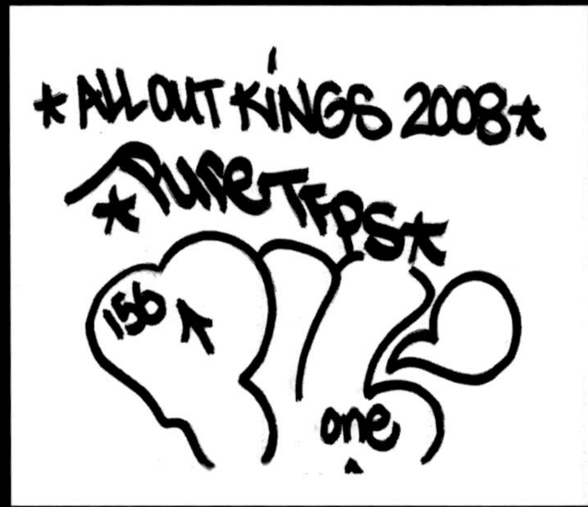


Pure

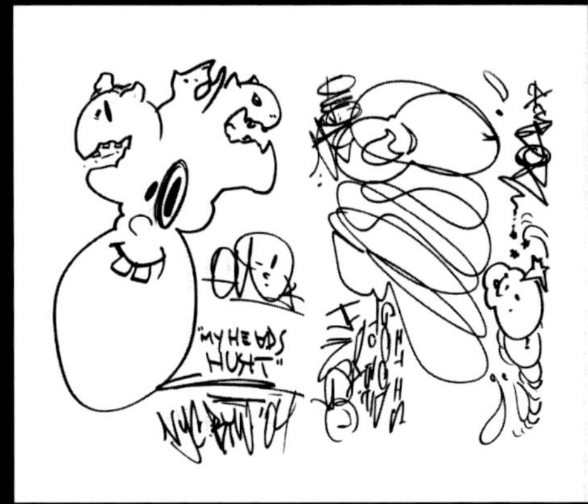


quik

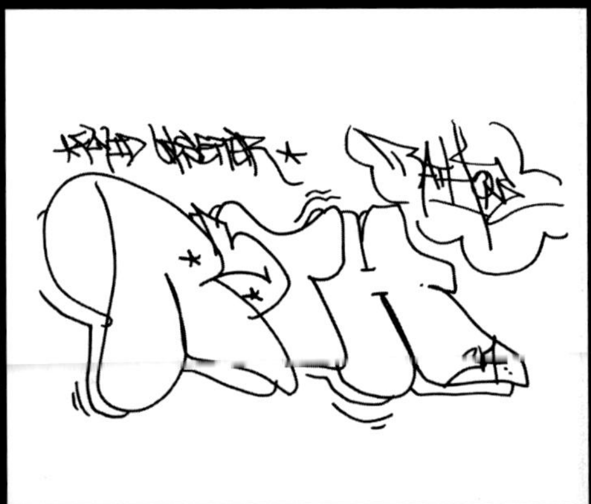

Rath

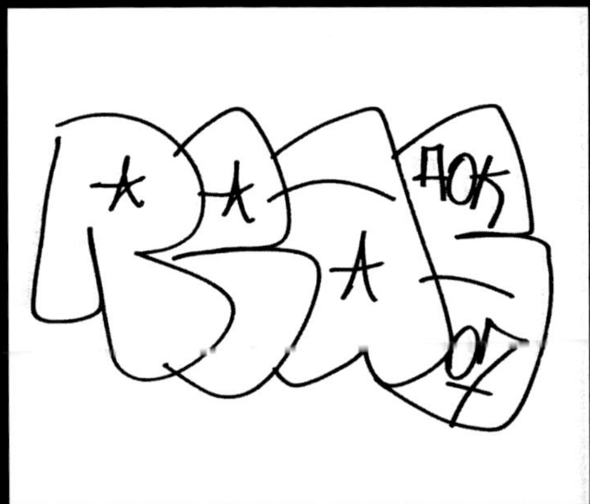

Reas

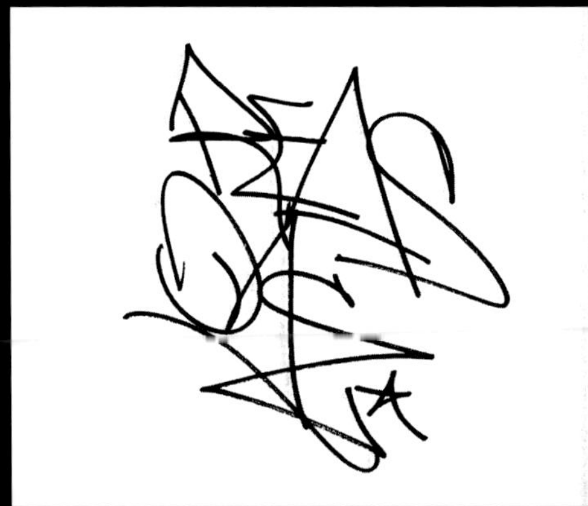

Reas

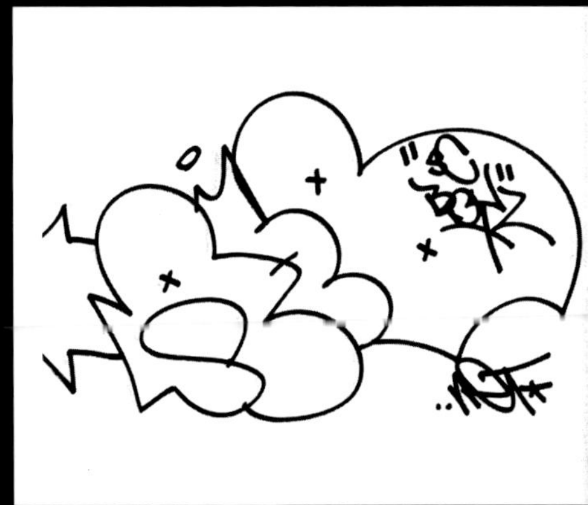

Rebel

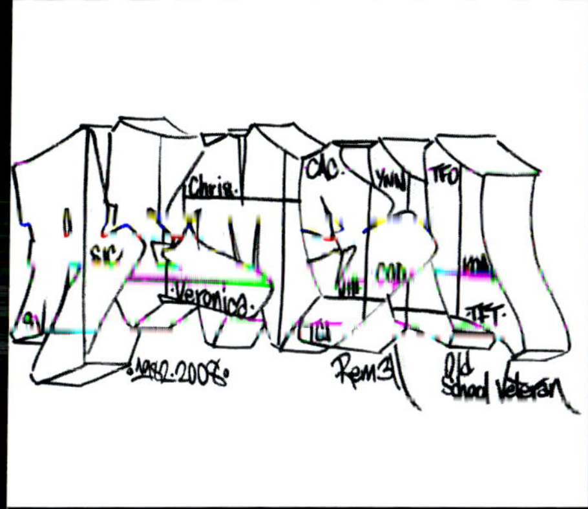


Rem311

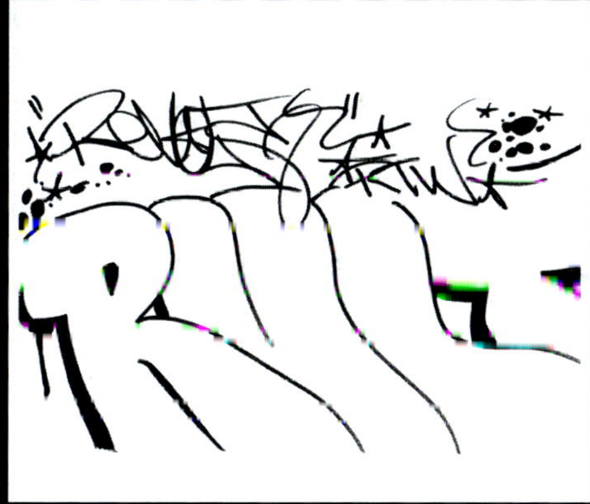

Revolt

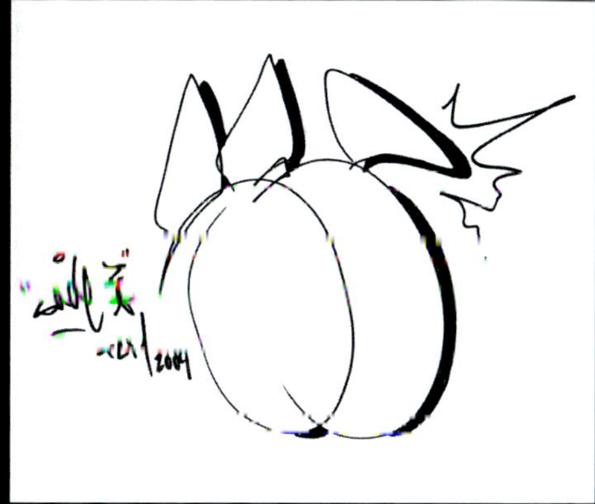

Sade

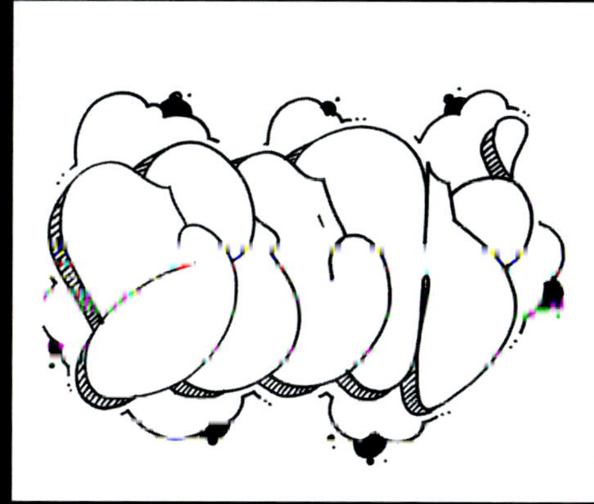

Siek

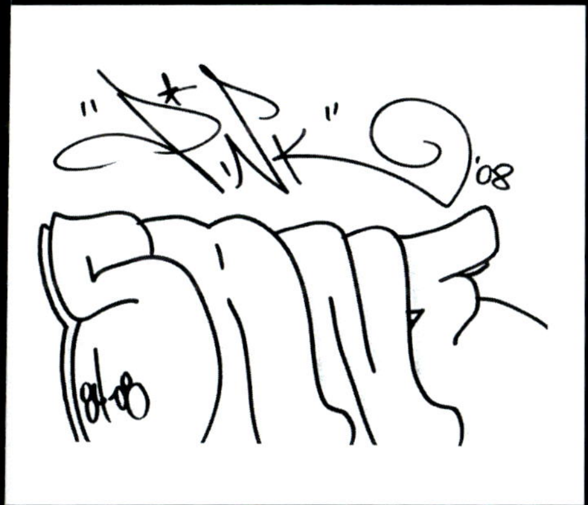

Smith

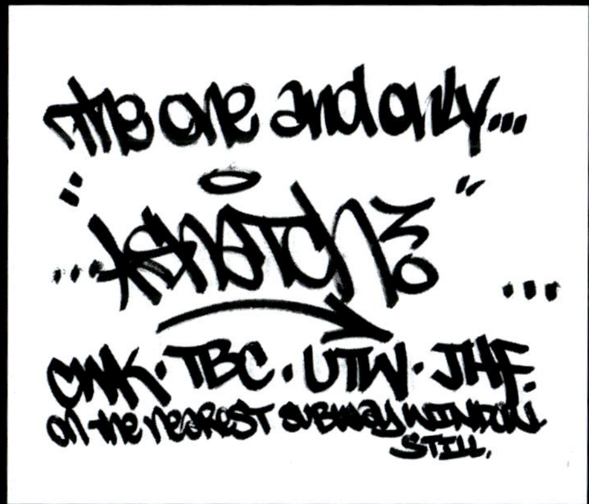


Snatch

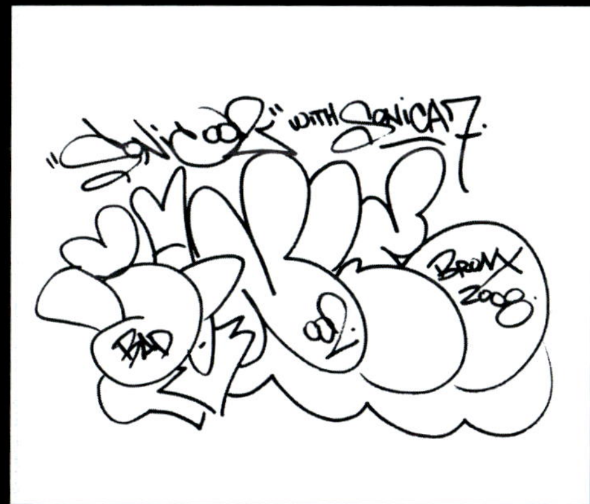


Sonic

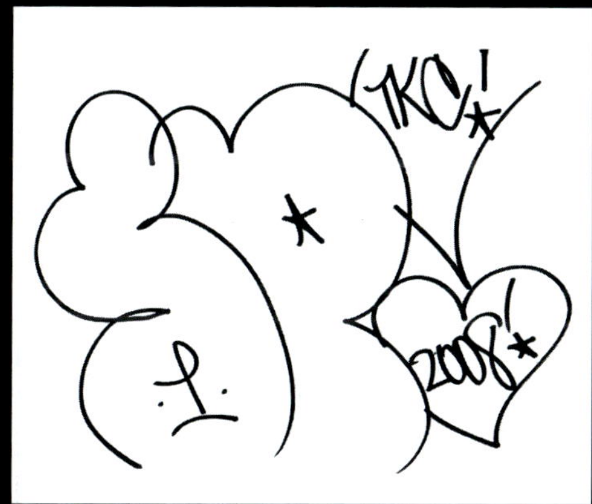


Sp

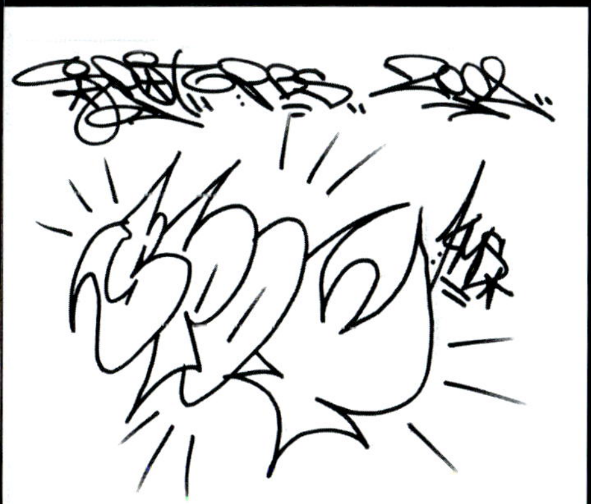

Spot

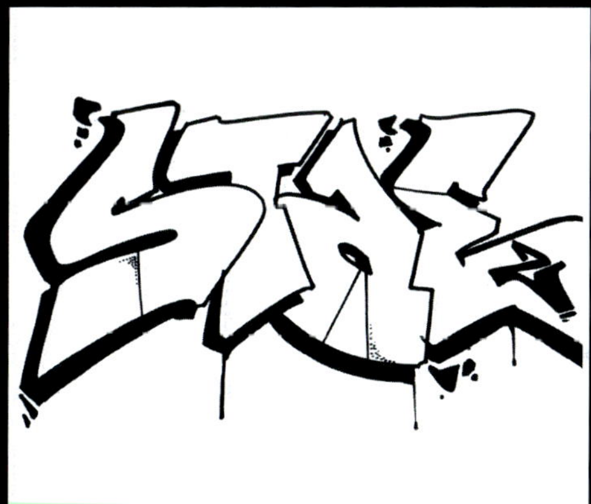

Stae

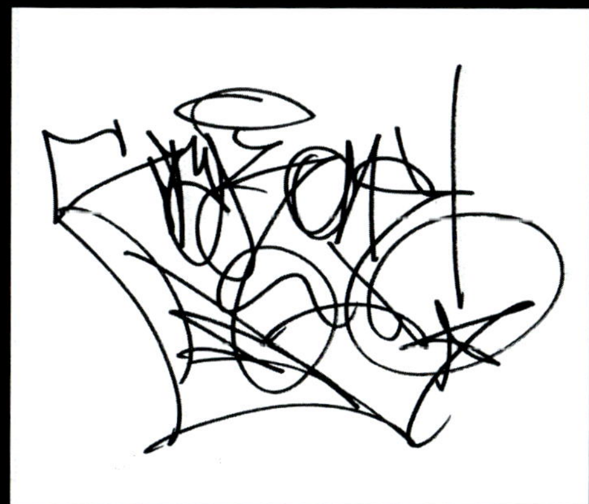

Stak

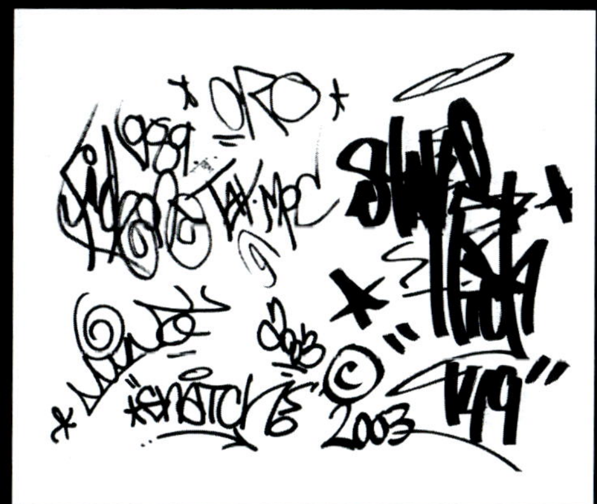


Stayhigh

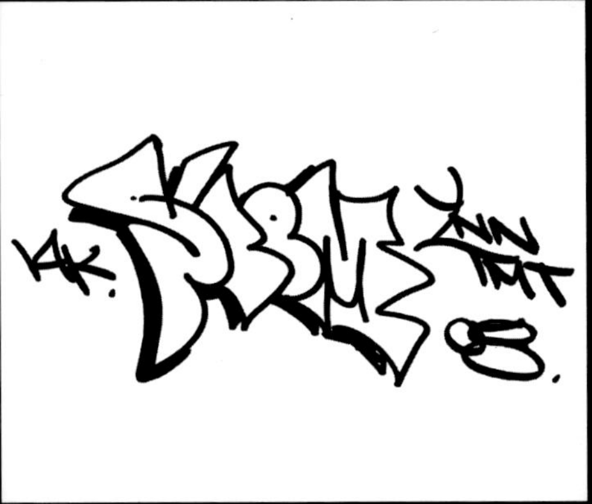
Stem

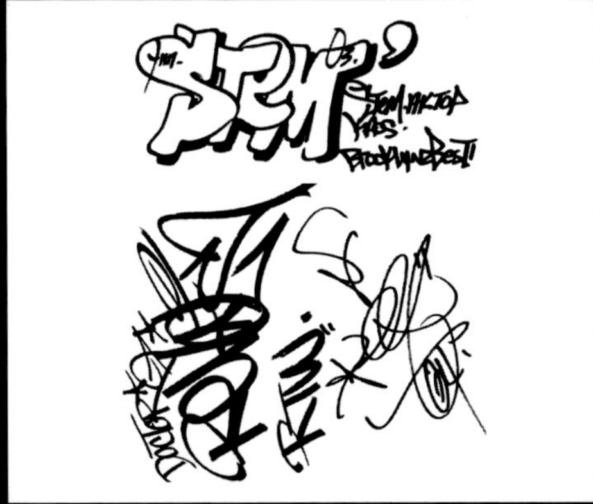
Stem

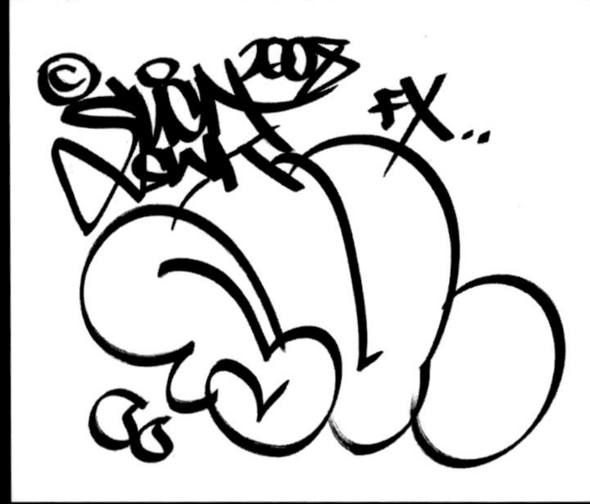
Such

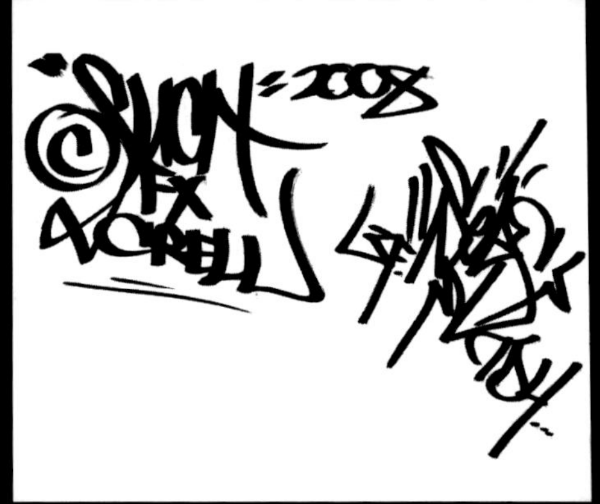
Such, Sebs

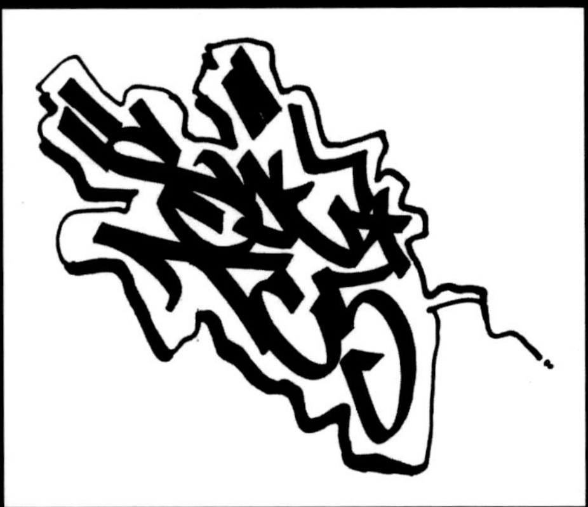
Sye

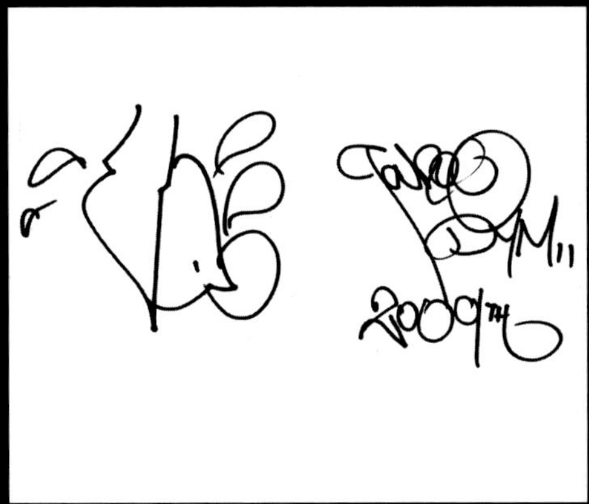
Taboo

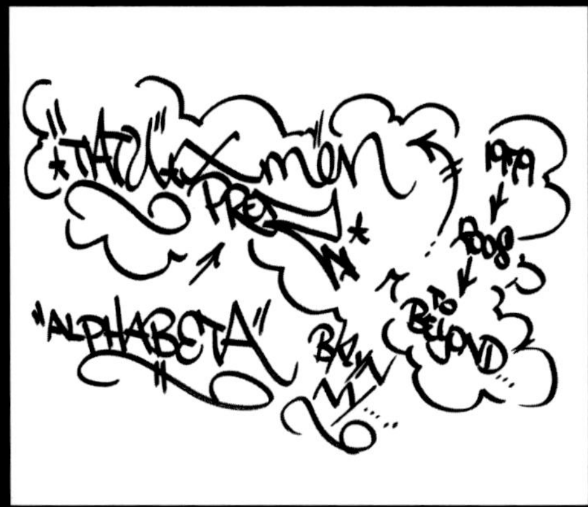
Tatu

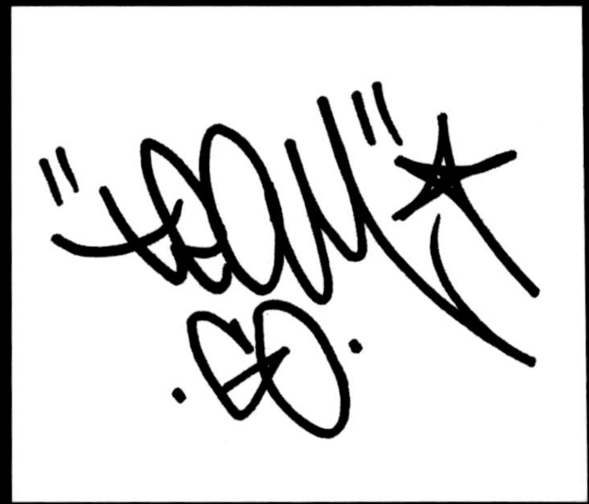
Team

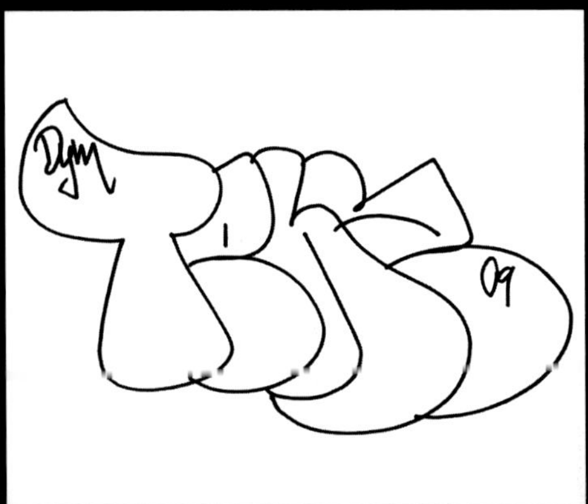
Tenz

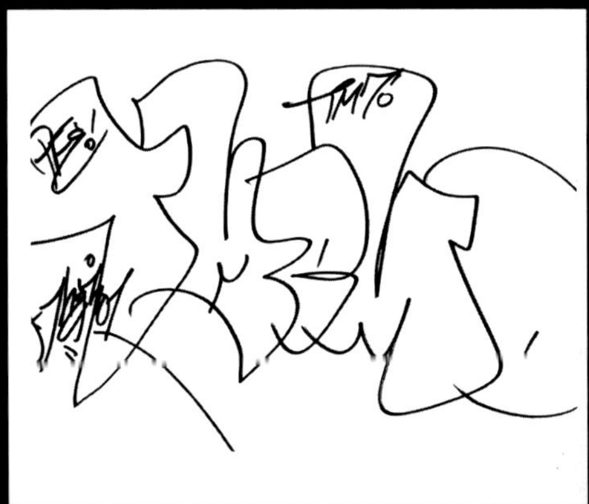
Themo

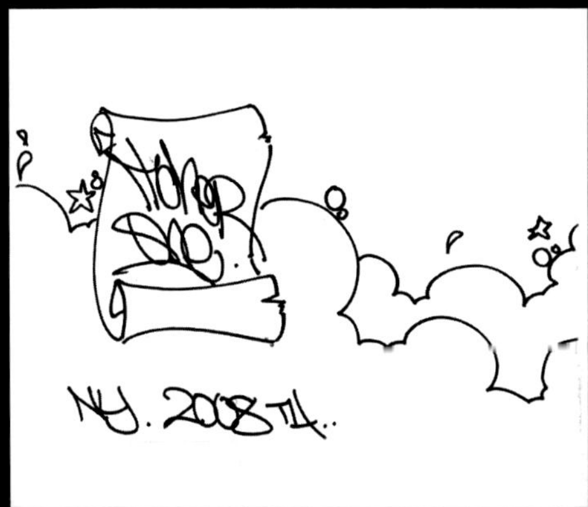
Tich

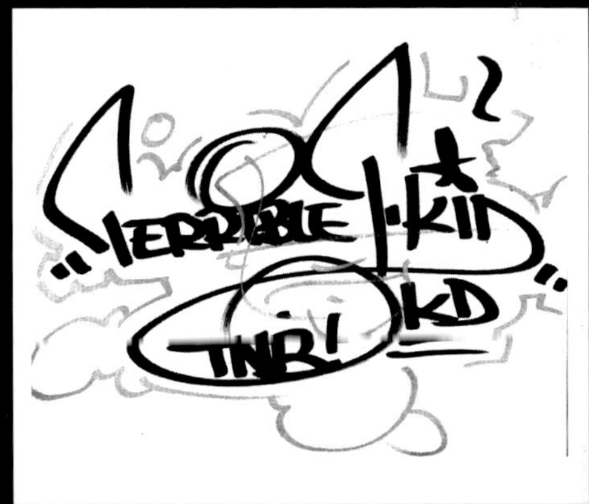
Tkid

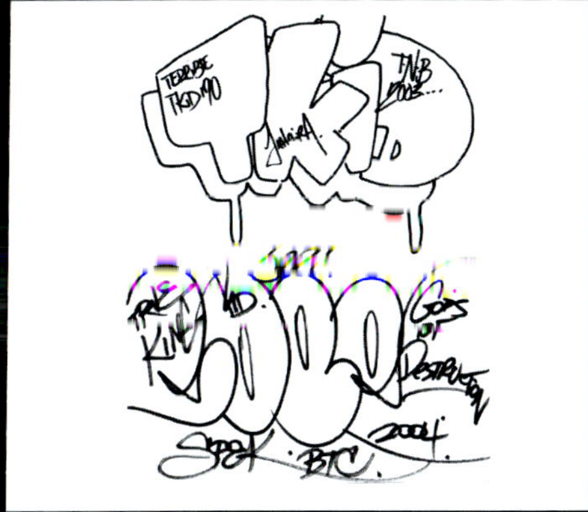

Tkid, Cope

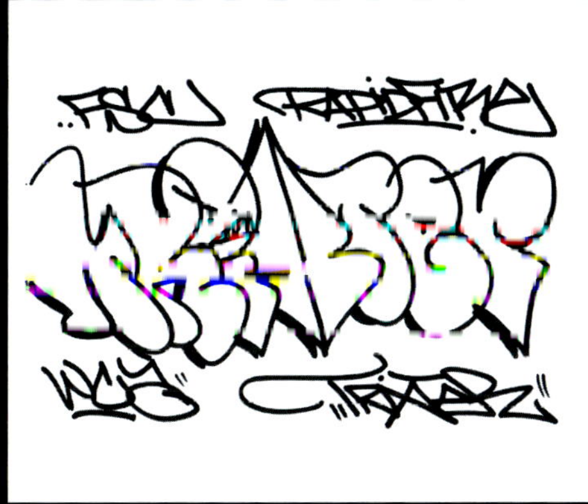

Trixter

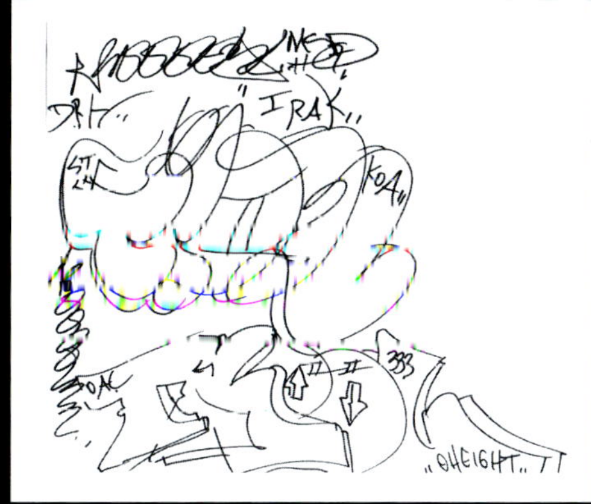

Trool22

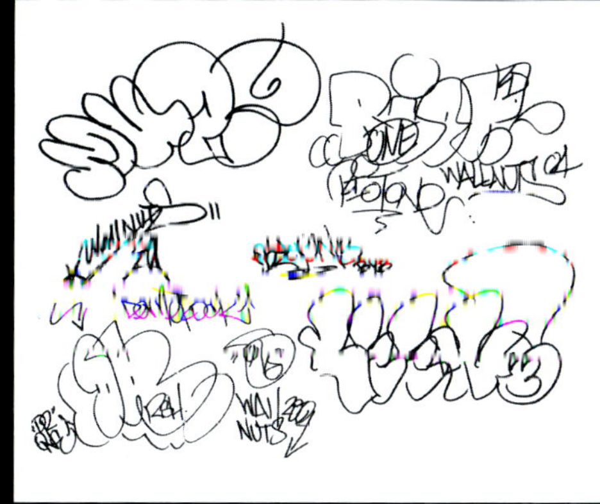

Wallnuts

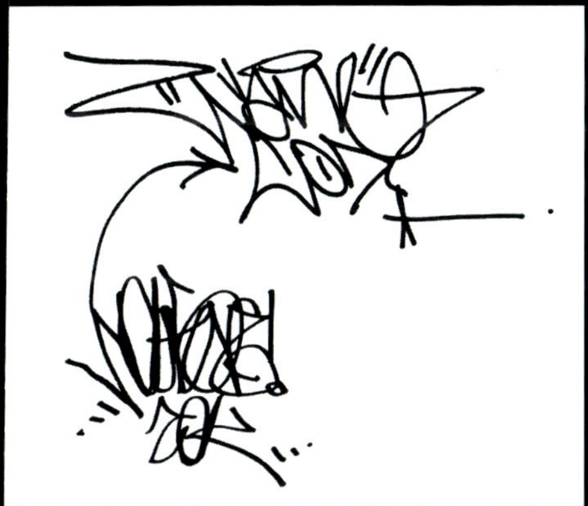

Wane, Wolf

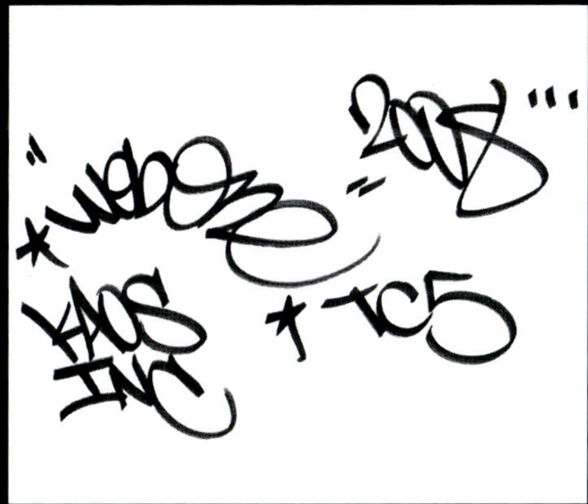

Web

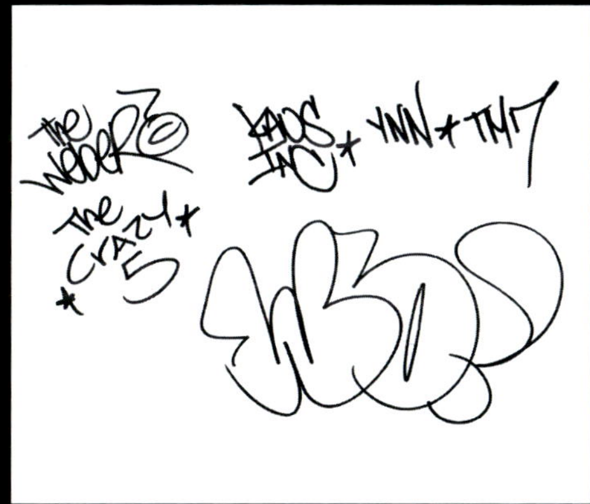

Web

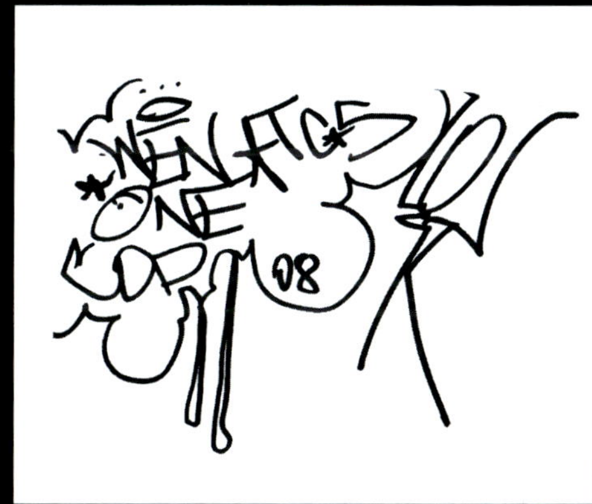

Wen

West

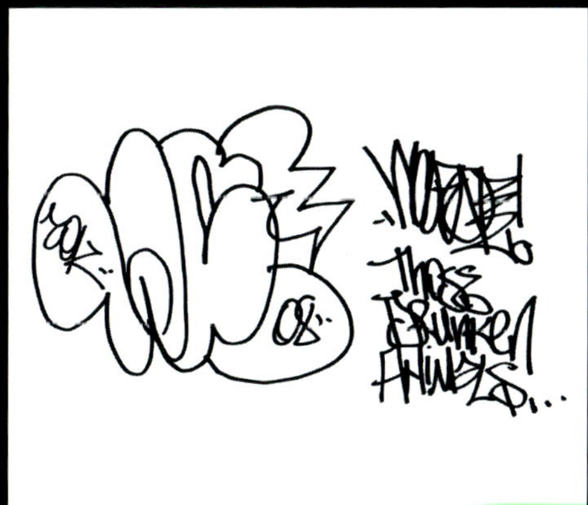

Wolf

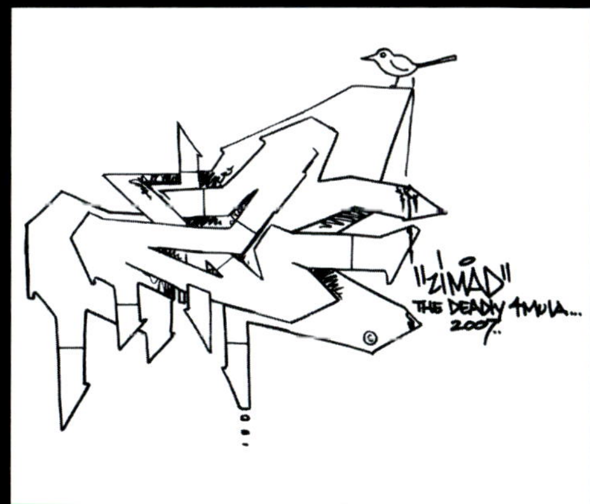


Zimad

# NYC GRAFFITI SHOPS

**Scrap Yard**
300 West Broadway
New York, New York
212-343-2557

**Tuff City Styles**
650 Forham Road
Bronx, New York
718-563-4157
www.tuffcitystyles.com

**Da Bakery**
1700 Southern Blvd – 174th St on the 2 & 5 Train
Bronx, New York
www.dabakerynyc.com

**All The Right**
35-61 Junction Blvd
Queens, New York
718-899-7685

**100 B**
100 B Forsyth St (between Broome and Grand)
New York, New York

**Graffiti Comix**

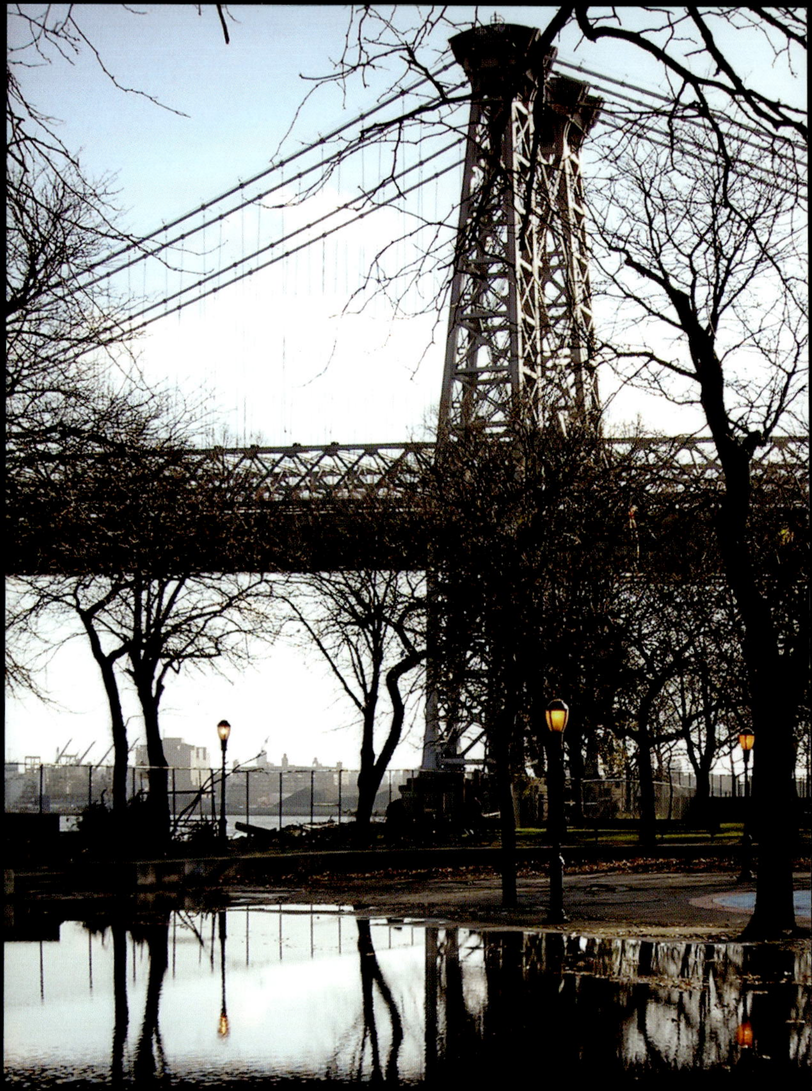